THE COUPLE'S GUIDE TO FERTILITY

THIRD EDITION

THE
COUPLE'S
GUIDE
TO
FERTILITY

THIRD EDITION

———

*Entirely Revised and
Updated with the Newest
Scientific Techniques to
Help You Have a Baby*

❈

Gary S. Berger, M.D.
Marc Goldstein, M.D.
Mark Fuerst

Broadway Books
New York

BROADWAY

This book is not intended as a substitute for professional medical advice on fertility, infertility, or gynecological disorders. The reader should regularly consult a physician in matters relating to health and particularly with respect to any symptoms that may require diagnosis or medical attention.

Visit our website at www.broadwaybooks.com

Library of Congress Cataloging-in-Publication Data
Berger, Gary S.
The couple's guide to fertility : entirely revised and updated with the newest scientific techniques to help you have a baby / Gary S. Berger, Marc Goldstein, Mark Fuerst.—3rd ed.
p.   cm.
Includes bibliographical references and index.
1. Infertility—Popular works. 2. Human reproductive technology—Popular works.
I. Goldstein, Marc.   II. Fuerst, Mark.   III. Title.
RC889 .B444 2001
616.6'92—dc21
2001025195

Illustrations by Jackie Aher

ISBN 0-7679-0548-2

03   04   05   10   9   8   7   6   5   4   3   2

*We dedicate this book
to our wives, Barbara, Frieda, and Margie,
and to all couples who want to
become parents.*

Acknowledgments

Many individuals—family, friends, patients, professional colleagues, and teachers—have contributed directly and indirectly to this book. It would be impossible to list them all by name. In particular, we would like to thank our wives and families for their support. Special recognition is due to our agent, Faith Hamlin, for her assistance through all phases of the book. We thank Frieda Goldstein, whose suggestion that we include a directory of fertility specialists immeasurably enhanced the value of this book.

Note on the Collaboration

From information supplied by Dr. Berger and Dr. Goldstein, Mr. Fuerst prepared the basic manuscript, and then interviewed other experts and patients across the country to add to Dr. Berger's and Dr. Goldstein's medical insights. The third-person references to Dr. Berger and Dr. Goldstein are used to differentiate their opinions and experiences from those of other fertility specialists.

CONTENTS

Contents

Contents

_____

PREFACE TO FIRST EDITION

To those of us who grew up in the 1960s and 1970s, it seemed a birthright to have two or three children by the time we reached our thirties. But for many among our generation, that's not the way it happened.

For various reasons, many of us put off even thinking about having kids until age thirty or beyond. Now it seems that some couples may have waited too long. The orchestration of events necessary to make babies has somehow fallen out of sync. A few discordant notes—a silent epidemic of sexually transmitted diseases, prolonged use of the Pill, sterilization operations, the stresses of making a living—have hindered many people's ability to produce babies.

Over the last twenty-five years, as today's childbearing generation has come of age, there has been a tremendous increase in couples seeking help for infertility. There are about 10 million infertile Americans, and this generation is the first in U.S. history that will not fully reproduce itself. The 73 million babies born between 1946 and 1965—known collectively as baby boomers—now face some new facts of life.

The irony is that the couples who have spent the last twenty-five years planning their lives so they could "have it all" now face the fact that the baby they thought they could delay may no longer be possible at all.

Infertility is pervasive. We all know someone or know of someone with a fertility problem. Even as new developments make the headlines and late-night news, infertility largely remains taboo. Most couples don't make cocktail conversation about their infertility. But let drop that you know of an infertility expert, and their ears perk up. Mention that you are writing a book about it, and they start to come out of the woodwork. Old college friends, next-door neighbors, and office colleagues all want to hear anything you have to offer—a new procedure, an article to read.

Today's infertile couples have more treatments available than in the past. Just twenty-five years ago, there were no drugs to induce ovulation, no microsurgical techniques to unblock fallopian tubes, the vas deferens, or epididymis. In vitro fertilization was only a dream. There is now a growing array of infertility therapies and providers of such services.

And infertile couples, possibly more than any other health consumers, shop around. They are highly informed and carefully weigh their doctor's advice, along with tidbits garnered through the grapevine. If they have the opportunity, they talk with other infertile couples about the kinds of tests and treatments they have received and what combinations of drugs they have tried. They are determined to find a way to have their own children.

And more men, who traditionally have found it difficult to express their feelings about infertility, are seeking help. Male feelings about producing an heir run deep, and the traditional view of infertility as a woman's problem is on the way out. Infertility is a couple's problem best treated with the full participation of the husband, who, like his wife, accounts for the fertility problem at least 25 percent of the time. The remaining 50 percent of cases are caused by a combination of male and female factors.

This is a book for couples. It examines how the *couple*, not just the husband or wife, can deal with the problems of infertility. It includes information from specialists in male and female fertility to show you how both husband and wife share the challenge of infertility. This way, you can understand what's happening to you as well as to your partner as you work through your fertility problems together.

We will lead you through the systematic, thorough evaluation and treatment of infertility. You'll find a detailed look at the step-by-step process by which infertility tests and treatments are conducted. You will see why certain tests should be performed at specific times so that you get the best use out of them and avoid visiting the doctor unnecessarily. You'll be taken on a day-by-day look at how your doctor determines where the baby-making problem lies and the treatments that will help produce healthy babies. Along the way, you'll learn about the multitude of new treatments and techniques now available to couples. At the end of most chapters, you'll find a list of questions to think about and discuss with your doctor if you are considering whether to have a particular test or to go through a particular treatment.

In instances where we believe one test or treatment is superior to another, we tell you so. We try to make it clear that this is our opinion based on our own experiences. That opinion may not necessarily be shared by all fertility specialists.

While doing our research, we contacted more than fifty of the top medical experts in their fields for the latest developments in infertility diagnosis and treatment. But this book is more than an up-to-date medical guide to fertility. We also consider social, psychological, religious, and legal perspectives on the latest fertility treatments, as well as recent statistics on treatment successes.

The Couple's Guide to Fertility seeks to show couples how they can restore the natural rhythms of life and fulfill their dreams of having a family. The book includes stories about real people who describe, in their own words, what it's like to go through the sometimes trying times of infertility diagnosis and treatment.

We wrote this book to help all couples understand the newest infertility treatments and techniques. In order to do this, we have translated medical terminology into ordinary language. We also include a directory of fertility specialists throughout the United States and fertility centers in Canada. Working with your doctor, you can use the directory to help you find a fertility specialist who may be the best for your particular problem.

PREFACE TO REVISED EDITION

In the five years since *The Couple's Guide to Fertility* was published, the fertility field has continued to make advances. We have included new developments and treatments that were not yet available when we wrote the first edition. Examples include a new method of evaluating the shape of sperm to better predict their fertilizing capability, and a technique to inseminate a single sperm directly into the egg that has revolutionized the treatment of severe male factor infertility. In vitro fertilization success rates have doubled, making this a more viable alternative for couples who need advanced treatment.

All of the statistics regarding fertility have been updated, as has the directory of fertility specialists. The directory includes more information about each doctor and clinic to help you locate the best treatment possible.

Feedback from readers helped us in planning this revision. They asked for more information about secondary infertility, the problem faced by couples trying to have a second baby. They also asked about pregnancy after fertility treatments, a concern for women who may face high-risk pregnancies and an area that Dr. Berger now addresses in his fertility practice. This edition contains two new chapters specifically on these topics.

We hope that couples will use this new edition as a guide to asking the right questions and gaining the information they need to enhance their chances of having a baby.

PREFACE TO THIRD EDITION

I t's time once again to revise *The Couple's Guide to Fertility*. Since the last edition was published seven years ago, the fertility field has made many significant advancements. To help readers keep up with this burgeoning area, we have included new developments and treatments, some of which were not even thought of when we wrote the original version of this book a dozen years ago. For example, advances in in vitro fertilization using a single sperm injected into the egg now lead to a 40 percent or better take-home-baby rate at some top fertility centers.

This edition also contains the latest research from Drs. Berger and Goldstein. Dr. Berger developed the technique of outpatient tubal reversals and has the most experience with this procedure in the world. He also has done extensive research with a tiny scope that is inserted into the fallopian tube, research that shows how previously unseen factors inside the tube lead to unexplained infertility. Dr. Goldstein has been focusing on the effect, other than infertility, of a varicocele (a varicose vein in the scrotum) on men's health. He has compelling evidence that men with varicoceles, whether fertile or infertile, are at risk for lower testosterone levels. Simple microsurgical varicocele repair increases their testosterone levels. He has also developed new microsurgical techniques to correct blockages that have increased success rates to as high as 99 percent.

The statistics regarding fertility have once again been updated, as has the directory of fertility specialists. The directory contains a comprehensive list of more than 1,000 fertility specialists, as well as a listing of Canadian IVF clinics, to help you find the best possible treatment. In addition, we have added an Internet Resources section as an aid in gathering information about fertility issues.

We also look at alternative approaches to fertility treatment, including herbal treatments, visualization, meditation, acupuncture, and other hands-on techniques, and tell you what we think is worthwhile and what isn't. The "Brave New World" of fertility now includes the possibility of cloning technologies, gene therapies, and women into their sixties having babies. Two new chapters in this edition deal specifically with these promising areas.

We hope this comprehensive new edition provides couples with information and insights that help them comfortably complete their families.

Note to the Reader

The stories throughout this book derive from interviews with dozens of infertile couples from around the country. Everything contained in them is real, except for the names and occupations, which have been changed to protect the couples' privacy.

Cynthia's Story

"We had decided early in our marriage that we didn't necessarily have to have children," says Cynthia, who owns a real estate agency with her husband. "I had been pregnant and had an abortion before I had met Doug. When we decided not to have children, he had a vasectomy. After seventeen years together, we had settled into our marriage, done everything that we wanted. Then we changed our minds about children." Cynthia, thirty-six, and Doug, thirty-seven, decided to try to have a baby through donor insemination, and on their second attempt she became pregnant.

"It's important to be surrounded in the doctor's office with people who really care. Dr. Berger and his staff made me and Doug feel real comfortable about the procedure we chose, even though both of us were embarrassed about it at first," Cynthia says. When she was five months pregnant, she went back to visit Dr. Berger to tell him how well the pregnancy was going. "Everything had fallen into place for us," she says.

As Cynthia left the doctor's office, a woman in the waiting area saw the spring in her step, as well as her obvious condition. "Did you get pregnant here?" she asked. Cynthia beamed and nodded, and the woman smiled in response. "Then there's hope for me too," she said.

Part One

WHAT'S GOING ON

1

THE ORCHESTRATION OF CONCEPTION

Like a good orchestra, reproduction requires an intricate combination of various parts synchronized to perform at just the right time. Reproductive organs produce the basic notes necessary for reproduction. Fertility hormones signal when and how long to play the notes that lead to fertilization.

The fertilization process begins with sperm entering through the vagina and swimming upstream through the cervix and uterus to the fallopian tubes. One sperm, one-thousandth of an inch long, swimming six inches to reach the egg, is analogous to a man swimming a hundred miles, or across the English Channel three times. No wonder, then, that among the millions that began the long journey, perhaps only a few dozen sperm will arrive at the egg. Only one will penetrate and enter it. As it is dividing, the fertilized egg must be transported into the uterus at just the right time to implant itself in a suitable spot for adequate nourishment, development, and growth over the months ahead.

Conception and Fertility

Before a couple can conceive naturally, several basic physiologic conditions must be met. The man must produce a sufficient number of normal, actively moving sperm. The woman must produce a healthy egg and must release the egg from one of her ovaries and have it picked up by the adjacent fallopian tube. The tube must be open and function normally so that the egg, after fertilization, can find its way into the uterus.

3

The man's sperm need open pathways so that they can pass from the testicles, where they are produced, out through the penis at the time of ejaculation. The man must be able to ejaculate and deposit the sperm into the vagina. The sperm have to travel up through fertile mucus produced by the cervix to reach the uterus and then through the fallopian tubes in order to reach the egg.

If the woman has ovulated and the egg has been released, the sperm must be able to penetrate and fertilize the egg. The woman's reproductive organs must be ready to receive the sperm and allow them to migrate from the vagina through the cervix and into a fallopian tube. Her tubes must be healthy and be able to help the sperm get to the egg. Then they will protect and nourish the fertilized egg to deliver it into the uterus, where it can develop fully.

The hormones that control production of sperm and eggs are called gonadotropins, which means they stimulate the gonads. These fertility hormones originate in the pituitary gland, a pea-sized extension of the brain located just behind the bridge of the nose. Men and women produce the same two pituitary gonadotropins, follicle-stimulating hormone (FSH) and luteinizing hormone (LH). In men, these hormones stimulate production of sperm and testosterone in the testicles; in women, they stimulate production of eggs, estrogen, and progesterone by the ovaries.

FSH governs the first half of the woman's menstrual cycle, stimulating the development of the egg and signaling the ovary to produce estrogen. On or about day fourteen of a normal twenty-eight-day cycle, the LH level suddenly rises to a sharp peak and then falls, stimulating release of the mature egg. Simultaneously, the egg-bearing sac, or follicle, begins producing progesterone. At this stage in the cycle, the follicle becomes known as the corpus luteum ("yellow body" in Latin).

Progesterone, along with estrogen, directs the lining of the uterus to produce a lush blanket of blood vessels and glands that secrete the nourishment needed for the fertilized egg to survive—like a seed sprouting in fertile soil. Unless an embryo has implanted, about two weeks after the corpus luteum is formed it stops making progesterone, and the woman menstruates, shedding the uterine lining, and the cycle starts over again.

It is not surprising, with such precise signals and directions, that these finely tuned reproductive instruments fail to perform exactly right from time to time. There is a relatively short period in each cycle during which the egg may be fertilized—probably only about eight to twelve hours. You don't have to make love precisely on the day of ovulation (the day the egg

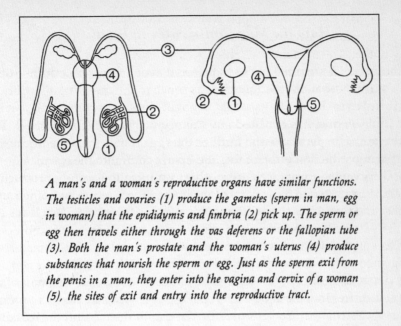

A man's and a woman's reproductive organs have similar functions. The testicles and ovaries (1) produce the gametes (sperm in man, egg in woman) that the epididymis and fimbria (2) pick up. The sperm or egg then travels either through the vas deferens or the fallopian tube (3). Both the man's prostate and the woman's uterus (4) produce substances that nourish the sperm or egg. Just as the sperm exit from the penis in a man, they enter into the vagina and cervix of a woman (5), the sites of exit and entry into the reproductive tract.

is released from the follicle) since healthy sperm may survive for days inside a woman's reproductive tract. The most fertile time in a typical twenty-eight-day cycle is most likely between days thirteen and fifteen.

Man and Woman: How They Are Similar

Everyone recognizes that a man and a woman have two distinct, separate reproductive physiologies, but they actually have many similarities (see diagram). A man's sperm (the male gamete) develops inside his testicles (1) and then enters the epididymis (2). Similarly, a woman's egg (the female gamete) first forms in the ovaries (1) and is picked up by the fringed ends, or fimbria (2), of the fallopian tube. As the sperm travels through the vas deferens (3) and the egg is transported through the fallopian tube (3), they both develop and grow during their time within these thin tubes. The man's prostate (4) and the woman's uterus (4), both about the same size and in the same approximate location within the body, produce nourishing substances for either the sperm or the fertilized egg. As the sperm exit from the penis (5), they enter the vagina and cervix (5)—the sites of exit or entry into the man's and woman's reproductive tract.

How the Man Contributes to Fertility

Although men are often not as expressive about the impact of infertility as women, husbands contribute just as much to the causes of infertility as do their wives. It can't be assumed, if a wife doesn't get pregnant, that it's her problem and that her husband's reproductive system is normal. The male side of the fertility issue must also be examined, from the beginning of sperm production through the release of sperm into the ejaculate.

The glands, organs, and tubes that comprise the male reproductive system are located in three parts of the body—the scrotum, abdomen, and penis. The scrotum is the sac that holds a man's testicles. Sperm leave the testicles bathed in testicular fluid, enter a cluster of microscopic tubules at the top of each testicle, and then move into a tightly coiled, fifteen-foot-long tube called the epididymis. From the epididymis, sperm enter the vas deferens, a fifteen-inch-long tube about as thick as a venetian blind cord, that rises into the abdomen. From the vas, sperm and testicular fluid enter the ejaculatory duct, formed by the end of the vas and the exit duct of the seminal vesicle, a gland that produces approximately 65 percent of the semen. The ejaculatory duct empties into the bulb of the urethra. Here, sperm from each testicle combine with a mixture of fluid produced in the prostate gland, which empties into the bulb of the urethra through a separate duct. Muscles surrounding the urethra contract rhythmically to cause ejaculation, the sudden spurt of semen from the penis.

Male Hormones

The male reproductive system takes its cues from male sex hormones (androgens). At puberty, these hormones trigger a man's testicles, penis, and pubic hair to grow, his beard to sprout, his voice to change, his muscles to bulk up, and his sex drive to escalate. Once he has matured, a continuous flow of testosterone and other androgens from his testicles helps maintain these secondary sexual characteristics.

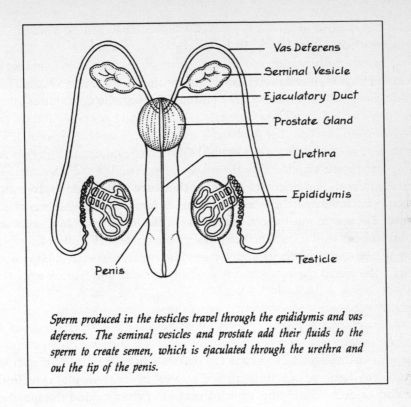

Sperm produced in the testicles travel through the epididymis and vas deferens. The seminal vesicles and prostate add their fluids to the sperm to create semen, which is ejaculated through the urethra and out the tip of the penis.

Sperm Production in the Testicles

The main instruments of the male reproductive system are the testicles, which manufacture sperm, the tailed microscopic cells that carry a man's genetic potential to a woman's unfertilized egg. The testicles typically produce 50,000 new sperm every minute of every day at puberty until a man is well into his seventies or older.

Mature sperm take roughly three months to evolve from primitive sperm cells. The early sperm forms divide several times while in the seminiferous tubules (the tiny tubes inside the testicles where sperm are produced) before they are fully mature. A mature sperm cell has one-half the chromosome content of all other body cells. About 50 percent of the sperm contain the genetic coding for maleness, the Y chromosome, and the other 50 percent contain the X chromosome, which specifies femaleness when paired with another X chromosome from the egg. A man has both an X and a Y chromosome, and a woman two X chromosomes. So a sperm determines a baby's sex.

When the fully mature sperm leave the testicles, they aren't yet able to swim on their own and aren't capable of fertilizing a woman's eggs. They acquire these abilities during their journey through the epididymis.

Epididymis

The epididymis is a tightly coiled, ultra-thin tube that fits into a two-inch space behind the testicle. The epididymis is like a swimming school for sperm. The sperm must spend some time in the epididymis to acquire the ability to swim well and attain their full fertilizing potential. As they take their two- to twelve-day journey through the epididymis, the special environment within the epididymis accelerates their ability to swim and fertilize eggs.

Vas Deferens

The now-mature sperm enter the vas deferens in preparation for ejaculation. A vas deferens (the tube cut and tied off in a vasectomy) runs from the end of each epididymis upward into the pelvis behind the bladder. Each vas is part of a bundle of veins, arteries, nerves, and connective tissues known as the spermatic cord.

Through its inner channel as thin as a hair on your head, the muscular vas carries sperm from the testicle to the ejaculatory duct. The vas, along with the epididymis, stores an estimated 700 million sperm at a time. During ejaculation, the two tubes (one from each testicle) contract to propel the sperm and testicular fluid into the ejaculatory duct and the urethra. There, the sperm join with the fluids, enzymes, and nutrients in the secretions of the seminal vesicles and prostate gland to form semen.

Seminal Vesicles and Prostate Gland

Each seminal vesicle secretes a fluid rich in the sugar fructose that nourishes the sperm and forms the major portion of the ejaculate. The seminal vesicles also make proteins that cause the normal ejaculate to come out white and lumpy. The prostate, a gland that surrounds the bladder and produces additional seminal fluid, has its own exit ducts leading to the urethra. The prostate makes enzymes that dissolve the lumpiness and cause the normal ejaculate to liquefy within ten to fifteen minutes after ejaculation. In preparing for an orgasm, the seminal vesicles and prostate pass most of their fluid into the urethra. That's why it takes a little while for most men to have a second ejaculation: the seminal vesicles and prostate need time to manufacture and emit more seminal fluid.

Ejaculation

Pleasurable sensations to the penis stimulate the muscles surrounding the base of the urethra to contract and convey semen out of the penis. The urethra also conveys urine from the bladder, but urine can destroy sperm, so semen and urine never mix in a healthy male. A sphincter muscle contracts during sexual stimulation, closing down the exit from the bladder to the urethra, which is why it's difficult for a man to urinate when he has an erection.

Sperm Penetration and Fertilization

Only a small number of rapidly moving sperm complete the journey to the egg; once sperm get to the egg, they also have to be able to penetrate it. Some men have normal sperm counts and motility (movement of the sperm or their ability to swim), yet their apparently normal wives don't become pregnant. The normal number and motility of the sperm provide no clues to the sperm's ability to penetrate eggs. The fertilizing potential of even the fastest swimming sperm varies from one man to another and, just as sperm counts do, from one ejaculate to the next from the same man.

Sperm need energy for their long journey to the egg. They pick up a boost of energy as they pass through the epididymis. The energized sperm can now swim up to and burrow itself into the egg. But just getting to the egg isn't enough; the sperm needs another burst of energy in order to penetrate the egg. The sperm sustains this high energy state for a few milliseconds, less than a blink of the eye, to attach to the outer layer of the egg and burrow its way inside.

When sperm leave the testicles, they don't yet have the ability to fertilize an egg. In the 1950s, reproductive scientists began studying the interaction of sperm and egg in the laboratory, and soon found that sperm have to spend time within the woman's reproductive tract to become fully capable of fertilization.

Developing the capacity to penetrate an egg is called capacitation. Only capacitized sperm that have gone through this final stage of maturing can penetrate the membrane that surrounds the egg. This final stage is called the acrosome reaction, during which the "stocking cap" on the sperm head, called the acrosome, dissolves, releasing enzymes that create a hole in the egg's cell wall so that the sperm can penetrate through the clear outer coat of the egg, known as the zona pellucida.

Once a sperm attaches to the zona pellucida, its tail begins to beat in a furious, whiplike motion, a sign of capacitation. Now the sperm can start penetrating the egg as it dissolves a tiny hole in the egg's outer membrane.

The egg doesn't just sit back passively. Once a single sperm has fused with the egg surface, the egg "grabs" the one sperm and helps bring it inside. At a certain point, the sperm's whiplike motion is no longer needed. Meanwhile, the egg immediately transforms its outer wall into an impenetrable barrier to all other sperm. (If more than one sperm fertilizes an egg, there would be too many chromosomes, since each sperm and egg carry one-half of the chromosomes needed for a new individual.)

Inside the egg, the chromosomes from the sole successful sperm fuse with those of the egg. The fertilized egg now has the genetic material needed to produce a new human being.

What the Woman Brings to Fertility

The woman's reproductive system complements the man's, but keeps time to a different schedule. Under the supervision of the gonadotropin hormones FSH and LH, one of the two ovaries normally produces a mature egg each month. Once released from the ovary, the egg must be gathered into the fallopian tube for its journey through the tube to each the uterus. If the egg meets healthy sperm on its way, it may become fertilized. When the fertilized egg implants in the uterus, pregnancy has begun.

The functions of the various parts of the female anatomy must harmonize with the male's for a couple to achieve a pregnancy.

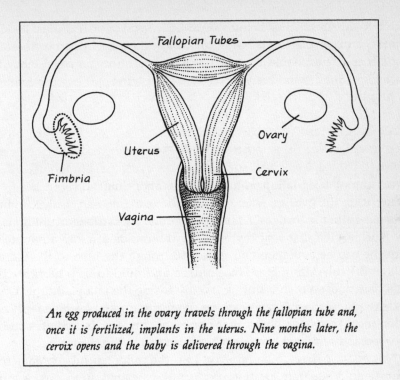

An egg produced in the ovary travels through the fallopian tube and, once it is fertilized, implants in the uterus. Nine months later, the cervix opens and the baby is delivered through the vagina.

Vagina

The vagina is a muscular, four-inch-long canal that provides an exit for menstrual blood and an entrance for semen. Normally flat, like a collapsed balloon, the vagina can stretch to accommodate a tampon, a penis, or a baby's head.

Cervix

The one-inch-long cervix lies at the top of the vagina and serves as the entrance to the uterus. In fact, it's more properly called the "uterine cervix." A mixture of powerful muscle and tough connective tissue, the cervix must remain closed throughout the pregnancy, but then has to expand to allow the baby's head to pass through during labor.

Most of the time, the cervix produces a barrier of sticky mucus that prevents the invasion of sperm, bacteria, and other organisms from the vagina to the uterus. Just before ovulation, however, sperm must be able to pass through the cervix. Only for a few days each month does the cervix become hospitable to sperm by changing the mucus consistency, allowing sperm to swim freely through to the uterus and enter the fallopian tubes.

Fallopian Tubes

The macaroni-sized fallopian tubes stretch about four to six inches from the uterus to the ovaries, where they feather out into ends called fimbria (which is Latin for "fringes"). Lining the fimbria and tubes are millions of tiny hairlike cilia that beat rhythmically thousands of times a minute to catch the egg at ovulation and move it through the tube to the uterus. Cells in the tube's lining produce mucus and fluid to help lubricate the egg's path and nourish it during its stay inside the fallopian tube. Once inside the tube, the egg meets sperm. If an egg doesn't become fertilized within eight to twelve hours after ovulation, the egg deteriorates and is absorbed and removed like any other dead cell in the body.

Not just a passive pipe or a conduit, the fallopian tube is an active organ with its separate locations performing separate functions. A muscular ligament, the fimbria ovarica, joins the end of the tube and the ovary; its contraction during ovulation pulls the fimbria immediately adjacent to the ovary. Like a vacuum cleaner, the fimbria then captures the egg and draws it into the tube. The middle section of the tube moves the egg and sperm toward each other by muscular contractions and the action of the beating cilia. The uterine end acts like a sphincter and prevents the egg from being released into the uterus until just the right time for implantation, which is about five to seven days after ovulation.

The Ovaries

The two almond-sized ovaries are perched just within the fallopian tubes' grasp. They are stocked with a lifetime of eggs at birth. Each month prior to ovulation, the brain triggers the release of follicle-stimulating hormone, which causes egg-bearing follicles to develop near the surface of each ovary.

Just as sperm struggle to survive the conception obstacle course, only one of the many eggs stimulated each month matures fully. The dominant follicle contains this egg and releases suppressor hormones to destroy all the other eggs that may be starting to mature each cycle. The egg in the dominant follicle matures fully; the rest shrivel and die.

The pinpoint-sized egg grows slowly its first week, then rapidly accelerates to about the size of a pencil point at the end of the second week as the cells lining the inner wall of the follicle produce estrogen. Subsequently, LH released from the brain stimulates the one dominant egg to burst forth from the grape-size follicle and be scooped up by one of the fallopian tubes. Most women ovulate about thirty-six hours after the surge of luteinizing hormone. (Ovulation-prediction test kits actually detect LH in the urine just after the LH surge.)

The fingerlike projections at the end of the fallopian tubes look a little like a catcher's mitt, but they don't always gather in an egg as easily as a catcher receives a pitched ball. Sometimes the egg isn't released near the end of the tube, but may gently drop from the surface of the ovary and float in a puddle of fluid in the bottom of the pelvic cavity (the cul-de-sac). The egg can float for several hours in this area and still be picked up by the tube and be fertilized, since the cul-de-sac has a smooth surface that allows easy movement of the egg and the fimbrial ends of the tubes also float in the fluid in the cul-de-sac.

The release of eggs from follicles month after month leaves the ovaries' surfaces wrinkled and full of pits. At ovulation, a hole appears in the surface of the ovary. Following ovulation, the corpus luteum forms and produces progesterone during the second half of the cycle to prepare the uterus for a pregnancy. The corpus luteum leaves a yellow stain on the ovary. In normally ovulating women, the ovaries have lots of depressions and yellow stains from previous ovulations.

Uterus

The uterus, the shape and size of a pear, sits at the top of the reproductive tract. It consists of a narrow inner mucus-membrane lining surrounded by a thick wall of muscle. Usually the cavity holds less than a quarter of a teaspoon of liquid, yet it can expand up to the size of a watermelon during pregnancy.

The lining of the uterus first proliferates, or thickens, under the influence of estrogen early in the menstrual cycle. Later, under the influence of progesterone, the lining secretes nourishing substances to support a fertilized egg that's ready to implant and develop into a fetus.

For Some, Things Have Gotten Out of Tune

Because of the intricate sequence of events required for conception, it's not surprising that many couples' ability to reproduce has somehow gotten out of tune. Most likely, you have tried to have a baby with no luck, maybe even for years, and you probably know other couples who have experienced similar difficulties. You have read about infertility in newspapers and magazines, or heard couples discussing their infertility on radio or TV talk shows. Infertility has even become a popular subject for TV dramas and sitcoms.

If you are just beginning to investigate your fertility problem, you may feel frustrated, depressed, or hopeless and may also be somewhat afraid of the workup necessary to diagnose your problem. If you have already begun fertility treatments, you know how stressful they can be at times, with the lack of privacy at the doctor's office, the grind of sex on schedule, and the time lost from work for tests and treatments. The people who love you, your family and friends, may make insensitive remarks that hurt because you haven't told them about your infertility. Once you have told them, they may come to pity you or make light of something you must face every day. The worst part is that empty feeling when you've done all that you can, but you don't succeed, and the menstrual period starts again. Then you have to go through the whole process for another month.

National Fertility Surveys

Although most couples coping with infertility feel isolated, there are in fact millions of others struggling with the same problem. Near the end of the baby boom in 1955, university researchers conducted the first national surveys to collect information on fertility, family planning, and maternal and child health. The surveys proved so useful that the federal government began funding similar studies.

The 1995 survey used personal interviews with nearly 11,000 women age fifteen to forty-four. The results show that 5.4 million women in this age group had an impaired ability to have children, or about one in eleven nationally. Government researchers concluded that there was an increase in the number of childless women due largely to delayed childbearing among the baby boomers who came of reproductive age.

About 2.1 million married couples with wives between fifteen and forty-four were considered infertile. One million of these women were childless (what doctors refer to as primary infertility), and 1.1 million had one or more children before they became infertile (secondary infertility).

But the survey's methodology vastly underestimates the true number of infertile couples. The survey defined impaired ability to conceive (fecundity) as the inability to become pregnant during a three-year period. However, fertility specialists and the American Society for Reproductive Medicine consider couples infertile if they have not conceived after twelve months of unprotected intercourse. In using a different definition of infertility, the government survey missed cases of infertility of less than three years in length.

The survey also may have missed other cases because most couples don't know that they have a fertility problem until they face it. Many couples are infertile and don't seek medical care or can't afford to pursue the many new solutions now available.

Even these underestimated numbers show that there are at least 2 million more infertile women today than in 1995 who are not going to conceive spontaneously and need fertility treatments. Data collected by the American Urological Association indicate that there are more than 2.5 million infertile or subfertile American men.

2

THE
MEDICAL
FACTS

---

*What Stands
in Our Way of Making
a Family*

Over the past few decades, we have witnessed an explosion in medical knowledge, including many exciting new ways to combat diseases and to control fertility through medications and operations. Unfortunately, not all of these advancements turn out to be as beneficial as originally intended.

Two Steps Forward, One Step Back

As the Pill came into widespread use in the 1960s, it became apparent that early versions had some serious side effects, including increasing a woman's risk of stroke and heart attack and, possibly, cervical cancer. So women in the 1970s began switching to intrauterine devices—until the reproductive risks associated with certain IUDs became widely publicized and most of the devices were taken off the market.

Another birth control method, sterilization, became widely available in the early 1960s and has become so popular that it is now the contraceptive method of choice among today's couples. As these operations grew more common, a select group of surgeons developed their microsurgical skills in order to reverse the operation if the individual later had a change of mind. Even so, some operations are so destructive that only a little more than half of the more than 20 million people who have had sterilization operations can have them successfully reversed if they want to be able to have children again.

In the late 1960s, nearly every American city had an epidemic of gon-

---

orrhea; at the time, the disease could be treated effectively by penicillin. By the late 1970s, cases of penicillin-resistant gonorrhea had become a new public health problem. Throughout this period, millions of men and women became infected with a then-obscure bacteria called chlamydia, also resistant to penicillinlike antibiotics. Unfortunately, treatment recommendations to doctors by infectious disease experts and the U.S. Public Health Service during the 1960s and 1970s did not include treatment with antibiotics that were effective against chlamydia. Not until the early 1980s did infectious disease experts realize the full extent of the insidious fertility problems caused by chlamydia.

Although gonorrhea and chlamydia led the venereal disease (VD) epidemic, a variety of other microorganisms also contributed to pelvic infections. These infections often led to scarring of fallopian tubes, which in turn led to a dramatic rise in ectopic (tubal) pregnancies. In addition, the sexually liberated lifestyle that often exposed people to sexually transmitted diseases may also have primed their bodies' immune systems to attack and kill sperm, which in turn led to infertility.

The advent of new, more powerful medications dominated the pharmaceutical scene of the 1960s and 1970s. Several of these drugs, including two of the top sellers—one for ulcers, the other for heart disease—have detrimental side effects on sperm that can impair a man's fertility. The introduction of specific cancer treatments has contributed to a high cure rate for certain cancers, such as cancer of the testicles. But, again, serious fertility-reducing side effects make most cancer treatments a problem for couples who want to have babies.

To keep tabs on all these new drugs, the federal government in the mid-1960s began requiring drug companies to provide medical evidence to support all new drug claims. But this was already too late for the sons and daughters whose mothers had taken the drug diethylstilbestrol (DES) in the 1950s in hopes of preventing miscarriages. The link between DES exposure and deformities of both daughters' and sons' reproductive organs came to light during the 1970s. Many DES daughters were unable to conceive or couldn't carry to term. Many DES men are subfertile.

The VD Epidemic

One of the primary causes of infertility among couples today, particularly among young men and women, is venereal infection due to a wide variety of sexually transmitted diseases (STDs). If left untreated, these STDs can infect a woman's upper reproductive tract, causing scar tissue and damage to the delicate membranes lining the fallopian tubes. In the man such infection can also cause scarring and damage to the delicate ducts of the epididymis, vas deferens, and ejaculatory ducts.

Even a single sexually transmitted infection can permanently damage the lining of the fallopian tubes or epididymis and partially or totally block them. With each episode of STD, the chances of blocked tubes in both men and women increase. A woman who has been infected is more likely to have chronic pelvic pain than other women, and she is more susceptible to repeated infections and ectopic (tubal) pregnancies if she does get pregnant.

The sheer number of these sexually transmitted infections is astounding. More than 65 million Americans are infected with one or more STDs. In the United States each year there are more than 3 million cases of chlamydia infection, 1 million cases of gonorrhea infection, and more than 10 million viral infections. Infections from common bacteria commonly found in the reproductive tract, such as streptococcus, and other organisms—mycoplasma, ureaplasma, trichomonas—and viruses such as cytomegalovirus can all lead to infertility.

These reproductive infections may affect the fertility of both women and men by scarring either the fallopian tubes or the sperm-carrying tubes. In women, the uterus, fallopian tubes, ovaries, and adjacent structures usually become infected by organisms traveling up from the vagina and cervix. The body's response to these infections tends to cause scars (adhesions) to form in and around the tubes. These scars may prevent sperm from meeting the egg inside the tube, or prevent the tube from transporting the fertilized egg to the uterus, which can lead to a tubal pregnancy. For men, the scar formation may close off the epididymis, the sperm-carrying tube on top of each of the testicles.

As described in the medical textbook *Pelvic Inflammatory Disease*, edited by Drs. Berger and Westrom, inflammation of the uterus, fallopian tubes, or ovaries seems to hit the upper reproductive tract with a one-two punch of infections. First, gonorrhea or chlamydia bacteria infections damage the immune-protective mechanisms of the tubes, leaving the tubes open to infections with other bacteria normally residing in the vagina or cervix. Bacteria from the vagina and cervix may ascend to the uterus during menstruation. Just as an open cut on your finger can become infected, the open blood vessels of the uterus are more susceptible to an attack by bacteria once the uterine lining has been sloughed off. Viral infections, such as cytomegalovirus, may also tax a woman's immune defenses, allowing bacteria to establish themselves more easily and do damage.

When a sexually active woman complains of lower abdominal pain or shows signs of pelvic tenderness, the diagnosis of pelvic inflammatory disease (PID) must be considered. Acute pelvic infections often begin with pain in the lower abdomen that becomes increasingly worse over two or three days. The pain may become so severe that a woman has trouble walking and urinating. If the condition is not treated properly, an abscess may form, and if the abscess ruptures, the infection may spread throughout the woman's abdominal cavity, requiring emergency surgery. But most PID infections have no symptoms, so they go undiagnosed and untreated, yet may leave their mark by forming scar tissue and damaging the tubal lining. The male equivalent of PID is epididymitis, which can also lead to chronic pain and permanently scarred and blocked ducts.

How Many Become Infertile from STDs

Infectious disease experts have shown that after one episode of PID, 35 percent of women become infertile. After two episodes, the infertility rate is 50 to 60 percent, and after three episodes, more than 75 percent.

More than 8 million American women have been diagnosed with PID. No one knows how many additional millions of cases go undetected. Studies have shown that at least as many women have had asymptomatic pelvic infections and didn't know it until they tried, unsuccessfully, to get pregnant.

"Silent" Symptoms

Because its symptoms are often "silent," chlamydia often cause more severe damage than other infections. Although men may notice a burning sensation during urination and a puslike discharge from the penis within a week of infection, most women don't feel any symptoms and consequently don't seek treatment. About 70 percent of women infected with chlamydia show no symptoms; the rest may notice only a yellowish color to the vaginal discharge. About half of the men with so-called NGU (non-gonococcal urethritis or inflammation of the urethra *not* due to gonorrhea) and nearly half of those with acute epididymitis are infected with chlamydia.

Both men and women can carry PID-causing organisms without showing symptoms. These infected carriers unwittingly pass the organisms on to their sex partners, who may carry the bacteria for weeks, months, or years. More than half of the women with closed fallopian tubes report no history of PID, which means either that they never had severe enough complaints to make them visit a doctor or that the doctor failed to make the correct diagnosis. Many women with PID symptoms are mistakenly diagnosed with a bowel infection.

Epidemiologists now recognize that a chlamydia infection often accompanies a gonorrhea infection. About half of the women who have an acute inflammation of the fallopian tubes harbor both chlamydia and gonorrhea infections, and 15 to 30 percent of heterosexual men infected with gonorrhea who have an inflamed urethra have a simultaneous infection with chlamydia. That is why during an initial workup, reproductive specialists who recognize the importance of these issues routinely order screening tests to detect the presence of both chlamydia and gonorrhea, as well as other potentially harmful, disease-causing bacteria.

Other Organisms

In women, gonorrhea and chlamydia infections are thought to cause about 75 percent of all cases of PID. The rest come from a variety of other bacteria in the vagina and cervix, which may be carried "piggyback" by sperm into the uterus. Insertion of an intrauterine device (IUD), a dilatation and curettage (D&C) operation, and other procedures that involve passing an instrument through the cervix into the uterus may also carry bacteria into the upper reproductive tract.

Infections with mycoplasma and a related organism, ureaplasma, are also associated with ectopic pregnancies, spontaneous abortions, and premature births. In males, mycoplasma or ureaplasma infections can cause urethritis and may impair sperm motility and fertilizing ability.

Sex and PID

In the 1960s and 1970s, more people started having sex at an earlier age than in prior decades. They were also more likely to have more sexual partners, which exposed them to more STDs. Since infertility often goes unrecognized until many years after the infection has occurred, much of today's increase in infertility is related to the increase in sexually transmitted infections acquired over the past three decades.

The sobering news for the victims of PID is that once an infection has damaged the tubes, medications can't repair the damage. (Surgery may be successful, depending on the extent of the problem.) So new antibiotics, even those active against chlamydia, cannot necessarily prevent the infertility once symptoms of the infection are recognized. To have a sizable impact on STD-related tubal infertility, infections have to be stopped before they reach the fallopian tubes. One way to accomplish this is to prevent the spread of infection from one partner to another by screening for "silent" infections of the lower reproductive tract before they can cause damage higher up.

Regular use of condoms significantly reduces the risk of acquiring sexually transmitted infections. Latex (rubber) condoms have proven effective in preventing not only bacterial infections, such as chlamydia and gonorrhea, but also viruses, including the herpes virus, human papilloma virus, cytomegalovirus, hepatitis B, and the AIDS virus.

Water molecules are much smaller than viruses, so if water can't get through a condom, then a virus can't either. The AIDS virus is much smaller, at 120 nanometers (billionths of a meter) in diameter compared with the much larger gonorrhea bacteria, at 1,000 nanometers. Sperm, in comparison, are huge, at 3,000 nanometers in diameter. The failure of condoms to protect against STDs is due much more often to not using the condom than to a defect in the condom itself.

The Risks of a Tubal Pregnancy

As the number of STDs and subsequent infertility has risen, so has the incidence of ectopic pregnancies, or pregnancies outside of the uterus, usually in the fallopian tubes. The primary reason for the increased incidence of tubal pregnancies is pelvic inflammatory disease. Because of damage to the delicate lining of the fallopian tube, which helps transport the egg to the uterus, PID can cause fertilized eggs to implant in the tubes before they reach the uterus. Women with a history of pelvic infection have at least four times the risk of ectopic pregnancy than women without a history of infection, and there is a tenfold increased risk of ectopic pregnancy among women with obvious tubal damage. About half of the women who have ectopic pregnancies become infertile.

The most common cause of ectopic pregnancy is previous salpingitis (fallopian tube inflammation). But other conditions that prevent the fertilized egg from reaching the uterus also predispose a woman to an ectopic pregnancy. Problems may arise from IUD use, fallopian tube surgery (such as plastic surgery to repair damaged tubes), surgery to remove all or part of a tube (salpingectomy), or tubal sterilization and previous tubal pregnancy. Other factors associated with a higher risk of tubal pregnancy include: abdominal or pelvic surgery, acute appendicitis, induced abortion, endometriosis, and exposure to DES in utero. Women who douche during the week after they ovulate, and cigarette smokers, too, appear to also have a higher risk of ectopic pregnancy.

Many women who have had abortions have obstructed fallopian tubes and pelvic scarring due to often "silent" infections following the abortions, and are therefore more likely to be infertile and have tubal pregnancies. This subtle problem of tubal infertility from asymptomatic infections has only recently become fully appreciated.

In the past, many early ectopic pregnancies weren't diagnosed before the fallopian tube ruptured and caused internal bleeding. Only those cases that progressed to a painful, serious, or life-threatening stage were diagnosed. Today early pregnancy testing (including highly sensitive, specific assays of the pregnancy hormone human chorionic gonadotropin, or hCG, and high-resolution ultrasound scans) and diagnostic laparoscopy have led to diagnosis of ectopic pregnancy within a week or two after a woman misses her period, leading to early treatment and less risk of tubal rupture.

Prolonged Use of IUDs and the Pill

New contraceptives introduced in the 1960s and 1970s added to fertility woes in the 1980s. While couples may have enjoyed new sexual freedom with highly effective contraceptives, they also may have contracted more

STDs by exposing themselves to more sex partners and by not using condoms, which could have helped prevent infection. The widespread use of intrauterine devices (IUDs) was also associated with an increase in pelvic inflammatory disease and infertility due to scarred fallopian tubes. And some women who took the Pill for years and then stopped once they planned to have a family have found that they are no longer ovulating and require fertility drugs to stimulate ovulation.

IUDs became the most popular form of birth control in the late 1960s and early 1970s when the safety of the Pill came into question. The high-dose oral contraceptives then available carried risks of increasing the chance of heart attack, stroke, and possibly cervical cancer. The switch to IUDs in the 1970s, along with a decrease in the use of condoms and diaphragms, may have unwittingly contributed to the rise in infertility.

An IUD works by causing an inflammatory reaction inside the uterine cavity, which prevents the embryo from implanting in the uterus.

Only after millions of American women were already using IUDs in the 1970s was the association between IUD use and an increased risk of PID fully appreciated. Thousands of women are believed to have suffered pelvic and uterine infections, ectopic pregnancies, and infertility while using the Dalkon Shield, which was removed from the market in 1974. Because of the legal problems encountered by the Dalkon Shield's manufacturer, most other IUD manufacturers withdrew their devices from the market. Now there are only two IUDs remaining, one copper IUD and one medicated, hormone-carrying IUD. These, too, carry the risk of PID.

Many studies have linked IUD use to tubal infertility. Two recent American studies report that childless women with tubal infertility were two to three times more likely to have used IUDs than women who have one child. IUD wearers with more than one sexual partner had a three to four times higher risk of tubal infertility, while IUD users with only one partner had no increased risk.

Inserting an IUD may increase a woman's risk of developing PID by giving bacteria and other organisms present in the vagina and cervix access to the upper reproductive tract. The bacteria may "wick" their way up on the tail of the IUD through the cervix and into the uterus, then move on into the fallopian tubes. The longer menstrual bleeding time associated with IUDs may also allow some bacteria easier entry to upper reproductive tract organs.

In the rare instance when an IUD user becomes pregnant with an IUD in place, the pregnancy is likely to be ectopic. The device is highly effective in preventing pregnancies within the uterus, but not those outside the uterus. IUD users have three to four times the rate of ectopic pregnancies, compared to women who don't use IUDs. (When several IUDs were available, women who used the steroid-containing Progestasert IUD appeared to have more tubal pregnancies than those who wore other IUDs.)

In contrast to the IUD, the Pill seems to protect women from developing PID to a certain extent. The hormones in oral contraceptives tend to reduce menstrual flow and produce a sticky cervical mucus that provides a barrier to infectious organisms, reducing their upward spread into the uterus.

Counterbalancing this possible protective effect is the increased risk of cervical infection, particularly with chlamydia, due to the growth of the cervical mucus membrane associated with Pill use. In addition, long-term Pill users may not menstruate or ovulate after they stop using the Pill. This condition, known as post-Pill amenorrhea, occurs because the Pill disrupts the natural rhythmic flow of hormones from the hypothalamus to the pituitary to the ovaries. This may pose a special problem for older women who have been on the Pill for many years because their ovaries may have become resistant to resuming ovulation.

Being on the Pill may make it harder to get pregnant once you go off, at least temporarily. The ongoing Nurses' Health Study of nearly 117,000 participants found about 2,000 former Pill users who did not become pregnant for one to two years after going off oral contraceptives. Eventually, 88 percent of them did become pregnant. This research may have the most significance for Pill users in their thirties. Women in this age group who are planning a pregnancy might want to switch to another form of contraception until they are ready to start trying to conceive, or it might take them longer than they expect.

Sterilization Operations

More than 25 million people have had sterilization operations over the past thirty years, some to gain more sexual freedom, others to curb the population explosion. Still others recognized the dangerous side effects of the high-dose Pill then in use and chose a more permanent form of birth control. Many individuals who chose sterilization now regret having been sterilized, and they want their fertility back.

Fortunately, with the advent of microsurgery, which uses high-powered magnification and surgical thread thinner than a hair, highly trained reproductive surgeons can now sew back together previously cut or tied-off fallopian tubes in women and sperm-carrying vas deferens in men, with up to 75 percent pregnancy rates in the best of hands.

Each year since around 1970, about 1.5 million people have opted for sterilization operations, the nation's most popular form of birth control. Yet as many as 10 percent each year not only regret having had these sterilizations but would like to have them reversed. Most do nothing about it, mainly because they don't know how successfully these "permanent" procedures can be reversed.

Couples are still choosing sterilization, and will continue to do so until a better, safer contraceptive is developed. And, concurrently, we can expect that the number of attempted sterilization reversals will continue unabated.

More Chances for More Miscarriages

The idea behind contraceptives is to prevent the sperm and egg from meeting, or to prevent the fertilized egg from implanting in the uterus. Even without contraceptives most fertilized eggs never develop into a live baby. About one-fourth of all pregnancies end in miscarriages, two-thirds of these within two weeks after conception—*before* a woman or her doctor becomes aware of the pregnancy.

Miscarriage has become an increasing problem for today's infertile couples. More women have postponed having children, and since the risk of miscarriage rises with the mother's age, miscarriages have become more common.

Traditionally, a woman had to have at least three miscarriages before a doctor would attempt to find the cause of "habitual spontaneous abortion." The rationale was that most women who have one or two miscarriages will eventually bear healthy babies without any need for treatment. However, for couples who delay having a baby until their thirties, many fertility specialists now investigate the problem of recurrent miscarriages sooner and won't arbitrarily make the couple wait until they have lost three pregnancies.

If a childless woman keeps miscarrying, this may suggest that she, her husband, or both of them are passing along a genetic defect. A chromosome analysis, called a karyotype, of each partner's blood can confirm a genetic problem. However, chromosome analysis is costly—as much as $1,000 for the couple—and provides an explanation for less than 2 or 3 percent of recurrent miscarriages. (Most repeat miscarriages are due to infections, hormone deficiencies, or immune system or anatomic problems, and not chromosome abnormalities.)

Combining sperm and egg to form a fetus is one of nature's most intricate processes, and it can go awry in many ways beyond incompatible chromosomes between husband and wife. An otherwise healthy woman can have a deficiency of the hormones she needs to sustain a growing fetus. A woman with an abnormally shaped uterus, for example with a septum (wall) in her uterus, may repeatedly lose pregnancies. Fibroids, or hard nodules, in the uterus can also lead to miscarriage by preventing the embryo from receiving an adequate blood supply after it has become implanted. Also, wearing an IUD or having an elective abortion or a D&C procedure can scar the uterus, making it difficult for a fetus to implant or grow.

Genital tract infections are also associated with miscarriage. Bacteria "piggybacked" on sperm can infect the lining of the uterus and sabotage the growing fetus. Viruses and bacteria from anywhere in a pregnant woman's body may also travel through the bloodstream and infect the fetus, or produce enzymes that trigger the release of prostaglandins and other chemicals that can cause her uterus to contract and send her into early labor. And recent experience from in vitro fertilization (IVF) clinics shows an increase in early miscarriages after embryo transfer when the husband has an unrecognized bacterial infection of the sperm or semen.

A woman's immune system can also malfunction, rejecting the embryo as a foreign body, since one-half of the fetus's genes come from the father. Normally, a pregnant woman's immune system must shield the fetus from her usual immune responses when she's not pregnant. If a woman has repeated miscarriages, her immune system may not recognize that she is pregnant and may fail to turn on its blocking response. This increases the chances that she will reject the pregnancy, often within days or weeks.

Sperm Busters

The immune system is like a night watchman prowling the spacious warehouse of our bodies from head to toe, checking out substances to see if they are friend or foe. Normally, friends are left alone, while foes get attacked by watchdoglike white blood cells and antibodies (blood proteins made by the immune system's white blood cells, to protect the body against invaders). Once the body has identified an invader, the immune system produces a specific antibody against it to help the white blood cells fight it off.

A man's body sometimes sees his own sperm as invaders and produces antibodies against them. These antisperm antibodies can attach to the sperm's surface and alter the sperm's ability to fertilize eggs. Women may also produce antibodies against sperm, interfering with sperm motility and fertilization.

Antisperm antibodies don't usually kill sperm, but more likely cause them to become vulnerable to attack by white blood cells. The antibodies can also interfere with fertilization by preventing sperm from penetrating through cervical mucus or by interfering with the sperm-egg interaction in the fallopian tubes, barring sperm from attaching to the egg or penetrating it.

Depending on where they attach themselves on the sperm, antibodies can interfere with sperm movement and fertilization. When antibodies attach to the sperm tail, the sperm can't swim as well. When antibodies attach to the sperm head, they are more likely to interfere with the sperm's ability to fertilize an egg.

No one knows why some women produce antisperm antibodies while others don't. Some women may be born with a genetic susceptibility that makes them react more to sperm, while others may turn on production of antisperm antibodies later in life.

A sexually active woman may be exposed to more than a trillion sperm in her lifetime. When too many sperm die within the reproductive tract or reach the abdominal cavity, the body acts to dispose of them by sending white blood cells to gobble them up. Once the immune system is turned on, it can produce antibodies against the sperm.

A woman who has had many sex partners is more likely to contract STDs. Her immune system reacts to these genital infections by producing antibodies against them. When the microorganisms attach to sperm, antibodies may form against both the bacteria and the sperm. In fact, some sperm antibody diagnostic tests give mixed results because they can't distinguish between antibodies against bacteria and antibodies against sperm with bacteria attached.

Animal studies suggest that anal intercourse may lead to antisperm antibody production whereas exposure to a healthy vagina or oral sex usually does not. When sperm come into contact with blood vessels in the rectum, the immune system may have a different response to sperm in the reproductive tract. Once discovered, the "invading" sperm may then have antibodies produced against them.

Antibodies might also play a role in miscarriages. Women who have recurrent miscarriages tend more often to have high levels of antisperm antibodies than women without a history of repeated miscarriages. Some doctors suspect that antisperm antibodies may interfere with normal embryo development. On the other hand, women who develop antibodies against sperm may also develop other immune system responses that may be involved in causing miscarriages.

Men produce antibodies against sperm only when their sperm come in contact with their own blood or fluids in tissues. When men are born, they have no sperm, and so their immune systems don't recognize sperm as "self" when they are produced later in life. Sperm develop within the testicles and are normally kept from exposure to the man's own blood (where antibodies could be produced against them) by a physical separation called the "blood-testis barrier." So, as far as the immune system is concerned, sperm develop "outside" the body and are "foreign."

When sperm get into body tissues—for example, after a vasectomy or trauma to the testicles, epididymis, or vas deferens—the body recognizes them as "foreign" and develops antibodies against them. These antibodies don't always impair a man's fertility, since men who have had vasectomies and then had them reversed have gotten their wives pregnant, but most men who have had vasectomies do develop sperm antibodies.

As in women, a genital infection can bring white blood cells into a man's genital tract and activate the immune system to fight off the infection. If the infection damages his genital tract, allowing sperm to come into contact with the blood, then antibodies may be produced against his sperm as well.

Two other conditions may also lead to antisperm antibody production in men. Cystic fibrosis, an inherited disease, is associated with missing sperm ducts. Twisting of the testicles, called torsion, can damage them. As with a vasectomy, these two problems may lead to antibody production by allowing sperm to escape into the bloodstream and be recognized by the immune system.

The location and number of antisperm antibodies also determines how damaging they may be. Antibodies attached to sperm cause more male fertility problems than antisperm antibodies circulating in the blood. And if less than 50 percent of the sperm have antibodies bound to them, the chances of a conception remain good if the sperm are otherwise normal.

New Medications, New Treatments

Many commonly used prescription drugs have been associated with infertility, mostly among men. Two popular drugs, the ulcer drug cimetidine (Tagamet) and the heart drug digitalis (Crystodigin), reduce a man's level of sex hormones and depress normal sperm formation. A medication used to treat ulcerative colitis, sulfasalazine, causes low sperm counts, decreases sperm motility, and increases the number of abnormally shaped sperm. Antibiotics also may affect male fertility, including nitrofurantoins (Furadantin), which are used to treat urinary tract infections that inhibit sperm formation. A class of drugs commonly used to treat high blood pressure, called alpha blockers, including prazosin (Minipress), may affect ejaculation. Propranolol (Inderal), used to treat high blood pressure and heart disease, has been shown to impair sperm motility. A very commonly prescribed class of drugs used to treat high blood pressure, called calcium channel blockers, such as nifedipine (Procardia) and diltiazem (Cardizem), interferes with the acrosome reaction, preventing sperm from fertilizing the egg. The antigout drug colchicine may lead to azoospermia (a zero sperm count). And the diuretic spironolactone (Aldactone) interferes with the synthesis of male hormones. (Every gray cloud has a silver lining: this action of spironolactone makes it a useful treatment for some infertile women who produce increased amounts of male hormones.)

Not as many medications lower a woman's fertility, but the use of decongestants in rare instances may impair a woman's ability to conceive. For example, one woman who was in the habit of taking oral decongestants for her sinus troubles reduced the flow of her cervical, as well as nasal, mucus. The lack of fertile cervical mucus over two years prevented her husband's sperm from reaching her eggs. Once she stopped taking the decongestants, she became pregnant.

More likely, a woman may have had a surgical treatment that interferes with her fertility. Freezing or burning the cervix to treat some cervical abnormalities detected by an abnormal Pap smear can damage the mucus-producing glands needed to promote sperm's ability to swim through the cervical canal into the uterus and limit a woman's ability to reproduce.

Cancer Therapies

When David began having constant back pains, he went to his doctor, who found a small mass on his back that turned out to be cancerous. A further investigation revealed that David had testicular cancer that had spread into his back. For the next year, he went through a series of chemotherapy and surgical treatments to cleanse his body of the cancer. Because of the treatment, David's sperm count was low, but gradually rose to nearly normal about two years after treatment. In that time, the single salesman met his future wife Judy, age thirty. "Now that I have been disease-free for three years, we are thinking about starting a family," says David, who adds that Judy plans to visit her gynecologist for a basic fertility workup.

Cancer treatments frequently cause infertility. Radiation and chemotherapy treatments can save the lives of 90 percent of men with testicular cancer. But the treatments that cure the cancer often cause the men to become permanently sterile. Even with careful shielding of a man's lymph nodes during radiation, his testicles often receive a dose of radiation that irreversibly damages his sperm-producing cells. Chemotherapy, designed to kill rapidly multiplying or dividing cancer cells, also damages the cells that produce the hundreds of millions of new sperm every day. Some men regain their fertility several years later if some of the sperm-producing cells survive the therapy.

Treatment for other cancers can also make a man sterile, at least temporarily. Some men treated for leukemias, lymphomas, and solid tumors who became sterile have shown renewed sperm production, some as early as seven months after their treatment stopped. The more drugs used in chemotherapy and the longer the treatment lasts, the greater the odds against the man becoming fertile again.

About half of all women who receive radiation and chemotherapy for Hodgkin's disease suffer from premature ovarian failure (menopause) because of damage to their eggs and egg-bearing follicles. Some women have only a temporary disruption in their menstrual cycles lasting from a few months to a few years. Those women treated with a combination of radiation and chemotherapy seem to have more damage than those exposed to either therapy alone.

The Damage Done by DES

Soon after Tina got pregnant the first time, she noticed she was spotting. She miscarried a few weeks later. Within five months, the thirty-two-year-old book agent was pregnant again and miscarried again. Her third pregnancy that year also ended in miscarriage. "I knew I had been exposed to DES. When I was fifteen, my mother told me she had taken the drug throughout her pregnancy with me because she had miscarried twice before," Tina says. "Since there was nothing I could do about it, and I was still young, it wasn't an immediate worry." Then she and her husband, Tom, a thirty-eight-year-old engineer, decided to make an appointment with a doctor who handles high-risk pregnancies.

She had an X-ray examination, which showed that Tina had a T-shaped uterus, probably caused by the DES exposure. The doctor told her to keep trying to get pregnant, and eventually an embryo would find a place to implant itself in her malformed uterus. "He told me he could put a stitch in my cervix to help prevent a miscarriage, and that I would have to stay in bed for the first six months of pregnancy," she says. "I told him, 'No way, I'd go crazy.'" Instead, Tina and Tom went through an adoption agency and now have a six-month-old son.

When women in the early 1950s took the synthetic estrogen diethylstilbestrol (DES) to prevent miscarriages, they never dreamed the drug could kink up their daughters' fallopian tubes, cause vaginal cancer and a malformed cervix and uterus, and cause their sons to have abnormal testicles. Prescribed for more than thirty years to women with high-risk pregnancies, DES was touted as a wonder drug. More than 8 million American daughters and sons were exposed to the drug in utero (during their development as a fetus inside their mother's uterus).

Most people know of the limb deformities caused by the drug thalidomide since the deformities are all on the outside of the body. With DES exposure, the deformities are on the inside, where they aren't so obvious. Some studies estimate that the reproductive organs of 40 percent of DES daughters are malformed, including deformities of the vagina or cervix, an abnormal, T-shaped uterus, and abnormal fallopian tubes. Some DES daughters have ovulation problems; others have an increased risk of ectopic pregnancy, repeated miscarriages, and premature delivery. A small number have also developed a rare form of cancer of the vagina, called adenocarcinoma. DES sons also have fertility problems, including low sperm counts, decreased sperm motility, and abnormal sperm forms.

Some have small penises, abnormally small testicles, undescended testicles (a risk factor for testicular cancer), or missing ducts.

In response to the drug's far-reaching effects, DES mothers, sons, and daughters founded a national consumer group called DES Action USA. With headquarters in New York and San Francisco and affiliates across the country, DES Action USA provides educational information and support to those exposed to DES as fetuses. A DES daughter who becomes pregnant is considered to have a high-risk pregnancy because of the increased risk of miscarriage or premature delivery. Since DES daughters are also at increased risk of an ectopic pregnancy, they need to confirm the location of the pregnancy as soon as possible to prevent the serious problem of a ruptured tube, which leads to internal bleeding.

As you can see, a variety of medical problems may lead to a couple's inability to conceive or bear a child. In addition, social factors play an important role. These various medical problems can be best understood within their social context, which we discuss in the next chapter.

3

THE
SOCIAL
FACTS

---

*Why Is This Generation
Different from All
Other Generations?*

With the first public sale of birth control pills in 1960, the sexual revolution was off and running, followed closely by the free-spirited drug culture and the rock 'n' roll music era. Those days of free love and hedonism may have taught us to live life to the fullest. But many former swinging singles who now want a family have learned—too late—that sexual freedom may have interfered with their fertility.

The 1960s was also an era of environmental consciousness. Rachel Carson's *Silent Spring* caused an uproar over pesticides, but the publicity did little to protect the fertility of pesticide workers and others exposed to harmful chemicals at the worksite.

Further dangers became known, including the risk of genetic damage to people who "dropped acid" (LSD) repeatedly. And although the Surgeon General warned us about the health hazards of cigarettes, he failed to mention that smoking can reduce fertility.

Social trends of the 1970s added a further variable to the fertility equation. Increasing numbers of women began building careers, and delayed childbearing. The equal rights movement encouraged women to take greater control of their own lives. The single, working woman became commonplace.

The "Me decade" also brought an increased emphasis on exercise and healthy eating habits. But some women who worked too hard at working out stopped menstruating, while others found that overly strict diets were detrimental to their reproductive function.

And in the 1980s, so-called yuppies, striving to one-minute manage their lives, found that a lack of control over their reproductive systems

---

can be frustrating. The factors that affect fertility have finally caught up with many of today's couples who are ready to reproduce, but find out that they can't. The first step is to cease potentially harmful behavior immediately. Then seek the help of a fertility specialist.

Pregnancy in Their Thirties or Forties, Not Their Twenties

One of the basic reasons why many of today's couples have trouble conceiving children is that they have waited until their thirties or forties before trying. As the body ages, conception becomes more of a gamble. Just how much of a gamble depends on your lifestyle, general health, and personal history. And just as most of us can run faster, stay up later, and eat more without gaining weight when we're younger, a woman's body is more apt to cooperate in conceiving a baby at age twenty than at thirty or forty.

Since the mid-1960s, the proportion of married women under thirty who have never had a baby has more than doubled, from 12 percent to 25 percent. The primary reason is that couples are marrying later and delaying childbearing. More than half of women age twenty to twenty-four and one-quarter of those twenty-five to thirty had never married in 1992, more than twice the percentages of never-marrieds among those age groups in 1960, according to the Office of Population Research at Princeton University.

Postponement of pregnancy represents a significant change by our generation. Women have their first child, on average, three years later than women did thirty years ago.

In addition to the natural decline in fecundability (the ability to become pregnant) with increasing age, the longer a woman puts off becoming pregnant, the more she risks having her fertility threatened for various other reasons—including sexually transmitted diseases and complications due to conditions like endometriosis. Since a woman carries all her eggs from birth, her eggs also have to survive all the drugs, chemicals, and X rays that she has been exposed to during her life. The extra years of exposure to different agents play a role in the increase in abnormal cell division seen in a woman's eggs as she ages. Older women, particularly those over age thirty-five, have a greater chance of bearing a child with birth defects, even though mother nature has a way of screening out most of these defective embryos in older women: she rejects them through miscarriages, which are also more common over age thirty-five.

Despite the body's changes, women in their thirties now account for an increasing percentage of births. Mothers older than thirty have more than one out of three U.S. births, more than four times as many as teenage mothers. And population experts anticipate a rising number of births to women over thirty-five.

Some of these older women are self-supporting singles who want a child before their biological clocks run down. The birth rates of unmarried women in their thirties and forties have increased steadily over the past twenty-five years, which may be a function of the increased number of unmarried women in their thirties today. In 1974, about one in seven women age thirty to thirty-four was unmarried; by the mid-1980s, the figure had risen to one in four.

Cohabitation without marriage has become a commonplace way of life for many couples. But the earlier days of free sex and swinging singles parties may have caused unwitting damage to a significant number of single people. Reluctant to settle for less than their ideal mates, many searched and searched, playing the field. Some women used repeated abortions as a means of birth control, which may have led in some cases to infection and scarring of the uterus and fallopian tubes.

A man's fertility may also decline with age. A promiscuous twenties can lead to a sterile thirties, due to the ravages of venereal diseases affecting the epididymis. Alcohol and marijuana are proven gonadotoxins (toxic to the testicles), and long-term substance abuse can reduce fertility. Also, men with varicoceles, a collection of abnormally enlarged veins draining the testicles, may be fertile when they are younger, but because a varicocele slowly damages the testicle's ability to make healthy sperm, they may become infertile later in life. Finally, as with older women, sperm from older men have more genetic defects and are more likely to contribute to abnormal embryos.

Economics

"Whatever I do, I feel I have to do well," says Ginger, a forty-two-year-old sales representative. "Everything I work hard at, I achieve. I worked at having a baby, but didn't achieve it. That's been hard to take." Ginger has wanted to have a baby with her second husband, Steve, since they were married two and a half years ago.

"I have read every book on fertility, and had a thorough history and practically every test conceivable," says Ginger, who has made notes about all of her fertility tests, treatments, and their outcomes "to see if I can shed some light. I feel that I have done all that I could, that I have left no stone unturned."

After three consecutive cycles of hormone stimulation with Pergonal without a pregnancy, Ginger has decided to take a break from treatment for a few months. "I will probably try to get pregnant until I'm fifty. I'm not going to give up until I'm sure we have exhausted all of our resources. I see it as a crapshoot—sometimes you win, sometimes you lose. Eventually, your number is going to come up. I'm going to rest up, and then go for it again."

Changes in the work world for women have led to more economic independence and postponed marriage and childbirth. Many couples have waited until both the husband and wife have established careers and they can afford to start a family. But the stress and anxiety of making a living in a competitive economic climate, even with two incomes, have taken their toll both on men's sperm counts and on the delicate balance of women's reproductive hormones.

Many infertile couples want to control their reproductive lives just as they do their business lives. With two incomes, these couples usually have the money and motivation to seek the top fertility experts. Women executives, for example, are more likely than other women to plan their pregnancies carefully. For these high achievers and technology believers, it is especially frustrating when a pregnancy doesn't happen on schedule. Those who thought they could overcome any obstacle in life keenly feel the disappointment of infertility.

Back in the 1940s, 1950s, and even the 1960s, newlyweds normally took a brief year to start a family. It was unusual for the wife to work. Today, it's not unusual for wives to earn more than their husbands, or for couples to wait ten years or more before trying to have a child. By postponing a family and having two incomes, these couples have found that they can achieve their high material aspirations.

Today's middle-class woman is used to having control over her life. So if something goes wrong and she can't have a child, she may face a profound sense of guilt and failure along with anger or depression. But most biological problems that cause infertility are not within her control. And the treatment of infertility adds stresses of its own.

Stress and Its Effects

"I tried all my life to prevent pregnancies, starting on the Pill when I was a teenager," says Jan, age twenty-eight. "I was in college a long time, then worked hard to save some money. I thought everything was in place. I had a good job as a nurse, a house, a good husband. After so many years of marriage, we were going to have a baby. It was all calculated."

What Jan and her husband Larry, age thirty, hadn't counted on was a combination of fertility problems. Her obstetrician-gynecologist ordered tests and found that her mucus was "hostile" to Larry's sperm, which had a high percentage of abnormal forms. An endometrial biopsy and hormone studies revealed that Jan had a luteal phase defect. After hormone treatments and artificial insemination failed, Jan decided to stop fertility treatments, and she and Larry have applied to an adoption agency.

"I had to stop. It was getting too stressful," says Jan. "I quit my job, even though I loved it, because I found myself slipping away from work, not giving 100 percent, thinking about having a baby. I'm trying to slow down, not put any pressure on myself. I've always been a go-getter. But when I got to the point of feeling like I was losing control, it scared me."

The infertile couple grapples with a variety of issues that are stressful for them physically, emotionally, and financially. Both husband and wife are naturally distressed by a loss of choice and control over their bodies' functions, and may feel they are damaged or defective.

Some sociologists attribute the high amount of emotional turmoil experienced by the current generation of prospective parents to their large numbers. Because of supply and demand, a large age group—baby boomers, who total nearly one third of all Americans—faces lower wages, higher unemployment, and less upward job mobility than smaller-size age groups. Most of today's younger couples have high material expectations because they grew up in prosperous times. To achieve their expectations in a highly competitive job market, many have stayed single or formed families with working spouses and few, if any, children.

Many people today feel more stressed and clinically depressed earlier in life than previous generations. Female baby boomers have a 65 percent greater chance than earlier generations of being clinically depressed at some time in their lives. The suicide rate among women age fifteen to twenty-four today is nearly three times that of a comparable age group 50 years ago. Depression has changed from a disease of people in their forties, fifties, and older to one of people in their twenties and thirties.

Chronic stress can have detrimental effects on the reproductive system, just as it can on any other organ system. It has been associated with lowering a man's sperm count, motility (how well sperm swim), and morphology (the percentage of normally shaped sperm). Depressed testosterone levels have been linked not only with the stress of combat or combat training but also with the stressful business climate today's men face every day.

Stress has been known to lower semen volume and raise the percentage of abnormal sperm forms. Without adequate counseling, the additional stress of an infertility evaluation and treatment—particularly for an in vitro fertilization (IVF) program—can further lower a man's semen quality.

Stress can also affect a woman's reproductive function and her ability to become pregnant. Chronic stress can reduce the output of gonadotropin-releasing hormone (GnRH) from the hypothalamus, which in turn causes the pituitary to reduce its output of the gonadotropins (FSH, LH). Because of the reduced signals to the ovaries from the pituitary gland, ovulation may not occur.

Women under acute stress may suddenly stop having their periods. For example, when a woman moves to a new city to change jobs or go to school, it's relatively common for her next period to be delayed.

Even extremely healthy people are susceptible to the reproductive ravages of stress. Both male and female athletes who put themselves through intense, stressful training periods may have disrupted reproduction.

Health Kicks

Even the obsession with fitness and health has had its reproductive repercussions. The search for the "runner's high" has led some female athletes to become prone to scanty or missed periods, and some highly trained male athletes to have lowered testosterone levels and impaired sperm production. Women who diet to become fashionably slim may run a risk of compromising their reproductive function since too little body fat can impair a woman's ability to ovulate.

Strict vegetarian diets may also have hurt today's fertility rates. Low-protein diets, particularly those lacking in meat, may affect a woman's fertility. Seemingly healthful vegetarian diets often lack essential nutritional requirements, such as zinc, which a man needs in sufficient amounts to produce sperm.

Once prevalent mainly among ballet dancers and models who felt the pressure to be thin, amenorrhea (no menstruation) has been spread by the exercise boom to runners, swimmers, and gymnasts. A decade of research has shown how exercise can disrupt a woman's hormonal balance and her menstrual cycle, particularly among competitive athletes: Regular exercise can delay a girl's first period or cause her to have irregular periods (oligomenorrhea) or no periods at all (amenorrhea). Older women athletes who become excessively thin can also experience menstrual irregularities or have no periods at all. Many women who began running in their mid-teens and have run long distances through their twenties have found that they are having trouble getting pregnant in their thirties.

Lack of body fat is one of the causes of this type of infertility. The body's fat tissues store and convert hormones, including reproductive hormones. To allow the natural rise and fall of hormones during the menstrual cycle, a woman must maintain a certain amount of body fat content. Too much exercise, along with an excessively rigorous diet, may reduce a woman's body fat and cause her to have ovulation problems.

Aside from body weight or fat content, exercise itself can disrupt the pattern of hormone pulses that initiate the menstrual cycle. Normally, the "master" regulatory gland in the brain, the hypothalamus, emits pulses of gonadotropin-releasing hormone every 90 to 120 minutes in women as a message to the pituitary to release luteinizing hormone (LH) and follicle-stimulating hormone (FSH). But during strenuous exercise, the brain signals to the hypothalamus are altered, so the pulse pattern of GnRH changes. As a result, the pituitary puts out less than normal amounts of FSH, and, in turn, the ovaries produce less estrogen (required for endometrial proliferation and for good cervical mucus production) and less progesterone (needed to make the uterine lining receptive for implantation). Also, a woman may not have a surge of LH during the middle of her menstrual cycle. Without these hormonal fluctuations, a woman may not ovulate or menstruate.

Another change in hormones found among competitive women athletes is an increased output of the stress-related adrenal hormone cortisol. The emotional stress of a strenuous training lifestyle, along with boosts in cortisol production, has led some women athletes to lose weight and stop having their periods.

The normal production of gonadotropins may also be hindered by increased production of endorphins in the brain. The release of these natural painkillers is thought to cause the so-called runner's high.

Men, Exercise, and Fertility

Strenuous exercise can cause a man's testosterone levels and sperm production to drop, also by interfering with the brain's signals that control hormones. It takes greater alterations in hormone levels to affect a man's fertility, however, and it usually takes a man longer than a woman to notice the symptoms of hormonal changes. If a man's testosterone level falls far enough over a long period, he will eventually lose his libido, and his sperm count will drop drastically.

Regular, intense long-distance running (more than 100 miles a week) may produce changes similar to those experienced by women long-distance runners. Prolonged periods of intense exercise can interfere with a man's rhythmic release of GnRH from the hypothalamus and, subsequently, the release of pituitary hormones LH and FSH, just as in women. For a man, the result can be reduced testosterone levels and a lower sperm count.

This may explain why men who run 200 or more miles each week often complain of a low sex drive. (They also may be tired from running nearly thirty miles a day!) New research shows that men who run twenty-five to thirty-five miles a week have a 20 to 30 percent drop in testosterone levels and a slightly impaired sperm count.

A study of competitive wrestlers shows that their testosterone levels were higher after the season, when they gained weight, than during the season, when they were fighting to make their weight class. This correlation between change in body fat combined with intense, stressful competition and falling hormone levels parallels that of women athletes striving to stay slim.

Food and Fertility

Coupling intense exercise with a severely restricted diet can add to a man's or woman's chance of reduced fertility. Anorexia, a psychological disorder in which a person loses his or her appetite and eats very little food, is rarely a problem for men. But a man may go on a low-calorie diet as he starts a strenuous exercise program in order to reduce his weight, which may reduce his testosterone level.

More often, it's fashion-conscious women pursuing to-the-bone thinness who compromise their fertility through dieting. Some of these extremely thin young women with unexplained infertility or menstrual problems have sex hormone levels that match those of anorexic women.

A woman's weight normally increases with age. Healthy women in their twenties and thirties who emulate teenage fashion models are trying to achieve an image that's not normal for their stage of life. As a result they are often underweight and may not ovulate or menstruate.

Young women in their twenties starving down to high-fashion figures may even hormonally repeat the experience of puberty. Researchers have found a general tendency for the LH level in the blood and the ratio of LH to FSH to increase as these underweight women begin to approach their ideal body weight. Just before a pubescent girl starts menstruating, the LH jumps way up and is maintained at this elevated level for several months, then drops down into the normal adult range. Women below their ideal body weight may become suspended in a hormonal state similar to puberty. Once they gain a few pounds, however, their pituitary gland function generally returns to normal.

Another factor may be what's in the diet. Nonmenstruating women athletes tend to consume less protein and take in fewer calories each day than menstruating women athletes. A Tufts University study shows nonmenstruating athletes consume an average of thirteen grams less protein per day than menstruating women athletes of the same height and weight. (One turkey sandwich and an eight-ounce glass of skim milk usually provide an adequate daily protein intake for an adult, say the Tufts nutritionists.)

A lack of meat in the diet can also affect ovulation. A German study of nine healthy young women on a balanced, meat-filled diet and nine women on a vegetarian diet found that seven of the vegetarian dieters stopped ovulating during a six-week weight-loss program compared to only two of the meat-eating weight watchers. In addition, the menstrual cycles of all the vegetarians became significantly shorter than those of the nonvegetarians. The researchers at the Max Planck Institute in Munich suggest that inadequate amounts of protein in the vegetarian diet may have contributed to the athletes' hormone problems.

A strict vegetarian diet has also been linked to male infertility due to a zinc deficiency. In fact, a low sperm count may be a tip-off to a mild zinc deficiency. Some men with low sperm counts and low zinc levels in their blood have been successfully treated with high doses of zinc. Men who lower their fat intake to about 10 percent also risk lowering their testosterone levels.

For men, eating too much meat, which has a high fat content, may lower the sex drive by reducing blood levels of testosterone. University of Utah researchers have found that blood testosterone levels dropped dramatically when a group of eight men drank a high-fat shake but not when they had a low-fat shake. The researchers suggest that a high-fat diet, over time, may curb a man's sex drive. A high-fat diet can also lead to clogged arteries, including the arteries in the penis, making it more difficult for a man to achieve an erection.

Free Radicals

The breakdown of oxygen as it passes through cells in the body results in substances known as free radicals. Cigarette smoke and other toxic compounds, such as air pollutants, heavy metals, and petrochemicals, can all increase the amount of free radicals in the body. Free radicals attack and destroy membranes, and they may play a role in male fertility by damaging the membrane surrounding sperm. While cells may be damaged by free radicals, substances dubbed free radical scavengers, or antioxidants, can combat these bad effects.

Infertile men have a higher concentration of free radicals in their semen compared to fertile men. Free radicals damage sperm and probably the genetic material within sperm, and therefore may also lead to more miscarriages. Free radicals can harm sperm any time during their development in the testicles. Sperm in the epidydimis are the most susceptible to free radical damage.

Seminal fluid contains high levels of free radical scavengers. Studies show that the concentration of free radical scavengers in seminal fluid varies from one man to another. A high volume of seminal fluid protects sperm because more scavengers exist. Therefore, a man with good semen concentration but low semen volume may be borderline fertile, because low semen volume allows for more free radical damage of sperm.

Substance Abuse

After nine years of using no birth control, Claire, a twenty-six-year-old account supervisor, still had not become pregnant. A laparoscopy when she was sixteen had revealed that Claire's left fallopian tube was severely scarred from chlamydia infections. Last year she had been rushed to the hospital with severe internal bleeding, and a doctor performed a laparoscopy and D&C. "The doctor told me I had no chance of becoming pregnant without in vitro fertilization," Claire says. She visited Dr. Berger. He performed surgery to clear scar tissue from her one healthy fallopian tube and prescribed a hormone to help regulate her ovulation.

Her husband, Ron, age twenty-nine, had a good number of sperm, but his sperm motility was low and he had many misshaped sperm heads. He reported that he had been smoking two to three marijuana joints a day for more than a dozen years. Dr. Berger advised Ron to stop smoking marijuana. A few months later, Ron's sperm quality showed a great improvement. On their second intrauterine insemination attempt, Claire became pregnant, and she gave birth to a healthy baby boy, Andrew. "We feel very fortunate to be able to have a baby," says Claire. "I don't think I would have become pregnant if Ron didn't quit smoking marijuana."

Drug abuse has so permeated our society that the use of nicotine, marijuana, alcohol, cocaine, and other mood-altering substances has become commonplace among young adults. An estimated 5 to 10 percent of women of childbearing age use illicit drugs on a regular basis, and another 5 percent have more than two drinks a day.

Drugs that affect the central nervous system (see accompanying list) will affect the control of gonadotropin secretion by the brain's pituitary gland. Because of their actions on the central nervous system, these drugs can modify the brain's output of hormones that control the production of reproductive hormones. Changes in concentrations of the pituitary hormones LH, FSH, and prolactin can result in reduced libido, sexual dysfunction, and infertility.

Marijuana's effects on reproduction have been well established. Studies show that women who smoke marijuana have shorter menstrual cycles and shorter luteal phases, particularly when they smoke during the late phase of the cycle. Men who are long-term marijuana smokers produce less sperm and tend to have lower testosterone levels, lower sperm motility, and more abnormally shaped sperm than nonsmokers. These men may even develop enlarged breasts due to an excess of estrogen. Chronic marijuana smokers may also have chromosome damage, affecting their sperm, which may lead to problems in conception, miscarriages, or birth defects.

Likewise, chronic use of cocaine inhibits gonadotropin production and elevates prolactin concentrations, resulting in impairment of a man's fertility by suppressing testosterone and sperm production, as well as his libido.

Alcohol, another commonly abused substance, may also adversely affect the reproductive system. As with other chemicals, alcohol's effects on fertility depend on the amount consumed. Chronic alcohol abuse in men can lead to reduced secretion of testosterone. In addition, chronic drinkers who have liver damage commonly have small sex organs, enlarged breasts, and irreversible impotence.

Both short- and long-term drinking can lead to abnormal sperm production. After a binge a man's sperm may have heads with deformities, curled tails, and swollen midpieces. Sperm from chronic alcoholics show a high percentage of abnormal shapes.

Women alcoholics also may suffer from infertility and menstrual disorders. And sexologists at Rutgers University have found that the intensity and frequency of orgasms among women drop rapidly as their alcohol level rises. Even moderate drinking has been linked to irregular ovulation.

In men with varicoceles, the adverse effects of drugs and alcohol are even worse because the varicocele weakens the testicle's ability to exclude toxic chemicals.

Moderate amounts of caffeine consumption also can lower a woman's chances of conceiving. From interviews with more than 1,000 women during early pregnancy, government-sponsored researchers found that women who consumed the amount of caffeine equivalent to that in three cups of coffee a day had a 27 percent lower chance of conceiving than caffeine abstainers. Women who drank the equivalent of one to two cups of coffee a day lowered their likelihood of becoming pregnant by about 10 percent. Caffeine may directly affect ovulation by reducing estrogen, which lessens a woman's chances of conceiving.

Drugs That Affect the Central Nervous System

Stimulants	Depressants
Amphetamines	Alcohol
Caffeine	Anesthetics
Cocaine	Barbiturates
Nicotine	Benzodiazepine tranquilizers
Phencyclidine	Heroin
("Angel dust")	Marijuana

Other drugs that affect the central nervous system—such as barbiturates and phencyclidine (PCP, or "angel dust")—also can impair fertility. Barbiturates inhibit both LH and FSH production, and therefore depress reproductive hormone secretion.

"Angel dust" affects many areas of the brain. PCP has been shown to depress both testosterone and LH levels in the blood of animals. Although there aren't any studies of PCP's effects on reproductive function in humans, its effects are probably comparable.

Smoking

Smoking tobacco can also affect the physiologic functions necessary for reproduction.

Smoking alters a woman's estrogen metabolism and depletes her egg production. It can lead to cervical problems since cervical mucus production depends on estrogen production. What's more, high levels of nicotine, found in female smokers' cervical mucus, can be toxic to sperm.

Inhaling tobacco smoke may also impair the ability of the lining of the fallopian tubes to fight off infections. Nicotine and other components in cigarette smoke affect the cilia lining the tubes and may alter the way the tubes' lining responds to inflammation. This may allow more infections of the tubes and pelvic inflammatory disease, which can lead to tubal damage and ectopic pregnancy.

Women who start smoking before age sixteen and smoke an average of more than half a pack a day show an increased risk of tubal infertility. If these women have used IUDs or had more than five lifetime sex partners, their infertility risk rises significantly. Women smokers have twice the risk of tubal pregnancy compared to women who have never smoked. They also have more frequent miscarriages and premature deliveries than nonsmokers.

Women who smoke may delay conception by about two months, increase the risk of miscarriage, and hasten menopause by about two years compared with nonsmokers. Studies on the impact of smoking on IVF outcomes show a small but significant reduction in the number of eggs retrieved.

Men who smoke are not immune to the harmful effects of tobacco on reproduction. They have significantly lower sperm counts and sperm motility and a significantly greater percentage of abnormally shaped sperm than nonsmokers.

New evidence shows the effects of cigarette smoke become even more obvious under the microscope. Men who smoke heavily show decreased sperm concentrations and damaged sperm DNA, and women smokers also show evidence of DNA damage.

Environmental and Workplace Hazards

A number of industrial chemicals have been implicated in fertility problems, especially in lowering a man's sperm count. In some instances, doctors and hospital personnel in contact with radioactive materials, radiation, and anesthetic gas have also suffered low fertility rates.

The testicles are the most sensitive organs in a man's body when it comes to exposure to environmental agents. Radiation, pesticides, and industrial solvents may all harm his sperm production. Many of these agents interfere with male hormone production and sperm formation, causing a loss of libido, impotence, or infertility.

Many toxic substances, including radiation and cancer drugs, have their greatest effect on cells with the highest metabolic rates, that is, cells in the process of growing and dividing. That's why the testicles, which make new sperm every day, are so prone to damage.

Of the 60,000 chemicals in widespread commercial use today, only three are regulated based on their documented effects on human reproduction: metallic lead, the pesticide dibromochloropropane (DBCP), and the pharmaceutical solvent ethylene oxide. Most of the remaining 59,997 chemicals haven't been thoroughly studied, so on one knows what their effects on sperm production might be. The National Toxicology Program (NTP) and the National Institute of Environmental Health Sciences have announced the establishment of a new center to evaluate whether specific chemicals play a role in reproductive and development problems. The NTP Center for the Evaluation of Health Risks to Human Reproduction will convene panels of scientists with expertise in reproduction, toxicology, and related areas to evaluate the information available on the effects of particular chemicals on reproduction.

Infertility due to occupational hazards has been less well studied among women, although women who work in the manufacture of oral contraceptives may have altered menstrual function. And pesticides may damage a woman's eggs, possibly leading to early menopause.

If a woman becomes pregnant, exposure to various chemicals may damage her developing embryo. Substances having the potential to cause early miscarriage include ethylene oxide, used in the chemical sterilization of surgical instruments; vinyl chloride, used in the plastics industry; chemical solvents used in manufacturing industries; nitrous oxide exposure among anesthetists, operating room nurses, veterinarians, dentists, and dental assistants; and metallic compounds of manganese, arsenic, and nickel.

What's more, the sex partners of men chronically exposed to lead, DBCP, vinyl chloride, and anesthetic gases, particularly nitrous oxide, may be at increased risk of a miscarriage. Several insecticides, including DDT, chlordecone, and methoxychlor, and metals, including organic lead, copper, cadmium, and zinc, can prevent implantation of the fertilized egg.

Heat and Infertility

Prolonged or repeated exposure to heat may cause significant fertility loss among men. Workers at risk of heat-provoked infertility include men involved in the smelting of metals and the manufacture of glass, those laboring in the engine rooms of ships, and possibly bakers, farm laborers, and long-distance truck drivers exposed to engine heat. Sitting at a desk with your legs crossed has also been shown to elevate testicular temperature significantly.

Normally, the temperature of the testicles is between 93 and 95 degrees Fahrenheit, or 34 and 35 degrees centigrade. Temperatures above normal body temperature (98.6 degrees F or 37 degrees C) can impair a man's sperm count and motility and cause him to produce abnormal sperm forms. Although the impact on sperm production is generally reversible, a worker exposed on a daily basis, year after year, could experience long-term or even permanent impairment.

A man's testicular temperature tends to be higher when he is sitting than when he is standing. The poor semen quality of paraplegics has been attributed, in part, to elevated testicular temperatures because they are forced to sit in a wheelchair. Others who sit for long periods, such as long-distance bus drivers and workaholic executives, may also be at increased risk of infertility.

The connection between exposure to heat and male infertility has also been noted outside the workplace. A high fever has long been associated with impaired sperm production. In tropical and subtropical climates, pregnancy rates decline during the hot seasons, when men have lower sperm counts.

How to Preserve Your Fertility

Although you or your mate might fit into one of the above categories, that doesn't mean that you won't ever have a baby. Even if your lifestyle or habits have led to some damage, you may still be able to prevent further damage to your fertility.

Obstetrics textbooks specify that a thirty-five-year-old woman who gets pregnant for the first time is considered to be an "elderly primigravida," which reflects the medical profession's concern with the medical and obstetric complications accompanying delayed childbearing. The ideal time, from a physical standpoint, for a woman to become pregnant is in her early or mid-twenties when her body is physically mature, her reproductive system is most responsive, and her chances of producing a genetically abnormal child are minimal.

From a socioeconomic view, however, delayed childbearing may be more advantageous. Studies supported by the National Institute of Child Health and Human Development have found that older mothers tend to have more education, higher status jobs, and better incomes than do mothers five or ten years younger. They also are likely to have higher aspirations for their children and more money to provide material goods and a quality education.

There have been many babies born to women in their late thirties and early forties, both naturally and through advanced reproductive technologies such as IVF. And now postmenopausal women or those with premature ovarian failure have borne children, thanks to donor eggs used with IVF.

When it comes to stress, a woman whose job or life circumstance places her under excessive pressure would be wise to delay pregnancy until she can reduce that stress, if at all possible. Stress reduction techniques have been shown to increase the chances of infertile women becoming pregnant. A Harvard study of fifty-four infertile women found that one-third became pregnant within six months of practicing relaxation techniques regularly.

A woman's intensity of exercise, her eating habits, the amount—and speed—of any weight loss, and the amount of stress she experiences during training and competition may all contribute to menstrual problems. But no one can say that running a certain number of miles a week or having a certain percentage of body fat causes amenorrhea, says Dr. Mona Shangold, a noted expert on athletic amenorrhea and an obstetrician-gynecologist at Hahnemann University in Philadelphia. She notes that a lot of thin women have perfectly normal periods, so each woman must be evaluated individually. Various disorders can interfere with menstruation, including a pituitary tumor, an underactive thyroid, or the overproduction of adrenal and male hormones.

The degree to which stress and exercise affect a man's testosterone level or sperm count depends on the individual man. Usually, hormonal changes in men who exercise regularly aren't severe enough to cause a loss in libido. For a man who exercises strenuously, is having difficulty fathering a child, and has a low sperm count, cutting back on exercise may help. Male athletes, particularly those involved in ever-popular "ultrasports," such as triathlons, may need to moderate their activity levels. Keeping body weight within normal limits and fat levels between 20 and 30 percent of the diet will likely maintain a man's fertility.

Strict vegetarians who want to father children may need zinc supplements to give their fertility some zest. Although some foods included in a typical vegetarian diet, such as whole grains, nuts, and legumes, contain some zinc, animal protein is considered the best source of this element. The widespread use of bran in nonmeat diets may counterbalance zinc intake: bran attaches itself to zinc in the intestine and stops it from being absorbed.

Natural antioxidants such as vitamins C and E, beta carotene (a precursor to vitamin A), and the trace element selenium can reduce free radical damage. Sperm also need to metabolize the minerals zinc and copper.

There are no definitive studies of antioxidants protecting against free radical damage of sperm. However, to protect against possible damage, we suggest that men take a daily multivitamin with minerals that includes 5,000 International Units (I.U.) of beta carotene and 2 milligrams (mg) of copper, and a total of 1,000 mg of vitamin C for several months (to cleanse semen of any toxins) and then 200 mg of vitamin C, 400 I.U. of vitamin E, 20 micrograms (mcg) of selenium, and 15 to 60 mg of zinc daily.

As much as possible, eat foods containing no chemicals, preservatives, or additives. These chemicals haven't been studied, and we don't know whether they have an effect on fertility.

Free radical damage is temperature-sensitive. You can halt the damage by keeping the testicle temperature at normal body temperature. A man who wears tight pants and sits most of the day in an office may have an increased testicle temperature that leads to free radical damage. Don't cross your legs when you sit, and get up to stretch your legs often during the day. Keep cool by wearing loose-fitting cotton undergarments or boxer shorts. Do not wear underwear to bed and do not use an electric blanket or very heavy covers.

People with an already damaged reproductive system will compound their fertility problems if they use illicit drugs. The type and amount of drug taken, how often it's taken, and the amount of active ingredient (which varies widely in street drugs), all affect the degree of reproductive, as well as general health, risks. Other factors include the user's age and the duration of use.

Fortunately, most drugs have only a temporary effect on the central nervous system pathways necessary for normal production of gonadotropins. So when you stop using drugs, the harmful effects on your reproductive function are likely to be reversed.

Alcohol and caffeine appear to damage reproductive function when taken in large quantities. Therefore, you would be wise to limit your intake to two alcoholic drinks per week and two cups of coffee per day.

Infertile couples who smoke cigarettes should quit if they want to improve their fertility potential, not to mention their general health and the health of their baby. The good news for smokers who have trouble conceiving is that quitting really does make a difference. It takes about three months for the levels of nicotine-related chemicals found in smokers' blood and follicular fluid to start dropping off when they quit. After about one year, their levels are the same as nonsmokers.

The problems of workplace reproductive hazards underscore the need to know the occupational history of each partner as part of the fertility workup. The history may also help in planning treatment. For example, it may take several months for a man to recover sperm production after an environmental insult, so periodic semen analyses are often useful in monitoring his response.

Assessing the significance of workplace exposures is often difficult. Occupational exposures are usually not isolated to one chemical, and the dosage may vary according to the particular job, tasks on the job, and accidents and spills. Exposure to potentially harmful agents is not routinely monitored in most workplaces.

One potential problem—excessive heat—can usually be overcome. If a man has sperm problems, he should minimize his exposure to heat.

When to Seek Help from a Specialist

You and your spouse may have been trying to have a baby for a few months and are wondering, "Do we have a fertility problem?" There are simple tests that your family doctor, ob-gyn, or urologist can perform to give you a clue about your fertility before you go through a full workup by a fertility specialist. With the ovulation predictor kits now available in drugstores, you can determine when you are ovulating, and can have sex around this most fertile time. Keeping a basal body temperature (BBT) chart may also help identify your normal ovulation days and hormonal cycles.

Remember that the odds of a woman getting pregnant are only about one in four each month, even under optimal conditions. That's why most couples should wait for at least six months before seeking medical help.

The American Society for Reproductive Medicine defines infertility as the failure to become pregnant after one year of regular unprotected intercourse for women under age thirty-five, and six months or more for women thirty-five and older. Many fertility specialists recommend an evaluation if the wife is over thirty and the couple hasn't conceived after six months of frequent intercourse without birth control. Couples under thirty should seek medical counseling if they haven't conceived after one year of unprotected intercourse or sooner if their history suggests that an infertility problem is likely.

When the woman is over thirty, or if either partner has reason to believe there is a risk factor in their background—a history of genital infections, an undescended testicle, a DES mother, irregular periods, cancer treatment, unusual sexual development—this certainly justifies an early evaluation. Women who have a history of two or more miscarriages and no live births may want to seek out a fertility specialist.

If you are over thirty or have clues from the past that you might have a fertility problem, and you still don't get pregnant after optimizing your chances by timing sex around ovulation, then you need not wait as long as six months before seeking medical help.

Part Two

WHAT
YOU CAN
DO

4

GETTING
STARTED WITH
A FERTILITY
SPECIALIST

Sandy, a thirty-five-year-old musician, was referred to a gynecologist who had recently helped her friend through a miscarriage. He found that Sandy had a hormone deficiency. Her writer-husband, Jeff, age thirty-six, had a normal sperm count. But after six months, Sandy and Jeff went looking for a fertility specialist. "My ob-gyn didn't treat me badly," says Sandy. "He picked up the ball, but he couldn't run with it. He wasn't able to do the more sophisticated tests we needed. His office was set up to provide care for pregnant women rather than deal with infertile couples."

Another friend recommended that Sandy see a doctor at a medical center, who suggested she and her husband try artificial insemination. "I asked him, 'What are the odds that this will work?' He said, 'I can't tell you that. Every patient is different.' So I went to the medical library. I found no evidence that artificial insemination made any sense in our situation. We could have done things nature's way without the stress of artificial insemination. Without a more thorough evaluation, artificial insemination was as sensible as having us do it standing on our heads."

Sandy and Jeff put their names on a waiting list at a big university hospital. Meanwhile, Jeff interviewed a doctor for a story. "I liked the sound of him. I knew he was running an in vitro fertilization (IVF) clinic, and was pretty sure he was a bona fide fertility specialist," Jeff says. "He was at a teaching hospital and was involved with federally funded research. By the way he spoke, I could tell he knew about Sandy's condition and that he could help us."

Finding the right fertility specialist can be a frustrating and confusing process. The American Society for Reproductive Medicine (ASRM), a medical society open to all doctors who have an interest in fertility, has more than eleven thousand members. But not all of these doctors specialize in treating infertility. With the information in this chapter, however, and the directory of fertility specialists in the back of this book, you should be able to find a doctor in your geographic area who will be likely to meet your infertility needs.

How to Find the Right Doctor

A couple should expect to see their fertility specialist frequently during a period of intensive testing and treatment, maybe even as often as they see their friends. If you don't feel comfortable with your doctor, you probably will not get the most out of your treatment. You should be able to ask questions and get answers that you can understand and that make sense to you. If not, you will probably not have a successful interaction with that doctor.

Some people find it hard to leave their primary care doctor or their gynecologist to look for a fertility specialist. They may feel disloyal about asking for a second opinion or transferring their care to another doctor. But it's your body and your future. Your relationship with your doctor is a professional, not a personal, one. Just because your previous doctor's treatments have not succeeded doesn't mean he is a bad doctor.

The first doctor you may talk with about wanting to get pregnant is your family doctor. *Family practitioners* (FPs) and *general practitioners* (GPs) are trained as generalists. They deal with a wide variety of diseases as well as health maintenance. Part of their training is to identify and treat a wide range of conditions and, if need be, make referrals to specialists. FPs and GPs may have you start a basal body temperature (BBT) chart or suggest a semen analysis.

Your primary physician may be an *internist,* whose training is in diagnosing and treating medical disorders. There are many subspecialties within internal medicine—cardiology to treat the heart, gastroenterology for intestinal organs, oncology for cancer treatments—but none specifically for fertility. The closest subspecialty is medical endocrinology, which requires an internist to take additional training in diseases that affect the endocrine system. A *medical endocrinologist* might treat a patient with excess hair growth (hirsutism), who may also have a coexisting fertility problem. Thyroid disorders often also affect fertility. But most medical endocrinologists, like general internists, FPs, and GPs, are neither specially trained nor often willing to provide reproductive health care.

Women who are having trouble getting pregnant usually go to their *obstetrician-gynecologist* (ob-gyn) for basic fertility studies. The ob-gyn is a specialist in the evaluation and treatment of diseases of women and in providing care for pregnant women, and has three or more years of residency training in these areas. If your ob-gyn has passed the required written and oral examinations and been in clinical practice for the additional years required by the American Board of Obstetrics and Gynecology, he or she will usually display a certificate or show on the practice's stationery that he or she is a certified specialist or diplomate of the American College of Obstetricians and Gynecologists. Sometimes, after a board-certified doctor's name, you will see the letters "FACOG," which stands for Fellow of the American College of Obstetricians and Gynecologists.

The basic tests performed by most ob-gyns include a pelvic exam, a check of basal body temperature charts, and the monitoring of some baseline hormone levels, such as prolactin and progesterone levels during the luteal phase. In addition, most ob-gyns will perform a postcoital test (PCT), endometrial biopsy, or diagnostic laparoscopy.

The *urologist* is the male's counterpart to the gynecologist. The urologist has completed a residency training of at least three years in the evaluation and treatment of disorders of the kidneys, urinary tract, bladder, and male reproductive organs, in addition to having at least two years of general surgical training. To become certified by the American Board of Urology, a urologist must also have practiced urology for eighteen months, including twelve months of urologic surgery. Board-certified urologists may become Fellows of the American College of Surgeons and use the initials "FACS" after their names.

For fertility patients, urologists will usually perform semen analyses, look for varicoceles (varicose veins in the scrotum), check hormone levels, and order lab tests to check sperm quality. Often, however, they see only the husband and have little idea about his wife's fertility problems, just as gynecologists see only the wife and have little knowledge of the husband's problems—which interferes with coordinating the couple's workup and treatment.

Some ob-gyns take additional subspecialty training and become certified as *reproductive endocrinologists*. The American Board of Obstetrics and Gynecology certifies reproductive endocrinologists who have completed two additional years of training beyond their ob-gyn residency, passed oral and written exams, shown they are competent in managing reproductive endocrinology problems in their practice, and published a report in a peer-reviewed medical journal. Most certified reproductive endocrinologists are also members of the ASRM's subspecialty group, the Society of Reproductive Endocrinologists. To join, a doctor must be an active member of the ASRM and be certified as a reproductive endocrinologist.

Reproductive endocrinologists primarily are subspecialists in the treatment of hormonal diseases of women, including disorders involving the pituitary, thyroid, and adrenal glands, as well as the ovaries. A reproductive endocrinologist is likely to use the full range of hormonal treatments available, including Pergonal, Metrodin, and gonadotropin-releasing hormone (GnRH).

A second group of subspecialists who deal with fertility problems is *reproductive surgeons*. A reproductive surgeon who is a gynecologist is specially trained and qualified to treat anatomical problems such as tubal obstruction, endometriosis, uterine abnormalities, and any other female reproductive organ disorder requiring surgery. For men, reproductive surgeons are urologists who have received special training in repairing obstructions, varicoceles, and other anatomic disorders of the testicles. A reproductive surgeon must be familiar with the principles of microsurgical reconstructive surgery, applying these principles to the reproductive organs.

Whether ob-gyns or urologists, reproductive surgeons look to conserve and restore reproductive potential. They are the most well-trained and experienced doctors to perform complicated reconstructive operations to restore fertility when it has been impaired by tubal blockage (including tubal ligation), scarring from pelvic inflammatory disease (PID), endometriosis, or blocked ducts in men.

Reproductive surgeons can also become members of an ASRM subspecialty group, the Society of Reproductive Surgeons. Since 1989, doctors must complete a fellowship either in reproductive endocrinology or reproductive surgery and be in practice for at least three years in order to become eligible to join the Society of Reproductive Surgeons. A minimum of half of their caseload must be reproductive surgery for infertility, and they must have been personally approved by two members of the society who have performed surgery with them. Physicians who became members of the Society of Reproductive Surgeons prior to 1989 were admitted based on their training and demonstrated experience in reproductive surgery before formal fellowship training was established.

Another type of specialist dealing with male fertility is the *andrologist*. The andrologist may be either a clinical or a basic scientist who studies various aspects of male reproductive function, such as the semen or hormones. Andrologists often are laboratory specialists rather than medical doctors (M.D.'s) and may have earned a Ph.D. (Doctorate of Philosophy) degree in biochemistry, endocrinology, or physiology. They direct the laboratory procedures for testing sperm in the most advanced fertility laboratories.

Andrologists are analogous to reproductive endocrinologists in the sense that these doctors focus on physiologic, hormonal conditions. Urologists are more like reproductive surgeons, since both deal mostly with anatomic problems. Some urologists are also andrologists.

Membership in the American Society of Andrology is open to qualified physicians and basic scientists who make contributions to the field of andrology. Currently, andrologists and embryologists are setting up criteria similar to other specialty groups, with both written and oral exams and clinical fellowships, as a prerequisite for board certification.

Once the sperm gets together with the egg, it has entered the bailiwick of the *embryologist*. Embryologists watch over the fertilization process through early embryo development. They collaborate with andrologists to work with sperm up to the point of fertilization. They are usually not medical doctors, but generally have advanced degrees, such as a Ph.D., and tend to work more in the laboratory than directly with patients. An embryologist is trained to handle sperm and eggs, monitor development of fertilized eggs in the lab until they are transferred back into the body, and study the development of the embryo.

There is a pyramid of access to the above fertility specialists. As you go from generalists to specialists, there are fewer to choose from. Of the more than 797,000 physicians in the country, about 214,000 are generalists, including FPs, GPs, and internists; about 39,000 are ob-gyns; and about 9,900 are urologists. The numbers drop off drastically when we get to the fertility subspecialists. In the United States there are currently about 590 reproductive endocrinologists, 450 reproductive surgeons, 500 andrologists, and 200 embryologists. There are, however, many other capable physicians who treat infertility problems and who are not members of one of these professional groups.

Getting to a Fertility Specialist

Sometimes a couple's primary care physician or ob-gyn may not refer them to a fertility specialist, even after prolonged, unsuccessful treatment.

In that case, the doctor is not acting in the couple's best interest. Sometimes couples want to stay with their primary care doctors even when they may be better off going to a specialist. That's all right as long as they are aware of available alternatives.

Your doctor may be an excellent physician and you may have a good relationship with him, yet he may not know how best to evaluate and treat your infertility, or may have ideas that don't fit with how you and your spouse envision your treatment. That's why you need to learn as much as you can about your condition. Listen carefully to what the doctor says and make sure his answers make sense to you.

If your doctor says, "Come in on day thirteen for a postcoital test—except if it's the weekend," then you are probably going to the wrong doctor for fertility treatment. A fertility specialist has to provide medical care at the right time of the cycle, *especially* when you are ovulating, which includes weekends, in order to check the cervical mucus, test hormone levels, and provide appropriate treatment when you are ovulating, not just when it's convenient. If your doctor is unavailable at the time these tests or procedures need to be done, find another doctor who takes these issues seriously enough to deal with them every day of the week, including weekends and holidays.

Your doctor should talk to you in a logical, unhurried fashion so that you can understand what he is thinking and develop confidence in him. You should also pay attention to your gut feelings. If you don't get "good vibes" when you see him, you may have a harder time with treatment.

You should recognize what's important to you in your relationship with your doctor. For example, do you want your doctor, who knows you and your history, to be on call (available to you) the majority of the time, or is a "covering" doctor or an associate acceptable? What do your friends, neighbors, colleagues, or any fertility patients you know like about their doctor? What don't they like about the doctor?

You may want to make initial appointments with more than one doctor to get a sense of what they are like, to learn about their staff, and to get a feeling for what it will probably be like to deal with them. Try to get a sense of how comfortable you will feel with the doctor. Listen carefully to the answers to your questions—not just the words, but also the feelings and messages behind the words.

It's best to arrange your first visit as a couple. If the doctor doesn't want you to do this, that's usually not a good sign. When you come for your initial visit, talk with other couples in the waiting room, if possible.

Ask how long they typically have to wait before being seen. Is the doctor available by phone? Does the doctor answer questions willingly? How much time does the doctor spend with each patient? Are there other physicians in the practice? If so, what are his associates like? Knowing what they now know, ask whether they would choose this doctor again if they were to start over with their fertility treatment.

Talk to the nurses, since they will probably interact with you the most. For example, in a private office setting, they draw the blood, perform various tests, and call you with test results and instructions.

If you feel your doctor is not listening to you, don't hesitate to make your concerns known. Ask the questions that are on your mind. According to Dr. Mack Lipkin, Jr., director of the National Task Force on Medical Interviews, studies have shown that patients who ask forthright questions receive better medical care than passive patients.

Here are some of the ways you can actually go about locating a fertility specialist:

- Get a recommendation from your primary care family doctor, obstetrician/gynecologist, or urologist.

- Check with the local medical society for names of specialists in your area.

- Contact the directors of private fertility clinics as well as those at nearby medical schools or hospitals.

- Ask a friend for a recommendation, and then check out the doctor yourself.

- Look in the phone book for doctors who limit their practice to fertility services.

- Consult the directory of fertility specialists in the back of this book.

- Contact the American Society for Reproductive Medicine or, in Canada, the Canadian Fertility and Andrology Society.

- Contact Resolve, a national organization run exclusively by and for infertile couples that has local chapters across the country.

- Call Fertilitext (900–884–PREGNANT), a national telephone service with information about fertility and fertility specialists.

As you embark upon your search for a specialist, keep in mind that fertility treatment is an ever-changing field. Your condition may now be treatable even though you were once told you had no chance. New treatment options continue to become available through private practices specializing in the treatment of infertility, as well as through university medical centers. Become familiar with doctors in your community whom you see, hear, or read about. They may have new techniques appropriate for treating your situation.

Insurance Issues

Betty and Bill had gone through a basic fertility workup, and after two artificial inseminations failed they were advised to try in vitro fertilization. Their first IVF attempt was unsuccessful. The second one worked and Betty, age thirty-two, became pregnant. Their joy was tempered somewhat when their insurance company failed to cover their second IVF procedure. "They told us we could bill for a total of three inseminations, whether they were artificial or in vitro," says Bill. He and Betty ended up paying out of pocket nearly the full amount for the last procedure.

Besides questioning the doctor, you should ask your insurance carrier or health care agent what types of fertility treatments, if any, are covered. Many companies resist covering new treatments, but several states have now passed laws mandating coverage of infertility and its often innovative procedures. It is up to you to know what your company does and does not cover.

With rapid changes in health care, patients may not have coverage or choice of doctors in most of the new managed care programs, such as those provided by health maintenance organizations (HMOs). You should elect to have access to your own choice of specialists outside of the program whenever possible.

Through appropriate testing, a knowledgeable fertility specialist will establish specific diagnoses underlying your infertility. Infertility is a symptom, not a disease. Make sure that your doctor submits the name and code for the disease or suspected disease causing the infertility to your insurance carrier. Some health insurance companies may not reimburse a couple for infertility but will cover the costs of diagnosis and treatment of a specific condition, such as endometriosis, polycystic ovarian disease, varicocele, blocked epididymis, or blocked vas deferens.

Usually, the underlying diagnosis comes only after tests of your reproductive physiology and anatomy. A woman with tubal infertility may have had salpingitis and developed tubal obstruction and/or pelvic adhesions due to a sexually transmitted infection, such as chlamydia. The further back in the chain of events the doctor goes in establishing the diagnosis, and the more specific the diagnoses he can make, the better chance he has of suggesting the best fertility treatment and the more likely your insurance company or health care plan may be to provide coverage for your tests and treatments.

Most insurance companies and health care organizations will require your doctor to use the standard diagnostic terms and number codes specified in the *International Classification of Diseases*, published by the National Center for Health Statistics. Similarly, for tests or treatments there is a standard book called *Current Procedural Terminology* published by the American Medical Association (AMA). The classifications change every year, so your doctor has to keep up with the codes to help you get the coverage and health care services you are entitled to.

If you are denied insurance coverage for an infertility treatment, ask your doctor to write a letter to your insurance carrier to help you receive the reimbursement and services you believe are due you. Insurance companies sometimes make mistakes and may deny a payment that you are entitled to. It's well worth your time to read your health insurance contract carefully and to stand up for your rights. You or your employer have paid the premiums for your coverage and you are legally entitled to what is specified in the contract. In most states, unless your contract specifically excludes coverage for a particular problem, you should be able to receive the necessary tests and treatments and be reimbursed for treatment of that condition.

But with the increasing emphasis on cost containment and overview of doctors by third parties, it will likely be more difficult to protect your rights to be treated for infertility, as many organizations do not believe it is "medically necessary" to treat infertility since it is not a life-threatening illness.

Doctors say that financial pressure is the main reason why half of all infertile couples never seek treatment. Even with insurance, most patients pay some, if not most, of the costs, and advanced treatments can run from $10,000 to $40,000.

Because of scant insurance coverage for both diagnosis and treatment of infertility, a group of doctors has organized a new approach. The

Advanced Reproductive Care (ARC) Network, which includes a large proportion of U.S. certified reproductive endocrinologists, provides financing, special treatment packages, and a money-back plan that refunds the treatment costs if a couple does not have a baby.

Many fertility clinics have offered money-back guarantees before. These doctors got paid only when the patient became pregnant, so some might have been tempted to take extra risks, for example, overstimulate the ovaries or implant too many embryos during IVF, to help guarantee a pregnancy. In the ARC Network plan, the participating physician gets paid whether the patient has a baby or not. ARC doctors are monitored through peer review, with fellow physicians checking on the number of implanted embryos and on live birth rates.

Patients who choose the money-back guarantee must pay an up-front premium. They can purchase a refund option that covers all or part of their infertility treatments. If the treatment fails, ARC refunds all but the costs of the refund plan. The cost of refund plans vary depending on a patient's age and medical history. Older patients pay more, and the plan seems most practical for women in their late thirties.

What to Expect

When Leslie and her husband, Lou, both age forty, decided to have a baby, they tried for six months, then went to their family doctor. He suggested they keep trying for a year on their own. Worried that she was running out of reproductive years, Leslie found a fertility specialist, who immediately put them both through a fertility workup.

The fertility specialist told Leslie she had endometriosis, and that she would have to undergo a diagnostic laparoscopy under general anesthesia. Leslie read all she could about endometriosis, including that the diagnostic surgery could be done under local anesthesia. She asked her doctor if he would perform the surgery under a local, and he told her, "Absolutely not." That's when Leslie went looking for another doctor who was comfortable with performing diagnostic laparoscopy using local, instead of general, anesthesia.

She found two other fertility specialists in the phone book, and called each one. Both said they could do her diagnostic surgery under local anesthesia, but one doctor offered to let her watch via video, which appealed to her. "He listened to all my questions, telling me my options, explaining how he made his choices," she says. She felt even more confident when she met the doctor and his staff. "I liked the way they treated me. He made an effort to be personable, and was responsive to details. He didn't seem too busy to talk."

It's important for you to understand as much as you can about your condition and the possibilities for treatment. If you know about your body and how it works, you can interact with, not just react to, your doctor. Well-informed, educated couples can discuss their situation more specifically with the doctor and his staff, which helps facilitate making the best choices in diagnostic tests and treatments.

A fertility workup does not have to be a long, drawn-out process. Within one or two months, a fertility specialist should be able to give you a diagnosis of what's wrong, tell you what can be done about the problem, and give you an idea of your chances of pregnancy.

For every diagnostic procedure the doctor suggests, you ought to know what to expect from the procedure and what alternatives are available. In the case of treatments, you ought to know the doctor's success with each one and, if it doesn't work, what the next step may be.

An infertility practice is not at all like a family practice or general ob-gyn or urology practice. A fertility specialist can't see thirty or forty patients a day, spending only five to ten minutes with each patient. Even if your doctor is busy and can't always be available to review your situation with you at each visit, this doesn't mean that your treatment should suffer. These doctors have to build up a staff around them to collect and disseminate information, answer questions, and perform certain procedures. But the doctor should always be available in the event that problems arise that only he can respond to appropriately. The clinic staff may screen the doctor's calls and provide routine information over the phone. You should be able to get in touch with a nurse or a counselor easily and, if need be, see or talk to the doctor.

Most fertility specialists do the least invasive, simplest procedures first, then go on to more complicated procedures. Yet some people want the most aggressive treatment right away. Your individual circumstances and needs help you and the doctor make the right choice. Your doctor should lay out all of the options available to you and discuss the pros and cons of each. There are almost always several treatment options possible.

Sometimes couples ask their doctor, "What would you do if you were in this situation?" Considering the medical facts, he may say, "I would do this." But he is not you. Besides physical concerns, emotional and social issues have to be considered. You and your spouse should be able to come to your own decisions about what seems best for you, given your particular circumstances. The doctor can help you make a decision, but if you ask him to make it for you, when you look back on your treatment later on you may wish you had actively participated in the decision-making process.

It's unrealistic for you to expect your doctor to take sole responsibility for your care. You have to take some responsibility for yourself. The first thing you can do is to learn about the diagnosis of your infertility and the available treatments so that you can discuss your care intelligently with your doctor.

Trust is an important element in your care. You needn't blindly trust your doctor. But if you don't have enough confidence or trust in your doctor, find one you do trust and have confidence in.

Learn as much as you can about your treatment, and don't lose sight of your goals. If you listen, think, and communicate well with your doctor, you will be able to decide when it's appropriate to question your doctor about his recommendations.

If the communication between you and your doctor is not going well, if you feel uncomfortable, or if you aren't getting what you want from the doctor or his staff, be explicit and say what's bothering you. If you still don't feel right, consider finding another doctor.

What Is a Good Fertility Center?

"When I visited my fertility doctor's office, I felt like I was in a living room, not a doctor's office," says Sandy. "I got a warm, cozy feeling, which helped me feel comfortable about being there."

A good fertility center will have an on-site fertility laboratory equipped with the latest medical technology. Some also offer on-site surgery. Typically, there will be several examination rooms, one of which may be reserved exclusively for ultrasound examinations. Another may be exclusively for artificial inseminations, keeping it separate and private from other patients. There should also be a "masturbatorium," a private room stocked with appropriate erotic materials for the collection of semen specimens. It should be quiet, where the man won't be disturbed, and be roomy enough for both the husband and wife if she wants to assist in obtaining the semen sample. Studies by the Chapel Hill Fertility Center and others show that this environment has an important effect on the number, motility, and shape of sperm provided in the sample.

To ensure that the laboratory provides high-quality tests and procedures, ask whether it is accredited by a national organization, such as the Commission on Laboratory Accreditation (COLA) or the College of American Pathologists (CAP), and whether the lab director has a doctorate degree (M.D. or Ph.D.) and is board-certified.

Federal legislation passed in 1988, the Clinical Laboratory Improvement Amendment (CLIA), calls for the accreditation of all laboratories based on strict guidelines. These guidelines call for better quality control, proficiency testing of equipment, and correlation of lab results with the doctor's findings. However, many doctors who provide infertility treatments such as artificial insemination do not have CLIA accreditation. Since treatment success depends largely on the quality of the laboratory, select a practice that can assure you of its laboratory's accreditation.

The clinic's professional staff, including the lab and operating room personnel, must be available *seven days a week*. This is critical, since certain tests and treatments have to be administered at precisely the right time of the woman's cycle. Such tests and treatments include hormone assays, ultrasound exams, cervical mucus exams, and sperm processing for artificial insemination. The doctor should also be able to perform a semen analysis and immunologic and microbiologic studies whenever he desires.

When a new couple comes into a fertility center, the doctor will perform certain basic studies in order to determine what treatment can help them have a baby. Ideally, both the man and woman should undergo prenatal screening for infectious diseases, including blood tests for the AIDS virus, hepatitis B virus, and documentation of immunity to rubella (German measles). If a woman lacks immunity to rubella, she should be given a vaccination to develop immunity before she becomes pregnant. This simple procedure eliminates the risk of her contracting rubella during pregnancy, which could result in the birth of a malformed baby.

Some basic equipment necessary for the appropriate laboratory procedures includes culture media, an incubator, and a high-quality microscope. Sperm banking should be available, with frozen husband and donor sperm stored in a liquid nitrogen tank.

If the clinic offers IVF or other assisted reproductive technologies, it needs a highly specialized embryology laboratory for handling human eggs outside of the body. This laboratory should be set up in or near the operating room where the egg retrievals take place. To become a member of the Society of Assisted Reproductive Technology of the American Society for Reproductive Medicine, an IVF clinic must have on staff a reproductive endocrinologist or a reproductive surgeon, and an embryologist familiar with human cell culture techniques. The clinic must have performed at least forty procedures and had at least three live births. An IVF laboratory must be more meticulous about every detail in performing procedures than a standard clinical laboratory.

A proper office waiting room will be designed for comfort and privacy, with several couches and easy chairs, some plants and paintings, maybe even colorful wallpaper. At Chapel Hill Fertility Center and at New York Hospital Cornell's Center for Reproductive Medicine, the waiting room also serves as a patient education area containing books and pamphlets on fertility, as well as a variety of popular magazines.

Most fertility specialists schedule sixty to ninety minutes for new couples in order to become acquainted with their histories and determine the course of their initial evaluation. Couples returning for, say, an ultrasound exam or a blood test require less scheduled time and may only need to see a trained nurse or technician. But if you need to discuss something with your doctor, make sure you ask for sufficient time on the appointment schedule for that day.

Besides the physician(s), the staff often includes nurses, lab technicians, a counselor, and various clerical personnel. If there is no reproductive urologist on staff, then the clinic should offer a referral to a urologist who treats male infertility.

The First Consultation

Before your first consultation, get all your medical records together, or have them sent ahead to your new doctor. The doctor should review with you the past records of tests and treatments at the initial interview. He may start by asking "What brings you here?" You can give specifics—"I have blocked fallopian tubes and my internist recommended seeing a fertility specialist." You should convey to your doctor whatever you feel are the most important issues or concerns on your mind.

Some standard questions the woman may be asked are: What cycle day is this for you? Have you kept a basal body temperature chart? Have you noticed any symptoms of ovulation? Do you develop premenstrual symptoms, such as fluid retention, tender breasts, or headaches, and how far in advance of your period? Have you used an ovulation predictor kit?

Some standard questions for the man may include: Have you ever fathered a child before or gotten anyone pregnant? Have you had an undescended testicle or surgery on the scrotum or groin? When you ejaculate, how much fluid comes out? Do you feel any sharp or aching pain in your testicles when lifting heavy objects? How many hours a week do you work (an indication of stress or possible on-the-job exposure to toxins that may impair fertility)?

For both partners, questions may include: How long have you been trying to have a baby? Are you taking any medications? Are you under treatment for any kind of medical problem? Do you feel any pain during intercourse? What kind of pain, and where is it located? Have you ever had any sexually transmitted diseases? How often do you have sexual intercourse?

After the initial interview, the couple is introduced to a counselor and a trained fertility nurse who listen to the doctor summarize and discuss the couple's history, and explain what tests he thinks need to be done and how to treat the problems already identified. Then they discuss with the couple what the tests and treatments mean in practical terms. The couple can start the diagnostic workup that day, or may choose to make another appointment or have a follow-up phone discussion, allowing them some time to discuss how they feel about their initial visit before taking any action.

You should never feel you are being pressured by your doctor into any particular treatment. The doctor's and his staff's role is to evaluate your situation, discuss it with you, and offer suggestions and recommendations. Your doctor should write letters to referring doctors, summarize test results, and give a copy to the couple so that the couple has a record of important test results and recommendations that they can refer to later, since it is quite common to forget certain points discussed during visits.

After the initial visit, Dr. Berger usually schedules the couple's next appointment at the fertile time of the wife's cycle, determined by having her run a simple home test that detects a surge in luteinizing hormone (LH). He likes to see couples on the day of the wife's LH surge since this is the optimal time to check the cervical mucus, perform a postcoital test, perform an ultrasound exam to document the presence of follicles, and draw blood to measure levels of LH, prolactin, and estradiol. In this single visit, he can diagnose many different conditions that cause infertility and begin to establish a treatment plan with the couple.

For the man's evaluation, Dr. Goldstein will complete the history, physical examination, semen analysis, cultures, and hormone tests on the first visit. Often a diagnosis plan can be formulated on this initial visit. If additional testing is needed, a follow-up phone discussion obviates the time and expense of an additional office visit.

Taking Your Medical History

The medical evaluation starts by focusing on the most common causes of infertility. Both partners should have a complete history and physical exam. The history and physical are important because general health problems involving weight, nutrition, and health habits can lead to infertility. Also, both work and play habits such as stress, excessive alcohol drinking, or cigarette smoking can contribute to infertility, as mentioned earlier.

The man's medical history begins with questions about childhood illnesses, especially any undescended testicles, current medical problems and their treatments, previous injuries or surgeries (including surgery on the testicles, for hernias, or vasectomy), and any family history of fertility problems. Infections of the reproductive tract can contribute to a male fertility problem, as well as common systemic infections that cause fevers, such as a flu or dental abscess. The doctor will also ask about the man's general health, whether he is under stress, has been exposed to toxic chemicals, uses any drugs, drinks alcohol, takes any long-term medications, or has been chronically exposed to heat, such as long baths, saunas, or Jacuzzis. A sexual history includes questions about the frequency of sexual intercourse and any problems with libido or ejaculation.

The woman's medical history will include questions about abdominal and pelvic surgery as well as any pregnancies. A menstrual history will include questions about when she began menstruating, what her cycles are like, when her last period started, and physical or emotional changes at ovulation or before or during menstruation. A sexual history will include questions about the frequency and timing of sex and if she experiences any discomfort during sex. Pain during intercourse, or dyspareunia, is a symptom that should always be taken seriously; it might be due to a pelvic infection or endometriosis. A careful history should elicit details about the pain and determine if it's related to a particular time of the menstrual cycle.

Endometriosis may cause pain with intercourse as well as pain immediately before and during menstruation and sometimes at ovulation. With endometriosis, tissue similar to the lining of the uterus (the endometrium) grows outside the uterus on or in other pelvic organs, and often leads to scar formation. During menstruation, the areas of endometriosis become engorged with blood. The more filled with blood and the closer the areas of endometriosis are to nerve endings in the reproductive tract, the more likely a woman is to feel pain.

Pain at ovulation may have to do with changes in the size of the ovary during ovulation. The microscopic follicle expands to about an inch in diameter during the week before ovulation as it fills with fluid. If scar tissue encloses the ovary, as the follicle expands it may push against the restricting scar tissue and cause pain.

Unfortunately, in many cases the diagnosis of endometriosis comes after the disease has been present for years and has advanced beyond its earliest stages. Frequently, the only symptom of endometriosis is infertility, and therefore this condition should always be considered during a fertility evaluation.

The Physical Exams

During the physical exams, general body appearance, fat and hair distribution, and breast development may reveal hormonal imbalances. For the man, the size and consistency of the testicles and ducts may indicate a blockage or poor sperm production. The physical may reveal a varicocele or an undescended testicle. For the woman, a pelvic exam may reveal infections of the vagina or cervix, or previous pelvic inflammatory disease, or suggest other abnormalities of the uterus, fallopian tubes, or ovaries.

The Man's Physical

A complete physical and detailed examination of the testicles can give a fertility specialist a good clue to a man's reproductive function. Hormonal deficiencies are often reflected by an abnormal or "feminized" body

71

shape, poorly developed pubic hair, or enlarged breasts. Sperm production is often reflected in the size and consistency of the testicles. Small, soft testicles generally denote a man has poor sperm production, while large, firm testicles usually mean he has good sperm production.

If a man has testicles of normal size and consistency, yet no sperm in his semen, this suggests that he is making sperm but they can't get out. On the other hand, a man with small, soft testicles who has a low sperm count or produces no sperm at all suggests a sperm production problem, which could be hereditary, hormonal, or due to a varicocele.

Just as cardiologists have their stethoscopes to listen to the heart and neurologists their rubber hammers to check the reflexes, male infertility specialists use orchidometers to measure the testicles. Like measuring spoons on a string, the orchidometer has various-size plastic orbs tied together. Your doctor simply matches each testicle to the appropriate-size orb hanging from the orchidometer. A normal testicle is about the size and shape of a small hen's egg.

If your doctor finds you have testicles of normal size and consistency, he will feel for the ducts that run behind them—the epididymis and vas deferens—to make sure they are present. About one in a thousand men is born without any vas deferens. This condition cannot be surgically corrected, but a new combination of procedures gives these men a good chance at fertility. These men have the sperm microsurgically extracted from the epididymis and injected into the wife's eggs in the IVF lab. With this revolutionary technique, a single sperm can be extracted and injected into the wife's egg to achieve a pregnancy. Dr. Goldstein has also been successful in microsurgically creating a sac made up of the man's own tissue so that sperm can accumulate and later be extracted with a fine needle.

VARICOSE VEINS IN THE SCROTUM • Once your doctor has determined that a man's testicles and ducts are normal, he will examine the scrotum for a varicocele. A varicocele is a mass of enlarged or dilated veins in the spermatic cord within the scrotum, like varicose veins in the leg. The enlarged vein causes pooling of blood and a rise in temperature in the testicles. This temperature rise is thought to inhibit sperm production and may affect fertility.

A varicocele is the most common, identifiable cause of male infertility. About 15 percent of all men, fertile or infertile, have a varicocele, so just having one doesn't mean that your sperm production will necessarily be impaired. Between 30 and 40 percent of men who have never fathered a child have a varicocele. But 80 percent of men who were once fertile and are now infertile have varicoceles. This means that men with varicoceles are at risk for a steady deterioration in fertility. Varicoceles are usually larger on the left side, since the vein on that side is longer and has a higher inner pressure than the vein on the right side. A varicocele in both testicles is common but is rare on just the right side alone.

No one knows why certain men with varicoceles are infertile, but recent research suggests that the pool of stagnant blood heats up inside the testicle's vein. In an animal model, varicoceles have been associated with increased testicular temperature and increased blood flow within the testicle. The high temperature impairs normal sperm production and motility, leading to infertility.

Dr. Goldstein has proven that, in humans, varicoceles do indeed raise testicular temperature. This had been suggested by temperature studies of the surface of the scrotum, but Dr. Goldstein has recently measured the temperature inside the testicle. His studies show that a varicocele in one testicle raises the temperature within both testicles. What's more, his data also document that repairing these varicoceles causes a drop in testicular temperature, confirming animal studies of varicocele repair.

The basic exam for a varicocele is similar to the simple "turn-your-head-and-cough" testicle check. The doctor has the man stand upright in a warm room (the warmth relaxes the scrotum) and cough to make the veins in the scrotum stand out. (By the way, the doctor has him turn his head only so he doesn't cough right on the doctor.) This will allow an experienced doctor to detect a large or medium varicocele. Then he has the man do what's called Valsalva's maneuver, in which the man strains as if he were having a difficult bowel movement. The squeezing makes the veins bulge out even more so that the doctor can detect smaller varicoceles.

A rectal exam completes the man's evaluation, allowing the doctor to detect abnormalities of the prostate and seminal vesicles, which contribute most of the fluid to a man's ejaculate.

The Woman's Physical

Following a general and complete physical exam, the woman's pelvic exam starts with a check for vaginal disorders. Examining the discharge from the vagina may help identify the presence of bacteria and other microorganisms that can contribute to infertility.

If an inflammatory discharge is present, a sample of vaginal secretion is checked for the pH (acidity level). A look through a microscope at the sample may reveal a high white blood cell count, which indicates that the woman has an inflamed vagina (vaginitis). The doctor can also perform a simple test, dissolving cells from the vaginal fluid in a salt solution of potassium hydroxide, to identify yeast organisms, and also perform a "wet prep," covering a slide with saltwater solution to identify the rapidly moving organism called trichomonas.

It's essential for you and your mate to know the specific causes of a vaginal infection. Some bacteria can damage the upper genital tract (the uterus, fallopian tubes, and ovaries); yeasts are more benign, although the symptoms of vaginitis from a yeast infection are just as irritating as from a bacterial infection. When pathogenic or potentially harmful bacteria may infect the lower genital tract (the vagina and cervix), a woman may notice a creamy gray or yellow discharge and an unpleasant odor. But more often, these lower tract infections produce no symptoms at all.

Viruses that cause vaginitis can be difficult to diagnose, except for the herpes virus, which typically causes blisters that become ulcers on the vulva. (Parasitic organisms, such as trichomonas, are usually more easy to diagnose than viral infections.) Another common viral infection of the vagina, human papilloma virus (HPV), causes genital warts, or condyloma. While genital warts can become quite large on the vulva (the outer part of the vagina), these lesions are often too small to see in the vagina or on the cervix except through a colposcopic examination. This exam involves using a magnifying instrument to get an enlarged view of the vagina and cervix.

The papilloma virus itself is not thought to cause pelvic inflammatory disease, but often is accompanied by other bacterial organisms that do. Women with genital warts are more likely to have infections with chlamydia, ureaplasma, gonorrhea, and anaerobic bacteria that can inflame the fallopian tubes and lead to infertility. (If a woman has genital warts, her partner should also be examined and treated for penile warts.) Papilloma virus has been implicated as a cause of cervical dysplasia, or abnormal cell growth, and cervical cancer.

Vaginal adenosis, a disorder related to exposure to diethylstilbestrol (DES) in utero, has also been associated with fertility problems. Even if you have no known history of DES exposure, if your fertility specialist sees adenosis (outgrowths of the cervical lining in the vagina) over the outer portion of the cervix in the vagina, you may have an anatomical defect higher up the reproductive tract, such as a ridge (septum) down the center of the cervix or uterus, an abnormally formed, T-shaped uterus, or cysts on your tubes.

CERVICAL EXAM • A cervical exam usually begins with the fertility specialist looking at the appearance of the cervix. If it looks red or bleeds when touched with a sterile Q-tip, this suggests an inflammation called cervicitis.

In Dr. Berger's opinion, it's important to make sure that you have no active infection of the lower genital tract before performing any invasive tests in the fertility workup. These tests include injecting dye into the uterus to take an X ray (hysterosalpingogram), pushing a solution through the fallopian tubes (hydrotubation), taking a fragment of the uterine lining (endometrial biopsy), or looking into the uterine cavity through a tiny telescope (hysteroscopy). These tests, often necessary to evaluate the extent of pelvic problems, can spread a lower tract infection farther up the woman's reproductive tract where it may cause damage to the uterus, tubes, and ovaries.

One of the most important tests is the postcoital test to see whether you are producing "fertile" mucus that allows your mate's sperm to swim through it. Dr. Berger performs this test at the most fertile time of the cycle, on the day of the LH surge, which can be determined using a simple at-home test kit.

Fertile mucus looks like the white of an uncooked egg: it's clear and transparent. It also is elastic and stretches about four inches, has a low viscosity (is not too gel-like) and a relatively high (alkaline) pH to allow sperm to survive in it. Nonfertile mucus is cloudy, sticky, not stretchy, may have white blood cells in it, is acidic, and will prevent sperm from entering the upper reproductive tract. (See illustration of fertile mucus.)

A woman may have scanty, inflamed, or no mucus due to an infection of the cervix that involves the mucus glands or possibly due to a treatment required after a previous abnormal Pap smear or a hormonal problem. Either cryocautery (freezing the cervix to treat cervical dysplasia or warts) or a cervical conization (surgery to cut out a cone-shaped portion of the cervix) may damage the mucus glands, causing them not to function properly.

The cervix, as well as the vagina, can be affected by in utero exposure to DES, causing cervical adenosis. The mucus membrane lining the cervical canal, or endocervix, grows on the outer surface of the cervix or vagina, creating an abnormality at the junction between the two. The growth of this mucus membrane where there should be epithelium can continue out into the vagina, causing vaginal adenosis.

If the same kind of thing happened to the lining of your respiratory tract, the mucus membrane that lines the inside of the nose would grow onto the outside of the nose. In many ways, the mucus in the reproductive and respiratory tracts functions similarly. Mucus in your nose protects the lungs by catching dust, smoke, bacteria, and viruses. In the cervix (which, incidentally, feels like and is about the size of the tip of the nose), mucus also traps microorganisms and foreign agents including sperm, except when the mucus changes consistency near ovulation to allow sperm to pass through it. Disorders such as infections, surgical trauma, hormonal deficiencies, and DES-related abnormalities can prevent the cervix from producing fertile mucus.

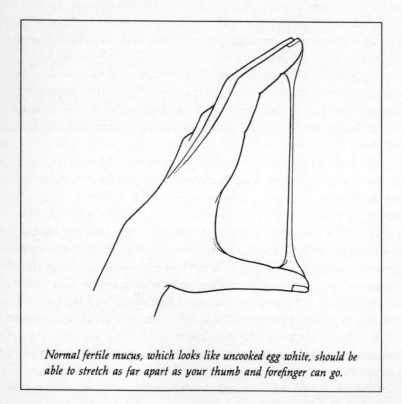

Normal fertile mucus, which looks like uncooked egg white, should be able to stretch as far apart as your thumb and forefinger can go.

THE UTERUS • A physical examination of the uterus may show whether its position, shape, or size is abnormal. In most cases, the uterus is in a mid or anterior (forward) position, tilted toward the bladder. If a woman's uterus is in a retroverted position—tilted backward—this may be normal, or it may be a suspicious sign of possible endometriosis or pelvic adhesions. If the area next to the uterus, called the adnexa, feels tender and the uterus isn't easily moved, this may mean that scars have formed between the pelvic organs, usually from previous pelvic inflammatory disease or endometriosis.

Occasionally, a physical exam alone can determine whether a woman's uterus has an abnormal shape—such as a double uterus, or an indentation in the top of the uterus—though this is more commonly picked up on an ultrasound scan, a hysterosalpingogram, or by laparoscopy.

The most common uterine abnormality is an enlarged uterus that feels firm to the touch and has an irregular shape. This often suggests uterine leiomyomas (fibroids) or adenomyosis (endometriosis of the uterine muscle). But it may also mean that the woman is pregnant. If the pelvic exam reveals that your uterus is enlarged, particularly if it's also soft, or if your period is late, the first thing to do is have a pregnancy test!

FALLOPIAN TUBES • Unlike the other female reproductive organs, normal fallopian tubes can't be felt on a physical exam even if a woman is very thin. If the doctor can feel a tubular structure, or thinks he can, this commonly indicates that the woman has fluid in the tube. This condition, called hydrosalpinx ("hydro" for water, "salpinx" for tube) is easily detected on a vaginal ultrasound scan, a hysterosalpingogram, or a diagnostic laparoscopy.

THE OVARIES • During a pelvic exam, your doctor feels for an enlargement on the ovaries, such as a cyst or firm nodules. If both ovaries are enlarged, you may have polycystic ovarian disease (PCOD), which is characterized by many enlarged, smooth ovarian cysts. This finding is easily diagnosed by an ultrasound scan and a check of hormone levels, which tend to show elevations of luteinizing hormone throughout the cycle as well as high amounts of androgens.

At the end of your pelvic exam, the fertility specialist should perform a rectovaginal exam. This involves inserting one finger in the vagina and one in the rectum in order to feel for any abnormalities in the space between these two organs. This is an important part of the exam since the presence of nodules in the rectovaginal space or on the lower back side of the uterus (cul-de-sac) is often the only finding on a physical examination that indicates endometriosis.

Once you have found a fertility specialist and had your initial history and physical, you and your doctor can sit down and discuss the tests and possible treatments to overcome your particular fertility problems.

Questions You May Have About Your Doctor

Is the doctor board certified in obstetrics and gynecology, reproductive endocrinology, or urology?

Has your doctor completed additional training in reproductive medicine and microsurgery? If so, is the doctor a member of the Society of Reproductive Surgeons?

Is he or she a member of the American Society for Reproductive Medicine? If so, then is the doctor a member of any ASRM specialty societies, such as the Society of Reproductive Endocrinologists, the Society of Reproductive Surgeons, or the Society of Assisted Reproductive Technology?

Does the doctor limit his or her practice to the treatment of infertility? If not, what percentage of his or her practice is related to the treatment of infertility?

How many infertile couples has he or she treated, and what is his or her overall success rate for your specific condition?

Questions You May Have About His or Her Practice

If I phone your office, will I speak with you or an assistant? When will I hear back from you?

Do you have special hours to answer phone questions? (Be prepared for a busy signal during these times.)

What are your office hours?

What are your fees?

Do you have (or use) a laboratory that is accredited by COLA, CAP, or CLIA?

If you examine and process sperm in your laboratory, is this performed by an andrologist? Does the laboratory director have a doctoral degree? Is the lab director board certified?

What medicines and diagnostic tests do you often prescribe?

How do you handle medical insurance?

(If the doctor is part of a large practice:) How often will I see you and how often will I see associates?

Will you see me for tests or treatments if I ovulate on a weekend or holiday?

Do you have a trained counselor on your staff to help couples deal with the stress and emotional impact of infertility?

Does your staff provide educational and written materials about tests and treatments?

Do you involve the infertile couple in the treatment?

Questions Your Doctor Is Looking to Answer in the Initial Workup

For the man

Is he producing enough sperm?

Are his sperm moving fast enough in a forward progressive fashion? Are they normally shaped?

Are his sperm passages clear and open?

Does he ejaculate high in the vagina near the woman's cervix?

Has he had or does he have any diseases, infections, operations, or congenital problems that may affect his fertility?

Does he have a varicocele?

For the woman

Is she ovulating?

Is the uterus in the normal position and of normal size?

Are the ovaries or fallopian tubes blocked, enlarged, or bound up with adhesions?

Does the cervix produce an adequate amount of favorable mucus to receive the migrating sperm?

Has she had or does she have any diseases, infections (particularly pelvic or cervical), or congenital problems that may affect her fertility?

5

THE
FERTILITY
EVALUATION

Initial Tests

Once you have found a fertility specialist and gone through a history and physical exam, the likelihood of your achieving a pregnancy depends largely on a full, coordinated evaluation involving both partners. In more than half of infertile couples, both the husband and the wife contribute to their infertility problem. So both partners need a complete, thorough fertility investigation, starting with a series of basic tests.

Before you start, let's recognize that there is no "perfect" score for these tests. There is a range of normal values for various diagnostic tests. Frequently, a man and a woman may each have "low-normal" test results, which, when put together, mean that they have been unable to have a baby. Improving, and, it is hoped, optimizing, each partner's low or abnormal fertility test scores will maximize your chance of becoming parents.

The probability of a pregnancy is based on a number of independent variables multiplied together. Consider the common situation where the husband and wife each have conditions that impair their fertility. For example, the husband's fertility, based on a reduced sperm count due to a varicocele, is 50 percent of normal values. His wife's studies show that she ovulates only in 50 percent of cycles and that one of her fallopian tubes is blocked. With only three relative infertility factors, their probability of conception is: 0.5 (varicocele) x 0.5 (ovulation factor) x 0.5 (tubal factor) = 0.125, or 12.5 percent of normal.

Now, realize that even normal, fertile couples have only a 25 percent probability of conceiving in any one cycle if they don't use contraception and make love at the wife's most fertile time of the cycle. So this couple's chance of conceiving in any given month, *without treatment,* is only 0.25 x 0.125 = 0.03125, or 3 percent! Thus, independent variables multiplied together can dramatically reduce the odds of a couple achieving a pregnancy. *In order to maximize the chances of conception, each partner's contributing infertility factors must be identified and corrected or improved as much as possible.*

In addition, some procedures, such as repair of a man's varicocele and treatment of a woman's endometriosis, create a "window" of optimal fertility. Therefore, both partners' treatments must be coordinated to ensure that their fertility problems have been evaluated and treated properly, and timed for the best possible results.

It makes sense to evaluate both partners' fertility potential before one undergoes major treatment, such as surgery, to improve fertility. For example, repairing a woman's blocked fallopian tubes surgically will do nothing to enhance a couple's fertility potential if her husband produces no sperm.

Initial Lab Tests for Women

Fertility testing for new couples begins with the most simple procedures to diagnose the most common and easily corrected problems. Each problem should be treated as soon as it's recognized. If the woman doesn't get pregnant within a specified number of cycles, then the "workup" moves on to the more difficult problems or conditions that require more invasive tests and more aggressive treatments.

At Chapel Hill Fertility Center, the workup begins with a prenatal blood screening of both partners. This includes testing for infection with hepatitis virus and the AIDS virus, typing their blood, checking for rubella (German measles) immunity, and a multichemistry panel to assess their general health. The screening checks heart, liver, and kidney function, cholesterol levels, and blood sugar, and provides a complete blood count.

Cervical Cultures

At the time of a woman's initial examination by Dr. Berger, the first laboratory tests usually include a variety of bacterial cultures of the cervix. After wiping the cervix with a sterile cotton pad soaked in sterile saline solution, samples from the cervical canal are obtained with sterile cotton swabs like Q-tips and examined to identify the various potentially harmful genital organisms, such as chlamydia, mycoplasma, ureaplasma, neisseria (gonorrhea), and gardnerella, as well as various other aerobic and anaerobic bacteria.

Few clinics offer such complete bacterial screening, although most now screen specifically for chlamydia and gonorrhea. Many physicians perform limited cultures only when a symptom is present, but most genital tract infections have no symptoms. Because infectious conditions are easy to diagnose and treat, it's usually the best place to start an infertility evaluation. If the tests reveal potentially harmful bacteria, then both partners should be treated simultaneously with appropriate antibiotics for the specific bacteria. Treating infections is one of the easiest ways to eliminate a problem of "hostile" cervical mucus—when a woman's mucus kills off her husband's sperm due to inflammation of the cervix (cervicitis).

A wide variety of bacteria may be found in a woman's vagina, including anaerobic bacteria (which survive with little or no oxygen) and aerobic bacteria (which need higher concentrations of oxygen to survive). The primary vaginal anaerobic bacteria include prevotella (previously called bacteroides), peptococcus, peptostreptococcus, and clostridia. If they find their way up through the cervix to the uterus or fallopian tubes, they may be especially dangerous since they can cause major pelvic infections and abscesses. For that reason, Dr. Berger believes that anaerobic bacteria in the cervical canal should be eradicated before they gain access to the uterus, tubes, or peritoneal cavity.

Potentially harmful aerobic bacteria frequently found in the cervix include group D streptococcus, or enterococcus, which may cause cervical bleeding and inflammation (a tip-off of infection) and may interfere with cervical mucus production; group B beta hemolytic streptococcus, which can infect, and even kill, a newborn baby if a mother carries the infection during the baby's birth; and staphylococcus aureus, which has been associated with toxic shock syndrome, a serious and potentially fatal form of blood infection first associated with the Rely superabsorbent tampon.

A culture of the man's semen is also appropriate at the time of the first semen analysis. (There's more about testing the husband later in this chapter.) In most cases, the same organisms that appear in the wife's cervix also are found in the husband's semen. This shouldn't be surprising, since sexual partners expose each other to bacteria in each of their genital tracts. That is why, in order to clear an infection in either partner, it is *essential that both sex partners be treated together.* (This is one example of why the *couple* is the infertility specialist's "patient.")

Cervical Mucus Tests

Warren and Bernadette tried to have a baby for more than a year before they were referred to a fertility specialist in New York City. "The doctor had all the up-to-date equipment and, being a real go-getter, he suggested we try an intrauterine insemination (IUI) before performing any tests," recalls Warren, age thirty-eight, a guidance counselor. Bernadette, a thirty-six-year-old teacher, did not get pregnant. After testing his sperm penetration in Bernadette's mucus, Warren says, "The doctor told us there was something in my sperm fluid that was preventing the sperm from being mobile, but he didn't know what it was." Two other IUI attempts failed.

Then the couple moved to North Carolina and were referred to Dr. Berger. "He systematically and thoroughly checked everything out before continuing with treatment," says Bernadette. He diagnosed irregular ovulation for her and low sperm motility for Warren. But a postcoital test timed around Bernadette's ovulation showed that Warren's sperm were unable to penetrate her mucus. "We had never done a home ovulation test, and had only estimated when Bernadette was ovulating, which was difficult to do with her irregular cycles," Warren says. "Our first doctor had timed the IUIs two or three days too early. Dr. Berger knew the right time for insemination almost down to the hour." After only one IUI attempt at Chapel Hill Fertility Center, Bernadette became pregnant.

"I was surprised she got pregnant the first try," says Warren. "After the IUI, I didn't want to lift my hopes up again. Then we did the home pregnancy test, and it was positive, and Dr. Berger confirmed it." Bernadette, who now has a healthy three-year-old says, "We're going to go for as many children as we can."

A cervical mucus examination should be performed when a woman is most likely to have fertile mucus, that is, on the day of the surge of luteinizing hormone (LH). (See the diagram of hormones through a normal menstrual cycle on page 86.)

This simple test samples the wife's cervical mucus to see whether the sperm are swimming freely. This basic test of sperm interaction is called the postcoital test (PCT). It indicates whether a man's sperm can penetrate and survive in his wife's mucus. It should be performed on the day before his wife ovulates, which she identifies by detecting her LH surge with a home urine test kit.

Your doctor should ask you when you last had intercourse before performing the test. For example, if a couple made love twelve to thirty-six hours before coming in for their visit, and the doctor sees sperm moving in the cervical mucus, that's an excellent sign that the wife's mucus isn't "hostile" to her husband's sperm. But if only a few sperm are moving only two hours after the couple had intercourse, then they have a sperm-mucus interaction problem.

Another mucus penetration test, called the Penetrak test, should also be performed. Sperm are allowed to migrate up thin tubes filled with bovine (cow's) cervical mucus to see how far they penetrate over a specific time (ninety minutes). If this test reveals normal sperm penetration but a properly timed postcoital test reveals only dead sperm, then the wife's cervical mucus is likely to be contributing to poor sperm survival or motility.

Yet another test places the husband's sperm and the wife's mucus side by side on a glass slide, and a laboratory technician checks whether the sperm can penetrate and swim freely in the mucus. The sperm-mucus mixture is kept at body temperature and looked at under the microscope periodically. A man with a good sperm count who hasn't been able to impregnate his wife might have good sperm survival for an hour, but then the sperm stop moving or die before they ever reach her eggs. A look at how quickly sperm die in this slide sperm-mucus interaction test may explain this couple's infertility.

If the postcoital and slide penetration tests reveal only dead sperm even though the wife's mucus appears to be fertile, and the Penetrak test reveals normal sperm penetration through the cow's mucus, this implies that there is something about the wife's mucus that's "hostile" to her husband's sperm. Infections and antibodies are frequently found to be the culprits. If sperm become immobilized both in the wife's mucus and cow's mucus, the sperm themselves are more likely to be the problem. Additional tests may use donor fertile mucus with the husband's sperm and donor sperm with the wife's mucus, placed together on a glass microscope slide, referred to as a "cross-match" test.

Since cervical mucus is receptive to sperm migration for a limited time during the menstrual cycle, these tests should all be performed when the mucus sample is most likely to reveal its actions upon the sperm, that is, on the day of the LH surge. Unfortunately, in many doctors' offices, *one of the most frequent causes for an abnormal PCT is that it was performed on the wrong day of the wife's cycle.* Remember that the mucus normally assumes

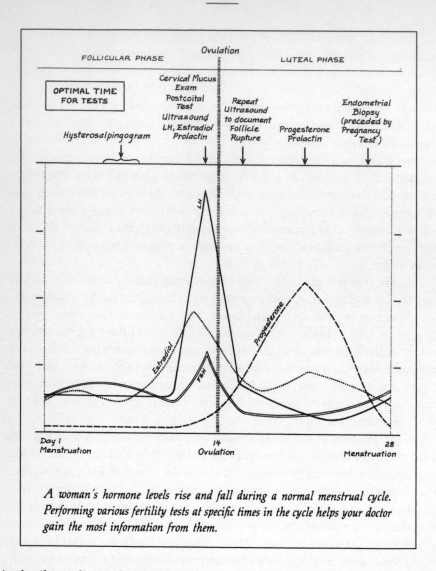

FOLLICULAR PHASE   Ovulation   LUTEAL PHASE

OPTIMAL TIME FOR TESTS

Hysterosalpingogram

Cervical Mucus Exam
Postcoital Test
Ultrasound
LH, Estradiol
Prolactin

Repeat Ultrasound to document Follicle Rupture

Progesterone Prolactin

Endometrial Biopsy (preceded by Pregnancy Test)

LH

Estradiol

FSH

Progesterone

Day 1 Menstruation   14 Ovulation   28 Menstruation

A woman's hormone levels rise and fall during a normal menstrual cycle. Performing various fertility tests at specific times in the cycle helps your doctor gain the most information from them.

its fertile quality and permits sperm survival only around the time of ovulation. Like any test, the PCT can provide extremely useful information, but only if it's performed at the proper time of the cycle.

Ultrasound Scans

The next step in the evaluation is an ultrasound (US) scan to look at the thickness and pattern of the endometrial lining and monitor follicle development to assure that a woman is ovulating. In the past, an ultrasound scan involved applying a probe to the outside of the woman's abdomen over a full bladder in order to scan the ovaries and assess the size of her follicles. Now, with newer vaginal ultrasound scans, the tip of the probe is placed into the woman's vagina near her cervix so that it comes closer to the pelvic organs.

The high-frequency sound waves, at this close distance, produce much clearer, sharper pictures, and can even enable imaging of the fallopian tubes if filled with fluid or blood. Although the images may look to you like a fuzzy weather map from a satellite scan, your doctor should be able to read them clearly and show you the findings during the exam.

For a vaginal scan, the US probe is covered with a clean condom and sterile lubricant (so as not to interfere with sperm motility). The woman's bladder should be empty (just the opposite of an abdominal scan, which requires a full bladder to enhance the ultrasound image), and the covered probe is inserted by a nurse or by the woman into the vagina like a tampon.

The vaginal US exam can reveal fibroids practically down to the size of the letter "o" on this page. These small benign tumors embedded in the uterine lining have a characteristic appearance: they are well-encapsulated, firm nodules that can appear in the uterine cavity (submucosal), in the muscle of the uterus (intramural), or on the uterus's outer surface (subserosal). A pea-size or smaller fibroid may not be evident on a physical exam but can be seen with a vaginal US scan.

A scan can determine how thick the uterine lining is, which is particularly useful on the day of the LH surge. A scan at that time can provide information about how well a woman's uterus is responding to hormone production. If the lining is thin, that indicates either that she is not producing adequate hormones or that her uterus is unable to respond to the amount of hormones she does produce.

Vaginal ultrasound is a safe, practical, noninvasive alternative to laparoscopy for diagnosing luteinized unruptured follicle (LUF) syndrome. From 5 to 30 percent of women with "unexplained" infertility have eggs that ripen but don't release from the follicle at ovulation. A vaginal ultrasound scan on the day of the LH surge enables a doctor to measure the size of the follicle, and a second scan two or three days later can confirm whether the follicle has ruptured or not.

In addition, this useful test can identify uterine abnormalities, such as a double horned uterus or a uterine septum. These abnormalities should be confirmed either with an X-ray dye study of the uterus (hysterosalpingogram) or a direct look through a telescopelike device placed into the uterine cavity through the cervix (hysteroscopy).

A US examination of the ovaries also helps diagnose one of the most common ovarian abnormalities—ovarian cysts, including those due to endometriosis (called endometriomas). The ultrasound scan can be used to measure the size of the ovaries and look at cysts or solid growths within the ovaries. US pictures of endometriomas, or blood-containing endometrial cysts in the ovaries, have a different appearance from the clear, fluid-containing follicles. A test for antiendometrial antibodies in a woman's blood is also helpful in screening for endometriosis.

Endometriosis afflicts as many as 10 million American women. It develops when tissue like that from the inner lining of the uterus, the endometrium, grows outside its normal location. The cells form patches and scars throughout the pelvis and around the woman's ovaries and fallopian tubes. The disease can cause severe menstrual cramps, painful intercourse, and abnormal menstruation. But frequently endometriosis causes no symptoms at all beyond infertility.

The longer the disease persists without treatment, the slimmer are a woman's chances of conceiving when she wants to. Often both women and their doctors overlook the warning signs. Fortunately, endometriosis is a treatable cause of infertility, especially if it is diagnosed early.

No one knows why some women, but not others, develop endometriosis. Most women experience "retrograde menstruation," in which some menstrual blood and tissue back up through the fallopian tubes and spill out into the pelvic cavity. The stray tissue from this retrograde menstruation may implant outside the uterus and continue to grow, reacting to each cycle of hormonal stimulation, just as the lining inside the uterus does. It isn't known why some women who experience retrograde menstruation have endometriosis while others don't, but the immune system clearly plays a role.

Another way endometriosis can arise is from misplaced cells scattered about a woman's abdominal cavity during her fetal development. According to this theory, beginning at puberty some of the cells become stimulated by the release of estrogen in each ovulatory cycle, and the "ectopic" cells grow and invade tissues outside the uterus.

Another condition similar to endometriosis is adenomyosis, in which endometrial tissue invades into the muscle of the uterus. It can be detected by a careful vaginal ultrasound study or by magnetic resonance imaging (MRI), and should be suspected in any woman with prolonged menstrual flow and pain during menstruation, especially if the uterus is somewhat enlarged on a pelvic exam.

Ovulation Monitoring

Because of her husband's male factor problems, Suzie, a forty-two-year-old caterer, went through five months of unsuccessful artificial insemination attempts by another doctor before going to see Dr. Berger. She had been testing her urine once a day with home kits but was unable to detect whether she was having an LH surge. On Dr. Berger's suggestion, she began running the test twice a day with an improved test kit (OvuKit).

The day before she had an artificial insemination, Suzie tested her urine in the morning (it was negative) and again that night. "I could tell from the weak color of the kit that I had not surged yet," she says. After an ultrasound exam confirmed that she had a preovulatory follicle present, and a blood hormone test run that day in Dr. Berger's lab indicated that the timing was right for ovulation, his nurse gave her an injection of hCG to release her egg. Because Suzie had fertile cervical mucus, Dr. Berger inseminated some of her husband Bob's sperm into her cervical canal later that day. The following day another scan showed that the egg had, indeed, been released by the follicle, and he inseminated some more of Bob's sperm into Suzie's uterine cavity and fallopian tubes. "I felt good knowing that some sperm had been put inside before the egg was being released, and then some after," says Suzie.

Most women have ovulation tests on the same day as their mucus exams and ultrasound scans. During their initial visit to his office, couples learn from Dr. Berger's staff how to use a simple, at-home ovulation testing kit. Dr. Berger then asks them to schedule their second office visit on the day of the wife's LH surge.

Another simple, widely used method to check on ovulation is the basal body temperature (BBT) chart. The basal body temperature is one's temperature upon waking up. First thing in the morning before getting up or doing anything else, the woman records her temperature on a daily chart. A special BBT thermometer with an expanded, easy-to-read scale is available at most pharmacies or fertility clinics. If you have been keeping a BBT chart at home, be sure to bring it with you to the doctor's office on your initial visit.

In a normal twenty-eight-day cycle, from day one of the cycle (the first day of menstruation) through days twelve to fourteen, a woman's BBT is usually between 97.2 and 97.6 degrees Fahrenheit (between 36.2 and 36.4 degrees centigrade). From just after ovulation, at midcycle, through to the onset of the next period, the BBT rises as much as one degree.

This temperature change results from fluctuations in hormone levels. Estrogen, predominant before ovulation, tends to lower body temperature. Progesterone, produced after ovulation by the corpus luteum (the structure left after the follicle releases the egg), tends to raise body temperature. So the temperature early in the menstrual cycle will be low, and when the woman ovulates and progesterone is released, the temperature will rise. The BBT chart should reflect this rise in temperature: the curve on the chart normally is low in the early part of the cycle, rises at, or right after, ovulation, and remains high until the woman's next cycle.

The rise in temperature at ovulation can happen suddenly in one day or slowly over several days. If a woman's temperature stays elevated for sixteen days or more, she may be pregnant, since the corpus luteum usually stops producing progesterone after thirteen to fifteen days.

The BBT pattern is useful *in retrospect*, but not too helpful in telling whether a woman is about to ovulate. Unfortunately, the temperature changes are obvious only *after* ovulation, so it's like someone telling you "Get off the bus the stop before me."

BBT charts aren't actually able to confirm ovulation, but they can be useful in making educated guesses about ovarian hormone production. If a woman's BBT chart shows no temperature rise, she probably does not have the typical hormone fluctuations through the cycle and is probably not ovulating. A BBT rise that lasts less than twelve days after the LH surge suggests luteal phase defect, in which the uterine lining fails to be maintained properly after ovulation.

In some cases your fertility specialist may order another ultrasound scan two or three days after the LH surge to confirm follicle rupture and ovulation. The advantage of US over the other methods used to detect ovulation—keeping a BBT chart or measuring the progesterone level in the blood—is that it can pinpoint the day of ovulation and document follicle rupture rather than simply reflect increased progesterone production (which can occur even without follicle rupture if a woman has luteinized unruptured follicle syndrome).

In addition, a series of US exams can provide valuable information about the progressive growth and development of the follicles. In a normal cycle, when the diameter of a woman's follicle reaches about 20 millimeters, she is about to ovulate. Eggs released from small follicles may not be healthy, fertilizable eggs. Ultrasound monitoring of the follicles' growth can help time artificial insemination or stimulation of egg release using hormone injections.

Most fertility experts use vaginal ultrasound not only to time ovulation but also to evaluate early pregnancy, specifically to rule out the possibility of ectopic (tubal) pregnancy. The vaginal scan is more sensitive than the abdominal exam, and can detect a pregnancy developing in the uterus within a week after a woman misses her period. If the US scan is clear, but blood hCG levels are high, then an ectopic pregnancy may exist.

Hormone Screening

On the day of the wife's first follow-up visit (the day of the LH surge), Dr. Berger also tests the woman's blood for hormone levels, including LH, estradiol (the major biologically active estrogen), and the pituitary hormone prolactin, to check her ovulation response. He asks the wife to return again to check hormone levels *exactly seven days later* during the mid-luteal phase of the woman's cycle. This is the best time to measure progesterone, which should be at its peak, and a second prolactin level.

Additional hormone studies depend on the woman's history and physical exam. For example, a baseline level of LH and FSH early in the cycle helps identify women with polycystic ovarian disease (PCOD), who have a high LH to FSH ratio, as well as a high production of male hormones (androgens). To correct PCOD, which includes no or irregular ovulation, these women may have to reduce their androgen production.

In the case of PCOD patients or other women with a suspected excess of androgens, the doctor will likely order an androgen panel to check the levels of free and total testosterone and dihydroepiandrosterone sulfate (DHEAS). DHEAS is an androgen produced primarily by the adrenal gland, and a high DHEAS level suggests too much adrenal androgen output. High production of testosterone along with normal DHEAS levels indicates that the ovaries are the probable source of the excess androgens.

Female Hormones—Normal Values

Phase of Cycle

	Follicular	Day of LH Surge	Mid-luteal
Luteinizing Hormone (LH)	<7 mIU/ml	>15 mIU/ml	—
Follicle Stimulating Hormone (FSH)	<13 mIU/ml	>15 mIU/ml	—
Estradiol	—	>100 pg/ml	—
Progesterone	—	<1.5 ng/ml	>15 ng/ml

	At any time
Prolactin	<25 ng/ml
Thyroid Stimulating Hormone (TSH)	0.4–3.8 uIU/ml
Free T3	1.4–4.4 pg/ml
Free Thyroxine (T4)	0.8–2.0 ng/dl
Total Testosterone	6.0–86 ng/dl
Free Testosterone	.07–3.6 pg/ml
DHEAS	35–430 ug/dl
Androstenedione	07.–3.1 ng/ml

< = less than
> = greater than
mIU = milli International Units
ml = milliliter
pg = picograms
ng = nanograms
uIU = micro International Units
dl = deciliter
ug = micrograms

Values from Chapel Hill Fertility Center laboratory. Normal values may vary in other laboratories.

Some PCOD patients produce excess androgens from the ovaries and the adrenals.

Almost all of a woman's hormone abnormalities can be picked up by doing the appropriate studies on these two specific days of the menstrual cycle—the day of the LH surge and seven days later in the mid-luteal phase. After two visits and two days of testing, Dr. Berger already has determined whether a woman has fertile cervical mucus, a normal preovulatory follicle, normal hormone levels accompanying ovulation, and a normal luteal phase of her cycle.

With these first two follow-up visits, he will not yet have evaluated all potential anatomic problems, but at this early point in the woman's workup he will have detected ovulation defects, hormone abnormalities, infectious problems, and male factor infertility. As soon as Dr. Berger gets all of this information, he can institute appropriate therapies to correct any abnormalities. Follow-up evaluation in the next cycle will confirm whether the abnormal conditions have, in fact, been corrected.

These tests—cervical cultures, cervical mucus tests, ultrasound scans, ovulation monitoring, and hormone screening—are the standard opening gambit in diagnosing a woman's fertility problems. Further testing and treatment recommendations depend on the results of these initial tests. Depending on the couple's history, the fertility specialist can go in several different diagnostic directions. For example, if a man's sperm score well on the Penetrak test but don't move easily through his wife's mucus, then the suspected diagnosis may be a cervical mucus abnormality, which could be due to an infection, a hormone deficiency, or an immunological problem, each of which needs to be investigated further.

Initial Lab Tests for Men

In addition to his wife's results, every husband should be evaluated to assess his fertility status. Initial evaluation of the male is simpler than of the female.

Certain male risk factors alert the physician to a potential problem in the man: a history of mumps as an adolescent or adult, an undescended testicle, previous urologic surgery, previous genital infections, and exposure to environmental toxins. A semen analysis and a hormone profile should be obtained on the man's initial office visit to the fertility specialist, or soon after, and, if warranted, his semen should be cultured as well.

Additional testing of sperm penetrating power, antisperm antibody levels, and a check of the testicles for sperm production may be reserved for specific situations. Usually additional testing isn't required if the man has at least two normal semen analyses, negative cultures, and a good score on the postcoital test. A more intensive evaluation by a male fertility specialist is advisable for men if these tests prove abnormal.

Don't Count on "Sperm Count"

The first person to see live sperm was Dutch scientist Anton van Leeuwenhoek, the inventor of the microscope. One of the first things he looked at in 1677 was sperm, which he believed carried the progenitors of humans inside them. More than three hundred years later, doctors still look at sperm through the microscope at the start of a fertility investigation to count the number of sperm in the ejaculate and to assess what the sperm look like and how well they move.

The volume of the semen, the sperm count, the concentration per milliliter of semen, sperm motility (the percentage of actively moving sperm), and sperm size and shape (morphology) remain the foundations of semen analysis. Yet these classic parameters are sometimes too crude to judge a man's fertility potential.

Sperm count properly refers to the total number of sperm in the ejaculate, while the number of sperm per milliliter is referred to as the sperm concentration. One way to take into account various factors—including the total sperm count, percentage of sperm with normal forward motility, and percentage of sperm with normal appearance (morphology)—is the "estimated total functional sperm count."

Although not too many doctors are accustomed to using it, at Chapel Hill Fertility Center the estimated total functional sperm count is considered the man's "bottom line." It's the one number that can be used accurately to compare different semen samples and compare a man's sperm quality to that of other men. The estimated total functional sperm count is calculated by taking the number of sperm in the entire ejaculate (the total sperm count) and multiplying that by the percentage of motile sperm, by the percentage of rapidly forwardly progressive motile sperm, and by the percentage of normal sperm forms determined by strict criteria.

Let's take an example. Both Allen and Bob have reports from their urologists that they had "normal" sperm counts. Each had a sperm concentration of 60 million sperm per milliliter, well above the normal lower limit of 20 million per milliliter. Both had been told they were fertile, but further analysis based on estimated total functional sperm count reveals that Allen was very fertile, while Bob was subfertile.

After getting a semen sample from each man, we calculate their estimated total functional sperm counts:

Allen	**Bob**
60 million sperm per milliliter	60 million sperm per milliliter
5 milliliters in the ejaculate	2.5 milliliters in the ejaculate
50% motility	25% motility
50% forward motility	25% forward motility
30% normal morphology	15% normal morphology

Allen: 60 million x 5 x .50 x .50 x .30 = 22.5 million estimated total functional sperm count

Bob: 60 million x 2.5 x .25 x .25 x .15 = 1.4 million estimated total functional sperm count

Allen's estimated total functional sperm count is more than fifteen times higher than Bob's. Bob's score of 1.4 million means that he needs evaluation and treatment and his wife may need artificial intrauterine insemination with his sperm to conceive. This example shows how a man's sperm count can be misinterpreted by physicians who are not familiar with calculating the estimated total functional count.

Sperm count alone can be a misleading indicator of fertility. Most infertile men who require hormone replacements have been able to father children, even though 75 percent have low sperm counts, because the quality of their sperm is often very good. Most men with low sperm counts not only have too few sperm, but often have sperm that don't function properly.

Although a man's fertility is related to the number of normal sperm in his ejaculate, researchers have found a surprisingly wide range of sperm counts among men with proven fertility. About 20 million sperm per milliliter used to be considered the minimum concentration needed in the ejaculate to produce a baby, but the necessary functional sperm count is lower, about 10 million sperm with normal shape and motility. And men with functional sperm counts lower than 1 million sperm per milliliter can father children with the help of new technologies such as intratubal insemination (ITI), gamete intrafallopian transfer (GIFT), IVF, and intracytoplasmic sperm injection (ICSI).

Knowing, as we now do, that sperm quantity does not necessarily equal sperm quality, how do we determine what are functioning sperm, that is, sperm capable of penetrating and fertilizing eggs? One measure is sperm motility. The proportion of sperm with rapid, forward progressive motility is more important in determining a man's fertility than is the total number of sperm in his ejaculate. Under the best conditions only a limited number of sperm with good tail movement get through the female reproductive tract to reach the egg.

But motility alone doesn't determine a man's fertility either. A high sperm count may compensate for a low motility. Like Allen and Bob, two men may produce the same concentration of sperm but with a widely different volume of semen, sperm count, and motility.

New computer-assisted sperm assessments may also help correlate motility with fertility. Using the computer to track sperm through the microscope, they can quantitatively assess sperm speed and how straight they swim. At present, computer-assisted semen analysis (CASA) is most useful as a research tool.

Semen Analysis

In a normal ejaculation, the total volume of semen is between a half and a whole teaspoon. It typically contains between 40 million and 300 million total sperm. A well-developed sperm can propel itself up a woman's reproductive tract at a rate of more than two inches an hour.

It takes about ten to twelve weeks from the initiation of new sperm formation for fully mature sperm to appear in the ejaculate. The urologist, andrologist, or fertility specialist must therefore consider any significant events in the man's history as far back as three months or more before the semen analysis.

The doctor usually advises a man who is scheduled for a semen analysis to abstain from sex for two to four days beforehand. Three days is consistent with the average frequency of intercourse—about two or three times a week for most couples. Also, studies have shown that bacteria attached to sperm or in the semen are more accurately detected after at least three days of abstinence. Bacteria attached to sperm or in the semen are now known to interfere with embryo development and implantation during IVF.

A man should have the results of the semen analysis back from the doctor the same or the next day. The first thing the doctor or laboratory technologist looks at is the appearance of the semen, the time it takes to liquefy, and the volume in the ejaculate. A normal volume is about 2 to 6 milliliters (ml). A very low volume, under 1 ml, may mean that the semen doesn't contain all of the normal components. The seminal vesicles make about 60 to 65 percent of the ejaculate, including the proteins that cause the coagulated ejaculate to coagulate and come out looking like a clotted gel. About 30 percent of the seminal fluid is made by the prostate gland, which produces enzymes that cause the coagulated ejaculate to liquefy.

If the semen doesn't come out as a clotted gel, this suggests that the man's seminal vesicles are malfunctioning or absent. If the semen doesn't liquefy, this suggests a prostate disorder. Only 3 to 5 percent of the seminal fluid comes from testicular fluid and sperm. Because so little comes from the testicles, there is often nothing noticeably different in the ejaculate of a man with a zero or very low sperm count compared with a man with a normal count.

If a man has an extremely low semen volume, the seminal vesicles may not be making enough fluid, or these ducts may be blocked. When the seminal vesicles are blocked, it usually occurs where they enter into the ejaculatory ducts. This commonly happens to men born with no vas deferens, a rare condition called aplasia of the vas deferens. These men may also be missing a kidney since the vas derives in the embryo from the kidney ducts. (Men without vas deferens should have an ultrasound scan or X ray to check whether they have both kidneys.)

A low semen volume may also signify a low testosterone output, with not enough testosterone available to stimulate the seminal vesicles to produce fluid.

A high semen volume also can have its drawbacks. An abnormally high semen volume is frequently associated with an infection. For example, when the prostate gland is inflamed, seminal fluid increases. This extra fluid will dilute the sperm concentration in the semen. Even normal sperm don't function as well when their concentration has been diluted, or when the seminal plasma contains a high concentration of white blood cells and other inflammatory components. The concentration of round cells (white blood cells or immature sperm) can be determined at the same time as the sperm concentration. There shouldn't be more than 1 million round cells in any one semen sample. Special stains must be performed to determine whether the high numbers of round cells represent white blood cells associated with inflammation and possibly infection, or immature sperm.

A pH test to determine the acidity of a man's semen can help detect an infection. The normal pH range of semen is 7.5 to 8.1. If the sperm sample has a pH higher than 8.1, then an infection may be present. If the pH is less than 7.5, and a man has no sperm in the sample, then his vas deferens, seminal vesicles, or epididymis may have developed improperly.

As part of the semen analysis, the doctor—or a certified laboratory technician or andrologist—will determine the number of sperm present in the ejaculate. A normal total sperm concentration falls between 20 million per ml and 200 million per ml. The lower normal limit of total sperm in the ejaculate should be at least 40 million. Between 20 million and 40 million sperm is considered a borderline low count, and under 20 million is definitely a low count. More than 1 billion total sperm, a rare condition, is abnormally high. In this situation, the sperm can clump together, causing a motility problem.

The technician looks at how well the sperm are moving and will count the total percentage of motile sperm by observing how many sperm per hundred are moving. At least 50 percent of any given sperm population should be moving. Then the sperm motion is qualified. The observer gives no movement a grade of 0. If the sperm stay in place and vibrate, that's considered Grade 1; if they are moving very slowly or meandering along, that's Grade 2. Sperm that are moving well in a straight line receive a Grade 3, and sperm that race across the microscopic field in a straight line are Grade 4. Normal, forwardly motile sperm are rated either Grade 3 or 4. More than half of all motile sperm should have forward, progressive motility of Grades 3 or 4 combined. A good andrology lab will specify the percentage of sperm in each of these categories rather than give an eyeball estimate of "2 to 3+" as an overall statement.

Finally, the shape, or morphology, of the sperm will be determined. Normal sperm heads are oval-shaped without irregularities. If the sperm are too narrow or thin, they are considered tapered. Men with an elevated testicular temperature, frequently due to a varicocele or exposure to excessive heat, often have tapered sperm. If the sperm have a large, round head, they may be missing the acrosome, the packet of enzymes at the tip of the sperm head that allow sperm to bore through the coating of the egg.

The midpiece, the part that connects the sperm head to the sperm tail, should also look normal. The tubular midpiece contains the mitochondria that provide the energy to make the tail move. The whiplike tail itself should be of normal size and have a wavelike motion.

Recently some fertility experts have begun using stricter criteria in assessing sperm morphology. They believe that a man must have 15 percent perfect sperm without any apparent defects in shape or motility, along with a normal count, to be considered to have normal fertility. It's important for you to know whether sperm were scored using these strict Kruger criteria (named after the doctor who proposed the stringent sperm requirements) so that you don't compare apples to oranges with different types of sperm analyses, that is, whether the percentage of sperm with normal morphology was determined using the older standard criteria or the newer stricter criteria.

Of all the parameters of semen analysis, shape is the most subjective. So assessment of morphology varies from one lab to the next. The same semen sample may be interpreted as normal in one lab and abnormal in another. Motility assessment is also somewhat subjective. The sperm count is the easiest to quantitate objectively. Semen analyses performed by or under the supervision of an andrologist are more detailed and more accurate than those by general lab technicians.

Even with computer-assisted semen analysis, there is a fair amount of error, particularly when a man's sperm count is low. The computer can rapidly assess the sperm count and sperm motility in men who have normal amounts of sperm to begin with. But computerized systems tend to overestimate the sperm count and underestimate motility, sometimes by as much as 30 percent. So a computer may interpret a man's sperm count as "normal" when it actually is low. At this time, computerized systems don't assess sperm morphology accurately, but they do show promise for the future.

Most experts recommend that men undergoing fertility evaluation have more than one semen analysis performed, with at least two to four weeks in between analyses. If a man has had a high fever or is under excess stress, he may have a temporarily reduced sperm count, abnormal motility, or abnormal morphology. Even a fertile man who has a semen analysis done every month for a year might have two or three analyses showing an abnormality in at least one of the three basic semen parameters—count, motility, morphology.

If a man has a zero sperm count, his semen should be tested for the presence of the fruit sugar fructose, which is produced by the seminal vesicles. If fructose is absent from the semen, this suggests a blockage along the reproductive tract—preventing sperm from getting into the ejaculate. The semen of a man with apparently no sperm at all should be centrifuged and the pellet in the bottom of the test tube examined to see whether it contains any sperm. A careful look at the pellet may turn up an occasional sperm. It's important to distinguish a blocked duct, with an occasional sperm in the ejaculate, from an absolutely zero sperm count caused by other conditions, such as hormonal or testicular abnormality. Most andrology labs spin down the semen from a zero count, but general clinical labs do not. What may be reported as a zero sperm count in a general lab, therefore, may not actually be so.

Sperm motility appears to be a more sensitive indicator of male fertility than sperm count. Time exposure photography through the microscope and videotaping through the microscope are now available to assess motility. The camera's eye accurately catches swimming speed and direction in a totally objective measurement. A video allows for simultaneous measurement of length and width of sperm heads, and can be analyzed by a computer within one minute for a closer inspection of sperm. This is mostly done for experimental purposes only.

The Hormone Profile

The next set of lab tests measures the hormones contained in a man's blood. Just as in women, the production of the key pituitary hormones—FSH and LH—is regulated by pulses of gonadotropin-releasing hormone (GnRH) from the hypothalamus. The bloodstream transports FSH and LH to the testicles where they stimulate the production of sperm and testosterone. The blood also is tested for testosterone itself. Testosterone is the male hormone that provides the sex drive, promotes hair growth and muscle development (the secondary sexual characteristics), stimulates the prostate and seminal vesicles to make their secretions, and provides the impetus for erections. Working in concert with FSH, testosterone helps produce sperm. So a man needs normal concentrations of both FSH and testosterone within his testicles to produce an adequate number of sperm.

General Semen Analysis Report*

Patient: Spouse:

Date of Specimen: Time Specimen Produced

Time Analysis Begun: Method of Collection:

Days Since Last Ejaculation: Any Portion of Specimen Lost?

Parameter	Results	Normal Values
Color		Gray/Translucent
Coagulate?		Yes
Liquefy?		Yes
If Yes, Time in Minutes		≤ 30
Volume (ml)		2–6
Viscosity (1, 2, 3, 4)		1
pH		7.5–8.1
% Motility		≥ 50%
% of 3–4 + Forward Motile Sperm		≥ 50
Sperm Concentration (x 1 Million per ml)		20–200
Total Sperm Count (x 1 Million per ml)		≥ 40
Total Motile Sperm (x 1 Million per ml)		≥ 20
White blood cells (x 1 Million per ml)		≤ 1
Agglutination (0, 1, 2, 3)		
Clumping of sperm to sperm		0
Clumping of sperm to round cells		0
% Normal Morphology		≥ 30 %
Penetrak Score (mm)		≥ 30

ml = milliliter

mm = millimeter

≤ = Less Than or Equal to

≥ = More Than or Equal to

* Based on World Health Organization criteria, 1992

Your doctor may assess both the total testosterone level as well as the level of testosterone free, or unbound, from a protein in the blood, called sex hormone binding globulin. Sometimes the total testosterone level is normal, but the free testosterone, which is the biologically active form, may be low.

Another pituitary hormone that an infertile man should have measured, as should his wife, is prolactin. High levels of prolactin (hyperprolactinemia) inhibit testosterone and, subsequently, sperm production. Microscopic-size pituitary tumors, called prolactinomas, are often associated with high prolactin levels. Hyperprolactinemia appears to be a less common disorder among men than women, but this may be due to the fact that tests looking for this disorder are obtained much less frequently among men than women.

The "female" hormone estradiol should be measured in men as well. All men produce this hormone, just as all women have some testosterone present in their blood. High levels of estradiol may lead to breast enlargement in men, which usually is associated with decreased sperm production. The estrogen feeding back to the brain turns off production of LH

Male Hormones—Normal Values

Testosterone, total	300–1,100 ng/dl
Testosterone, free	50–210 pg/ml
Prolactin	0.1–15.2 ng/ml
Luteinizing Hormone (LH) (<50 years)	0.5–10 mIU/ml
Follicle Stimulating Hormone (FSH)	0.8–9 mIU/ml
Estradiol	<60 pg/ml

ng = nanograms
dl = deciliter
ml = milliliter
mIU = milli International Units
pg = picograms
< = less than

Values from the Endocrinology Laboratory at New York Hospital.
Normal values may vary in other laboratories.

and FSH, which in turn halts production of testosterone and sperm. High levels of estrogen often occur among men with testicle or adrenal gland tumors or those with liver diseases that prevent the normal metabolism of estrogen.

Because the hypothalamus sends pulses of GnRH to stimulate FSH and LH release frequently during the day, it may be necessary to sample a man's blood and measure his gonadotropin levels more than once to assess accurately the function of his hypothalamus or pituitary.

At the minimum, men with abnormal semen analyses should have blood tests to measure testosterone, FSH, and prolactin.

Semen Culture and Antisperm Antibodies

In addition to these initial studies, the fertility specialist may recommend more sophisticated tests. If the man has sperm clumping (agglutination) or signs of a reproductive tract infection, the doctor should obtain bacterial cultures. It is crucial that semen cultures be obtained *before* any form of artificial insemination or assisted reproductive technology like IVF is performed with the husband's sperm.

A man should wash his hands and genital area with an antiseptic solution before he produces a semen specimen for culture. This avoids contamination with normal skin bacteria that have nothing to do with infertility.

Some semen is placed in growth media and incubated at body temperature to check for any potentially harmful bacteria, such as chlamydia, mycoplasma, ureaplasma, or gonorrhea bacteria, that may affect fertility. Other bacteria, such as those that cause staph infections or a strep throat, may also be detected.

If the man's sperm agglutinate, and he has no signs of infection, then the doctor may recommend an antisperm antibody test. Until recently, tests to detect sperm antibodies relied on measuring sperm clumping or immobilization. New tests have been developed that can localize and quantify specific antibodies in the blood, in the semen, and on the sperm's surface. Greater availability and standardization of these highly specific tests should help clarify the role of antisperm antibodies in male infertility. One particular test, the immunobead test, is currently the best commercially available one for looking at antibodies attached to sperm.

It is important to know where the antibodies attach to the sperm, since antibodies stuck to the head of the sperm can prevent penetration or fertilization of an egg; antibodies coating the sperm tail can prevent the sperm from moving properly to get to the egg. Antibody assays may also be performed in the blood and seminal fluid, as well as in the wife's blood and her cervical mucus.

Sperm antibody tests are also in order if a man has consistently poor sperm motility even if he shows no sperm agglutination, particularly if his doctor suspects a blockage along the reproductive tract ducts or if he has a varicocele. Some fertility specialists, like Dr. Goldstein, check for sperm antibodies routinely. His Cornell group discovered that varicoceles are often associated with sperm antibodies in the blood by testing all infertile men who appeared at the clinic.

Questions to Ask Your Doctor About Basic Lab Tests for Women

Do my cervical cultures show any harmful bacteria?

Does my cervical mucus appear to be fertile? (It should look like raw egg white.)

Is my cervical mucus receptive or "hostile" to my husband's sperm?

Did my ultrasound exam reveal any abnormalities (fibroids, ovarian cysts, fluid-filled fallopian tubes)?

Does my BBT chart show normal temperature fluctuations?

Does the ultrasound exam show I am ovulating normally and that I have normal-size follicles?

Are the hormone levels in my blood within normal ranges?

Does my blood or cervical mucus contain antisperm antibodies?

Questions to Ask Your Doctor About
Basic Lab Tests for Men

Is my total sperm concentration within the normal range (20 million to 200 million sperm per milliliter)?

What is my total sperm count (normal = 40 million to 300 million sperm)?

Is the volume (amount) of my semen within the normal range (2 to 6 milliliters)?

Do I have a high white blood cell count in my semen (a sign of inflammation and possibly infection)?

Was a special stain applied to tell the white blood cells apart from immature sperm cells?

What percentage of my sperm are actively moving (more than 50 percent is normal)?

Do my sperm look like they have normal shapes (more than 30 percent should have normal shapes)?

Are the hormone levels in my blood within normal ranges?

Does my semen culture show any harmful microorganisms?

Do I have sperm antibodies in my blood or seminal fluid, or attached to my sperm?

6

THE
EVALUATION
CONTINUES

Additional Tests

Affter you have gone through the basic fertility evaluation, your fertility specialist will have an idea of how best to proceed to begin treatment and complete your workup. Some doctors, once they discover an abnormality, will put off further testing and begin treating that one particular problem. But this approach can be ineffective since, in most cases, a couple has more than one factor contributing to their fertility problem.

Although the husband's fertility evaluation may be simpler than his wife's (because his reproductive organs and sperm are more accessible for examination than her reproductive organs and her eggs), this doesn't mean that there are more or better infertility treatments available for men. In fact, the reverse is true. Although semen analysis allows a simple evaluation of several aspects of a man's reproductive potential, only a pregnancy or observing fertilization in the IVF lab can prove with certainty whether a man's sperm actually fertilize his wife's eggs. Even with all of the sophisticated technology available today, no fertility test can absolutely predict a couple's ability to conceive or maintain a pregnancy. Actually having a baby is the only way of verifying your fertility as a couple.

Testing the Woman

Tests using X rays and telescopes, and examining a woman's endometrial development in the late luteal phase, can give the doctor more information about exactly where a woman's fertility problem may lie.

The Dye Test (Hysterosalpingogram)

When a couple has completed the basic, initial tests, the fertility evaluation often proceeds with a study of the wife's upper reproductive tract. This study is called a hysterosalpingogram (HSG), which is an X ray of the uterus (hystero) and tubes (salpinges). Basically, this involves injecting radiopaque dye, which appears white on an X ray, through the cervical canal into the uterus and fallopian tubes.

The hysterosalpingogram shows the shape of the internal cavity of the uterus and whether the fallopian tubes are patent (open). As the uterus fills and the dye moves out through the fallopian tubes, the X ray can reveal different types of abnormalities, such as blocked areas due to adhesions (scar tissue) and growths, polyps, or tumors. In normal, healthy fallopian tubes, the dye fills the lengths of the tubes and quickly spills out through the far end. If a tube is blocked at its fimbrial end near the ovary, then the tube will enlarge as the dye is pushed into it, just as a balloon grows larger when it is blown up with air.

Unless the dye test is performed carefully, it can be painful, particularly if there is a blockage of the fallopian tubes. Dr. Berger recommends that a woman take 600 mg of ibuprofen (three Advil or Nuprin tablets) thirty to sixty minutes prior to the HSG to minimize her discomfort.

The major risk of an HSG—the possibility of spreading an unrecognized infection from the cervix to the upper reproductive tract—can be avoided by making sure that cervical cultures show no pathogenic bacteria before scheduling the HSG. If the woman has a cervical infection, then Dr. Berger postpones the exam, and she and her partner are put on appropriate antibiotic treatments. Only once the lower tract infection has cleared does he proceed to a hysterosalpingogram. In addition, for two days before the HSG and two days afterward, the woman routinely receives a broad spectrum prophylactic antibiotic, such as doxycycline. She also uses a betadine douche to cleanse her vagina immediately before going in for her X ray, as an added precaution. (Betadine is a powerful antiseptic preparation used by most doctors to kill any bacteria on the skin prior to surgery.)

Hysteroscopy

If the HSG suggests an abnormality of the uterus, further evaluation may be performed with a hysteroscope, a thin, fiber-optically lighted telescope inserted through the cervical canal into the uterus. Through the hysteroscope's eyepiece, the doctor can see abnormalities inside the uterine cavity, such as fibroid tumors, adhesions, a septum, a double shaped uterus, or the T-shaped uterine cavity associated with DES exposure while in utero. Pictures taken through the hysteroscope can document the condition of the uterine cavity, and are filed in the woman's permanent medical record.

Hysteroscopy is a simple procedure that can be performed using local anesthesia. The doctor places the hysteroscope through the woman's cervical canal and then distends her uterus with either a gas, such as carbon dioxide, or a liquid medium to push the walls of the uterus apart and allow a panoramic view of the uterine cavity.

In many situations, Dr. Berger will combine hysteroscopy and laparoscopy to confirm the exact location and type of uterine abnormality, as well as to determine if the woman has any other abnormal conditions involving the uterus, fallopian tubes, and ovaries, such as pelvic adhesions or endometriosis.

The hysteroscopic examination is often performed early in a woman's menstrual cycle before her uterine lining (endometrium) has become fully developed. At that time, the doctor can get the clearest view of the uterine cavity, including the opening into each fallopian tube. (Later in the cycle, the exam may be more difficult to perform because the endometrium thickens and can obscure the view of the openings of the fallopian tubes.)

However, the decision when to perform hysteroscopy during the woman's cycle also depends on whether the doctor wants to obtain an endometrial biopsy to study the maturation of her uterine lining. In this case, the hysteroscopic examination is best performed late in the luteal phase of the cycle when an endometrial biopsy is most useful.

Before proceeding to diagnostic laparoscopy and endometrial biopsy, the woman should always have a blood pregnancy test to make sure that she isn't already pregnant. For fear of harming the early pregnancy, no couple or doctor would want to perform an invasive examination of the uterus for infertility only to find out that a fertilized egg had already implanted itself.

Laparoscopy

Several cycles after Wendy had a hysteroscopy and still wasn't pregnant, her doctor suggested that the thirty-year-old skin care specialist undergo a diagnostic laparoscopy as a further investigation. While she watched on a television monitor in the operating room, he inserted the laparoscope through a small puncture in her abdomen. "It was amazing. I could see streams of adhesions pulling the tube out of position," says Wendy, who had received a local anesthetic and intravenous sedation. "I couldn't feel the instruments inside me, but I saw him pick up my ovary and examine it. I never realized how small the ovaries really are."

The single procedure that provides the most information about a woman's reproductive anatomy is diagnostic laparoscopy. A diagnostic laparoscopy involves inserting a narrow fiber optic telescope into the woman's abdomen to get a direct view of her pelvic organs—the uterus, fallopian tubes, and ovaries—and to look for endometriosis or pelvic adhesions.

Dr. Berger usually schedules diagnostic laparoscopy in the late luteal phase, two or three days before the woman is expected to menstruate and late enough after the LH surge (eleven to thirteen days later) to check her hormone levels in the blood to make sure she isn't already pregnant before proceeding with the examination.

A "second look" diagnostic laparoscopy is also sometimes performed to check the results of reconstructive surgery. In cases where extensive scarring has been corrected through microsurgery, the laparoscope may be used for a second look at the pelvic organs between three and six weeks after reconstructive surgery to assess the results and to remove any new adhesions that may have developed after the surgery.

The fiber-optic laparoscope, introduced into the abdominal-pelvic cavity through a half-inch or smaller incision just below the navel, comes in different types and sizes. A thin, 4 millimeter (mm) diameter laparoscope (about as thick as a darning needle) is adequate for most examinations, but an intermediate-size laparoscope 6 to 8 mm in diameter (about as thick as a ballpoint pen) provides more light, which is required for video or photographic recording of findings. A larger, 10 to 12 mm diameter operating laparoscope (about as thick as a fountain pen), which has a channel that can be used to introduce instruments into the abdominal cavity, is usually required to correct any abnormalities. With the larger scope, the doctor can cut away adhesions with scissors or burn away endometriosis with an electric probe or a laser beam.

To enhance his view of the woman's reproductive organs, the doctor will place gas (carbon dioxide) into the abdominal cavity to lift up the abdominal wall (the skin, muscles, and other soft tissues). Then the woman lies on the operating table so that her head is lower than her pelvis, which helps the bowel fall away from the pelvic organs so that the reproductive organs can be clearly seen.

Frequently, the doctor needs to insert a second instrument through the lower abdomen to move various organs while he looks through the eyepiece of the laparoscope. Another instrument placed inside the woman's uterine cavity through the cervical canal allows him to move the uterus for a thorough pelvic inspection.

Dr. Berger follows a routine during a laparoscopic exam, beginning with a look at the uterus, then moving along systematically to the fallopian tubes and ovaries. Using the laparoscope and a probe as extensions of his fingers, Dr. Berger traces along the right fallopian tube adjacent to the uterus. First, he looks for an enlargement, thickening, or obstruction in the segment of the tube adjacent to the uterus (the isthmic segment). He then examines the rest of the tube, tracing it out to its fimbrial end near the ovary. This end, which has the bell-like shape of a trumpet and fringed ends, normally is open and its lining appears lush and healthy.

Sometimes the fimbrial end of the tube is partially closed. Think of the tube as an arm with the hand and fingers (fimbria) at the end. Pelvic inflammatory disease (PID) or salpingitis can cause the tube's fingers to close (which helps prevent the spread of infection out into the abdominal cavity). If the fingers draw together completely like a shut fist, then dye can't pass through the end of the tube, and the tube becomes enlarged with the accumulation of the distending dye, giving it the shape of a "clubbed tube."

The laparoscopic examination also involves inspection of the ovaries. Ovulation requires the rupture of a follicle from the ovary's surface, which subsequently leaves a small pit or depression in the ovary. Ovaries that have very smooth surfaces indicate that a woman hasn't been ovulating. When laparoscopy is performed in the postovulatory phase of the cycle, a yellow stain can be seen in the corpus luteum due to the production of progesterone, which occurs after ovulation. The ovary also is examined for endometriosis, adhesions, cysts, and other abnormalities.

After examining the right fallopian tube and ovary thoroughly, Dr. Berger points the instrument down behind the uterus in the cul-de-sac and along the broad ligaments on both sides of the uterus, looking for endometriosis. If the cul-de-sac contains fluid, he removes the fluid and continues the search for endometriosis. Then he moves along to the woman's left side and performs a similar evaluation on the left fallopian tube and ovary.

Hydrotubation

If there is any doubt about whether one or both tubes are open, Dr. Berger injects a sterile solution of indigo carmine dye diluted in saline up through the cervical canal and uterus to check for the free spill of the dye from both tubes. This procedure is called hydrotubation.

The doctor places a cone-shaped instrument up against the woman's cervix to help prevent the flow of the dye solution back out through the cervical canal. When dye comes out of the fimbrial end of the fallopian tube, that proves that the entire length of the tube is open. If a recent HSG shows both tubes are open and appear to be normal at laparoscopy, this step is not necessary.

Tuboscopy

An infection can destroy the cilia, or tiny hairs, lining the fallopian tube, transforming the tube's inner lining into a glassy, polished—and nonfunctioning—tube. Without the hair propellant, the egg may enter the tube and be stopped short, like a car stuck in a car wash with no power to the conveyor belt. If the egg is fertilized, it may not be transported into the uterus, resulting in a tubal pregnancy.

The problem of cilia damage is insidious because infections of the fallopian tubes frequently produce no symptoms. Many infertile women are found at laparoscopy to have scarred fallopian tubes, but had no history to suggest when the infection happened. A high percentage of these women have antibodies to chlamydia, indicating that they have been infected with this organism in the past.

The longer and more severely the tube has been damaged, the less likely the cilia will return. The earlier the infection is diagnosed and treated with antibiotics, the less damage to the tube's lining and cilia.

For the first time, internal examination of the fallopian tube allows assessing tubal health and disease to permit optimal treatment. Falloposcopy is the visual examination of the inside of the fallopian tube. This procedure involves inserting a tiny flexible catheter through the cervical canal and uterine cavity into the fallopian tube. An even smaller flexible fiber optic endoscope is threaded through the catheter into the fallopian tube. The inside of the tube can then be thoroughly examined on a TV monitor via a camera attached to the outer end of the falloposcope.

Abnormalities of the tube, including obstruction, scar formation, and damage to the inner lining, can be identified. As soon as abnormalities are identified, the doctor can repair the tubes at the same time if that is the best method of treatment. The forward-unfurling balloon at the front of the falloposcope has been shown in clinical trials in Japan to unblock obstructions in the fallopian tube, particularly in the proximal end near the uterus. If tubal damage is too severe to repair surgically, then the recommended treatment is IVF. In many cases, the tubes can be repaired through outpatient microsurgical techniques.

Falloposcopy takes between thirty and forty-five minutes to perform. If followed by tubal reconstructive surgery, the total operating time is one to two hours. The procedure can be performed with local anesthesia or with intravenous sedation. When combined with reparative tubal surgery, general anesthesia is used.

General risks of any invasive diagnostic procedure include the possibility of infection or bleeding. The risk of infection is avoided by first obtaining bacterial cervical cultures and treating any possible infectious microorganisms with appropriate antibiotics before falloposcopy is performed. Perforation of the fallopian tube can occur, although this is uncommon and generally does no harm. In rare cases, bleeding at the perforation side may require laparoscopic treatment.

Endometrial Biopsy

An endometrial biopsy involves scraping a small amount of tissue from the endometrium for examination by a pathologist. A woman can have the endometrial biopsy right in the doctor's office to monitor her endometrial development in the luteal phase and to determine the presence of a luteal phase defect (LPD). But to avoid any discomfort associated with the procedure, Dr. Berger prefers to perform an endometrial biopsy at the time of hysteroscopy or laparoscopy, when the woman already has received suitable anesthesia.

An endometrial biopsy is most helpful in diagnosing luteal phase defect. The doctor should suspect this condition when a woman's luteal phase of the cycle lasts for twelve days or less (from the surge of luteinizing hormone to onset of the next menstrual period) or her mid-luteal progesterone level is low (less than 10 nanogram [ng]/ml). The pathologist studies the fragment of endometrium removed at biopsy to see how the tissue has developed. To ensure proper interpretation, the biopsy material must be related to the date of the LH surge and to the time of the next period. The biopsy should be performed eleven to thirteen days after the LH surge (one to three days before the next expected period), and only after a negative pregnancy test of blood hormone levels.

Some doctors perform endometrial biopsies in the mid-luteal phase of the cycle when implantation occurs, but a pregnancy test can't detect pregnancy this early. So a biopsy at this time of the cycle causes a possible risk of interrupting a pregnancy that is just beginning. For this reason, Dr. Berger does not perform mid-luteal biopsies except in unusual cases and then only if the couple has not been sexually active during the fertile time of the cycle.

Integrin Testing

Researchers may have found one answer to the mystery of why apparently healthy women can't get pregnant. Many of these women may lack a protein that makes embryos stick to the uterine wall.

Proteins called integrins must be present when the embryo arrives for it to implant in the uterus. Integrins are cell adhesion proteins that project from the surface of all cells (except red blood cells). About two dozen different integrins have now been identified. In certain infertility patients with luteal phase defect, one particular beta integrin is almost always absent. The same one may also be missing from the endometrium of some women with mild endometriosis.

Testing for this specific beta integrin may help diagnose endometriosis and identify patients who may benefit from treatment. An endometrial biopsy timed to the LH surge at six to ten days after ovulation is all that's required. This beta integrin is usually present during the window of implantation, so if it's not there, this test is easy to interpret.

A large number of women with tubal disease and fluid in the tubes (hydrosalpinges) also appear not to have this integrin. This corroborates reports that patients with tubal disease with hydrosalpinges do poorly during IVF cycles. Implantation failure may represent a major cause of unexplained infertility, and more research may elucidate the role of beta integrins in implantation and infertility.

Testing the Man

Paralleling the woman's tests, the continuing analysis of a man's fertility may include X-ray studies and examination of his sperm-producing tissues, as well as several tests of the health of his sperm.

Beyond Semen Analysis

Since semen analysis doesn't measure sperm function—only the quantity of sperm, what they look like, and how they move—other tests of sperm function have been developed to aid the male fertility investigation. Some tests check for components of the seminal fluid that the sperm swim in; other tests measure the sperm's ability to survive in and move through cervical mucus. Still others determine whether a sperm can penetrate the coating around an egg and fertilize it.

THE SUGAR TEST • If a man has no sperm in his semen at all—that is, a zero sperm count—the doctor should perform a simple test for the presence of fructose (fruit sugar) in his semen. If he has no fructose in the semen, then his seminal vesicles are not functioning properly or, more likely, the ducts along the semen's path are blocked or absent, preventing the secretions from the seminal vesicles from mixing with his sperm.

To do the test, the seminal fluid is mixed with chemical reagents. If the mixture turns a pink-orange color (a positive test), then fructose is present and the secretions of the seminal vesicles are getting into the semen. If there is no color change (a negative test), then there is no sugar in the semen. Since the majority of the fluids in semen are made by the seminal vesicles, a negative test usually means that nothing is coming out of the seminal vesicles, or that ducts from the seminal vesicles are blocked or not working properly. A negative sugar test almost always parallels low semen volume of less than 1 ml. Further investigation of the man's reproductive tract ducts is necessary to try to locate blockages and determine whether they can be repaired.

THE "HAMSTER TEST" OR SPERM PENETRATION ASSAY

Lucy and Bill came to Chapel Hill Fertility Center after many years of trying, unsuccessfully, to have a baby. They already knew that Bill, a forty-three-year-old writer, had a low sperm count. Lucy, a psychotherapist, wanted to have his sperm penetration checked out right away. "We did not want to use donor sperm, and if Bill's sperm were not able to penetrate my egg, I didn't want to continue treatment," says Lucy. Bill's sperm penetration assay showed good penetrating ability. "That renewed my interest in treatment. I couldn't go on not knowing," Lucy says.

The best lab test currently available that correlates with the fertilizing ability of a man's sperm, besides IVF, is the sperm penetration assay, or hamster egg penetration test. It is like a trial run of in vitro fertilization, using a hamster's egg instead of the woman's eggs. This test determines one thing: whether human sperm placed immediately adjacent to hamster eggs can penetrate them. To penetrate an egg, sperm must have a healthy acrosome, the packet of enzymes at the head of the sperm. These enzymes dissolve the coating around the egg. The sperm head must also be free of antibodies and have an intact energy factory so that it has the power to move.

Instead of using human eggs, which are difficult to obtain, fertility researchers have turned to hamster eggs. Hamster egg penetration generally correlates with how well sperm can penetrate human eggs. Using enzymes, a lab technician removes the outer coat around the hamster egg (zona pellucida). This coat, also found on a human egg (ovum), prevents interspecies fertilization and must be removed before human sperm can penetrate the hamster egg. (That's also why you may hear the test called a hamster zona-free ovum or HZFO test.) Once the zona is removed, the sperm are mixed with hamster eggs; the technician then collects the eggs and checks to see how many have been penetrated by sperm and how many sperm penetrated each hamster egg. (Without the protective coating, more than one sperm can penetrate an egg.)

The hamster test is most valuable when the man has an apparently normal semen analysis and his wife has no defined fertility problem, yet they have failed to conceive. It also has been used to check whether an artificial insemination attempt may be worthwhile for men with very low sperm counts. If his sperm can't penetrate an egg when they are placed immediately beside it, then intrauterine or intratubal insemination will probably be of little value.

Like any test, the hamster test is not perfect. Although there is a good correlation between a sperm's ability to penetrate a hamster egg and its ability to penetrate human eggs, about 5 to 10 percent of men who have negative hamster tests still can father children with assisted reproductive technologies. So human eggs may be easier for human sperm to penetrate than hamster eggs.

On the other hand, some men who score well on the hamster test don't impregnate their wives and show no evidence of fertilizing their wives' eggs during IVF treatment. Perhaps this is due to some abnormality in the wife's eggs. The hamster test provides a good, but not perfect, correlation with human fertility.

Also, there may be problems with the hamster test as most laboratories currently perform it. Performing the test with different types or concentrations of albumin to supplement the media will produce different penetration results from the same ejaculate. So it's often difficult to compare results from one lab to the next. An international reference standard needs to be developed for this test. Also, results may vary from one ejaculate to the next from the same man. One hamster test, like a single semen analysis, may not tell the whole story and may mislead a doctor to draw the wrong conclusion about a man's fertilizing potential.

THE ULTIMATE FERTILITY TEST • The ultimate fertilization question is "Can a man's sperm fertilize his wife's egg?" Aside from a pregnancy, a couple can get an answer only during treatment by in vitro fertilization. Since the couple's sperm and egg are placed together directly in a petri dish, this minimizes fertilization problems caused by mucus barriers, moderately low sperm counts, and low sperm motility (although some sperm with normal motility must be able to move to and attach to the egg within the dish).

Other sperm penetration tests, such as the hamster egg test, can provide clues about a couple's fertilization potential, but IVF uses both of the couple's gametes (sperm and egg), not just the man's sperm and a hamster's egg.

Therefore, IVF can be viewed as both a diagnostic and a therapeutic procedure. As a diagnostic test, it determines whether the husband's sperm will penetrate his wife's egg. If the sperm penetrate and the egg divides, but the embryo doesn't implant, then it's worth trying another standard IVF procedure after determining possible causes of the IVF failure. If his sperm don't penetrate her eggs, there is little point in further standard IVF attempts, and further IVF attempts should be done with direct sperm injection.

If sperm fertilize eggs in vitro (outside the body in a laboratory environment), that's good evidence that sperm *can* fertilize, that the eggs are fertilizable, and conception could happen naturally as well. In fact, IVF programs report a high spontaneous pregnancy rate. As many as 30 percent of women who become pregnant in IVF programs conceive during a non-IVF cycle! The success of IVF procedures relates to the care that's taken to regulate induction cycles, the maturation of more than one egg, optimal timing of insemination, and support of the luteal phase with hormones, as well as fertilization outside of the body. If a woman ovulates and has functional tubes, she may be able to get pregnant without having to mix sperm and egg in a laboratory environment. As long as the man's sperm fertilizes her egg, the couple can be reassured that IVF or other treatments offer them the potential for having children.

As a diagnostic test, IVF holds most value for couples with unexplained infertility (which represents only 1 percent of infertile couples who have gone through a fertility workup). If all other tests fail to explain why a couple is infertile, then an IVF attempt may provide the explanation. If eggs can be successfully retrieved from the woman, and her husband's sperm penetrate them, then they have a good chance of having a child together, possibly through an IVF procedure. If his sperm don't penetrate her eggs, then it is time to consider more advanced treatments, such as microinjection of a single sperm (see Chapter 9) or donor insemination or stopping treatment altogether.

In addition to the cervical mucus, other secretions from the female reproductive tract also play a role in how well sperm function. The fluids found in the uterus and follicles are potent inducers of the acrosome reaction, the biological change the sperm must go through to become "capacitated" and be able to penetrate eggs. The ability of sperm to undergo the acrosome reaction can be tested in the laboratory.

Testicular Biopsy

A man with a zero sperm count either isn't producing sperm or the sperm he produces can't get into the ejaculate. If his testicles are small and soft, and his FSH level is high—more than twice normal—his doctor can presume he is not manufacturing sperm. If examination by an experienced male fertility specialist reveals that his vas deferens are absent from birth, he knows the sperm are being blocked. Sometimes a testicular biopsy may be necessary to find out whether he is producing sperm.

If a man has no sperm in the ejaculate but has a normal semen volume along with normal FSH levels, a vas deferens on each side, and normal-size testicles, then a testicular biopsy is definitely indicated. The doctor removes a small sample of tissue from each testicle and examines it under a microscope to see whether adequate numbers of sperm are being produced. If they are, but no sperm are present in the semen, then an obstruction exists somewhere along the tubes between the testicle and the penis.

Microscopic examination of the testicular sample allows the doctor to identify sperm in their various stages of development. This is a simple outpatient procedure. When Dr. Goldstein does a testicular biopsy, the cuts in the testicle are so small that no stitches are required. Most patients are back to work in one or two days. A preliminary biopsy report is available immediately. The final biopsy results are usually ready in four to seven days.

The biopsy isn't painful if it's done under general anesthesia, but is somewhat uncomfortable if the doctor uses only local anesthesia. (Some men who have had a biopsy under local anesthesia wish they had never had it done that way.) A cord block is the only way to anesthetize the testicle accurately with a local. This involves injecting the anesthetic directly into the spermatic cord. But placing a needle in the cord, where all of the testicle's blood vessels and nerves are located, runs the risk of injuring these tiny structures and worsening, rather than improving, a man's fertility.

If the biopsy shows that a man is making sperm, the next step is to find the blocked duct and repair it microsurgically. But if the biopsy shows no signs of sperm production, then the man may have arrested sperm maturation or a condition called "Sertoli-Cell-Only" syndrome, which is characterized by slightly smaller than normal testicles and a zero sperm count. Presuming that his reproductive hormone levels are normal, no current treatment can stimulate his sperm production.

The doctor must make sure not to miss a hormonal cause of azoospermia, such as hypogonadotropic hypogonadism. With this condition, a man's pituitary doesn't signal the testicles to produce sperm. This is analogous to a woman not ovulating because she lacks the proper hormonal signals from the brain to the ovaries. A man can be treated with the same drugs used to induce ovulation in women—Pergonal, human chorionic gonadotropin (hCG), or GnRH.

Karyotyping

Another test that is sometimes performed is a chromosome study (karyotyping). In men who have abnormally small testicles and a feminine body shape, a chromosome analysis may reveal a congenital, nontreatable condition, such as Klinefelter's syndrome (in which the man has an extra X chromosome), which halts sexual development.

Vasogram

A urologist or male fertility specialist should be able to diagnose a blockage with a testicular biopsy. If the biopsy shows a man has normal sperm production, but no sperm in the ejaculate, then it's obvious that the man has a blockage somewhere. The man's reproductive surgeon can explore the vas and epididymis under the microscope and, if nee a vasogram to find out exactly where the vas is blocked.

A vasogram involves making a small incision in the posing the vas deferens. Contrast dye is injected into the latory duct, and X rays are taken from various angles. This is particularly useful in locating the exact spot of an obstruction since it gives an outline of the sperm transport system.

A vasogram isn't quite the same as an X-ray study of the fallopian tubes. The vas's tiny ducts are only one-third of a millimeter in diameter. Even the smallest needle placed in the vas to inject the X-ray dye can injure the pinpoint-size duct. The needle itself can end up blocking the vas, and doing the vasogram before or at the time of a testicular biopsy can damage a man's vas ducts. Yet some urologists routinely perform a biopsy and vasogram together. If your doctor suggests doing the vasogram along with a biopsy, obtain a second opinion from a reproductive surgeon who specializes in male fertility.

A vasogram should be performed only by a physician experienced in the technique, with an operating microscope available and only when the blocked ducts can be repaired immediately. That way, if the vas is damaged during the test, the reproductive surgeon can repair the damage right away by cutting out the segment of vas and sewing the two ends together.

In most cases, a vasogram is rarely indicated. To check for a blockage, the doctor can make a microscopic opening in the vas and take a sample of fluid to see if it contains sperm. If there are sperm in the fluid, then he knows there's a blockage. He can also inject saline into the vas. If it flows easily through the vas, then he knows the vas is open. When the saline doesn't flow easily, he can pass a thin catheter up into the vas. Where the catheter stops is where the vas is blocked. Only when these tests are inconclusive is a vasogram necessary to find the blocked spot.

Transrectal Ultrasound

This involves putting a fingerlike ultrasound probe into the rectum to obtain images of the prostate gland and seminal vesicles. It is indicated in men with low semen volume and/or no fructose associated with either a low or zero sperm count and poor sperm motility. It can detect blockages in the ejaculatory ducts or seminal vesicles.

Questions to Ask Your Doctor About Additional Fertility Tests for Women

Does my hysterosalpingogram show any abnormalities of my uterus or fallopian tubes (uterine adhesions, polyps, tumors, malformation, or blocked tubes)?

Does my hysteroscopic exam show any abnormalities (uterine adhesions, fibroids, a septum, or abnormally shaped uterus)?

What did my laparoscopic exam reveal about my uterus, fallopian tubes, and ovaries?

Do I have endometriosis or pelvic adhesions?

Did hydrotubation show that my fallopian tubes are both open?

Did my endometrial biopsy show I have a luteal phase defect?

Questions to Ask Your Doctor About Additional Fertility Tests for Men

In general

How well did my sperm do on the hamster egg test?

Do my wife and I need to try in vitro fertilization to learn whether my sperm can fertilize her eggs?

Is my sperm so poor that we should try in vitro fertilization with single-sperm injection?

Does my chromosome analysis reveal any abnormalities?

For men with low sperm motility

Do my sperm appear to be sticking to each other?

Are my sperm coated with antibodies?

For men with no sperm in the semen

Does my sugar test show I have fructose in my semen?

Is my semen volume low? Do I need transrectal ultrasound to look for ejaculatory duct blockages?

If my FSH is normal, do I need a testicular biopsy to determine whether my ducts are blocked?

Can you feel any vas on both sides?

7

HORMONE TREATMENTS

As one important step during their fertility workups, both partners will have their hormone levels checked and, if need be, take fertility drugs designed to stimulate ovulation or sperm production. Hormones are chemical messengers produced in one organ, an endocrine gland, and released into the bloodstream, which carries them to another (target) organ, where they have their effect.

Hormones and Feedback

Hormone regulation is analogous to the way a thermostat and heater feed information back to each. As the temperature increases, the thermostat shuts off, signaling the heater to reduce its heat output. When the temperature falls below the thermostat's setting, the thermostat signals the heater to turn up the heat again.

A similar signaling relationship exists between the pituitary gland and the ovaries in women, and testicles in men. As the concentration of gonadotropin hormones in the blood rises, this signals the woman's ovaries or the man's testicles to increase hormone output. When the hormone levels of estrogen (for women) or testosterone (for men) reach a certain point, the pituitary gland slows its production and release of gonadotropins.

Just as you work the gas and brake pedals on your car, the body steps up or holds back hormone production when appropriate. When the body's hormone production or regulation breaks down, or becomes slug-

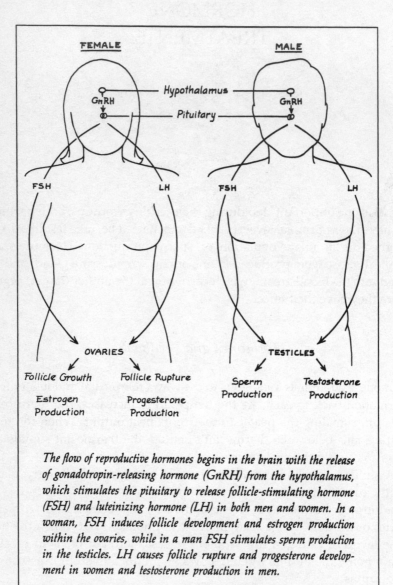

The flow of reproductive hormones begins in the brain with the release of gonadotropin-releasing hormone (GnRH) from the hypothalamus, which stimulates the pituitary to release follicle-stimulating hormone (FSH) and luteinizing hormone (LH) in both men and women. In a woman, FSH induces follicle development and estrogen production within the ovaries, while in a man FSH stimulates sperm production in the testicles. LH causes follicle rupture and progesterone development in women and testosterone production in men.

gish, powerful fertility drugs can move it into action. Up to 75 percent of couples with fertility problems that are correctable by hormone treatments eventually achieve pregnancies.

Hormone Treatments for Women

When there is an imbalance in the interaction of hormones between the hypothalamus, pituitary, and ovary, a woman may ovulate irregularly or not at all. This is a frequent cause of infertility. Various hormone treatments for women can now correct the flow of hormones along the ovulation pathway. Other fertility drugs can help time exactly when to release the egg to become fertilized and, once the woman becomes pregnant, help maintain and support the pregnancy to prevent an early miscarriage.

A woman can also take medications that affect hormone production to treat such conditions as endometriosis, fibroids, and polycystic ovarian disease (PCOD).

Clomiphene Citrate (Clomid, Serophene)

Some women can't get pregnant because they don't secrete enough LH and FSH at the right time during the cycle and, as a result, they don't ovulate. For these women, the first drug doctors often prescribe is clomiphene citrate (Clomid, Serophene). This synthetic drug stimulates the hypothalamus to release more GnRH, which then prompts the pituitary to release more LH and FSH, and thus increases stimulation of the ovary to produce a mature egg.

Clomiphene is a good first-choice drug when a woman's ovaries are capable of functioning normally and when her hypothalamus and pituitary are also capable of producing their hormones. In short, the woman's reproductive engine is in working order, but needs some revving up.

Structurally like estrogen, clomiphene binds to the sites in the brain where estrogen normally attaches, called estrogen receptors. Once these receptor sites are filled up with clomiphene, they can't bind with natural estrogen circulating in the blood and they are fooled into thinking that the amount of estrogen in the blood is too low. In response, the hypothalamus releases more GnRH, causing the pituitary to pump out more FSH, which then causes a follicle to grow to produce more estrogen and start maturing an egg to prepare for ovulation. Typically, a woman taking clomiphene produces double or triple the amount of estrogen in that cycle compared to pretreatment cycles.

If a woman is menstruating, even if irregularly, clomiphene is usually effective, particularly if she develops follicles that aren't reaching normal size. Usually a mature follicle is about 20 millimeters in diameter, or about the size of a small grape, just before it ruptures and releases its egg. Clomiphene may help small, immature follicles grow to maturity.

A low estradiol level in a woman's blood correlates with an inadequately stimulated, small follicle. A woman having a spontaneous ovulation cycle (that is, ovulating without the aid of fertility drugs) generally has peak estradiol levels ranging from 100 to 300 picograms (pg; one trillionth of a gram)/ml. A woman may have enough hormones to produce an egg, but if her estradiol production by the follicles is low (less than 100 pg/ml), she may not adequately stimulate her cervix to produce fertile mucus or stimulate her endometrium to get ready to accept a fertilized egg for implantation. Clomiphene could boost her weak signals from the hypothalamus to the pituitary to the ovaries.

A woman who ovulates infrequently—say, at six-week intervals or less often—is also a good candidate for clomiphene therapy, since clomiphene will induce ovulation more frequently. The more a woman ovulates, the more opportunities her mature eggs have to be exposed to her husband's sperm and, therefore, the greater her chance to become pregnant.

Clomiphene is also often effective for a woman with luteal phase defect (LPD). A woman with LPD may begin the ovulation process properly, but her ovarian function becomes disrupted, resulting in low production of the hormone progesterone in the luteal phase of the menstrual cycle. Following ovulation, the ovary produces progesterone, the hormone needed to prepare the uterine lining for implantation of the fertilized egg, which has divided and entered the uterine cavity. A fall in progesterone levels in the blood during this critical time can interfere with early embryo implantation or, even if a fertilized egg has already implanted, cause a woman to menstruate too early and end a pregnancy within a few days after implantation.

Using an LH-urine detector kit or keeping a basal body temperature (BBT) chart can help a woman taking clomiphene to determine whether the luteal phase of her cycle is shorter than the normal fourteen days. The luteal phase of the cycle, the length of time from ovulation until she menstruates, has a normal range of thirteen to fifteen days. Clomiphene often can "tune up" the hypothalamus and pituitary so they keep producing the hormones the ovary needs to manufacture progesterone throughout the luteal phase.

Of women whose only fertility problem is irregular or no ovulation at all, about 80 percent will ovulate and about 50 percent will become pregnant within six months of clomiphene treatments. About 3 percent of women on clomiphene have a multiple pregnancy, usually twins, compared with about 1 percent in the general population.

If a woman responds to clomiphene and develops a mature follicle (determined by adequate estrogen production and ultrasound examination), but has no LH surge by cycle day fifteen, then injection of the hormone human chorionic gonadotropin (hCG), which acts like LH, can be given to stimulate final egg maturation and follicle rupture, releasing the egg. The woman tends to ovulate about thirty-six hours after the LH surge or hCG injection, which can be confirmed by further ultrasound scans.

Clomiphene is a relatively inexpensive drug, and is taken orally for only five days each month. The doctor attempts to initiate clomiphene therapy so that the woman ovulates on or around day fourteen of a regular twenty-eight-day cycle. The simplest, most widely used dose starts with one daily 50 mg tablet for five days starting on either cycle day three or five. If a woman ovulates at this dose, there is no advantage to her increasing the dosage. In other words, more of the drug isn't necessarily better. In fact, more may be worse, producing multiple ovulation, causing side effects such as an ovarian cyst or hot flashes, and, most commonly, interfering with her fertile mucus production.

If a woman doesn't ovulate after taking one clomiphene tablet for five days, then her doctor will usually double the daily dose to two tablets (100 mg) in her next cycle. If she still doesn't respond, the doctor will usually triple the daily dose to 150 mg or add another fertility medication, such as human menopausal gonadotropin (hMG) in the next cycle. (Some doctors increase the dose up to 250 mg a day, but this is not recommended by either of the drug's two manufacturers.) Women tend to have side effects much more frequently at higher doses.

If the dose of clomiphene is too high, the uterine lining may not respond completely to estrogen and progesterone stimulation, and may not develop properly. As a result, a woman's fertilized egg may not be able to implant in her uterus. So clomiphene may actually result in luteal phase defect in a woman who was ovulating spontaneously. For this reason, clomiphene should be prescribed only when indicated.

SIDE EFFECTS • Because clomiphene binds to estrogen receptors, including the estrogen receptors in the cervix, it can interfere with the ability of the cervical mucus glands to be stimulated by estrogen to produce fertile mucus. Only "hostile" or dry cervical mucus may develop in the days preceding ovulation. If this occurs, adding a small amount of estrogen beginning on cycle day ten and continuing until the LH surge may enhance cervical mucus production.

Some women taking clomiphene experience hot flashes and premenstrual-type symptoms, such as migraines and breast discomfort (particularly if they have fibrocystic disease of the breasts). Visual symptoms such as spots, flashes, or blurry vision are less common and indicate that treatment should stop.

The hot flashes are just like the hot flashes women experience at menopause when the level of estrogen circulating in the blood is low. The clomiphene fools the brain into thinking that blood estrogen levels are low.

Clomiphene is a safe medication with relatively few contraindications. Preexisting liver disease is one contraindication since clomiphene is metabolized by the liver. Enlarged ovaries also are a relative contraindication since clomiphene may occasionally produce hyperstimulation of the ovaries.

CLOMIPHENE ABUSE • Too often, doctors give clomiphene to women with unexplained infertility before the couple has a fertility workup, or even after they have a workup, but there is no evidence of an ovulation disorder. This empiric therapy may create new problems, such as interfering with fertile mucus production or luteal phase defect, and often delays further evaluation that would lead to a specific diagnosis and proper treatment.

For a woman who has normal, spontaneous ovulation, driving the pituitary harder with clomiphene won't make ovulation any more normal. If a woman has taken clomiphene for several cycles without becoming pregnant, then clomiphene should be discontinued and she and her fertility specialist should investigate other conditions that may be preventing her pregnancy.

After noting a good postcoital test (PCT) during a fertility workup, some doctors fail to repeat the test after placing a woman on clomiphene. A PCT definitely needs to be repeated to check the quality of the woman's cervical mucus while she is on clomiphene, since 25 percent or more of women who take the drug develop cervical mucus problems. It's important for a woman to monitor her cervical mucus production during every cycle while trying to become pregnant, including her cycles while taking clomiphene.

Human Menopausal Gonadotropin

Women who fail to respond to clomiphene become candidates for treatment with human menopausal gonadotropin (hMG, Pergonal, Humegon, Repronex). This fertility drug is made from equal amounts of FSH and LH. These natural gonadotropins are produced in very high amounts by women after menopause, and are extracted from the urine of women who have stopped menstruating. Unlike clomiphene, hMG induces ovulation by directly stimulating the ovaries, and can be used in women who don't have normal hypothalamic or pituitary function.

hMG therapy is effective for a woman who has ovaries that are capable of responding normally to FSH and LH, but who doesn't have a normal flow of hormones from the hypothalamus to the pituitary to the ovaries. The FSH provided through a hMG injection goes through her blood into the ovaries to stimulate follicle growth.

These drugs offer the advantage over clomiphene of producing fertile cervical mucus (if the woman's mucus glands are normal) since they don't interfere with the body's estrogen receptors.

Two other less common indications for hMG include a woman with two ovaries but only one normal healthy fallopian tube, and the 5 to 10 percent of women with regular menstruation who have luteinized unruptured follicle (LUF) syndrome. For a woman with two ovaries and one healthy tube, hMG can enhance the probability that both of her ovaries ovulate simultaneously in the same cycle, which facilitates egg pickup by the normal tube. For LUF, in which an egg matures but the follicle doesn't rupture and release it, hMG plus hCG to stimulate ovulation seems to be more effective than either hCG alone or clomiphene plus hCG.

A woman with long-standing "unexplained" infertility may have abnormal FSH and LH levels despite normal estrogen and progesterone secretions. hMG may allow her to conceive by overriding these abnormal gonadotropin patterns.

Like clomiphene, hMG can also be taken along with hCG to induce ovulation to time artificial insemination. In addition, hMG is the primary fertility drug used for "superovulation": intentionally stimulating a woman's ovaries to produce multiple eggs during a cycle. Also called controlled ovarian hyperstimulation, this concept was originally developed for IVF. It has now been applied to other assisted reproductive technologies, most commonly combined with timed insemination techniques. The rationale is simple: Any time a woman produces more than one egg, she increases her chances of having a pregnancy, since more eggs are available to become fertilized.

For the proper candidates, about 90 percent will ovulate and about 50 percent will become pregnant through hMG therapy. The main drawback of hMG is the increased risk of multiple pregnancy. The multiple pregnancy rate is higher than with clomiphene-induced cycles because of the larger number of eggs produced by hMG stimulation. The risk of bearing three or more babies has been about 5 percent, but by careful monitoring of estrogen levels and using ultrasound scans, that risk can be reduced to 2 percent or less.

Gauging the amount of hMG that will properly stimulate ovulation without overstimulating the ovaries is an intricate process. The amount of hormone that must be given each day, and the number of days of treatment, varies greatly not only from one woman to the next, but may vary from one course of treatment to another for the same woman. Usually, however, once an adequate dose is established, a woman will generally respond to a similar dose in subsequent cycles.

A new hMG that can be administered subcutaneously has been approved for patients undergoing ovulation induction and for those participating in IVF protocols. Both subcutaneous and intramuscular administrations of Repronex, which contains equal amounts of FSH and LH, have been approved. The subcutaneous injection provides more convenience and has a low cost. Adverse effects associated with the drug are comparable to other gonadotropins, including the risk of ovarian hyperstimulation. Injection site reactions are more frequent among patients who receive the drug by subcutaneous administration, but the reactions are mostly mild and occur early in treatment.

HYPERSTIMULATION • Because of its potency, hMG stimulation must be carefully monitored during each cycle to avoid the risk of hyperstimulation syndrome, in which too many follicles are stimulated and the ovaries become enlarged.

The majority of women become only mildly hyperstimulated, experiencing pelvic discomfort and ovaries enlarged to about the size of golf balls. Moderate hyperstimulation will enlarge the ovaries to baseball size and cause a woman to gain weight and have a tender tummy.

A severe case may enlarge a woman's ovaries to grapefruit size or even larger, and may require that she spend time in the hospital to monitor her fluids and electrolytes. This is a rare but potentially serious complication. Just as the most potent heart drugs should be prescribed by cardiologists, hMG should be prescribed only by experienced fertility specialists.

Once a woman's ovaries begin responding to hMG, the fertility specialist will monitor her with frequent, often daily, estradiol blood tests, ultrasound scans, and cervical mucus examinations. Dr. Berger starts administering hMG on cycle day two or three after obtaining a baseline ultrasound scan to ensure that the woman has no ovarian cysts. By cycle day eight, he takes daily measurements of her estradiol and progesterone levels in the blood, monitors the number and size of her developing follicles, and examines her cervical mucus to determine whether she needs more hMG or if the conditions are right to induce ovulation with an hCG injection.

If the woman responds too much to hMG stimulation, he takes her off the drug and forestalls giving her hCG to prevent hyperstimulation. Her ovaries are allowed to rest until they completely return to normal size before another attempt at ovulation induction occurs.

The risk of hyperstimulation is related to the number of developing follicles and to the blood level of circulating estrogen produced by these follicles. Since each stimulated follicle puts out its own estrogen, blood levels of estradiol will be noticeably higher if there is an excess number of follicles.

Ultrasound examinations will tell a woman how many mature follicles she is developing. Dominant follicles during hMG treatment are generally 16 mm, or the size of a plump raisin, in diameter, or larger. Follicles that reach 12 mm in diameter should be monitored daily, with the woman returning to the fertility specialist's office to decide when to stop the hMG and give her the final injection of hCG.

The risk of multiple pregnancies is directly related to the number of dominant follicles. When two follicles exceed 16 mm in diameter, a woman has about a 2 to 4 percent chance of having twins. If she has three or four large follicles, the risk increases. The couple should understand the risks of multiple pregnancies before hMG treatment is administered. (Many couples go ahead with ovulation induction by hMG even though there may be an increased risk of twins or triplets because it's so effective in increasing the couple's chances of achieving a pregnancy.)

Examining the cervix also provides a method of rapidly monitoring the amount of circulating estrogen. Women often notice an abundance of cervical mucus while taking hMG because each follicle puts out estrogen, which in turn stimulates cervical mucus. As the blood level of estradiol increases, the cervix becomes soft, opens up, and produces copious amounts of watery, clear, fertile mucus. This indicates that the cervix has shifted into a fertile time of the woman's cycle, and is called the "clinical shift." Once a woman has undergone the clinical shift, she can usually expect to receive an hCG injection within one or two days to induce ovulation.

In addition to estradiol, Dr. Berger monitors a woman's progesterone levels to check for "premature luteinization." Luteinization is the process by which an ovarian follicle transforms into the corpus luteum, which produces the progesterone needed to mature the endometrial lining for pregnancy. About 20 percent of women taking hMG luteinize their follicles before, and not after, an hCG injection, frequently due to a spontaneous surge in LH production. If this happens, the woman's eggs may not fertilize, or if they do, her endometrium may not be receptive for implantation at the right time of her cycle.

Dr. Berger also has a woman use a home urinary LH kit to learn when she is having a spontaneous LH surge, particularly if she has to time an artificial insemination attempt. If a woman starts to develop an LH surge on her own while taking hMG, she is instructed to take an hCG injection, and the insemination is timed from the onset of the LH surge.

THE COMMITMENT TO PERGONAL

Emma, a forty-year-old actress, went to a fertility specialist because she hadn't had her period in six months. After reviewing her history and physical examination, the doctor found she had low gonadotropin production, and put her on clomiphene. When clomiphene alone failed, she added Pergonal to her drug treat-

ment. Once her follicles began to approach maturity, she began daily ultrasound exams.

"When you make a commitment to go on Pergonal, you have to plan your life around the treatment," says Emma. "My husband, Fred, wanted to make plans to go off together one weekend when I was taking Pergonal, and I told him I was sorry, we couldn't go because I had to go in for an ultrasound exam."

When monitored properly, Pergonal is a highly effective and relatively safe drug. But without precise monitoring and controlled use, it can be dangerous. Pergonal stimulation requires much more time and commitment on a woman's, and her doctor's, part than ovulation induction with clomiphene. While she is being monitored, a woman can expect to make four or five office visits during a cycle to evaluate the drug's effects.

The couple should thoroughly discuss Pergonal treatments with their fertility specialist. To minimize the number of office visits, a nurse may train the husband to give his wife the injections. This ability to receive injections at home comes in handy, especially since the hCG injection is usually given late at night. For the couple to time an insemination procedure at 10 A.M. the wife has to receive the hCG injection at 10 P.M., thirty-six hours before the scheduled insemination.

Pergonal treatment is expensive, with each vial costing $60 or more. The cost adds up quickly when a woman takes two or more vials a day for seven to ten days in each treatment cycle. Fortunately, most insurance companies cover treatment of ovulation disorders with Pergonal.

Pure FSH

The success of Pergonal treatments to induce ovulation mostly results from the action of FSH. So its manufacturer, Serono Laboratories, has recently developed a purified form of FSH (Metrodin) free of the LH that is also present in Pergonal preparations. Another pure FSH, called Fertinex, is also available.

Pure FSH helps induce ovulation in some infertile women who have too high an output of LH compared to the FSH they produce. It is specifically approved by the Food and Drug Administration (FDA) for clomiphene-resistant women with polycystic ovarian disease, who characteristically have an elevated LH to FSH ratio and are also prone to hyperstimulation. For these women, it can successfully initiate adequate follicle growth and reduce the risk of hyperstimulation associated with Pergonal.

A woman takes pure FSH by injection starting early in the cycle and continuing daily until her follicles start to respond, usually within six to ten days. She must be closely monitored during stimulation just as with hMG. And as with hMG, when pure FSH is used to stimulate ovulation, a woman usually won't have a spontaneous LH surge, and an hCG injection is usually given to cause her eggs to mature and her follicles to rupture.

Synthetic FSH

Recombinant FSH brands Gonal F and Follistim were the first genetically engineered drugs available for fertility treatment. They vary little from batch to batch and are generally well tolerated following subcutaneous injection, which may cause a slight stinging sensation. They seem to produce comparable results to first-generation hMGs and pure FSH.

While it certainly is more pure, recombinant FSH costs more to produce, and ultimately these costs are passed on to patients. The genetically engineered versions cost about twice as much as hMG preparations. Pharmacy prices for these drugs may vary widely, so it may be possible to shop around for the best possible price.

The Egg Releaser—Human Chorionic Gonadotropin (hCG)

Once Pergonal or Metrodin have stimulated the growth and maturation of a woman's follicles, she then takes an injection of human chorionic gonadotropin (hCG) to stimulate release of the eggs from the follicles. Human chorionic gonadotropin is structurally similar to luteinizing hormone. Its primary function is to support the corpus luteum, which is what remains of a follicle after its egg has been released. The corpus luteum produces progesterone, which prepares the uterine lining for implantation of the fertilized egg and maintains the pregnancy. Once a woman is pregnant, she produces her own hCG, which stimulates the corpus luteum to produce progesterone to keep the pregnancy going and prevent her from menstruating.

Purified LH is not yet available for injection in large enough amounts to trigger ovulation. However, since hCG has a structure similar to LH, it can be given to women to stimulate the release of an egg from a mature follicle. In ovulation-induced cycles, releasing the egg from the follicle usually requires an injection of hCG (5,000 to 10,000 units), most often given one day after the last dose of Pergonal. A woman ovulates, on average, about thirty-six hours after taking the hCG injection.

Some fertility specialists also provide repeated hCG injections to a woman with luteal phase defect as a means of stimulating her ovaries to keep producing progesterone late in the cycle so that menstrual bleeding doesn't occur prematurely, before the pregnancy can establish itself adequately in the uterus.

CONFUSED PREGNANCY TESTING • Since hCG is the same hormone detected by pregnancy tests, one problem with treating a luteal phase defect with hCG is that the injections can cause confusion. When a woman has a pregnancy test of the hormone levels in her blood, and hCG is identified, it's not known whether the hCG derives from the injections or pregnancy.

Not being able to differentiate the source of the hCG makes it more difficult to detect repeated, early miscarriages. When repeated hCG injections are given, it takes at least two blood tests—the second showing an increase in hCG over the earlier one—to establish that a woman is pregnant. If the initial test simply measures hCG left in the blood from a previous injection, then the second test will show a fall, not a rise, in the hCG level.

SIDE EFFECTS • If a woman has developed a large number of mature follicles, then an hCG injection may cause her to feel some tenderness in her lower abdomen due to enlarged ovaries. Occasionally, women complain of redness and tenderness at the site of injection or experience hot flashes.

Gonadotropin-Releasing Hormone (GnRH)

When a woman's hypothalamus fails to produce pulsating bursts of gonadotropin-releasing hormone (GnRH) to signal the pituitary to secrete LH and FSH, she will fail to ovulate. One solution is to provide supplementary GnRH, which mimics what happens naturally in the body. The drug can be administered through a vein or just under the skin in pulses (one every ninety minutes) delivered by a controlled-rate infusion pump, about the size of a cigarette pack, worn on a belt around the waist.

GnRH therapy is generally indicated for women who have failed to ovulate on clomiphene or Pergonal. The best response has been found among women with a weak signal within the hypothalamus–pituitary–ovary system. Less common indications include women who have underdeveloped ovaries due to lack of hormone stimulation (hypogonadotropic hypogonadism), delayed puberty, and PCOD. GnRH can also stimulate ovulation in physically active women whose menstrual cycles have ceased due to excess exercise and occasionally in women whose reproductive years have been cut short by premature menopause.

Pulses of GnRH infused throughout the menstrual cycle can also be used to treat a luteal phase defect that is unresponsive to clomiphene and progesterone. This treatment has quite successfully corrected hormonal deficiencies at both the beginning and the end of the cycle, promoting normal follicle development and normal luteal function after ovulation occurs.

An alternative to pulses of GnRH is to have the woman inject the drug into a muscle every other day, which seems to increase responsiveness to clomiphene. Some women who don't respond to clomiphene and take several GnRH injections may then respond to clomiphene and ovulate without the need for any more GnRH. This seems to be more effective for women who haven't menstruated for under one year than it is for women who are in a later stage of ovarian failure and have gone longer than one year without menstruating.

Among women who can tolerate a needle in a vein for a few weeks and are appropriate candidates for GnRH therapy, two out of three become pregnant within four months, assuming there are no other uncorrected fertility factors. GnRH administered subcutaneously carries about a 40 percent pregnancy rate. Most women find subcutaneous administration more acceptable and easier to manage. Intravenous infusion can be effective for some women who have failed to respond to subcutaneous GnRH.

Unlike Pergonal and Metrodin, which produce multiple follicles, GnRH-induced cycles usually result in the development of a single, dominant follicle accompanied by an LH surge. But these cycles need continual hormonal support through the luteal phase. The GnRH must be provided through the luteal phase, or low doses of hCG must be injected after the pump is withdrawn. Or progesterone itself can be given. If the drug is discontinued, the corpus luteum will promptly wither, ending the pregnancy.

Therapy with GnRH is at least as expensive as treatment with Pergonal. An infusion pump costs $2,000, but can usually be rented from the pump's manufacturer or from the physician providing treatment.

SIDE EFFECTS • GnRH therapy has few contraindications. As with any ovulation-inducing agent, it shouldn't be used if a woman is already pregnant. Meticulous monitoring of estradiol levels and ultrasound evaluations is less important than in Pergonal– or hCG–induced ovulation, since ovarian hyperstimulation is not as much of a problem with GnRH treatment.

Side effects may include pain, swelling, drainage, and infection at the injection site. Intravenous infusion carries a risk of phlebitis (inflammation of the vein) and requires careful inspection and frequent changes of the infusion site to prevent this potential problem.

GnRH Agonists

Scientists have developed synthetic versions of gonadotropin-releasing hormone that are sixty times as potent as the natural hormone. These chemical copies of GnRH, called GnRH agonists, are similar in structure and action to the natural hormone. Initially, they cause greater release of LH and FSH from the pituitary gland. But with continued use, and due to their longer duration of action than the natural hormone, GnRH agonists quickly deplete the pituitary gland of LH and FSH. They therefore have an advantage over Pergonal alone in controlled ovarian hyperstimulation by preventing a spontaneous LH surge that interferes with the proper timing of egg retrieval in an IVF or gamete intrafallopian transfer (GIFT) cycle.

The most widely used GnRH agonist currently in the United States is leuprolide acetate (Lupron). The woman takes Lupron as a once- or twice-daily injection just under the skin. Lupron is also available for injection in a depot form, which requires only one injection a month. Other versions of GnRH agonist can be given as a nasal spray taken twice a day (Naferelin or Synarel) or as a thirty-day skin implant (Goserelin or Zoladex).

Currently, the main use of GnRH agonists for infertility is to suppress pituitary function. As an aid in ovulation induction, GnRH agonists can, in effect, wipe the hormone slate clean before a woman takes ovulation-inducing drugs.

GnRH agonists also may assist ovulation induction for women with polycystic ovaries. After GnRH agonist treatments reduce excess LH secretion and shut down ovarian function, GnRH infused by a pump or Metrodin stimulation allows a woman to produce more acceptable estrogen levels and develop follicles with less chance of hyperstimulation.

ENDOMETRIOSIS AND FIBROIDS • Many physicians now use GnRH agonists to treat endometriosis and shrink uterine fibroids. The growth of endometriosis and fibroid tumors is stimulated by estrogen, and GnRH agonists stop estrogen production.

About 40 to 50 percent of women with endometriosis who receive monthly injections of Lupron for six months will become pregnant, about the same percentage as those who take Danazol, which in the past has been a common medical treatment for endometriosis. But GnRH agonists do not cause the masculinizing side effects of Danazol.

Some doctors biopsy endometriosis lesions to determine their drug binding capability. If the endometriosis lesions show no receptor binding with Danazol, a GnRH agonist may be a more useful treatment than Danazol.

GnRH agonists are also effective in reducing the size of uterine fibroid tumors. Some physicians advocate using Lupron to reduce the size of fibroid tumors before removing them surgically. Other doctors say that pretreatment with GnRH agonists makes it more difficult to remove the tumors because of fibrosis forming around them.

The side effects of GnRH agonists parallel those of menopause: calcium loss, hot flashes, decreased sex drive, and vaginal dryness.

Some studies show that GnRH agonists also cause some loss of bone mass, although the loss appears to be reversible once a woman stops the drug.

GnRH ANTAGONISTS • Another way to shut off pituitary gonadotropin output is with gonadotropin-releasing hormone (GnRH) antagonists. These synthetic drugs cause a very rapid decrease in circulating gonadotropin levels, even faster than their chemical cousins, the GnRH agonists. While GnRH agonists lead to low GnRH by depleting the pituitary gland of the hormone, the antagonists block the effect of GnRH at the level of the pituitary gland and prevent further production of GnRH by the hypothalamus. Thus, the antagonists work more quickly (within four to eight hours) than the GnRH agonists (within a week) to lower gonadotropin levels. They may be used along with FSH to induce ovulation since they probably would be effective in preventing a woman's spontaneous LH surge or premature luteinization.

Ganirelix acetate (Antagon) or cetrolix acetate (Cetrotide) injections are indicated for the inhibition of premature LH surges in women undergoing controlled ovarian hyperstimulation. This new treatment will help reduce the number of days of medication necessary to suppress LH surges and therefore maintain eggs in the ovaries. In contrast to GnRH agonists, which take up to twenty-six days, ganirelix or cetrolix achieves the same goal within five days, while reducing unpleasant side effects such as headaches and hot flashes. This long-anticipated addition to the armamentarium of fertility specialists can be self-administered as a subcutaneous injection.

Bromocriptine Mesylate (Parlodel)

Excess production of another pituitary hormone, prolactin, can interfere with normal production of LH and FSH and disrupt a woman's menstruation and ovulation. Suppressing prolactin with the drug bromocriptine (Parlodel) allows the hypothalamic–pituitary–ovarian relationship to return to normal.

Elevated levels of prolactin in the blood (hyperprolactinemia) have been associated with a variety of fertility dysfunctions. A woman may not ovulate, or may ovulate infrequently, have a luteal deficiency, decreased production of estrogen by her ovaries, and irregular or no menstruation (oligomenorrhea/amenorrhea). As prolactin levels become more highly elevated, she may become stimulated to produce breast milk. Any woman who produces breast milk and isn't pregnant should be checked for hyperprolactinemia.

Bromocriptine, the same drug used to treat Parkinson's disease, is effective in suppressing prolactin secretion. The drug is useful for women who have elevated prolactin levels and don't menstruate or ovulate. From 60 to 80 percent of women with an ovulation problem caused by higher than normal prolactin levels become pregnant after bromocriptine treatments if they have no other fertility problems. Parlodel may also be used in conjunction with other fertility drugs, such as clomiphene, Pergonal, Metrodin, and hCG.

Some fertility specialists advocate using the drug to treat women who are ovulating spontaneously, but have only mild or intermittent elevations of prolactin levels in their blood. If a doctor orders a prolactin level test randomly during a menstrual cycle, he may miss a transient prolactin elevation. These occur most frequently about the time of ovulation or in the mid-luteal phase. That's why Dr. Berger routinely tests for prolactin levels on the day of the LH surge and seven days later. If he identifies an elevated prolactin level, he prescribes the smallest dose of bromocriptine that will correct the problem.

Blood tests for prolactin are best performed in the morning before eating. A woman's levels of prolactin in the blood fluctuate throughout the day and may increase in response to stress. The stress of an office visit may be enough to elevate prolactin levels. Other things can stimulate prolactin elevations, such as breast stimulation. A woman shouldn't have blood drawn for a prolactin measurement following a breast examination by the doctor or herself.

In most cases, a high prolactin level can be easily corrected. Dr. Berger puts his patients on a small dose of bromocriptine, usually from 1.25 to 3.75 mg daily, which is half or less of the standard dose for women with high prolactin levels. As with most drug treatments for a hormone abnormality, rather than use a standard dose for all patients, he individualizes the amount of drug needed to achieve normal blood levels. A mild prolactin elevation may inhibit follicle maturation and is frequently seen among women with luteal phase defect, who usually have low estrogen and progesterone production. Side effects, frequent during the first few days after drug treatment has begun, include nausea, headache, dizziness, fatigue, and nasal congestion.

BROMOCRIPTINE VS. SCANNING • Many medical textbooks say that all women with elevated prolactin levels should have a brain scan, such as a computerized tomogram (CT scan) or magnetic resonance imaging (MRI) scan, to look for prolactin-secreting, benign pituitary tumors. This aggressive monitoring and heightened awareness of pituitary tumors is a function of our advanced medical technology. Only within the past twenty years have doctors been able to measure prolactin levels in the blood. And only within the past fifteen years have newer, more accurate brain scans been available to detect these tiny tumors. So doctors have "discovered" a condition that probably existed long before these diagnostic techniques were available.

Small pituitary tumors, less than 10 mm in diameter (microadenomas), are best treated with bromocriptine, and can be safely monitored with blood levels of prolactin. If the tumor is growing, the level of prolactin in the blood will increase. The doctor can follow these blood levels and treat the woman with bromocriptine without subjecting her to repeated X-ray examinations or MRI scans. If the levels rise substantially, imaging studies can then be performed to look for tumor growth. A sudden rise in prolactin may also indicate that the woman has been taking another medication—such as a phenothiazine for anxiety, or a high blood pressure medication—that shuts off the prolactin-inhibiting factors in the brain.

A woman with high prolactin levels should also have her level of thyroid-stimulating hormone (TSH) and thyroxine (T4) checked, since an underactive thyroid (hypothyroidism) can result in increased brain production of TSH, which leads to increased prolactin release. If the underlying problem is hypothyroidism, administering synthetic thyroid hormones is the correct treatment. Sometimes bromocriptine must be added to bring a woman's high prolactin levels down to normal.

Progesterone

Becoming and staying pregnant requires a delicate balance of hormones. A progesterone deficiency may explain why some women fail to become pregnant despite adequate egg development, or why they fail to maintain a pregnancy to term. Without the right levels of progesterone, a fertilized and dividing egg may be unable to implant itself successfully in the walls of the uterus. Or if it does implant, the uterine lining may be shed via menstruation, resulting in a pregnancy loss so early that the woman may not even know that she was pregnant.

A woman may safely take progesterone supplements (by oral capsules, suppositories, or injections) to support an implanted embryo and maintain an early pregnancy. The supplements can also prevent a miscarriage due to inadequate corpus luteum function.

If a luteal phase defect is found after a woman with normal preovulatory hormones ovulates, then progesterone supplementation is in order following ovulation. Also, if a woman develops spotting or cramping during pregnancy and she has low progesterone levels, then progesterone administration plus other medications that stop uterine contractions may help prevent a threatened miscarriage.

Although the Food and Drug Administration hasn't approved progesterone supplementation during the first trimester of pregnancy, most fertility specialists prescribe the hormone for women with inadequate luteal phase function to reduce their risks of miscarriage. The progesterone supplements may mask a miscarriage, but monitoring with hCG assays will detect a pregnancy that has stopped developing. If the pregnancy stops developing normally, the woman should stop taking progesterone supplements. She usually will begin to bleed from the uterus, aborting the pregnancy, or a D&C can remove the abnormal pregnancy from the uterus.

A hormone deficiency in the follicular (preovulatory) phase of a woman's cycle requires a different type of treatment, and here clomiphene or Pergonal with hCG are most helpful. Even with these drugs, a woman may still need additional progesterone in the luteal or postovulatory phase of the cycle to achieve and maintain a pregnancy.

Unfortunately, some women with problems beginning in the follicular phase are treated only with progesterone late in their cycles, which usually ends up being a wasted effort. If these women don't ovulate, then late progesterone supplementation is just that—too late to do any good. They need early hormonal therapy first to get them ovulating and to prepare the endometrial lining for progesterone's action later in the cycle.

New Progesterones

New oral and gel formulations of progesterone are now available. The oral dosage form of progesterone (Prometrium) is synthesized from yams and is structurally identical to natural progesterone. The micronized formulation increases its absorption. It has been approved for secondary amenorrhea.

Patients who may be allergic to peanuts, suffer from severe liver disease, or who have known or suspected breast cancer or are pregnant should not take Prometrium capsules. The most common side effects are dizziness, abdominal cramping, headache, and breast pain.

A progesterone gel (Crinone) has been used as a supplement for women undergoing assisted reproduction with excellent clinical pregnancy rates. It also is indicated for secondary amenorrhea. Its unique administration allows patients the convenience and benefits of progesterone therapy without taking injections.

Danocrine (Danazol)

One of the most frequently prescribed drugs to treat endometriosis has been danocrine (Danazol). Danazol is a synthetic derivative of testosterone that counteracts the effects of estrogen and decreases its synthesis by interfering with the production of FSH and LH. By putting the body into a "pseudomenopausal" state, Danazol inhibits buildup of the endometrium, and thereby reduces the growth and spread of endometriosis.

A woman typically takes 200 mg of Danazol three or four times a day for three to nine months. The pregnancy rates quoted for Danazol treatments range from as high as 75 percent for mild endometriosis, to 50 percent for moderate endometriosis, to 25 percent for severe disease. These pregnancy rates may be optimistic for women with severe disease, who usually have such widespread endometriosis that they require surgery as well as medication. It's unclear whether treatment with Danazol is truly superior to treatment with a variety of other drugs, such as the synthetic progestins medroxyprogesterone acetate (Provera) or megestrol acetate (Megace), or to treatment by surgical methods alone. Many doctors also use GnRH agonists to treat endometriosis.

SIDE EFFECTS • Although doctors consider Danazol an effective treatment for endometriosis, more than half of the women who take it develop side effects. A woman may grow facial hair, gain weight, develop acne, hear a deepening of her voice, show a decrease in breast size, experience muscle cramps and muscle enlargement, and have a raised blood cholesterol level. Basically, Danazol produces masculinizing effects, since it is an anabolic steroid.

Androgens

Women and men both produce the steroid hormones called androgens in their adrenal glands, and in the ovaries for women and testicles for men. They are often thought of as "male" hormones because androgens are the primary hormones circulating in a man's blood, leading to masculine sexual characteristics, while estrogens are the primary circulating hormones in women.

In some women, the ovaries or adrenal glands produce more than normal amounts of androgens. In exceptional cases, androgens can reach such high levels that they may cause clinical masculinization of a woman—her voice deepens, her muscle mass increases, she grows hair on the face and chest, and she may even lose hair on her head in a male baldness pattern. In dramatic cases like this, it's important for the physician to perform appropriate tests to determine whether the woman has an androgen-producing tumor of either the adrenal glands or the ovaries.

Much more frequently, androgen levels are only mildly elevated in women, but can still interfere with a woman's normal reproductive cycles. Since androgens tend to block the actions of estrogen, they can prevent normal follicle development, ovulation, and cervical mucus production. Increased androgens are frequently seen in women with prolonged anovulation, such as in women with polycystic ovarian disease.

The most commonly measured androgens are testosterone and dihydroepiandrosterone sulfate (DHEAS). If testosterone levels are elevated but DHEAS levels are normal, this suggests that the ovaries are the source of the excess androgens. A high DHEAS level suggests that the adrenal glands are responsible.

When the adrenal glands are the source of high androgens, adrenal gland activity should be reduced by treatment with steroid medications, such as prednisone or dexamethasone. These medications reduce the secretion of adrenocorticotropic hormone (ACTH) from the pituitary, which in turn reduces the adrenal production of hormones.

If the source of excess androgens is the ovaries, then medical treatment consists primarily of administering the drug spironolactone (Aldactone). This drug binds to the androgens and therefore reduces the amount of androgens available to affect the ovaries, uterus, and cervix.

When ovaries and adrenal glands are both producing excess androgens, a combination of spironolactone and steroid treatment may be required. Medical management of high androgen production usually requires continued treatment, month after month, until a woman gets pregnant. In some cases, a GnRH agonist like Lupron may be used to reduce stimulation to the ovaries, and then ovulation is induced with pure FSH.

Diabetes Drugs for Polycystic Ovarian Disease (PCOD)

Oral insulin-lowering agents generally prescribed for diabetes appear to improve hormonal and metabolic function in PCOD patients and to induce ovulation and improve pregnancy rates. The most studied drug is metformin (Glucophage), which has been used for more than two decades to lower insulin levels in diabetics. It appears to also lower insulin levels among PCOD patients and allows their bodies to respond better to a program of diet and exercise. Even PCOD patients who are very resistant to fertility drugs seem to ovulate while taking metformin.

Usually a woman starts on low doses of metformin that are increased gradually. The most common side effects are nausea, vomiting, diarrhea, bloating, and abdominal cramping. Women with kidney disease, circulatory problems, liver disease, pancreatitis, or severe infection may be a high risk for a serious condition called lactic acidosis. Long-term results are not yet available on this treatment.

Other diabetes drugs that reduce insulin levels even more than metformin may also be effective for PCOD. Troglitazone (Rezulin) effectively treated PCOD, but it was removed from the market by the FDA because of concerns about serious side effects. The similar, safer agents rosiglitazone (Avandia) and pioglitazone (Actos) now available may work as well for PCOD, but require liver enzyme testing. Another promising insulin-lowering agent—D-chiro-inositol—appears to be well tolerated by PCOD patients.

Risks of Ovarian Cancer

Despite an intense media focus on the possibility of fertility drugs causing ovarian cancer, it appears that there is no link. Many studies have found that infertile women are at increased risk for ovarian cancer compared to fertile women but that there is no increase in ovarian cancer risk among women who take ovulation drugs. Infertility itself is a risk factor for ovarian cancer. And giving birth appears to protect women from ovarian cancer, with each birth reducing a woman's lifetime risk by 20 percent. Several case-controlled studies of women with ovarian cancer and long-term follow-up studies of women treated with injected gonadotropins have not shown a connection between fertility drugs and the development of ovarian cancer.

Even so, it seems appropriate to limit the duration of exposure to fertility drugs. The American Society of Reproductive Medicine recommends clomiphene be used for no more than six months. Also, infertile women who have never conceived or have a strong family history of reproductive cancer should be followed closely and have frequent pelvic and breast examinations. Dr. Berger now includes a vaginal ultrasound examination of the ovaries for his patients taking hormones to see whether they are at high risk of developing ovarian cancer. A pelvic exam is not sensitive enough since a doctor cannot usually feel a small cyst or tumor in the ovaries. If a vaginal ultrasound suggests the possibility of an ovarian abnormality, additional screening tests (such as the blood test CA-125) or diagnostic tests (such as laparoscopy) can be performed.

Hormone Treatments for Men

Although urologists have traditionally focused on the surgical management of male infertility, most infertile men have disorders that don't lend themselves to surgery. Disorders interfering with hormone flow from the hypothalamus to the pituitary to their testicles comprise about 10 percent of male infertility but are among the most treatable causes.

Men and women produce the same sex hormones, but in different concentrations. Men make testosterone in their testicles and adrenal glands and women make it in their ovaries and adrenals. Men have about ten times as much testosterone as women, which is what gives them their secondary sexual characteristics. (It follows that testosterone is considered a "male" hormone.)

The same hormones that induce ovulation in women also occur naturally in men and play a role in male reproduction. LH and FSH stimulate the testicles to produce testosterone. Men with inadequate amounts of FSH and LH may produce insufficient testosterone, resulting in too few sperm or sperm of poor quality.

And just as men and women share reproductive hormones, the same hormonal therapies can be used to cure a man's infertility due to hormonal deficiencies—although the doses and lengths of treatment may differ.

Clomiphene

Clomiphene is one of the most commonly prescribed drugs for infertile men. The drug increases a man's levels of LH and FSH, which stimulate his testicles to produce testosterone and sperm. Men with low FSH or LH levels often show increased sperm counts after clomiphene treatments, but clomiphene alone hasn't been proven effective in increasing pregnancy rates.

The group of men who seem to benefit the most from clomiphene have low sperm counts and low or low-normal gonadotropin levels and low levels of testosterone in their blood. They usually receive a dose of 12.5 to 25 mg per day for twenty-five days per month for three to six months. While taking clomiphene, a man should have a semen analysis and testosterone, LH, FSH, and estrogen levels checked every three months. If his estrogen level rises above normal, his sperm production may slow down. Too much estrogen in the blood signals the pituitary to stop gonadotropin secretion, which will worsen, rather than improve, the man's situation. In these cases, lowering the clomiphene dose or using tamoxifen, a drug similar to clomiphene, may be effective.

hCG and Pergonal

If a man's hypothalamus or pituitary gland is malfunctioning, and he is secreting inadequate amounts of FSH and LH, the quality or quantity of his sperm may not be sufficient to fertilize his wife's egg. Treatment with hCG, followed by Pergonal, is the most direct way to correct the problem. hCG treatment stimulates the testicles to produce testosterone. Pergonal can be added to increase sperm production.

This combination therapy is effective only for men with hypogonadotropic hypogonadism. Men with this rare condition lack production of GnRH, and are diagnosed by finding very low levels of LH, FSH, and testosterone in the blood, along with physical findings such as small testicles, breast enlargement, and often the lack of a sense of smell (Kallman's syndrome).

Initially, a man takes hCG injections three times each week for six months. If the size of his testicles increases and his testosterone levels reach normal, then he adds FSH, in the form of Pergonal or Metrodin, by mixing in two ampules with his hCG injections three times each week. If he doesn't respond after four months, then his doctor will double the Pergonal dosage. Once he has achieved adequate sperm output, he often can stop taking Pergonal and will continue with hCG treatments alone. The Pergonal can be added again when the couple wants to maximize his sperm output to achieve a pregnancy.

Although inconvenient, there are few side effects with this combination therapy. Almost 50 percent of the treated men will impregnate their wives even though their sperm counts are rarely above 10 million per ml. The sperm produced, however, usually have good motility and normal morphology.

GnRH

Since men with hypogonadotropic hypogonadism lack GnRH, the ideal replacement is GnRH itself. However, GnRH must be delivered subcutaneously or intravenously through a pump in pulses every 120 minutes (compared to every ninety minutes for women).

For men who can tolerate the portable infusion pump, the therapy is highly effective. About 75 percent who have had three to thirty months of therapy with natural GnRH show sperm in their ejaculates, and 50 to 60 percent of these men have impregnated their wives. Once the couple has achieved a pregnancy, the husband can return to hCG or testosterone therapy to maintain his secondary sexual characteristics. If the couple wants another child, he can use the GnRH pump again.

Bromocriptine

High prolactin levels can also affect a man's fertility. A high prolactin output inhibits LH and FSH secretion, probably because it inhibits secretion of GnRH. The lack of these reproductive hormones usually leads to impotence and a low sex drive, as well as a lowered sperm count and low testosterone levels. In other words, elevated prolactin can adversely affect both sexual performance and fertility.

High prolactin levels among men can be due to a pituitary tumor, hypothalamus disorders, hypothyroidism, or drug treatments. In most cases, bromocriptine can reduce blood levels of prolactin to normal, restoring testosterone levels as well as a man's potency and fertility. Bromocriptine also shrinks pituitary tumors that secrete prolactin.

For men with high prolactin levels, bromocriptine often succeeds in restoring potency and fertility where testosterone therapy has failed. This is believed to be due to the increases in FSH levels after bromocriptine treatments. (Testosterone often doesn't increase FSH levels.)

Bromocriptine's side effects for men are the same as those for women. They include nausea, dizziness, headache, and fatigue, usually experienced only during the first few days of treatment.

Other Drugs

Hypothyroidism can be associated with low LH, FSH, and testosterone concentrations, in addition to a low sperm count and decreased sperm motility. A man with low thyroid levels should be treated with thyroid replacement, which may correct his infertility without any other treatment being required.

Testosterone has been prescribed for infertile men, but this is now known to be ineffective. In fact, giving a man testosterone will reduce sperm production, and testosterone has even been used successfully as a contraceptive. Testosterone is sometimes administered to impotent men, but never to men with desires for fertility. Other, more successful, treatments include eliminating medications and recreational drugs that lower the libido and, as a last resort, penile implants. Tamoxifen, a drug similar to clomiphene, is an antiestrogen that increases sperm counts but has shown no clear improvement in pregnancy rates for the partners of infertile men.

Antioxidant vitamins (such as vitamin C and E) and minerals (zinc and selenium), as well as amino acids can be recommended for the treatment of unexplained male infertility in doses indicated on page 50. Amino acids such as L-arginine have been proven ineffective.

Future Drugs

Several new drugs, some still experimental, are on the horizon as infertility treatments for hormonal problems.

PURE LH • A pure version of luteinizing hormone has recently been produced through genetic engineering. The hormone is purer than hormones extracted from the pituitary gland or the urine of postmenopausal women.

Pure LH could have value for both women and men. Instead of receiving hCG on the day of the LH surge, a woman would receive pure LH to stimulate ovulation induction. The drug may also stimulate sperm production.

PROGESTERONE ANTAGONISTS • Progesterone antagonists, or antiprogestins, are a new class of steroids that compete with progesterone within the body. The most well known is the controversial abortion pill RU486 (mifepristone). Experts predict that within the next decade progesterone antagonists will be available to obstetrician-gynecologists to help control hormone-dependent tissue growth such as endometriosis.

ACTIVIN • Exciting possibilities have emerged with the recent discovery of a new hormone called activin. First, researchers looking into the action of FSH identified a hormone called inhibin in women's ovarian follicular fluid and in men's testicular fluid. This hormone inhibits FSH secretion.

Then researchers found a potent activator of FSH secretion, which they termed activin.

Activin may have a role in increasing egg production. It has led to a doubling of the number of eggs produced in animal experiments. In addition, it may be useful in lowering the levels of androgens and the high LH-to-FSH ratio found among women with polycystic ovaries, which may then permit these women to have normal ovulation. Since activin also increases progesterone and hCG levels, it may also be useful in rescuing pregnancies in women with poor luteal function. For men, activin may be able to stimulate the body to produce more FSH, which in turn stimulates sperm production.

A limited supply of man-made activin produced in the lab is now available to a few researchers. Even after we have a larger supply, it will likely take some years for it to become available to clinicians for infertility treatment.

RELAXIN • A recently identified component of semen is the hormone relaxin. This hormone enhances sperm motility. If and when more tests confirm its usefulness, relaxin may be a tool for the treatment of male infertility, especially for men with poor motility.

Women also produce relaxin, which helps to reduce the strength of uterine contractions during pregnancy. Relaxin may also play a role in the relaxation, or "softening," of the cervix in preparation for labor. Its potential for therapeutic uses, such as to stop premature labor, has not yet been determined.

Questions to Ask Your Doctor
About Hormone Treatments

Both women and men may want to ask some basic questions about the hormones they are taking, including:

Are my blood hormone levels abnormal?

Why am I a good candidate for this hormone treatment?

How much of the hormone do I need to take each day, and for how many days?

What are the potential side effects of the hormone?

How much does the treatment cost?

In your experience, what are our chances of conceiving?

Specific Questions for Women About Specific Hormones

Clomiphene

Do I have any contraindications that make clomiphene an inappropriate drug for me?

How will I know if the drug is working or not working?

Is the drug interfering with my cervical mucus production?

hMG

How will you monitor my drug taking to know how much I need to ovulate and to avoid hyperstimulation?

What are my risks of multiple pregnancy?

Do I have any contraindications that make hMG an inappropriate drug for me?

Human Chorionic Gonadotropin

How will I know the proper time for an hCG injection?

Will you teach me (or my husband) how to administer the injection?

Gonadotropin-Releasing Hormone

Will I have the needle under my skin or in a vein?

How do I know whether I am developing a blood clot in the vein or an infection where the needle enters my body?

Where do I get an infusion pump?

Bromocriptine

Do I have an elevation in my prolactin levels, even a mild or intermittent one?

Do I need a brain scan to rule out a pituitary tumor?

Progesterone

Am I at risk of an early miscarriage?

Do I need progesterone supplements after I ovulate?

Danazol

Why do you recommend Danazol, and how does it compare with other treatments available for endometriosis?

Diabetes Drugs

With my polycystic ovarian disease, am I a candidate for diabetes drugs?

Specific Questions for Men

How often will I need a semen analysis and blood tests while on hormone therapy?

Will the hormones I take affect my potency or sex drive?

Clomiphene

Are my blood testosterone level and sperm count low?

Are my LH and FSH levels normal?

Human Chorionic Gonadotropin and/or Pergonal

Do I have hypogonadotropic hypogonadism?

Are all my hormone levels (LH, FSH, testosterone) below normal?

How often will I get shots? How long will treatment take?

Bromocriptine

Is my prolactin level high on at least two tests?

Is my testosterone low?

Do I need an MRI of my pituitary gland?

8

OTHER MEDICAL
AND SURGICAL
TREATMENTS

After your situation has been adequately evaluated, your fertility specialist may recommend certain other medical and surgical treatments. Once you have a diagnosis of your fertility problem, you should sit down with your doctor and discuss how to try to resolve it. Consider your treatment options as carefully as you chose your doctor. Ask your doctor why he or she has decided this is the best treatment. Find out how to learn more about your diagnosed problem and the particular therapies available to you.

Antibiotics

If the early part of the infertility evaluation reveals that either partner has a genital tract infection, both partners should be treated with antibiotics and then have follow-up cultures taken to be sure that the bacteria have been eradicated. Once the infection has been cleared from both the man's and woman's genital tracts, then it's safe to proceed with other treatments, including surgical or advanced laboratory methods.

There are several antibiotic treatments for chlamydia for men and nonpregnant women: tetracycline four times a day, doxycycline twice a day, or a once-a-day antibiotic, azithromycin.

A new class of antibiotics called quinolones are also highly effective against chlamydia, mycoplasma, and most other bacteria associated with infertility. Treatment with these antibiotics (Floxin, Cipro) is usually given to both partners twice a day for two to three weeks.

Erythromycin is the first choice for treating chlamydia infections in pregnant women, and offers the advantage of being effective against tetracycline-resistant ureaplasma organisms that may also be involved. Acute infection can be treated with a ten- to fourteen-day course of antibiotics; chronic cases, however, may require longer treatment with more than one course of antibiotics.

Mycoplasma and ureaplasma infections can be more difficult to eradicate with antibiotics than gonorrhea and chlamydia. Couples often receive an inadequate dosage or duration of treatment with tetracycline, or the organism may be resistant to the medication used. About 85 percent of mycoplasma organisms appear to be resistant to erythromycin. Don't assume that you are free of mycoplasma until you have negative cultures at least three months after your last antibiotic dose.

Aggressive antibiotic treatment may prevent the complications of PID if therapy is begun very early, perhaps within days of an acute symptomatic infection, or better, if the infection is discovered and treated before it causes symptoms. With PID, the fallopian tubes may close partially or totally, or scar tissue may form around the tubes and ovaries, impeding the egg's journey to the tubes and uterus. Antibiotics can help the body's immune system eliminate bacteria, but they have no beneficial effect on already damaged tubes and ducts or on scar tissue.

Even today, many doctors don't recognize the importance of routine screening to diagnose and treat asymptomatic lower genital tract infections to prevent salpingitis and subsequent infertility. Most doctors tend to treat patients only *after* they have developed symptoms, and even then may treat for a presumed chlamydia infection without the benefit of appropriate, simple tests that tell them exactly what organisms may be causing the infection.

Treating the Woman

Treatments for fertility problems in women have grown by leaps and bounds lately. The advent of microsurgical techniques in the 1970s allowed reproductive surgeons to remove adhesions, including the scars formed by endometriosis or PID, from a woman's upper reproductive tract. In addition, microsurgeons began performing delicate operations on the fallopian tubes, including reconnecting tubes "tied," burned, or cut during sterilization procedures. In the 1980s and 1990s, the movement toward surgery through laparoscopes and hysteroscopes helped transfer delicate reproductive surgery from the hospital to the outpatient surgicenter.

Microsurgery

Spectacular advances in microsurgery since the mid-1970s have helped restore many women's fertility. Just as the invention of the microscope opened up new horizons to scientists more than three hundred years ago, the development and application of special microscopes and magnifying lenses vastly expanded the horizons of modern surgery. Microscopes were first used in human surgery in the 1920s. Although the magnification of the microscope gave doctors a better view of tiny structures, the lack of microscopic-size needles and surgical thread held back further development of microsurgery.

By the 1960s, surgical manufacturers were producing needles as thin as a human hair and surgical thread virtually invisible to the naked eye. With the new technology came the need for new skills. Surgeons had to learn how to sew using a specially adapted jeweler's forceps or tweezers while looking through the eyepieces of a microscope. After practicing for hundreds of hours in the lab, microsurgeons began performing previously impossible surgical feats, such as repairing ultrathin nerves and blood vessels and removing tiny tumors from the brain.

Reproductive surgeons adapted microsurgery to meet their patients' fertility needs. For women, microsurgery can remove the scar tissue from the ovaries or other pelvic locations, destroy active areas of endometriosis, and repair damaged fallopian tubes.

TUBAL SURGERY • If a woman has an obstruction in the middle of the fallopian tube, most often due to a tubal ligation, she must have that portion of the tube removed. A skilled microsurgeon can remove the obstruction and stitch together the adjacent open ends of the tube in what's called an anastomosis.

The most common operation on the fallopian tube is a fimbrioplasty. The fimbria, the flared ends of the tubes near the ovaries, can become inflamed and scarred, and may need reconstruction. If the fimbria become tied up with adhesions, the adhesions must be removed or the tube cannot pick up eggs released from the ovary. If the fimbrial end of the tube is blocked and the fallopian tube is enlarged with fluid (a hydrosalpinx), then reconstructive surgery through an open incision (laparotomy) may be necessary.

The portion of the tube that enters the uterus is often a more difficult area to repair, and requires a different surgical approach from a blocked fimbria. If this portion of the tube is damaged or diseased, a woman may need to have the portion removed and the remaining section of the normal tube placed in a newly created opening into the uterine cavity, a procedure called a tubouterine implantation. After the damaged part is removed, if the damage is in one small area, the tube can be rejoined microsurgically.

A condition called salpingitis isthmica nodosa causes an outpouching of bumps (diverticulae) at the junction of the tube with the uterus. This part of the tube controls when the fertilized egg is delivered into the uterine cavity. These inflamed nodules in the fallopian tube can prevent sperm from passing through the tube to meet the egg or, after the egg has been fertilized, can prevent the fertilized egg from traveling into the uterus for implantation. The affected portion of the tube has to be surgically removed to restore normal function.

Shortening an elongated ligament between the fallopian tube and the ovary back to its normal length using microsurgery may allow the ligament to move the fimbrial end of the tube over the ovary, pick up an egg when released at ovulation, and, eventually, lead to a pregnancy.

STERILIZATION REVERSAL

The month after Jenny's divorce from her first husband was final, she married Peter, a thirty-seven-year-old engineer. "I thought we wouldn't want any more children," says Jenny, age forty, who had been sterilized after she bore two sons. But a few years into their marriage, they decided they would like to have a baby. A surgeon at a fertility clinic told Jenny it might take several operations in the hospital to reverse her sterilization, and "I didn't want to go through that," she says.

Later that year, she read an article in Redbook *magazine about Dr. Berger's success with outpatient sterilization reversals. "He told me he could do the procedure, and I decided to go right ahead," Jenny says. "On the day of the surgery, I came into the outpatient center at ten o'clock, walked out to meet Peter in the car at noon, and was home before one." Their daughter Deborah is now three years old, and Jenny is pregnant again.*

One of the most dramatic ways microsurgeons apply their skills is to reverse sterilization operations. As many as 10 percent of women who choose to be sterilized have second thoughts about it later on and want a reversal to make them fertile again. Most sterilized women don't know how simple and effective sterilization reversal surgery can be.

The women most likely to want a sterilization reversal and have a child are in the thirty- to forty-year-old age bracket. In general, women who were sterilized in their twenties want a reversal more often than those who were thirty or older when they were sterilized. Also, women who had a tubal ligation only a short time ago may be more likely to want a reversal than those who had the surgery many years ago.

Women whose lives have changed due to separation, divorce, or death of a husband and who are considering remarrying also want reversals much more often than women who have remained married to the same spouse. And when sterilized partners divorce and remarry, they, too, are highly motivated to seek reversals. More than 90 percent of the couples who ask Dr. Berger to reverse a sterilization have remarried and want to start a second family.

In addition to using microsurgical techniques, Dr. Berger pioneered the development of new surgical and anesthetic techniques and adapted the concept of out-of-hospital surgery to sterilization reversals. Instead of the usual three- to five-day hospital stay and four- to six-week recovery period, Dr. Berger's patients recuperate at home a few hours after surgery and are back at work in one to two weeks.

So far, of the more than 150 women Dr. Berger has operated on in this manner and followed for one year or more after the procedure, 95 percent have clear and open tubes and more than 70 percent have become pregnant.

Outpatient Surgery

Janice, age thirty-six, had been sterilized for ten years when she and her forty-two-year-old husband, Mark, decided they wanted to have a child together. When Dr. Berger examined her fallopian tubes, he found that each tube had been divided in two places. Using local anesthesia around an incision in Janice's abdomen, as well as a regional nerve block in her pelvic area, he gently and bloodlessly used microsurgical techniques to reconnect her tubes. Janice was at home recuperating the same day as surgery and back to full activities within one week. Three months later she became pregnant.

Besides reversing sterilizations, outpatient surgery can now be used to treat virtually all anatomical disorders that cause infertility in women. Gynecologists in the 1970s popularized "Band-Aid" sterilization operations, performing same-day surgery through a small slit in the woman's abdomen near her belly button after injecting local anesthesia into the incision site. Outpatient surgical centers offering these and other simple surgeries flourished in the 1980s and 1990s, partly due to a change in attitude among doctors and their patients.

Doctors are increasingly realizing that surgery doesn't always mean that the patient has to be hospitalized. Although many fertility specialists who perform surgery are hospital-based, more of them have begun adopting the concept of outpatient surgery in their practices.

Outpatient surgery costs less than the same operation performed in the hospital. You don't have to pay for a hospital room or lose as much time from work, since you recover faster than from in-hospital surgery. Instead of being in the hospital for up to one week and out of work for six weeks, women who have major pelvic reconstructive surgery using outpatient methods are back home the same day and usually back to work within ten days.

Almost all reconstructive operations for a woman's or a man's fertility problems can be performed safely and effectively on an outpatient basis. For the man, these procedures include testicular biopsy, microsurgical repair of varicoceles, surgical lowering of a testicle from the abdomen into the scrotum (orchidopexy), and microsurgical correction of blocked ducts.

Most gynecologic surgeons associate laparoscopy (surgery through the laparoscope) with minor, outpatient surgery, and laparotomy (surgery through an open incision) with major, in-hospital surgery.

But Dr. Berger's experience of more than two decades of performing outpatient surgery has shown that this simplified rule doesn't really apply. Even when he performs microsurgical repairs with the woman asleep under general anesthesia, he incorporates outpatient surgery techniques, such as employing local anesthesia and avoiding the use of traumatic instruments to lessen postoperative pain. This dramatically reduces the woman's pain and speeds her recovery. Less than 1 percent of his patients require hospital stays.

Reproductive surgery is really a form of plastic surgery applied to the reproductive organs. Like plastic surgery on the face, the objective is to restore normal anatomy, in this case in the pelvic region. As a result, patients feel better, heal faster, and have better surgical results in the outpatient setting, with no need for hospitalization at all.

Dr. Berger knows it is essential to meticulously control blood loss. Every time he cuts through tissue, he seals it with heat or sutures and examines it under magnification to be certain all bleeding has stopped. To feel confident about letting women go home the same day as surgery, he has to be absolutely certain that there is no bleeding internally.

To control postoperative pain, in addition to the general anesthesia he injects a long-lasting local anesthetic into the tissues being operated on. Immediately blocking the acute sensation of pain allows his patients to wake up pain-free, get dressed, and go home.

He backs this up with a take-home pain-killing machine, called a Transcutaneous External Nerve Stimulation (TENS) unit. The TENS machine is a battery-operated box about the size of a Walkman. Instead of headphones, it has electrodes that attach to the skin near the incision.

When she's home, the woman controls the strength of the electrical stimulation to activate nerve endings in her skin, which in turn causes the nerve endings to release endorphins, the body's natural pain-killers. In more than four hundred outpatient open surgeries, most of Dr. Berger's patients have needed no narcotic medications after surgery. Instead, they may use the TENS machine or a simple ice pack to reduce pain.

In addition, he avoids using traumatic "self-retaining" skin retractors and only exposes the site of surgery when he is operating on it. Each of these steps leads to less traumatic surgery and less postoperative pain than the more customary techniques used by most gynecologists.

Besides the many outpatient sterilization reversals he has performed, Dr. Berger treats other anatomic problems using the same techniques. For salpingitis isthmica nodosa, he cuts out the damaged portion of tube as it exits from the uterus. He can remove adhesions from the bowel, the fallopian tube, the area between the fallopian tube and ovary—virtually anywhere in the pelvis where there is scar tissue. He also performs tuboplasties to open up the end of a tube that has been closed due to PID; excises ovarian cysts, mostly due to endometriosis; performs uterine myomectomies, removing tumors from the surface of the uterus, the wall of the uterine muscle, or inside the uterine cavity; and occasionally performs an ovarian wedge resection in very large polycystic ovaries—surgically removing a section of the ovary to reduce it to normal size—to spark spontaneous ovulation.

To be successful, outpatient surgery requires cooperative, well-informed patients. Dr. Berger maintains daily contact with anyone who has had major outpatient surgery to make sure that her postoperative course is proceeding normally at home. The woman should know what kinds of complications may occur and how to contact her doctor at any time should a problem or question arise. For example, if the woman has a fever after surgery, with a temperature that reaches 100 degrees Fahrenheit, she must call the doctor immediately, since this may be a sign of an infection.

So far, none of Dr. Berger's patients has developed a major postoperative infection during the years he has been performing outpatient surgery, mostly due to thorough preoperative testing for infections and treating any existing infections before performing surgery.

Laparoscopic Surgery

While microsurgery came into its own in the 1970s, the 1980s witnessed a surge in operations through the laparoscope. In the 1990s, laparoscopy has become the most frequently performed gynecological procedure in the United States. Laparoscopy courses are taught all across the country, and procedures such as removing adhesions, endometriosis, and even ectopic pregnancies have become common one-day, outpatient procedures using laparoscopy.

The main advantage of surgery through the laparoscope is that the doctor can see into the abdomen without the need for a wide incision, performing the surgery by passing instruments through the thin telescope's operating channel or a second laparoscope. Before the laparoscope, a woman might have had to undergo exploratory surgery if she felt acute abdominal pain. Now she can have a laparoscopic exam that may reveal the nature of the problem and lead to an immediate, less traumatic operation than standard laparotomy.

Laparoscopic surgery has its drawbacks, however, and can't replace the exquisite suturing technique of microsurgery through an open incision. Although most women recover more rapidly from surgery through the laparoscope, the potential for serious complications is actually higher than for surgery through an open incision. For example, if the surgeon accidentally nicks a blood vessel during laparoscopic surgery, he may have problems controlling bleeding as the blood blocks his view through the laparoscope. For this reason, many fertility surgeons limit the extent of reconstructive operations through a laparoscope. Instead, they make a larger incision in the woman's abdomen and perform microsurgery for more difficult surgical procedures and for reconstructions requiring more delicate, precise techniques.

Through the laparoscope, an experienced doctor can see abnormalities of the size and shape of the uterus, fibroids, tumors, ovarian cysts, pelvic adhesions, and endometriosis (commonly found in front of or behind the uterus in the cul-de-sac) and any other abnormality involving the outside of the uterus, tubes, and ovaries.

Surgery through the laparoscope can remove scar tissue in a woman's pelvis or around her tubes or ovaries, or correct a narrowing at the tube's end. Forceps passed through the laparoscope's operating channel can be introduced into a partially blocked end of the tube and pulled out to reopen the end.

In general, the risks of an operation through the laparoscope—bleeding, infection, and anesthesia-related complications—are the same as for any other surgical procedure. Specific risks of laparoscopy include possibly injuring a woman's intestine, urinary tract, or internal blood vessels. These are rare but potentially serious complications that require immediate laparotomy to repair.

The most common problem a woman encounters after laparoscopy is abdominal, chest, or shoulder pain. Most often, this pain is due to the carbon dioxide gas used during laparoscopy, which irritates the respiratory system's diaphragm. The pain usually disappears in a day or two.

Hysteroscopic Surgery

When a radiologist read Judith's hysterosalpingogram, he thought the X ray showed a normal uterus. But the fertility doctor saw a shadowing that didn't appear normal, and he recommended that she undergo a hysteroscopic exam for further evaluation.

The outpatient hysteroscopy showed that Judith, a thirty-year-old dentist, had a septum dividing her uterus. The doctor removed the septum through the hysteroscope's operative channel, avoiding the need for abdominal surgery. "I went out to dinner that night with my husband and was back to normal activities the next day," says Judith. She had a follow-up hysterosalpingogram a month later to ensure that the operation had worked. "The exam showed a real difference. My uterus looked normal," she says.

Just as your doctor uses the laparoscope as both a diagnostic and therapeutic tool inside the abdomen, the hysteroscope can be used to correct some abnormalities within the uterus as soon as they are found. By passing tiny scissors through an operating channel in the scope, the doctor can treat such abnormalities as intrauterine adhesions; benign growths, such as polyps or small fibroid tumors growing into the uterine cavity; and abnormal development of the uterus, such as a uterine septum (excess connective tissue distorting the normal shape and volume of the uterus).

The operating hysteroscope allows removal of adhesions that may have formed in the uterus after a woman had a previous D&C, an abortion, from IUD use, or a uterine infection. Before hysteroscopy was available, it was difficult to recognize and treat uterine adhesions. Through the hysteroscope, fertility surgeons can now easily remove this scar tissue with no, or very infrequent, recurrence.

Although hysteroscopy is a minor operation, it's not always simple. It is often more technically difficult to perform than laparoscopy and requires an experienced doctor who will know what he is looking at as he peers into small spaces. As with other specialized techniques, proficiency requires experience and repeated use.

The potential complications of hysteroscopy include those associated with any surgery, such as bleeding, infection, and anesthesia-related complications (such as a possible allergic reaction), as well as the risk of perforation of the uterus with the hysteroscope or scissors. (This is an infrequent complication and usually causes no harm.)

Endometriosis

Jane, age thirty-four, had cysts on her ovaries from long-standing endometriosis. Her doctor suggested that she have the cysts removed laparoscopically under local anesthesia. The cysts were more extensive than the doctor thought, and it took him four hours of laparoscopic surgery to destroy them. After a rough postop course, including two weeks of severe pain and discomfort, Jane's doctor suggested he do another laparoscopy to check his results. "No way I'm going to let you put another tube in me," Jane told him. Instead, she went to see a fertility specialist, who successfully performed microsurgery through an open incision to clear up remaining adhesions. Jane went home the same day in little pain, and she was back at work by the end of the week.

Doctors have widely different ideas about how to treat endometriosis. Some doctors use medical treatment, often with the steroid drug Danazol (danocrine) or similar drugs that cause the endometrium to shrink in size, which relieves the pain of endometriosis. Others prefer laparoscopic surgery, sending a small electrical probe or laser beam down a laparoscope to burn away the diseased tissue. Still others choose surgery through an open incision. These approaches all have similar success rates.

Most surgeons use either medical treatment or laparoscopic surgery for stage one (minimal) or stage two (mild) endometriosis, which includes implants on the woman's ovaries and other parts of the pelvic area, such as the bladder, but no obstructions in her fallopian tubes. One consideration in choosing a therapy is the timing. Since medical treatment suppresses a woman's ovulation and menstruation, she can't get pregnant during the months she's on the medication. After surgery to remove the implants, the couple can attempt a pregnancy as soon as the wife has recovered from the operation.

A woman may need a combination of medical and surgical treatments for stage three, or moderate, endometriosis, which causes endometrial cysts, tubal abnormalities, and a partial obliteration of the cul-de-sac from adhesions. To remove large endometrial "chocolate" cysts in the ovaries, some surgeons advocate draining the cysts and destroying them with a laser through the laparoscope. This can be potentially hazardous since some of the endometriosis may leak out and spread to other parts of the woman's abdominal cavity. Dr. Berger prefers to remove large endometrial cysts with microsurgery through an open incision in the abdomen.

Stage four, or extensive, endometriosis that has destroyed a large portion of the ovaries, obliterated the cul-de-sac, and left dense, vascular adhesions in the pelvic area often warrants treatment with both conservative reconstructive surgery and medication. In some cases, a woman has so much dense scar tissue from stage four endometriosis that even microsurgery can't repair the damage. In these severe cases, especially when a woman's pelvic pain can't be controlled with suppressive hormones, the only way to achieve pain relief is a total hysterectomy and removal of the ovaries. Fortunately, this radical approach can usually be avoided by an early diagnosis and management of endometriosis before it reaches this stage.

Unfortunately, many women with advanced endometriosis are given no choice but a hysterectomy by their gynecologist. In most (but not all) cases, endometriosis can be controlled through conservative surgery and medical treatment so that a woman can retain her ability to get pregnant. Endometriosis is a chronic disease, but if recognized, followed, and treated properly, it doesn't have to develop into an extensive condition. Instead of a hysterectomy, in vitro fertilization may be an option, particularly if a woman has obstructed tubes and extensive adhesions on her ovaries and fallopian tubes.

As with pelvic inflammatory disease, many times the only symptom of endometriosis is infertility. Most women with endometriosis, however, experience pain just before they get their period. If you begin to feel less pain while taking endometriosis medication, that's good sign that the underlying endometriosis is resolving.

Adenomyosis

Cindy, age thirty-eight, had been to several fertility specialists over three years trying to become pregnant before she saw Dr. Berger. After several intrauterine insemination (IUI) attempts failed, he did a hysteroscopy and laparoscopy and found that Cindy had endometriosis, which he corrected surgically, as well as what he believed to be adenomyosis, endometriosis implanted in her uterine muscle.

Dr. Berger put Cindy on synthetic gonadotropin-releasing hormone (Lupron) for several months, as well as prednisone, aspirin, and pentoxi-fylline. Six months later, Cindy became pregnant, and delivered a healthy boy.

Endometriosis implants within the uterine muscle, called adenomyosis, may also cause severe pain when a woman menstruates, as well as enlarge her uterus. The treatment, according to most medical textbooks, is a hysterectomy. But adenomyosis, too, can often be treated by medication and conservative surgery by a trained fertility expert.

Ectopic Pregnancies

Ectopic pregnancy also has several treatment options. The ability to diagnose ectopic pregnancy earlier has led to a trend toward more conservative surgery for the condition. Conservative surgery involves making an incision in the fallopian tube (salpingostomy) to remove the ectopic pregnancy or removing the portion of the fallopian tube containing the tubal pregnancy (partial salpingectomy).

Some gynecologists now advocate performing conservative surgery through an open incision to remove the growing fetus from the woman's fallopian tube. Others prefer surgery through a laparoscope with a laser. A few doctors advocate medical treatment with the cancer drug methotrexate, which causes the woman to abort the tubal pregnancy spontaneously. This chemical treatment, however, carries a risk of damaging the liver and of causing an incomplete miscarriage, which might lead to scarring of the tubes.

Treating the Man

Microsurgery has also benefited men greatly. Microsurgical techniques are now applied to repair varicose veins in the testicles, to open up blocked ducts along a man's reproductive tract, and to sew back together the ends of the vas deferens severed in a vasectomy.

Novel designs of penile implant devices and other innovative treatments have helped impotent and infertile men become fathers. And better sperm processing techniques combined with artificial insemination now allow couples to overcome sperm-mucus and antisperm antibody problems. Finally, IVF with the injection of only one or a few sperm can help a man fertilize his wife's eggs.

Varicocele Repair

Nathan and his wife, Mary, had no success in conceiving a child eight months into their marriage. A semen analysis showed that Nathan's sperm concentration was low, between 2 million and 3 million per milliliter. His motility was only 30 percent. His urologist put him on hormone therapy and suggested that Mary go for a fertility evaluation. Six months later Mary, who tested normal, still wasn't pregnant. Together they went to see Dr. Goldstein, who found varicoceles on each of Nathan's testicles, and suggested they be repaired microsurgically.

During Christmas week, Nathan checked into the hospital ambulatory unit the morning of his scheduled surgery. He took some pain-killing medication one hour before Dr. Goldstein successfully repaired the varicoceles. "I had some pain when I woke up, and I was still a little uncomfortable when I went home that night," says Nathan, a twenty-nine-year-old accountant. He was up and around and back at work in three days. By the end of the week, he felt normal. He and Mary, age twenty-six, went on vacation to Europe that summer, and just as they were returning, Mary noticed her period was about five days late. When they got home, Mary did a home pregnancy test; it was positive. Their daughter, Clare, is now seven years old.

Varicoceles—varicose veins in the scrotum—cause steady damage to the process of sperm formation starting from the time they appear. The majority of men with varicoceles are fertile when they are young, but their fertility gradually declines. More than 80 percent of men with secondary infertility—that is, those who have previously fathered a child—have a varicocele. This suggests that varicoceles cause a progressive decline in fertility.

Fortunately, this most common cause of male infertility also is one of the most treatable. At least 80 percent of men will have improved sperm counts and better sperm motility after a varicocele repair, and can expect to increase their chance of fathering a child. An average of 50 to 60 percent of the wives of men who have had a varicocele repaired will become pregnant within two years of the repair. A successful varicocele repair virtually assures a halt to any further damage to the testicle, although it doesn't absolutely guarantee a pregnancy.

Both large and small varicoceles can be repaired equally well through surgery. A larger varicocele does more damage to the testicle than a smaller one. After repair, however, a man with a large varicocele generally shows a bigger increase in sperm count.

Several ways to repair varicoceles are available: conventional surgery, microsurgery, balloon occlusion, and laparoscopic surgery.

The conventional method of treating varicoceles involves making a three- to four-inch incision in the groin, under general anesthesia, and lifting the spermatic cord out of the scrotum. The spermatic cord is the lifeline to the testicle; it provides all nourishment through the blood vessels and contains the testicles' nerves and lymph glands, as well as the vas deferens. The surgeon looks for the bundle of enlarged veins attached to the cord, exposes them, and ties them off with sutures, relieving the pressure on the swollen vein. After a day or two in the hospital, the man goes home and returns to the doctor's office the next week to have the stitches removed. It may take a few weeks to recover fully from the surgery. Most urologic surgeons use this method to repair varicoceles. However, 15 to 20 percent of the men who have their varicoceles repaired in this fashion have recurrences and may need additional surgery.

One potential problem with this conventional operation is the formation of a hydrocele—a collection of fluid around the testicle. This occurs in 4 to 10 percent of men who undergo a conventional operation. If the tiny lymph ducts that run close to the veins also become tied off accidentally, then a hydrocele forms, and the temperature inside the testicle can remain high. This type of surgery may also damage the even tinier artery that runs into the testicle, which may cut off the blood supply to the testicle, causing it to waste away and lose its potency.

By performing the operation under magnification, experienced urologic microsurgeons can virtually eliminate the complications of recurrence, hydrocele, or injury to the testicle. Using an operating microscope, the surgeon can identify the lymph ducts and also find and isolate the tiny veins that, if left untied, can slowly enlarge and cause the varicocele to recur. In addition, he can more easily identify the testicular artery and avoid injuring it, and thereby prevent damage to the testicle from loss of its blood supply.

With a less than one-inch cut in the groin, the reproductive surgeon can bring the whole testicle out of the body, enabling him to identify and tie off the accessory veins that don't go into the spermatic cord. This markedly reduces the recurrence rate. Then, under microscope guidance, he cuts into the cord with a tiny knife, preserving the testicular artery and lymph ducts, and individually ties off the enlarged veins with ultrathin thread or titanium clips.

Microsurgery is gaining popularity because of its great success. In 2,975 cases, Dr. Goldstein has had but nineteen varicocele recurrences. None of his patients has formed a hydrocele or has had his testicles injured.

Microsurgical varicocele repair also is less stressful on the patient than conventional surgery. The procedure only requires spinal anesthesia, or possibly light general anesthesia similar to the nitrous oxide given at the dentist's office. The patient can go to an ambulatory surgical center, have the operation, and go home the same day. What's more, there are no stitches to remove later since all the stitching is done beneath the skin and dissolves on its own. About ten days after the operation, the man simply removes the tiny strips of tape, called steri-strips, that hold the skin in place over the incision, and resumes his normal activities.

An even less traumatic, less painful varicocele repair uses small, silicone balloons to block off the veins. After making a half-inch incision in the groin, the operating surgeon or a radiologist snakes a tiny catheter into a large vein in the thigh under the guidance of a fluoroscope. A balloon is passed through the catheter, moved through the femoral vein into a kidney vein and finally the testicular vein. After checking an X ray to make sure the balloon is in the right place, the surgeon inflates the balloon to the size of a jellybean and leaves it in place permanently to block off the vein. Occasionally, two balloons are needed to help block off the vein. This minor surgical approach requires only local anesthesia at the site of the incision, and is also performed on an outpatient basis.

But the potential complications of the balloon technique are more serious than those of the two other procedures. If the balloon gets lodged in the wrong place, such as the kidney vein, the man can lose a kidney. If it floats loose, it can lodge in a lung and produce a potentially life-threatening blood clot, called a pulmonary embolism. These complications are rare, but disasters can happen.

The balloon repair also takes longer to perform than surgery. Positioning the balloon takes about ninety minutes, so the entire procedure can last much longer than the thirty minutes required by the other methods. Varicoceles recur in about 10 to 15 percent of balloon repairs, slightly less than conventional surgery, but much more than microsurgical repairs.

Varicoceles also are being repaired through the laparoscope, but there appears to be no advantage to laparoscopic surgery in this case. With hopes of quick recovery and less pain for their patients, urologic surgeons hopped on the laparoscopy bandwagon for varicocele repairs. However, an open procedure using local anesthesia and microsurgery through a small incision offers better results than laparoscopy, according to a recent study. Men who had open surgery needed the same amount of pain-killing pills as those who had laparoscopic surgery, and they were back at work within three days, half the time of those who had laparoscopy, report Brown University researchers. There have also been reports of deaths from laparoscopic repair of varicoceles.

A controversial issue regarding varicoceles involves repairing tiny ones that can't be seen or felt on examination, but can be detected with devices that measure blood flow. To detect these so-called subclinical varicoceles, some doctors use either a Doppler stethoscope, which magnifies the sound of the blood flowing through the testicle's veins, or a thermogram, a sophisticated thermometer that indicates pockets of heat in the testicles.

The Doppler device bounces sound waves off the blood vessels. The way the sound reflects indicates if there are any flow abnormalities inside the vessel, such as a varicocele. The thermogram measures the surface temperature of the scrotum, which reflects the temperature inside the testicle. This way the doctor can measure any heat buildup in the testicles, another indication of a varicocele.

Once detected, these subclinical varicoceles can be repaired like any other varicocele. But the results of repairing subclinical varicoceles are less dramatic than repairing varicoceles the doctor can feel. And subclinical varicoceles are extremely common even among fertile men. Their importance in reducing fertility is uncertain.

One problem in particular with the thermogram is that a single temperature measurement can't determine whether a varicocele is definitely present. To be reliable, a man should have multiple thermogram measurements taken at different times. If the doctor can't see or feel the varicocele, the diagnosis isn't certain; so varicocele surgery should not be scheduled based only on a single abnormal thermogram.

Although there is no specific medication for varicocele treatment, many fertility experts prescribe the drugs clomiphene citrate (Clomid, Serophene) or tamoxifen (Nolvadex) after surgery in an attempt to increase the sperm count. These drugs stimulate the production of follicle-stimulating hormone (FSH) and luteinizing hormone (LH) to drive the testicles to work harder. Sometimes a man receives repeated hormone injections of human chorionic gonadotropin. This stimulates maximal sperm output from the testicle. Combining varicocele surgery with drug therapy may slightly increase the sperm count, but may not improve a couple's chances for pregnancy any more than varicocele repair alone. These drugs are most useful for men with low blood testosterone levels.

Impotence

When George married Marian she wanted to have children, and he agreed, though he already had two sons from a previous marriage. Ever since his divorce, however, George, fifty-six, had been impotent. A urologist found that "it wasn't all in my head," says George. Hardening of the arteries, which had caused a heart attack a few years earlier, had begun to narrow the blood vessels in his penis. Tests also showed that he had a reduced sperm count and motility, probably due to a varicocele.

George went to Dr. Goldstein to see what could be done for him. After conducting some tests, the doctor suggested a penile prosthesis. George chose a flexible cable type "mainly because I had more control over it," he says. "It was painful for a few weeks after the surgery, but well worth it." Five months later, he went back to Dr. Goldstein to have the varicocele removed. After spending a few days in the hospital, he went home and began taking clomiphene. In three months, a semen analysis showed that his sperm count was four times higher and his sperm motility was much better. "Dr. Goldstein told me there's a good chance we can have children," George says.

About 10 percent of male infertility is due to impotence, or the inability of a man to ejaculate inside the vagina. An estimated 10 to 15 million American men are impotent. The majority of them have wives beyond their childbearing years, but impotence involves men of all ages. Impotence and infertility are generally signs of disease, not age. A careful search must be made to uncover the origins of the impotence if a man is to receive the proper treatment.

Most cases of impotence in the prime reproductive years are due to environmental factors. A man may take drugs such as cocaine, smoke marijuana, smoke cigarettes, or drink lots of coffee. All of these chemicals constrict blood vessels, including those in the penis, and therefore counteract a man's ability to open up his blood vessels and achieve an erection. Alcohol abuse can also lower a man's hormone levels and injure the nerves in the penis necessary to produce an erection.

A wide variety of medications has also been implicated in impotence. The most common offenders are high blood pressure medications, antidepressants, tranquilizers, narcotics, and estrogens. Going off medication for a month is a good test of medication-induced impotence. Substituting another drug with a different mechanism of action frequently restores potency. When drugs can't be withdrawn or substituted, and psychological factors have been ruled out, then a penile prosthesis may be the solution.

Increased secretion of the pituitary hormone prolactin, often due to a pituitary tumor, can cause impotence and a low sex drive. Men with kidney disease on chronic dialysis are often impotent due to high prolactin levels. The extra prolactin seems to decrease secretion of gonadotropin-releasing hormone (GnRH) from the hypothalamus, resulting in lower levels of FSH and LH by the pituitary, which in turn reduces testosterone output. The best treatment is therapy with the drug bromocriptine

(Parlodel) to lower prolactin levels and reduce the size of a tumor, if present, that's producing the excess prolactin.

About half of the impotent men taking bromocriptine become potent again. Surgery to remove pituitary tumors within the man's brain has been tried, but can be dangerous, and generally is no longer recommended.

As much as two-thirds of all impotence may be traced to physical problems. This includes diseases that reduce blood flow to the penis, such as hardening of the arteries, high blood pressure, diabetes, or Peyronie's disease (scar tissue in the penis); and diseases that interrupt the nerve supply to the penis, such as a stroke, spinal cord injury, kidney disease, diabetes, or pelvic surgery.

As recently as a few years ago, doctors commonly believed that 90 percent of impotence was psychological. But improved diagnostic methods, including monitoring for the normal nighttime erections, measuring flow through the arteries of the penis, and careful psychiatric evaluations, have helped to distinguish physical and psychological causes of impotence. Often an impotent man has a combination of physical and psychological factors. He may require evaluation by both a urologist and a psychologist or psychiatrist, who must collaborate closely to determine his best therapy.

For example, it may be difficult to tell the difference between an impotent man whose hormone cells in the testicles, called Leydig cells, don't function properly from a man who is clinically depressed. Both men feel like their energy has been sapped and have low sex drives.

Clinical depression seems to interrupt the brain's signals of chemical messengers, which can cause a man to lose sleep, feel irritable and lethargic, and lower his sex drive. Antidepressant medications can often correct the imbalanced signals in his brain and restore a man's potency.

A man with another type of depression, situational depression, may show the same symptoms, including impotence. He is responding to stress—on the job, in his marriage—which in turn increases his anxiety over getting an erection. His potency usually improves following treatment with antidepressants or psychotherapy.

Performance anxiety, which arises in all men on occasion, can also cause impotence if it persists. Misinformation about sexuality can feed stress, performance anxiety, and impotence. Macho attitudes about how a "real man" should perform can backfire and contribute to impotence.

Reassurance, marital counseling, or both are often all that men with psychological impotence need. Sex therapy results in a 75 to 80 percent cure rate for men impotent for less than one year due to a psychological cause.

Another similar syndrome—premature ejaculation—also can be treated with sex therapy. In this case, the problem isn't getting an erection, but maintaining one long enough to ejaculate in the vagina. If therapy fails, then the couple may be able to achieve a pregnancy through artificial insemination, as long as the man is capable of ejaculating. (Most men can ejaculate through masturbation even if they have a soft penis.) For artificial insemination, the doctor places a sperm sample inside the vagina and into the cervical canal through a syringe. Or the man can be taught how to draw the sperm up into a syringe and gently inject the sperm into his wife's vagina at home.

Men with combined causes of impotence should first try medical or sex therapy, or both. When all the treatable medical causes have been excluded, and when a man with psychological impotence doesn't respond to sex therapy, then he still has other options.

Viagra: The Magic Bullet?

Nearly 1 million prescriptions were written for Viagra in its first month for sale in early 1998, and the highly touted impotence drug grabbed 95 percent of the existing sexual disorder market. Compared to vacuum pumps, inserting suppositories into the tip of the penis, or injecting prostaglandin into the penis's base, Viagra does seems like a magic bullet. For men who truly are impotent, more than 60 percent who take Viagra no longer have dysfunction.

Viagra works through a chemical called sildenafil citrate, which blocks an enzyme that allows blood to flow in and out of the penis. This enables the veins that hold blood in the penis to stay shut and cause an erection. But the drug doesn't raise a man's desire. Even if it did, it is not much help in a troubled relationship. No pill is going to solve root problems that are more emotional than physical.

Viagra is a new, important treatment for impotence, but it's not a miracle drug. Men with erectile dysfunction may have undiagnosed diabetes, early heart disease, or even testosterone deficiency, and should have a complete medical evaluation before taking the drug. Men who use Viagra should make lifestyle changes, including losing weight, exercising, quitting smoking, and controlling stress, which may help with their impotence.

Adverse effects associated with Viagra include headache, diarrhea, blurred vision, changes in blue and green vision, and increased light sensitivity. What's more, men taking heart medication containing nitrate, such as nitroglycerin for chest pains, should steer clear of Viagra. Viagra and nitrates both dilate the blood vessels, which in turn lowers blood pressure. Taken together, they can cause dangerous pressure drops. Also, men taking the ulcer drug Tagamet, the antifungal medications ketoconazole and itraconazole, or the antibiotic erythromycin should start with a lower dose of Viagra because these drugs interfere with Viagra's metabolism.

The drug's manufacturer, Pfizer, added a warning to labeling shortly after the drug was first approved at the request of the Food and Drug Administration that states: "There is a potential for cardiac risk of sexual activity in patients with preexisting cardiovascular disease." This action was taken after 128 people died after taking the medication, including 77 due to cardiovascular events. A large British postmarketing study has found no evidence that men with erectile dysfunction who were taking Viagra were at an increased risk of heart attack or death due to a cardiovascular event, according to Pfizer. The best-selling drug is now approved in more than 100 other countries.

The first of the Viagra "me-too" drugs, called Cialis, is now being tested in large clinical trials. The drug also relaxes smooth muscles in the penis to allow blood to flow in to help achieve and maintain an erection. It is said to be more potent than Viagra and does not appear to induce blue-vision side effects.

Viagra for Women?

While the FDA has not approved Viagra for use by women, a number of physicians reportedly are treating female sexual dysfunction with the drug. A small, placebo-controlled, crossover study shows that Viagra helps to thicken the uterine lining in women who have poor blood flow. It apparently improves blood flow, which allows more estrogen to reach the lining. As many as 100,000 American women who can't conceive because their endometrium is too thin to support an implanted embryo might benefit from Viagra, since only about 40 percent of these women become pregnant with estrogen supplementation or fertility drugs.

But besides the potential side effects of Viagra, the drug's effects on a woman's reproductive health have not been carefully studied. It might adversely affect eggs, chromosomes, or fetal development. And only a small percentage of women with sexual dysfunction have inadequate pelvic blood flow.

Penile Prostheses

The Chinese implanted pieces of ivory into the penis more than three thousand years ago to treat impotence. More recently, doctors have successfully implanted a variety of prosthetic devices in thousands of impotent men.

There are two basic types of prostheses, rigid or semirigid devices and inflatable prostheses. The rigid or semirigid devices contain two silicone rods that are implanted under local anesthesia in a relatively easy operation that does not require a hospital stay. Earlier versions gave the man a permanent erection, which was a problem to conceal. More recent devices are either hinged or malleable, permitting easier concealment. A newer version of the malleable prosthesis has a silver wire core or a series of segments held together by a cable. These prostheses have several advantages: They are simple, inexpensive, reliable, always ready to use, and provide good erections. The disadvantages: The penis is always the erect size, although the prostheses do bend down for easier concealment.

The newest, more sophisticated prostheses are inflatable. One type, the self-inflatable prosthesis, consists of two hollow silicone tubes implanted in the penis with a pump reservoir near the tip. To achieve an erection, the man squeezes just behind the head of his penis. To deflate the device, he squeezes the release valve located just behind the reservoir. These devices may be implanted with a local anesthetic, and require an overnight stay and a longer recovery than for a malleable prosthesis. These devices can also break or fail—the liquid filling the reservoir may leak out—and they require some skill and dexterity in inflating and deflating.

Fully inflatable prostheses also consist of two hollow silicone tubes connected to a reservoir containing fluid and a pump to inflate and deflate the tubes. The two cylinders are implanted in the penis, the reservoir is placed behind the bladder, and the pump is placed in the scrotum. A complex network of tubing connects the various parts.

To achieve an erection, the man gently squeezes the pump in the scrotum. This produces the most natural and hardest erection of all the prostheses. He presses the release valve on top of the pump to deflate the device. The shape and feel of this implant also best approximates the normal, nonerect state of the penis, which makes it the easiest to conceal. But because of the complexity of the device, it requires extensive surgery under general anesthesia, and also has a higher failure rate. About 25 percent of men with fully inflatable devices will require another operation, usually to repair mechanical failure of the device, within ten years.

Malleable prostheses have been around for more than thirty years and have a good track record. A man can move them up and down easily, and they give a good erection, particularly the cable-and-segment type prostheses. All of the inflatables eventually have problems due to the complicated hydraulic systems that pump the fluid. Some surgeons shy away from inflatables, particularly for younger men, to avoid having to do repeated replacement operations over the man's lifetime.

Self-Injections

Another way to promote an erection for men with physical causes of impotence is self-injection of drugs directly into the penis. The drugs papaverine, a chemical derived from papaya, and prostaglandin E1, a chemical found throughout the body, cause blood vessels to dilate and increase blood flow to the penis. Some men with impotence due to a partial narrowing of blood vessels or nerve damage to blood vessels can inject one of these drugs directly into the penis before sex to stimulate an erection. The drugs bypass the damaged nerves and directly open up the blood vessels. The prostaglandin injection seems to produce less scarring inside the penis than papaverine.

The downside is that the man has to inject chemicals into his penis every time he wants an erection. Also, rarely, these injections result in serious complications, such as the development of scar tissue inside the penis from the constant injections. With severe scarring, these men may no longer be capable of erections, and the only treatment available to them is a prosthesis.

Since the late 1970s, surgeons have made attempts to reconnect or bypass damaged arteries to bring blood flow into the penis. To determine the integrity of the arteries in the penis, papaverine is injected directly into the spongy tissue of the penis. In the presence of normal blood vessels, a man will achieve a full erection within ten minutes. If he has no erection, the test may be repeated using an ultrasound scan to measure the arteries in his penis, which should double in diameter. The Doppler stethoscope can also measure changes in penile blood flow. To achieve an erection, the blood flow in a man's penis must increase six to eight times over the normal baseline blood flow.

If these tests reveal that the penile arteries are blocked or damaged, the man may need surgery to correct the damage. One surgical procedure brings arteries from the back of a muscle in his rectum and connects them to the penis. Another operation attaches arteries to veins to bring blood into the penis in a backward fashion. The problem with these procedures is that the disease that causes impotence usually damages the small blood vessels of the penis as well as the large ones. So bringing new arterial blood to the penis may not increase local blood flow significantly. These operations work best in young, healthy men who have had trauma to the genital area that damaged the penile arteries. For these patients, about 40 to 50 percent have successful reconstructions, and they become potent again.

Some impotent men are able to get an erection, but lose it too quickly. They may have good blood flow into the penis, but are unable to obtain or maintain an erection because of a leaky vein inside the penis. Ten to 20 percent of impotence due to physical causes is due to these leaky veins.

To diagnose this type of impotence, the doctor first checks for blocked arteries in the penis with a papaverine injection. If a man has no erection, then saline is injected into his penis at a high infusion rate to determine how quickly it takes the saline to leak out. Normally, the saline will produce a full erection, just as if blood were filling the vessels in the penis. If the arteries dilate, but he doesn't get an erection, the veins may be leaking and failing to trap blood in the spongy tissue of his penis.

By injecting dye into the penis, a urologist can see where the leak is and perform an operation to tie off the abnormal veins causing the leak. For men with good blood flow into the penis but a big leak going out, between 50 and 70 percent will have their potency restored.

Retrograde Ejaculation

A small number of men who have a small volume of semen have backward, or retrograde, ejaculation. About 10 percent of infertile men have zero sperm counts, and 10 percent of them have retrograde ejaculation. This condition, most commonly due to diabetes, is caused by nerve damage. Because of the nerve damage, the bladder sphincter doesn't close down at orgasm and ejaculation, as it normally would. The bulk of the semen takes the path of least resistance, which in this case is backward into the bladder.

A simple way to test this is to examine a man's urine after he ejaculates. If there are sperm in the urine instead of his semen, then he has retrograde ejaculation. If a man has no sperm in his semen or a very low volume of sperm, the doctor should look for retrograde ejaculation.

Drugs similar to decongestants used to treat a head cold can minimize retrograde ejaculation by tightening the bladder neck. If drugs fail to work, then a man's sperm can be retrieved from his urine by putting a catheter into the bladder. The catheter contains a buffer solution to reverse the acidity of urine, which usually kills sperm. Or the man can alkalinize his urine by drinking bicarbonate of soda and then urinate immediately after ejaculation. Recovered sperm are washed and artificially inseminated. Pregnancy rates, however, are low, only about 10 percent, because the sperm recovered are generally not of good quality.

Unblocking Ducts

Blocked ducts in a man's reproductive tract contribute to another 10 percent of male infertility. Half of these men are born with abnormal or missing ducts, such as an absent vas deferens or an abnormal epididymis. The other half have acquired blockages, most commonly due to scarring from infections with gonorrhea or chlamydia. If the epididymis becomes infected on both testicles, or if a man has only one healthy, functioning testicle and its epididymis becomes infected, this tiny tube may become blocked and the man may become completely sterile.

New microsurgical techniques have dramatically improved the results in repairing a blocked epididymis. In Dr. Goldstein's latest studies, sperm reappear in the ejaculate in 83 percent of men, and 40 percent will father a child naturally. Those who don't father a child naturally can be helped with assisted reproductive technologies. Lower fertility rates have to do with how the epididymis functions. When sperm first enter the epididymis, they can't swim and won't penetrate an egg. As the sperm come out the other end of the epididymis, they can swim and penetrate an egg. If the epididymis is damaged and repaired microsurgically, it may still not allow sperm to mature fully and develop their full swimming and fertilizing abilities. IVF with injection of sperm directly into the egg (intracytoplasmic sperm injection, or ICSI) can now help these men impregnate their wives.

Another cause of blocked ducts includes injury to the vas deferens from a hernia repair. From 5 to 17 percent of males who have a hernia repaired suffer a blocked vas. Fortunately, the blockage is usually on only one side. But if hernias are repaired on both sides, or a hernia on the side of the only functioning testicle is repaired, it could damage the vas deferens and cause infertility. These blocked tubes can be repaired microsurgically, and more than half of these men's wives become pregnant.

Vasectomy Reversal

"I thought I never wanted any more kids," recalls Roy, age forty-six, who had a vasectomy at thirty after fathering three children. Then he divorced his first wife and married Dawn, age thirty-seven, and after "spending a lot of time talking about having a child together, we decided to give it a try." A little apprehensive about the vasectomy reversal, Roy had the delicate surgery with no major trouble. He was in the hospital on a Wednesday, rested at home for a few days, and went back to his job at the phone company the next Monday.

Although Roy's reversal operation was a technical success—his tubes were open and healthy—his sperm count remained low a year later. "The doctor told me I had one strike against me since it had been so long since my vasectomy," he says. He and Dawn kept trying anyway, and she got pregnant about a year later, but lost the baby to a miscarriage. "I thought that was our one and only shot," says Dawn. Six months later, Roy was started on hormone treatments. His sperm count rose sharply, and within four months, Dawn was pregnant. Their son, Andy, is now seven and a half years old.

"I'm experiencing more with Andy than when I watched my first three kids grow up," says Roy. "I can enjoy him more. I'm looking forward to being a Little League coach again."

A vasectomy causes sterility by blocking the vas deferens. Each year, about half a million American men choose vasectomy as their primary form of birth control. It can be safely performed as an outpatient procedure with minimal discomfort using local anesthesia. The doctor removes about a one-inch segment of the vas deferens and seals the cut ends of the vas with stitches, heat, or clips.

Inevitably some of the men who had vasectomies have reconsidered and regret their earlier decision. Most men who have had vasectomies and want them reversed are in their late thirties or early forties. These men had children, then divorced, and have now remarried, usually to younger women who do not have children of their own.

Another group of men who regret having undergone vasectomy are those in their early thirties who put off marriage and having children. Now these socially conscious men have married and they want children.

Still others want their fertility restored in response to improved financial status, allowing the couple to afford more children, or the improved health of either the man or the woman.

Urologic microsurgeons can perform the delicate sterilization reversal surgery. Before the introduction of microsurgery, less than 25 percent of the approximately three thousand men who had vasectomy reversals were able to impregnate their wives. Microsurgical repair of the vas has more than doubled the success rate. With recent publicity about greater successes, more of the nearly 17 million men who have had vasectomies are seeking reversals.

The length of time since the vasectomy has some effect on the success of a reversal operation. The more years that have passed since vasectomy, the lower the natural pregnancy rates after microsurgery. If the reversal is performed within a decade of vasectomy by an expert reproductive microsurgeon, more than 90 percent of men have sperm return to their ejaculate. In the more than 1,250 vasectomy reversals he has performed, Dr. Goldstein's overall return of sperm rate is 96 percent and the pregnancy rate is 63 percent for all men who have fertile wives. This includes men who have blockages of the epididymis. For those who had the sterilization procedure less than five years ago, the pregnancy rate is 73 percent. A man who had a vasectomy more than ten years ago should know that his odds of success are good but lower.

A new technique for vasectomy reversal developed by Dr. Goldstein increases the chances for fertility. The Microdot technique facilitates more accurate placement of sutures, which, in turn, helps to secure a leak-proof reconnection of the vas deferens. Like an architect making a blueprint before building a building, Dr. Goldstein makes a blueprint before performing the microsurgery. Using an operating microscope that magnifies this tiny duct thirty times and a microscopic marking pen, he places six dots at 1, 3, 5, 7, 9, and 11 o'clock positions. Then he reattaches the vas deferens by lining up the dots with six sutures for each of four separate layers.

The challenge faced by microsurgeons for a vasectomy reversal is to reattach two widely discrepant sides of the vas deferens without gaps in order to prevent sperm leakage. The Microdot technique facilitates this process. As a result, Dr. Goldstein's overall success rate for return of sperm to the semen after vasectomy reversal has increased to 99.5 percent using the Microdot technique for men who have sperm found in at least one vas at the time of the surgery.

Dr. Goldstein also has imported a Chinese technique to do a quicker, less painful vasectomy without a scalpel that also is highly reversible. He makes a tiny puncture in the scrotum, pulls the vas deferens out, cuts it and seals both ends with heat, then slips the tube back in. There are no stitches and little blood. The no-scalpel vasectomy takes ten minutes or less and the man can return to work the same day.

In contrast, a crudely performed vasectomy can damage the nerve supply of the vas deferens and possibly compromise its function, making a vasectomy reversal less successful. Also, if too much of the vas has been removed, a reversal is more difficult.

In addition to blocking the vas deferens, a vasectomy may also later result in a block of the epididymis. Between 30 and 50 percent of vasectomies ultimately result in ruptures of the epididymis and a secondary obstruction in that tiny tube. In order to repair the obstruction, the urologic microsurgeon must open up the epididymis to allow a free flow of fluid and sperm through it and reconnect it to the vas deferens. This is a much more difficult procedure than the standard microsurgical vasectomy reversal because the epididymis is considerably thinner and more delicate than the muscular vas deferens. Nevertheless, in the hands of a skilled microsurgeon using newer microsurgical techniques, the damaged epididymis can be repaired with more than 80 percent return of sperm to semen. Pregnancy rates, however, are in the 40 to 50 percent range, lower than that of men who have a vasectomy reversal and no epididymis obstruction.

In some men after vasectomy, sperm leak from the vas, provoking an inflammatory reaction. The immune system responds by forming a nodule, called a sperm granuloma, at the vasectomy site. The end of the vas forms a network of pockets and channels that trap the sperm. This small knot of tissue, from pea to grape size, relieves the pressure on the epididymis and protects that delicate tube. Men with a sperm granuloma have a better chance of pregnancy after a reversal.

Vasectomy may also lead to the production of antisperm antibodies, which play a significant role in those men who have reasonably good sperm counts after reversal surgery, yet can't get their wives pregnant. Up to two thirds of vasectomized men develop antibodies that can interfere with sperm motility and fertilizing capability. This problem can sometimes be overcome by treatment with steroid medications to reduce antibody production and with sperm washing and separation procedures, followed by artificial insemination into the uterus. If this doesn't work, then ICSI is a very successful treatment for sperm antibodies.

Sperm Processing and Artificial Insemination

Several methods for preparing sperm for artificial insemination are available to couples, the purpose being to select the most actively swimming sperm, the ones most likely to fertilize an egg.

Different approaches for separating sperm from semen include dilution and washing, sperm migration, and adherence methods for the elimination of dead sperm and debris. Depending on the specific characteristics of the semen sample, one or more of these methods can recover the best sperm population possible. Since there are advantages and disadvantages to each method, it takes special training and experience to determine which sperm processing method, or combination of methods, is best in a particular situation. In addition, there are different types of culture media to enhance sperm vitality, as well as different types of columns or gradients for the sperm separation.

In most clinical laboratories across the country, simply washing and centrifuging the sperm is the standard approach. But this often does not give the best results. Centrifuging the sperm may damage them, and the "pellet" at the bottom of the test tube after centrifugation contains all of the sperm (including the abnormal and dead sperm) and other cells in the final sperm population used for insemination.

Instead, Dr. Berger's lab uses a selective filtration (Sephadex or Percoll) method in which sperm are separated from the seminal plasma in columns filled with special beads that trap white blood cells, debris, and dead sperm. The healthy sperm swim between the beads and through holes in a filter just large enough to let the healthy sperm through yet keep back the debris. An ejaculate with a high concentration of abnormal sperm is best processed using a selective filtration method.

Sperm washing also removes prostaglandins found in the seminal plasma. (These chemicals, found in practically all types of tissue, were first isolated from the prostate gland, and so were named prostaglandins.)

183

In the past, before sperm were separated from seminal plasma, prostaglandins in the semen restricted the amount of semen that could be inseminated into a woman's uterus because the chemicals caused painful, intense uterine contractions at the time of insemination. Now, with sperm processing techniques, doctors can eliminate the prostaglandins, white blood cells, and a variety of other chemicals and debris to gather as many motile sperm as possible for insemination.

Unfortunately, most men who have significant antisperm antibodies have the antibodies attached to their sperm—not just in the seminal fluid—so that sperm washing can't remove them. These sperm-bound antibodies often cause the sperm to clump together. If the sperm clump, they can't swim, and if they can't swim, they can't get to the egg to fertilize it. And when antibodies attach to the sperm's head, they may prevent fertilization even if the sperm can swim to the egg.

Treating Sperm-Bound Antibodies

When the husband or wife, or both, have been diagnosed as having antisperm antibodies, several treatment options are available to them. If a wife's mucus is "hostile" to her husband's sperm, the woman can be treated with hormones to change the mucus's composition, or she can use a sperm nutrient douche at the fertile time of her cycle to reduce the mucus's acidity and to enhance sperm vitality. If she has antibodies in her mucus, the doctor may recommend steroid treatments.

To reduce the immune reaction that produces antisperm antibodies, both the husband and wife may need to take steroid pills. These medications, such as prednisone and dexamethasone, can lower antisperm antibody levels and improve fertility in some men without altering their sperm count or percentage of normally shaped sperm. These potent drugs, which suppress the immune system, may produce serious complications, including raising the blood pressure, causing hip deterioration, and activating an already existing ulcer. In contrast to men, women usually take lower, continuous doses of steroids rather than high, intermittent doses. It's the high doses used for men that are more risky.

If the wife, but not her husband, tests positive for antisperm antibodies, the couple can use condoms during intercourse to try to reduce the stimulation of her immune system. Treatment is often required for at least six months, always using condoms during intercourse except during the fertile time of her cycle.

Although sperm processing doesn't dislodge antibodies from the sperm, it does permit separation of the most healthy, rapidly swimming sperm. The couple can then have artificial insemination to deliver the healthy sperm high in the woman's reproductive tract. The fewer the number of healthy sperm, the closer the sperm must be placed to the egg.

The most common treatment for sperm antibodies is intrauterine insemination (IUI) with processed sperm. The sperm are injected directly into the uterus, bypassing the cervix and enabling more sperm to travel a shorter distance to the fallopian tubes. The pregnancy rate of IUI is about 20 to 25 percent after six to eight months of inseminations with washed sperm, if all other fertility conditions are normal. That's about one half the normal pregnancy rate for fertile women. If IUI is unsuccessful, then IVF with ICSI is a very successful treatment for all anti-sperm antibody problems.

The fertility specialist helps the couple time an intrauterine insemination around the wife's ovulation. In most cases, the couple uses an at-home test kit to detect the wife's surge of luteinizing hormone in midcycle, and the insemination takes place the day following the LH surge. When ovulation is induced, such as with clomiphene or gonadotropins, insemination can be timed at thirty-six hours after an hCG injection. The woman lies on an examining table with her hips slightly elevated. A speculum is placed into her vagina to allow the doctor to see her cervix, and after cleansing the cervix with a sterile sperm nutrient solution, a narrow catheter is passed through her cervical canal and into the uterine cavity. The husband's sperm, prepared for insemination, are injected through the catheter into the uterus. After forty-five minutes of rest, the woman may resume her normal activities.

IUI using processed sperm is also one of the most helpful treatments for a cervical mucus problem. If tests show that a husband's sperm can't survive in his wife's cervical mucus, an IUI can help the couple achieve a pregnancy simply by allowing sperm to bypass the mucus. After six cycles of IUI, about 60 percent of women with only cervical problems will become pregnant.

IUI is also an effective treatment for male factor infertility problems besides immunologic infertility, with about 20 to 30 percent of couples achieving a pregnancy after six months of inseminations. When IUI with

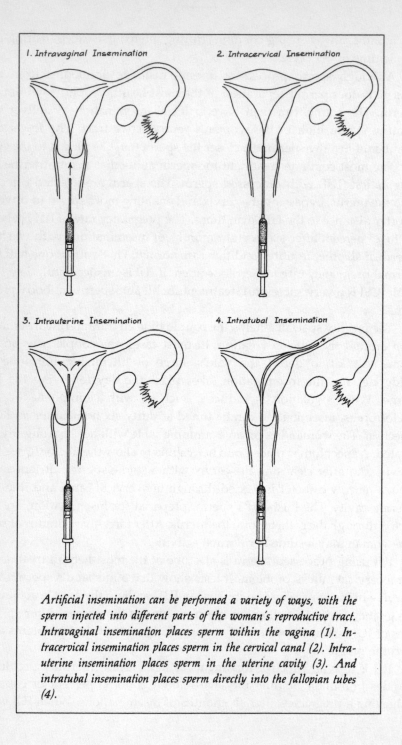

1. Intravaginal Insemination

2. Intracervical Insemination

3. Intrauterine Insemination

4. Intratubal Insemination

Artificial insemination can be performed a variety of ways, with the sperm injected into different parts of the woman's reproductive tract. Intravaginal insemination places sperm within the vagina (1). Intracervical insemination places sperm in the cervical canal (2). Intrauterine insemination places sperm in the uterine cavity (3). And intratubal insemination places sperm directly into the fallopian tubes (4).

frozen donor sperm is used to treat azoospermia, 80 percent of couples conceive after twelve months.

Questions to Ask Your Doctor About Other Medical and Surgical Treatments for the Woman

Does my uterus have a normal or abnormal size and shape? If it's not healthy, what can I do to correct the problem?

Are my fallopian tubes open? Are both fimbria healthy?

Do you see any signs of infection? If so, what antibiotics do you recommend for us?

Are my ovaries and follicles of normal size? Am I ovulating?

For women with endometriosis

What stage of disease do I have?

What are my options for endometriosis treatments?

What is your experience with different treatments?

If you prefer certain types of treatment over others, please tell me why.

Do you ever refer women to other specialists for treatment? If so, under what circumstances?

For women who want sterilization reversal

Do you perform sterilization reversal operations? If you do, how many have you performed? What are my odds of becoming pregnant after a reversal? What is your complication rate? Will you do this as an outpatient procedure? If you don't, can you refer me to someone who does?

Questions to Ask Your Doctor About Other Medical and Surgical Treatments for the Man

Do my ducts feel normal?

If my ducts are blocked, what are the chances that surgery will improve my sperm count? Will surgery help us achieve a pregnancy?

Do I have healthy vas deferens on both sides?

Do I have a varicocele on either side? If I do, how do you suggest I have it repaired?

Will my disease or its treatment affect my potency?

Do I have antibodies attached to my sperm, in my blood, or in my semen?

Does my wife have antibodies to my sperm in her cervical mucus or in her blood?

Will sperm processing help us conceive? Is your lab certified in andrology procedures and directed by a board-certified andrologist?

Based on my sperm count, do you recommend we try an intrauterine insemination?

For impotent men

Can we use artificial insemination to overcome an impotence problem?

What type of penile implants do you offer?

For men who want a vasectomy reversal or reversal of blockages

Do you perform vasectomy reversals with a microscope? How many have you done? If you do, what are my chances of a successful reversal? What are our chances of having a baby after the reversal? If you don't, can you refer me to someone who does?

Do you do repairs of the epididymis if blockage is found at reversal? How many have you done?

What are your pregnancy rates?

Can you freeze sperm found during an operation for future use with IVF?

If my blockage is uncorrectable, do you aspirate sperm for injection with IVF?

9

MORE
ADVANCED
TREATMENTS

If you and your partner have gone through fertility evaluations and your doctor has attempted standard medical and surgical treatments, all to no avail, then it may be time to consider the more advanced treatments now available to infertile couples. New, aggressive approaches are enabling three out of five persistently infertile couples to fulfill their dreams of conceiving a child.

Most couples won't need these newer advanced treatments. Many of them are available only in select centers or through a handful of fertility specialists. Check the directory of fertility specialists in the back of the book to see which ones might provide the therapy you're looking for. To help you get a sense of which therapies might be more available, we begin with those that hold out the most promise for the greatest number of infertile couples.

Superovulation Plus Insemination

To improve the chances of couples with unexplained infertility, many fertility specialists give women hormones to produce more than one egg during a menstrual cycle, and then perform intrauterine insemination (IUI) timed to take place near ovulation. Superovulation improves the chances of pregnancy by producing more than one egg, and IUI brings concentrated numbers of motile sperm into close proximity with the greater number of eggs. The greater the number of sperm (up to a certain level) and eggs, and the closer they are brought together, the better the couple's chances of achieving a pregnancy.

Most doctors stimulate superovulation with Pergonal and human chorionic gonadotropin (hCG). Pure FSH (Metrodin) and hCG can also be used to induce the woman to produce and release more than one egg.

If a woman has poor cervical mucus and isn't ovulating, treating her with Pergonal or Metrodin usually stimulates her to ovulate and improves the quality of her cervical mucus. A postcoital test (PCT) performed during the stimulation cycle will determine whether intracervical insemination (ICI) or intrauterine insemination is necessary. If the couple has a good PCT, artificial insemination may not be necessary.

At Chapel Hill Fertility Center, the decision to attempt an ICI or IUI or to inseminate the sperm higher up the genital tract directly into the fallopian tubes (intratubal insemination) or into the follicles (intrafollicular insemination) depends on the estimated total number of functional sperm available from the husband. That decision can be made as the time of ovulation approaches, based on the quality of the wife's mucus and husband's sperm at that time. Some couples want to know beforehand which type of insemination will likely be most successful, and Dr. Berger provides them his best estimate based on previous semen analyses and the wife's hormonal responses in previous induction cycles.

Some fertility specialists combine clomiphene, Pergonal, and FSH early in the cycle. Others also provide additional progesterone—in vaginal suppositories, oral capsules, or injections—later in the cycle to support the luteal phase. Follicle growth is usually monitored by ultrasound scans and a series of hormone measurements. Women who have ovulation induced with hCG will receive the insemination thirty-four to thirty-six hours after the hCG injection.

Many fertility specialists now believe that superovulation plus IUI is an effective treatment for couples with unexplained infertility. Some believe that women with ovulation problems and endometriosis are also good candidates. Others show good results for couples with antisperm antibodies carried by the wife, particularly if less than 50 percent of her husband's sperm are affected by the antibodies.

Before couples with unexplained infertility opt for the more invasive and costly gamete intrafallopian transfer (GIFT) or in vitro fertilization (IVF) procedures, IUI with superovulation is often recommended, since pregnancy rates with these procedures rival the 30 to 40 percent pregnancy rates of GIFT, although multiple attempts may be necessary. When a man's estimated total sperm count is under 1 million, the couple may be better off trying intratubal or intrafollicular insemination. If they are unsuccessful, they can move on to GIFT or IVF procedures that mix the sperm and egg and then place them into the fallopian tubes or incubator to fertilize. Instead of IUI, some fertility researchers have attempted to inseminate washed sperm directly into the peritoneal (abdominal and pelvic) cavity, which is called intraperitoneal insemination.

Couples with unexplained infertility who fail to conceive following repeated cycles of superovulation combined with IUI may still conceive with GIFT or IVF procedures.

Intratubal Insemination (ITI)

When Pam's pelvis was crushed in an auto accident, doctors told her she would never carry a baby to term. Even after reconstructive surgery, her cervix and uterus were blocking sperm from getting up into the reproductive tract. Pam, a thirty-three-year-old payroll clerk, tried to get pregnant for more than ten years before she saw Dr. Berger. He put her on fertility drugs to stimulate ovulation and tried one cycle of IUI, which did not result in a pregnancy. When that failed, he suggested that Pam and her homebuilder husband Don, also age thirty-three, try an intratubal insemination. At Pam's most fertile time, Dr. Berger placed Don's processed sperm into her fallopian tubes.

"When I found out that Pam was pregnant, it floored me. I had already decided that nothing was going to work, that we were just wasting our time," says Don. "We were in Dr. Berger's waiting room, and he was on the phone behind a glass partition when he flashed a piece of paper at us that read, 'Congratulations, you're pregnant.' It took about a week before I believed it."

Intratubal insemination has successfully placed sperm within the fallopian tubes at the time of ovulation. Dr. Berger was the first to report performing ITI. He did so during spontaneous and induced ovulation cycles. Most cycles are induced with Pergonal, some with a combination of Pergonal and clomiphene, and others with clomiphene alone, depending on the woman's particular history. The timing of hCG injections to induce ovulation is based on ultrasound evaluation of ovarian follicle size, tests of blood levels of estradiol and progesterone, and cervical mucus exams. Sperm processing is performed just before the insemination since sperm normally become capacitated during their passage through the woman's reproductive tract, and placing sperm directly into the fallopian tube would bypass this essential step.

About thirty-four to thirty-six hours after the hCG injection, Dr. Berger inseminates the husband's sperm into the wife. This can be done either through a laparoscope or by using ultrasound guidance to go through the cervix. When using a laparoscope, Dr. Berger places it into her abdomen, inserts a blunt-tipped needle through a second site to help trace out her fallopian tube, and passes a catheter down through the needle just into the opening of the fimbrial end of her tube. Then Dr. Berger slowly injects sperm through the catheter—first into one, then into the other fallopian tube. About one hour after the procedure, the woman can go home. The ultrasound approach is done as an office procedure but is not always successful in guiding the catheter into the small openings of the fallopian tubes. For women who have positive pregnancy tests ten to fourteen days later, Dr. Berger follows up with hCG and progesterone assays and ultrasound exams until he documents a normal pregnancy.

Dr. Berger has performed ITI on approximately fifty women—those who have had unsuccessful standard infertility treatments (such as IUI) as well as those who were undergoing diagnostic laparoscopy for evaluation of infertility. He has performed the latter in hopes of achieving a pregnancy regardless of the underlying diagnosis.

So far, he has had moderate success with couples with long-standing infertility of more than five years, achieving an overall pregnancy rate of roughly 20 percent, although the live birth rate has only been 15 percent.

Since it doesn't require an egg retrieval or an egg laboratory with an embryologist, ITI can be provided by any gynecologist who administers infertility treatment and has experience with ovulation induction, a certified lab for sperm processing, and access to the operating room at the proper time of the woman's menstrual cycle.

ITI through the laparoscope does require a minor operation. But the advantage is that the doctor can be certain that the sperm are placed directly where they need to be for fertilization—in the fallopian tubes. Therefore, intratubal insemination requires fewer normal sperm than intracervical or intrauterine insemination. This is a particular advantage for a man with an estimated total functional sperm count of between 500,000 and 1 million after sperm processing. ITI, however, works only for women who have at least one healthy, open fallopian tube.

ITI can also be performed through a narrow, flexible-tipped hysteroscope, which can be passed through the cervix and into the uterus. This enables the doctor to see the opening into the fallopian tube and insert the catheter into it. Applying this approach to ITI avoids the need for laparoscopy but is more invasive than ultrasound-guided transcervical ITI and therefore is not widely used.

Lasers Through the Laparoscope

The introduction of the laser has opened up the laparoscope to even more uses. The laser has many features that make it an ideal instrument to cut and remove tissue cleanly, with minimal bleeding.

Albert Einstein postulated the theory of laser energy in the early 1900s. The first working laser was developed in 1961 at Bell Laboratories, and was first used in gynecology in 1973 to treat cervical lesions. Doctors first put a laser through the laparoscope in 1979.

Laser light has greater energy focused in a smaller area than ordinary light. Just as a magnifying glass captures and focuses sunlight to make a fire, the surgeon focuses a laser beam to burn away tissues.

Each type of laser has a single specific wavelength that gives it unique properties. The types of lasers now in use include the CO_2 laser, the most commonly used laser, which acts as a surgical knife to vaporize tissue; the Argon laser, whose red light is selectively absorbed by red pigment, such as endometriosis, and has the advantage of being able to move through flexible fibers; the Nd-YAG laser, which creates its beam from ordinary electrical power and has proven useful in hysteroscopy, particularly in endometriosis treatments; and an offshoot of the YAG, the KTP laser, which has properties much like those of the Argon laser but at a different wavelength.

The laser can be adjusted to destroy tissue just to a certain depth—as little as a millimeter thick—causing little or no damage to surrounding or underlying normal tissues. Because the laser beam seals off small blood and lymph vessels in the surgical area, there is minimal loss of blood and other body fluids. There is also less risk of infection since the heat of the laser light can sterilize the area, destroying infectious organisms.

Gynecological surgeons are using the intensely concentrated light beams from lasers to remove cervical lesions, including condyloma and precancerous conditions; to correct malformations of the uterus; to open up blocked fallopian tubes; to remove adhesions; and to reduce the size of polycystic ovaries.

Lasers and Endometriosis

Laser laparoscopists have led the way in tackling more severe endometriosis. The secret of the CO_2 laser for vaporizing endometriosis is that the surgeon can direct the laser beam with great precision to the areas of endometriosis, wherever it is located. The surgeon can remove endometriosis on thin tissues, such as the bladder and bowel wall, more safely with the laser than by electrocautery.

Because of the large amount of smoke created by laser vaporization of tissue, the laser laparoscope requires two operating channels, one to remove smoke that can block the surgeon's vision, the other to aim the laser beam. A small microchip camera attached to the laparoscope provides a high-resolution view of the pelvic organs during surgery, a procedure called videolaserlaparoscopy.

In the hands of an experienced endoscopic laser surgeon who is comfortable operating while watching the video monitor, videolaserlaparoscopy is precise, safe, and effective. One advantage of combining the video camera with the laser is that the surgeon can apply the camera's magnification and zoom capabilities to operate on very small areas, according to Dr. Camran Nezhat of the Fertility and Endocrinology Center in Atlanta, Georgia, and Stanford University, who has pioneered the use of videolaserlaparoscopy for the treatment of endometriosis and adhesions.

If the surgeon diagnoses endometriosis laparoscopically, he can treat it right away. By completely removing the endometriosis at that time, the surgeon avoids the need to treat the woman for months with medications that prevent her from ovulating and therefore delay the couple's attempts to conceive. The 40 to 65 percent pregnancy rates reported for laser laparoscopic surgery compare favorably with those for medical treatment and microsurgery through an open incision (laparotomy). Follow-up studies of women with endometriosis treated by laser so far haven't determined if these women have fewer recurrences than those treated with drugs or conventional surgery.

Although the benefits of lasers have been publicized over the past ten years, the laser laparoscope isn't a panacea. In the presence of extensive adhesions and a large amount of ovarian disease, a surgeon may choose not to treat endometriosis at initial laparoscopy. These women may do better with medical pretreatment, followed by laparotomy. In addition, lasers can't replace microsurgery for dense adhesions between the fimbria of the fallopian tube and the ovary.

Laser surgery also has its disadvantages. Lasers can be dangerous if not used exactly correctly, and there have been reports of injuries to patients and medical staff during laser surgery. The equipment is expensive, more than $100,000 for an operating room laser, and costly to maintain, and the cost of using the laser is of course passed on to the patient either directly or indirectly.

A surgeon accustomed to hands-on surgery with a scalpel or microsurgical instruments must undergo different training before he feels comfortable with a laser. Just as a plastic ski boot doesn't transform a nonskier into a championship racer, using a laser doesn't itself impart improved skills to a surgeon. The surgeon must gradually develop new laser skills by first performing simpler operations under supervision and then constantly practicing these newly learned skills.

Lasers and Fibroids

A new, experimental technique called laser ablation may allow doctors to zap and shrink painful fibroid tumors. Until just a few years ago, women with these tumors faced either invasive surgery or hysterectomies, both requiring lengthy hospital stays. A far less invasive procedure introduced about three years ago, called uterine artery embolization, offered similar results without any hospital stay. Now laser ablation, done under light sedation as an outpatient procedure, may speed up the treatment and lessen the pain.

British doctors have used magnetic resonance imaging to guide the insertion of four needles through the abdominal wall into the center of the fibroid. The centers of the needles are removed, and the laser fibers encased in a sheath are advanced into the tumor. Then the laser heat is used to liquefy the fibroid. Scar tissue forms, and the fibroid starts to shrink within six weeks and continues shrinking for about six months.

Women who have laser ablation are mildly sedated and generally experience only mild discomfort. They can go home after about four hours; they may experience mild, menstrual-like cramps for a few days. Tumors typically shrink by about one-third. Early studies show that laser ablation does not appear to damage the uterus or its lining and preserves fertility, but more studies are necessary.

Uterine artery embolization also involves shrinking tumors, but by cutting off their blood supply. Fibroid tumors have many blood vessels feeding them. Doctors can maneuver a catheter into the artery that supplies blood to the uterus and inject small particles that block the artery. This deprives the tumor of its blood supply, which causes it to scar over and shrink. More than five thousand American patients have had the procedure done, and it is the most widely used surgical treatment for fibroid tumors. Many insurance companies still consider it experimental and will not pay for it. The main side effect of embolization is the possibility of an artery becoming blocked, but that is rare.

Unblocking Fallopian Tubes

The same balloon treatment used to clear clogged arteries in the heart has been adapted by fertility specialists to open blocked fallopian tubes. The technique, called transcervical balloon tuboplasty, represents a safe way to achieve pregnancy for some of the estimated 10,000 women treated each year to clear obstructions within the fallopian tubes.

The procedure is attractive because it can be performed through a hysteroscope, making it a minor operation compared with abdominal surgery, and it costs about as much as other minor, outpatient procedures. The surgeon guides a catheter with an internal guide wire and a balloon at the tip through the operating channel of the hysteroscope and into the fallopian tube. Once the tip of the catheter has reached the site of the obstruction, he inflates the balloon, stretching the fallopian tube and opening it up. Then he pushes the guide wire farther into the fallopian tube to perforate an obstruction and advances the catheter over the guide wire, inflating the balloon again. Step by step, the surgeon opens up the tube along its entire length.

Unlike the heart technique, called coronary balloon angioplasty, transcervical balloon tuboplasty has much less risk of serious complications. A few women have had the guide wire perforate their fallopian tubes or uterus, but this hasn't caused any apparent harm.

Hundreds of women have had the balloon procedure. The technique may well open new opportunities for the treatment of obstructed fallopian tubes. But it is not appropriate for women who have blocked tubes due to extensive scar tissue or gaps in the tubes from tubal ligation.

Another balloon tuboplasty technique involves guiding the catheter into the tube under X-ray visualization rather than through a hystero-scope. With the aid of fluoroscopy, the doctor injects a radiopaque dye (which shows up on an X ray) directly into the woman's fallopian tube. If the dye passes out the tube's other end, then there may have only been a temporary spasm in the tube or the dye may have flushed out a mucus plug or some menstrual debris that was blocking the tube. If the dye stops inside the tube, then the tube is still blocked and the doctor applies the balloon technique just as through a hysteroscope.

Nearly 80 percent of the women who have had the procedure have had their tubes unblocked, sparing them major surgery, and scores of women who have had the procedure have conceived.

When the tube is blocked by scar tissue, the doctor may advance the guide wire beyond the obstruction and then push a catheter over the guide wire to try to open up the blockage. Once the guide wire is with-drawn, a second dye flush confirms whether the tube has been cleared. This procedure causes only minor discomfort, including cramping and spotting over the next few days. The guide wire has perforated the tube in a few cases, but the tube heals without any apparent harm.

A few doctors use the transcervical catheterization technique to place gametes or embryos directly into the fallopian tubes through the uterus, thus avoiding the need for laparoscopic surgery. An experimental instru-ment, the falloposcope, may also help clear blocked fallopian tubes. The tiny instrument is an endoscope small enough to navigate even the nar-rowest passages of the fallopian tube. The falloposcope is inserted through the vagina and up into the first portion of the fallopian tube. To make navigation easier, an artificial membrane is first unrolled to line the fallopian tube's walls. The doctor can see blockages and lesions along the tube, and may be able to reopen blocked tubes just by clearing debris as the falloposcope moves along. The doctor also may be able to detect and treat ectopic pregnancies.

The instrument has been used worldwide and has been approved by the FDA for use in the United States, but only a handful of American re-searchers have used the device so far. Dr. Berger probably has more expe-rience with the device than any other American doctor.

Electroejaculation

Today's infertility technology has allowed scores of men who were told they would never father children to do just that. An electroejaculation technique to obtain sperm from men who can't ejaculate now offers renewed hope for some of the estimated 250,000 men in the United States with spinal cord injuries. In addition, it can help men with other problems that prevent ejaculation, such as multiple sclerosis (MS), diabetes, and testicular cancer treated by dissection of lymph nodes.

The best candidate for electroejaculation is a man who is healthy, exercises regularly, eats well, has normal-size testicles, and has had few urinary tract infections.

Electroejaculation is currently enjoying a renaissance. The earliest attempts at this procedure date back to 1948. The first reported births occurred in Australia and France in the 1970s. U.S. researchers began experimental programs in 1985. Now there are more than a dozen fertility clinics across the country that have combined electroejaculation with new advanced reproductive technologies such as IUI and IVF to increase pregnancy rates. More than 1,000 American babies have been born through the use of electroejaculation.

The doctor inserts a probe into the man's rectum and attaches the probe to a boxlike device that delivers mild electrical stimulation to the prostate in a gradually increasing fashion to induce an ejaculation. Stimulation starts at a low voltage and increases slowly; the man usually attains an erection and ejaculates within four minutes.

If the man has an adequate number of moving sperm, they are inseminated into his wife's cervix or her uterus. The electroejaculation procedure, therefore, must be timed around his wife's ovulation. Some of his sperm may be inseminated into her cervix on the day of her LH surge and more sperm inseminated into the uterus the next day after sperm washing and "swim-up."

Men with injured spinal cords have dysfunctional nerves running from the back down to the testicles and the epididymis. "Jump-starting" the nerves by electroejaculation in effect rewires the circuitry that disease, an accident, or surgery has short-circuited. The electric probe stimulates nerves that make it possible to obtain an ejaculate in about 80 percent of these men.

Most men with spinal cord injuries feel only a slight discomfort and a tightening in the testicles during treatment. If they feel pain, they receive anesthesia. Since they usually feel little pain, electroejaculation can be performed in an outpatient setting. Men without spinal cord injuries must have general anesthesia, since the electric current causes pain.

Each year, an estimated eight thousand men under age thirty-five injure their spinal cords and another three thousand are diagnosed with testicular cancer. Fortunately, if testicular cancer is diagnosed early, chemotherapy, radiation therapy, and lymph node dissection, when needed, can keep virtually 100 percent of these men alive. Between 30 percent and 50 percent of these men have their sperm counts return to normal within two years, but some of them fail to ejaculate after lymph node dissection, since nerve tissues are frequently affected by the surgery. Electroejaculation can help these men.

The overall pregnancy rates following insemination after electroejaculation are only about 10 percent per attempt, since the motility of electrojaculated sperm rarely exceeds 10 to 20 percent. Success depends on a well-coordinated medical team using the most up-to-date techniques developed to separate and harvest the best available sperm.

Since the quality of these men's sperm varies, some fertility clinics increase the chances of fertilizing at least one egg by superovulating the man's wife with hormones. About one quarter of the men who undergo electroejaculation produce sperm of such compromised quality—less than 5 percent motility and less than 5 million sperm per milliliter—that the realistic potential for pregnancy with IUI is extremely low. It's particularly important in the case of combined therapies that the reproductive urologist and reproductive gynecologist work together as a team.

If insemination by IUI doesn't produce a pregnancy, then IVF with ICSI can be successful. In fact, men with sperm counts as low as 2 million sperm per ml have fathered children by these types of techniques. Sperm recovered from the urine of men who have retrograde ejaculation (where ejaculation occurs into the bladder) has also been inseminated after electroejaculation. In fact, the first North American baby born following electroejaculation resulted from insemination of sperm recovered from retrograde ejaculation.

The potential damage of electroejaculation is injury to the rectum from excessive electrical stimulation, which is most likely to occur if an inexperienced operator attempts the procedure.

A new hand-held vibrator has recently become available, which puts the reproductive control back into the couple's hands. The home model is used to apply stimulation on the underside of the penis for a few minutes until the man ejaculates. He collects the semen sample in a cup and brings it to a fertility center for sperm processing and insemination into his partner. Using this vibrator leads to a 20 percent risk of hyperreflexia, or very high blood pressure, which puts the man in danger of a stroke, so this technique should be practiced first under a doctor's guidance. Several dozen babies have been born in Canada and the United States using this technique.

Miscarriage Immunotherapy

When Iris became pregnant for the first time, she excitedly let her family know. Eight weeks later she miscarried and felt guilty that she had done something wrong. "I remember spotting and wondering whether I should have gotten off of my feet," says Iris, a thirty-six-year-old store manager. "But my doctor told me that it wouldn't have made a difference, that something was wrong genetically and this was just Nature's way."

Iris got pregnant twice more over the next two years, and miscarried each time at about eight weeks. Her fireman husband, Fred, age thirty-four, heard about a couple who had gone successfully through immune therapy with Dr. Berger for repeat miscarriages, and they made an appointment to see him. Dr. Berger discovered that Iris wasn't producing the blocking antibodies necessary to protect a pregnancy from her own immune system. She received infusions from Fred's white blood cells, and within six weeks she was producing the blocking antibodies.

She then received Lupron and Metrodin to help regulate her ovulation, and she became pregnant the next month. When a pregnancy was confirmed, Iris began taking daily steroids, baby aspirin, and progesterone in separate tablets to help maintain the pregnancy. "I started having cramps about the seventh week, so at Dr. Berger's suggestion I stopped working and got off my feet," Iris says. "Now I'm in my fifth month and everything is progressing normally. I know I wouldn't have been able to carry this far without the immune therapy."

Certain women, such as DES daughters, are at increased risk of miscarriage—signaled by bleeding or spotting, cramping, less breast tenderness, and the symptoms of premature labor, regular contractions of the uterus, a dull, low backache, menstrual-like cramps, and leaking fluid from the vagina due to rupture of membranes. Obstetrician-gynecologists have learned to treat these women from the beginning as having high-risk pregnancies.

Only in the early 1970s did doctors gain the ability to measure reproductive hormones that could detect a pregnancy as soon as (and even before) a woman's period was late. Now such routine hormone measurements allow doctors to know early on when a woman has miscarried. In addition, ultrasound scans can detect the normal growth and development of the fetus, and can see a fetal heartbeat, or the lack of one, as early as five to six weeks from the last menstrual period, or three to four weeks after conception.

Since one half of the fetus's genes are from the father and can be recognized as "nonself" by the mother's immune system, in order to be successful the pregnancy must signal the mother's immune system to shield the pregnancy from its usual rejection of any foreign tissue.

Researchers at several centers, including Dr. Berger, are attempting to influence a mother's immune response to prevent her body from rejecting her pregnancy. In one experimental treatment, a woman may receive injections of a type of her husband's white blood cells. Or a woman may receive blood cells from a donor to produce a similar protective response.

About 75 percent of couples with unexplained recurrent spontaneous abortion have achieved a live birth after immunotherapy with white blood cells. The results of immunotherapy are promising. But, in fact, half of the women who have recurrent abortions achieve successful pregnancies with no treatment at all. Doctors are beginning to use immunotherapy as a treatment of choice for recurrent spontaneous abortion, but acceptance awaits further evaluation of its effectiveness and safety. In addition, long-term follow-up of mothers and their offspring is needed to evaluate completely the potential long-term effects of immunologic therapy.

Another immune system dysfunction that may lead to recurrent abortion is found among women with autoimmune disorders. In these diseases, such as rheumatoid arthritis and systemic lupus erythematosus, the body mistakenly redirects the immune system against itself. The antibodies made to fight off invaders such as infections get sent to destroy the body's own tissues and organs. Most women with repeated miscarriages do not have these diseases.

Autoantibodies may interfere with fertilization, implantation, and the normal progress of pregnancy. They have been found in greater numbers among women who have repeated miscarriages. They also have been found among women with unexplained infertility and have been associated with endometriosis as well. There seems to be a further correlation between autoantibodies and antibodies produced against sperm, which can prevent the sperm from ever reaching the egg or fertilizing it.

Having the mother take the blood-thinning drug heparin along with a baby aspirin daily may be a simple treatment for repeat miscarriages related to autoantibodies. A subtle blood-clotting disorder may induce miscarriage due to autoantibodies: vital nutrients can't reach the fetus because of blood clots in vessels that supply nutrients through the placenta. Blood tests can detect whether the mother has these antibodies, and if she does, she can take heparin and aspirin therapy. If strong, multiple autoimmune antibodies are present, then steroids may also be used for immune therapy.

Other Miscarriage Therapies

After specific treatments to correct identified problems, a woman's first line of defense against miscarriage or premature delivery is bed rest. If bed rest doesn't help delay the premature opening of her cervix, then other treatments are available. One involves putting a stitch around the cervix to hold it closed. This technique, called cerclage, has become a common practice for women who have an "incompetent cervix," in which the cervix opens too early as the baby's weight increases. Cervical cerclage usually is reserved for women who already have lost a pregnancy, had a premature birth, or have signs of an incompetent cervix on physical or X-ray examination. The stitch must be removed when labor begins in order to permit a normal vaginal delivery.

A woman can take the hormone progesterone during the first trimester to suppress her uterine contractions and reduce the risk of a miscarriage. When progesterone levels are low or falling early in pregnancy, the woman may receive progesterone to augment her ovaries' supply of the hormone to maintain the pregnancy until the placenta is large enough to manufacture a sufficient amount of progesterone on its own. Some fertility clinics and IVF centers also use hydroxyprogesterone caproate, a synthetic version of progesterone, given as a once-a-week injection to prevent miscarriage.

The use of a class of prostaglandin inhibitors, such as aspirin or ibuprofen, also reduces uterine contractions early in pregnancy. Another group of drugs, called tocolytics (labor inhibitors), relax the body's smooth muscles, including the uterus, to stop the contractions of premature labor. Most commonly ritodrine and terbutaline, these drugs also increase the mother's heart rate, however, and may decrease her blood pressure. Pulse and blood pressure must be monitored carefully when a woman takes these drugs.

Unfortunately, we have limited knowledge of the short- and long-term effects of tocolytics on the fetus. They do reach the fetal circulation, and the fetal heart rate increases during treatment. Preliminary studies show that these drugs can delay premature births if used in time, but the data on their long-term safety isn't completely in yet.

Cancer Therapies

While some medications can help preserve fertility, other drug treatments, such as for cancer, can reduce fertility potential. A cancer with one of the best cure rates—Hodgkin's disease—has led cancer specialists to devise ways to preserve the fertility of both men and women who survive treatments. About 80 percent of Hodgkin's disease patients are cured. Most are still in their prime reproductive years once therapy ends, and they may want to have children.

Two methods are now in use to preserve the fertility of women who have had Hodgkin's disease. One involves surgically moving a woman's ovaries higher and more to the sides, away from the areas to be irradiated, and shielding the transposed ovaries with lead during radiation treatments. The second provides women with birth control pills during radiation and chemotherapy treatments. The pills suppress ovarian function and may minimize the damage to inactive follicles.

For a man who has had Hodgkin's disease, the amount of damage to his reproductive system depends on the amount and type of his treatment. Most men become sterile within ten weeks of either single or multiple drug treatments. Radiation also lowers a man's sperm count. The higher the radiation dose, the longer it takes a man to recover sperm production, if he recovers it at all.

To preserve a man's reproductive ability, researchers at the M. D. Anderson Hospital and Tumor Institute in Houston, Texas, have devised an effective and shorter, less intensive treatment for Hodgkin's disease than the standard six cycles of chemotherapy. The Texas team uses only two cycles followed by low-dose radiation, and when possible, they avoid radiation to the man's pelvis. Men treated in this way have been recovering their sperm counts about 80 percent of the time. Other researchers have developed effective chemotherapies with different combinations of drugs that seem to protect the testicles from extensive injury.

In addition, most men with newly diagnosed Hodgkin's disease have a chance to freeze their sperm before starting therapy. The sperm can then be used later for artificial insemination in case the man doesn't recover his fertility. The physicians at M. D. Anderson also offer an experimental approach, treating men with testosterone before and during chemotherapy. The testosterone suppresses the man's sperm production and may protect his testicles from the toxic effects of chemotherapy by rendering them inactive. This is analogous to the use of birth control pills to inactivate a woman's ovaries before she undergoes treatment. In the future, a synthetic version of GnRH may also be used to suppress the function of both sexes' gonads during chemotherapy to preserve fertility. The overall fertility rate after any kind of cancer treatment is about 50 percent.

Questions to Ask Your Doctor About the Newest Fertility Treatments

As for any medical treatment, the couple should ask questions about how appropriate the recommended procedure is for them. These questions may be even more important for a couple contemplating undergoing a new, and possibly experimental, fertility treatment.

Are we good candidates for this treatment?

What are our chances of achieving a pregnancy and delivering a live, healthy baby?

How many patients have you treated with our particular problem?

What is your success rate for couples like us using this treatment?

What other treatment options are available to us?

Why do you recommend this procedure over other available treatments?

How long will the treatment take? How much will it cost?

If surgery is required, can it be performed on an outpatient basis? What type of anesthesia will I need?

What are the potential side effects or complications? How likely are they?

Do you perform these new procedures, and if not, can you refer us to someone who does? (The directory at the back of this book lists doctors who offer some of these advanced treatments.)

10

IVF
AND ITS
"COUSINS"

When Miriam and Roberto married six years ago, they wanted above all else to have a baby. They were heartbroken when they found out it wasn't going to be easy. Miriam, a thirty-five-year-old policewoman, had conceived while taking Pergonal, but the pregnancy was ectopic. The diagnosis did not come until after the fallopian tube ruptured, causing internal bleeding that required emergency surgery. By that time, the fallopian tube was severely damaged. With more fertility drugs, she conceived again and had another ectopic pregnancy. To avoid yet another ectopic pregnancy, Miriam had her remaining tube sealed off completely.

With her ovaries still functioning, but no healthy fallopian tube, Miriam became an ideal candidate for in vitro fertilization. She again took Pergonal to stimulate her ovaries, and had three eggs retrieved and fertilized with Roberto's sperm.

When her pregnancy test was positive, Miriam says, "We were ecstatic, overwhelmed." She went back to work as a detective, but took a leave of absence shortly afterward. Nine months later, with Roberto present, she gave birth to their son, Omar. "I was happy to hear him cry so loud," says Roberto, a thirty-nine-year-old teacher. "I was happy but at the same time relieved that we had finished the whole thing."

Someday, Miriam and Roberto plan to tell their son the miraculous story of how he was conceived. "We plan to show him the pictures taken through the microscope only forty-eight hours after the eggs were retrieved, and the ultrasound pictures taken at twenty-one days and at about fifteen weeks from the transfer into the uterus," says Roberto. "We will tell him exactly what happened, about the whole exciting process of seeing his total development."

Somewhere in the world, a "test-tube" baby is born every day. The miracle of babies born through in vitro fertilization (IVF) no longer seems so

---

miraculous. In fact, fertilization outside the human body is now available throughout the Western world. In North America, four hundred centers perform IVF, and the best report pregnancy rates of more than 30 percent per cycle after embryo transfer. That's even better than the 20 to 25 percent chance of natural pregnancy in any given month under ideal conditions.

What Is In Vitro Fertilization?

Simply stated, IVF involves removing eggs from a woman, fertilizing them in the laboratory (in a culture dish, actually, not a test tube), and then transferring the fertilized eggs, or zygotes, into the uterus a few days later.

More specifically, after superovulation with hormones to produce multiple eggs, the IVF team places the retrieved eggs in sterile culture media along with processed sperm and keeps them at normal body temperature inside an incubator, where fertilization and early cell division take place. Then the team returns the fertilized and dividing eggs to the uterus. From that point, if the zygotes implant successfully and become embryos, the pregnancy progresses as it would naturally.

What to Look for in an IVF Clinic

There are more than four hundred IVF clinics in the United States and Canada, and finding the right one for you is just as important as your search for the right fertility specialist. Some, but not all, are members of the ASRM's Society of Assisted Reproductive Technologies (SART), which has established criteria to asses the quality of IVF clinics and also monitors clinic results. SART now requires its members to adhere to a set of strict standards, which include yearly pregnancy outcome data collection and reporting; validation (a modified audit) of these data by a SART/Centers for Disease Control (CDC) inspection team; embryology laboratory inspection and certification every two years by an outside agency; and adherence to all SART/ASRM ethical practice, laboratory, and advertising guidelines.

Inquire about the program's patient selection process, including any age limitations and the types of infertility patients it accepts. Most programs won't accept a woman over the age of forty. You should know the number of cycles the clinic has performed and how soon you can be seen. Waiting for your IVF cycle usually takes a few months.

Ask straightforwardly about your chances of achieving a pregnancy at *that* clinic. How does this compare with your chances at other IVF centers? How does it compare with that of other couples with similar diagnoses at that particular clinic?

Reputable IVF centers report only clinical pregnancy rates and do not include "chemical" pregnancies in their statistics. Chemical pregnancy refers to a rise in hCG levels about ten to fourteen days after hCG administration, but many chemical pregnancies never make it to the more advanced stage at which the pregnancy can be seen with an ultrasound exam of the uterus.

The clinical pregnancy rate is a more important statistic. A clinical pregnancy continues at least until it can be documented with an ultrasound exam showing the presence of a fetus. But even pregnancies that reach this stage can miscarry, and—as after natural conception—up to one fourth of all clinical pregnancies established through IVF don't progress to a live birth. The most important statistic, of course, is the clinic's live birth rate. The live birth rate should be calculated by taking into account all of the couples who have had treatment there over a specified length of time. Ask what your chances are of taking home a baby, based on the clinic's past experience.

There are various ways to calculate the outcome of IVF. A program will report its pregnancy rate, which is the number of couples who conceived clinical pregnancies divided by the total number of couples treated, regardless of how many treatment cycles they had. A program may also report its pregnancy ratio per treatment cycle or per embryo transfer. Find out how many cycles were done before the clinic had its first pregnancy and what the success rate has been since then.

It may also help you evaluate a program to find out the canceled cycle rate. A canceled cycle means the woman began ovarian stimulation but never got to the stage of attempting egg retrieval. A high rate of dropped cycles (30 percent or more) may reflect a poor ovulation induction technique, or it may just mean that the clinic has stringent criteria before proceeding to egg retrieval.

Cost is obviously important. Does your health insurance policy cover any of the costs incurred during the IVF cycle? Most clinics now offer transvaginal ultrasound-guided egg retrieval instead of laparoscopy, which decreases the cost of the egg retrieval.

Other Options

Another way to assess a clinic's suitability for you is to examine the variety of services and support systems it offers. For example, most IVF clinics provide embryo freezing. The clinic may also provide adjuncts to IVF as well, such as embryo or egg donor programs.

Embryo freezing—actually freezing and storing fertilized eggs or zygotes—allows preservation for transfer in future spontaneous ovulation cycles. This is an advantage if many eggs are retrieved and fertilized, since most centers transfer back only a limited number of zygotes per IVF cycle due to the increased risk of multiple pregnancy. If the center offers freezing, ask whether any basic research, using animal models, has been performed to assess the viability of the freezing and thawing technique. This quality-control measure is required of all SART member clinics.

There should be a clear-cut policy regarding any remaining frozen embryos that are left after a woman becomes pregnant. What happens to them? How long will they be kept in storage? Would you consent for them to be donated to other couples after you have your child? These issues should all be clearly addressed and approved by the couple in a written consent form provided by the clinic.

IVF is an exceedingly difficult technique to perform with good results. Launching and maintaining an IVF program is an expensive, time-consuming process. Strict quality-control standards need to be established and met. A team of committed professionals, each with a specialized expertise, is essential. Besides a reproductive surgeon and reproductive endocrinologist, the team will probably include an embryologist, andrologist, IVF lab technician(s), nurse-coordinator, and counselor. Familiarize yourself with the qualifications and previous experience of the staff of the program. It's okay to ask about their credentials and experience. You should receive a written document from the clinic regarding the training and experience of the staff, and their success rates.

Patient Education and Support

Before you decide to undergo treatment at any clinic, you should understand the entire IVF process, step by step, including when drug therapy
begins, how often the woman needs blood tests and ultrasound monitoring, and when egg retrieval will likely take place. If you have traveled
from out of town, the clinic should help arrange for a place for you to stay
during the IVF treatment. Also, a doctor in your area should be contacted
to assist in follow-up tests after you have returned home following embryo transfer.

Your first set of tests may duplicate the general fertility workup—
blood tests for both partners to rule out immunological problems and to
confirm that the woman is ovulating; a complete physical exam for the
woman, including a measurement of her uterine cavity; and a semen
analysis, sperm antibody assay, and semen cultures for the man. You
should also receive instructions on how to administer the fertility drugs
the wife will take to induce multiple egg production.

Ovulation Induction

*"It was odd giving my wife the injections," says Sam, age forty, a local council-
man. He and his wife, Jennifer, also forty, had tried to have a baby for nearly four
years before they went to see Dr. Goldstein. He found that Sam had a low sperm
count, probably due to a varicocele, which was repaired microsurgically. In the
meantime, Jennifer's gynecologist could find nothing wrong with her after a fertility workup. Sam's postop semen analysis showed that his sperm count was still
low. He tried clomiphene for three months, but his sperm count did not rise, so he
and Jennifer decided to try IVF.*

*At the start of their first IVF cycle, Sam gave Jennifer an injection of
Pergonal in the buttock every night for a week. "I thought, 'I can't stick a needle
in there.' But she said she hardly felt any pain."*

The goal of any IVF program is to maximize the couple's chances of having a baby. To achieve pregnancy, there must be successful responses to
ovulation medication, egg collection, fertilization, embryo replacement,
and subsequent implantation. Failures can occur at any step along the
way.

For example, of thirty women who start ovulation induction, six may have the cycle dropped because of inadequate stimulation. Of the remaining twenty-four women who undergo egg retrieval, only twenty-one may get to the point of embryo transfer, with three having eggs that didn't fertilize and divide. Of the twenty-one who have embryo transfers, only five might achieve a clinical pregnancy if the clinic's pregnancy rate is 25 percent per embryo transfer. One of those five is likely to miscarry, leaving only four couples that may have a live-born infant. This means the live birth rate is 4 out of 30, or 14 percent.

To maximize a couple's chances of pregnancy, most IVF programs use some combination of ovulation-inducing agents to make multiple fertilizable eggs available at the time of scheduled egg retrieval.

The first attempts at IVF, a concept developed and made successful by the late British gynecologist Dr. Patrick Steptoe and his co-researcher, embryologist Robert Edwards, had little success because only one egg was recovered during a spontaneous ovulation cycle. These unstimulated cycles required the IVF team to detect the very beginning of the woman's LH surge and then closely monitor her to find the best time to retrieve her egg. Following her spontaneous LH surge, Steptoe and Edwards often had to perform egg retrievals very late at night or during early morning hours.

The success of IVF improved dramatically with the use of superovulation with Pergonal, first advocated by the Norfolk, Virginia, group headed by Drs. Georgianna and Howard Jones. Larger numbers of eggs could be recovered, and the IVF team could better time egg retrieval. Now the use of superovulation has become routine with IVF. In addition, gonadotropin-releasing hormone (GnRH) agonists have also been introduced prior to or when beginning controlled ovulation to prevent the woman from having her own spontaneous LH surge so that egg retrieval timing can be strictly controlled and the chance of a canceled cycle minimized.

Generally, the woman begins taking ovulation-inducing drugs between the first and fifth days of her cycle to stimulate the development of multiple follicles. Several eggs are stimulated to develop at the same time so that a group of eggs will be available for fertilization. This "superovulation" is usually accomplished with combinations of the same hormone medications used to stimulate ovulation in other treatment cycles, such as for IUI: clomiphene citrate, Pergonal, pure follicle-stimulating hormone (Metrodin), and human chorionic gonadotropin (hCG).

Many couples are already familiar with these medications since they may have used them in previous treatment cycles, before ever considering IVF. Usually a member of the IVF team teaches the husband how to give his wife the daily injections so that she doesn't have to go to the doctor's office for her medication. Although this may be difficult to do at first, it gives the couple some control over their own treatment.

There are almost as many individual stimulation regimens as there are IVF programs. Most IVF clinics start providing high doses of hormones, either alone or in combinations, early in a woman's cycle—when more follicles can be recruited to progress and mature. The woman's response to stimulation is carefully monitored by estradiol levels, ultrasound exams, cervical mucus examination, and, possibly, progesterone and LH levels to determine how the follicles containing the eggs are developing. Blood hormone levels may be obtained intermittently during the first week of stimulation, then daily, along with ultrasound exams and cervical mucus monitoring, as the follicles grow. The doctor adjusts the stimulation schedule to maintain a steady growth in the size of ovarian follicles and a steady rise of estradiol levels. When the follicles reach maturity, usually after seven to ten days of medication, an hCG injection is administered to trigger egg maturation in anticipation of egg retrieval from the follicles.

At first, most IVF clinics had one standard way to induce ovulation. If a woman's follicles weren't stimulated sufficiently, she had no egg retrieval, and the cycle was canceled. Today many programs individualize ovulation induction, which has reduced IVF cancellation rates.

Since some women do better with larger amounts of hormones, and others with lesser amounts, hormone stimulation often needs to be individualized. Doctors often determine individual hormone doses based on the woman's response to previous cycles of hormone therapy or to previous IVF cycles.

IVF researchers have learned that excessively high amounts of gonadotropins can often disrupt and shorten a woman's luteal phase, making it difficult for implantation to occur or for her to carry the pregnancy to term. To help support the luteal phase, most IVF teams now provide progesterone daily from the day of egg retrieval until a pregnancy test is performed two weeks later. Others also provide repeated injections of hCG in the luteal phase of the cycle to keep the ovaries producing progesterone.

Unfortunately, between 10 and 20 percent of women attempting IVF have a poor ovarian response to ovulation-inducing drugs and never reach the stage of egg retrieval. Increased doses of gonadotropins at the beginning of the menstrual cycle may enhance egg recruitment for such poor responders.

Most IVF teams use GnRH agonists such as leuprolide acetate (Lupron) at the beginning of gonadotropin ovulation induction. GnRH agonist pretreatment, followed by FSH or hMG, increases the number of mature eggs collected, the fertilization rate, the length of the luteal phase, and pregnancy rates. After pretreatment with a GnRH agonist, however, it usually takes larger amounts of Pergonal to produce ovulation than when no GnRH agonist is used.

This more controlled stimulation with GnRH and FSH or hMG or Metrodin has the advantage of fewer canceled IVF cycles due to a spontaneous LH surge than with Pergonal alone. If a woman has an LH surge, most programs now cancel cycles because it's difficult to predict ovulation accurately, and retrieval of the eggs may be performed either too early or too late. Cycles may also be canceled due to a low number (less than four) of mature follicles, inadequate estradiol production, or poor follicle development.

Some women respond too much to ovulation-inducing drugs. They are given the lowest dose possible in subsequent cycles. The Cornell IVF team also adds birth control pills along with Lupron to help control a high response.

Egg Retrieval

Married for two years, Marilyn, age thirty-six, and Edward, age forty-six, wanted a baby. Since they had been unsuccessful after trying for a year, they each went to fertility specialists. Even though he had fathered two children in his first marriage, Edward showed a borderline low sperm count. Marilyn had intermittent high prolactin levels and elevated androgen levels. The following years were fraught with frustration as they both tried hormone treatments and numerous artificial inseminations without success. Their next alternative was an IVF procedure.

In their first IVF attempt, Marilyn had her eggs retrieved laparoscopically. "I didn't feel a thing when I was asleep, and I remember having a pleasant dream. In fact, I was annoyed that they had awakened me when it was over," says Marilyn. "Then my belly hurt where they had made the incision for the laparoscope, my hand hurt where the IV tube had been in place and I felt nauseous."

214

Although three of her eggs were fertilized and transferred into her uterus, the attempt failed.

During her next IVF attempt, Marilyn had her eggs retrieved, with ultrasound guidance, through her vagina. "I felt a little uncomfortable when they were rinsing my ovaries, but it wasn't bad," she says. "I hardly felt when they stuck the needle into my follicles. After it was over, I didn't feel any pain."

If a woman doesn't take GnRH agonists, then as she nears the middle of her cycle she usually begins to monitor herself with a home test kit several times a day to check for her LH surge. The IVF team retrieves her eggs based on the prediction of when she will ovulate naturally after the LH surge or after administering hCG, which is usually more accurate. In most cases, after taking gonadotropins, the woman receives an hCG injection and the IVF team retrieves her eggs thirty-four to thirty-six hours later.

The team normally retrieves the woman's eggs with an ultrasound-guided needle placed through the vagina. She may receive either general anesthesia or only intravenous sedation and possibly takes mild analgesics.

For ultrasound-guided retrieval, the IVF team covers an ultrasound probe, specifically designed for pelvic imaging, with a sterile covering glove and inserts the probe into the woman's vagina. With the aid of a needle guide attached to the probe, the doctor harvests her eggs by puncturing the follicles and removing the follicular fluid. The embryologist immediately identifies and places the eggs in nutritive media in an incubator.

Ultrasound-guided egg retrieval has made the most physically demanding part of the IVF procedure in the past (the laparoscopy) less traumatic. In some centers, husbands can be with their wives during the egg retrieval. The procedure is easier on the woman than laparoscopy and is equally effective in retrieving eggs. It is also usually less costly, faster, and leads to a quicker recovery than laparoscopic retrieval.

Laparoscopic retrieval is reserved for women who need a simultaneous assessment of pelvic anatomy through a diagnostic laparoscopy. IVF clinics should have both retrieval methods available to pick the best method for a particular woman.

Semen Collection

"At first, it was embarrassing providing the sample because of all those people in the waiting room," recalls Sam. "They all knew what I was there for. But then I realized that all the guys were there for the same reason."

Before the start of the IVF cycle, the husband makes an appointment to give a semen sample for evaluation. The clinic should provide a quiet, private place for optimum semen collection, since studies show that this may contribute to the success or failure of the cycle. In some cases, the husband's sperm can be frozen as a backup for the day of egg retrieval. As with a semen analysis, he is asked to refrain from ejaculation for two or three days beforehand to increase the number of sperm in the semen. On the day of egg retrieval, he provides a semen sample through masturbation, and the sample undergoes a standard semen analysis along with the best sperm processing method for this particular situation to recover the healthiest sperm.

Egg Fertilization

For men with normal semen, about 50,000 to 100,000 of the most motile sperm are incubated with each of his wife's eggs. An embryologist inspects the eggs, allows them to incubate in culture media, and then mixes the sperm with mature eggs. Assisted fertilization techniques, such as partial zona dissection, may be performed before the eggs are mixed with the sperm for fertilization. The embryologist places the mixture in an incubator overnight and the following morning checks the eggs for fertilization.

There are four basic steps to fertilization: the egg's metabolism must be turned on, the sperm must be incorporated into the egg, a barrier must be erected to keep other sperm out, and the nuclei and chromosomes from the egg and the sperm must be united inside the egg.

Generally, about 60 to 80 percent of eggs become fertilized at this stage. Eggs penetrated by more than one sperm (polyspermy), which produces an abnormal embryo, are not transferred back to the wife's uterus.

By about thirty hours after fertilization, the sperm and egg have become a two-celled pre-embryo. By forty-eight hours after fertilization, the pre-embryo should have four cells, and by sixty hours it should have divided into eight cells. The pre-embryo is usually transferred into the wife's uterus anywhere from the two-cell to the eight-cell stage.

If 60 to 80 percent of the retrieved eggs become fertilized, why do only 40 to 50 percent of women at most successful IVF clinics become pregnant? The answer may lie with several factors. The uterus may not be properly prepared for implantation. A woman's hormonal support after embryo transfer may be inadequate. With IVF, embryos are transferred into the uterus more quickly (after two days) than they would normally appear in the uterus in a natural cycle (five to seven days after ovulation). That is because after the first few days in incubation outside of the body, the pre-embyros won't keep dividing at the normal rate as inside the woman's reproductive tract.

Blastocyst Transfer

A recent advancement in embryology enhances the timing of embryo transfer and has led to improved pregnancy rates. Embryos can now be cultured in a special medium beyond the typical two to three days and be transferred on day five—closer to what happens in the body during natural conception—at the blastocyst stage. This allows for the selection of only the healthiest embryos and improved pregnancy rates. What's more, transferring two blastocysts leads to pregnancy just as often as transferring three blastocysts, which lessens the risks of multiple births.

The development of new culture media was the driving force behind the widespread use of blastocyst transfer. Fertility clinics switch embryos to a culture medium that mimics uterine fluid around the third day after retrieval and maintain them in culture until day five. The blastocysts are then transferred into the uterus.

A blastocyst is the final stage of the embryo's development before it hatches out of its shell (the zona pellucida) and implants in the uterine wall. Only the most viable embryos reach this stage of development at about day five. Delaying the transfer of the embryo a few days allows a longer observation of embryo development and later assessment of embryo quality. One reason blastocyst transfer may increase pregnancy rates is that embryos with abnormal chromosomes that might have been transferred at day two or three typically do not develop to the blastocyst stage.

217

The incidence of implantation of blastocysts is about double that of embryos on day two or three. So fertility clinics may now transfer half as many blastocysts as they did embryos and achieve roughly twice the implantation rate. In the future, clinics may be able to transfer only one blastocyst to avoid multiple pregnancies altogether.

Blastocyst transfer has been used successfully for standard IVF, for ICSI, for IVF with donor eggs, and for frozen embryo transfer. Implantation and pregnancy rates are higher in fertility patients with a history of IVF failure who utilize blastocyst transfer. Babies born through blastocyst transfer have a similar birth weight to babies born through spontaneous conception.

While blastocyst transfer is certainly appropriate for younger women who produce many eggs, it's not that clear whether the overall pregnancy rate will be better for all patients since some eggs won't make it to the blastocyst stage in the culture. Fewer patients reach transfer than with conventional embryo transfer on day three. And while blastocyst transfer can theoretically lead to fewer multiple pregnancies, some IVF programs still transfer three blastocysts, and this technique has been used as a marketing ploy.

Embryo Transfer

Of the six eggs retrieved from Jennifer's follicles, three became fertilized by Sam's sperm and were transferred into her uterus. "We were ecstatic about the three fertilizations after spending a tense weekend waiting to hear about the results," Sam says. "We came in early Sunday morning for the embryo transfer. Two other couples were also in the office for the same thing, so we shared bagels and lox together. It was the most unusual Sunday brunch I have ever had."

When the fertilized eggs have divided and become pre-embryos, the woman returns to the IVF clinic for the transfer procedure. The reproductive endocrinologist or surgeon threads a thin plastic catheter through the vagina, through the cervical canal, and into the uterus, and transfers the fertilized egg through the catheter. The patient's husband may be allowed to stay with his wife during the transfer process.

This ten-minute, outpatient procedure requires no anesthesia. After resting for a few hours, the woman returns home and usually can resume normal activities in a day or two.

To enhance the embryo transfer rate, the Cornell IVF clinic has the woman go through a mock embryo transfer using radiopaque dye in a pre-IVF cycle. A fluoroscope reveals where the dye (which is like the fluid that will contain the embryo) ends up. In certain body positions, such as with the woman on her back, the dye may run out of her vagina. She may be better off having her embryos transferred while she is in a knee-chest position (on her stomach, not her back). Other clinics have devised equipment that holds the uterus tilted downward, hoping to use gravity to help the transferred embryos implant in the uterus.

The chances of having a child through IVF are improved by transferring several embryos into the uterus. The more transferred, the higher the pregnancy rate, but also the greater the likelihood of multiple pregnancy. Most IVF teams like to transfer three or four embryos during each IVF cycle. If more than four eggs are retrieved, all mature eggs are fertilized and the extra embryos may be frozen. If freezing is unavailable, the couple may be asked to donate the eggs to another infertile couple or to allow the IVF team to use them to refine culturing methods and embryo handling techniques. IVF centers are increasingly using larger numbers of embryos to maximize their pregnancy rates, in part under pressure from competition to maintain high pregnancy rates.

Embryo Freezing

If an IVF procedure fails, the couple should wait at least one month while the wife recovers before undergoing superovulation and egg retrieval again. Saving eggs for future use by fertilizing them with sperm and then freezing them as pre-embryos can be helpful. Frozen pre-embryos can be transferred during subsequent spontaneous (natural) ovulation cycles without subjecting the wife to any additional medications and another egg retrieval.

At the right time during succeeding treatment cycles, the frozen pre-embryos are thawed and transferred into the uterus as with any IVF attempt.

The ability to preserve pre-embryos for future use lowers the total cost of repeated IVF treatments since the most costly first few stages (ovulation induction, egg retrieval, fertilization) don't have to be repeated. Another advantage is that one or more pre-embryos can be transferred during a natural ovulation cycle when the woman's uterus is naturally ready for implantation.

Only about half of frozen pre-embryos survive thawing, and less than 20 percent lead to pregnancies. Most U.S. centers now freeze pre-embryos. Improved freezing and thawing techniques are currently being developed and will almost certainly lead to more centers offering pre-embryo freezing in the future.

If a couple has pre-embryos frozen, they should expect to pay the IVF clinic a storage fee. After a certain length of time, the couple must decide what to do with any unused frozen pre-embryos, such as whether to donate them to another infertile couple.

Some IVF clinics, such as the one at Cornell University, have the couple sign an agreement stating that the frozen pre-embryos are the joint property of the couple. Upon the woman's forty-fifth birthday, the frozen pre-embryos become the property of the Cornell IVF team. This ethical dilemma of survivorship gained worldwide attention when a wealthy California couple died in a plane crash without designating what to do with their frozen pre-embryos left in Australia. After a lengthy court battle, the rights to the frozen pre-embryos were transferred to the couple's estate.

Other ethical issues also may come up concerning frozen pre-embryos. If one of a pair of twin pre-embryos is frozen while the other is implanted immediately, twins could be born years apart. With techniques now available to clone animal eggs, cloning human eggs may someday become a reality, which would greatly expand the supply of pre-embryos to be frozen and transferred later on.

Post-Transfer

"The first seven days after the embryo transfer were exciting," says Sam. "Jennifer's eggs were implanted in her womb and in a way she was pregnant. Everything was going well." As it got closer to two weeks and the pregnancy test, they spent more time together, nurturing each other. The pregnancy test result came back as borderline, and Sam and Jennifer had to wait another two days. In that time, her hCG levels crashed, and Jennifer got her period.

"That was hard for us to take. We started to think again that we would never have a baby," says Sam. "I told Jennifer that this was only our first IVF cycle, that she should keep her spirits up. Although they told us we only have a 20 per-

cent chance, I reminded her that even though we have a male fertility problem, we had fertilizations. We're looking forward to the next attempt."

The two weeks of waiting after pre-embryo transfer often become the most difficult part of the IVF treatment emotionally. After the transfer, the woman may continue to take hCG or progesterone to help support the uterine lining built up in the first half of the cycle. During this period, various blood hormone levels are measured to track the wife's progress. If necessary, she receives more progesterone to help maintain the endometrial lining and prevent premature menstruation. Two weeks following embryo transfer, she returns for a pregnancy test.

If her pregnancy test is negative, the IVF team usually encourages the couple to schedule a follow-up visit with the clinic's doctor and a counselor, usually a social worker or psychologist, for treatment, to ask any questions, and to discuss their options. The couple may decide to try another IVF attempt. A woman who goes through the IVF procedure three times has about a 50 percent chance of taking home a baby.

If her pregnancy test is positive, the woman still has a 15 to 20 percent chance of miscarrying (women over forty tend to have a higher miscarriage rate) and about a 5 percent chance of an ectopic pregnancy, also higher than for the general population. Within two weeks after a positive pregnancy test, she returns for an ultrasound scan to confirm the presence of a fetal heartbeat and to see whether she is carrying more than one baby.

There is no evidence of an increased risk of birth defects or premature births from IVF. Most IVF clinics don't consider IVF pregnancies high-risk pregnancies, except for the risk of early miscarriage, for which many provide progesterone supplements to help maintain the pregnancy to term. Any multiple pregnancy is considered high risk, especially for premature delivery.

If the woman becomes pregnant, she will be referred back to her obstetrician. If she doesn't have an obstetrician, the clinic usually helps her find one. Genetic counseling and amniocentesis are usually recommended for any woman over thirty-five; a genetic abnormality, however, can occur at any age. Chorionic villus sampling (CVS) is a newer alternative to diagnose a genetic disorder in the first trimester, but it carries a higher risk of miscarriage than amniocentesis, which is performed in the second trimester. Dr. Berger has performed amniocentesis about ten to eleven weeks from the last menstrual period, which avoids the risks of miscarriage and limb deformity associated with CVS. As always, you should discuss the need for and risks of genetic testing with your doctor.

Cancellation of a Cycle

Occasionally, an IVF team will decide not to attempt to retrieve a woman's eggs, but rather to cancel the treatment cycle. Sometimes the woman doesn't respond optimally to the medications, and the blood tests and ultrasound exams don't reveal successful follicle growth. Her eggs may be immature, or too mature, to be fertilized. Or the eggs may fertilize but not continue to divide, in which case they will not be transferred back into the uterus.

You have to realize that your chances for success in any one IVF cycle, even at the best clinics, is no higher than about one in three once you have gotten to embryo transfer. Of all the couples who start IVF treatment, only 15 to 20 percent take home a baby. These percentages are likely to increase as fertility specialists gain more experience with IVF.

Who Are the Candidates for IVF?

The couple with the best chances for a successful IVF procedure involves a woman younger than thirty-five who has normal menstrual cycles and a good response to controlled ovarian hyperstimulation, and a man with any live sperm.

IVF with ICSI can bypass most causes of infertility, including irreversibly blocked fallopian tubes, antisperm antibody problems, endometriosis, a cervical factor problem, very low sperm counts, and even unexplained causes of infertility. IVF is a particularly good alternative for a woman who produces mature eggs but can't conceive naturally because of blocked fallopian tubes and for a woman with luteinized unruptured follicle syndrome, who develops but doesn't release mature eggs from her follicles.

The Age Factor

The chances of an IVF birth depend heavily on the wife's age. Younger women have higher pregnancy rates than older women. At Cornell, about 50 percent of couples take home a baby if the woman is under age thirty-four and the husband has any live sperm. As women reach their late thirties, only 40 percent take home babies, and by age forty, 33 percent deliver babies. After that, the take-home-baby rate drops to 20 percent at age forty-two and only 5 percent at age forty-six. Yet even knowing the odds, many women over forty say they want to go through at least one IVF cycle before giving up their search for a fertility treatment.

One way to determine whether a woman over forty has a good chance of success is to measure her FSH level on day three of her menstrual cycle. Researchers at the Jones Institute were the first to recognize a trend toward higher pregnancy rates and fewer canceled cycles for women over forty when their FSH level was low on cycle day three. That now has become an accepted prognostic tool regarding IVF outcome.

Another predictor is an elevated estradiol level on cycle day three. A high estradiol level appears to be associated with a poor response to ovarian stimulation and a greater chance of canceling an IVF cycle. So doctors and patients can use this information to decide whether it's best to cancel a cycle rather than move on to more gonadotropins. An early cancellation can save a couple the expense of further medication and monitoring for that cycle.

In older women who produce fewer than half a dozen eggs per egg retrieval, ICSI is often indicated to assure that enough eggs will be fertilized to allow embryo transfer.

PCOD Patients

While an abnormal day three FSH or estradiol level can mean a diminished ovarian reserve and a poor prognosis for IVF, that's not the case for patients with polycystic ovarian disease (PCOD). These patients are often younger and have elevated estradiol levels, so an elevated day three estradiol level may predict a high response to stimulation with drugs.

The PCOD patient poses a unique problem. This group of women will often display an exaggerated response to gonadotropins and have an increased risk of hyperstimulation and cycle cancellation. These patients often develop very high estradiol levels without an adequate number of mature follicles. Administration of hCG places them at risk for severe ovarian hyperstimulation syndrome. These high responders tend to have fewer implanted embryos and reduced pregnancy rates.

The Cornell IVF team has developed a successful approach to controlled ovarian hyperstimulation of high responders. The protocol consists of oral contraceptive pretreatment before administration of GnRH agonists in a long protocol in combination with low-dose gonadotropins. This protocol normalizes the LH/FSH ratio and lowers ovarian androgens in PCOD patients. It appears to be useful for both PCOD patients and non-PCOD patients who are high responders.

The Male Factor

For four years, Diane and John tried to have a baby with no success, even after a dozen attempts at intrauterine insemination. A loan officer in a bank, John, age forty-eight, had a borderline low sperm count, low sperm motility, and poor sperm morphology. When an IVF clinic opened near their home, their fertility specialist suggested they give it a try.

"Our first attempt, with all the injections I had to give her every night, brought us closer together," John says. Four of Diane's healthy eggs were fertilized and transferred, but the attempt failed. They decided to try again. "This time we knew the routine, but we were both feeling bad since we didn't expect to have to go through the procedure twice," he says. That attempt also failed. John and Diane, a thirty-eight-year-old school counselor, took some time off and came back for another attempt three months later.

This time the test showed that Diane was pregnant. "We were scared because we thought it might be a false positive pregnancy test," she says. Then they had an ultrasound exam. "We actually saw a tiny, beating heart. It was a beautiful moment, so exciting to see the fruits of our labor," John says. Their daughter, Doreen, is now six years old.

Intracytoplasmic Sperm Injection (ICSI)

One of the true wonders of today's infertility treatments is the way sperm and eggs can be handled with very fine tools called micromanipulators.

The most exciting new development that has revolutionized male factor infertility treatment is the direct injection of a single sperm, called intracytoplasmic sperm injection (ICSI). The doctor holds the egg on the end of a micromanipulator while placing a single sperm on the tip of an extremely thin needle. It takes a steady hand and a powerful microscope to inject the sperm successfully through the zona into the egg.

Direct sperm injection seems to work no matter how low the sperm count, no matter what their shape, and no matter how slowly the sperm move. At Cornell, researchers have selected the only sperm found in an entire testicle and achieved a pregnancy.

Based on work originally done in Belgium, the method has resulted in thousands of pregnancies and births. About 75 percent of eggs are successfully fertilized. For women age thirty-five or under, the pregnancy rates are about 50 percent, and about 40 percent deliver live, healthy babies. By the age of forty, the pregnancy rates have dropped to 40 percent and the live delivery rate to 25 percent at the best centers. Currently, IVF with ICSI is indicated for all cases where male factor infertility is suspected and for women over age forty to minimize the risks of failed fertilization. The number of birth defects among their children has been no greater than that of the general population.

In the future, IVF with ICSI may be preferred for all fertility treatments. However, handling the micromanipulation equipment can be difficult, and ICSI requires considerable training to master the procedure. It also adds about $2,000 to $3,000 to the cost of an in vitro fertilization procedure.

All of these advanced fertility treatments are being evaluated to help infertile couples with the most severe and persistent problems achieve a pregnancy. While some of these treatments are in the experimental stage, the basic technique of in vitro fertilization has become an accepted clinical procedure throughout the world and may be a viable option when conventional treatments fail.

IVF with ICSI offers new hope to couples with severe male factor infertility. With new techniques to insert sperm directly into an egg, a man who has just a few viable sperm recovered from appropriate separation techniques can achieve a pregnancy through IVF with ICSI.

Besides a semen analysis, the IVF clinic should also check the man and his wife for sperm antibodies, which reduce the chances of fertilization of both normal and oligospermic men. Many centers now routinely culture the semen to detect bacteria, since infected semen samples have been associated with reduced clinical pregnancy rates (although not reduced fertilization rates) in IVF.

Sperm from men with male factor infertility can have difficulty both in getting the sperm to the egg and in penetrating the egg. Once the eggs become fertilized in the IVF lab by ICSI, however, these couples with a male factor problem have pregnancy rates equal to infertile couples with no male factor problem. In other words, once a sperm fertilizes the egg, its mission has been accomplished and the outcome of pregnancy is just as good as for eggs fertilized by sperm from men with no known male factor problem.

ICSI is the biggest breakthrough in the treatment of male factor infertility since the development of IVF. The success rates for direct sperm injection are comparable to or even better than those for non–male factor patients. It has become the treatment of choice for otherwise untreatable male factor infertility. However, it can take several years for IVF teams to become proficient in the technique.

Assisted Hatching

Another micromanipulation technique known as assisted hatching can help an embryo implant. Normally, the embryo sheds its outer layer about one week after fertilization so that it can attach to the uterus. Some older women have problems with this embryo "hatching," so embryologists may cut a small hole in the embryo's outer layer just before transfer, which is called assisted hatching.

The embryo transfer after assisted hatching occurs a day or two later than a traditional IVF cycle. The clinic performing the procedure must have a good laboratory since embryos spend more time there. In addition, if an embryo has too large a gap in the outer layer, it can fall out during transfer. So assisted hatching requires a high degree of skill and a very high-quality laboratory.

More than one hundred American IVF programs use this procedure, and thousands of babies have been born after assisted hatching. Assisted hatching is generally reserved for the most difficult cases, and has an implantation rate of about 20 percent per embryo.

Sperm Aspiration

Sometimes perfectly healthy sperm get stranded inside the epididymis. Scar tissue from sterilization or cancer surgery can block the vas deferens, or the vas may simply have been missing from birth. For the 100,000 couples facing this problem, sperm aspiration may help.

For this technique, the doctor, using an operating microscope, sucks sperm from the epididymis through an incision in the scrotum. The procedure is performed under local, regional, or light general anesthesia, and the man can go home the same day. After sperm have been microsurgically removed, they are placed in a nutrient solution that mimics those found in the fallopian tubes. This fluid helps sperm mature and develop good motility. Once prepared, the sperm are divided into a dozen or more tiny vials and frozen for future use with IVF with ICSI. At Cornell, using this technique, called microsurgical epididymal sperm aspiration (MESA), almost 100 million sperm are collected, and the pregnancy rate using frozen sperm for future ICSI is 63 percent.

Sperm can also be removed from the epididymis in the doctor's office with a needle, but far fewer sperm are obtained this way, and the pregnancy rates are significantly lower, about 30 percent. This is called percutaneous epididymal sperm aspiration (PESA). This technique might be used at centers that do not have reproductive urologists with microsurgical training.

MESA and PESA can only be used in men with normal sperm production inside the testicles, but who have blocked ducts that can not be fixed, which is known as obstructive azoospermia. For men who have blockages, some centers aspirate sperm directly from the testicle for IVF with ICSI. This technique, called testicular sperm aspiration (TESA), is often used during a sperm retrieval in men who are unable to give a specimen on the day of IVF, or on men who have unexpectedly developed a blockage before the IVF attempt. In another scenario, a man's sperm, frozen before undergoing vasectomy, may show only dead sperm when thawed. In each of these cases, with TESA, enough sperm can be obtained to salvage what would have been a canceled IVF cycle. Since testicular sperm have not had a chance to mature, pregnancy rates are lower, about 25 percent.

Testicular Extraction

For men with a zero sperm count and no blockages (non-obstructive azoospermia), a few sperm can be found hiding in the testicles of half of these men. Using an operating microscope with high power, a reproductive surgeon can access the four hundred U-shape tubules in each testicle that carry sperm and take out a tiny pea- to small-grape-size piece of tissue from the testicle with a needle. Operating under the microscope allows the surgeon to avoid blood vessels on the surface of the testicle; in this way the surgeon avoids injury, takes the least amount of tissue, and can choose the thicker tubules that are more likely to contain sperm.

The technique, known as testicular sperm extraction, can be used as backup to retrieve sperm if problems occur during an IVF procedure. At Cornell, a laboratory technician with a microscope immediately searches the testicular tissue for sperm so that the IVF team does not have to wait long for the results.

About 50 percent of all IVF procedures at Cornell involve male factor infertility, and about 25 percent of them now use TESE. So about 10 percent, or 120, of the 1,200 IVF cycles per year at Cornell involve TESE. If the woman is under age forty, the overall pregnancy rate at Cornell is 50 percent for regular IVF and 25 percent for IVF with TESE because sperm are located in only half of all men. However, if sperm is obtained through the TESE procedure, then the couple's chance of pregnancy is again 50 percent. But because of higher miscarriage rates, the live delivery rate is 39 percent.

Using this technique, the Cornell IVF team achieved the first live births from men with Klinefelter's syndrome (who have an extra X chromosome) with a combination of ICSI and TESE. Couples should know that if a man has a genetic defect, such as a microdeletion of the Y chromosome, then he will pass the defect along to any male children he has.

Competition

In their third IVF attempt, Marilyn and Edward had only one two-cell embryo that degenerated, and they never got to the embryo transfer stage. "We had gone to a big place that sent couples through like herds of cattle," Marilyn says.

"They tried to tell us what was 'best' for us without stopping to understand our needs. They kept saying my eggs would never be fertilized with Edward's sperm, and that donor insemination was for us. But I told them that donor sperm was difficult for me to accept. I'm adopted, I don't know who my father was, and I didn't want my baby not to know who his or her father was. They didn't bother to listen. I was so frustrated, that evening I went home and smashed several boxes of light bulbs, one at a time, in our backyard. It was very therapeutic."

As IVF has become one of the fastest-growing areas of infertility treatment, it has also become ripe for exploitation. Couples desperate for a baby may be lured by IVF clinics promising results they can't achieve.

Entrepreneurs are cashing in on a surging fertility industry, and the most controversial aspect of this commercialization of conception is IVF, which by some estimates is itself a $100 million industry.

Of the more than four hundred U.S. and Canadian IVF clinics, about one third are at university centers and the rest have private funding or are associated with for-profit hospitals. The bulk of IVF births comes from a small number of large programs. Those infertile couples who have gone through IVF treatment have found that IVF can cost them tens of thousands of dollars or more, with no money-back guarantees and stiff odds against success. Unfortunately, after all the expenses, heartache, poking, and prodding, most couples go home childless.

Doctors at the larger centers say that a high volume of patients is necessary to establish a track record, to perfect techniques, to maintain a level of competency, and to support the necessary staff specialists. They claim that a commitment of at least two years and an expenditure of $1 million is necessary for a new program to establish itself, and that physicians who dabble in IVF won't have comparable results if they don't make similar investments. But large programs aren't trouble-free. Some couples at large clinics feel as if they are being put through an assembly line.

It's difficult to pinpoint the right balance. If a clinic performs too many cycles, it may be impersonal. Too few cycles, and the clinic staff may not have the experience to give couples the best chances of having a baby.

As the number of IVF clinics has grown, so has the professional and public pressure to regulate them. Exaggerated estimates of success have led doctors, insurance companies, members of Congress, and infertile couples to push for stronger regulation.

The American Society of Reproductive Medicine has an IVF registry about individual IVF clinics and their success rates. A couple can check with the ASRM to see the registry. Membership in the Society for Assisted Reproductive Technology (SART) is restricted to IVF programs that can account for at least forty patients and three live births and that adhere to strict quality control and proficiency testing. Many of these centers are listed in the directory of fertility specialists at the end of this book.

Scientists have also been urging the federal government to take a more active role in IVF research to improve a couple's odds. The government now has lifted a moratorium on federal funding for any research involving human embryos or fetuses, which allows federal funding for IVF research. The National Advisory Board for Ethics and Reproduction reviews proposals for reproductive research.

The federal government now requires all IVF programs to report their pregnancy rates and live birth rates to the Centers for Disease Control. These results are available by phoning the CDC at 1-800-311-3435 or through the Internet at www.cdc.gov/nccdphp/drh/arts/.

IVF "Cousins"

Once considered a last-chance technology, IVF has spawned the development of other procedures that use variations of the same assisted reproductive techniques. These technologies offer couples the advantages of the years of experience that went into making IVF a viable infertility treatment. They carry IVF technology along to the next logical step in an attempt to help more infertile couples have babies.

Gamete Intrafallopian Transfer (GIFT)

In addition to IVF as a treatment, many IVF clinics offer another approach to fertilization, called gamete (for egg and sperm) intrafallopian (within the fallopian tube) transfer (GIFT). This combines eggs with sperm and then places the egg/sperm combination directly into the fallopian tubes, where, it is hoped, conception will occur naturally.

The GIFT procedure requires a woman to have at least one normal fallopian tube. The ovulation induction and monitoring procedures for GIFT are basically the same as for IVF. After the surgeon retrieves the eggs, the embryologist draws up small amounts of sperm for each egg and places eggs and sperm into each fallopian tube. If the sperm fertilize the egg, it happens as it would naturally—inside the fallopian tube rather than in an incubator outside the body, as in IVF.

Except for women with two damaged fallopian tubes, candidates for IVF are also candidates for GIFT, which in some centers has a higher pregnancy rate (25 to 35 percent) than IVF. It is most suitable for couples with unexplained infertility, cervical or male factor problems, mild endometriosis, or luteinized unruptured follicle syndrome. GIFT also seems to offer women over forty a better chance at live birth than IVF.

GIFT has some disadvantages when compared to IVF. At present, GIFT usually requires laparoscopy to transfer the eggs and sperm into the fallopian tubes, making it a more major procedure than an IVF embryo transfer through the vagina and cervix into the uterus. Newer developments have led to successful GIFT procedures by placing gametes in the fallopian tube through a tiny catheter threaded through the cervix and uterus. But this technique is more difficult to perform successfully than direct visualization through a laparoscope. More important, if the GIFT procedure fails, there is no way of knowing whether the woman's eggs were fertilized, which is readily apparent with IVF.

ZIFT

Because of the lack of knowledge about fertilization from GIFT, some couples with a male factor problem may be treated with zygote intrafallopian transfer (ZIFT), also known as pronucleus transfer. The wife's eggs, retrieved with ultrasound guidance, are exposed to her husband's sperm in the lab. Within twenty-four hours, the fertilized egg (known as a zygote) is transferred to her fallopian tube, usually by laparoscopy.

ZIFT has an advantage over a GIFT procedure, particularly for male factor couples, because the embryologist will know whether the wife's eggs have been fertilized by her husband's sperm. If his sperm don't fertilize her eggs, then the couple may decide at that point to accept donor insemination rather than pursue further efforts to achieve a pregnancy with the husband's sperm.

At Cornell, the pregnancy rate for standard IVF is higher than GIFT or ZIFT pregnancy rates at other centers, so Cornell does not do either of these procedures. At Chapel Hill Fertility Center, GIFT and IVF are combined to allow evaluation of fertilization in the lab, with a 43 percent pregnancy rate.

Endometrial Cell Co-culture

Another technique that takes advantage of the body's own environment is endometrial cell co-culture. Before doing the IVF procedure, a woman's uterine lining (endometrium) is biopsied. The endometrial cells removed are grown in a culture disk. Then, at the time of IVF, the fertilized eggs are placed in the dish of growing endometrial cells to allow them to develop into healthier embryos or blastocysts. This technique has been used for couples who have had consistently poor quality embryos using conventional IVF or for women who repeatedly have embryos that fail to implant into the uterus. The indications are for slow-growing embryos, fragmented embryos, and embryos with an exceptionally thick coating around them.

With the advent of endometrial cell co-culture, the indications for assisted hatching are limited. At Cornell, the pregnancy rates with endometrial cell co-culture approach those with conventional IVF. This experimental technique is used by only a few centers, and promising early results may take years to substantiate.

Ultrasound GIFT

To avoid the surgery involved in GIFT, some clinics perform the procedure entirely with ultrasound guidance, both for egg retrieval and tubal transfer of the eggs and sperm. This new technique, first reported from Australia, is gaining popularity in North America.

As IVF techniques become more refined, researchers are learning more and more about the miracles of conception. By sampling the fluids and protein substances found inside the fallopian tube, they are getting a better understanding of the tube's normal environment.

If what's happening inside the fallopian tube and the conditions leading to successful implantation can be better understood, then more couples will have babies through IVF and related treatments. At the best IVF clinics, researchers can do even better than the 20 to 25 percent natural

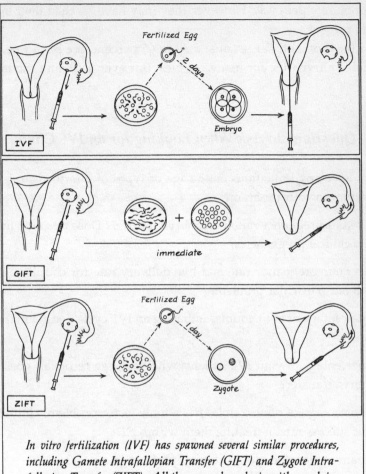

In vitro fertilization (IVF) has spawned several similar procedures, including Gamete Intrafallopian Transfer (GIFT) and Zygote Intrafallopian Transfer (ZIFT). All three procedures begin with eggs being retrieved from the woman's follicles. In IVF, the eggs are mixed with sperm in a culture dish in the lab, and two days later the doctor transfers the growing embryo into the woman's uterus. For GIFT, eggs are combined with sperm and immediately placed in the woman's fallopian tubes, where sperm fertilize the eggs. ZIFT is a combination of IVF and GIFT: the sperm and egg are mixed in a culture dish, and one day later the doctor places the developing zygote into the fallopian tube.

conception rate per cycle. However, they may have reached their limit at 30 to 40 percent.

For the moment, IVF, even at a 30 to 45 percent live birth rate, is an acceptable alternative for many couples. But even IVF isn't the last resort.

Questions to Ask When Looking for an IVF Clinic

Do you have any limitations on the age or types of infertile couples you accept into your program?

What is your pregnancy ratio per embryo transfer? Does this ratio include only clinical pregnancies?

What is your pregnancy rate and live-delivery rate for couples our age with our particular problem?

What percentage of your couples initiating an IVF cycle doesn't make it to transfer?

What percentage of your IVF patients who have egg retrievals goes on to embryo transfer?

What percentage of your couples has a male factor problem, and what is your success rate in treating them with ICSI?

How many cycles does your program perform in a year?

How much does the procedure cost, including hormone treatments? (Costs generally range from about $10,000 to $15,000, including the drugs.)

Do you freeze embryos and blastocysts?

What happens to frozen embryos and blastocysts after we achieve a pregnancy?

Do you have an egg donation program?

Do you do intracytoplasmic sperm injection (ICSI)? How many have you done? What is your pregnancy rate and live-delivery rate?

What is your live birth rate among all couples who have started an IVF cycle in your program?

Is your clinic a member of the Society of Assisted Reproductive Technologies (SART)? Have your results been reported to the Centers for Disease Control?

Are your andrologist and embryologist certified?

Part Three

ALTERNATIVES

11

DONATING
SPERM, EGGS,
EMBRYOS

When you have struggled through fertility treatments, possibly even in vitro fertilization or other assisted reproductive technologies, and still have not had a baby, you may become increasingly frustrated and desperate. By this time, you have to come to grips with the idea that you may never have a child together.

But that doesn't mean that one or the other partner can't contribute to the birth of a baby that carries his or her genes by donating sperm, eggs, or embryos.

Donor Insemination

If a thorough physical evaluation reveals that a man has an untreatable fertility problem and that his wife has no known fertility problems, then the couple should consider donor insemination. It currently is far and away the most popular and successful method for treating severe male factor problems. More than thirty thousand babies are conceived by donor insemination each year in the United States.

In most cases, donor insemination simply involves placing donor sperm in the wife's cervical mucus at the fertile time of her cycle. If the wife also has fertility problems, more advanced insemination methods may be necessary. If her cervical mucus is hostile to the donor sperm, the donor sperm can be processed and placed inside a narrow catheter and safely inserted through the cervical canal into the uterus (IUI) or fallopian tubes (ITI) at the time of ovulation. Donor sperm can also replace or be used in addition to the husband's sperm in any of the assisted reproductive technologies, including IVF or its "cousins."

Finding a Donor

If you are considering donor insemination, your fertility specialist can help you select a suitable anonymous donor. The donor should be carefully screened and selected to resemble the husband as closely as possible, including his age, education, race, height and weight, hair and eye color, blood group and type, occupation, religion, and nationality.

Because of the widespread availability of frozen donor sperm from a number of sperm banks throughout the country, a suitable donor match for most men can almost always be found. At some fertility centers, couples can examine lists of donor characteristics and themselves make the selection of the sperm donor.

When a doctor orders donor sperm from a sperm bank, he requests that the donor have particular characteristics. Often the characteristics of several donors closely resemble those of the husband. Your doctor should give you information about the available donors so that you can select the most appropriate one. The donor's identification by a code number will be kept as a part of your permanent record.

In the recent past, many practitioners of donor insemination did little to protect couples from genetic disorders and infectious diseases, such as acquired immune deficiency syndrome (AIDS), that might be passed through donor semen. Now sperm banks that provide donor sperm routinely test donors for antibodies to the AIDS virus or for infections with syphilis, gonorrhea, hepatitis, and chlamydia. Still, don't take it for granted that these safeguards are being used without asking for, and obtaining, written information about the screening of potential donors.

How Good Are the Sperm?

Rhonda, age thirty-seven, and Owen, age thirty-eight, chose their frozen semen from a large national sperm bank. Their first attempt at donor insemination failed because Rhonda's cervical mucus was hostile to the donor's sperm, killing off most of them very rapidly. The doctor suggested they try an intrauterine insemination the next month. The day following her urine LH surge, Rhonda came in for an IUI. But upon thawing, the donor sperm showed a very low motile sperm count, "so low that the doctor didn't want to use that sperm sample. But I felt close to the donor. He sounded so much like Owen," says Rhonda. The frozen donor sperm were washed and inseminated into her uterus.

You should ask your doctor whether the donated sperm came from a commercial sperm bank that is a member of the American Association of Tissue Banks, which has set standards for screening donors. If possible, try to find out the sperm bank's success rate. This is often hard to obtain, since many sperm banks often don't collect information from their physician-clients regarding the number of pregnancies achieved. Ask the doctor how many pregnancies he has had from this bank and how successful donor insemination has been, in his experience, for couples with similar fertility problems.

You should know how many rapid, forwardly progressing motile sperm with normal morphology are contained in the donor samples *after* they are thawed and used in the insemination. The success of donor insemination correlates with the number of normally shaped, motile sperm inseminated. A quality sperm bank will provide straws or vials containing at least 20 million motile sperm or more per ml. The andrologist should check the sperm count, the rapidly progressive forward motility, and sperm morphology upon thawing the sample and preparing it for insemination.

It is important that the couple not only select their own anonymous donor but choose from sperm banks that have the highest quality control. Dr. Fernando Rodriguez at the Chapel Hill Fertility Center has studied donor sperm samples provided by various nationally known sperm banks and found that semen quality varies greatly from what sperm banks claim, and that some provide better specimens than others.

The couple should be actively involved in the process. To be sure about the quality of the donor sperm and the lab that prepares them for your doctor to inseminate, you should ask to see the analysis results on the sperm after they have been thawed and prepared for your insemination. You should also know the unique identification code for the donor sample you have selected to ensure that you are being inseminated with the donor sperm you selected.

The Medical Aspects of Donor Insemination

"At our second attempt, Owen and I were both really excited," Rhonda says. "The ultrasound exam showed that I had four follicles. Everything felt right." An IUI was performed on the day of the LH surge. The following day, Rhonda came back for an insemination of more sperm into her uterus and, after lying on her back with her hips elevated for about forty-five minutes, she and Owen went home. Four days after the inseminations, she felt sick to her stomach, and "I knew I was pregnant," Rhonda says. A few days later, Owen suggested she take a home pregnancy test, which was positive. She went to the doctor's office the next day, and he confirmed the pregnancy by checking her blood hormone levels. A week later, a vaginal ultrasound examination showed that her pregnancy was developing normally. She and Owen plan to name their baby girl Terri.

If you have chosen donor insemination to overcome a male factor problem, your chances for a pregnancy will correlate with the number of fertility problems the wife has. Women who have two healthy fallopian tubes, no endometriosis, need no medication to stimulate ovulatory cycles, and are under age thirty-five have an 80 percent chance of pregnancy success with donor insemination of frozen sperm after six cycles. Women with ovulation problems during donor insemination cycles may take longer to conceive. If a woman hasn't conceived within four to six well-timed donor insemination cycles, she should consider another donor and further fertility evaluation of herself.

Detection of the luteinizing hormone surge leads to the best timing for insemination. Most doctors inseminate sperm either once or twice each cycle near the expected time of ovulation.

Before Dr. Berger performs donor insemination, the woman undergoes basic screening blood tests and Dr. Berger obtains cervical cultures to check for infection or bacteria in the wife's reproductive tract. (If she does not have immunity to rubella, she is offered a vaccination and waits three months to develop immunity before proceeding with insemination.) Some couples prefer donor insemination without any further fertility evaluation; others will have a hysterosalpingogram and ovulation monitoring to check that the wife has open tubes and normal hormone levels and follicle development.

The donated sperm can cost the couple from $125 to $250 per sample.

Most insurance companies will not reimburse for donated sperm. They maintain that this isn't a treatment for an infertile man.

Frozen Semen

Since the ever-growing epidemic of AIDS, virtually all couples undergoing donor insemination use frozen semen. (Donor insemination has also been called artificial insemination by donor, or AID, in the past. To avoid confusion with the disease AIDS, most fertility specialists now use the terms "therapeutic donor insemination" or "donor insemination" instead.) Before being used, frozen donor semen should be quarantined for at least six months to ensure that the donor hasn't developed antibodies to the AIDS virus during that time.

To prevent the possible transmission of the AIDS virus (as well as other infectious conditions such as gonorrhea, chlamydia, and hepatitis) through donated semen, the American Society for Reproductive Medicine, the Food and Drug Administration, and the Centers for Disease Control collaborated on guidelines for donor insemination. The guidelines call for a potential donor to be interviewed to determine whether he has a history of risk factors for infection with the AIDS virus; to have a physical exam to document any obvious signs of AIDS infection; and to have a blood test for infection with the AIDS virus or the development of antibodies to the virus—both when he donates semen and six months later before the frozen semen is released for use.

Frozen semen can be shipped anywhere, be stored in a liquid nitrogen tank, and be immediately available at the fertile time of the woman's cycle. Freezing and thawing a semen sample reduces the number of rapidly motile sperm. Taking into account lower numbers of functionally normal sperm, some fertility specialists perform IUI with thawed frozen semen. Dr. Berger performs an intracervical insemination on the day of the wife's LH surge, if she has fertile mucus that day. The following day, he can also perform an IUI with a second thawed sample, which has been processed and concentrated into a small volume. He has found that more women become pregnant with both inseminations in a single cycle than with either insemination alone.

Tracking Down a Donor's Identity

Typically, your doctor receives a code number for the donor semen from the sperm bank. The sperm bank usually has no information about you. At least two sperm banks that have held so-called extraordinary sperm from intellectually or athletically outstanding donors screened the couple, but in a manner that still kept the identities of the sperm donor and the couple from each other.

Most doctors who keep records that could lead to identification of the donor will not release this information, unless the couple or a court order instructs them to do so. This may be necessary if, for example, the child needs to know about his or her chances of having a hereditary disease.

Emotional Factors

"The most difficult thing for me was the way I was informed that I had a low sperm count," recalls Phil, a forty-four-year-old government employee who lives in New York. "One of the urologist's staff came out to the waiting room and, in front of everyone there, said, 'You have practically no sperm.' That attacked my foundations as a man." Once Phil and his wife, Ann, a thirty-eight-year-old tennis pro, decided to try donor insemination, Phil says, "I didn't feel so humiliated as when I first got the semen analysis results. Once the decision was made, it felt okay."

Even though his family's blood line faced extinction, Phil had no problem accepting donor insemination. "It all depends on how crucial it is to have a genetic link to the future," he says. "Neither my sister nor I could have our own biological children, but I felt that a child was a child."

Over a three-year period, Phil and Ann tried donor inseminations, with all the ups and downs of starting a new cycle of treatment over and over again. During that time, they took a break for six months while Ann took medication for endometriosis. Then their fertility specialist found that she had sperm antibodies in her mucus, and Phil began wearing condoms during sex. Meanwhile, they tried more donor inseminations without success. When they finally concluded that donor insemination would not work for them, they decided to stop trying to have a baby.

Donor insemination is readily accepted by many couples, but it can be stressful for them. How you may feel depends on you and your spouse's personalities, attitudes, values, and upbringing. Studies of couples who attempt donor insemination have found them to be as well adjusted psychologically and sexually as "normal" fertile couples, whether they achieve a pregnancy or not. Most couples who have gone through donor insemination say that they are satisfied with their marriages and that the procedure even helped bring them closer together. Yet for some couples the experience of uncorrected infertility adds such a strain to the relationship that their marriage may not survive.

Being conceived through donor insemination doesn't appear to affect the child's emotional development. The children conceived through donor insemination most often are well adjusted, do well in school, and don't seem to have identity crises. More and more, children born through donor insemination are requesting information about the donor when they become adults. Although revealing a donor's identity was once thought to be undesirable, more couples now believe that it is healthy for a grown child to want information about the donor. However, most couples do not tell others, including their own family or their children, about the use of donated sperm.

Social and Ethical Issues

Donor insemination raises many complex issues for the couple. You may wonder whether the decision to let friends and family know may someday cause your child to ask about his or her biological father. You also have to consider insensitive things family and friends might say to you and the child. Essentially, you have to address the question, "If we let people know now, are we likely to regret it later?"

Your decision to use donor insemination carries implications that reach far into the future. Some other questions you must consider: What if our child is born with a birth defect? Will we regret our decision? Can our marriage stand the strain?

There are no pat answers to such questions. Certainly, there are no answers applicable to everyone. Each couple must be able to explore these questions freely with each other and answer them as best they can. If you are having difficulty, a professional counselor at or outside the fertility clinic may be able to help.

Some people compare children born through donor insemination to children who were adopted. But the experience a couple goes through in conceiving a child, and the actual nine months of pregnancy with donor insemination offspring, is quite different from that of an adoptive couple, who don't experience the process of pregnancy. And a child conceived through donor insemination is legally the natural child of the woman who gives birth and her legal husband. This is not at all like adopting a child.

Legal Issues

If you choose donor insemination, clearly, you want the maximum protection under the law for you and your child. Yet only a few states require that donors be screened for disease, and many states have no laws at all regulating donor insemination.

The legal issue of paternity is firmly established. Most states have laws covering paternity with donor insemination and provide that the offspring is the legal child of the birth mother and her husband. Many laws specifically state that a man who provides his semen to a doctor for use in donor insemination isn't the child's legal father. In all states, the husband of the woman who delivers the child is presumed to be the child's legal father. This legally makes donor insemination a much more straightforward procedure than surrogate motherhood or adoption.

Egg Donation

Egg donation, analogous to sperm donation, is the process by which the doctor uses the husband's sperm to fertilize eggs donated by a woman other than his wife—usually through an assisted reproduction technique, such as IVF or one of its "cousins." In the case of IVF, the doctor transfers the fertilized egg (pre-embryo) into the wife's uterus, which has been primed with hormones to allow them to implant successfully.

This technique is particularly useful for women who don't produce eggs, such as after premature menopause, or women who have had their ovaries removed or have had radiation therapy for cancer that destroyed their ovarian function. It also has become an alternative for women who want to avoid passing along a genetically defective trait in the wife's family, such as hemophilia. Recently, women in their forties and even fifties who have gone through menopause have conceived using donated eggs.

More than 150,000 women in the United States can't bear children because of premature ovarian failure. Premature menopause has become more of a problem in recent years with many women deferring pregnancy until their thirties. In some cases, women with premature menopause can be treated hormonally and ovulate again. For those who don't ovulate, even after hormone treatments, fertility specialists can now offer the egg donation alternative.

Donor egg programs, once on the outer edge of infertility research, are growing in popularity and availability. About one hundred U.S. clinics have a pool of potential egg donors from healthy young women age eighteen to thirty-five who have no known genetic or sexually transmitted diseases and have normal menstrual cycles, enabling doctors to match the physical characteristics of recipients with those of carefully selected donors.

The donor eggs can be retrieved by laparoscopy or, more commonly, by using a transvaginal ultrasound guided approach. While the egg donors take superovulatory hormones for seven to ten days to increase their egg production, the recipient also receives hormones—first to synchronize her cycle with that of the donor and then to prepare her uterus for pregnancy. These hormones include estrogen, which can be taken orally or administered in patches that attach to the skin, and progesterone administered by pills, vaginal suppositories, or injections.

Fertilization of the donor eggs with the husband's sperm usually takes place in the IVF lab. As with IVF, several fertilized eggs may be transferred to increase the couple's chances of pregnancy.

Donor eggs can also be fertilized in the recipient woman's fallopian tubes via gamete intrafallopian transfer (GIFT). Also, fertilized eggs or zygotes have been transferred to a recipient's fallopian tubes, known as zygote intrafallopian transfer (ZIFT).

More than one thousand babies have been born in the U.S. through egg donation, the majority of eggs coming from anonymous donors. The live birth rate is 30 to 40 percent for women. About 30 percent up to age 37, and about 20 to 30 percent up to age 40. It then falls dramatically. About 30 percent have multiple pregnancies, a contingency that the contract should provide for. Even women in their fifties are conceiving through egg donation. Their pregnancy rates and safe deliveries rival those of women in their thirties. In fact, some fertility experts recommend egg donation as a first-line treatment for a woman who is over age forty-three and wants to bear a child. Among women older than 46, more than 70 percent of assisted reproductive technology cycles now use donor eggs.

Finding Egg Donors

The usual sources of donated eggs have included women undergoing an IVF or GIFT procedure who have an overabundance of eggs, the wife's sister, other relatives, or a woman having a tubal ligation. For older women, the eggs may come from their daughters from a previous marriage.

Some egg donation programs accommodate only recipients who provide their own donors. Others rely on women who are having tubal ligations—during which eggs can be retrieved without additional surgery. Most egg donation programs offer donors $2,500 and up for their time and inconvenience, which usually includes undergoing psychological screening, blood tests, and ultrasound exams, as well as superovulation and egg retrieval.

Embryo freezing allows the doctor to synchronize the donor and recipient cycles more easily. If the recipient's uterus isn't ready to receive the fertilized eggs, the donated eggs can be fertilized and then frozen and transferred at a more appropriate time. The extra eggs retrieved from IVF and GIFT cycles are now often fertilized and the embryos frozen for later use by the infertile couple, who may decide, after they have had their own successful treatment, to donate their embryos to another infertile couple.

In this era of new reproductive technology, if you are seeking an egg donor, you should know your state laws. Some states forbid payment for eggs or pre-embryos recovered through IVF. Others specifically forbid freezing pre-embryos even if it is for clinical treatment and not for research purposes.

Emotional Issues

Most egg donation programs accept only married couples in good mental and physical health who have a stable marriage. You may undergo a psychological evaluation that usually includes a screening interview and psychological testing. If you provide your own donor, then the psychological evaluation looks at the possible effects on a child who grows up in a family where a relative or a friend is the child's genetic mother.

Like sperm donation, egg donation from an anonymous donor offers you the possibility of concealing the fact of the egg donation from friends and relatives as well as the child. You should openly discuss with each other your feelings about what to tell others before undertaking egg donation, and then stick to your decision, revealing as much information as you wish in whatever way suits you best.

The Couple's Concerns

If you are seeking an egg donor, you probably have a long history of infertility and have tried a wide range of fertility treatments. You may choose egg donation over adoption or surrogate motherhood to give the wife the opportunity to become pregnant and deliver the baby.

There are no uniform standards for screening egg donors. Just as with sperm donors, you should be informed about various characteristics of the donor to determine how closely she matches the wife's characteristics, that she is in good health and has no known family history of genetically transmitted diseases. You may ask a donor for an AIDS antibody test before allowing her eggs to be fertilized with the husband's sperm. You should also consider whether you agree as a couple about egg donation and have the personal and financial resources to cope with the stresses of the treatment.

If you receive eggs from a known donor, you should have a consent form signed by the donor stipulating that she may never pursue any legal action seeking access to any child resulting from the egg donation. If the egg donor is anonymous, as with sperm donation, neither the donor nor the recipient knows the other's identity. This probably provides the best protection for the child against the possibility of a custody dispute later on.

Egg Donors and Their Concerns

Egg donors, often recruited through announcements in the media and on line, generally are younger, less affluent, and less well educated than egg recipients. They may volunteer to donate eggs to help another couple have a child. Some egg donors also use the experience as a way of dealing with their own unresolved fertility issues; they previously may have had an induced abortion, which also is a reason why some women volunteer to become surrogate mothers.

The primary concern of most potential donors is whether you can provide a good home environment for a baby. Donors want assurance that the recipients of their eggs are physically healthy and psychologically well adjusted, that their marriages are stable, and that the husband and wife are committed to being good, supportive parents.

Ethical Principles

Some people fear that compensating egg donors will lead to commercialization, and tempt women to sell their eggs, as is often the case with sperm donors. (Some sperm banks, however, don't pay donors for their samples.) Others, including the Catholic church, contend that egg donation and sperm donation violate the sanctity of marriage by bringing a third party into the conjugal relationship.

A great deal of debate has arisen about third-party collaboration in reproduction. The ethical and legal ramifications become murky when the collaboration breaks down and the donor wants to claim "rights" to the child. There's more confusion regarding egg donation than sperm donation, although the two situations are analogous and future laws probably will specify that an egg donor, like a sperm donor, is not the legal parent of any offspring conceived.

Host Uterus

The availability of a host uterus may enable you to have your own genetic offspring even though the wife may be unable to carry a child to term. Her eggs can be fertilized by her husband's sperm in the IVF laboratory and the embryo transferred into another woman's uterus, where it is carried until birth.

This may provide a solution for women with one or both ovaries but without a uterus, those who can't risk pregnancy because of a health problem, and those with conditions that would put a fetus at severe risk, such as Rh incompatibility with a mother who has high levels of anti-Rh antibodies.

The Host Uterus Contract

At the outset, you sign a contract with a carefully screened woman to be the life-support system for your growing embryo. Since this other woman is carrying the husband's and wife's baby, there is a reduced risk of her refusing to hand the child over to the true biologic parents—one of the dangers of surrogate motherhood. Even though you are the genetic parents, you will likely have to adopt the baby legally from the woman who carries and delivers it. In most states, the woman who gives birth is legally presumed to be the child's mother and, if she is married, her husband is considered the child's legal father.

The "host uterus" gives a woman who has ovaries but is incapable of carrying her own baby a chance to have a child that is genetically her own and her husband's by having another woman carry the pregnancy. This differs from surrogate motherhood, in which the wife is neither the genetic nor the birth mother.

The ethical and legal issues regarding the host uterus are different from those regarding surrogate motherhood, where the woman who is inseminated by the husband's sperm contributes half of the genes to the baby, which she then carries to birth. While the host may form an emotional bond with the baby she has carried for nine months, she is likely to feel less of a loss than a surrogate mother, who has to give up her own genetic baby for adoption to the infertile couple.

Naturally, any woman who carries a baby to term for you is likely to develop a close relationship with the baby. A woman who provides a host uterus, and changes her mind and wants to keep the child, could argue that her contribution was just as vital to the child's development and birth as you and your mate's sperm and egg. The contract between you and the woman providing the host uterus should address this issue. But if either party breaks the contract, you probably will be embroiled in legal confusion.

A woman offering to carry another couple's pregnancy may be placing herself at physical and psychological risk. It's important for you that she receive counseling to ensure that she fully understands the risks and voluntarily consents.

With the uncertain legal situation across the country regarding these new varieties of third-party reproduction, including the host uterus technique, you should think carefully about this type of "frontier" baby and seek professional and legal counseling before entering into a relationship with a woman who is willing to serve as a host uterus or surrogate mother.

About two hundred U.S. centers report using a host uterus program, and they have helped dozens of women to become mothers. Most of the recipients are over age forty, with about 20 percent of them taking home a baby. Overall, including women in their thirties, the live birth rate is almost 30 percent. There is a high risk (37 percent) of multiple births, and contracts should spell out how to handle this situation. The cost is nearly $50,000, including about $20,000 to a lawyer to set up the contract.

Surrogate Motherhood

One of the most controversial areas of the new reproductive technology has been surrogate motherhood. Brokers across the country have established surrogate counseling centers offering infertile couples a "womb for rent." Despite the highly publicized Baby M case, most surrogate motherhood arrangements go smoothly when the parties involved take the proper precautions and have the surrogate mother thoroughly evaluated.

A surrogate mother is inseminated with the sperm of a man whose wife can't conceive or carry a child to term. Once the baby is born, the surrogate allows the biological father and his infertile wife to adopt the baby.

Who Are the Candidates?

Surrogate motherhood is usually reserved for rare circumstances. For some couples, it represents the last hope of having a child who's genetically related to at least one spouse. In particular, surrogate motherhood may be suitable for women who don't produce eggs, whose eggs aren't fertilized by their husband's healthy sperm because of an egg problem, who are afraid of passing on a genetic defect, who have been advised not to get pregnant because of a medical condition, or who have had a hysterectomy.

How to Find a Surrogate

You can explore various avenues to find an appropriate surrogate. One way is to ask family members or friends if they are willing to become a surrogate. Remember the case of the mother who carried a triplet pregnancy conceived via IVF with her daughter's eggs and her son-in-law's sperm. She ended up giving birth to her own grandchildren! Some couples advertise in the newspaper for surrogates; others go to their fertility expert or a lawyer or a center that specializes in finding surrogates.

Surrogate agencies look for physically and psychologically healthy women who would like to serve as a surrogate for an infertile couple. These agencies put the potential surrogate through a battery of psychological and medical tests, match her with a prospective couple, negotiate a contract, acquire informed, legal consent of the surrogate and the infertile couple, and work with the doctors who will perform the insemination.

Who Becomes a Surrogate?

A typical surrogate mother is a woman in her late twenties or early thirties, married with children of her own, who has at least a high school education and a full-time job. These women usually become surrogates because they want to help infertile couples to have a child. Being a surrogate may provide some women with a sense of altruism. Some do it because they had a previous abortion and believe that creating a child for someone else may help them resolve their own feelings. Some may be motivated by financial considerations, since the surrogate may receive as much as $20,000 for her involvement. But most women decide to become surrogates for altruistic reasons.

Meeting the Surrogate

Whether you meet the surrogate depends on your individual choice. Some couples feel that keeping the surrogate anonymous or distant puts them in a better frame of mind to develop a strong relationship with the newborn, with less likelihood of interference by the surrogate. They feel better about communicating with the surrogate only through their doctor, lawyer, or surrogate center. Others want to have frequent contact with the surrogate before, during, and after the pregnancy and birth. If the surrogate is a friend or family member, you already have a very close relationship with her.

You should ascertain whether the potential surrogate can cope with carrying the baby and giving it up. Even if she does have her family's and friends' support, the surrogate should have counseling arranged for her after the baby is born (as well as before she becomes a surrogate and during the pregnancy). Once they have given the baby to the adoptive couple, most surrogates say they feel fulfilled and more satisfied about themselves.

Both the surrogate and the adoptive couple usually say that they perceive the child as the couple's, not the surrogate's. But this isn't always the case, and various disputes have arisen over who should be the legal guardians of the child born through surrogate motherhood.

The Surrogate Motherhood Contract

The rights of the genetic father, his infertile wife, the surrogate, and the surrogate's husband should be agreed upon in writing beforehand.

The clear, detailed surrogacy agreement should specify that the child will become the legitimate, adopted child of the infertile couple, the intended parents. Despite this safeguard, late changes of mind occasionally occur. Some legal experts have suggested that after the child is born, the surrogate should be given a limited grace period, similar to those provided in many adoption laws, in which she can give notice that she has changed her mind. If there is a dispute between the surrogate and the intended parents, then legal proceedings will probably determine who keeps the child. That decision should be guided by the child's best interests.

To provide the contract and find an appropriate surrogate, a lawyer may charge a fee of about $20,000. Add in the fee to the surrogate herself plus about $8,000 in medical costs, and surrogate motherhood ends up costing about $40,000.

Legal Issues

The highly publicized Baby M case set the legal precedent in New Jersey. Other states may follow suit or decide the issue on their own. Most state laws view a woman who bears a child as the mother, and the baby born by a surrogate must be given up willingly by the surrogate mother (and her husband, if she is married) for adoption to the infertile couple, even though the infertile woman's husband is the true biological father.

Other laws that have been applied to surrogate motherhood cases include those concerning artificial insemination, private adoption, family laws, stepparent laws, even antislavery laws. It's now possible for couples to skirt some state laws by choosing a surrogate from a state with a more favorable legal climate.

The legal waters of surrogate motherhood will continue to be murky. Many states in the country are considering legislation to legalize, regulate, or ban surrogate motherhood. Among the pending laws, some states would ban surrogacy altogether, while others would ban only paid surrogacy—allowing unpaid surrogacy, but regulating the practice.

When problems arise, the courts will have to decide on the appropriateness of the various aspects of the surrogacy contract. The competing rights of the biological father (the sperm provider) and the biological mother (the surrogate), their spouses, and the child must be sorted out. Surrogate motherhood court cases have had mixed results, some ruling in favor of the surrogate, others for the biological father and his wife.

Counseling the surrogate mother beforehand may help to avoid subsequent custody disputes. Surrogate screening should provide the surrogate with information about her own health status and the risks of surrogacy. The counseling should ensure that both the surrogate mother and the intended parents know what they are getting into. The directors of surrogate motherhood centers are attempting to develop some standards, including criteria for the screening and testing of couples and surrogates.

Surrogate Publicity

In the United States about one hundred babies are born to surrogate mothers each year. Although the publicity surrounding the Baby M decision has caused some couples to reconsider surrogate motherhood, others still consider it their best option. There was a similar heated reaction—and publicity—years ago about donating sperm. Despite the adverse publicity surrounding surrogate motherhood, infertile couples are still calling surrogacy centers. There is also a growing underground market aimed at infertile couples wishing to hire surrogate mothers.

There remain many questions and issues—legal, ethical, medical, religious—that need clarification. Surrogate motherhood and other reproductive technologies invite doctors, lawyers, and legislators to intrude on the private, intimate experience of conception and birth. Advocates of women's rights have had to confront whether the cost of gaining this fertility option may cause women to lose reproductive control. Some fear that motherhood will be denigrated by separating a woman's genetic and birth functions, and that this may make it more difficult for a woman to retain control over her body.

Many are concerned about the possibility that a poor woman might be coerced into carrying a rich man's child. They think commercial arrangements reduce surrogates to paid baby-carriers. Yet if sperm donors are paid and surrogates aren't, this might be considered another example of women doing more work for less money than men.

Surrogate motherhood is a dramatic example of how medical technology has outrun society's established definitions and laws. We currently have a crazy quilt of state laws concerning who controls decisions about the family, how to deal with surrogates who have second thoughts, and what is best for the children produced by these technologies. New hybrid family relationships, often the last hope of infertile couples, deserve your careful consideration but also require close scrutiny.

Questions to Ask Your Doctor About Artificial Insemination by Donor

How are the potential semen donors screened? (Such screening should include tests for the AIDS virus, hepatitis virus, and other sexually transmitted diseases and genetic disorders.)

What choice of sperm banks do we have? Are the sperm banks members of the American Association of Tissue Banks?

How many normal, rapidly forward motile sperm are available after thawing and sperm processing for the insemination?

What are our chances of a pregnancy, given our fertility problems?

How many attempts do you expect it will take us to achieve a pregnancy?

Do you use frozen or fresh semen? (Accept only frozen semen from a donor that has been tested for the AIDS virus or antibodies to the AIDS virus, with the semen quarantined for at least six months until the donor has been retested.)

How can you assure us that no error can be made in the sample used for insemination?

How much will the donor semen cost us?

Will we be able to track down the identity of the sperm donor if necessary for medical reasons?

What is the medical and genetic history of the donor?

What is the law in our state regarding donor insemination?

Can you provide us with a licensed counselor to talk to?

Questions to Ask Your Doctor About Egg Donation

Can you provide us with donor eggs, or refer us to an IVF program that can?

Can we provide our own egg donor?

How will the donor be screened?

What hormones will I (the wife) have to take, and how will they be administered?

What are our chances of achieving a pregnancy, given our particular fertility problems?

Does our state have any laws prohibiting egg donation?

How much will we have to pay for donor eggs?

Do you have a contract for us to sign with the egg donor?

Can you provide us with a licensed counselor to talk to?

Questions to Ask Your Doctor About Host Uterus or Surrogate Motherhood

Are we candidates for this procedure?

Will you perform this procedure, or refer us to a specialist who will?

How do you recruit potential donors or surrogates? How are they screened?

What is the donor's or surrogate's fee?

What are the laws in our state regarding this procedure?

Do you have a contract for us and the donor or surrogate to sign?

Can you provide us with a licensed counselor to talk to?

12

COPING WITH INFERTILITY, AND ALTERNATIVES TO FURTHER TREATMENT

"I really believed that if I was a good person and took care of myself, didn't abuse drugs, wasn't too fat or too thin, then my body would work the way it was supposed to. I was truly surprised when I didn't get pregnant," says Robin, a twenty-nine-year-old biologist.

Most infertile couples believe that if they understand the causes of their fertility problem, dedicate themselves to treating it, and persevere in their pursuit of pregnancy, they will eventually have a baby. Unfortunately, this isn't always true. Frequently, there are factors beyond your or your fertility doctor's control that determine the outcome of fertility treatments. When things don't work out, your frustrations and fears of not having a child can become intensified.

You will have to cope with the emotional impact of infertility before, during, and after your treatment. If, like most couples treated by a fertility specialist, you are fortunate enough to have a baby, dealing with the emotional crises of infertility may be easier than if you have made heroic efforts but failed to produce a child.

When fertility treatments do not succeed, you have to be able to work through your feelings, and either choose to end fertility treatment and accept life without a child, or pursue other options, such as adoption. At some point, you must be able to resolve the emotional issues involved so that your unfulfilled desire to have your own baby will not remain your life's main focus.

Infertility and Your Emotions

The emotional challenges of infertility change during the different phases of recognition, evaluation, treatment, and resolution of your problem. Many factors may influence your emotional responses, including the causes of your infertility, the types of treatment you have been receiving, how long you have been dealing with infertility, how well you and your spouse cope with the usual stresses of life, and the emotional support you receive from others.

You may feel anxious before and during your initial interview with a fertility specialist and whenever the specialist makes a specific diagnosis of your fertility problem. This is especially true for the partner who may feel guilty or angry about being identified as the source of the problem. If both you and your mate contribute to your fertility problem, as is often the case, then one won't be as quick to take blame for causing the infertility.

Don't be surprised if you feel emotionally unsettled at the beginning of your fertility evaluation. The workup is intrusive both physically and emotionally. During your treatment, you will likely become more accustomed to the rigors of therapy. But if the treatment drags on, you may find your stress level rising as you become increasingly aware of the possibility that your treatment may not be successful.

Losing Control

Pam, age twenty-eight, and her husband Jeff, age thirty-four, went to see a fertility specialist after three years of trying unsuccessfully to have a baby. Her ovulation monitoring showed an ovulation and luteal phase defect, which was treated with hormones. After several months, she and Jeff, who had a low sperm count and poor sperm morphology, also tried artificial insemination, but without success.

Then Pam got a new job for a pharmaceutical company, and they stopped treatment for several months while she was traveling out of town. "It was a great career opportunity, but I had to quit after six months because it was so stressful. Being on the road, visiting doctors' offices full of pregnant women—all this grief that I had been pushing down came up again."

Although she's a go-getter and has worked all of her life, Pam is trying to slow down and not put so much pressure on herself. "When I got to the point where I felt like I was losing control, it scared me. I felt like a lost soul, as if I had died and was just floating." Through counseling, she came to realize that "the worst thing was that I kept saying to myself, 'Be thankful you have a house, your health, a good husband.' I kept belittling my infertility, trying to convince myself that it wasn't as bad as I thought. But it's all right to feel sad. It's normal to feel that way."

One of the most important emotional issues of fertility treatment is loss of control. You may often feel as if you have lost control over your bodies and your lives. You may never before have been confronted with a problem that not only challenges your concept of your own health but also makes you feel dependent on your doctor and the medical care system.

You may sleep, drink, and think infertility all day long, from the minute the wife wakes up to take her basal body temperature until the husband and wife go to bed knowing that "tonight's the night" to make love. The intrusion into your lives of fertility drugs that require repeated ultrasound scans, blood tests, and examinations also puts daily pressure on your relationship.

In addition, infertility can strike at the very core of your identities. Children were supposed to be a part of life's plan. Marriage and family are a universal dream. But the dream may seem more like a nightmare to the infertile couple who hasn't been able to conceive.

Regaining Control

One way you can regain control is to understand and take an active role in your particular fertility problem. You need detailed information about the infertility workup, reasonable treatment options, and your chances of success. Only then can you make well-informed decisions regarding the course of your treatment.

Both partners should think about and discuss the extent to which they want to pursue fertility treatment. How far are you willing to go in achieving a pregnancy, knowing that no treatment is guaranteed to be successful? Would you consider adoption, and if so, how quickly? How do you feel about the prospect of living without your own biologic child, or any child at all?

Once the evaluation begins, the fertility team should provide you with as much information as you need to make these decisions. If you fail to achieve a pregnancy or carry a pregnancy, the doctor and his staff should also help you understand and accept what has happened. This means spending adequate time with you to talk about what you have gone through and its impact, and the doctor making himself available to answer any questions that you may have.

Each time a treatment fails, you may experience a period of mourning, which includes sadness accompanied by grief, anger, and jealousy. After many failed treatment cycles, you may experience numbness and disbelief, often replaced by a period of questioning, as you look for more answers, more treatments. Because of the significant recent advances in infertility treatment, most infertile couples believe that fertility specialists can work wonders. But medical science doesn't have the solution to every fertility problem. Of all couples who experience infertility, about 70 percent will eventually have their own biological child.

Emotions Through Assisted Reproduction

Stuart, a forty-year-old printer, and his computer programmer wife, Jane, thirty-two, are now going for their second IVF attempt to try to compensate for his very low sperm count. "I feel like I'm depriving her of the experience of being pregnant," he says. "We've thought about adoption, but we want to keep trying IVF. We're lucky we don't have to worry about the money.

"Sometimes it's hard to deal with all the emotions. We stopped visiting with old friends who had a child because it was just too painful for us to see them," Stuart says. "It's also hard for us to see people playing with their children in the park, or even just walking with them on the street."

Of all fertility treatments, in vitro fertilization (IVF) and other assisted reproductive techniques tend to be the most intense emotional experiences for husbands and wives. Almost all couples fear these highly involved procedures, not only for what they have to go through, but also because they are afraid that they will fail. They know this may be their last chance to achieve a pregnancy.

Despite the known probability of success, most couples are overly optimistic about the likelihood of achieving a pregnancy via IVF. Although they may intellectually acknowledge that they have less than a 30 percent chance of success with each cycle, most couples undergoing IVF believe that they will be the ones to beat the odds. In some ways, they may need to have these positive beliefs in order to endure the treatment.

If the treatment fails, your immediate reaction may include depression and anger. But most couples can work through these emotions, becoming more optimistic again and ready to try another cycle. IVF patients seem to be the self-selected infertility "survivors." They seem to have the emotional, physical, and financial resources to tolerate the treatment procedures and keep trying.

Following unsuccessful treatment cycles, many wives feel intense anguish. They often feel sad, empty, hopeless. Husbands report similar feelings, although they may not demonstrate them as graphically.

The husband may feel separated from his wife during the treatment process. His wife may be the one most involved in treatment, even if the diagnosis is male factor infertility. He can be more involved by participating in her treatment: giving his wife her hormone injections and going with her for blood tests and ultrasound scans. This enhances his sense of involvement, and he may be better able to explore his feelings if the treatment fails. His presence and support also help his wife get through the treatment process.

Some infertile couples become closer as they prepare for assisted reproduction. They may support and nurture each other through the arduous treatment, sharing what the procedure means to them and what they will do if they fail to conceive. Most IVF teams provide counseling before as well as during an IVF cycle. You should be forewarned about stressful events in the cycle, such as those two weeks after embryo transfer while you wait to hear the results of the pregnancy test.

Your fertility specialist and his or her team usually bring up the possibility of your not having your own child, and should encourage you to think about alternatives. The team may discuss adoption as an option, provide information and contacts at agencies, and help you explore your feelings about not having children at all. Because an assisted reproduction procedure is often the last treatment option, if you fail to achieve a pregnancy the team's counselor may be able to help you accept your loss and talk about your feelings and future options.

Emotions Through a Miscarriage

Abby had had several miscarriages before she saw a fertility doctor, who found that she wasn't ovulating regularly and wasn't producing enough progesterone after ovulation to support a pregnancy. He treated the thirty-three-year-old financial analyst with clomiphene and Pergonal to induce ovulation and supplemental progesterone in the luteal phase of the cycle. "Just when I got to the point when I couldn't take the hormone treatments any more, that's when something came through for me," Abby says. "I ran into a friend who had heard that I had miscarried, and she told me she had been through the same thing last year and now was pregnant. She told me it was a matter of keeping up the treatments. I'm glad I didn't give up."

Women who have miscarried are caught in an emotional gray area between the ongoing frustration of infertility and the pain of losing an unborn child. Many people believe that a miscarriage isn't as important as the death of a newborn or older child. But the death of an unborn child has a similar emotional impact on the couple who experiences the loss. Grieving and mourning are the normal psychological reactions to any loss. If you minimize or deny these emotions, it may be harder for you to come to terms with your experience and eventually resolve your feelings about the miscarriage.

Miscarriage can throw a couple's emotions into turmoil. Individuals typically feel sad, depressed, angry, or even helpless and hopeless. For some, the fear of yet another disaster can turn off the sex drive, while others increase their sexual contact in their desire for another pregnancy.

Recognizing the intense emotional pain an infertile couple goes through after a miscarriage, some doctors have changed their attitudes about how best to help the couple. In the past, the couple would have been automatically "protected" from seeing their unborn child. Now some hospitals provide pictures or a lock of hair as something tangible for the infertile couple to take with them. Many couples have burials or memorial services for their unborn child.

Seeing the miscarried fetus helps many people to substantiate the reality of their loss, which in turn helps them grieve for the lost child, according to Sister Jane Marie Lamb, founder of SHARE, a national support group for couples who have experienced miscarriage.

Infertility: Like (and Not Like) a Death in the Family

In many ways, infertility is like a chronic illness that uses up a great deal of the couple's resources, demanding the expenditure of time, money, and physical and psychological energy. Even when you achieve a pregnancy and have a child, you may still feel that you are infertile. (This often arises when you attempt another pregnancy.) The infertility has been such a major component of your lives that it is not easily forgotten.

Infertility may be felt as an invisible stigma: the emotional scars are usually more significant than the physical manifestations of infertility. Although a childless marriage is obvious to your family and friends, you may choose not to reveal exactly why you haven't had children. But you can never escape your own knowledge of the facts.

When someone dies, the death usually brings family and friends together to grieve the loss. In contrast, infertility leads to a very private form of grief. There is no service each month when the woman starts her period. No one sends cards or flowers. Family and friends often feel uncomfortable and may be reluctant to broach the subject, and as a result, you often grieve without the same type of support that sustains the family grieving a death.

Infertility and Stress

Through two years of marriage, Helen and Arnie had failed to achieve a pregnancy due to infrequent ovulation, manifested by her irregular menstrual periods. Helen, a thirty-seven-year-old sculptor, feels her infertility as a private, personal loss. "I have a sense of failing my husband because I'm the one with the fertility problem," says Helen. "I was in the Y exercising when I saw a woman breastfeeding. Her baby was making loud sucking noises. I had to get out, get away from that very graphic, sensual sound. I cried in the locker room, thinking that I would never feel a baby at my breast."

Trying to live with infertility while still attempting to become pregnant can put you on an emotional roller coaster. Psychotherapists who specialize in grief say that it's emotionally easier finally to lay someone to rest after a death than it is to grieve and simultaneously maintain hope, as most infertile couples do month after month. At some point, if you remain infertile despite the best treatments available, you have to learn how to let go of the baby you never had.

The frequent visits to the doctor's office, daily temperature charts, and sex on schedule can tax any couple. The costs and time involved can be emotionally and financially draining. Getting time off from work and making excuses to your employers and family may add to your burden. Besides the daily stresses and physical demands of medical treatment, infertile couples must adjust emotionally to their constantly thwarted hope for a child. The emotional frustration you feel isn't necessarily accompanied by depression or physical symptoms, but it's there nonetheless.

Minimizing Stress

"Sometimes it feels as if all the burden falls on me. I'm the one who goes to the doctor to get tested, who had the surgery, and who drives forty miles each night to see a nurse friend for hormone injections during a treatment cycle," says Helen. During her last cycle, Helen didn't have to carry the burden alone. "Arnie charted my temperature, he ran the LH urine kits to help time the insemination, and he called the doctor's office for the pregnancy test result, which unfortunately was negative.

"The most important thing has been recognizing the need to keep living our lives," Helen says. Even though it means they will lose a few cycles of treatment, she and Arnie, a thirty-eight-year-old television producer, are going on vacation for six weeks. "You set yourself up for a fall if the only thing that's important is achieving a pregnancy," she says. "A lot of things in my life are exciting, including my marriage. If we don't have a child, then we will still have a great marriage. There are lots of friends' and relatives' children to love, or we may consider adoption."

Arnie adds, "I think it's important not to drive yourself crazy trying everything under the sun. Also, you have to either support each other or get support from someone else."

The couple involved in the evaluation and treatment of infertility can help support each other through the process. The husband can record his wife's temperature on a BBT chart, learn how to give his wife hormone injections, or be with her during inseminations. His participation helps his wife avoid feeling alone and isolated.

You should arrange to have someone available who can help answer your questions, show sensitivity to your feelings, and address your "lack of control" during fertility treatment. Some couples express a need to know if their thoughts and feelings about infertility are normal, and want to share their questions and fears with other couples. The husband or wife may also want to talk to someone other than each other. For these couples, either a counselor on the fertility specialists's staff or an infertility self-help group, such as those under the umbrella of Resolve, may help fill these needs.

Men and Women and How They Cope

Clara and her husband, Carl, each had children in previous marriages but have been unable to have a child together. Clara, age forty-two, the owner of a bake shop, had several miscarriages before visiting a fertility specialist. The doctor diagnosed an ovulatory problem and, after considering her age, treated her with Pergonal. After three treatment cycles without pregnancy, Clara and Carl, a thirty-nine-year-old plumber, have decided to take a break from treatment for a few months. "I really got tired of being poked and prodded," she says. "I feel drained after three tries and no success."

Clara has told Carl that "sometimes I want a baby so bad I can't stand it," she says. "But it's hard for me to get him to talk about our therapy. The most I can get out of him is 'Don't worry. If we don't have children, it's okay.' "

Men and women tend to react differently to their infertility. A man's infertility may affect his sense of self-esteem and self-image, his feelings of adequacy and masculinity. He may feel that he has a damaged body, that he is biologically incompetent to carry on the species. Women tend to focus more on wanting to be pregnant and give birth; men want their bloodline carried on.

It's probably easier for a man to block out or minimize some of his feelings because he doesn't have to go through a monthly menstrual cycle and doesn't have to feel all the changes in his body. Part of the difference in this response also relates to the fact that many men have been educated to keep a stiff upper lip, to hold their feelings inside.

Also, the husband doesn't feel all the physical and psychological changes that accompany pregnancy. Men may feel sad and disappointed about not achieving a pregnancy or losing one through miscarriage, but they don't experience it in the same way as their wives.

Some infertile men compensate by treating themselves like their only child, getting intensely involved in activities such as body building, health foods, and macho sexuality. Others become more socially involved in such child-rearing activities as leading a youth group, teaching Sunday school, or coaching a Little League team. Many infertile men deal with their inability to father children by lavishing parentlike devotion on their homes, pets, gardens, or cars, often going so far as to refer to them as "my baby."

Women generally seem to believe that infertility can harm more areas of their lives than men do. Women who remain infertile often say that they originally had intended to make motherhood their primary occupation, but subsequently returned to school or devoted more energy to their careers as a result of infertility.

If the "motherhood mandate" remains intact, women may believe that they are somehow inadequate as women if they can't have children, and may feel bad about themselves because of their infertility. Perhaps men simply are less willing to admit to negative emotions, or infertility may on average be more distressing for women than for men.

Each partner copes with the stresses of infertility by using those mechanisms that have been honed in the past by life's other traumas and crises. It's important that you listen to each other and understand your differences. Too often, partners blame one another or take their anger out on their spouse. A couple should be able to approach their fertility problem as a team, not as adversaries.

The Dreaded Bed

The impact of infertility inevitably reaches the infertile couple's deepest intimacy. One or both partners may feel less attracted to the other. With the initial reactions of shock, grief, anger, denial, and depression, the sex drive diminishes. When this happens, sex becomes a chore associated with attempts to get pregnant rather than the spontaneous expression of love that was experienced previously.

The feeling of inadequacy can extend to other areas, including the husband's and/or wife's job performance and relationships with others. Infertile men and women who experience sexual dissatisfaction and who already have low self-esteem are most vulnerable to emotional problems such as persisting anxiety and depression that spread to other parts of their lives. The "go-getter" types may also feel bad about themselves because they thought everything was possible if they worked hard enough. Attempting to have a baby may be the first time they have experienced "failure," finding that no matter how diligently they try, there are forces at work beyond their control.

Family and Friends

Robin, twenty-nine, and her husband, Leon, thirty-nine, went to a specialist after one year of a barren marriage. The routine fertility workup found that Robin had endometriosis. After Robin had undergone surgery and medical treatment to remove her endometriosis, Robin and Leon wrote letters to their parents and siblings explaining their infertility problems. "We couldn't keep saying that Robin needed minor surgery. We had to give them some explanation," says Leon, the manager of a sportswear outlet. "We thought we had to clue them in."

"Once they knew what we were going through, they were sympathetic, but I don't believe they really understood," says Robin. "My sister Beth has three children, the third one conceived when she wasn't trying to become pregnant. We had just been through a GIFT procedure and found out I didn't get pregnant. Beth delayed telling us about her third pregnancy because she knew it would be difficult for us. As the years have passed, our families know we've come to accept our infertility, and they, too, have become more comfortable with that."

Family and friends often unintentionally add to your sense of inadequacy or isolation. You may be reluctant to talk about or even reveal your problem because others might not take your situation seriously and may offer false reassurances or bad advice.

You have to realize that your family and close friends may not know exactly how to support you when it comes to dealing with infertility, and they may, unintentionally, make insensitive and unhelpful remarks. That's not to say that family and friends don't want to help, or that they don't care or aren't interested in you. It may mean that they are uninformed about infertility and they don't know how to help, or that their own feelings about your infertility (denial and anxiety) interfere with their ability to help. It may be too painful for them to face the pain of infertility in someone they love.

Family, friends, and even strangers may respond inappropriately due, in part, to the stress they feel being around someone else who is suffering. Your friends and family may also feel angry about the way infertility has disrupted their usual ways of relating to you. Even when your friends know what they want to say, they may feel awkward saying it.

So sharing your infertility with family and close friends can yield mixed results. They may give you support, but your interactions may still be constrained. Once you feel you are ready and have gotten over the initial shock of infertility, you have to figure out whom to tell and what to tell them.

You can help your family and friends be more supportive. Talk to them openly about how you feel and what you are going through. Tell them what you need from them. Saying "Be supportive" may not be clear enough. You may need to define this better, by saying, for example, "Be aware of sensitive topics of conversation, like baby showers" or "Let me cry when I'm upset."

Common Myths About Infertility

"Before learning that we were infertile, we enjoyed getting together with my family for Mother's Day and attending church," says Robin. "In my parents' church on Mother's Day, the mothers in the congregation wear corsages and the sermon is usually related to motherhood. One year the message I received from the sermon was that you're worthless unless you're a mother. I remember looking around the congregation for other women not wearing corsages and wondering how they were feeling. Leon and I then decided that we preferred not to attend church on Mother's Day. That was our way of coping."

When they find out that you have a fertility problem, many people, even loved ones, may blithely toss off a comment that has no factual basis. They may be covering up their own discomfort in dealing with infertility, or they may not know any better. You may have to educate them about the common myths of infertility.

Give them specific feedback, such as "I feel frustrated when you say I should just relax and I'll get pregnant." Ask them not to judge your emotions by saying things like "You ought to feel better by now" or "It's just Nature's way." Don't be afraid to tell others what you don't need from them or what isn't helpful.

Here are some of the common infertility myths you may hear from others, and why they are false:

- "Infertility is all in your head." Infertility is due to disorders of the reproductive system, and while emotions can affect all body functions, one or more physical causes are identified in 95 percent or more of infertile couples.

- "You're thinking about it too much. Why don't you go on a vacation?" Getting away from it all is important for everyone, but while it may soothe your jangled nerves, it won't help you treat a physiologic or anatomic disorder.

- "Go to another doctor and you're sure to get pregnant." A second opinion may be a good idea, especially if both partners have not had appropriate fertility workups or if communicating with your doctor is a problem. But just switching doctors doesn't guarantee success.

- "If you work at it and want it enough, you'll get pregnant." Unlike many other parts of your lives, infertility may be beyond your control. While new methods of diagnosing and treating infertility have improved most couples' chances of having a baby, there's no guarantee, and some problems remain unsolvable.

- "Just pray and have faith." Believing in your treatment can help you get through often demanding fertility procedures and help you maintain a positive outlook, even when all hope seems lost. But sheer will and blind faith won't overcome a physical problem, such as blocked tubes.

- "There are plenty of children for adoption." While this may be true for black and Hispanic couples, there are fewer white children being put up for adoption relative to the number of white couples who want to adopt white children. For a white couple, the chances of adopting a healthy newborn baby are much less than the chances of achieving a pregnancy through IVF or other assisted reproductive techniques.

- "Adopt a child, and you'll get pregnant." Besides the fact that it is increasingly difficult to adopt these days, only about 5 percent of couples who do adopt later become pregnant, a similar percentage to those who don't adopt and who become pregnant without further treatment.

Statements like these indicate a certain amount of ignorance about infertility and are counterproductive. To help dispel these myths, ask your family and friends what they experience as they try to be supportive. Do they feel sad, anxious, helpless? What is it like for the friend or relative? You can educate those close to you about what it's like to go through infertility, the emotional roller coaster, the demands on your time, patience, and money. Tell them not to be afraid of hurting your feelings by asking questions. Answering questions and telling your story may be painful, but in the process your relationship may grow stronger.

Pay attention to what you feel when a friend or sister tells you she is pregnant. Some feelings like jealousy and resentment are hard to accept. You may be feeling that you deserve a child more than she does, or that, if you had children, you would be a better parent. Admitting those feelings even to yourself may be hard to do. You may feel at a loss for what to say. Work together, learn how to deal with each other. Explain which situations are painful, and avoid them or at least be aware of them. Holiday times, when the family all gathers together to exchange gifts, may be among the most difficult.

Infertility Support Groups

"I was sleeping a lot, I felt on edge," says Clara. "My family doctor put me on an antidepressant for a month. He and his wife had gone through fertility treatments, so he knew what was going on with me. His wife shared some of her feelings, and told me about a local Resolve group. I sent them my money right away, and they told me about their monthly meetings and newsletter. Now I have other infertile people to talk to. I tell my fertile friends what's going on with my treatment, but they can't empathize. They haven't experienced infertility firsthand."

You may find that some of your emotional needs can best be met by other infertile couples. No one really understands better what it feels like to be unable to bear a child. You may find it helpful to participate in an infertility support group where you can talk about your experiences and feelings in a sympathetic, understanding atmosphere. Then you can begin to feel that you aren't so alone. Having the group listen to you and accept you for who you are may help you to accept yourselves and stop feeling so isolated.

The national self-help group for infertile couples, Resolve, based in Massachusetts, now has more than 25,000 members in fifty chapters across the country. By becoming a basic member (for $45), you become part of a national network of members with similar problems, including a twenty-four-hour hotline that puts you in touch with volunteers who provide support and answer questions. You also receive a national newsletter, journal articles, and up-to-date fact sheets. Local Resolve chapters have regular programs on medical and emotional issues, newsletters, information on local services (including adoption), and support groups.

Many fertility clinics also offer their own support groups to facilitate sharing, or newsletters with articles and letters from infertile couples. These groups and newsletters provide information and emotional support for infertile couples who are going through, or have gone through, fertility treatments. They also address coping strategies and specific needs of the doctor's patients.

It's natural, if you have had no success in achieving a pregnancy, to seek out other infertile couples. Infertile couples can't avoid interacting with fertile people if they are to maintain family relationships or friendships. Support groups may help you ease your way back into social networks where you can feel comfortable living your lives without children, either temporarily or permanently.

When to Stop Treatment

"Nothing we had done had worked, and the only thing left was IVF," says Leon. "Robin and I had already spent thousands of dollars, and we were looking at spending much more, which would have been a financial burden. With the information we had, given what we had been through, we felt our chances of success were minimal, and no better with IVF than the other treatments we had pursued.

"We discussed adoption, but my age was a consideration. I was concerned that I'd be over sixty by the time my child was out of high school. Besides, the public adoption agency had a long waiting list for a baby of the same race and an age cutoff at thirty-eight. We decided not to consider a foreign or private adoption, and didn't want to risk adopting through a 'baby broker.'

"The decision not to have children was almost inevitable," Leon continues. "We had been staring at the possibility for a long while. Once you can't achieve a pregnancy easily, there's always the possibility that you never will. Robin and I weren't willing to subject our bodies, emotions, and pocketbooks to the endless varieties of treatment once we believed that treatment wasn't likely to succeed."

"Leading up to the time to stop, we began thinking about it a little at a time," recalls Robin. "We needed a new car, and had to choose between a two-seat sports car or a sedan with a backseat. We really wanted the sports car, and so we bought it,

telling ourselves that if we had a child, we'd sell it. We were already thinking that the treatment wouldn't work. Earlier in our treatment, we wouldn't have done that.

"I'm competitive. I don't remember quitting anything. It was hard for me to say 'Let's stop,'" Robin says. "But the treatment becomes such a routine that it controls your life. When we first quit, I didn't know what else to do with my time. But quitting also changes your life. Either it makes you closer or drives you further apart. It can't be the way it was before. Leon and I definitely feel closer and enjoy our time together. A few years before, I would have thought of ourselves as being lonely without children. Occasionally, I think about what would happen if Leon was gone, but you get through that, too. You feel the grief. It's like burying a dream. You have to lay it to rest and get on with your life, put it behind you."

One of the most difficult times is when treatment hasn't worked. Your doctor may tell you, "The treatment has failed. I can't offer you any other medical treatments that are more likely to work." (More often, there is always something else to try, even if that means repeating the same treatment.) But it's not up to the doctor to say "It's time for you to stop." *You* have to make that decision. It should be a well thought out decision that you make freely and feel comfortable with.

Your fertility specialist may feel that he has failed you. Doctors don't like to admit they can't help everyone who comes into their office. This may make it difficult for him to advise you when you should consider stopping treatment. A sensitive physician, however, can help make you aware of the signals you may be sending that indicate perhaps one or both partners is ready to stop trying. One partner may appear emotionally drained or exhausted. One or both partners may seem immobilized, unable to function normally or to make clear decisions. You may become obsessed with your goal of achieving a pregnancy, or have unrealistic expectations about treatment, falling prey to the seduction of every new technology.

Other signals that you are not coping effectively may include repetitive calls to ask the same questions, complaints of anxiety, depression, sleeplessness, and marital conflict. Or you may demonstrate your ambivalence about fertility treatment by missing appointments or not adhering to the treatment regimen.

The financial toll of prolonged, unsuccessful fertility treatments can be heavy as well. You must also take this into consideration when you discuss how much longer you will keep trying to have a baby.

When to stop treatment is a major decision for any couple. Once the decision is made, it's usually made for good, and it is rarely a sudden decision. Infertile couples tend to think about stopping throughout their treatment.

Sometimes the decision not to pursue further treatment is made passively for an infertile couple who has exhausted all treatment options. As each successive treatment fails, another option is lost. One by one, the doors close until the only one open is not to have children.

When appropriate therapies have been tried for a sufficient duration of time, and have failed, your fertility treatment will come to an end. If and when this happens, you will have to adopt or live without children. You may not feel that you are able to accept either of the two choices. Feelings of vulnerability and desperation may make you unable to assess your situation clearly. This is the time for you to rely on all the support you have—doctor, family, friends, local support groups—to help you work through your emotions to reach a sound decision.

Ultimately, you must make a personal assessment about what's best for you. You may need to wrestle with the idea of not having children for a long time before you come to accept the inevitable. Each partner has to face it alone, but you also have to deal with it together if you are to remain a couple. Some marriages can't withstand the strain, but many couples draw closer together. They have been through a lot together, and somehow the struggle and self-examination make them more intimate.

If and when you decide to stop treatment, it's important for you really to give up infertility treatment and get on with your lives. There are alternative solutions to fertility problems, but they can't really be developed while you are still counting on getting pregnant.

Fertility specialists like to quote their pregnancy rates—the "bottom line" for fertility treatments. But pregnancy isn't the only way to measure success. Couples who don't conceive after treatment are not failures as human beings. You needn't denigrate your self-worth by defining a successful life only as having children.

Adoption

Society's values have fostered the idea that infertile couples are somehow not complete because they can't conceive. Implicit in this message is the idea that blood is thicker than water, that biological babies are "better," and that adoption is second best. You probably have received perplexing messages about creating families. The challenge is to sort out the messages and to make some sense of them for your own lives and the family you seek to create.

For every hundred American couples seeking adoption, only two or three children are available. This illustrates the practical obstacles to the adoption option. These statistics are worse than continuing treatment even after several unsuccessful IVF cycles!

Fewer young women, particularly white women, are placing babies for adoption. There are, however, other options, including adopting an older child waiting in an institution or foster home, or a nonwhite or foreign-born baby. Many couples bypass traditional adoption agencies in favor of an independent adoption.

About 2 million Americans are competing each year to adopt 55,000 domestic children and about 18,000 foreign-born babies, according to the National Council for Adoption. That makes for poor odds for the couple who want to adopt. About two-thirds of domestic adoptions are arranged through agencies, the rest independently. Half of newborns are adopted independently and half through agencies. The couples most likely to adopt successfully are middle class, between the ages of thirty-three and forty-two, earning incomes of $25,000 to $50,000, the council says.

Although there are no good records about the number of adoptions of older American children, the best estimates, based on annual placement rates from the largest U.S. agencies, suggest that 10,000 to 12,000 older children are adopted each year. Check the resources in the back of this book for agencies that help couples with various types of adoptions.

When you do decide to adopt, let people know. Contact as many people as you possibly can, and put your name on as many agency waiting lists as possible. Also, find out about an adoptive parent support group in your area to help you through the adoption process. Your doctor or fertility specialist may also be able to help you with this process.

Private Agency Adoption

Last fall, Pam and Jeff applied to a private adoption agency. After they were accepted, the social worker told them it would probably take two years before they had their adopted baby. "I'm glad we decided to adopt," says Pam. "I want to have a baby, but I was ready to stop treatment. I couldn't go on forever. I didn't think I could ever stop trying to have a baby. But after I had to give up my dream job because of the stresses of fertility treatments, I knew I had had enough. I'm happy to relax and wait for the agency to come through for us." Nine months later, they took home their son, Ben.

Licensed private adoption agencies usually seek homes for American or foreign infants and toddlers. They screen and counsel pregnant women who contact them about placing babies for adoption. The agency frequently provides for medical care to the mother during the pregnancy, and gives the couple a complete social and medical history of the baby. The identity of the birth mother is ordinarily kept confidential from the adoptive parents.

The agency also has social workers who screen the potential adoptive couple with visits to the couple at home. These agencies often reject adoptive parents who are over age forty-two or under age twenty-five, who have their own biological children, or who have no proof of infertility.

Waiting lists for private adoption are generally two to five years for a white baby, less than a year for a non-white baby. There are more white couples who want to adopt and, although these agencies generally have more non-white babies available, some do not allow white couples to adopt non-white babies.

Public Agency Adoption

Run by counties or states, public adoption agencies seek parents for children who have been removed from the custody of their biological parents. Public agencies have newborns, but most of their children are school age or teen age. They may have a physical or emotional handicap.

Adoptions through public agencies are inexpensive, but the process is arduous. If either you or your spouse has been divorced, if you are of different religions, or if you are well over age forty, you may be rejected.

Independent (Open) Adoption

After four private agencies failed to locate a baby for them, Patricia and Jack were contacted by a couple from their church about a pregnant girl who wanted to place her baby for adoption. Teresa had just graduated from college in Iowa and returned to North Carolina to have her baby. "We met Teresa when she was five months pregnant, and spent a lot of time getting to know her. We had been burned many times by agencies who said they had babies for us, so we didn't let ourselves believe that this time was really it," says Patricia, age thirty-six.

Through a doctor who had adopted a baby, Patricia and Jack, age thirty-nine, were introduced to an attorney to represent them. They went through a Social Services home study, received medical records on Teresa (none were available for the birth father), and Teresa signed papers so that Patricia and Jack would become the baby's guardians as soon as he was born.

"We were outside the hospital room when Richard was born," Patricia says. "Within a few minutes, we were all there together like one big family." Two weeks later, Teresa went back to work in Iowa. On Mother's Day, Teresa and Patricia exchanged gifts, and "we have sent her pictures of Richard about four times over the past six months," Patricia says. "The first picture in his adoption book is Teresa holding him in her arms. We felt very close to her. He's going to know he was adopted. We want him to know how special he is."

For independent adoption, a couple contacts an attorney, doctor, or religious leader who works directly with a pregnant woman. While most adoption agencies prohibit direct contact between the birth mother and adoptive parents, an independent adoption may give the infertile couple a chance to contact the birth mother before delivery, which is called an open adoption.

An attorney or the couple typically places classified ads in newspapers and locates a pregnant woman willing to place the baby at birth. The attorney may also send her to a state with lenient adoption laws, where the woman delivers and surrenders her newborn. For his work, the attorney receives a fee of about $3,000 to $5,000. Some states permit reimbursement to the birth mother for reasonable expenses, and the adoptive couple frequently pays for her lost wages, counseling, food, rent, and medical care during the pregnancy. Some birth mothers have demanded cars, tuition, and trust funds in exchange for babies.

Independent adoption is a speedier route, from three months to two years for a healthy white baby. But it's also vulnerable to ethical, legal, and emotional risks. Many attorneys have no training in social work or psychology. Adoption experts express concern that some prospective parents aren't properly screened and that birth mothers may not receive adequate counseling. The couple also runs the risk that an unscrupulous attorney may raise the price just before they adopt the baby. Problems may also arise if the birth mother wants further contact with the child and the couple opposes it.

You're likely to find a qualified adoption attorney among the members of the American Academy of Adoption Attorneys. This national organization of about 250 adoption attorneys requires that a member have participated in at least twenty-five adoptions recently. Members of this group specialize in adoptions, and they should be familiar with state adoption laws and the many special regulations needed in adoptions. You also can find an adoption attorney by asking your local Resolve chapter, adoptive parents' association, private adoption agency, or other couples who have adopted. Call your state bar association to see whether any disciplinary actions have been taken against the attorney. Find out how long most of the attorney's clients wait before adopting, what methods are used to locate and screen birth mothers, and the fees involved.

The birth mother should be free of any pressure from the couple or the intermediary, and usually doesn't sign any binding adoption agreement until at least three days after she gives birth. Independent adoption is now illegal in six states, and others are tightening their laws.

Identified Adoption

Because of the increasingly smaller numbers of newborns placed for adoption, private adoption agencies and attorneys have come up with a new form of adoption, called identified adoption. In this scenario, the agency or attorney aids the couple in placing classified ads in newspapers to identify a prospective birth mother. The couple learns where prospective birth mothers are most likely to live, how to present themselves to the birth mother, and how to manage the relationship with the birth mother. Once the couple has made the connection with the birth mother, then the agency or attorney helps provide the support services necessary to complete the adoption.

By doing the legwork to identify the birth mother, the couple can speed up the adoption process. An identified adoption usually takes, on average, about one year. However, the couple also is subjected to the abuses of fraudulent telephone calls and must take an active role in dealing with the birth mother, at least at first. The couple needs to hire an adoption attorney to help them through the legal aspects of the adoption.

Foreign Adoption

For some couples, the best option is to adopt a foreign child. They may have been shut out of American adoption agencies because of their age or due to the reluctance of agencies to allow white couples to adopt a minority baby. (There is no shortage of black and American-born Hispanic babies for minority couples to adopt.) The infertile couple may not feel capable of accepting an older or handicapped child, or they may not want to go through an independent or identified adoption.

More infertile white couples are looking into foreign adoption. To meet this demand, government-licensed adoption agencies have proliferated and made foreign adoption more available. American couples adopt about 7,000 foreign children each year, with most of them coming from China and South America, as well as Eastern Europe and Southeast Asia. It usually takes a couple about one year to adopt a foreign baby after they have applied to an agency.

The rules of foreign adoption vary from country to country. To find out the current adoption laws in a particular country, contact the federal Immigration and Naturalization Service near you. An adoption agency or attorney who handles foreign adoption should also know the rules in various countries.

The Hague Treaty on International Adoption approved in 1993 and ratified by 40 countries defines a set of minimum norms and procedures that will be uniform to all countries. Legislation to implement the treaty was passed in the United States in the fall of 2000, and then President Bill Clinton signed it into law. Adoption experts expect that the current avenues to adopt foreign children will now remain clear and open.

Foreign adoption begins with a home study by a licensed social worker, just as in domestic adoptions. Once the couple has been approved by the agency, they can start their search for a foreign baby. The simplest approach is to locate an adoption agency that has overseas contacts. Or the couple may want to use an intermediary, such as an attorney who specializes in foreign adoptions. The couple should choose an agency or attorney who can demonstrate experience in foreign adoptions. If possible, they should try to speak to people who have adopted babies from the agency or through the attorney.

Adoption Costs

Agency, independent, and identified adoptions range from $1,500 to $30,000. Foreign adoptions range from $5,000 to $30,000. So adopting a child isn't necessarily less expensive than going through infertility treatment. The money goes toward paying for social worker fees, medical care and counseling for the birth mother, legal fees, and travel for foreign children.

All employee-based insurance companies must offer adoption benefits, such as time off from work and a limited reimbursement of expenses from the time of placement. This includes preexisting conditions. The requirement applies even before the adoption has become finalized. Most adoptions aren't finalized until six to twelve months after a couple takes custody of the child.

What Agencies and Birth Mothers Look for in a Couple

Whatever route you go in search of an adopted child, the adoption agencies, brokers, or birth mothers look for certain characteristics in the adoptive couple. In general, they look for a stable marriage and a couple who can afford to take care of the child. Also, they want to know if you have come to terms with your problem—that, for example, one partner doesn't blame the other for the couple's infertility.

Some agencies have taken to interviewing prospective adoptive parents in groups. This gives them the opportunity to see how you interact with other people. The adoption study by a social worker in your home also weighs heavily in an agency's decision to accept a couple. You can use this home study with the social worker to express your feelings about your infertility and why you want to adopt. It may even help you work out any uncertain feelings about adoption.

Making Use of Waiting Time

Once you have made the commitment to adopt, you may want to use your time to think about and prepare for the arrival of your new family member. This parallels the preparation time couples have during pregnancy, although it may last longer than nine months. Like the couples who have a natural child, adoptive couples aren't innately endowed with child care skills, and must also go through a learning phase. If you have applied for adoption, you need to consult baby books and seek out friends and relatives just as other expectant parents do.

Questions may run through your minds about preparing for the child: "What can we do to prepare emotionally for the instantaneous transformation from a twosome to a threesome?" If you are adopting a foreign baby, you may wonder, "What can we do to make the baby feel welcome in a strange environment?" Or if you are adopting a toddler or older child, "What kind of transition problems can we expect when our child arrives?"

The waiting period may be difficult and frustrating, but you should cherish your moments together. Being alone together will someday be a precious commodity. This may be the time to take a vacation or second honeymoon; it could be your last chance for a long time.

Answering Questions About Adoption

You can also think about what to say when strangers ask questions about the adoption. This may be a good time to open up with your relatives, who may still be having trouble accepting either your infertility or your decision to adopt.

You may decide to learn as much as you can about the baby's background. For newborns, the mother's state of health during pregnancy is important since her habits and health affect the baby's condition. Any information about the birth mother's and father's family histories may be important to the child later.

In addition, you can decide how, and when, to tell the infant or young child about the adoption. Sooner or later, someone is bound to bring up the subject. Since the 1960s, most parents have heeded expert advice and have told children early in life that they were adopted. But parents almost universally overestimate their child's ability to comprehend his or her own adoption. Adopted children need to be retold more fully as they get older. You may later have to decide whether to aid the adopted child in a search for his or her natural parents.

Whether you choose to adopt or not, you should feel satisfied that you have done all you could about your fertility problem. After the adversity of infertility, you probably know yourself better, you may feel like a stronger person, and your marriage may be stronger, too.

Once you have resolved your feelings about your infertility, you can realize that it's not, in and of itself, a major part of your life. Infertility doesn't loom nearly so large any more. You can accept that your personality and identity do not revolve around your ability to have children.

Still, like most infertile couples, somewhere in the back of your minds you may think of yourselves as "infertile," even if you have a baby. Once you have a child, he or she is a constant reminder of your infertility. And you may treat your child as "precious" since you know how hard it can be to have a baby.

You will probably remember when everything seemed to be a crisis while you were going through fertility treatments. Like any other life crisis, you can gradually put it into better perspective as time goes by. Whether you have a baby or not, you will have learned that there is life after infertility.

Questions for the Infertile Couple to Ask Themselves About Their Fertility Treatments

How far are we willing to go in order to have a baby?

Do we feel we have to have our own biologic child?

Would we accept adopting a baby? How quickly would we want to adopt?

Would we consider living without children?

What should we tell our family and friends about our infertility?

What can we do to make it easier for them to accept?

What should we tell them about what is and what isn't helpful to us?

Questions for Each Partner Undergoing Infertility Treatment

Am I willing to talk to my spouse about how I really feel about our infertility and the treatments we're going through?

How easily can I talk with my fertility specialist or one of his team members about how I really feel?

How can I help my spouse get through fertility treatments?

Questions for the Infertile Couple to Ask Their Doctor

In general

Do you know of any local patient support groups? How can I contact them?

How do we know when it may be time to stop fertility treatments?

Are there any of the signs that it may be time to stop (emotional exhaustion, obsession with achieving a pregnancy, wanting indiscriminately to try any new treatment)?

After a miscarriage

Can we see the baby we've lost or take home his or her picture or lock of hair?

Can you help us arrange for a burial or memorial service? What caused the miscarriage? How can another be prevented?

Questions for the Infertile Couple to Ask Themselves About Adoption

Can we afford to adopt a baby?

Will the child come between us or interfere with our relationship?

Are we talking openly to each other about how we feel about adoption?

Do we want to apply to a public or private adoption agency, or opt for an independent, identified, or foreign adoption?

What should we tell our friends and relatives about the adopted baby?

Can we find out about the birth mother's or father's medical history?

What was the birth mother's health during her pregnancy and delivery?

When, and how, should we tell the child that he or she was adopted?

Should we aid the child in the search for his or her natural parents?

Sue's Story

For four years, Sue and her husband, Frank, both age thirty-five, have had a strong interest in adopting a Korean child. They had a son, Grant, now age five, after antibiotic treatments cleared up a genital infection. Yet after nearly two years of various surgeries to remove scar tissue and endometriosis, Sue still hadn't conceived again, so they put themselves on a waiting list to adopt a foreign baby.

"A year ago, the most important thing in my life was having a baby," says Sue. "Every time I got my period, it was a major catastrophe." Now Frank, an insurance executive, and Sue have decided to take a few years off from fertility treatments, and she has decided not to work as a respiratory therapist. Instead, Sue says, "I'm going into 'baby-raising mode,' loving my toddler, taking him to preschool. And if we adopt, I'll have another one on my hands.

"I have blind faith that I will get pregnant again," she says. "Three of my friends had kids after age forty, so I know it's doable. I'll be patient and persevere. Grant keeps asking, 'Mommy, when are we going to get pregnant?' He knows I never gave away his crib. One way or another, we're going to use that crib again."

Part Four

PREGNANCY SUCCESS

13

PREGNANCY AFTER FERTILITY TREATMENTS

Andrea, age thirty-seven, and Kenny, age thirty-eight, wanted to have a baby quickly, so Andrea's gynecologist sent her to see Dr. Berger. A fertility workup found that her menstrual cycles were irregular, her cervix was abnormal, and she had a mild urinary tract infection. Antibiotics cured the infection, but several intrauterine insemination attempts in hormone-stimulated cycles failed. Dr. Berger drained a cyst from Andrea's right ovary, and she continued to take Pergonal to prepare for another IUI attempt.

Ten days after the IUI, Andrea had blood drawn in Dr. Berger's office. "He had said if my hCG was negative, I might need a biopsy of my uterine lining, and that's what I was expecting to hear when he told me 'You're pregnant,'" says Andrea. She immediately called Kenny at his office to share the news and took one of the prenatal vitamins the nurse had given her.

Two weeks later, an ultrasound scan revealed Andrea was carrying twins. She drove home to show Kenny the ultrasound video. "He took a close look and said, 'My God, there's two.' All he could say for five minutes was 'Two.' I'm glad he was sitting down." She stayed under Dr. Berger's care for the next two months. "He and his staff took extra special care of us. They treated us like family," she recalls.

As her pregnancy progressed, Andrea's nose became congested and she became nauseous; simple remedies alleviated these problems. But at six months, she started having uterine contractions. Her obstetrician put her on a fetal monitor, asked her to stop working in a print shop, and told her to rest in bed for the remainder of her pregnancy. "I was miserable at night, and tired and nauseous during the day," she says. "When my precious girls, Heather and Helen, were born, I knew it was all worthwhile."

After what may well have been many fertility treatments, you are finally going to be parents. Congratulations! You may be feeling a wide range of emotions at the same time, including disbelief, elation, anxiety, and fright. This is just the beginning of many changes to follow.

This chapter will assist you through the early critical weeks of your pregnancy by outlining the care offered through the first trimester (first twelve weeks) at the Chapel Hill Fertility Center. Since many obstetricians-gynecologists do not see pregnant patients until they are twelve weeks pregnant, Dr. Berger began an early pregnancy care program for them. Because of the nature of pregnancies after fertility treatments, he and his staff carefully follow pregnant patients and intervene when necessary early on. By carefully monitoring and preventing early pregnancy complications, they have prevented women from falling through the cracks of the medical system.

After the first trimester, Dr. Berger refers his pregnant patients back to the care of their primary obstetrician-gynecologist, or if they do not already have one, to an ob-gyn or one of the perinatal specialists at the University of North Carolina who specialize in caring for women with high-risk pregnancies. Most of his patients return to his office to visit as their pregnancy progresses and, once they deliver, to show off their babies.

High-Risk Pregnancies

About 600,000 of the more than 4 million women who give birth each year in the United States are considered to have a high-risk pregnancy. With more women waiting to start families and more advances in technology to help women get pregnant, the chances of multiple pregnancies, premature birth, and miscarriages have risen, leading to more high-risk pregnancies.

Every pregnancy following fertility treatment should be considered high risk until proven otherwise. Most studies show that women who have had fertility treatments and those who have a history of previous miscarriage or of bleeding early in the first trimester of pregnancy have a higher percentage of pregnancy complications than the general public. Multiple pregnancies are more common after fertility treatments, and carrying more than one baby is more risky for both the mother and her children. Other women considered likely to have a high-risk pregnancy are those with prior repeated miscarriage and systemic diseases such as diabetes and high blood pressure.

The Value of Bed Rest

An effective way to help a woman with a history of premature deliveries to prolong pregnancy is bed rest. Bed rest reduces the amount of adrenaline and other steroid hormones the pregnant woman produces, increases circulation to her uterus and placenta, and reduces gravity's force against the cervix. Early bed rest has proven to be even more effective than drugs (tocolytics) that help prevent uterine contractions. Each year about 300,000 women with high-risk pregnancies are sent to bed to avoid a premature delivery.

Dr. Berger prescribes bed rest even very early in pregnancy for a woman with uterine bleeding or contractions, particularly if she has a history of miscarriage. He often prescribes bed rest in combination with natural progesterone during the first trimester to help maintain the pregnancy. She may also receive baby aspirin if she has a history of miscarriage (see p. 203 about miscarriage therapy) or the drug terbutaline (Ritodrine) if she is having uterine contractions.

If a pregnant patient starts to have contractions or to bleed from the uterus, then Dr. Berger attempts to find the cause in order to treat the problem. The bleeding might be caused by cervical infection, which can be eradicated with antibiotics; an abnormal implantation, which is otherwise known as a low-lying placenta; or bleeding from within or at the placenta or at the attachment to the uterus.

No one knows exactly what causes early uterine contractions. A decline in progesterone levels, loss of amniotic fluid, or inflamed or infected cervical polyps or uterine fibroids may all have some effect. All these conditions can be detected and treated early on. Also, psychological stress or even orgasms may increase the chemicals that affect uterine contractions.

"Bed Rest Buddies"

Across the country, groups are forming to help women who need bed rest get through high-risk pregnancies. The Sidelines National Support Network provides counseling and pairs a pregnant woman with phone counselors who have similar medical histories and understand their problems. Other groups of "Bed Rest Buddies" also offer friendship and support to bed-ridden pregnant women.

Also, a Web site offers help for expectant mothers on bed rest. Pregnancy Bed Rest: Information and Support for Families and Caregivers armstrong.son.wisc.edu/~son/bedrest/ provides comprehensive information, including easy-to-print resources defining conditions for which bed rest is often recommended, discussing common medications, and describing expected changes in mothers and fetuses during development; exhaustive lists of resources for families and caregivers, including citations of relevant research; dozens of cross-referenced answers to frequently asked questions; and personal stories by women and their husbands and links to support groups and other online resources.

When Can You Expect the Arrival of Your Bundle of Joy?

Last Menstrual Period (LMP) and Gestation

You may feel confused by all of the calculated dates related to your baby's development. If so, you are not alone! A full-term pregnancy is based on an average of thirty-eight weeks of development (gestation), and it is divided into three trimesters. The first trimester encompasses the first twelve to thirteen weeks. For most women, ovulation and conception usually occur around two weeks after the last menstrual period (LMP). Conventionally, obstetricians speak of your pregnancy from the date of your last menstrual period ("menstrual age"), because in the past only the date of the LMP, rather than the date of actual ovulation or conception, was known. In keeping with this convention, obstetricians continue to talk about gestational age relative to the LMP.

This is often confusing since most people talk about gestational age in terms of weeks from conception ("conception age"). This refers to the time elapsed from the day of conception or when fertilization occurs. Gestational age (or conceptual age) is usually two weeks less than the age based on the LMP. However, when ovulation or your LH surge (or injection of human chorionic gonadotropin [hCG]) occurred after cycle day fourteen, your baby's conceptual/gestational age may be more than two weeks behind the age based on LMP. And if you had an LH surge or hCG injection before cycle day fourteen, your baby's conceptual/gestational age may be less than two weeks ahead of the age based on LMP. Dr. Berger calculates a pregnant patient's estimated date of delivery (due date) based on her LH surge or hCG injection, as this gives a more accurate determination than the last menstrual period.

How Is Your Pregnancy Confirmed?

Your pregnancy is first confirmed after the nurses draw blood and send it to the laboratory to test for the presence of the pregnancy hormone hCG, which is produced by the earliest cells of the pregnancy. If the result is positive, Dr. Berger's nurses make sure that the patient is taking her prenatal vitamins, which she was instructed to start taking at the beginning of fertility treatments, and that she starts taking an extra 1 mg a day of folic acid, a vitamin that reduces the chances of abnormal development of the neural tube in the spine. Most women find that these one-a-day prenatal vitamins are easier to tolerate at bedtime.

Once the pregnancy is confirmed, the same blood sample usually will be stored in a lab to measure the exact level of hCG. Early in pregnancy, the hCG level normally doubles every two to three days.

Additional Reading

When pregnancy is confirmed, Dr. Berger gives the couple a copy of *Planning for Pregnancy, Birth and Beyond* to read. This excellent source is published by the American College of Obstetricians and Gynecologists. At your local library or bookstore, you should be able to find a copy of *What to Expect When You're Expecting* (Workman Press), another source of reliable information. Also available through Dr. Berger's office is an order form for the magazine issue of "As Your Baby Grows," published by *American Baby* magazine. It provides pictures of the baby's development from conception through infancy.

What Will Be Done During Ob Visits?

Depending on hCG and progesterone results, the progress of the pregnancy will be followed with blood tests in Dr. Berger's office once or twice a week until the development of the baby can be seen within the lining of the uterus (endometrium) by a transvaginal ultrasound exam. The first scan is usually performed one to two weeks after the first positive pregnancy test.

Each week, the pregnant woman provides a urine specimen for analysis. She also has her blood pressure monitored, her weight checked, and a tube of blood drawn to be sent to the lab for hCG and progesterone tests. If she is taking supplemental progesterone capsules, she omits her morning dose until after her blood is drawn. Progesterone is the hormone secreted from the corpus luteum to keep the pregnancy from miscarrying. The normal level is usually greater than 15 mg/dl while pregnant.

Urine Analysis

The pregnant woman's urine is analyzed in Dr. Berger's lab by microscopic examination each week. The first urine specimen is sent for a culture to detect a possible bladder or urinary tract infection (UTI). An infection, if undetected and untreated, can increase the risk of miscarriage or premature delivery. Laboratory personnel check for red and white blood cells, sugar, protein, bacteria, and any other abnormalities that might affect the pregnancy and need follow-up care.

Blood Pressure

Blood pressure is assessed for major changes. Women are told to alert the nurses if they experience any headaches, lightheadedness, dizziness, ringing in the ears, or fainting, or see spots or halos around objects. These symptoms are sometimes due to blood pressure elevations.

Weight

Your weight usually remains stable during the early part of pregnancy. It is rare to gain more than five pounds in the first trimester. Your obstetrician will guide you in the amount of weight you can expect to gain during the remainder of your pregnancy. Some women may even lose a pound or two during the earliest weeks of their pregnancy because of nausea. While this does not pose a problem, you should not try to lose weight by dieting during your pregnancy. If a woman loses too much weight due to nausea early in pregnancy, she may have to be given fluid and nutritional supplements intravenously. Fortunately, this is a rare problem.

Blood Test Results

The hCG and progesterone levels indicate the progress during the early stages of pregnancy. Below is a listing of normal ranges of hCG levels according to cycle day or weeks based on last menstrual period. More important than the absolute level is the rate of increase, with doubling expected every two to three days early in the first trimester

Normal Values

Menstrual age	hCG level (mIU/dL)
Week 3–4 =	25–100
Week 4–5 =	100–4,000
Week 5–9 =	4,000–130,000
Week 9–12 =	30,000–200,000

Dr. Berger's nurse plots out the results of hCG levels on a curve. If the hCG levels fall outside the normal curve, it may be an early indication that the woman will miscarry or that the pregnancy has some other abnormality.

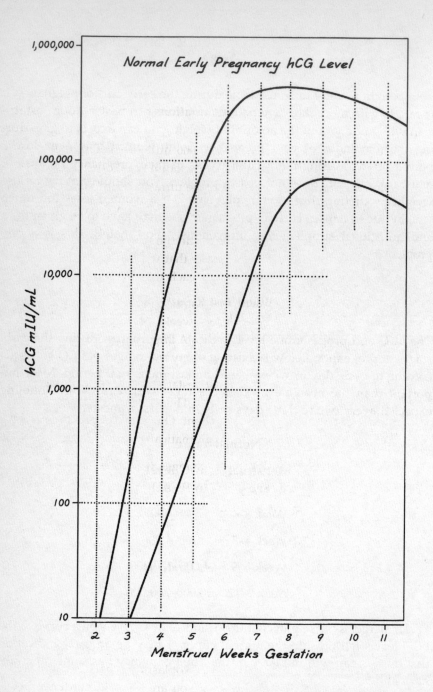

Normal Early Pregnancy hCG Level

hCG mIU/mL

Menstrual Weeks Gestation

Expect a plateau, then a slight decline in the level just prior to the end of the first trimester.

Ultrasound Examinations

The hCG level usually reaches 1,500 to 3,000 mIU/dL before the gestational sac can be seen on a transvaginal ultrasound scan. Your doctor may use the following terms associated with the ultrasound to describe your developing baby.

- Gestational sac: a fluid-filled circle inside the endometrium. This sac will grow and become the bag of water that will break while you are in labor. The size should increase with each scan performed.

- Yolk sac: a ball-like object inside the gestational sac that manufactures blood cells for the baby in the earliest weeks of pregnancy. The yolk sac rarely grows larger than 6 x 6 mm. (A large yolk sac often signals a pregnancy that is more likely to miscarry.)

- Fetal pole: a tubelike shape inside the gestational sac with a pulsation. The pulsation is your baby's heartbeat! This is a critical developmental milestone in embryonic development. Once the fetal pole is seen, the likelihood of miscarriage drops dramatically.

- Embryo/fetus: your baby. Dramatic changes will take place week by week, which can be documented by photographs or videotape taken from the ultrasound.

Common Concerns About Early Pregnancy

Animals

If you have household cats as pets, do not empty the litter box while pregnant because used kitty litter can contain toxoplasmosis bacteria, which is harmful to the developing baby. Also, if you are an avid gardener, use gloves when digging in the soil, for the same reason. If a woman becomes infected from contaminated animal feces during pregnancy, her baby may have birth defects.

Backache

Use a heating pad for no more than twenty minutes to help relieve the discomfort of backaches. Doing so may lead to a rise in your body temperature, which could affect the baby's metabolism.

Breast Soreness

Because of an increase in the hormone progesterone, your breasts will be tender to touch, be firm, and may feel stretched. To prevent dryness and cracking, avoid using soap on the nipples, especially if you intend to breastfeed. You will notice the nipple area (areola) enlarge, and the blue veins on the skin surface may appear darker. When showering, turn your back toward the shower spray so that the pulsation of the water does not cause increased discomfort.

Tannic acid in tea helps to toughen the nipples. A good home remedy for the relief of nipple tenderness is to make a strong cup of tea and let the bag steep until the water cools. Dip two extra-large cotton balls into the strong tea and squeeze out the excess liquid. Place one cotton ball over each nipple, then rest a breast pad on top of the cotton ball. Take a small piece of plastic wrap and put it on top of the breast pad to prevent the solution from staining your bra. Wear the cotton balls for fifteen minutes three times each day to help toughen the nipples in preparation for lactation (breastfeeding) and to help relieve nipple tenderness.

Some pregnant women will find comfort by rubbing vitamin E oil into the nipples. Avoid lanolin-based creams; some women are allergic to wool, and there may be trace amounts of pesticides in the extracted lanolin.

Constipation

Many pregnant women experience constipation. You should increase your fluid intake by drinking between eight to ten eight-ounce glasses of fluid per day, including milk, fruit juice, and water. Limit your intake of coffee, tea, and cola soft drinks because they all have a high caffeine content. You should also avoid Nutrasweet and saccharin unless you are diabetic. Prenatal vitamins with iron often cause constipation because the iron has a tendency to reduce the amount of fluid in the stool. Metamucil and Colace are over-the-counter preparations that you may take safely if you become constipated. Metamucil adds bulk to the stool. Colace is a stool softener that may be taken once or twice a day. If you have a severe bout of constipation, an occasional dose of Milk of Magnesia is also safe.

Cramping

Some lower abdominal cramping can be expected in the early weeks of pregnancy; however, the cramps should not be as uncomfortable as menstrual cramps. If you experience cramping, minimize your activity, preferably by lying down, and inform your doctor. You may take ibuprofen, such as in Advil or Motrin, or aspirin, if directed by your doctor. Ibuprofen and aspirin inhibit the synthesis or prostaglandins, chemicals that stimulate uterine contractions.

Cravings

If you crave certain foods during the early weeks of your pregnancy, your body needs them. So go ahead and eat or drink those foods. Common cravings include fruits, juices, and other nourishing foods. Avoid alcohol, cigarettes, any drugs not prescribed by a physician, and nonhealthful items such as candy and extremely salty foods.

Fatigue

Fatigue is a common side effect experienced during the first several weeks of pregnancy. Take naps if your schedule permits you to do so. When relaxing in the evening, lie down on the couch. Elevate your feet whenever possible. You should become less tired by the beginning of your second trimester.

Fumes

Avoid painting and refinishing furniture while you are pregnant. Some research indicates that fetal brain development may be impaired by exposure to chemical fumes. Women also should avoid having their hair permed or color treated during the first trimester, because the inhaled chemicals can travel throughout the expectant mother's bloodstream.

Gas/Indigestion

Nibbling on crackers or eating small frequent meals will help eliminate gastrointestinal disturbances. If you feel you need antacids, take Tums, Mylicon, or Mylanta.

Headache

Some women will experience more headaches than usual. Please notify your doctor if this occurs. If your headaches are severe, two Tylenol or aspirin every four to six hours as needed may help relieve the discomfort. You also may try putting a small ice pack at the nape of your neck to help ease the pain.

Hemorrhoids

Many pregnant women experience hemorrhoids even if they have never experienced them before. Try using Tucks pads after a bowel movement instead of dry tissue. Preparation H Ointment and Anusol cream also help to shrink the swelling. Do not insert suppositories into the rectum; just apply creams externally on the irritated skin. A&D Ointment or Desitin Cream also helps relieve irritation.

Hot Tubs

Avoid soaking in hot water. Raising your internal body temperature higher than 100.4 degrees Fahrenheit for an extended period of time can adversely affect your baby's metabolism and brain development.

Intercourse

Your sexual activity should not harm your developing baby. If you experience cramps after sexual activity, avoid nipple stimulation and orgasm. These activities tend to increase uterine contractions. Avoid intercourse if you notice active bleeding. The use of condoms during pregnancy may be recommended to reduce the risk of uterine contractions, which may be caused by enzymes in seminal fluid called prostaglandins. The use of a condom will prevent seminal fluid from contacting the cervix. For women who have had one or more previous miscarriages in the first trimester, Dr. Berger recommends avoiding unprotected vaginal intercourse during the first trimester.

Leg Cramps

Some pregnant women may experience leg cramps, particularly at night. If you are meeting your recommended dietary intake of dairy products, try taking your prenatal vitamin at bedtime. Walking or other nonstrenuous exercise will also help relieve the cramps. Constant pain, swelling, or redness in your calves should be reported to your doctor and evaluated since thrombophlebitis (blood clot and inflammation) may occur during pregnancy.

Linea Nigra

You may see a dark line of skin pigment (linea nigra) form from the base of your navel to the pubic hair line. This line in your abdomen is thought to be where your own development began at conception and may become darker and prominent during pregnancy, depending on your skin coloring. However, it will fade after delivery.

Mood Swings

Many pregnant women experience mood swings. This may be related to fluctuation in hCG levels, which may double every day up to the ninth week of pregnancy before they plateau. You may find that you cry easily for no apparent reason, or you may experience feelings similar to premenstrual syndrome. Expect to be a little more emotional during this time.

Nasal Stuffiness

Use saline drops if you experience nasal congestion. Actifed and Sudafed are the only over-the-counter remedies that are known to be safe during pregnancy. Avoid other nonprescription sinus preparations. The best rule is to check with your physician prior to taking any medication.

Nausea

Most pregnant women experience nausea and sometimes vomiting. This is common in the first trimester and early part of the second trimester and usually disappears when the hCG level begins to decline. (See graph on normal hCG levels on p. 295.) Some suggestions on limiting nausea include: Eat small frequent meals (six small meals rather than three large ones), take your prenatal vitamin at night right before you go to sleep, and take an additional 1 mg of folic acid. This requires a doctor's prescription. Not only is extra folic acid helpful in relieving nausea, but it also protects the baby by reducing the chances of neural tube defects due to immature development of the spinal column.

Many women will find that eating a bedtime snack consisting of cheese, milk, or yogurt lessens nausea because the increased fat content takes longer to digest. Also, have a pack of crackers available at all times to nibble on and keep a few crackers at your bedside to eat even before you get up out of bed in the morning.

Nausea and Increased Sensitivity of Smell

Many pregnant women experience a queasy feeling whenever smelling strong aromas, such as perfume and coffee. Although this is unpleasant, it is normal.

Nutrition

Pregnant women need increased amounts of calories to nourish their growing babies. A good general guideline for pregnant women is to include at least four servings daily from each of the following food groups: milk/dairy, breads/cereals, and fruits/vegetables. Pregnant women also need at least two servings per day of the meats/protein food group.

Rare Meats

Make sure that the meat you eat is cooked well. You should not eat meats that are not thoroughly cooked because of the potential for developing a toxoplasmosis infection, which could make you ill and potentially infect the fetus, causing a miscarriage.

Exercise and Weight Lifting

Avoid initiating any new strenuous activities or a new exercise program once you find out that you are pregnant. Walking and low-impact aerobics, such as swimming or riding a stationary bicycle, are the best forms of exercise. When you exercise, do not raise your pulse rate above 120 beats per minute. There is no reason for a pregnant woman to avoid lifting heavy objects. Strengthening muscles through a regular weight-lifting program using light weights will help a woman deal with the low-back pain and other problems encountered during pregnancy due to weight gain and an altered center of gravity.

Warning Signs

Certain warning signs need to be reported to your doctor immediately. They include the following.

Absence of Pregnancy Symptoms

Contact your doctor if you no longer experience breast tenderness and/or swelling that you noticed before; are no longer fatigued or sleepy although you had been all of the time; or suddenly are not nauseous when several days before you were frequently nauseous.

Bleeding

Call your doctor immediately if you notice any bright red bleeding. This does not necessarily mean that you will miscarry; however, it requires medical evaluation. The bleeding may be from the cervix, most often due to an inflammation. Bleeding from the uterus is more worrisome. In most cases of bleeding in the first trimester, the pregnancy will not be affected.

Inability to Tolerate Food and Fluids

Dehydration could result if you are experiencing severe nausea. Cramping could also increase. If your inability to eat or drink becomes severe, Dr. Berger generally recommends Gatorade. Those rare patients who can't tolerate any fluids may need to receive intravenous fluids. More conservative management includes antinausea medication, changing the way you take your prenatal vitamins, changing the pattern of snacks, and eating smaller, frequent meals rather than fewer large ones.

Right- or Left-Sided Pain in the Lower Abdomen

This type of pain could alert your doctor to the possibility of an ectopic or tubal pregnancy. If your ultrasound scans early in pregnancy do not show the gestation sac within the uterus, then your doctor may recommend further evaluation, such as laparoscopy, to determine the cause of your pain. The possibility of tubal pregnancy is increased for women who have previously had a tubal infection (pelvic inflammatory disease). Tubal pregnancy occurs in approximately one out of every ninety pregnancies in the overall U.S. population. Dr. Berger's routine early pregnancy monitoring is designed both to minimize the risk of miscarriage and to diagnose and treat ectopic pregnancy as early as possible, before complications occur.

Questions to Ask Your Doctor About Pregnancy After Fertility Treatments

Do you provide early pregnancy monitoring through the first trimester? If not, where can I find a doctor who provides this care?

Should I expect to have a high-risk pregnancy?

Do you know of any "Bed Rest Buddy" programs in my area?

What is my baby's gestational age?

What is my due date based on the day of ovulation/conception?

How will my pregnancy be monitored to minimize the risk of complications?

Will you show me my growing baby on an ultrasound scan? Can I videotape the ultrasound scans?

What common symptoms might I notice during early pregnancy?

What warning signs should I report to you immediately?

14

SECONDARY INFERTILITY

Ever since their daughter, Melanie, was three years old, Mary, age thirty-eight, and Ron, age forty, had tried to conceive another child. Mary, a school nurse, had been to several fertility specialists, who told her repeatedly and confidently that she would never have another child. She had had diagnostic surgery, and they had tried intrauterine insemination several times unsuccessfully over six years. When they saw Dr. Berger, he found that Mary had endometriosis and adenomyosis, and treated it through surgery and drugs. He also confirmed, for the first time, that Ron had healthy sperm. After a year of drug therapy and inseminations, Mary still had not conceived.

"We visited Dr. Berger's office and told him we were going to stop treatments," says Mary.

"We had always wanted another child, but we had sunk a fortune into fertility treatments. For Melanie's sake, we gave up our dream," adds Ron, a chemist.

One month later, Mary recalls "feeling hot flashes, like I was going into menopause. My period was late, and I'm never late. I called Dr. Berger's office, and the nurse suggested I get a home pregnancy test kit. Sure enough, it was positive." Mary went to a nearby clinic to have blood drawn for a confirming pregnancy test. "She called me and said it cost $125. I said, 'Go ahead, we've spent this much, what's another $125,'" says Ron. An hour later, Mary received a phone call from the clinic—she was pregnant. "I had to sit down. I'm six months pregnant now, and I still don't believe it at times," she says.

More than 1 million couples who know the joys of parenthood also know the frustrations of infertility. They have children but they want to have more, and, for various reasons, they cannot have them.

Although they may have one child, these couples with what is known as secondary infertility often mourn the lack of a second child. They have been denied the choice that most parents take for granted—the choice of when to bear children and of how large their families will be.

By definition, a couple with secondary infertility has achieved a pregnancy (with the present or a previous partner) and delivered a child in the past, but is unable to do so again. Both partners' reproductive systems may be intact, but since the first pregnancy one or both of them may have developed a problem that caused their current infertility. Or they may be having trouble conceiving together as a couple even though one or both of them may have had a child with a previous partner.

Who Has Secondary Infertility?

The number of couples with secondary infertility has declined since the mid-1960s, from 2.5 million married women of childbearing age to 1.3 million, according to the latest government statistics from the National Survey of Family Growth, while primary infertility, the inability to conceive or carry a child to term, has increased.

Primary infertility becomes more prevalent as women age, according to the fertility survey. One in five married women in her late twenties and early thirties has difficulty conceiving; the odds of delivery decrease to only one in three between the ages of thirty-five and forty-four.

Once a woman has delivered a baby, her chances of not being able to deliver again are just under 10 percent, according to the government statistics. So a woman who has delivered one child is more likely to deliver a second child than a woman who has never been pregnant and carried a child to term. A woman age thirty-five and up who has never had a child has a one-in-three chance of an impaired ability to get pregnant and carry a child to term. She should move faster toward a fertility consultation than a thirty-five-year-old woman who already has had a child.

Despite the slightly better odds, couples who are having trouble having a second child are subject to all the same conditions that can cause primary infertility. In addition, they have to deal with added problems of increasing age, fewer eggs and sperm, and a potential for more damage from sexually transmitted diseases.

The government's definition of infertility (it uses the term "fecundity") is a difficulty in conceiving or delivering a child after three years or more of unprotected, regular sexual intercourse. This three-year time frame is three times as long as most fertility specialists use, which means the survey may have missed many women with both primary and secondary infertility. (For more interpretation of the fertility survey, see p. 14.)

This definition also may wrongly classify some women. Is a woman who miscarries repeatedly or has had more than one ectopic pregnancy considered to have secondary infertility? Some would say so, but the survey puts these women in the primary infertility classification.

Emotional Turmoil

Dana and her husband, Alan, waited three years after April was born to try to have another baby, and then suffered through five years of infertility. After visiting several doctors and fertility specialists, they went through dozens of artificial inseminations, including two in vitro fertilization (IVF) attempts, all to no avail. "I had saved a spot in my heart for another child," says Dana. "Some days I can handle it. Some days I just cry."

"It still hurts and it's been two years since we stopped trying to have another baby," she says. "I can't go to the mall without seeing someone with twins and wondering why couldn't we have another one." Adds Alan, "The healing never stops. I still hope that one day Dana may become pregnant again." In the meantime, he showers his love on April, who is now eleven. "I call April three, four times a day. She says, 'You call me even more than Mom does.' I tell her I love her a lot and just worry about her."

While some people may not perceive secondary infertility as stressful, the emotional turmoil of being unable to have a second child can be as severe as that of never having been pregnant.

Most couples who experience secondary infertility probably used contraception for a period of time before trying for a second pregnancy. The last thing they anticipated was a fertility problem, making secondary infertility an even more unpleasant surprise.

Friends and family may unknowingly ask insensitive questions, wondering when the couple is going to have another child. Or they may ask, "Why do you only have one?" They may think that not having more children is a conscious decision, implying that the couple is selfish or self-centered. People tend to believe that the couple's inability to conceive is a result of not wanting more children or is a psychological disorder.

Guilt

"My daughter Becky really wanted us to have another child," says Ella, a thirty-seven-year-old telephone consultant. "When Becky was about four, she realized that all of her friends had families with more than one child. She kept asking "Why can't I have a brother or sister like everyone else?' She didn't know Sam and I had been trying desperately for two years."

Some couples feel incredibly guilty for not being able to have a second child. They may search their souls or believe they must have done something wrong in their lives to have only one child. Having a child also raises the hopes of having another child and possibly delays the acceptance of secondary infertility. It may not be as easy to conceive the second time around, and not all infertility problems can be corrected.

Others feel guilty about not providing a sibling for their only child. People look at the couple as not being fair to the child the couple already has. The child may feel left out of conversations when other children talk about their siblings. The parents can reassure the child that they are doing everything they can and hope that someday they will have another child. It may help to let the child get to know a family member or a friend's baby and have the experience of hugging or holding a younger child.

If the couple had a difficult time conceiving the first time, trying again may bring up all of the emotional issues they dealt with before. The pressure may be even greater to have a second child since the couple knows that having a baby is possible. Unfortunately, the same infertility myths to "just relax" or "take a vacation" persist not only among friends but physicians as well. Couples who suspect that they may have secondary infertility should not waste crucial time before beginning an infertility workup.

Diagnosing Secondary Infertility

The infertility investigation of the couple with a previous pregnancy is the same as that of a couple who has not had a baby. This includes evaluation of the man with a semen analysis and sperm function tests and of the woman with a hysterosalpingogram or documentation of ovulation and preparation of the uterine lining for implantation, and a laparoscopic examination looking for tubal blockage, adhesions, and endometriosis.

Specific hormone tests should be done when appropriate—for example, when the woman has abnormal periods or breast secretions. A thorough, efficient investigation minimizes the potential for overlooking reproductive problems and the cause or causes of the couple's secondary infertility.

Couples who have had a previous pregnancy tend to think of themselves as having "normal" fertility. But this is not always the case. A woman may have had minimal endometriosis in past years, and it may become more advanced, lowering her probability of conceiving from the normal 20 percent each month to 2 to 4 percent without appropriate treatment. And if a woman had a baby with a different partner, then her new partner needs to be evaluated as soon as possible.

The time it took to conceive the first child should not be overlooked. Some doctors often are reluctant to send a couple for a fertility evaluation if they already have a child. But it may have taken the couple several years before they conceived their first child, indicating that there were fertility-limiting factors even then.

Men who have fathered a child previously may be reluctant to have a semen analysis. They feel that they have proven they are functionally "normal." But a semen analysis is essential because sperm quality can vary greatly. Generally several semen analyses are recommended to account for the normal variation in sperm count and quality. In addition, some functional assessment of sperm quality may be in order, such as a test of how well the man's sperm swim in his wife's cervical mucus and how well his sperm penetrate hamster eggs, a good predictor of how well his sperm might penetrate his wife's eggs.

Even though he fathered a child, he may not have had a "normal" semen analysis in the first place. About 20 percent of all infertility is due to a combination of both male and female factors. A man with a borderline low sperm count who has a very fertile wife may be able to father a child. If he remarries a woman who is also only borderline fertile, they may not be able to conceive together.

Treating Secondary Infertility

"After I had Karen, my menstrual cycles became irregular," says Liz, a thirty-nine-year-old housewife. "When Barry and I decided to have another baby, I tried taking Clomid on my doctor's advice, but that didn't work. He referred me to a fertility specialist who raised the dose, but still nothing happened."

Liz decided to visit the Chapel Hill Fertility Center, where Dr. Berger diagnosed polycystic ovaries and put her on Metrodin for one month. When she didn't get pregnant, he added Pergonal. Liz conceived the next cycle. "We had been talking about the possibility of IVF," she says. "We would have done anything we had to, that's how desperately we wanted to have another baby."

A wide array of fertility treatments is now available, including techniques to induce ovulation through fertility drugs. Other treatments can stimulate a woman to produce more than one egg each month. These hormone treatments often are combined with insemination techniques to place sperm closer to the eggs to enhance the possibility of fertilization. These often complicated, expensive treatments usually are applied only after a comprehensive search for the cause of the couple's fertility problem.

The Age Factor

"We had tried for six or seven years, on and off, to have a second child," Liz says. "Now that we finally have Brent, who is two years old, we want to have as many as we can before the clock runs out."

Time is of the essence to most couples who have been dealing with infertility for years or are already in their mid- or late thirties. Both a man's and woman's fertility decline as they get older, with a woman having a more rapid reduction in her mid- to late thirties. Couples with secondary infertility often are in their thirties and therefore need to act quickly.

Even the latest improvements in fertility treatments will not necessarily compensate for the inevitable age-related decline in sperm and egg number and quality. For example, the success of IVF drops drastically after a woman turns thirty-five. At New York Hospital–Cornell Medical

Center, about 50 percent of couples take home a baby if the woman is under age thirty-four and her husband has no fertility problems. As women reach their late thirties, only 30 percent take home babies. After that, the delivery rate drops to 15 percent for those women forty and up and to only 5 percent for those over age forty-two.

Couples with secondary infertility are not only more likely to be older but, with the nearly 50 percent divorce rate, possibly divorced and remarried. Therefore, each partner may have had more exposure to sexually transmitted diseases (STDs) that may affect fertility. Pelvic inflammatory disease (PID) or an undetected, "silent" chlamydia infection may obstruct a woman's fallopian tubes or a man's sperm-carrying tubes, reducing the chances of conception. A woman may also develop a uterine infection, adhesions that scar the uterus, or cervical trauma associated with a complicated labor and delivery.

The Vagaries of Varicoceles

Ella and Sam decided to have a second child when Becky was two years old. After six months of timed intercourse, Ella went to her doctor. "He kept telling me to relax, don't worry, it will happen," says Ella. "Every six months I went back for a checkup, and he told me the same thing."

After two years with no results, both Ella and Sam had fertility workups. She had no problems, but Sam was diagnosed with varicoceles on both sides. He sought out Dr. Goldstein, who operated on both varicoceles. Within three months, Ella was pregnant.

"Once I found out what was wrong, I felt better that we could do something positive instead of just being in limbo. I also was mad at myself for waiting for so long," Ella says. She doesn't even mind that their son Jake is now going through "the terrible twos."

New research shows that men with varicoceles who have fathered a child may have future fertility problems. These varicose veins in the scrotum are a major risk factor for secondary infertility. The enlarged veins occur in at least 35 percent of infertile men with prior infertility. Typically, the veins increase the temperature in the testicles. This rise in temperature impairs normal sperm production as well as the sperm's swimming ability.

Men with secondary infertility appear to have a particularly high incidence of varicoceles. Dr. Goldstein has found that more than 80 percent of men with secondary infertility have varicoceles compared to 35 percent with primary infertility and 15 percent of the general population. These men with secondary infertility and a varicocele are generally slightly older and have significantly lower sperm counts and more abnormally shaped sperm.

The long-term effects of drugs, alcohol, and the environment in lowering a man's fertility are also worse for men with varicoceles.

If a varicocele is diagnosed and corrected surgically at an early stage, a man's future fertility can be saved, says Dr. Goldstein. Between 50 and 60 percent of men who have microsurgery to remove the varicocele will impregnate their wives within two years.

Obstructed Ducts

Men who have had vasectomies reversed also may suffer from secondary infertility. About 6 percent of men who have had vasectomies request reversals, most often after they have divorced one wife and remarried a woman who wants to have a baby. Using microsurgery, surgeons can reverse vasectomies and more than 90 percent will get sperm back in their semen, and more than half of these men can father children using IVF with ICSI. The majority of men will be able to father a child again. Any man who has had a vasectomy and wants to father another child should be evaluated to make sure that he still potentially is fertile and, if so, is a candidate to undergo microsurgical reversal.

Interestingly, men who have had a vasectomy while married to the same partner and who decide to have a reversal due to loss of a child or a change of heart have the highest chance of success. In a study by Dr. Goldstein, after microsurgical vasectomy reversal, the pregnancy rate is more than 90 percent. He believes that this could be due to the couple's proven fertility or, perhaps, higher power intervention. A man's sperm-carrying ducts may be unintentionally obstructed from an STD infection or after an abdominal operation (especially hernia repairs), which is another reason why any man who has difficulty fathering a second child should have a thorough fertility evaluation.

While the ability to conceive a second child is not always a given, most couples with secondary infertility can have another child, if they have the appropriate clinical workups and treatments. The frustrations of not conceiving may remind the couple of prior problems in conceiving their first child. The emotional turmoil can be ameliorated by the caring staff at a fertility clinic while the couple undergoes treatment. Knowing that they have conceived once helps most couples remain patient as they go through fertility treatments yet again.

Part Five

TWENTY-FIRST-CENTURY FERTILITY

15

ALTERNATIVE
THERAPIES

"I've been in the health field for thirty years," says Lilly, a health food store owner, "so using alternative therapies was a natural outgrowth of my understanding that certain foods are better than others and certain supplements make you feel stronger." Lilly and her husband Richard waited until she turned forty before they tried to have a baby. "I tried many natural ways to increase my fertility, using muscle testing and working with nutritionists, including saliva testing to determine my hormone levels on a daily basis. I used natural thyroid hormone, natural progesterone cream and oil, and a natural cortisol."

When the natural methods and supplements didn't work, they tried conventional fertility treatments. One fertility specialist put her on Clomid, but that didn't stimulate her ovaries enough. A second specialist suggested a GIFT procedure, which produced four eggs, two of which were viable, but her chemical pregnancy ended after three days. "I insisted that Richard not take the antibiotics that were part of the protocol," says Lilly. "I surrendered to the artificial forces of medicine, kicking and screaming all the way. The whole process was humiliating and impersonal. The team of doctors and staff were not talking to each other or integrating our therapy," Lilly recalls.

The specialist who performed the GIFT procedure found endometriosis had left scar tissue around her fallopian tubes, which Lilly thought validated her decision to take natural cortisol. "Cortisol helps autoimmune diseases, such as endometriosis, and the saliva testing showed I had an uneven adrenal output," she says.

With her advancing age, her doctor recommended egg donation, and Lilly searched the Internet for three months to find an appropriate egg donor program. "I connected with a doctor, but he said he wouldn't work with me because I was taking cortisol. Then I heard about a nearby program, which found an egg donor within six months," she says. Lilly became pregnant on Labor Day and the next May, at age forty-seven, gave birth to her son Clay, who's now a healthy 21-month-old.

317

Millions of Americans have become disenchanted with some of today's conventional medical treatment approaches. Indeed, more than one third of all Americans say they have tried an alternative therapy. People pace the aisles of health food stores and pharmacies with a newfound self-reliance to self-diagnose and self-treat with over-the-counter drugs and dietary supplements. This disenchantment is apparent even in the prevention and treatment of fertility problems.

The past few decades have witnessed the increasing involvement of health-conscious consumers in their own fertility treatment decisions. For about thirty years, high-tech fertility medicine has rapidly progressed with an increasing array of synthetic drugs and surgical interventions. But we are experiencing a revolution in health care, and natural remedies are here to stay.

Alternative fertility treatments have their attractions. In general, the cost of care is often a fraction of conventional medicine. Alternative medicine practitioners usually offer their full, undivided attention for lengthy periods, unlike many busy fertility doctors. Perhaps the most important reason that more than 83 million Americans embrace alternative medicine is that they have more control over their own health care.

However, the alternative medical community tends to accept anecdotal evidence as reality, and this may, in some cases, mislead patients in terms of what they may expect from their results. Alternative practitioners need to diligently demonstrate the safety and efficacy of what they claim. Patients like to know that what they are being offered will work safely. The conventional fertility doctor is armed with the convincing double-blind controlled trial. Many theories or applications of natural medicine are flawed or are empiric. Alternative medical practitioners need to start to search more for a scientific basis for their recommendations. Miracle cures may exist, but they are few and far between.

What we need is a new breed of fertility doctor who seeks to integrate conventional and alternative medical practices. The new millennium will see more practitioners willing to seek out what works, without concern for its medical origins. Today's health care consumers have learned to question the validity of some fertility treatments, for example, transferring too many embryos into the uterus during IVF. Educate yourself about what treatments are helpful, then make your selections with appropriate insight.

Who Uses Alternative Therapies, and Why

Well-educated, high-income patients are turning to alternative therapies, despite little or no scientific proof of their value, according to a survey of Resolve members in New York City. The one-page survey distributed in the monthly newsletter received seventy-two responses, mostly by women, average age thirty-nine, who were college-educated, had been married for six years, had been trying to conceive for about three and a half years, and had a median household income of $100,000. Nearly half of the respondents reported that they had been helped by alternative treatments; the most frequently used alternative treatments were vitamins (71 percent), counseling and/or support groups (61 percent), exercise (50 percent), mind-body techniques (49 percent), and herbal supplements (49 percent). Most of them said that they used alternative treatments because of dissatisfaction with conventional medical treatment. Others looked to alternative approaches to regain control and reduce stress, to make themselves healthier or to feel better, to make sure to "try everything," and because they truly believed in alternative medicine, according to Joann Paley Galst, Ph.D., who conducted the research.

While the survey represents an uncontrolled sampling of infertility patients, it shows the growing use of alternative therapies and why they are so attractive. Galst suggests that the appetite for alternative therapies stems from needs that are unmet by conventional fertility treatments, including "a need for control, a less invasive, less costly, and gentler approach that may be viewed as more natural, and a treatment of the whole person, including their emotional needs for attention and compassion. The most attractive feature of alternative medicine for infertility patients may be its holistic treatment of people, serving as an antidote to the depersonalizing effect of being treated like a body part, a test result, or a statistic."

Stress and Conception

With the cycles of hope and crashing disappointment, the scheduled sex and strain between partners, infertility certainly creates stress. But does stress cause infertility? By far, the majority of fertility problems are due to physiological causes, but it's becoming more apparent that the mind plays a role in infertility.

It's not uncommon for women to grow frustrated, develop anxiety, or suffer from stress by their prolonged inability to conceive. Research shows that stress can disrupt ovulation and diminish IVF success rates, and that IVF may be less effective for women who are easily stressed. Female lawyers who work long hours at their jobs are five times as likely to experience great stress at work and three times as likely to suffer miscarriages as female lawyers who work fewer than thirty-five hours a week. Women who have extensive fertility treatments or a high-risk pregnancy may also be susceptible to post-traumatic stress disorder.

There is evidence that stress can cause hormonal imbalances and tubal spasms, both potential factors in infertility. The hypothalamus, which controls the flow and timing of reproductive hormones, is keenly sensitive to stress. Without enough estrogen, an egg will never be released or will be too immature to grow. Not enough progesterone and an embryo can't be implanted or stay implanted.

Men also show the stresses and strains of infertility treatments. Sperm counts in the normal range may fall to barely fertile after a long workup and months and months of trying to achieve a pregnancy. Chronic stress in rats can reduce sperm counts dramatically and make some of them sterile. Stress has also been shown to impair sperm motility and morphology. High levels of stress hormones can reduce testosterone production and probably impair fertility.

Relaxation and meditation have been proven to reduce stress, blood pressure, and levels of stress hormones in the blood. Relaxation techniques such as acupuncture and acupressure have been known to regularize a woman's menstrual cycle as well as to improve the quality of a man's sperm counts.

Research from the Harvard Medical School's Mind/Body Medical Institute suggests that stress reduction may aid conception. Since 1987 Alice Domar, Ph.D., has taught groups of infertile women relaxation skills, stress management, yoga, and better nutrition as ways to cope with infertility. The ten weekly sessions also give women and their spouses a chance to commiserate about what many describe as the worst experience of their lives. The average conception rate for couples who have gone through the program is 36 percent compared to 18 percent for couples with a similar history who did not receive any relaxation training.

The program has no formal studies to confirm the theory that stress is to blame for infertility. It may work for several reasons. Women who feel better about themselves might have sex more often. They may be more aggressive in seeking medical treatment, or stick to treatments long enough for them to work. Networking could help women find out about other doctors and treatments that lead to success. Or relaxation and stress management may be making a real difference.

Most fertility specialists have problems working with the ideas of stress and infertility because it's so difficult to prove. They would rather use high-tech medicine and quantify their results. Fertility doctors need to pay attention to the psychological as well as medical needs of fertility patients. That means helping them schedule injections and blood tests to be as convenient as possible and suggesting coping skills and relaxation techniques. Most large fertility centers now offer psychological counseling as part of the fertility treatment process.

We can't tell couples that stress is going to cause their treatment to fail because we don't know whether stress is actually the cause of the failure or whether it's simply related to it. Biology is still the most important factor in infertility. But if a couple keeps their stress levels low, they seem to have a better chance of achieving a pregnancy than if they are stressed.

Mind/Body Therapy

Many alternative medicines feature a harmonious existence with nature, and anxiety, stress and depression are seen as the cause of many medical problems, including infertility. The natural substance purveyors and practitioners of natural health suggest that you direct your attention to total body wellness by achieving a peaceful mind combined with the utmost personal care and nutrition. They say the answer to fertility problems rests in combining nutrition, natural healing processes, and the power of the mind over the body.

There is more and more evidence that spirituality affects health. Transcendental meditation, yoga, and biofeedback are ancient concepts now applied by modern mind/body therapies. Various styles of bodywork, from acupuncture to acupressure to Jin Shin Jyutsu, claim to harmonize and balance the body's energy flows, which promote optimal health and well-being, and may be valuable complements to conventional treatments.

The overall goal of mind/body therapy is to use psychotherapy, relaxation, counseling, and spiritual methods to protect the body by releasing repressed emotions and resolving conflict. The use of psychospiritual interventions, breathing exercises, sharing, love, intimacy, prayer, visualization, and meditation are all examples of techniques that may exert powerful healing effects. These novel approaches to general wellness can be considered a sophisticated extension of stress reduction and behavioral therapy. Some alternative practitioners believe these techniques, in themselves, are a complete treatment approach to infertility. However, since most fertility problems can be traced to a physiological cause, it's prudent to get a full workup for an appropriate diagnosis and treatment of fertility problems and to use these mind/body therapies as adjuncts.

Treating the Female

Traditional Chinese Medicine

Traditional Chinese medicine (TCM) views infertility as a state of weakening, aging, disease, or imbalances in the body. To improve your fertility, TCM practitioners try to slow down or reverse the aging process and restore the body's functions.

Like fertility specialists, TCM practitioners usually begin a couple's infertility investigation with an evaluation and consultation. Depending on the diagnosis, the treatment may last from three months or longer, and patients may be referred to a fertility specialist for a clinical workup.

Most major American cities now have licensed acupuncturists or Doctors of Oriental Medicine who specialize in reproductive medicine. To find one, contact the American Association of Oriental Medicine at (610) 433–2448.

A major component of TCM is acupuncture, which is now practiced by more than 10,000 licensed acupuncturists who treat more than 1 million Americans each year. Despite its five thousand–year history, nobody knows exactly how acupuncture works as a healing technique. The Chinese believe that a balanced flow of vital life energy, called qi or chi, is necessary for good health. According to the Chinese, qi can become imbalanced by heat, cold, dampness, emotions, diet, exercise, and the spirit. Acupuncture rebalances the flow of qi by inserting special needles at 360 points along energy pathways, or meridians. Acupuncture to kidney points is said to release psychological blocks that interfere with reproduction.

For female infertility, acupuncture has in some studies been as successful as hormone therapy in helping women become pregnant. Acupuncture may be effective because it triggers chemicals, including pain-killing endorphins, and brain-altering neurotransmitters and neuropeptides, which influence the endocrine system. Acupuncture is also used to promote healing and hormonal regulation in uterine fibroids, anovulation, and premature menopause. Chinese clinical studies also show acupuncture to be effective in promoting ovulation in secondary amenorrhea.

Electro-acupuncture is a specialized version of acupuncture. It uses electric impulses sent through acupuncture needles for such conditions as anovulation and fallopian tube obstruction, and to improve implantation during assisted reproduction procedures.

Another common addition to acupuncture is moxibustion, which involves burning an herb known as mugwort to create heat. This is said to increase circulation throughout the pelvic cavity and promote healing and follicle development, and is used to treat pelvic pain and infertility.

For couples who lead stressful lives, TCM practitioners may prescribe qi gong, a form of meditative exercise. Qi gong is a combination of gentle movements, breathing, and imagery that assists the body to relax, and is said to improve the implantation of embryos.

Chinese Herbs

Infertility treatments have been studied extensively in China, in particular immunologically based infertility treated with herbal remedies. Chinese herbs are usually used in combination and prescribed for specific conditions. Raw herbs, taken in a brewed tea over several weeks, are mostly prescribed for infertility conditions. The herbs can also be prescribed in powder, capsule, pill, or tincture form.

The TCM Guyin Decoction has been used to treat women with infertility attributed to an antisperm immune response. Herba epimeti is an aphrodisiac used to tone renal/adrenal function because the Chinese believe that reproductive function is related to the kidney. Deer antler helps women over forty trying to extend their egg-producing years. Wormwood creates more circulation in the pelvic cavity and is used along with daughter seed and fructose litchi. Dong quai and cortex cinnamon help the circulation in the pelvic cavity.

Endometriosis

While the cause of endometriosis is unknown, it is clearly a hormonally related condition. Some holistic medicine specialists recommend a low-fat, high-fiber diet to decrease estrogen levels and, it is hoped, decrease pain and shrink fibroids. Phytoestrogens, such as soy food sources, also lower estrogen levels by blocking estrogen receptor sites.

Various vitamins, minerals, and supplements are recommended for endometriosis by holistic practitioners, including B-complex vitamins; the amino acid methionine; magnesium; a multivitamin-and-mineral supplement; vitamin E; omega-3 oils or flaxseed oils; gamma linolenic acid; and quercetin, which is a potent flavonoid found in many fruits that has anti-inflammatory effects. Other holistic remedies recommended include the TCM Dong Quai, licorice root extract, alfalfa extract, homeopathic remedies, acupuncture (for pain and endometrial dysfunction), and massage therapy. Biofeedback, meditation, and guided imagery are among the mental and emotional health recommendations for endometriosis.

Enhancing Endocrine Function

A long list of herbs may have an effect on fertility by enhancing endocrine function. Chaste berry increases luteinizing hormone, which increases progesterone and may help women with low progesterone levels; the herbs beth root, false unicorn root, and black cohosh may promote estrogen production; and Dong Quai can supposedly improve the rhythm of the menstrual cycle.

Naturopathy

Naturopathic physicians believe that natural treatments can turn on the self-healing mechanisms of the body. For example, if a woman's hormones are out of balance, a natural approach might help. Naturopathic physicians have an extensive background in botanical sciences, including the use of herbs and tinctures with a wide variety of immune-stimulating properties.

A couple going for a fertility evaluation with a naturopath may be asked to fill out a comprehensive questionnaire, including personal, nutritional, and hormonal information. Naturopaths believe that the body needs to dispose of toxins to prepare for pregnancy, and may develop an individualized metabolic detoxification program for each patient. The program generally involves a variety of dietary changes, along with herbal or antioxidant supplements, and natural hormones, such as natural progesterone. The program may take several months to complete. At that time, the couple's health will, it is hoped, have improved enough to allow them to conceive.

A natural approach to infertility tends to be less physically invasive and less expensive than conventional fertility treatments. It also is complementary to conventional approaches, and couples may try both methods. Hard medical evidence, however, is lacking for naturopathy. Unless there's proven data to support it, it could be a waste of time and money.

Fallopian Tube Obstruction

The herbs phytolacca decandra and calendula have been used to decongest the fallopian tubes, and thuja might help reduce growths, cysts, and adhesions. One naturopathic treatment for pelvic infections that have scarred fallopian tubes is the old-fashioned sitz bath. The woman sits in a tub of hot water, with arms and legs out of the tub, for five minutes, then in cold water for one minute, and alternates back and forth. This supposedly helps the body throw off scar tissue and toxic material in the ovaries. Some practitioners of natural hygiene believe that a fast of several days followed by a good nutritional regimen helps in the case of fallopian tube obstruction. Colloidal silver is a supplement that purportedly helps clean a woman's system of chlamydia, one of the most common causes of pelvic infection.

Treating the Male

Traditional Chinese Medicine

The Chinese formula Tze Pao San Pien is said to increase potency and treat male infertility. *Panax ginseng* (Chinese or Korean ginseng) and *Eleutherococcus senticosus* (Siberian ginseng) have a history of use as male tonifiers. The herbal preparation Zhibai Dihuang Wan, a traditional formula for autoimmune disorders, has been found to decrease autoimmunity measures and allow sperm to become more viable. Astragalus may also build up the immune system. Other Chinese herbal formulas that may be useful are deer antler, Rehmannia Eight and Rehmannia Six, Wu Zi Wan (the Five Herbs of Creation), ashwagandha, and fo-ti.

When Chinese herbalists find "blood deficiency and stagnation, arising from poor circulation," they often recommend Dong Quai. When they think impotence is due to an androgenic hormone deficiency, they might suggest rehmannia and eucommia, which are regularly taken together to augment each other, as are many Chinese herbs. Deer antler, Rehmannia Six, *Schisandra chinensis*, and *Epimedium grandiflorum* may also be helpful.

The Chinese believe that premature ejaculation can be treated with a combination of rehmannia and eucommia called you qui wan, or with Rehmannia Six or astragalus. You qui wan can be brewed as a tea or taken as a dried extract.

Other Herbs

Other herbal remedies said to correct imbalances and enhance fertility are gota kola, stinging nettles, green oats, dandelion, and blue vervain. The traditional Indian herb tribulus, often used by body builders, is used to counter infertility by increasing testosterone as well as sperm count.

L-Carnitine—Fertility Booster?

Many couples can't have children because the man's sperm does not swim well enough. L-carnitine, a naturally occurring substance similar to an amino acid, has been touted for its ability to boost sperm motility. It has been found in very high concentrations in the epididymis, the ducts that transport sperm from the testes to outside the body, and has been reported in low levels in men with below normal sperm motility.

L-carnitine producers, including the highly promoted product Proxeed, would like to claim their product energizes sperm, but they have yet to prove it. The natural supplement has been around for twenty years, but there is no convincing evidence that it's effective. Half of carnitine studies show a slight benefit, and the other half show no benefit. None of the studies is controlled, nor are the results published in high-quality journals. While carnitine is a carrier molecule of fatty acids, we don't know whether it plays a critical role in sperm maturation and sperm metabolism. We don't know whether the carnitine in supplements gets into semen or whether the amount is enough to have a beneficial effect on sperm. Therefore, consider it of unproven value until it has been subjected to controlled studies against a placebo. It probably does no harm, except to your pocketbook, since it costs about $90 for a month's supply. That money may be better spent in a proper diagnosis to find out why a couple hasn't been able to conceive.

Before trying carnitine supplements, men should see their doctors rather than medicate themselves. A man may have a more serious condition that can usually be treated. Men with wives approaching forty are especially encouraged to consult a fertility specialist. L-carnitine is thought to take about four months to work. In the meantime, a woman in her late thirties is fast losing her fertility and may require more aggressive treatment.

Impotence

The most valuable nutritional supplement for impotence may be zinc. Clinical studies show that zinc supplements may help increase testosterone levels. Some holistic doctors recommend 30 to 60 mg of zinc daily along with 1 or 2 mg of copper daily for impotent men. Other recommendations include beta carotene, magnesium, essential fatty acids, as well as lycopene (the flavonoid found in tomatoes and other red fruits and vegetables) and arginine (an amino acid found in nuts and meats). The hormone DHEA, a very popular over-the-counter medication touted for anti-aging and to improve testosterone naturally, has also been suggested as an impotence treatment. It supposedly is converted into testosterone naturally by the body, but no one knows its effects on sperm production.

Herbal remedies for impotence usually begin with yohimbe, a powerful stimulant that helps maintain erections by increasing blood flow to the penis. It is often taken with damiana (considered an aphrodisiac in Central and South America), stinging nettles, and green oats. Other herbs and supplements that are purported to enhance sexual potency include: ginkgo biloba (to increase circulation); ashwagandha (an Ayurvedic herb); *Panax ginseng* (to stimulate the endocrine system); and Siberian ginseng (to support the adrenal glands). However, in contrast to an uncontrolled pilot study of oral ginkgo biloba, a placebo-controlled, double-blind evaluation could not prove any benefit from treatment with the extract for patients with erectile dysfunction.

Once Viagra hit the market, and the demand for it soared, other herbal products and enhancers soon followed. The offerings range from drugs that promise similar results to herbal alternatives, such as L-arginine and ginkgo, which help relax blood vessels in the penis and allow an erection to occur, similar to the way Viagra works. If holistic doctors find poor penile blood flow, they may use niacin or chelation therapy to increase the blood flow. The Viagra frenzy also inspired "Viagra-enhanced" subliminal tapes aimed at increasing sexual performance. Try them at your own risk.

Some of the alternative products for impotence caught the attention of the Federal Trade Commission, which in May 1999 imposed an $18.5 million judgment on several companies for falsely advertising products. The FTC also has published a brochure to help consumers identify bogus treatments for impotence. For a copy, call 877-FTC-HELP (877–382–4357).

Threats to Fertility

Some of the more popular botanical therapies appear capable of inhibiting conception or damaging sperm. Laboratory tests show that high concentrations of echinacea (touted as a cold remedy), ginkgo biloba (recommended as an energy and memory booster), and St. John's wort (used to treat depression) impair the ability of sperm to penetrate hamster eggs. What's more, echinacea and St. John's wort damaged the sperm's outer membrane when sperm were bathed for one week with dilute solutions of the herbal preparations. While these tests are preliminary, they warrant attention for couples trying to conceive who regularly take these common herbal products.

Melatonin is another popular supplement, used as a sleep aid or for jet lag. Claims have been made that melatonin is a powerful antioxidant that helps with aging and immunity and reduces the risk of cancer and heart disease. However, research on melatonin is still very preliminary, and often not in controlled studies. Some preliminary data suggest that it may cause constriction of blood vessels, inhibit fertility, and suppress the male sex drive. And as a powerful hormone, it should not be taken by pregnant women.

While the trace mineral selenium is essential to sperm development, some claims have been made that selenium supplements can treat infertility. Selenium is a powerful antioxidant that is found in many foods, including brown rice, seafood, enriched white rice, and whole wheat flour. Despite studies in randomized controlled trials, there is no conclusive data that shows selenium works as a fertility aid.

The FDA lists yohimbe as an unsafe herb, primarily due to the risks of low and high blood pressure. It can potentiate elevated heart rates and cause anxiety, hallucinations, headache, and skin flushing. It should not be taken by anyone with high blood pressure, heart or liver disease, diabetes, or kidney problems, or by anyone who uses alcohol, tranquilizers, or antihistamines.

While moderate doses of vitamins C and E may enhance the ability of sperm to fertilize an egg, high levels of these vitamins can be toxic to sperm, rapidly decreasing their motility and eventually killing them, according to research by Dr. Goldstein. He recommends daily dosages of about 250 mg of vitamin C and 400 IUs of vitamin E.

A mixture of herbs can have adverse effects on sperm. Couples trying to conceive need to be cautious when taking herbal remedies. Unlike prescription medications, which are FDA approved, they are not required to have toxicity testing. Since herbal remedies don't come under FDA review, there is no way of knowing whether they have adverse effects. For example, a medication sold in Israel contains ground-up bull's testicles. Any medication that contains testosterone, as this one does, will suppress sperm production and be harmful to couples trying to have a baby. The brain senses the testosterone as from outside the body and sends a signal to the testicles to turn off testosterone production, which shuts down sperm production as well.

Also, some herbs are contraindicated once a woman becomes pregnant, such as black cohosh. If a couple wants to use herbs, they should consult an herbalist or naturopathic doctor experienced with infertility for the right combination in the right amount at the right time. Although anecdotal evidence provides occasional success stories, there is no medical research to prove that herbs and natural hormones can improve a couple's ability to conceive. If you do opt for an alternative treatment, make sure it won't interfere with your goal of having a baby.

16

THE BRAVE
NEW WORLD
OF FERTILITY

In the brave new world where a sixty-three-year-old woman has a baby and sperm is retrieved from dead men, fertility patients and specialists must wrestle with ethical quandaries almost daily. Assisted reproductive techniques now help people with complex problems involving sperm and eggs who would have been told just a few years ago that they were sterile. Researchers are manipulating sperm and poking and prodding eggs, taking single cells out of embryos and testing them for genetic defects, taking cytoplasm out of one egg and adding it to another, and moving chromosomes from one egg to another.

An irrevocable change has occurred in how humans reproduce. Technology continually provides new choices that help couples have a baby, continue a pregnancy, attempt to overcome infertility, and genetically shape babies, including possibly choosing their sex. Some of the thorniest issues include genetic engineering; fetal rights; access to technology by the wealthy and the potential exploitation of the poor "hired" for their reproductive capacity; and creating a fetus for research. While some detractors describe any manipulation of the human embryo as "morally unacceptable," scientists in the field say it's an "immoral waste" to destroy embryos that could lead to potential treatments.

A couple's fertility may be in the future—young men and women may eventually deposit high-quality sperm and eggs into a reproductive bank for use when they are older. Later, when they are ready to have a baby, they will simply go to the bank and withdraw what they need. This kind of scenario will move legal, ethical, and moral issues from the laboratory and the fertility clinic into the forefront of public debate.

Eventually society must take the lead in deciding how to deal with issues like these. Right now, whatever fertility clinics are willing to offer and whatever couples are willing to pay for gets done. Since the first IVF success in 1977, more than 300,000 babies have been born to women who, without IVF technology, would be infertile. IVF is now taken for granted. ICSI, fertilization of an egg by direct injection of a single sperm under the microscope, was an even greater technological achievement. It has become a powerful tool for the treatment of male infertility, and more than 10,000 ICSI babies have been born since 1992. "Miracle" births from IVF and ICSI may just be the tip of the iceberg if other new, cutting-edge technologies become commonplace.

Cloning

The cloning of Dolly the sheep by Scottish researchers in 1997 clearly signaled that, after a lot more exploratory work with animals, humans could be cloned. Policymakers in America and Europe found this dangerous and alarming enough that they immediately proposed a ban on human cloning, although Americans are having second thoughts.

Dolly was cloned not from an embryo, which is what happens naturally with twins when an embryo splits, but from an adult sheep. This cloning does raise some curious possibilities. It might be possible to have identical twins separated by a number of years, or to clone an infant copy of an existing adult. The cells that were cloned from Dolly were very early embryonic cells that had not started on the path to being defined tissues, as happens naturally in the case of identical twins. Many fertility specialists are convinced that such cloning will have great human benefits, such as the production of several potential embryos for implanting during fertility treatments.

The first-ever human cloning experiment further fueled the cloning debate in 1998. A Korean fertility doctor produced a four-cell embryo from genetic material extracted from a thirty-year-old woman. He removed the nucleus of an ordinary cell taken from an infertile woman and substituted it for the nucleus of one of her eggs. It grew into a four-cell embryo, but the experiment was stopped at that point because of an adopted code of conduct that banned inserting a cloned embryo into a womb. Although the egg started to divide, a developing embryo does not actually use its DNA until the fourth or fifth round of cell division. So the

Korean experiment ended before researchers could evaluate whether the DNA transfer was a success.

While Dolly was cloned using nuclear transfer, the rhesus monkey Tetra was made by splitting a very early embryo into four pieces, making her the first nonhuman primate to be cloned. This method, called artificial twinning, is commonly used in animals such as cattle but had never been used to create a monkey. Tetra came from one-fourth of an embryo. Scientists have learned that animals like Dolly cloned by nuclear transfer are not 100 percent clones since they have genetic material both from the adult cells they were taken from and from the egg that is hollowed out to make the clone. Each of Tetra's cells contain all the same genetic material.

New cloning techniques are being developed all the time. Japanese researchers have cloned calves from skin cells, which are easy to obtain, in contrast to earlier efforts that have used udder cells (for Dolly) or embryos. Experts believe this technique should work in other species, including humans. The British government now allows the "therapeutic cloning" of human embryos for research using embryonic stem cells, which has sparked a heated debate over the ethical limits of medical research. Opponents of cell-based techniques say it will effectively give scientists the green light to create new human beings, use them for "spare parts," and throw away the remains.

It seems just a matter of time before human cloning becomes an acceptable way to conceive children. Several groups claim to be on the verge of cloning a human. But numerous experiments will need to be done to prove that human cloning can produce a healthy, normal birth. Attempting to clone a human would pose unknown risks to a mother and her cloned child. Technically, there is no doubt that cloning can be done in any animal. But there is no data to show that human cloning would be safe. In particular, because a clone is derived from an adult cell, there are questions whether it would live a normal life span. Also, animal cloning experiments have resulted in a high rate of miscarriages.

Embryonic Stem Cells

Exciting opportunities will emerge from studies and research on embryonic stem cells, the so-called master cells that can develop into any kind of cell in the body. This technology could ultimately provide the basis for controlled production of stem cells for transplantation and gene therapy, a concept that would revolutionize medicine. Although embryonic stem cells can't develop into a human being, they can grow into many types of cells, such as muscle cells, nerve cells, heart cells, and blood cells. Researchers envision cultivating the cells into replacement nerve cells for patients with Parkinson's disease, insulin-secreting cells for diabetics, and heart muscle cells for heart attack victims. Or the genes of embryonic stem cells might be altered to ensure that they will not be rejected by the immune system, in effect creating universal donor tissue.

This research raises the tricky question of the source of the stem cells. Some scientists have derived them from aborted fetuses, while others get them from leftover embryos donated by couples who had gone through IVF at a private fertility clinic. Abortion-rights activists say destruction of an embryo means destruction of an organism, and early stem cell research has been conducted without any federal funding.

New guidelines from the National Institutes of Health (NIH) suggest that research on embryonic stem cells be allowed, but restricts the source of the cells. Researchers must obtain them from privately funded researchers or companies, and must be able to document that the embryonic stem cells lines meet certain conditions. Those conditions include that the stem cells must have been derived from "extra" frozen embryos left over after fertility treatments; embryo donors may not receive payment or other compensation and are not allowed to specify recipients of the cells; companies or laboratories supplying the cells must document that donors were informed that their cells may be used indefinitely and for commercial purposes. While NIH has recommended that American scientists receive federal funding for research on stem cells from human embryos, Congress may not allow it, with some in Congress and President George W. Bush arguing that stem cells taken from adults work just as well as embryonic cells.

Society has much to gain from research on human embryos, including insights into various genetic diseases and cancer. Fetal tissue transplants have already reversed the ravages of Parkinson's disease, yet researchers may never get enough of this precious tissue to meet the demand for such therapy. Patients and their families faced with life-threatening and chronically disabling diseases want science to move as quickly as possible, which has helped change public opinion about this emotionally charged issue.

Frozen Embryos

About 10,000 unused frozen IVF embryos a year have been piling up in private fertility clinics since 1992. Stem-cell researchers would love to adopt these orphan frozen embryos, and the ethics of allowing researchers to obtain the embryonic cells continues to trigger debates. Couples going to IVF are generally asked to sign consent forms about how to handle extra embryos, which can be frozen. The practice of having couples sign contracts developed because so many frozen embryos were ultimately abandoned.

Couples undergoing IVF should be counseled by the fertility clinic about the possibility of having spare or leftover embryos. Couples should be asked to make a decision about what to do with these embryos when they are no longer wanted for purposes of reproduction, and both members should agree on that decision. When they decide they no longer want their frozen embryos stored, either because they have had all the children they want or because they have abandoned attempts at IVF, then they should be asked about how to handle the embryos. If the embryos are to be donated to stem-cell research, then the couple should know that. If either member of the couple disagrees with donating them to research, then the embryos should be destroyed. Couples should not be offered financial compensation for their frozen embryos.

Who Owns the Embryos?

Disputes in a handful of states have arisen over control of frozen embryos created through IVF after couples had gotten a divorce. While each state has had its own legal interpretation in these cases, a nonbinding consensus of sorts has emerged. Embryos are considered neither children nor property, but rather a "special entity" with the potential for life. Whenever possible, the agreement a couple signed with an infertility clinic about what to do with their embryos if the couple divorce or die should be considered a contract. The special rights that abortion law gives a woman over the embryo growing in her body do not apply when the embryo has been frozen, so the father and the mother should have equal rights over what is done with it. State courts have ruled that those equal rights can shift if the embryos seemed to be a potential parent's only chance to have a biological child.

Embryo Adoption

Another way for couples to handle extra frozen embryos is to put them up for adoption. A number of fertility clinics are quietly offering couples the option to do so, either openly or anonymously. Embryo adoption allows expectant parents to experience pregnancy and control prenatal care. They also can get more information about the child's genetic parents. However, only a handful of states have laws governing the donation of embryos.

Fertility clinics usually match embryo donors and recipients from within their own patient pool. Specialists who help arrange embryo adoptions say they screen the genetic parents for AIDS and other diseases, and provide psychological counseling to all involved.

Embryo adoption turns out to be an inexpensive alternative for couples who can't conceive. Because fertility clinics do not want to become caught up in state laws about selling babies, they typically require embryo donors to give the embryos as a gift. The only fee is the cost of the in vitro fertilization procedure, which runs about $3,000. With the exceeding demand to do something with the growing number of frozen embryos, embryo adoption may turn out to be a viable alternative.

Older Mothers

"Egg donation is a volatile topic in our family, causing lots of stress and strain," says Rick, fifty, who runs a computer company. He and his wife, Shelly, a forty-four-year-old therapist, went through two unsuccessful IVF cycles. "Shelly had a slightly elevated FSH level, and my sperm seemed to swim in circles, so we used ICSI and assisted hatching. Each time, the transferred embryos didn't take, so our fertility specialist recommended a donor egg," says Rick.

About one year later, the fertility center located an appropriate donor, who was "intelligent, athletic, and attractive, according to the nurses," says Rick, who notes that an eight-page summary described the donor's characteristics, family and medical history, but contained no picture of her. Right before the embryo transfer, the donor dropped out of the program, which "was very hard on us emo-

tionally. The center said this was very rare, and put us on top of the waiting list,"
recalls Rick.

Two months later, the center located a second donor, "a Russian immigrant,
very intelligent, upbeat, and attractive, who had a marginal high hepatitis B
test," Rick says. "We were all set for the embryo transfer. The center retested her
for hepatitis B and found a higher reading, and canceled the cycle. They wouldn't
risk transferring hepatitis to our baby." Another donor was available immedi-
ately, so Shelly stayed on Lupron, even though she hated the hot flashes and mood
swings it induced. "Everything was fine with this donor—she had produced lots
of eggs for harvest. The day before the embryo transfer, the center cut back on her
medication to avoid overstimulation. All of her eggs were absorbed," says Rick.

For the third time, they didn't even get to the embryo transfer stage. "I was
beside myself," says Shelly. "I felt that maybe I wasn't meant to have a baby this
way or to have a baby period. The center offered to try again with the same egg
donor, but I said, 'No more.' I couldn't handle this psychologically or physically.
I'm not saying I won't do donor egg again, but I need time to sort things out." In
the meantime, Rick and Shelly feel the longing for a child whenever they see a
young baby, including their friend's son, who was born through a donor egg pro-
gram about the time they were going through their first donor egg attempt.

A woman's fertility changes with age, but improved treatments such as
donor eggs are helping more women in their forties, fifties, and even sixties become mothers. For older women trying to get pregnant, every
month counts. The major regret of older infertility patients is that they
took a wait-and-see approach while their chance of conceiving was getting smaller every month. After menopause, a woman's ovaries are unable to produce viable eggs. But her uterus ages much less rapidly and
still offers a hospitable environment. If a woman had frozen some embryos when she was younger, she could withdraw some from a reproductive bank and increase her chances of conceiving later in life.

Faulty egg production is the major age-related infertility issue. As she
ages, a woman's egg production declines, particularly after age forty.
What's more, more of the eggs she produces contain abnormal chromosomes, reducing the chance of pregnancy and raising the risk of miscarriage or birth defects. At the moment, there are no treatments to improve
egg quality.

Older eggs, once fertilized, may divide abnormally, leading to a high
proportion of embryos with chromosomal problems. Women thirty-five
and older run the risk of having a child with Down syndrome, which is
caused by the presence of an extra chromosome 21. A Cornell team has

targeted women age thirty-nine and older undergoing IVF, looking at their embryos for the correct number of chromosomes before transferring them. The hope is to increase their fertility chances and to reduce older women's risks of having a genetically defective child. If it works, the method could offer thousands of older women who are having trouble conceiving the hope of having a healthy child.

Many older women go through initial fertility treatments unsuccessfully, and must go to IVF as the next step. For IVF to work, a woman must still be able to produce usable eggs. Some IVF programs have strict age cutoffs, usually between forty-one and forty-three. Others rely on a woman's day three FSH results. As women approach menopause and their ovaries become increasingly unresponsive, FSH levels begin to climb. Measuring FSH levels on day three of a woman's cycle has become a crucial test for aging eggs.

Fertility specialists are learning how to adjust every step in the IVF process to maximize the chances for forty-plus women. Aggressive stimulation with higher doses of fertility drugs can compensate for the ovaries' lower ability to respond. Assisted hatching can create a small opening in the outer shell of the egg, which is thicker and harder in older women, before embryo transfer. More embryos may be transferred for a woman in her forties since she may not be making as many eggs and has a lower chance of success in freezing extra embryos for later use. On the positive side, a woman over forty is only about half as likely to have a multiple pregnancy as a woman under thirty-five but the possibility still exists of a dangerously high number of embryos being implanted.

For some older women, the only hope is to use donor eggs, using a younger woman's eggs that are fertilized, either with her husband's or donor sperm, and the resulting embryo transferred to the older woman's uterus. While IVF success rates go down drastically after age thirty-four, the success of donor eggs remains high, with a live-birth rate of about 40 percent overall, though some recipients may require several cycles before becoming pregnant. Donor egg programs have begun to set age limits, starting at forty-five and up. Most programs insist that a woman over forty-five be tested to ensure that she is healthy enough to carry and deliver a baby. If no available donor fits the recipient's immediate requirements, a prospective mother or couple simply has to wait until an acceptable donor turns up. The average wait is a few months, but it can take as long as a year.

There are health risks associated with late-in-life pregnancies. A woman over thirty-five is twice as likely to develop high blood pressure or gestational diabetes during pregnancy as a woman in her twenties. Developing diabetes during pregnancy about doubles a woman's chances of becoming diabetic later in life. Obstetrical complications are more common among even healthy forty-year-olds, including preeclampsia, which causes high blood pressure after the twentieth week of pregnancy, and placental abruption, where the placenta detaches from the uterine wall. Almost all pregnancies in women forty-five and older are delivered by cesarean section. Also, a woman in her forties may have a marginal, undiagnosed heart condition that reveals itself during the physical stress of pregnancy. Even so, a healthy older woman with no underlying, chronic condition has only minimal risks of harming her health during pregnancy.

Ultimately, there is no guarantee that forty-plus women will be able to reproduce. The natural reduction in eggs continues until the ovaries are depleted around age fifty. For most women, fertility begins to decline in their early thirties, drops again at age thirty-five, and plunges steadily at age thirty-nine and beyond. A thirty-year-old is three times more likely to conceive using IVF than is a forty-year-old. While science may push back the envelope to help some women breach biology's barriers, the question of whether these sophisticated technologies should be used to turn back time remains.

Young Egg Donors

Some ethicists worry that young, inexperienced women may be jeopardizing their health and future fertility by becoming egg donors. An egg donor must take powerful hormones and undergo invasive medical procedures. In rare cases, fertility drugs may overstimulate the ovaries, requiring hospitalization. The egg retrieval process may cause scarring or bleeding of the ovaries. Some infertility programs provide inadequate information to prospective egg donors, who may be given less information than infertility patients who go through IVF. Some refer the donor to psychologists for pretreatment evaluations, but others simply rely on intuition to screen out indigent or unstable donors.

Others believe that egg donation has become too commercial. The fees paid to donors have risen along with the demand for donor eggs, most of which come from white, middle-class women. This coincides with a decline in the number of adoptable American infants born to white, middle-class women. Because so many recipients are looking for certifiable intelligence in their donors, many fertility programs are placing ads in student newspapers at Ivy League schools, offering as much as $50,000. Marketing strategies by egg donation programs include advertisements in cinemas and in *Backstage* magazine, which is used by actors to get work. Many agencies direct would-be recipients to Internet sites to browse pictures of donors, accompanied by detailed profiles of health history, education, and interests. Donors are often selected for their marketability as well as their general health. One Web site even offered an "auction" to sell eggs donated by fashion models to the highest bidder in the hopes of providing potential parents with more attractive children.

Although it is difficult to precisely quantify appropriate levels of compensation to egg donors for time and trouble, an Ethics Committee of the American Society of Reproductive Medicine has determined that "sums of $5,000 or more require justification and any amount of more than $10,000 would be inappropriate." ASRM guidelines say a donor should not be paid for her eggs, but, according to the Ethics Committee, rather for her "inconvenience and physical and emotional demands," and her fee should be fixed regardless of how many eggs she produces. As a safety precaution for donors, most clinics limit them to four or five cycles. The ASRM guidelines say that donors should contribute to no more than ten live births, and suggest that all donors be offered psychological counseling before they begin the treatment.

Donor brokerage agencies typically charge $2,500 for their matching services, but high-end agencies charge each recipient more than $6,000 to cover the agency's fee for recruiting and screening donors as well as the donor's basic fee, which can be as high as $18,000. Most donors receive about $2,500. Most health insurance policies do not cover egg donation costs, so infertile couples must have the means to cover the entire cost of the donor's drugs and fees themselves, which typically cost about $20,000, but can exceed $50,000.

Some lawyers familiar with egg donation have suggested that fertility clinics adopt American Bar Association guidelines devised to cover contracts with surrogate mothers. These guidelines call for $100,000 worth of life insurance coverage for every surrogate and require recipients to cover any medical expenses that arise from the procedure. The guidelines mandate that a professional counselor discuss any possible psychological risks with both the surrogate and prospective parents, and suggest that the surrogate get legal counsel.

Donors sign consent forms releasing them from any parental rights or responsibilities. More than thirty states have laws that guarantee sperm donors their independence from any offspring, but only a handful so far have comparable laws for egg donation. Sometimes the couple meets with the egg donor, akin to an open adoption; in other circumstances, the egg donor remains anonymous.

Multiple Pregnancy Problems

An epidemic of multiple pregnancies has seen the incidence of twin births nearly double and triplet births triple over recent decades. Much of this is related to older women wishing to have babies, and fertility clinics have transferred as many as ten embryos at once during IVF procedures. For women over forty, transferring three rather than two embryos seems to have no effect on the pregnancy rate. But it does increase the rate of multiple births.

The birth of seven and even eight babies challenges medical practitioners to think about how many babies is too many. Multiple pregnancy imposes additional financial, emotional, and logistical burdens on families. They increase the risk of injury to mothers and babies, and are considered the greatest potential hazard of medically assisted reproduction. They also present some parents with the difficult choice of selectively reducing one or more fetuses.

Currently, two is the magic number for IVF embryo transfer, according to revised guidelines by the ASRM. As long as women have a good prognosis for the procedure, such as being young and with no past IVF failure, research shows that only two healthy embryos achieve the best outcomes. In England, Australia, and most of Europe, regulations have for years forbidden fertility specialists to transfer more than two or three embryos. The result has been fewer multiple pregnancies than in the United States, but IVF success rates have been about 20 percent lower.

A shift in thinking is occurring in American IVF practices. Triplets used to be regarded as a necessary disadvantage, a compensation for low IVF pregnancy rates. Now they are considered an avoidable complication. The trend toward reducing the number of embryos transferred has led some fertility clinics to go back to natural cycle treatments, noting that Louise Brown, the world's first test-tube baby, was born after IVF during a natural menstrual cycle. They suggest that couples with unexplained fertility or women with regular monthly cycles with fallopian tube problems might be suited for natural IVF.

The pressure on IVF providers is to maximize pregnancy rates. Doctors want to get their patients pregnant. Doctors know that a low pregnancy rate can spell doom for their clinic, so some clinics take a whatever-it-takes attitude. They know that patients shop for doctors who have the best pregnancy rates. And the way to get the best rates is to transfer more embryos, which increases the risks of multiple pregnancy. Basically, there is a built-in disincentive to resolve the multiple pregnancy problem.

And patients want to be pregnant, and often pressure fertility specialists for success. Since many patients have to pay out of pocket for fertility treatments, they often pursue a more aggressive treatment plan than their physicians might recommend. Financial pressures often lead couples into high-risk treatments without regard to the risk of multiple pregnancies. Many couples are prepared to accept the risks of multiples, especially against the background of the costs and stresses of further IVF cycles. Most fertility clinics explain the risks of multiple pregnancies, but many patients who are desperate to become parents simply cannot envision them.

The risks are real. Babies born in groups of three or more are more likely to die as infants or to be dangerously small, which can lead to vision and hearing impairment, mental retardation, and developmental delays. Twins are almost five times as likely to die in their first year as single births, and babies from triplets, quadruplets, or larger groups are more than ten times as likely to die as infants.

Many hope that technology will come to the rescue. The three-versus-two embryo debate may be superseded by research aimed at improving culture conditions and embryo selection so that fewer but better-quality embryos can be transferred. Delay of transfer until the blastocyst stage at day five or six yields implantation rates of up to 50 percent, and should also allow for selection of better embryos. Avoiding triplets may someday become straightforward, but the ultimate goal should be the transfer of only one embryo.

Fertility on Ice

New technology may make it possible for a woman to preserve her future fertility and have a baby after her peak reproductive years. Embryo freezing—having eggs retrieved, fertilized, and frozen—gives a couple the option of thawing and implanting the embryos when they are ready to have a baby. Not all of the embryos are likely to survive, and they are legally bound to the male partner or donor who fertilized them.

Egg freezing and later thawing for use in IVF is another approach. Mature eggs are notoriously tricky to freeze safely. Newer freezing media rely on higher concentrations of coolants and faster cooling times. This results in glasslike solutions rather than icelike frozen ones that can damage the egg. A few births have been reported using unfrozen mature eggs or immature eggs that were frozen and treated in the laboratory.

Women may be able to stop their biological clocks by having one ovary surgically removed, sliced, and frozen. The thawed slices may someday be reimplanted and, it is hoped, resume producing hormones and eggs. This process has produced pregnancies in sheep, but not in humans as yet.

Ovarian Tissue Transplants

A thirty-year-old ballet dancer is the first human to have received an ovarian tissue transplant. She had an ovarian cyst removed when she was seventeen, and her other ovary excised when she was twenty-nine due to a benign disorder. After the second operation, some of the ovarian tissue was frozen and banked. The next year she had a chain of segments of the tissue stitched into her pelvic wall close to the ovary's former site. Four months later, after a dose of fertility drugs, she ovulated and had a normal menstrual period, like any fertile woman. If she wants to become pregnant, doctors will have to stimulate the ovarian tissue again, retrieve eggs, and perform IVF.

This procedure may be an insurance policy for young women with severe endometriosis or cancers in remission, but it cannot stop menopause in older women and cannot be done for women with ovarian cancer. Women close to menopause are not candidates because their ovaries do not have enough eggs to restore fertility after freezing and thawing. And no doctor would put a cancerous ovary back into a patient.

Transplanting ovaries from one woman to another is not practical yet. Immunosuppressive drugs needed to prevent rejection cannot be taken during pregnancy. But that could change with more research. At the moment, it does not make sense for a woman to take immunosuppressive drugs to keep an ovary just so she does not have to take hormone replacement therapy.

Some fertility clinics have begun offering to remove an ovary before a cancer patient undergoes treatment and to reimplant part of it later. Ovarian tissue slices are easier to obtain than eggs, and the immature eggs within survive freezing better. The freezing and reimplanting technique has great potential, but doctors need to study it to find out how much of the grafted tissue survives, how many eggs it can produce, and how long a woman's apparent fertility will last. Also, mouse studies have raised a concern that frozen ovarian tissue from a cancer patient might harbor roaming tumor cells. However, researchers have transplanted both fresh and frozen ovarian tissue into monkeys and restored ovarian function and produced mature eggs.

Germ Cell Transfer

Researchers have reported transferring germ cells taken from virile male mice to the testes of infertile mice. Those cells matured to form sperm and allowed some of the mice to father offspring. This leads to the intriguing concept for humans—take germ cells from a man with a low sperm count, culture them in the laboratory, and use them to replenish the man's testes. Such research could also pave the way for germ-line gene therapy, the technique of replacing a disease-causing gene with a healthy gene.

Theoretically, researchers could obtain germ cells from a man who carried a genetic flaw, snip out the mutant gene, and replace it with a normal one. Then the corrected germ cells could be transferred to the man's testes. None of his children would carry the genetic flaw. Currently, gene insertions remain risky, and it's premature to think about germ-line gene therapy in humans. But if researchers can iron out the glitches, it would offer tremendous benefits.

Oocyte Nuclear Transfer

This technique involves removing the nucleus of an egg from an infertile woman and transplanting it into a fertile woman's donor egg that has had the nucleus removed. The resulting egg is then fertilized with sperm donated by the infertile woman's husband and reimplanted into her uterus. For many infertile women, particularly those forty and older, the only options are adoption or conception through IVF using a donor egg. This technique, called oocyte nuclear transfer, provides another alternative. Many older women are considered infertile not because of problems with DNA in their eggs but because of deterioration through aging of the cytoplasm that contains the structures, chemicals, and nutrients needed to support the egg's development. This assumption that defects lie in the cytoplasm has never been proven. This research combines genes from two women, and raises questions of what blood line and kinship means.

Pre-implantation Genetic Diagnosis

Analyzing embryos for genetic flaws now is available for certain women and certain disorders. Despite no federal funds, studies of pre-implantation genetic diagnosis (PGD) have forged ahead. This technique involves gently sucking one or two cells out of an embryo, which can then be analyzed for such diseases as cystic fibrosis, Tay-Sachs, and Down syndrome. Embryos can also be sorted to avoid X-linked disorders, such as hemophilia or muscular dystrophy, and couples can choose to have only female embryos transferred to the uterus during IVF. In X-linked disorders, female children may carry the mutant gene on one of their X chromosomes, but generally only male children will actually develop the disease.

About one thousand couples have now used PGD, and about two hundred PGD-babies have been born. The multiple pregnancy rate after PGD is quite high at 33 percent. The average birth weight of these babies is similar to that of other babies born through IVF, and there is no increased risk of birth defects compared to the general population. Over the next decade, researchers predict that PGD will help improve efficiency of IVF by allowing doctors to choose the best embryos to transfer.

A team of Cornell University researchers led by Dr. Zev Rosenwaks has used a method of PGD to ensure the birth of healthy children born to parents who both carried the trait for sickle cell disease, an inherited red blood cell disorder. The procedure involves fertilizing the woman's egg with the man's sperm in the laboratory, then analyzing the resulting embryos for evidence of the disease. Genetic analysis indicated that four embryos were normal, one embryo's sickle-cell status was uncertain, and two embryos had sickle-cell disease. The three healthy embryos were transferred, two developed to full term, and healthy twin girls were born.

This powerful technology ensures that the immediate offspring and any future offspring do not carry the sickle cell trait, and avoids the difficult decision of whether to abort an affected fetus. As the Human Genome Project identifies many more positions on chromosomes occupied by specific genes, the same methods can be applied to other devastating or lethal diseases.

A Colorado couple used PGD tests to create a IVF baby that would have the exact type of cells desperately needed to save their six-year-old daughter. This was the first time a couple knowingly screened their embryos before implanting one in the mother's womb for the purpose of saving a sibling's life. Doctors collected cells from the newborn's umbilical cord and infused them into the circulatory system of his sister, who suffers from an inherited bone marrow deficiency, called Fanconi anemia. With the cell transplant, the girl now has a good chance of being free of the disease, which is fatal without treatment. The procedure is a harbinger of where scientific advances are taking human reproduction in the near future. The case also raises questions about parents' ability to choose the traits of their children, for whatever practical, or capricious, reason they may have.

Sex Selection

The new wave of assisted reproductive technologies includes the potential to choose a baby's sex. PGD allows couples to choose the sex of their babies as well as screen out diseases, which has caused controversy over the potential to produce designer babies. PGD is relatively uncontroversial when it is used to prevent genetic diseases. Much more contentious is the use of the technology by couples who want a child of a particular sex for nonmedical reasons, for example, to balance out their family—they already have a child of one sex and want to have another of the opposite sex.

The slippery slope fertility clinics must navigate comes when a couple pretends to have concerns about genetic disease and asks for PGD, while all they really want to know is the baby's sex. This has happened in the past with other sex selection techniques that used sperm swimming speed to sort X-bearing from Y-bearing sperm (usually unsuccessfully). Some couples who found out they had the "wrong"-sex baby would abort the fetus. This also was apparent in the first report of a successful sperm-sorting technique by researchers at the Genetics & IVF Institute in Fairfax, Virginia. This technique, which exploits the natural difference in the amount of DNA in X and Y chromosomes, was offered as a way for families to avoid dangerous sex-linked genetic diseases. However, the overwhelming majority of families who used the technique wanted it for family balancing.

Some ethicists worry that sex selection may open the way for designer babies, where couples not only choose the sex they prefer but other characteristics such as height, eye color, or other factors largely under genetic control. Many people feel sex selection is tampering with Nature, and the concept has not really caught on. Sex selection is not the most important ethical issue facing medicine, but it may be the beginning of an important debate over whether couples should be allowed to select or enhance nondisease genetic traits.

DIRECTORY OF U.S.
AND CANADIAN FERTILITY SPECIALISTS

The following Directory of Fertility Specialists derives from a questionnaire sent to all members of three subsocieties of the American Society for Reproductive Medicine—the Society of Reproductive Endocrinologists, the Society of Reproductive Surgeons, and the Society for Assisted Reproductive Technology—plus the Society for the Study of Male Reproduction, a subspecialty society of the American Urological Association.

The information included in the directory was provided by those physicians who responded to our questionnaire. Only board-certified doctors who responded to our mailings are included here. Other qualified fertility specialists may have been omitted. While this directory can help you find a nearby fertility specialist, or one who has a particular clinical interest, it is not an endorsement of any physician. In all cases, you should use the same careful deliberation that you normally would employ when choosing a physician.

UNITED STATES

ALABAMA

Birmingham

Ricardo Azziz, M.D., M.P.H.
618 South 20th Street, OHB-549
Birmingham, AL 35233-7333
Phone (205) 934-5708
Fax (205) 975-5732
E-mail razziz@uabmc.edu
Specialty Certification Ob/Gyn
Subspecialty Certification Reproductive Endocrinology
Practice Setting academic
Clinical Interests polycystic ovary syndrome and androgen excess; operative endoscopy in pain and infertility; endometriosis
Research Interests polycystic ovary syndrome; adrenal hyperplasia; androgen excess
Member Society of Reproductive Surgeons

Richard E. Blackwell, Ph.D., M.D.
Department of Obstetrics & Gynecology 555 OHB
University of Alabama at Birmingham
Birmingham, AL 35233
Phone (205) 934-6050
Fax (205) 975-5731
E-mail R.Blackwe@VAB.MC.EDU
Specialty Certification Ob/Gyn
Subspecialty Certification Reproductive Endocrinology
Practice Setting academic
Clinical Interests ovulation induction; surgery
Research Interests pituitary tumors; ovulation induction
Member Society of Reproductive Surgeons

Kathryn L. Honea, M.D.
2006 Brookwood Medical Center Drive, Suite 508
Birmingham, AL 35209
Phone (205) 870-9784
Fax (205) 870-0698
Specialty Certification Ob/Gyn
Subspecialty Certification Reproductive Endocrinology
Practice Setting private
Clinical Interests IVF; ovulation induction; infertility surgery—endoscopic (endometriosis, etc.)
Research Interests blastocyst culture for IVF
Member Society of Reproductive Surgeons
Comments Visit our Web site, www.artprogram.com. Our mission is to help couples achieve a pregnancy with a cost-effective, compassionate plan of care focused on reducing the chance of occurrence of higher-order multiple birth

William A. Leitner, M.D.
2700 10th Avenue S, Suite 406
Birmingham, AL 35205

Phone (205) 930-0920
Fax (205) 939-8939
Specialty Certification Urology
Practice Setting private
Clinical Interests male infertility; microsurgery
Member Society for Male Reproduction and Urology

Mobile

George T. Koulianos, M.D.
3 Mobile Infirmary Circle, Suite 312
Mobile, AL 36607
Phone (334) 438-4200
Fax (334) 438-4211
Specialty Certification Ob/Gyn
Practice Setting private
Clinical Interests IVF ovulation induction; tubal reversal
Research Interests IVF; polycystic ovaries
Member Society for Assisted Reproductive Technology
Comments Visit our Web site www.infertilityalabama.com.

ALASKA

Anchorage

Robert G. Thompson, M.D., FACOG
4001 Dale Street, Suite 117
Anchorage, AK 99508
Phone (907) 562-5328
Fax (907) 562-4363
E-mail robert_thompson_md@MSN.com
Specialty Certification Ob/Gyn
Subspecialty Certification Reproductive Surgery
Practice Setting private
Clinical Interests advanced laparoscopic surgery and hysteroscopy; endometriosis and pelvic pain
Research Interests health and nutrition
Member Society of Reproductive Surgeons

ARIZONA

Gilbert

Joseph H. Worischeck
Casa Blanca Medical Group
4001 E. Baseline
Gilbert, AZ 85234
Phone (480) 926-6237
Fax (480) 926-6206
E-mail Wapiti1@1x.netcom.com
Specialty Certification Urology
Practice Setting private
Clinical Interests vasectomy reversal; sperm aspiration and ICSI; laparoscopic varix ligation
Member Society for Male Reproduction and Urology

Phoenix

Sujatha Gunnala, M.D.
Southwest Fertility Center
3125 N. 32nd Street, Suite 200
Phoenix, AZ 85018
Phone (602) 956-7481
Fax (602) 956-7591
Specialty Certification Gyn
Practice Setting private
Clinical Interests endometriosis; uterine fibroids; Infertility, microsurgery
Research Interests endometriosis; depot Lupron
Member Society of Reproductive Surgeons

John H. Mattox, M.D., FACOG
Arizona Reproductive Medicine Specialists
1300 N. 12th Street, Suite 520
Phoenix, AZ 85006
Phone (602) 343-2767
Fax (602) 343-2766
E-mail jhm@samaritan.edu
Specialty Certification Ob/Gyn
Subspecialty Certification Reproductive Endocrinology
Practice Setting academic
Clinical Interests andrology; menopause; Mullerian anomalies
Research Interests position emission tomography and postmenopausal dysfunction disorder; position emission tomography and hormone replacement therapy
Member Society of Reproductive Surgeons

Drew V. Moffitt, M.D., FACOG
Arizona Reproductive Medicine Specialists
Edwards Medical Specialists
1300 N. 12th Street, Suite 520
Phoenix, AZ 85006
Phone (602) 343-2767
Fax (602) 343-2766
E-mail dmoffitt@arizonarms.com
Specialty Certification Ob/Gyn
Subspecialty Certification Reproductive Endocrinology
Practice Setting private
Clinical Interests IVF
Research Interests treatment protocols for IVF
Member Society of Reproductive Surgeons, Society for Assisted Reproductive Technology, Society of Reproductive Endocrinology and Infertility

Robert Tamis, M.D.
3411 N. 5th Avenue, #207
Phoenix, AZ 85013
Phone (602) 468-3840
Fax (602) 468-2449
E-mail: geninfo@conceive.com
Specialty Certification Ob/Gyn
Practice Setting private
Clinical Interests infertility
Research Interests habitual pregnancy loss

Member Society for Assisted Reproductive
Technology

Tucson

Scot M. Hutchinson, M.D.
6365 E. Tanque Verde, #230
Tucson, AZ 85715
Phone (520) 733-0083
Fax (520) 733-0771
E-mail rhc@azstarnet.com
Specialty Certification Ob/Gyn
Subspecialty Certification Reproductive
Endocrinology and Infertility
Practice Setting academic/private
Clinical Interests infertility; endometriosis
Research Interests sperm function/preparation;
uterine blood flow
Member Society for Male Reproduction and
Urology, Society of Reproductive
Endocrinology and Infertility

Sheldon H. F. Marks, M.D.
2355 N. Wyatt Drive, Suite 111
Tucson, AZ 85712
Phone (520) 881-5429
Fax (520) 326-7841
E-mail reverse@azstarnet.com
Specialty Certification American Board of
Urology
Practice Setting private
Clinical Interests vasectomy reversal—
microsurgical; male infertility
Member Society of Reproductive Surgeons
Comments Medical director of the
International Center for Vasectomy Reversal
in Arizona. Successful reversals as far out as
thirty-five years from vasectomy. See our
website www.dadsagain.com.

ARKANSAS

Little Rock

Dean Moutos, M.D.
4301 W. Markham, Slot 518
Little Rock, AR 72204
Phone (501) 296-1783
Fax (501) 296-1710
E-mail: MoutosDeanM@exchange.uams.edu
Specialty Certification Ob/Gyn
Subspecialty Certification Reproductive
Endocrinology
Practice Setting academic
Clinical Interests endometriosis; polycystic
ovarian disease; IVF
Member Society for Assisted Reproductive
Technology, Society of Reproductive
Endocrinology and Infertility

CALIFORNIA

Berkeley

Ferdinand J. Beemink, M.D.

2999 Regent Street
Berkeley, CA 95746
Phone (510) 843-7722
Fax (510) 841-5535
Specialty Certification Ob/Gyn
Practice Setting private
Clinical Interests infertility; sex preselection;
treatment of endometriosis
Research Interests sex preselection
Member Society of Reproductive Surgeons

Ryszard J. Chetkowski, M.D., FACOG
2999 Regent Street, Suite 101-A
Berkeley, CA 94705
Phone (510) 649-0440
Fax (510) 649-8700
E-mail abivf@pacbell.net
Specialty Certification Reproductive
Endocrinology
Subspecialty Certification Ob/Gyn
Practice Setting private
Clinical Interests ART; donor egg; infertility
surgery
Research Interests implantation; egg donation;
polycystic ovarian syndrome
Member Society for Assisted Reproductive
Technology, Society of Reproductive
Endocrinology and Infertility

Beverly Hills

Mark W. Surrey, M.D.
450 N. Roxbury Drive, 5th Floor
Beverly Hills, CA 90210
Phone (310) 277-2393
Fax (310) 274-5112
E-mail rmsasurrey@msn.com
Specialty Certification Reproductive Surgery
Practice Setting academic/private
Clinical Interests microendoscopic evaluation
of tubal ovarian hiatus; transvaginal
hydrolaparoscopy
Research Interests endometriosis;
salpingoscopy; microhysteroscopy
Member Society of Reproductive Surgeons

Sharon A. Winer, M.D.
9400 Brighton Way, Suite 206
Beverly Hills, CA 90210
Phone (310) 274-9100
Fax (310) 273-6191
E-mail saw@ucla.edu
Specialty Certification Ob/Gyn
Subspecialty Certification Reproductive
Endocrinology
Practice Setting private
Clinical Interests ovulation disorders;
menopause; amenorrhea
Research Interests menopause; oral
contraceptives
Member Society of Reproductive Surgeons
Comments Practice limited to gynecology,
reproductive endocrinology, and infertility
workup through ovulation induction.

Glendale

Charles M. March, M.D.
   1560 E. Chevy Chase Drive
   Glendale, CA 91206
   Phone (818) 242-9933
   Fax (818) 242-9937
   E-mail cmarchmd@earthlink.net
   Specialty Certification Ob/Gyn
   Practice Setting academic/private
   Clinical interests hysteroscopic surgery;
   ovulation induction; recurrent abortion
   Research Interests ovulation induction;
   endometriosis; leiomyomas
   Member Society of Reproductive Surgeons

Laguna Niguel

Paul W. Zarutskie, M.D.
   25500 Rancho Niguel Road, Suite 280
   Laguna Niguel, CA 92677
   Phone (949) 448-7818
   Fax (949) 448-7819
   E-mail Zinstitute@yahoo.com
   Specialty Certification Ob/Gyn
   Subspecialty Certification Reproductive
   Endocrinology
   Practice Setting private
   Clinical Interests male factor infertility; IVF;
   menopause
   Research Interests progesterone support to
   endometrium; insulin and androgen excess
   Member Society of Reproductive Surgeons

La Jolla

Jeffrey S. Rakoff, M.D.
   Director, IVF & Fertility Center
   Scripps Clinic
   10666 N. Torrey Pines Road
   La Jolla, CA 92037
   Phone (858) 455-9100
   Fax (858) 554-8727
   E-mail jrakoff@scrippsclinic.com
   Specialty Certification Ob/Gyn
   Practice Setting private
   Clinical Interests IVF; endoscopic surgery
   Research Interests IVF; endometriosis,
   polycystic ovaries
   Member Society of Reproductive Surgeons,
   Society for Assisted Reproductive Technology
   Comments Completed full fellowship training
   in reproductive endocrinology and infertility
   at UCSD School of Medicine. We provide all
   aspects of clinical infertility care.

Phillip G. Wise, M.D.
   9850 Genesec Avenue, #460
   La Jolla, CA 92037-1228
   Phone (858) 452-8845
   Fax (858) 535-8364
   E-mail pwise@ucsd.edu
   Specialty Certification Urology
   Practice Setting private
   Clinical Interests vasectomy reversal; testicular
   sperm extraction; effects of varicocele
   surgery, laparoscopic
   Member Society for Male Reproduction and
   Urology
   Comments I am in the solo private practice of
   urology. I work closely with gynecologists in
   the community to give the optimum care for
   the couple.

Samuel H. Wood, M.D.
   4150 Regents Park Row, Suite 280
   La Jolla, CA 92037
   Phone (858) 625-0125
   Fax (858) 625-0131
   E-mail Swood@fertile.com
   Specialty Certification Ob/Gyn
   Subspecialty Certification Reproductive
   Endocrinology
   Practice Setting private
   Clinical Interests IVF
   Research Interests implantation; assisted
   fertilization
   Member Society for Male Reproduction and
   Urology, Society for Assisted Reproductive
   Technology, Society of Reproductive
   Endocrinology and Infertility

La Mesa

Martin D. Bastuba, M.D.
   8851 Center Drive, Suite 501
   La Mesa, CA 91942
   Phone (619) 697-2456
   Fax (619) 697-2494
   Specialty Certification Urology
   Practice Setting private
   Clinical Interests infertility; impotence
   Research Interests infertility; impotence
   Member Society of Reproductive Surgeons
   Comments Completed fellowship in
   impotence and infertility at Boston University
   in 1993.

Loma Linda

Steven C. Stewart, M.D.
   11370 Anderson Street, Suite 1100
   Loma Linda, CA 92354
   Phone (909) 558-4830
   Fax (909) 558-2602
   Specialty Certification Urology
   Practice Setting academic
   Clinical Interests impotence/male infertility
   Member Society for Male Reproduction and
   Urology

Long Beach

Bill Yee, M.D.
   701 E. 28th Street, Suite 202
   Long Beach, CA 90806
   Phone (562) 427-2229
   Fax (562) 427-2751
   Specialty Certification Ob/Gyn
   Subspecialty Certification Reproductive
   Endocrinology

Practice Setting private
Clinical Interests ART laparoscopic surgeries; pelvic ultrasound
Research Interests embryo culture techniques
Member Society for Assisted Reproductive Technology, Society of Reproductive Endocrinology and Infertility

Los Angeles

Alan H. DeCherney, M.D.
10833 Le Conte Street
Los Angeles, CA 10092
Phone (310) 794-1884
Fax (310) 367-0024
Specialty Certification Ob/Gyn
Subspecialty Certification Reproductive Endocrinology
Practice Setting academic
Clinical Interests infertility; IVF; reproductive surgery
Research Interests IVF; infertility
Member Society of Reproductive Surgeons

Jaroslav J. Marik, M.D.
Tyler Medical Center
921 Westwood Boulevard
Westwood Village
Los Angeles, CA 90024
Phone (310) 208-6765
Fax (310) 208-3648
E-mail jjmarik@aol.com
Specialty Certification Ob/Gyn
Practice Setting private
Clinical Interests endometriosis and infertility; polycystic ovarian syndrome; preimplantation diagnosis
Research Interests preimplantation diagnosis; investigation of etiology and possible treatment of oligoastheno-azoospermia
Member Society of Reproductive Surgeons, Society for Assisted Reproductive Technology, Society for Male Reproduction and Urology

Richard J. Paulson, M.D.
1245 Wilshire Boulevard, Suite 403
Los Angeles, CA 90017
Phone (213) 975-9990
Fax (213) 975-9997
E-mail rpaulson@uscivf.org
Specialty Certification Ob/Gyn
Subspecialty Certification Reproductive Endocrinology
Practice Setting academic
Clinical Interests oocyte donation; IVF; fertility in menopausal women
Research Interests implantation; blastocyst culture; natural-cycle IVF
Member Society of Reproductive Surgeons, Society for Assisted Reproductive Technology, Society of Reproductive Endocrinology and Infertility
Comments Visit our Web site: www.uscivf.org.

Cappy Rothman, M.D.
2080 Century Park East
Los Angeles, CA 90272
Phone (310) 277-2873
Fax (310) 286-2139
Specialty Certification Urology
Practice Setting private
Clinical Interests andrology (male infertility); microsurgery
Research Interests cryopreservation
Member Society of Reproductive Surgeons

Charles E. Shapiro, M.D., FACS
Chief, Department of Urology
4900 Sunset Boulevard, 2nd Floor
Los Angeles, CA 90027
Phone (800) 954-8000
Specialty Certification Urology
Practice Setting academic
Clinical Interests infertility
Member Society of Reproductive Surgeons

Rebecca Z. Sokol, M.D.
1245 Wilshire Boulevard
Los Angeles, CA 90017
Phone (213) 975-9990
Fax (213) 975-9997
Specialty Certification Internal Medicine
Practice Setting academic/private
Clinical Interests male reproduction; sperm function; male infertility
Research Interests reproductive toxicology; genetics of infertility; androgen replacement
Member Society for Male Reproduction and Urology

Orange

Moon H. Kim, M.D.
Department of Obstetrics & Gynecology
University of California Irvine Medical Center, Bldg. 22A
101 The City Drive
Orange, CA 92868
Phone (714) 456-7204
Fax (714) 456-8360
E-mail kimmh@uci.edu
Specialty Certification Ob/Gyn
Subspecialty Certification Reproductive Endocrinology
Practice Setting academic
Clinical Interests infertility; hyperandrogenism/polycystic ovarian syndrome; ovulatory dysfunction
Research Interests menopause
Member Society of Reproductive Surgeons

Palo Alto

David Adamson, M.D.
540 University Avenue, Suite 200
Palo Alto, CA 94301
Phone (650) 322-1900
Fax (650) 322-1730
E-mail fpnc@aol.com
Specialty Certification Ob/Gyn

Subspecialty Certification Reproductive
Endocrinology
Practice Setting private
Clinical Interests ART; endometriosis;
endoscopic surgery
Research Interests endometriosis; endoscopic
surgery; ART
Member Society of Reproductive Surgeons
Comments We provide all aspects of advanced
reproductive care in a supportive and caring
environment in Palo Alto and San Jose.

Valerie Baker
540 University Avenue, Suite 200
Palo Alto, CA 94301
Phone (650) 322-1900
Fax (650) 322-1730
Specialty Certification Ob/Gyn
Subspecialty Certification Reproductive
Endocrinology and Infertility
Practice Setting academic
Clinical Interests ART
Member Society of Reproductive
Endocrinology

Alexis Kim, M.D.
540 University Avenue, Suite 200
Palo Alto, CA 94301
Phone (650) 322-1900
Fax (650) 322-1730
E-mail fpnc@aol.com
Specialty Certification Ob/Gyn
Subspecialty Certification Reproductive
Endocrinology and Infertility
Practice Setting private
Clinical Interests IVF; basic infertility;
endometriosis
Member Society for Assisted Reproductive
Technology

Deborah A. Metzger, Ph.D., M.D.
780 Welch Road, Suite 206
Palo Alto, CA 94304
Phone (650) 833-7900
Fax (650) 833-7909
E-mail drdebmetz@pol.net
Specialty Certification Ob/Gyn
Subspecialty Certification Reproductive
Endocrinology
Practice Setting private
Clinical Interests low-cost/high-yield
approaches to infertility treatment;
endometriosis; chronic pelvic pain
Research Interests adhesion treatment and
prevention; endometriosis and fatigue
Member Society of Reproductive Surgeons
Comments I do not do IVF and therefore my
orientation is directing the couple toward the
best treatment for them.

H. Preston Nelson, M.D.
540 University Avenue, Suite 200
Palo Alto, CA 94301
Phone (650) 322-1900
Fax (650) 322-1730

E-mail fpnc@aol.com
Specialty Certification Ob/Gyn
Subspecialty Certification Reproductive
Endocrinology and Infertility
Practice Setting private
Clinical Interests IVF, basic Infertility;
endometriosis
Member Society for Assisted Reproductive
Technology

Camran Nezhat, M.D.
900 Welch Road, Suite 403
Palo Alto, CA 94304
Phone (650) 327-8778
Fax (650) 327-2794
E-mail cnezhat@leland.stanford.edu
Specialty Certification Ob/Gyn
Practice Setting academic/private
Clinical Interests laparoscopic management of
endometriosis; laparoscopic management of
myomas of the uterus; laparoscopic
management of ovarian endometriomas
Research Interests endometriosis; myoma;
ovarian cysts
Member Society of Reproductive Surgeons

Gene Naftulin, M.D.
520 N. Prospect Avenue, Suite 201
Redondo Beach, CA 90277
Phone (310) 374-9670
Fax (310) 376-9474
Specialty Certification Urology
Practice Setting private
Clinical Interests microsurgery; andrology
Member Society for Male Reproduction and
Urology
Comments Feel strongly about medical and
emotional need for male partner evaluation.

Roseville

Carlos Soto-Albors, M.D.
406½ Sunrise Avenue, Suite 3A
Roseville, CA 95661
Phone (916) 773-2229
Fax (916) 773-8391
E-mail c.soto@ncfmc.com
Specialty Certification Ob/Gyn
Practice Setting private
Subspecialty Certification Reproductive
Endocrinology
Clinical Interests IVF; carbon dioxide laser
surgery—endometriosis; tubal
reconstruction—anastomosis
Research Interests habitual abortion; polycystic
ovarian syndrome
Member Society for Assisted Reproductive
Technology, Society of Reproductive
Endocrinology and Infertility

Sacramento

Ellen J. Snowden, M.D.
New Life Fertility Center
2288 Auburn Boulevard, Suite 204
Sacramento, CA 95821

Phone (916) 568-2125
Fax (916) 567-1360
E-mail drsnowden@newlifefertility.com
Specialty Certification Ob/Gyn
Subspecialty Certification Reproductive
Endocrinology
Practice Setting private
Clinical Interests IVF
Member Society of Reproductive Surgeons

San Diego

Steven A. Brody, M.D.
6719 Alvarado Road, #108
San Diego, CA 92120
Phone (619) 265-1800
Fax (619) 265-4055
E-mail sbrodymd@cts.com
Specialty Certification Ob/Gyn
Subspecialty Certification Reproductive
Endocrinology
Practice Setting private
Clinical Interests blastocyst transfer for IVF;
assisted reproduction; laser laparoscopy and
hysteroscopy
Research Interests IVF and micromanipulation;
male infertility; neuroendocrine control of
ovarian function
Member Society of Reproductive Surgeons
Comments (1) Coauthor with Professor Bob
Edwards of the textbook *Principles and
Practice of Assisted Human Reproduction.*
(2) Assistant Clinical Professor, Division of
Endocrinology and Metabolism, UCSD
School of Medicine, La Jolla, CA

Wendy Buchi, M.D.
9339 Genesee Avenue, Suite 220
San Diego, CA 92121
Phone (858) 455-7520
Fax (858) 554-1312
Specialty Certification Ob/Gyn
Practice Setting private

William Cass, M.D.
3250 Fordham Street
San Diego, CA 92110
Phone (619) 221-0350
Fax (619) 221-6442
Specialty Certification Ob/Gyn
Practice Setting private
Clinical Interests reproductive endocrinology;
infertility
Member Society for Assisted Reproductive
Technology, Society for Male Reproduction
and Urology, Society of Reproductive
Endocrinology and Infertility

Laurie Greenberg, M.D.
9339 Genesee Avenue, Suite 220
San Diego, CA 92121
Phone: (858) 455-7520
Fax: (858) 554-1312
Specialty Certification Ob/Gyn
Practice Setting private

Stephen Hebert, M.D.
9339 Genesse Avenue, Suite 220
San Diego, CA 92121
Phone (858) 455-7520
Fax (858) 554-1312
Specialty Certification Ob/Gyn
Practice Setting private
Clinical Interests infertility; endometriosis;
obstetrics
Member American Society of Reproductive
Medicine

William P. Hummel, M.D.
San Diego Fertility Center
11515 El Camino Real
San Diego, CA 92130-2045
Phone (858) 794-6363
Fax (858) 794-6360
Specialty Certification Ob/Gyn
Practice Setting private
Clinical Interests IVF; low sperm counts;
blastocyst embryo transfer
Research Interests treatments for low sperm
counts; reproductive immunology; age and
improved reproductive outcomes
Member Society of Reproductive Surgeons
Comments We provide a team of specialists to
help each and every couple to achieve the
success they deserve. Visit our Web site:
www.sdfertility.com.

L. Michael Kettel, M.D.
11515 El Camino Real, Suite 100
San Diego Fertility Center 92130
Phone (858) 794-6363
Fax (858) 794-6360
E-mail mkettel@ucsd.edu
Specialty Certification Ob/Gyn
Subspecialty Certification Reproductive
Endocrinology
Practice Setting private
Clinical Interests IVP; blastocyst transfer; egg
donation
Research Interests pelvic adhesion reduction/
prevention; blastocyst culture;
ovulation induction
Member Society of Reproductive Surgeons

Jon H. Lischke, M.D.
9339 Genesee Avenue, Suite 220
San Diego, CA 92121
Phone (858) 455-7520
Fax (858) 554-1312
Specialty Certification Ob/Gyn
Practice Setting private
Clinical Interests Infertility—ART and IVF;
perimenopause; gynecologic surgery
Member Society for Assisted Reproductive
Technology

Benito Villanueva, M.D.
9339 Genessee, Suite 200
San Diego, CA 92121
Phone (858) 455-7520
Fax (858) 554-1312

Specialty Certification Ob/Gyn
Practice Setting private
Clinical Interests laparoscopic surgery; IVF; intracytoplasmic sperm injection; egg/sperm donation
Member Society of Reproductive Surgeons, Society for Assisted Reproductive Technology

Philip E. Young, M.D.
9339 Genesee Avenue, Suite 220
San Diego, CA 92121
Phone (858) 455-7520
Fax (858) 554-1312
Specialty Certification Ob/Gyn
Practice Setting private
Clinical Interests general infertility and ART
Member Society for Assisted Reproductive Technology

San Francisco

Philip E. Chenette, M.D.
San Francisco Center for Reproductive Medicine
390 Laurel Street, Suite 205
San Francisco, CA 94118
Phone (415) 771-1483
Fax (415) 771-8421
E-mail chenette@sfivf.com
Specialty Certification Reproductive Endocrinology and Infertility
Subspecialty Certification Ob/Gyn
Practice Setting private
Clinical Interests IVF; pregnancy in women over forty; oocyte donation
Research Interests corpus luteum function; ovarian cancer; data systems
Member Society of Reproductive Surgeons, Society for Assisted Reproductive Technology, Society for Male Reproduction and Urology, Society for Reproductive Endocrinology and Infertility

Carolyn Givens, M.D.
Pacific Fertility Center
55 Francisco Street, Suite 500
San Francisco, CA 94133
Phone (415) 834-3000
Fax (415) 834-3099
E-mail cgivens@pfmc.com
Specialty Certification Ob/Gyn
Subspecialty Certification Reproductive Endocrinology
Practice Setting private
Clinical Interests IVF; male factor infertility; genetics of infertility
Research Interests role of progesterone in the luteal phase and early pregnancy
Comments I have recently joined Pacific Fertility Center (now owned by San Franscisco Center for Reproductive Medicine) after seven years on the faculty at the University of California, San Franscisco.
Member Society for Assisted Reproductive Technology

Simon Henderson, M.D.
390 Lavrel Street, Suite 200
San Francisco, CA 94118
Phone (415) 921-6100
Fax (415) 563-0922
E-mail henderson@sfivf.com
Specialty Certification Ob/Gyn
Subspecialty Certification Reproductive Endocrinology and Infertility
Practice Setting. private
Clinical Interests IVF, ICSI, blastocyst transfer; tubal microsurgery, conservative surgery; laparoscopy, hydroscopy, myomectomy
Research Interests blastocyst freezing; women in their forties; maximizing pregnancy rates/IVF
Comments Solo practice

Carl M. Herbert, M.D.
390 Laurel Street
San Francisco, CA 94118
Phone (415) 771-1483
Fax (415) 771-6924
E-mail herbert@sfivf.com
Specialty Certification Ob/Gyn
Subspecialty Certification Reproductive Endocrinology
Practice Setting private
Clinical Interests ART; endoscopic surgery
Member Society of Reproductive Surgeons
Comments Recently acquired Pacific Fertility Center in San Francisco and merged practice with Drs. Eldon Schrioch/Carolyn Givens, who were previously at the University of California, San Francisco.

Ira D. Sharlip, M.D.
2100 Webster Street, Suite 222
San Francisco, CA 94115
Phone (415) 202-0250
Fax (415) 202-0255
E-mail iSharlip@aol.com
Specialty Certification Urology
Practice Setting private
Clinical Interests general male infertility; reproductive microsurgery; varicocele
Research Interests sperm retrieval techniques
Member Society of Reproductive Surgeons

Paul J. Turek, M.D.
Department of Urology
University of California, San Francisco
2330 Post Street, 6th Floor
San Francisco, CA 94115-1695
Phone (415) 353-7344
Fax (415) 353-7252
E-mail mrvas@itsa.ucsf.edu
Specialty Certification Urology
Subspecialty Certification Male Reproductive Medicine and Surgery
Practice Setting academic
Clinical Interests male infertility— endocrinology; microsurgery; genetic male infertility

Research Interests molecular genetics of infertility; epidemiology of infertility; diagnostic assays of genetic infertility
Member Society for Male Reproduction and Urology
Comments I am program leader of a new program called Progeni, TM or the Program in the Genetics of Infertility, that serves to diagnose, counsel, and possibly treat genetic infertility.

San Jose

Robert W. Andonian, M.D.
123 DiSalvo, Suite D
San Jose, CA 95128
Phone (408) 279-0742
Specialty Certification Urology
Practice Setting private
Clinical Interests vasovasostomy; micro-epidydimal sperm aspiration, testicular sperm aspiration
Member Society for Male Reproduction and Urology
Comments Approximately 150 new male infertility patients annually.

Carmelo S. Sgarlata, M.D.
2505 Samaritan Drive, Suite 208
San Jose, CA 95124
Phone (408) 358-1776
Fax (408) 358-9287
E-mail Csgarlata@aol.com
Specialty Certification Ob/Gyn
Subspecialty Certification Reproductive Endocrinology
Practice Setting private
Clinical Interests ovulation induction; ART; perimenopause
Member Society of Reproductive Surgeons

San Ramon

Louis N. Weckstein, M.D.
3160 Crow Canyon Road, Suite 150
San Ramon, CA 94583
Phone (925) 939-0773
Fax (925) 275-0933
Specialty Certification Ob/Gyn
Practice Setting private
Clinical Interests oocyte donation; IVF/ART; infertility surgery
Member Society of Reproductive Surgeons
Comments Visit our Web site: www.ihr.com/bafertil.

Santa Monica

Richard P. Marrs, M.D.
1245 16th Street, #220
Santa Monica, CA 90404
Phone (310) 828-4008
Fax (310) 828-3310
Specialty Certification Ob/Gyn
Subspecialty Certification Reproductive Endocrinology

Practice Setting private
Clinical Interests ovulation dysfunction; endometriosis; surgical infertility
Research Interests embryo growth; in vitro culture environment; sperm function
Member Society of Reproductive Surgeons

Ingrid Rodi, M.D.
1450 Tenth Street, #404
Santa Monica, CA 90401
Phone (310) 451-8144
Fax (310) 451-3414
Specialty Certification Ob/Gyn
Subspecialty Certification Reproductive Endocrinology
Practice Setting private
Clinical Interests IVF; endometriosis; fibroids
Research Interests ectopic pregnancy
Member Society of Reproductive Surgeons

Tarzana

Michael Vermesh, M.D.
18370 Burbank Boulevard, Suite 301
Tarzana, CA 91356
Phone (818) 881-9800
Fax (818) 881-1857
Specialty Certification Ob/Gyn
Subspecialty Certification Reproductive Endocrinology
Practice Setting private
Clinical Interests ART; laparoscopic surgery; endometriosis
Research Interests ectopic pregnancy
Member Society of Reproductive Surgeons

Thousand Oaks

Richard P. Buyalos, Jr., M.D.
325 Rolling Oaks Drive, Suite 110
Thousand Oaks, CA 91361
Phone (805) 778-1122
Fax (805) 778-1199
Specialty Certification Ob/Gyn
Subspecialty Certification Reproductive Endocrinology
Practice Setting private
Clinical Interests ART; polycystic ovarian syndrome; endometriosis
Research Interests reproductive aging; biochemical markers of ovarian reserve
Member Society of Reproductive Surgeons
Comments IVF laboratory on-site. Clinical Associate Professor, University of California, Los Angeles, Department of Obstetrics/Gynecology

Dean L. Moyer, M.D.
Medical Director
Gene Choice
2955 East Hillcrest Drive, Unit 102
Thousand Oaks, CA 91362
Phone (805) 230-3155
Fax (805) 230-3153
E-mail novaxx@frontiernet.net

Specialty Certification Anatomical and Clinical Pathology
Practice Setting private
Clinical Interests fertility assistance; genetic disease; sperm and ova donation
Research Interests laboratory testing of genetic disease
Member Society of Reproductive Surgeons
Comments Gene Choice offers sperm and ova banking with an emphasis on the reduction of genetic disease to the intended parent.

Upland

Bert J. Davidson, M.D.
510 N. 13th Avenue, Suite 201
Upland, CA 91786
Phone (909) 949-8300
Fax (909) 985-7137
E-mail drdavidson@sach.org
Specialty Certification Ob/Gyn
Subspecialty Certification Reproductive Endocrinology
Practice Setting academic/private
Clinical Interests ART; infertility surgery; polycystic ovaries
Research Interests menopause; infertility
Member Society of Reproductive Surgeons, Society for Assisted Reproductive Technology, Society of Reproductive Endocrinology and Infertility

COLORADO

Aurora

J. Joshua Kopelman, M.D.
1550 S. Potomac, Suite 330
Aurora, CO 80012
Phone (303) 369-1050
Fax (303) 337-0671
E-mail jgooddr@aol.com
Specialty Certification Ob/Gyn
Practice Setting private
Clinical Interests endometriosis; surgical repair of fallopian tubes; anovulation
Member Society of Reproductive Surgeons

Colorado Springs

Eric Silverstein, M.D.
125 Medical Center Point, #290
Colorado Springs, CO 80907
Phone (719) 636-0080
Fax (719) 636-3030
E-mail csrh@aol.com
Specialty Certification Ob/Gyn
Practice Setting private
Clinical Interests ART; endometriosis; polycystic ovarian syndrome
Member Society for Assisted Reproductive Technology

Denver

Sam Alexander, M.D.
Colorado Reproductive Endocrinology
4600 E. Hale Parkway, #350
Denver, CO 80220
Phone (303) 321-7115
Fax (303) 321-9519
E-mail crecares@concentric.net
Specialty Certification Ob/Gyn
Practice Setting private
Clinical Interests IVF; polycystic ovarian syndrome; reproductive surgery
Research Interests oocyte/embryo developmental abnormalities
Member Society of Reproductive Surgeons, Society for Assisted Reproductive Technology, Society of Reproductive Endocrinology and Infertility

William D. Schlaff, M.D.
University of Colorado Health Sciences Center, Box E198
Denver, CO 80262
Phone (303) 315-7128
Fax (303) 315-8889
Specialty Certification Ob/Gyn
Subspecialty Certification Reproductive Endocrinology
Practice Setting academic/private
Clinical Interests congenital abnormalities of the reproductive tract; abnormal bleeding; infertility
Research Interests myoma of the uterus; endometriosis; ovulatory dysfunction
Member Society of Reproductive Surgeons, Society for Assisted Reproductive Technology, Society of Reproductive Endocrinology and Infertility

Englewood

Eric S. Surrey, M.D.
Colorado Center for Reproductive Medicine
799 E. Hampden Avenue, #300
Englewood, CO 80111
Phone (303) 788-8300
Fax (303) 788-8310
E-mail ccrm@colocrm.com
Specialty Certification Ob/Gyn
Subspecialty Certification Reproductive Endocrinology
Practice Setting private
Clinical Interests ART, poor responders; blastocyst transfer; endometriosis; tubal endoscopy
Research Interests ovulation induction and poor responders; endometriosis and infertility; blastocyst development; tubal endoscopy (salpingoscopy, falloposcopy)
Member Society of Reproductive Surgeons

Littleton

Bruce Albrecht, M.D.
7720 S. Broadway, Suite 580

Littleton, CO 80122-2624
Phone (303) 794-0045
Fax (303) 794-2054
Specialty Certification Ob/Gyn
Subspecialty Certification Reproductive
Endocrinology
Practice Setting private
Clinical Interests IVF; ovulation induction
Practice Setting private
Clinical Interests infertility; endometriosis;
obstetrics
Web site: www.sdfertility.com

CONNECTICUT

Danbury

Jeffrey Gorelick, M.D.
The Center for Male Reproductive Medicine
73 Sand Pit Road, Suite 304
Danbury, CT 06810
Phone (203) 748-0330
Fax (203) 797-0255
Specialty Certification Urology
Practice Setting private
Clinical Interests male infertility, erectile
dysfunction
Comments We are the exclusive specialists in
male infertility for our local population of
250,000+ and receive referrals from all the
local female infertility specialists.

Farmington

Claudia Benadiva, M.D.
The Center for Advanced Reproductive
Services
University of Connecticut Health Center
263 Farmington Avenue
Farmington, CT 06030
Phone (860) 679-4580
Fax (860) 679-1499
E-mail Benadiva@up.uchc.edu
Specialty Certification Ob/Gyn
Subspecialty Certification Reproductive
Endocrinology
Practice Setting academic
Clinical Interests IVF; ovulation induction;
endoscopic surgery
Research Interests new ovulation induction
drugs
Member Society of Reproductive
Endocrinology and Infertility

Donald Maier, M.D.
The Center for Advanced Reproductive
Services
University of Connecticut Health Center
263 Farmington Avenue
Farmington, CT 06030
Phone (860) 679-4580
Fax (860) 679-1499
E-mail Maier@NS01.UCHC.edu
Specialty Certification Ob/Gyn

Subspecialty Certification Reproductive
Endocrinology
Practice Setting academic
Clinical Interests Recurrent pregnancy losses;
infertility; hysteroscopic surgery
Research Interests recurrent pregnancy losses
Member Society of Reproductive Surgeons,
Society of Reproductive Endocrinology
Infertility

John Nulsen, M.D.
The Center for Advanced Reproductive
Services
University of Connecticut Health Center
263 Farmington Avenue
Farmington, CT 06030
Phone (860) 679-4580
Fax (860) 679-1499
Specialty Certification Ob/Gyn
Subspecialty Certification Reproductive
Endocrinology
Practice Setting academic
Clinical Interests IVF; ovulation induction;
evaluation and treatment of infertility
Research Interests evaluation of parameters
that influence success rates for IVF
Member Society for Assisted Reproductive
Technology, Society of Reproductive
Endocrinology and Infertility

Hartford

Matthew G. Ely III, M.D.
85 Seymour Street, Suite 416
Hartford, CT 06106
Phone (860) 947-8500
Fax (860) 524-8643
Specialty Certification Urology
Practice Setting private
Clinical Interests male infertility; vasectomy
reversal; vasectomy

Bernard Kosto, M.D.
85 Seymour Street, Suite 416
Hartford, CT 06106
Phone (860) 947-8500
Fax (860) 524-8643
Specialty Certification Urology
Subspecialty Certification American College of
Surgeons
Practice Setting private
Clinical Interests general urology
Member Society for Male Reproduction and
Urology

August C. Olivar, M.D.
100 Retreat Avenue, Suite 900
Hartford, CT 06106
Phone (860) 325-8283
Fax (860) 525-1930
Specialty Certification Ob/Gyn
Subspecialty Certification Reproductive
endocrinology
Practice Setting private
Clinical Interests laparoscopic surgery—

hysteroscopic; endometriosis; androgen
excess
Research Interests lasers; endometriosis;
polycystic ovarian syndrome—CAH
Member Society of Reproductive Surgeons

New Britain

Anthony Luciano, M.D.
100 Grand Street, Suite N3
New Britain, CT 06050
Phone (860) 224-5469
Fax (860) 224-5764
E-mail aluciano@nbgh.org
Specialty Certification Ob/Gyn
Subspecialty Certification Reproductive
Endocrinology
Practice Setting academic (hospital based)
Clinical Interests reproductive surgery;
infertility; menopause/endocrinology
Research Interests hermone replacement
therapy; adhesion prevention;
superovulation—IVF
Member Society of Reproductive Surgeons

New Haven

Stanton Honig, M.D.
Male Reproductive Medicine/Surgery
60 Temple Street
New Haven, CT 06510
Phone (203) 789-2222
Fax (203) 624-3697
E-mail shonig@urologycenter.com
Specialty Certification Urology
Practice Setting academic/private
Clinical Interests sperm retrieval; vasectomy
reversal; male infertility
Research Interests sperm retrieval;
electroejaculation; intracytoplasmic sperm
injection
Member Society of Reproductive Surgeons,
Society for Male Reproduction and
Urology

Norwalk

Michael A. Werner, M.D.
148 East Avenue, Suite 1GI
Norwalk, CT 06851
Phone (914) 997-4100
Fax (914) 683-0979
E-mail mwerner@wernermd.com
Specialty Certification Urology
Practice Setting private
Clinical Interests male infertility; male sexual
dysfunction; microscopic varicocelectomy
and vasectomy reversal
Member Society for Male Reproduction and
Urology

Stamford

Frances W. Ginsburg, M.D.
The Stamford Hospital
P.O. Box 9317
Stamford, CT 06904
Phone (203) 325-7559
Fax (203) 325-7259
E-mail Frances_Ginsburg@Stamhosp.Chime.
org
Specialty Certification Ob/Gyn
Subspecialty Certification Reproductive
Endocrinology
Practice Setting private
Clinical Interests infertility/IVF; uterine
fibroids; endometriosis
Member Society for Assisted Reproductive
Technology, Society of Reproductive
Endocrinology and Infertility

Gad Lavy, M.D.
1275 Summer Street
Stamford, CT 06905
Phone (203) 325-3200
Fax (203) 323-3130
E-mail NEFertility.com
Specialty Certification Ob/Gyn
Subspecialty Certification Reproductive
Endocrinology
Practice Setting private
Clinical Interests ART; ovulation induction;
surgery
Member Society for Assisted Reproductive
Technology, Society of Reproductive
Surgeons

DELAWARE

Newark

Jeffrey B. Russell, M.D., FACOG
4745 Ogletown-Stanton Road, Suite 111
Newark, DE 19713
Phone (302) 738-4600
Fax (302) 738-3508
E-mail Russ98JRBI@aol.com
Specialty Certification Reproductive
Endocrinology
Subspecialty Certification Ob/Gyn
Practice Setting private
Clinical Interests IVF; immature oocyte
retrieval and maturation; embryo donation
and adoption
Member Society of Reproductive Surgeons,
Society for Assisted Reproductive
Technology, Society of Reproductive
Endocrinology and Infertility

DISTRICT OF COLUMBIA

Paul Gindoff, M.D.
2150 Pennsylvania Avenue, NW
Washington, DC 20037
Phone (202) 994-4614
Fax (202) 994-0815
E-mail obgprg@gwumc.edu
Specialty Certification Ob/Gyn
Subspecialty Certification Reproductive
Endocrinology
Practice Setting academic

Clinical Interests ART; blastocyst transfer; intracytoplasmic sperm injection (ICSI)
Research Interests preimplantation genetic diagnosis
Member Society of Reproductive Surgeons, Society for Assisted Reproductive Technology, Society of Reproductive Endocrinology and Infertility

Beth Hartog, M.D.
2150 Pennsylvania Avenue NW, 6A-410
Washington, DC 20037
Phone (202) 994-4614
Fax (202) 994-0815
E-mail obgbcn@gwumc.edu
Specialty Certification Ob/Gyn
Practice Setting academic
Clinical Interests blastocyst culture and transfer; advanced laparoscopy/hysteroscopy; advanced ART
Research Interests preimplantation genetic diagnosis; antiprogestins and role in reproduction
Member Society of Reproductive Surgeons, Society for Assisted Reproductive Technology, Society of Reproductive Endocrinology and Infertility

James A. Simon, M.D.
2021 K Street NW, #500
Washington, DC 20006
Phone (202) 293-1000
Fax (202) 785-1570
Specialty Certification Ob/Gyn
Subspecialty Certification Reproductive Endocrinology
Practice Setting private
Clinical Interests assisted reproduction, surgical infertility, menopause/osteoporosis
Research Interests menopause/osteoporosis, contraception, implantation
Member Society of Reproductive Surgeons

Craig A. Winkel, M.D., M.B.A.
Department of Obstetrics & Gynecology
Georgetown University Medical Center
3800 Reservoir Road, NW, 3 PHC
Washington, DC 20007
Phone (202) 687-8531
Fax (202) 687-1472
Specialty Certification Ob/Gyn
Subspecialty Certification Reproductive Endocrinology
Practice Setting academic
Clinical Interests endometriosis; polycystic ovaries; ovulation induction
Research Interests endometriosis; menopause
Member Society of Reproductive Surgeons

FLORIDA

Boca Raton

Moshe R. Peress, M.D.
875 Meadows Road

Boca Raton, FL 33486
Phone (561) 368-5500
Fax (561) 368-4793
E-mail nurse@bocafertility.com
Specialty Certification Ob/Gyn
Practice Setting private
Clinical Interests IVF; Laparoscopic CO_2 laser—endometriosis
Member Society of Reproductive Surgeons, Society for Assisted Reproductive Technology

Brandon

James E. Alver, M.D.
500 Vanderburg Drive, Suite 201E
Brandon, FL 33511
Phone (813) 685-0827
Fax (813) 685-0968
E-mail Alverje@aol.com
Specialty Certification Urology
Practice Setting private
Clinical Interests microsurgical epididymal sperm aspiration; male factor infertility; surgical correction of male factor infertility
Member Society for Male Reproduction and Urology

Clearwater

Edward Andrew Zbella, M.D.
2454 McMullen Booth Road, Suite 601
Clearwater, FL 33759
Phone (727) 796-7705
Fax (727) 796-8764
Specialty Certification Ob/Gyn
Subspecialty Certification Reproductive Endocrinology
Practice Setting private
Clinical Interests endometriosis; assisted reproduction; tubal anastomosis
Research Interests endometriosis
Member Society of Reproductive Surgeons, Society for Assisted Reproductive Technology, Society for Male Reproduction and Urology, Society of Reproductive Endocrinology and Infertility
Comments Currently assistant clinical professor at University of South Florida and division director at Bayfront Medical Center residency program in obstetrics and gynecology.

Fort Myers

William Evans, M.D.
12651 Whitehall Drive
Ft. Myers, FL 33901
Phone (941) 939-4444
Fax (941) 939-5977
Specialty Certification Urology
Practice Setting private
Clinical Interests microsurgery and vasectomy reversal

Craig R. Sweet, M.D.
12611 World Plaza Lane

Fort Myers, FL 33907
Phone (941) 275-8118
Fax (941) 275-5914
Specialty Certification Ob/Gyn
Subspecialty Certification Reproductive
Endocrinology
Practice Setting private
Clinical Interests male and female infertility;
IVF; pediatric and adolescent gynecology
Research Interests polycystic ovarian
syndrome; endometriosis; embryo transfer
techniques
Member Society for Assisted Reproductive
Technology, Society of Reproductive
Endocrinology and Infertility

Gainesville

Simon Kipersztok, M.D.
Park Avenue Women's Center at the
University of Florida
807 N.W. 57th Street
Gainesville, FL 32605
Phone (352) 392-6200
Fax (352) 392-6204
E-mail skiper@obgyn.ufl.edu
Specialty Certification Ob/Gyn
Subspecialty Certification Reproductive
Endocrinology
Practice Setting academic/private
Clinical Interests IVF and other ART;
endometriosis and advanced laparoscopy;
reproductive surgery including microsurgery
Research Interests ART; preimplantation
genetic diagnosis; contraception
Member Society of Reproductive Surgeons
Comments on-site full-fledged state-of-the-art
infertility services by fellowship-trained
subspecialists in a private practice setting.

R. Stan Williams, M.D.
Park Avenue Women's Center at the
University of Florida
807 N.W. 57th Street
Gainesville, FL 32605
Phone (352) 392-6200
Fax (352) 392-6204
E-mail williams@obgyn.ufl.edu
Specialty Certification Ob/Gyn
Subspecialty Certification Reproductive
Endocrinology
Practice Setting academic
Clinical Interests infertility; IVF; laparoscopic
surgery
Research Interests preimplantation genetics;
endometriosis; adhesion prevention
Member Society of Reproductive Surgeons,
Society for Assisted Reproductive
Technology, Society of Reproductive
Endocrinology and Infertility
Comments Patients are seen at the private
office of the University of Florida with one-
to-one personal care.

Gulf Breeze

Robert C. Pyle, M.D.
1110 Gulf Breeze Parkway, Suite 202
Gulf Breeze, FL 32561
Phone (850) 934-3900
Fax (850) 932-3753
Specialty Certification Ob/Gyn
Practice Setting private
Clinical Interests infertility; reproductive
surgery; assisted reproductive
technologies/ICSI
Member Society for Assisted Reproductive
Technology
Comments Medical director of Fertility
Institute of Northwest Florida since 1983.

Jacksonville

Patrick L. Blohm, M.D.
836 Prudential Drive, Suite 902
Jacksonville, FL 32207
Phone (904) 399-5620
Fax (904) 399-5645
Specialty Certification Ob/Gyn
Subspecialty Certification Reproductive
Endocrinology
Practice Setting private
Member Society of Reproductive
Endocrinology and Infertility, Society for
Assisted Reproductive Technology
Comments Please visit our Web site at:
www.firmjax.com.

Michael D. Fox, M.D.
1820 Barrs Street, Suite 358
Jacksonville, FL 32204
Phone (904) 388-4695
Fax (904) 387-1497
Specialty Certification Ob/Gyn
Subspecialty Certification Reproductive
Endocrinology
Practice Setting private
Clinical Interests ART; ultrasound/imaging;
endometriosis
Research Interests Polycystic ovarian
syndrome (insulin resistance)
Member Society of Reproductive Surgeons

Marwan M. Shaykh, M.D.
3627 University Boulevard South
Jacksonville, FL 32216
Phone (904) 398-1473
Fax (904) 399-3436
Specialty Certification Ob/Gyn
Subspecialty Certification Reproductive
Endocrinology
Practice Setting private
Clinical Interests IVF; tubal surgery
Member Society of Reproductive Surgeons

Kevin L. Winslow, M.D.
836 Prudential Drive, Suite 902
Jacksonville, FL 32207
Phone (904) 399-5620
Fax (904) 399-5645

Specialty Certification Ob/Gyn
Subspecialty Certification Reproductive
Endocrinology
Practice Setting private
Member Society of Reproductive
Endocrinology and Infertility, Society for
Assisted Reproductive Technology
Comments Please visit our Web site
www.firmjax.com.

Margate

David I. Hoffman, M.D.
2825 N. State Road 7, Suite 302
Margate, FL 33063
Phone (954) 247-6200
Fax (954) 247-6262
E-mail dhncire@attglobal.net
Specialty Certification Ob/Gyn
Subspecialty Certification Reproductive
Endocrinology
Practice Setting private
Clinical Interests ART; perimenopause/
menopause
Research Interests ART
Member Society of Reproductive Surgeons

Wayne S. Maxson, M.D.
2825 N. State Road 7, Suite 302
Margate, FL 33063
Phone (954) 247-6200
Fax (954) 247-6262
Specialty Certification Ob/Gyn
Subspecialty Certification Reproductive
Endocrinology
Practice Setting private
Clinical Interests ART; all areas of infertility;
hormone problems in menopause
Research Interests natural hormone
replacement; ART
Member Society of Reproductive Surgeons

Steven J. Ory, M.D.
2825 N. State Road 7, Suite 302
Margate, FL 33063
Phone (954) 247-6200
Fax (954) 247-6262
Specialty Certification Ob/Gyn
Subspecialty Certification Reproductive
Endocrinology
Practice Setting private
Clinical Interests ART; estrogen replacement
therapy; endometriosis
Research Interests ectopic pregnancy
Member Society of Reproductive Surgeons,
Society for Assisted Reproductive
Technology, Society of Reproductive
Endocrinology and Infertility

Marvin Stein, M.D., FACS
5800 Colonial Drive, #404
Margate, FL 33063
Phone (954) 979-2949
Fax (954) 979-2263
E-mail stoneman12@netscape.net

Specialty Certification Urology
Practice Setting private
Clinical Interests male infertility;
Vasvasostomy
Member Society for Male Reproduction and
Urology

Miami

Nancy Brackett, Ph.D., HCLD
The Miami Project to Cure Paralysis
University of Miami School of Medicine
1611 N.W. 12th Avenue
Miami, FL 33136
Phone (305) 243-6226
Fax (305) 243-4427
E-mail nbrackett@miami.edu
Practice Setting academic
Clinical Interests ART for couples with male
factor infertility secondary to spinal cord
injury
Research Interests cause of poor semen quality
in men with spinal cord injury
Member Society for Male Reproduction and
Urology
Comments We evaluate semen quality in men
with spinal cord injury and we retrieve
semen from these men for insemination and
for study. For a man with neurogenic
anejaculation, our center is one of the most
experienced in the world.

Maria Bustillo, M.D.
6250 Sunset Drive, #202
Miami, FL 33143
Phone (305) 662-7901
Fax (305) 662-7910
E-mail IVFMD@aol.com
Specialty Certification Ob/Gyn
Subspecialty Certification Reproductive
Endocrinology
Practice Setting private
Clinical Interests assisted reproductive
technologies; oocyte donation; ovulatory
disorders
Research Interests ovulation; gametes

Gordon Kuttner, M.D.
Department of OB/GYN
University of Miami School of Medicine
PO Box 016960 (R-116)
Miami, FL 33101
Phone (305) 682-7000
Fax (305) 324-8558
E-mail gkuttner@obgyn.med.miami.edu
Specialty Certification Ob/Gyn
Subspecialty Certification Reproductive
Endocrinology and Infertility
Practice Setting academic
Clinical Interests ART; endoscopic surgery
Research Interests ART; progesterone/
implantation
Member Society for Assisted Reproductive
Technology, Society of Reproductive
Endocrinology and Infertility

George D. Mekras, M.D.
  Miami Urologic Institute, Inc.
  7051 S.W. 62 Avenue
  Miami, FL 33143
  Phone (305) 661-8977
  Fax (305) 662-9123
  E-mail gmekras@miauroinst.com
  Specialty Certification Urology
  Practice Setting private
  Clinical Interests male factor infertility;
  microscopic vasovasostomy and
  vasoepididymostomy sperm aspiration for
  intracytoplasmic sperm injection
  Member Society for Male Reproduction and
  Urology

Arthur Shapiro, M.D.
  Department of Obstetrics & Gynecology
  Division of Reproductive Endocrinology
  University of Miami
  PO Box 016960 (D-52)
  Miami, FL 33101
  Phone (305) 243-9150
  Specialty Certification Ob/Gyn
  Subspecialty Certification Reproductive
  Endocrinology
  Practice Setting academic
  Clinical Interests ovulation induction; intrauter-
  ine insemination; laser surgery, laparoscopic
  and hysteroscopic surgery; endometroisis
  Research Interests menopause; polycystic
  ovarian disease and insulin resistance
  Member Society of Reproductive Surgeons

Kimberly Thompson, M.D.
  6250 Sunset Drive, #202
  Miami, FL 33143
  Phone (305) 662-7901
  Fax (305) 662-7910
  E-mail IVFMD@aol.com
  Specialty Certification Ob/Gyn
  Subspecialty Certification Reproductive
  Endocrinology
  Practice Setting private
  Clinical Interests ART; egg donation and sperm
  donation; general female and male infertility
  Member Society for Assisted Reproductive
  Technology, Society of Reproductive
  Endocrinology and Infertility

Miami Beach

Bernard Cantor, M.D.
  4302 Alton Road, Suite 900
  Miami Beach, FL 33140
  Phone (305) 531-1480
  Fax (305) 531-1496
  E-mail drcantor@drcantor.com
  Specialty Certification Ob/Gyn
  Subspecialty Certification Reproductive
  Endocrinology
  Practice Setting private
  Clinical Interests all aspects of infertility
  diagnosis and treatment; habitual abortion
  Member Society of Reproductive Surgeons

New Port Richey

Ramon Perez-Marrero, M.D.
  Urology Health Center
  5652 Meadow Lane
  New Port Richey, FL 34652
  Phone (727) 842-9561
  E-mail rperezl6@gte.net
  Specialty Certification Urology
  Practice Setting private
  Clinical Interests male infertility; obstructive
  infertility; prostatitis
  Member Society for Male Reproduction and
  Urology

Orlando

Mark Jutras, M.D.
  615 E. Princeton Street, Suite 225
  Orlando, FL 32803
  Phone (407) 896-7575
  Fax (407) 894-2692
  E-mail mjutras@gte.net
  Specialty Certification Ob/Gyn
  Practice Setting private
  Clinical Interests IVF; sterilization reversal;
  donor ovum
  Member Society of Reproductive Surgeons
  Comments Refund IVF available.

Mark Trolice, M.D.
  22 Underwood Street
  Orlando, FL 32806
  Phone (407) 649-6995
  Fax (407) 841-3367
  E-mail rhi@orhs.org
  Specialty Certification Reproductive
  Endocrinology
  Subspecialty Certification Ob/Gyn
  Practice Setting academic
  Clinical Interests IVF; recurrent pregnancy
  loss; polycystic ovarian syndrome
  Research Interests predictive markers of
  abnormal pregnancies; thrombophilias and
  pregnancy loss
  Member Society of Reproductive Surgeons,
  Society for Assisted Reproductive
  Technology, Society of Reproductive
  Endocrinology and Infertility

Pensacola

Barry Ripps, M.D.
  5147 N. North Avenue, Suite 402
  Pensacola, FL 32504
  Phone (850) 857-3733
  Fax (850) 807-0670
  E-mail baripps@aol.com
  Specialty Certification Ob/Gyn
  Subspecialty Certification Reproductive
  Endocrinology
  Practice Setting academic
  Clinical Interests endometriosis; polycystic
  ovaries and insulin; laparoscopic
  management of endometriosis infertility

Research Interests osteoporosis prevention; endometriosis causes
Member Society for Male Reproduction and Urology, Society for Assisted Reproductive Technology, Society of Reproductive Endocrinology and Infertility

Plantation

Mick Abae, M.D.
6738 West Sunrise Boulevard, Suite 106
Plantation, FL 33313
Phone (954) 584-2273
Fax (954) 587-9630
E-mail carelife@bellsouth.net
Specialty Certification Ob/Gyn
Subspecialty Certification Reproductive Endocrinology
Practice Setting private
Clinical Interests assisted reproductive technologies; laparoscopic/hysteroscopic surgery; reproductive endocrinology
Research Interests embryonic and endometrial implantation; endometriosis and polycystic ovaries
Member Society for Assisted Reproductive Technology

Eliezer J. Livnat, M.D.
Fertility Institute of Ft. Lauderdale
4100 S. Hospital Drive, Suite 209
Plantation, FL 33317
Phone (954) 791-1442
Fax (954) 791-1887
Specialty Certification Ob/Gyn
Practice Setting private
Clinical Interests endoscopic reproductive surgery; ART
Member Society of Reproductive Surgeons

Tampa

Marc A. Bernhisel, M.D.
2919 Swann Avenue
Tampa, FL 33609
Phone (813) 870-3553
Fax (813) 872-8727
E-mail repromedgroup@msn.com
Specialty Certification Ob/Gyn
Subspecialty Certification Reproductive Endocrinology
Practice Setting private
Clinical Interests ART; laparoscopic surgery; polycystic ovarian disease; hirsutism
Research Interests polycystic ovarian syndrome; hirsutism; sperm penetration assays
Member Society of Reproductive Surgeons, Society for Assisted Reproductive Technology, Society of Reproductive Endocrinology and Infertility

Samuel Tarantino, M.D.
3450 E. Fletcher Avenue
Tampa, FL 33613
Phone (813) 971-0008

Fax (813) 972-1508
Specialty Certification Ob/Gyn
Subspecialty Certification Reproductive Endocrinology and Infertility
Practice Setting private
Clinical Interests ART; endometriosis; pelvic pain
Member Society for Assisted Reproductive Technology, Society of Reproductive Endocrinology and Infertility

Barry S. Verkauf, M.D.
2919 Swann Avenue, #305
Tampa, FL 33609
Phone (813) 870-3553
Fax (813) 872-8727
Specialty Certification Ob/Gyn
Subspecialty Certification Reproductive Endocrinology
Practice Setting private
Primary Interests myomectomy; endometriosis; infertility, female
Member Society of Reproductive Surgeons, Society for Assisted Reproductive Technology, Society of Reproductive Endocrinology and Infertility

Stephen Welden, M.D.
4801 N. Habana Avenue
Tampa, FL 33614
Phone (813) 876-4731
Fax (813) 877-7813
Specialty Certification Ob/Gyn
Practice Setting private
Clinical Interests IVF; endometriosis; sterilization reversal
Research Interests endometriosis; age-related infertility; sex preselection
Member Society of Reproductive Surgeons
Comments IVF/GIFT, ovulation induction, IUI, artificial insemination, laser and microsurgery.

West Palm Beach

Georgis Patsias, M.D.
10111 W. Forest Hill Boulevard, Suite 224
West Palm Beach, FL 33414
Phone (561) 753-3787
Fax (561) 753-3793
Specialty Certification Urology
Practice Setting private
Clinical Interests male infertility; male sexual dysfunction
Member Society of Reproductive Surgeons

GEORGIA

Atlanta

Joe B. Massey, M.D.
5505 Peachtree Dunwoody Road, Suite 400
Atlanta, GA 30342-1713
Phone (404) 257-1900
Fax (404) 257-0792

E-mail JBMassey@mindspring.com
Specialty Certification Ob/Gyn
Practice Setting private
Clinical Interests endoscopic surgery; IVF
Research Interests egg cryopreservation (human)
Member Society of Reproductive Surgeons

Dorothy E. Mitchell-Leef, M.D.
5505 Peachtree Dunwoody Road, Suite 400
Atlanta, GA 30342
Phone (404) 250-6852
Fax (404) 256-6999
Specialty Certification Ob/Gyn
Practice Setting private
Clinical Interests IVF—preimplantation genetics/ICSI; endometriosis; habitual abortion
Research Interests endometriosis—genetic aspects/therapy; effects of age and reproduction; ovarian tissue removal in patients with carcinoma
Member Society of Reproductive Surgeons

Ana A. Murphy, M.D.
Isobel Frazier OPC, 4th Floor
20 Linden Avenue
Atlanta, GA 30308
Phone (404) 686-8095
Fax (404) 686-4956
E-mail amurphy@emory.edu
Specialty Certification Ob/Gyn
Subspecialty Certification Reproductive Endocrinology
Practice Setting academic
Clinical Interests endometriosis; surgical infertility/laparoscopy and hysteroscopy; IVF
Research Interests endometriosis; leiomyomata/fibroids; reproductive surgery
Member Society of Reproductive Surgeons, Society for Assisted Reproductive Technology, Society of Reproductive Endocrinology and Infertility

Anne Namnoum, M.D.
Emory Center for Reproductive Medicine
20 Linden Avenue, Suite 4701
Atlanta, GA 30308
Phone (404) 686-8095
Fax (404) 686-4956
Specialty Certification Ob/Gyn
Practice Setting academic
Clinical Interests ART; polycystic ovarian disease; unexplained infertility
Member Society for Assisted Reproductive Technology; Society of Reproductive Endocrinology and Infertility

Andrew A. Toledo, M.D.
5505 Peachtree-Dunwoody Road, Suite 400
Atlanta, GA 30342
Phone (404) 256-6972
Fax (404) 256-8375
E-mail Fertman790@aol.com
Specialty Certification Ob/Gyn

Subspecialty Certification Reproductive Endocrinology
Practice Setting private
Clinical Interests IVF and embryo transfer; microsurgery and advanced laparoscopic surgery; treatment of recurrent pregnancy loss
Research Interests blastocyst transfer results; use of GnRH antagonists in IVF and ovulation induction treatment preimplantation genetics
Member Society of Reproductive Surgeons

J. Maxwell White, M.D.
1938 Peachtree Road, NW, Suite 408
Atlanta, GA 30309
Phone (404) 355-8141
Fax (404) 355-8583
Specialty Certification Urology
Practice Setting private
Clinical Interests microsurgery/reconstruction; varicocele
Member Society of Reproductive Surgeons, Society for Male Reproduction and Urology

Michael A. Witt, M.D.
5505 Peachtree-Dunwoody Road, Suite 550
Atlanta, GA 30342
Phone (404) 256-6987
Fax (404) 256-8376
E-mail mwittmd@mindspring.com
Specialty Certification Urology
Practice Setting private
Research Interests sperm retrieval; vasal reconstruction
Member Society for Male Reproduction and Urology

Augusta

Lawrence C. Layman, M.D.
Department of Obstetrics & Gynecology
Section of Reproductive Endocrinology, Infertility & Genetics
Medical College of Georgia
1120 15th Street
Augusta, GA 30912-3360
Phone (706) 721-3831
Fax (706) 721-6830
E-mail Llayman@mail.mcg.edu
Specialty Certification Ob/Gyn
Subspecialty Certification Reproductive Endocrinology, Clinical Genetics
Practice Setting academic
Clinical Interests ovulation disorders; hypogonadism; infertility
Research Interests genetics of puberty; physiologic functions FSH
Member Society for Assisted Reproductive Technology, Society of Reproductive Endocrinology and Infertility

Paul G. McDonough, M.D.
Department of Obstetrics & Gynecology, BBR-7514

Medical College of Georgia
1120 15th Street
Augusta, GA 30912
Phone (706) 721-3832
Fax (706) 721-6830/0574
E-mail pmcdonou@mail.mcg.edu
Specialty Certification Ob/Gyn
Subspecialty Certification Reproductive
Endocrinology, Cytogenetics and Clinical
Genetics
Practice Setting academic
Clinical Interests genetics—reproductive
endocrinology
Research Interests molecular biology of sexual
differentiation
Member Society of Reproductive Surgeons,
Society for Assisted Reproductive
Technology, Society of Reproductive
Endocrinology and Infertility

Edouard T. Servy, M.D.
812 Chafee Avenue
Augusta, GA 30904
Phone (706) 724-0228
Fax (706) 722-2387
E-mail ARBA@CSRAnet.com
Specialty Certification Endocrinology and
Metabolic Diseases (France)
Subspecialty Certification Ob/Gyn (U.S.)
Practice Setting academic/private
Clinical Interests reproductive endocrinology
Research Interests endocrinology; Ob/Gyn
Member Society for Assisted Reproductive
Technology
Comments Associate professor in obstetrics
and gynecology and physiology/
endocrinology at the Medical College of
Georgia.

Scott Slayden, M.D.
Department of Obstetrics & Gynecology, BB-
7514
Medical College of Georgia
1120 15th Street
Augusta, GA 30912
Phone (706) 721-3832
Fax (706) 721-6830/0574
E-mail sslayden@mail.mcg.edu
Specialty Certification Ob/Gyn
Practice Setting academic
Clinical Interests infertility
Research Interests menopause
Member Society of Reproductive
Endocrinology and Infertility

Sandra P. T. Tho, M.D.
Department of Obstetrics & Gynecology,
BBR-7514
Medical College of Georgia
1120 15th Street
Augusta, GA 30912
Phone (706) 721-3832
Fax (706) 721-6830
E-mail stho@mail.mcg.edu

Specialty Certification Ob/Gyn
Subspecialty Certification Reproductive
Endocrinology
Practice Setting academic
Clinical Interests delayed puberty; recurrent
abortion; sexual differentiation disorders
Research Interests gonadal dysgenesis;
azoospermia
Member Society for Assisted Reproductive
Technology, Society of Reproductive
Endocrinology and Infertility

Macon

Douglas E. Ott, M.D., M.B.A.
250 Charter Lane
Macon, GA 31210
Phone (912) 477-8996
Fax (912) 471-6862
E-mail gabiomed@mindspring.com
Specialty Certification Ob/Gyn
Practice Setting private
Clinical Interests laparoscopy; microsurgery
Research Interests peritoneal cavity;
macrophages
Member Society of Reproductive Surgeons
Comments Adjunct professor of biomedical
engineering, Mercer University.

Marietta

Joseph Wheatley, M.D.
833 Campbell Hill Street, Suite 300
Marietta, GA 30060
Phone (770) 428-4475
Fax (770) 426-1499
E-mail GWAR@mindspring.com
Specialty Certification Urology
Practice Setting private
Clinical Interests male infertility; varicocele
Member Society of Reproductive Surgeons
Comments Private practice setting after
academic career.

HAWAII

Honolulu

Kenneth Vu, M.D.
1319 Punahou Street, Suite 1010
Honolulu, HI 96826
Phone (808) 941-3322
Fax (808) 941-2522
Specialty Certification Ob/Gyn
Subspecialty Certification Board eligible for
Reproductive Endocrinology and Infertility
Practice Setting academic
Clinical Interests ART; leiomyomata;
endometriosis
Research Interests apoptosis of leiomyoma
Member Society for Assisted Reproductive
Technology, Society of Reproductive
Endocrinology and Infertility

ILLINOIS

Burr Ridge

John Rinehart, M.D.
160 Circle Ridge Drive
Burr Ridge, IL 60521
Phone (630) 856-3535
Fax (630) 856-3545
Specialty Certification Ob/Gyn
Subspecialty Certification Reproductive
Endocrinology
Practice Setting private
Clinical Interests IVF; infertility; ovulatory
dysfunction
Research Interests IVF; ovulation induction;
embryo culture conditions
Member Society of Reproductive Surgeons

Chicago

Eric J. Bieber, M.D.
University of Chicago
5841 S. Maryland
Chicago, IL 60637
Phone (773) 702-6642
Fax (773) 702-5848
Specialty Certification Ob/Gyn
Subspecialty Certification Reproductive
Endocrinology
Practice Setting academic
Clinical Interests infertility; fibroids;
endometriosis
Research Interests adhesion reduction;
endometriosis; menopause
Member Society of Reproductive Surgeons

Jan Friberg, M.D., Ph.D.
845 North Michigan Avenue,
Watertower Place
Suite 935 E
Chicago, IL 60611
Phone (312) 642-6777
Fax (312) 642-8383
Specialty Certification Ob/Gyn
Subspecialty Certification Reproductive
Endocrinology
Practice Setting private
Clinical Interests reproductive immunology;
habitual abortion; IVF
Research Interests reproductive immunology
Member Society of Reproductive Surgeons

Ralph R. Kazer, M.D.
333 E. Superior Street, Suite 1578
Chicago, IL 60611
Phone (312) 926-8244
Fax (312) 926-6643
E-mail rkazer@nwu.edu
Specialty Certification Ob/Gyn
Subspecialty Certification Reproductive
Endocrinology
Practice Setting academic
Clinical Interests polycystic ovarian syndrome;
IVF

Research Interests endocrinology of breast
cancer; polycystic ovary syndrome
Member Society of Reproductive Surgeons

Laurence A. Levine, M.D.
1725 W Harrison Street, Suite 917
Chicago, IL 60612
Phone (312) 829-1820
Fax (312) 829-9365
Specialty Certification Urology
Practice Setting academic/private
Clinical Interests male infertility; sperm
retrieval techniques; male sexual erectile
function
Research Interests Peyronie's disease; repair of
varicocele—efficacy; new drugs for erectile
dysfunction
Member Society for Male Reproduction and
Urology

Magdy P. Milad, M.D.
333 E. Superior Street, Suite 1564
Chicago, IL 60611
Phone (312) 695-7269
Specialty certification Reproductive
Endocrinology
Practice Setting academic
Clinical Interests IVF; ovulation induction;
male infertility
Research Interests implantation in ART cycles;
male infertility; endometriosis
Member Society of Reproductive
Endocrinology and Infertility

Craig Niederberger, M.D.
University of Illinois at Chicago
840 South Wood Street, 515CSN
Chicago, IL 60612
Phone (312) 996-2779
Fax (360) 838-0335
E-mail craign@uic.edu
Specialty Certification Urology
Practice Setting academic
Clinical Interests male infertility; erectile
dysfunction
Research Interests sperm retrieval;
spermatogenesis
Member Society of Reproductive Surgeons,
Society for Male Reproduction and Urology,
Society of Reproductive Endocrinology and
Infertility

Gail Prins, Ph.D, HCLD
University of Illinois at Chicago
Department of Urology, M/C 955
820 South Wood Street
Chicago, IL 60616-7316
Phone (312) 413-9766
Fax (312) 966-1291
E-mail gprins@uinc.edu
Specialty Certification High Complexity Lab
Director
Practice Setting academic
Clinical Interests andrology; client deposit
sperm bank

Research Interests cancer of prostate
Member Society for Assisted Reproductive
Technology, Society for Male Reproduction
and Urology, Society of Reproductive
Endocrinology and Infertility

Elizabeth Puscheck, M.D.
Northwestern University Medical School
675 N. St. Claire, Suite 14-200
Chicago, IL 60611
Phone (312) 695-7269
Fax (312) 908-8500
E-mail epuschec@nmh.org
Specialty Certification Ob/Gyn
Subspecialty Certification Reproductive
Endocrinology
Practice Setting academic
Clinical Interests infertility, all aspects;
laparoscopy and microsurgery; reproductive
endocrinology; IVF
Research Interests male infertility; ovarian
paracrine interactions and implantation;
menopause studies
Member Society of Reproductive Surgeons

Ewa Radwanska, M.D.
1725 West Harrison Street, Suite 408
Chicago, IL 60612
Phone (312) 997-2229
Fax (312) 997-2354
E-mail eradwans@rush.edu
Specialty Certification Ob/Gyn
Subspecialty Certification Reproductive
Endocrinology
Practice Setting academic/private
Clinical Interests ovulation; endometriosis; IVF
Research Interests endometriosis; IVF;
amenorrhea
Member Society of Reproductive Surgeons,
Society for Assisted Reproductive
Technology, Society of Reproductive
Endocrinology and Infertility
Comments three locations in Chicago area:
downtown and two suburban; all include on-
site IVF program.

Lawrence S. Ross, M.D.
University of Illinois
Department of Urology, M/C 955
820 South Wood Street
Chicago, IL 60612-7316
Phone (312) 996-9330
Fax (312) 996-1291
E-mail lsross@uic.edu
Specialty Certification Urology
Practice Setting academic
Clinical Interests male infertility;
microsurgery; ICSI/IVF
Member Society of Reproductive Surgeons

Downers Grove

Amos E. Madanes, M.D.
Midwest Fertility Center
4333 Main Street

Downers Grove, IL 60515
Phone (800) 244-0212
Fax (630) 810-1027
E-mail midfert@aol.com
Specialty Certification Ob/Gyn
Subspecialty Certification Reproductive
Endocrinology
Practice Setting private
Clinical Interests infertility; polycystic ovary
syndrome; IVF with micromanipulation
techniques
Member Society of Reproductive Surgeons
Comments additional locations in Chicago and
Northwest Indiana

Glenview

Aaron S. Lifchez, M.D.
3703 West Lake Avenue
Glenview, IL 60025
Phone (847) 998-8200
Fax (847) 335-9927
E-mail ASL1943@aol.com
Specialty Certification Ob/Gyn
Practice Setting private
Clinical Interests IVF; ICSI; polycystic ovaries;
endometriosis
Research Interests preimplantation genetic
diagnosis
Member Society of Reproductive Surgeons,
Society for Assisted Reproductive Technology

John Rapisarda, M.D.
Fertility Centers of Illinois
3703 W. Lake Avenue, Suite 106
Glenview, IL 60025
Phone (847) 998-8200
Fax (847) 998-6880
Specialty Certification: Ob/Gyn
Practice Setting private
Clinical Interests endometriosis; irregular
periods; infertility
Member Society for Assisted Reproductive
Technology

Gurnee

Raza Khan
202 S. Greenleaf, Suite D
Gurnee, IL 60031
Phone (847) 599-1111
Fax (847) 599-1148
Specialty Certification Urology
Practice Setting private
Clinical Interests prostate cancer; urinary
incontinence

Highland Park

Edward Marut, M.D.
Fertility Centers of Illinois
750 Homewood Avenue, Suite 190
Highland Park, IL 60035
Phone (847) 433-4400
Fax (847) 433-6245
E-mail embryo@hotmail.com

Specialty Certification Ob/Gyn
Subspecialty Certification Reproductive
Endocrinology
Practice Setting private
Clinical Interests ART; ovulation induction;
medical treatment of fibroids and
endometriosis
Research Interests novel gonadtropins; new
technologies in ART
Member Society for Assisted Reproductive
Technology, Society of Reproductive
Endocrinology and Infertility

Jorge A. Valle, M.D.
750 Homewood Avenue, Suite 190
Highland Park, IL 60035
Phone (847) 433-4400
Fax (847) 433-6145
Specialty Certification Ob/Gyn
Practice Setting private
Clinical Interests infertility; reproductive
surgery; gynecologic endocrinology
Research Interests hyperinsulinemia in
reproductive medicine
Member Society of Reproductive Surgeons

Hinsdale

Andrew Ruiz, M.S.T.S.
Hinsdale Center for Reproduction
121 N. Elm Street
Hinsdale, IL 60521
Phone (630) 856-3535
Fax (630) 856-3545
E-mail HCRAndrew@aol.com
Specialty Certification Lab Supervisor
Subspecialty Certification Embryology/
Andrology
Practice Setting private
Clinical Interests reproductive medicine;
embryology; andrology
Research Interests cell culture; cell
development; micromanipulation
Member Society for Assisted Reproductive
Technology, Society for Male Reproduction
and Urology

Hoffman Estates

Reeva Jabamoni, M.D.
1585 N. Barrington Road, Suite 401
Hoffman Estates, IL 60523
Phone (847) 843-7090
Fax (847) 843-0584
Specialty Certification Ob/Gyn
Subspecialty Certification Reproductive
Endocrinology
Practice Setting private
Clinical Interests IVF; endoscopic surgery
(laparoscopy/hysteroscopy); microsurgery;
endometriosis
Research Interests polycystic ovarian disease
Member Society of Reproductive Surgeons

Naperville

Oladapo A. Ashiru, M.D., Ph.D.
1465 Terrance Drive
Naperville, IL 60565
Phone (630) 717-9508
Fax (312) 996-7176
E-mail denrele@tigger.ucc.edu
Specialty Certification Reproductive
Endocrinology
Subspecialty Certification Embryology
Practice Setting academic/private
Clinical Interests infertility; ART
Research Interests embryo implantation
Member Society for Assisted Reproductive
Technology, Society of Reproductive
Endocrinology and Infertility

Oak Brook

W. Paul Dmowski, M.D., Ph.D.
2425 W. 22nd Street, Suite 102
Oak Brook, IL 60523
Phone (630) 954-0054
Fax (630) 954-0064
E-mail wpdmowski@oakbrookfertility.com
Specialty Certification Ob/Gyn
Subspecialty Certification Reproductive
Endocrinology
Practice Setting private
Clinical Interests reproductive
endocrinology/infertility; endometriosis; IVF
Research Interests pathophysiology of
endometriosis; identification of new,
noninvasive diagnostic tests;
evaluation of new therapeutic agents and
new treatment methods and clarifying
association between endometriosis and
infertility
Member Society of Reproductive Surgeons
Comments Practice affiliate—the Institute for
the Study and Treatment of Endometriosis, a
not-for-profit organization; conducts basic
and clinical research on endometriosis and its
management.

Reeva Jabamoni, M.D.
100 Oak Brook Center, Suite 308
Oak Brook, IL 60523
Phone (630) 574-3633
Fax (630) 574-3660
Specialty Certification Ob/Gyn
Subspecialty Certification Reproductive
Endocrinology
Practice Setting private
Clinical Interests IVF; endoscopic surgery
(laparoscopy/hysteroscopy); microsurgery;
endometriosis
Research Interests polycystic ovarian disease
Member Society of Reproductive Surgeons

Nasir Rana, M.D. MPH
2425 W. 22nd Street, Suite 102
Oakbrook, IL 60523
Phone (630) 954-0054

Fax (630) 954-0064
E-mail nasirrana@msn.com
Specialty Certification Ob/Gyn
Subspecialty Certification Reproductive
Endocrinology/Infertility
Practice Setting private
Clinical Interests pelvic endometriosis;
infertility; laparoscopic surgery
Research Interests endometriosis
Member Society of Reproductive Surgeons,
Society for Male Reproduction and Urology,
Society of Reproductive Endocrinology and
Infertility

Rockford

Chiravudh Sawetawan, M.D.
Reproductive Health & Fertility Center
2350 N. Rockton Avenue, Suite 408
Rockford, IL 61103
Phone (815) 971-7234
Fax (815) 971-7425
Specialty Certification Ob/Gyn
Subspecialty Certification Reproductive
Endocrinology
Practice Setting private
Member Society for Assisted Reproductive
Technology; Society of Reproductive
Endocrinology and Infertility
Comments Visit our Web site:
www.reprohealth-fertility.org. We are a full-
service ART center serving northern, western,
and north-central Illinois as well as southern
Wisconsin, eastern Iowa, and far northwest
suburbs of Chicago.

Springfield

Phillip C. Galle, M.D.
340 West Miller Street
Springfield, IL 62702
Phone (217) 523-4700
Fax (217) 523-9025
E-mail reproend@worldnet.att.net
Specialty Certification Ob/Gyn
Subspecialty Certification Reproductive
Endocrinology
Practice Setting private
Clinical Interests IVF; infertility surgery;
recurrent abortions; menopause
Research Interests menopause—hormone
replacement
Member Society of Reproductive Surgeons,
Society for Assisted Reproductive
Technology, Society of Reproductive
Endocrinology and Infertility

Mary Ann McRae, M.D.
Reproductive Endocrinology Associates, S.C.
340 W. Miller Street
Springfield, IL 62707
Phone (217) 523-4700
Fax (217) 523-9025
Specialty Certification Ob/Gyn

Subspecialty Certification Reproductive
Endocrinology
Practice Setting private
Clinical Interests infertility; reproductive
surgery; endometriosis
Member Society of Reproductive Surgeons,
Society for Assisted Reproductive
Technology; Society of Reproductive
Endocrinology and Infertility

INDIANA

Fort Wayne

Shelby Cooper, M.D.
7910 West Jefferson Boulevard, Suite 301
Fort Wayne, IN 46804
Phone (219) 432-6250
Fax (219) 436-7220
E-mail scooper@afg-ivf.com
Specialty Certification Ob/Gyn
Practice Setting private
Clinical Interests IVF; micromanipulation and
ICSI; reproductive surgery
Member Society for Assisted Reproductive
Technology

Indianapolis

Robert E. Cleary, M.D.
8091 Township Line Road, #109
Indianapolis, IN 46260
Phone (317) 872-0582
Fax (317) 876-0115
Specialty Certification Ob/Gyn
Subspecialty Certification Reproductive
Endocrinology
Practice Setting private
Clinical Interests reconstructive pelvic surgery
including congenital anomalies; newer
approaches to operative laparoscopy and
hysteroscopy
Research Interests chlamydia
Member Society of Reproductive Surgeons

Donald L. Cline, M.D.
2020 W. 86th
Indianapolis, IN 4620
Phone (317) 872-1515
Fax (317) 879-2784
E-mail dcline@mem.po.com
Specialty Certification Ob/Gyn
Subspecialty Certification Reproductive
Endocrinology
Practice Setting private
Clinical Interests IVF; endometriosis—laser;
microsurgery
Research Interests cervical mucus
Member Society of Reproductive Surgeons,
Society for Assisted Reproductive Technology

Robert M. Colver, M.D.
Midwest Reproductive Medicine
8081 Township Line Road
Indianapolis, IN 46260

Phone (800) 333-1415
Fax (317) 872-5063
Specialty Certification Ob/Gyn
Subspecialty Certification Reproductive Endocrinology
Practice Setting private
Clinical Interests ovulation induction; reproductive surgery
Member Society for Assisted Reproductive Technology
Comments Visit our Web site: www.fertilitymrm.com

John C. Jarrett, II, M.D.
8081 Township Line Road
Indianapolis, IN 46260
Phone (317) 875-5978
Fax (317) 872-5063
Specialty Certification Ob/Gyn
Subspecialty Certification Reproductive Endocrinology
Practice Setting private
Clinical Interests ART; polycystic ovaries; endometriosis
Research Interests polycystic ovaries
Member Society of Reproductive Surgeons

David S. McLaughlin, M.D.
8040 Clearvista Parkway, Suite 280
Indianapolis, IN 46256
Phone (317) 841-2255
Fax (317) 841-2265
Specialty Certification Ob/Gyn
Practice Setting private
Clinical Interests endometriosis; polycystic ovaries; fibroids
Research Interests oocyte cryopreservation; ovarian tissue cryopreservation; monozygotic twins following day five blastocyst transfer
Member Society of Reproductive Surgeons
Comments I recently published *Atlas of Reproductive Surgery & Assisted Reproductive Technology Procedures* through Martin Dunitz Publishers.

Samuel Tanner Thompson, M.D.
1801 North Senate Boulevard, Suite 655
Indianapolis, IN 46202
Phone (317) 929-1100
Fax (317) 924-7791
E-mail sthompson2@clarian.com
Specialty Certification Urology
Practice Setting private
Clinical Interests sperm aspiration; microsurgical vasectomy reversal; treatment of hormonal abnormalities
Research Interests varicocele repair; infection of semen; prevention of male infertility
Member Society of Reproductive Surgeons

Munster

Anthony Caruso
800 MacArthur Boulevard, Suite 23
Munster, IN 46410

Phone (219) 769-0556
Fax (219) 769-0572
E-mail midwfert@aol.com
Specialty Certification Reproductive Endocrinology
Subspecialty Certification Ob/Gyn
Practice Setting private
Clinical Interests IVF; endometriosis; tubal reversal
Member Society of Reproductive Surgeons
Comments All new patient inquiries should be directed to our toll-free number at 1(800) 244-0212.

South Bend

A. Philip DePauw, M.D.
707 Cedar, Suite 450
South Bend, IN 46617
Phone (219) 234-4100
Fax (219) 282-1739
Specialty Certification Urology
Practice Setting private
Member Society for Male Reproduction and Urology

IOWA

Ames

Marvin L. Swanson, M.D.
McFarland Clinic
1215 Duff Avenue
PO Box 3014
Ames, IA 50010
Phone (515) 239-4414
Fax (515) 239-4786
E-mail mswanson@mcfarlandclinic.com
Specialty Certification Ob/Gyn
Subspecialty Certification Reproductive Endocrinology and Infertility
Practice Setting private
Clinical Interests infertility; IVF; menopause
Research Interests reproductive surgery
Member Society for Assisted Reproductive Technology, Society of Reproductive Endocrinology and Infertility

Iowa City

Jay Sandlow, M.D.
University of Iowa Hospitals & Clinics
Department of Urology
200 Hawkins Drive
Iowa City, IA 52242
Phone (319) 353-7035
Fax (319) 356-3900
E-mail jay-sandlow@uiowa.edu
Specialty Certification Urology
Practice Setting academic
Clinical Interests male infertility; vasectomy reversal; vasectomy
Research Interests genes involved in spermatogenesis

Member Society for Male Reproduction and Urology

Brad Van Voorhis, M.D.
Department of Obstetrics & Gynecology
University of Iowa Hospitals & Clinics
Iowa City, IA 52242
Phone (319) 356-4536
Fax (319) 353-6659
E-mail brad-van-voorhis@uiowa.edu
Specialty Certification Ob/Gyn
Subspecialty Certification Reproductive Endocrinology
Practice Setting academic
Clinical Interests infertility; reproductive endocrinology
Research Interests cost-effective infertility treatment; ovarian function
Member Society for Assisted Reproductive Technology

Valery Montgomery-Rice, MD
Department of Ob/Gyn
Women's Reproductive Center
3901 Rainbow Boulevard
Kansas City, KS 66160
Phone (913) 588-6261
Fax (913) 588-6271
E-mail vmontgomery-rice@kumc.edu
Specialty Certification Ob/Gyn
Subspecialty Certification Reproductive Endocrinology
Practice Setting academic
Clinical Interests repetitive pregnancy loss; premenstrual syndrome; endometriosis and menopause
Research Interests use of purified hormones to induce ovulation; postoperative adhesion prevention; role of tumor necrosis factor in ovarian steriodogenesis; role of gonadotropins in ovarian cancer
Member Society for Assisted Reproductive Technology, Society of Reproductive Endocrinology and Infertility
Comments Along with her colleagues at the Women's Reproductive Center, Dr. Montgomery-Rice provides complete diagnostic and treatment programs for all aspects of infertility and reproductive endocrine disorders, including ovulation induction, endometriosis management, inseminations and in IVF with assisted hatching and ICSI as required.

Wichita

David A. Grainger, M.D.
2903 E. Central
Wichita, KS 67214
Phone (316) 687-2112
Fax (316) 687-1260
E-mail grainger@southwind.net
Specialty Certification Ob/Gyn
Subspecialty Certification Reproductive Endocrinology

Practice Setting academic
Clinical Interests polycystic ovarian syndrome/insulin resistance; endometriosis; IVF
Research Interests techniques of endometrial ablation; embryo transfer techniques
Member Society for Assisted Reproductive Technology, Society of Reproductive Endocrinology and Infertility

Bruce Tjaden
The Center for Reproductive Medicine
2903 E. Central
Wichita, KS 67214
Phone (316) 687-2172
Fax (316) 687-1260
E-mail cvmblt@southwind.net
Specialty Certification Ob/Gyn
Subspecialty Certification Reproductive Endocrinology and Infertility
Practice Setting academic
Clinical Interests Mullerian anomalies; ectopic pregnancy; DCD
Member Society of Reproductive Surgeons, Society for Assisted Reproductive Technology, Society of Reproductive Endocrinology and Infertility

KENTUCKY

Lexington

James W. Akin, M.D.
1780 Nicholasville Road, Suite 201
Lexington, KY 40503
Phone (606) 260-1515
Fax (606) 260-1425
Specialty Certification Ob/Gyn
Subspecialty Certification Reproductive Endocrinology
Practice Setting private
Clinical Interests endometriosis; IVF
Research Interests endometriosis
Member Society for Assisted Reproductive Technology, Society for Male Reproduction and Urology,
Society of Reproductive Endocrinology and Infertility

Shona Murray, M.D.
1780 Nicholasville Road, Suite 201
Lexington, KY 40503
Phone (606) 260-1515
Fax (606) 260-1425
Specialty Certification Ob/Gyn
Subspecialty Certification Reproductive Endocrinology
Practice Setting academic/private
Clinical Interests IVF; ovulation induction; polycystic ovaries
Member Society for Assisted Reproductive Technology, Society of Reproductive Endocrinology and Infertility

Louisville

Arnold M. Belker, M.D.
  250 E. Liberty Street, Suite 602
  Louisville, KY 40202
  Phone (502) 584-0651
  Fax (502) 587-6434
  E-mail 102704.2733@compuserve.com
  Specialty Certification Urology
  Practice Setting private
  Clinical Interests microsurgical vasectomy
  reversal; male infertility
  Research Interests clinical results of male
  reproductive surgery
  Member Society of Reproductive Surgeons

Christine L. Cook, M.D.
  601 S. Floyd Street, Suite 300
  Louisville, KY 40202
  Phone (502) 629-3830
  Fax (502) 629-3841
  E-mail christine-cook@louisville.edu
  Specialty Certification Ob/Gyn
  Practice Setting academic
  Clinical Interests menopause; perimenopause;
  polycystic ovarian syndrome
  Research Interests menopause; perimenopause;
  polycystic ovarian syndrome
  Member Society of Reproductive Surgeons

Ronald L. Levine, M.D.
  University of Louisville
  Department of Obstetrics & Gynecology
  550 S. Jackson Street
  Louisville, KY 40202
  Phone (502) 852-1371
  Fax (502) 852-1911
  E-mail rllevi01@guise.louisville.edu
  Specialty Certification Ob/Gyn
  Practice Setting academic
  Clinical Interests endoscopic surgery
  Research Interests endoscopic surgery
  Member Society of Reproductive Surgeons

Marvin A. Yussman, M.D.
  601 S. Floyd Street
  Louisville, KY 40202, Suite 300
  Phone (502) 629-3830
  Fax (502) 629-3841
  E-mail mayoss01@gwise.louisville.edu
  Specialty Certification Ob/Gyn
  Subspecialty Certification Reproductive
  Endocrinology
  Practice Setting academic/private
  Clinical Interests endoscopy; tubal anastomosis
  Research Interests induction of ovulation
  Member Society of Reproductive Surgeons

LOUISIANA

Baton Rouge

Philip Hindelang, M.D.
  451 East Airport, Suite A
  Baton Rouge, LA 70806
  Phone (225) 924-9080
  Fax (225) 924-9060
  Specialty Certification Ob/Gyn
  Practice Setting private
  Clinical Interests routine infertility workup;
  endoscopic surgery; ovulation induction
  Member Society of Reproductive Surgeons

Bobby W. Webster, M.D.
  9000 Airline Highway, Suite 670
  Baton Rouge, LA 70815
  Phone (225) 926-6886
  Fax (225) 922-3730
  E-mail MDBW@womans.com
  Specialty Certification Ob/Gyn
  Subspecialty Certification Reproductive
  Endocrinology
  Practice Setting private
  Clinical Interests ART; microsurgery;
  polycystic ovarian syndrome
  Research Interests ART; microsurgery;
  polycystic ovarian syndrome
  Member Society of Reproductive Surgeons

Lafayette

William D. Pelletier, M.D.
  4540 Ambassador Caffery, C-220
  Lafayette, LA 70508
  Phone (318) 989-8795
  Fax (318) 989-8766
  Specialty Certification Ob/Gyn
  Practice Setting private
  Member Society of Reproductive Surgeons

John Storment, M.D.
  4540 Ambassador Caffery, C220
  Lafayette, LA 70508
  Phone (318) 989-8795
  Fax (318) 989-9728
  E-mail storment@fertilityinstitute.com
  Specialty Certification Ob/Gyn
  Subspecialty Certification Reproductive
  Endocrinology
  Practice Setting private
  Clinical Interests recurrent pregnancy loss;
  infertility; advanced laparoscopic surgery;
  conservative treatment of fibroids; pelvic pain
  and endometriosis
  Member Society of Reproductive
  Endocrinology, Society of Reproductive
  Surgeons

John Tolson III, M.D.
  1016 Coolidge Boulevard
  Lafayette, LA 70503
  Phone (337) 233-6665
  Fax (337) 233-0327
  Specialty Certification Urology
  Practice Setting private
  Clinical Interests male infertility
  Member Society for Male Reproduction and
  Urology

James L. Zehnder, M.D.
  4540 Ambassador Caffery, C-220

Lafayette, LA 70508
Phone (318) 989-8795
Fax (318) 987-8766
Specialty Certification Ob/Gyn
Practice Setting private
Clinical Interests infertility—surgical and nonsurgical; menopause management; endometriosis
Member Society of Reproductive Surgeons

Lake Charles

Thomas P. Alderson, M.D., FACS
Urology Center of Southwest Louisiana
234 South Ryan Street
Lake Charles, LA 70601
Phone (318) 433-5282
Fax (318) 433-1159
E-mail tald234@iamerica.net
Specialty Certification Urology
Practice Setting private
Clinical Interests male infertility; reconstructive male infertility; surgery/vasovasostomy
Member Society for Male Reproduction and Urology
Comments Interest in male factor infertility and assisted reproductive techniques is limited by community interest and economic support.

Metairie

Joseph H. Bellina, M.D.
2525 Severn Avenue
Metairie, LA 70002
Phone (800) 535-4177
Fax (504) 832-4200
E-mail jbellina@omega-institute.com
Specialty Certification Ob/Gyn
Practice Setting private
Clinical Interests pelvic reconstructive surgery; endometriosis; pelvic pain
Research Interests endometriosis
Member Society of Reproductive Surgeons
Comments Omega Institute of Health and Hospital is a complete women's facility treating all aspects of women's diseases.

Heber E. Dunaway, Jr., M.D.
4720 I-10 Service Road, Suite 100
Metairie, LA 70002
Phone (504) 454-2165
Fax (504) 888-2250
E-mail HeberD@aol.com
Specialty Certification Ob/Gyn
Subspecialty Certification Reproductive Endocrinology
Practice Setting private
Clinical Interests endometriosis; pelvic pain; uterine anomalies
Research Interests recombinant luteinizing hormone
Member Society of Reproductive Surgeons, Society for Assisted Reproductive

Technology, Society of Reproductive Endocrinology and Infertility
Comments Two full-service centers located in Metairie and Baton Rouge, Louisiana.

Robert W. Kelly, M.D.
2525 Severn Avenue
Metairie, LA 70002
Phone (504) 832-4200
Fax (504) 832-4209
E-mail Rkelly@Omega-Institute.com
Specialty Certification Ob/Gyn
Subspecialty Certification Reproductive Endocrinology
Practice Setting private
Clinical Interests endometriosis; pelvic pain; leiomyomata uteri
Research Interests endometriosis; pelvic pain
Member Society of Reproductive Surgeons

New Orleans

David N. Curole, M.D.
Ochsner Clinic
1514 Jefferson Highway
New Orleans, LA 70121
Phone (504) 842-4155
Fax (504) 842-4141
E-mail dcurole@ochsner.org
Specialty Certification Ob/Gyn
Practice Setting academic
Clinical Interests fertility; pelvic pain and endometriosis; uterine fibroids
Research Interests pelvic adhesion prevention
Member Society of Reproductive Surgeons

Richard P. Dickey, M.D.
6020 Bullard Avenue
New Orleans, LA 70128
Phone (504) 246-8971
Fax (504) 246-9778
E-mail Info@FertilityInstitute.com
Specialty Certification Ob/Gyn
Subspecialty Certification Reproductive Endocrinology
Practice Setting private
Clinical Interests IVF; ovulation induction and intrauterine insemination; recurrent pregnancy loss
Research Interests ovulation induction for IUI and IVF uterine blood flow in infertility and recurrent pregnancy loss
Member Society of Reproductive Surgeons

Harold Fuselier, Jr., M.D.
Ochsner Clinic
1514 Jefferson Highway
New Orleans, LA 70121
Phone (504) 842-4083
Fax (504) 842-2009
E-mail hfuselier@ochsner.org
Specialty Certification Urology
Practice Setting private
Member Society for Male Reproduction and Urology

Wayne J. G. Hellstrom, M.D.
Department of Urology, SL-42
Tulane University School of Medicine
1430 Tulane Avenue
New Orleans, LA 70112
Phone (504) 587-7308
Fax (504) 588-5059
E-mail whellst@tmcpop.tmc.tulane.edu
Specialty Certification Urology
Practice Setting academic
Clinical Interests male infertility—
endocrinology; microsurgical surgery—
gamete retrieval; erectile dysfunction
Research Interests varicocele studies; sperm
stimulation protocols; nitric oxide effects on
spermatogenesis
Member Society for Male Reproduction and
Urology

Phillip H. Rye, M.D.
2633 Napoleon Avenue, Suite 805
New Orleans, LA 70115
Phone (504) 895-7717
Fax (504) 891-0619
Specialty Certification Ob/Gyn
Practice Setting private
Clinical Interests recurrent pregnancy loss;
unexplained infertility; IVF
Member Society of Reproductive Surgeons;
Society for Assisted Reproductive Technology

Steven N. Taylor, M.D.
6020 Bullard Avenue
New Orleans, LA 70128
Phone (504) 246-8971
Fax (504) 246-9778
Specialty Certification Gynecology
Practice Setting private
Clinical Interests infertility; fibroid surgery;
endometriosis surgery
Research Interests ovulation induction
medication; adhesion prevention
Member Society of Reproductive Surgeons

Dennis D. Venable, M.D.
Department of Urology
Louisiana State Univeristy Health Science
Center
P.O. Box 33932
Shreveport, LA 71130
Phone (318) 675-5600
Fax (318) 675-5665
E-mail Dvenab@LSUMC.Edu
Specialty Certification Urology
Practice Setting academic
Member Society for Male Reproduction and
Urology

MAINE
South Portland

Buell Muller, M.D.
Coastal Women's Healthcare
260 Western Avenue

South Portland, ME 04106
Phone (207) 774-5941
Fax (207) 761-2441
Specialty Certification Ob/Gyn
Practice Setting private
Clinical Interests operative laparoscopy;
ovulation induction; IUI, operative
hysteroscopy; sonohysteroscopy
Member Society of Reproductive Surgeons
Comments Also satellite site for monitoring
ART program, Boston IVF, Reproductive
Science, Brigham & Women's, Mass. General.

Joseph L. Wilkis, M.D.
Coastal Women's Healthcare
260 Western Avenue
South Portland, ME 04106
Phone (207) 774-5941
Fax (207) 761-2441
Specialty Certification Ob/Gyn
Practice Setting private
Clinical Interests microsurgery; laparoscopic
surgery for endometriosis and adhesions;
controlled ovarian hyperstimulation/
intrauterine insemination;
polycystic ovarian syndrome (medical and
surgical treatment)
Member Society of Reproductive Surgeons
Comments Also satellite site for monitoring
ART program, Boston IVF, Reproductive
Science, Brigham & Women's, Mass, General.

MARYLAND
Annapolis

Gilbert Mottla, M.D.
116 Defense Highway, Suite 203
Annapolis, MD 21401
Phone (410) 224-5500
Fax (410) 224-4272
Specialty Certification Ob/Gyn
Subspecialty Certification Reproductive
Endocrinology
Practice Setting private
Clinical Interests ovulation induction in
polycystic ovarian syndrome patients; IVF in
the low-responder patient
Research Interests blastocyst evaluation by
morphologic and biochemical markers
Member Society of Reproductive
Endocrinology and Infertility

Baltimore

Theodore A. Baramki, M.D.
6569 N. Charles Street, Suite 307
Baltimore, MD 21204
Phone (410) 828-2753
Fax (410) 512-8050
Specialty Certification Ob/Gyn
Subspecialty Certification Reproductive
Endocrinology
Practice Setting private
Clinical Interests infertility; operative

laparoscopy; genetic counseling,
amniocentesis, chorionic villus sampling
Member Society of Reproductive Surgeons

Marian Damewood, M.D.
Greater Baltimore Medical Center
6565 N. Charles Street, Suite 314
Baltimore, MD 21204
Phone (410) 769-8953
Fax (410) 769-8951
Specialty Certification Ob/Gyn
Subspecialty Certification Reproductive
Endocrinology
Practice Setting academic/private
Clinical Interests endometriosis; ovulation
dysfunction; reproductive surgery
Research Interests premature ovarian failure;
autoimmune—endometriosis association;
assisted technologies
Member Society of Reproductive Surgeons

Alan Geringer, M.D.
5406 Spring Lake Way
Baltimore, MD 21212
Phone (410) 323-4797
Fax (410) 323-4446
E-mail agering@charm.net
Specialty Certification Urology
Practice Setting private
Clinical Interests male infertility; erectile
dysfunction
Member Society for Male Reproduction and
Urology

Jonathan P. Jarow, M.D.
601 N. Caroline Street
Baltimore, MD 21287
Phone (410) 955-3617
Fax (410) 614-8487
Specialty Certification Urology
Practice Setting academic
Clinical Interests male infertility; sexual
dysfunction
Member Society of Reproductive Surgeons

Eugene Katz, M.D.
Greater Baltimore Medical Center
6569 N. Charles Street, Suite 406
Baltimore, MD 21204
Phone (410) 828-2484
Fax (410) 828-3067
E-mail ekatz@gbmc.org
Specialty Certification Ob/Gyn
Subspecialty Certification Reproductive
Endocrinology
Practice Setting private
Clinical Interests IVF/ICSI reproductive
surgery; prolactin disorder
Research Interests in vitro egg maturation;
recombinant follicle-stimulating hormone for
ovulation induction; male infertility
Member Society of Reproductive Surgeons,
Society for Assisted Reproductive
Technology, Society of Reproductive
Endocrinology and Infertility

Howard D. McClamrock, M.D.
University of Maryland School of Medicine
405 W. Redwood Street, 3rd Floor
Baltimore, MD 21201
Phone (410) 328-2304
Fax (410) 328-8389
E-mail hmcclamr@ummc001.ummc.
umaryland.edu
Specialty Certification Ob/Gyn
Subspecialty Certification Reproductive
Endocrinology
Practice Setting academic
Clinical Interests assisted reproductive
technology
Research Interests ovarian stimulation
protocol; predictors of success
Member Society of Reproductive Surgeons

Edward E. Wallach, M.D.
Department of Gynecology and Obstetrics
Johns Hopkins Medical Institutions
600 N. Wolfe Street
Baltimore, MD 21153
Phone (410) 955-7800
Fax (410) 955-9138
E-mail ewallach@jhmi.edu
Specialty Certification Ob/Gyn
Subspecialty Certification Reproductive
Endocrinology
Practice Setting academic
Clinical Interests ART; IVF; infertility;
myomectomy
Research Interests ovarian physiology—
mechanism of ovulation
Member Society of Reproductive Surgeons

Howard A. Zacur, M.D., Ph.D.
The Johns Hopkins Institutions
600 N. Wolfe Street, Houck 247
Baltimore, MD 21287
Phone (410) 955-7295
Fax (410) 614-9684
Specialty Certification Ob/Gyn
Subspecialty Certification Reproductive
Endocrinology
Practice Setting academic
Clinical Interests hormone replacement
therapy; oral contraceptives; endometriosis
Member Society of Reproductive Surgeons

Bethesda

Frank E. Chang, M.D.
10215 Fernwood Road, Suite 301A
Bethesda, MD 20817
Phone (301) 897-8850
Fax (301) 530-8105
E-mail Fchang362@aol.com
Specialty Certification Ob/Gyn
Subspecialty Certification Reproductive
Endocrinology
Practice Setting private
Clinical Interests ART—IVF, GIFT, ZIFT;
endometriosis; male factor
Member Society of Reproductive Surgeons

Brad Miller, M.D.
National Naval Medical Center
Bethesda, MD 20889
Phone (301) 295-4394
Fax (301) 869-0396
E-mail Btmrepro@hotmail.com
Specialty Certification Ob/Gyn
Subspecialty Certification Reproductive
Endocrinology
Practice Setting academic
Clinical Interests reducing high-order
multiples; ART; blastocyst transfer
Research Interests estrogen receptor function;
GnRH agonist and antagonist function
Member Society for Assisted Reproductive
Technology, Society for Male Reproduction
and Urology, Society of Reproductive
Endocrinology and Infertility

Kensington

Ruben Alvero, M.D.
3106 Homewood Parkway
Kensington, MD 20895
Phone (202) 782-3680
Fax (202) 782-3492
E-mail ruben.alvero@na.amedd.army.mic
Specialty Certification Ob/Gyn
Subspecialty Certification Reproductive
Endocrinology and Infertility
Practice Setting academic
Clinical Interests ART; exercise physiology;
polycystic ovarian disease
Member Society of Reproductive Endocrino-
logy and Infertility

Rockville

Burt Littman, M.D.
9711 Medical Center Drive, #214
Rockville, MD 20850
Phone (301) 424-1904
Fax (301) 424-1902
Specialty Certification Ob/Gyn
Subspecialty Certification Reproductive
Endocrinology
Practice Setting private
Clinical Interests IVF; endometriosis;
male/female infertility
Member Society of Reproductive Surgeons

Arthur Sagoskin, M.D.
15001 Shady Grove Road, Suite 400
Rockville, MD 20850
Phone (301) 340-1188
Fax (301) 340-1612
Specialty Certification Ob/Gyn
Practice Setting private
Clinical Interests IVF; endometriosis
Research Interests hydrosalpinges and IVF;
endometriosis
Member Society of Reproductive Surgeons

Timonium

Janet L. Kennedy, M.D.
2405 York Road, Suite 304
Timonium, MD 21093
Phone (410) 252-6633
Specialty Certification Ob/Gyn
Subspecialty Certification Reproductive
Endocrinology
Practice Setting private
Clinical Interests all forms of infertility;
menopause; hirsutism, amenorrhea,
polycystic ovarian disease; uterine fibroids;
Mullerian anomalies
Member Society of Reproductive Surgeons

Towson

Brad D. Lerner, M.D.
7505 Osler Drive, Suite 508
Towson, MD 21204
Phone (410) 296-0166
Fax (410) 828-7275
Specialty Certification Urology
Practice Setting private
Clinical Interests male reproductive medicine
and surgery; microsurgery and vasectomy
reversal; sperm retrieval procedures
Member Society for Male Reproduction and
Urology

Santiago L. Padilla, M.D.
110 West Road, Suite 102
Towson, MD 21204
Phone (410) 296-6400
Fax (410) 296-6405
Specialty Certification Ob/Gyn
Subspecialty Certification Reproductive
Endocrinology
Practice Setting private
Clinical Interests ART; operative laparoscopy;
endometriosis
Member Society of Reproductive Surgeons,
Society for Assisted Reproductive
Technology, Society of Reproductive
Endocrinology and Infertility

MASSACHUSETTS
Boston

Robert L. Bordicui, M.D.
Department of Obstetrics & Gynecology
Brigham & Women's Hospital
75 Francis Street
Boston, MA 02115
Phone (617) 732-4222
Fax (617) 277-1440
E-mail Rbarbieri@partners.org
Specialty Certification Ob/Gyn
Subspecialty Certification Reproductive
Endocrinology
Practice Setting academic
Clinical Interests endometriosis; polycystic
ovarian syndrome

Research Interests endometriosis; polycystic ovarian syndrome
Member Society of Reproductive Endocrinology and Infertility

Antonio Gargiulo, M.D.
Center for Reproductive Medicine
Brigham and Women's Hospital
75 Francis Street, A5B1-3
Boston, MA 02115
Phone (617) 732-4222
Fax (617) 232-7625
E-mail argargiulo@partners.org
Practice Setting academic
Clinical Interests ART; minimally invasive pelvic surgery; reproductive endocrinology
Research Interests implantation failure; luteal physiology
Member Society for Assisted Reproductive Technology, Society of Reproductive Endocrinology and Infertility

Elizabeth Ginsburg, M.D.
Brigham & Women's Hospital
75 Francis Street
Boston, MA 02115
Phone (617) 732-4285
Fax (617) 566-7752
E-mail esginsburg@partners.org
Specialty Certification Ob/Gyn
Subspecialty Certification Reproductive Endocrinology
Practice Setting academic
Clinical Interests IVF
Research Interests IVF outcomes; alcohol effects on estrogen metabolism
Member Society for Assisted Reproductive Technology, Society of Reproductive Endocrinology and Infertility

Michael Guarnaccia, M.D.
Department of Obstetrics & Gynecology
Center for Reproductive Medicine
Brigham & Women's Hospital
75 Francis Street
Boston, MA 02115
Phone (617) 732-4285
E-mail Mguarnaccia@partners.org
Specialty Certification Ob/Gyn
Practice Setting academic
Clinical Interests ART; infertility; endometriosis
Member Society of Reproductive Endocrinology

Joseph A. Hill, M.D.
Center for Reproductive Medicine
Brigham & Women's Hospital
75 Francis Street
Boston, MA 02115
Phone (612) 732-4222
Fax (612) 566-7752
Specialty Certification Ob/Gyn
Subspecialty Certification Reproductive Endocrinology

Practice Setting academic
Clinical Interests recurrent pregnancy loss; infertility
Research Interests immunology of reproduction; recurrent pregnancy loss; implantation
Member Society of Reproductive Surgeons, Society for Assisted Reproductive Technology, Society of Reproductive Endocrinology and Infertility

Mark D. Hornstein, M.D.
Department of Obstetrics & Gynecology
Brigham & Women's Hospital
75 Francis Street
Boston, MA 02115
Phone (617) 732-4222
Fax (617) 232-7625
E-mail Mhornstein@partners.org
Specialty Certification Ob/Gyn
Subspecialty Certification Reproductive Endocrinology
Practice Setting academic
Clinical Interests infertility; assisted reproduction; endometriosis
Research Interests endometriosis; assisted reproduction
Member Society for Assisted Reproductive Technology, Society of Reproductive Endocrinology and Infertility

Robert B. Hunt, M.D.
319 Longwood Avenue
Boston, MA 02115
Phone (617) 731-6111
Fax (617) 738-6161
E-mail rbhunt@pol.net
Specialty Certification Ob/Gyn
Practice Setting private
Clinical Interests tubal microsurgery; advanced laparoscopic surgery for infertility
Member Society of Reproductive Surgeons, Society for Male Reproduction and Urology
Comments No ART please!

David Keefe, M.D.
New England Medical Center
750 Washington Street
Boston, MA 02111
Phone (617) 636-0053
E-mail Dkeefe@WIHRI.org
Specialty Certification Ob/Gyn
Subspecialty Certification Reproductive Endocrinology
Practice Setting academic
Clinical Interests IVF; infertility
Research Interests aging and infertility; improving IVF outcomes; reducing triplet gestations
Comments I also direct the laboratory for reproductive medicine at the Woods Hole Marine Biological Laboratory,

Marc R. Laufer, M.D.
  Department of Obstetrics & Gynecology
  Brigham & Women's Hospital
  75 Francis Street
  Boston, MA 02115
  Phone (617) 732-4222
  E-mail MRLaufer@Bics.bwh.harvard.edu
  Specialty Certification Ob/Gyn
  Practice Setting academic
  Clinical Interests endometriosis; fertility issues
  for cancer patients; congenital anomalies of
  reproductive tract
  Research Interests endometriosis;
  congenital anomalies of reproductive tract
  Member Society of Reproductive Surgeons

Robert D. Oates, M.D.
  DOB Suite 606
  720 Harrison Avenue
  Boston, MA 02118
  Phone (617) 638-8485
  Fax (617) 638-8487
  Specialty Certification Urology
  Practice Setting academic
  Clinical Interests male reproductive medicine
  and surgery; vasectomy reversal;
  microsurgical sperm aspiration
  Research Interests genetics of azoospermia;
  congenital absence of the vas
  Member Society of Reproductive Surgeons

Michael P. O'Leary, M.D., M.P.H.
  Brigham & Women's Hospital
  Department of Urology
  45 Francis Street
  Boston, MA 02115
  Phone (617) 732-6325
  Fax (617) 566-3475
  E-mail moleary1@Bics.bwh.harvard.edu
  Specialty Certification Urology
  Practice Setting academic
  Clinical Interests sexual dysfunction; infertility
  (male); prostate disease
  Research Interests sexual dysfunction
  Member Society of Reproductive Surgeons

Isaac Schiff, M.D.
  Obstetrics & Gynecology Department
  Massachusetts General Hospital
  55 Fruit Street, VBK 113
  Boston, MA 02114
  Phone (617) 726-3001
  Fax (617) 726-7548
  Specialty Certification Ob/Gyn
  Subspecialty Certification Reproductive
  Endocrinology
  Clinical Interests infertility
  Research Interests premature menopause
  Member Society of Reproductive Surgeons

Danny Schust, M.D.
  Department of Obstetrics & Gynecology
  Division of Reproductive Endocrinology &
  Fertility
  Brigham & Women's Hospital

75 Francis Street
  Boston, MA 02115
  Phone (617) 732-4648
  Fax (617) 566-7752
  E-mail dschust@hms.harvard.edu
  Specialty Certification Ob/Gyn
  Practice Setting academic
  Clinical Interests recurrent spontaneous
  pregnancy loss; infertility
  Research Interests placental immunology;
  implantation

Elizabeth S. Stewart, M.D.
  Center for Reproductive Medicine
  Brigham & Women's Hospital
  75 Francis Street
  Boston, MA 02115
  Phone (617) 732-4285
  Fax (617) 566-7752
  Specialty Certification Ob/Gyn
  Subspecialty Certification Reproductive
  Endocrinology
  Practice Setting academic
  Clinical Interests uterine fibroids; abnormal
  uterine bleeding
  Research Interests mechanisms of uterine
  bleeding; innovative treatments for uterine
  fibroids; alternatives to hysterectomy
  Member Society of Reproductive
  Endocrinology and Infertility
  Comments I am the clinical director for the
  Center for Uterine Fibroids. We have a Web
  site—www.fibroids.net—with resources for
  patients and physicians.

Thomas L. Toth, M.D.
  Massachusetts General Hospital, Vincent 213
  55 Fruit Street
  Boston, MA 02114
  Phone (617) 724-3513
  Fax (617) 724-8882
  E-mail TLToth@partners.org *or*
  Toth.Thomas@MGH.harvard.edu
  Specialty Certification Ob/Gyn
  Subspecialty Certification Reproductive
  Endocrinology
  Practice Setting academic
  Clinical Interests assisted reproductive
  technologies
  Research Interests oocyte cryopreservation
  Member Society for Assisted Reproductive
  Technology, Society of Reproductive
  Endocrinology and Infertility

Elena Yanushpolsky, M.D.
  Center for Reproductive Medicine
  Brigham & Women's Hospital
  75 Francis Street
  Boston, MA 02115
  Phone (617) 732-4222
  Fax (617) 566-7752
  E-mail ehyanushpo@bics.bwh.harvard.edu
  Specialty Certification Ob/Gyn

Subspecialty Certification Reproductive
Endocrinology
Practice Setting academic
Clinical Interests infertility; minimally
invasive (endoscopic) gynecologic surgery
Research Interests novel approaches to
gynecologic surgery; new techniques in IVF

Brookline

Merle J. Berger, M.D.
Boston IVF—The Brookline Center
One Brookline Place, Suite 602
Brookline, MA 02445
Phone (617) 735-9000
Fax (617) 738-8993
E-mail merle.berger@bostonivf.com
Specialty Certification Ob/Gyn
Subspecialty Certification Reproductive
Endocrinology
Practice Setting private
Clinical Interests DES; IVF
Member Society for Assisted Reproductive
Technology, Society of Reproductive
Endocrinology and Infertility

Abraham Morgentaler, M.D.
One Brookline Place, #624
Brookline, MA 02445
Phone (617) 277-5000
Fax (617) 277-5444
E-mail amorgentaler@worldnet.att.net
Specialty Certification Urology
Practice Setting private
Clinical Interests vasectomy reversal—
microsurgical; varicocele—microsurgical
repair; epididymal/testicular sperm harvest
Research Interests temperature and testis
function
Member Society for Male Reproduction and
Urology

Chelmsford

Paul R. Feldman, M.D.
228 Billerica Road
Chelmsford, MA 01824
Phone (978) 250-6200
Fax (978) 244-6665
Specialty Certification Ob/Gyn
Practice Setting private
Clinical Interests infertility, female and male;
infertility psychosocial aspects
Member Society of Reproductive Surgeons

Danvers

Mitchell S. Rein, M.D.
One Hutchinson Drive
Danvers, MA 01923
Phone (978) 777-1070
Fax (978) 774-9635
E-mail Rein@nsmc.partners.org
Specialty Certification Ob/Gyn
Subspecialty Certification Reproductive
Endocrinology

Practice Setting academic
Clinical Interests uterine fibroids; infertility
Research Interests uterine fibroids; infertility
Member Society for Assisted Reproductive
Technology, Society of Reproductive
Endocrinology and Infertility

Dedham

Machelle M. Seibel, M.D.
333 Elm Street, 3rd Floor
Fertility Center of New England
Dedham, MA 02026
Phone (781) 326-9732
Fax (781) 726-9651
E-mail mseibel@mediaone.net
Specialty Certification Ob/Gyn
Subspecialty Certification Reproductive
Endocrinology
Practice Setting private
Clinical Interests endometriosis; assisted
reproduction; general infertility
Research Interests nutrition and
infertility/women's health
Member Society of Reproductive Surgeons
Comments Performed first IVF in
Massachusetts; first to use FSH (performed
clinical trials and testified before FDA); first
to use ultrasound for follicle size and egg
retrieval.

Quincy

Richard H. Reindollar, M.D.
Boston IVF—The South Shore Center
300 Congress Street
Quincy, MA 02169
Phone (617) 479-7461
Fax (617) 479-5948
E-mail rreindol@caregroup.harvard.edu
Specialty Certification Ob/Gyn
Subspecialty Certification Reproductive
Endocrinology
Practice Setting private
Clinical Interests infertility/ART;
pathophysiology of amenorrhea, delayed
puberty, intersex disorder; contraception
Research Interests molecular search for genes
involved in Mullerian development;
molecular basis for reproductive disorders;
congenital absence of the uterus and vagina,
intersex disorders
Member Society for Assisted Reproductive
Technology, Society of Reproductive
Endocrinology and Infertility

Waltham

Michael M. Alper, M.D.
Boston IVF—The Waltham Center
40 Second Avenue, Suite 300
Waltham, MA 02451
Phone (781) 434-6500
Fax (781) 434-6501
E-mail michael.alper@bostonivf.com
Specialty Certification Ob/Gyn

Subspecialty Certification Reproductive
Endocrinology
Practice Setting private
Clinical Interests IVF
Research Interests IVF
Member Society for Assisted Reproductive
Technology, Society of Reproductive
Endocrinology and Infertility

Samuel C. Pang, M.D.
Reproductive Science Center of Boston
Hope Avenue
Waltham, MA 02453
Phone (781) 647-6263
Fax (781) 647-6323
Specialty Certification Ob/Gyn
Subspecialty Certification Reproductive
Endocrinology
Practice Setting private
Clinical Interests ART; male factor infertility;
anovulatory infertility
Member Society for Assisted Reproductive
Technology, Society for Male Reproduction
and Urology, Society of Reproductive
Endocrinology and Infertility

Alan S. Penzias, M.D.
Boston IVF—The Waltham Center
40 Second Avenue, Suite 300
Waltham, MA 02451
Phone (781) 434-6500
Fax (781) 434-6501
E-mail Alan.Penzias@bostonivf.com
Specialty Certification Ob/Gyn
Subspecialty Certification Reproductive
Endocrinology
Practice Setting private
Clinical Interests ART; advanced operative
laparoscopy and hysteroscopy; recurrent
miscarriage
Research Interests multiple pregnancy and IVF;
outcome-oriented research
Member Society for Assisted Reproductive
Technology, Society of Reproductive
Endocrinology and Infertility

Kim L. Thornton, M.D.
Boston IVF—The Waltham Center
40 Second Avenue, Suite 300
Waltham, MA 02451
Phone (781) 434-6500
Fax (781) 434-6501
E-mail kimthornton@bostonivf.com
Specialty Certification Ob/Gyn
Subspecialty Certification Reproductive
Endocrinology
Practice Setting private
Clinical Interests ovulation induction; assisted
reproductive technology, IVF, GIFT;
endometriosis, fibroid uterus
Research Interests ART
Member Society for Assisted Reproductive
Technology, Society of Reproductive
Endocrinology and Infertility

Woburn

Steven R. Bayer, M.D.
Boston IVF—The Woburn Center
23 Warren Avenue
Woburn, MA 01801
Phone (781) 994-5600
Fax (781) 994-5608
Specialty Certification Ob/Gyn
Subspecialty Certification Reproductive
Endocrinology
Practice Setting academic/private
Clinical Interests ART; reproductive surgery;
menstrual irregularities
Research Interests outcomes research
Member Society for Assisted Reproductive
Technology, Society of Reproductive
Endocrinology and Infertility

MICHIGAN

Ann Arbor

Dana A. Ohl, M.D.
Section of Urology, Box 0330
1500 E. Medical Center Drive
Ann Arbor, MI 48109-0330
Phone (734) 936-5770
Fax (734) 936-9127
E-mail dana.ohl@umich.edu
Specialty Certification Urology
Practice Setting academic
Clinical Interests microsurgical reconstruction
of vas/epididymis; varicocele surgery;
electroejaculation/penile vibrating
ejaculation
Research Interests spinal cord injury and fertility;
sperm function; antisperm antibodies
Member Society for Male Reproduction and
Urology
Comments Board of directors for Society for
Male Reproduction and Urology.

John F. Randolph, Jr., M.D.
University of Michigan
1500 E. Medical Center Drive
L4100 Women's Hospital
Ann Arbor, MI 48109-0276
Phone (734) 936-7401
Fax (734) 647-9727
E-mail jfrandol@umich.edu
Specialty Certification Ob/Gyn
Subspecialty Certification Reproductive
Endocrinology
Practice Setting academic
Clinical Interests perimenopause; osteoporosis;
ovulatory infertility/polycystic ovarian
syndrome
Research Interests perimenopause
Member Society of Reproductive Surgeons

Birmingham

Michael S. Mersol-Barg, M.D.
 Center for Reproductive Medicine and
 Surgery
 300 Park Street, Suite 460
 Birmingham, MI 48009
 Phone (248) 593-6990
 Fax (248) 593-5925
 E-mail mersol-barg@reproductive-
 medicine.com
 Specialty Certification Ob/Gyn
 Subspecialty Certification Reproductive
 Endocrinology
 Practice Setting private
 Clinical Interests ovulation induction; ART;
 minimally invasive surgery
 Member Society of Reproductive Surgeons

Dearborn

Maria F. Hayes, M.D.
 18181 Oakwood Boulevard, Suite 109
 Dearborn, MI 48124
 Phone (313) 593-5880
 Fax (313) 593-8837
 Specialty Certification Ob/Gyn
 Subspecialty Certification Reproductive
 Endocrinology
 Practice Setting private
 Clinical Interests assisted reproductive
 technologies—IVF; uterine fibroids;
 endometriosis
 Member Society of Reproductive Surgeons

Detroit

Michael P. Diamond, M.D.
 Department of Obstetrics & Gynecology
 4707 St. Antoine Boulevard
 Detroit, MI 48201
 Phone (313) 993-8331
 Fax (313) 745-7037
 E-mail mdiamond@med.waynes.edu
 Specialty Certification Ob/Gyn
 Subspecialty Certification Reproductive
 Endocrinology
 Practice Setting academic
 Clinical Interests postoperative adhesions and
 endometriosis; polycystic ovarian syndrome;
 ART
 Research Interests peritoneal healing and
 adhesions; glucose metabolism; endoscopic
 surgery
 Member Society of Reproductive Surgeons

Grand Rapids

William Dodds, M.D.
 630 Kenmore, Suite 100
 Grand Rapids, MI 49546
 Phone (616) 988-2229
 Fax (616) 988-2010
 Specialty Certification Ob/Gyn
 Subspecialty Certification Reproductive
 Endocrinology

Practice Setting private
 Clinical Interests IVF; endometriosis; operative
 laparoscopy

James E. Young, M.D.
 221 Michigan Street, Suite 406
 Grand Rapids, MI 49503
 Phone (616) 391-2550
 Fax (616) 391-2552
 Specialty Certification Ob/Gyn
 Subspecialty Certification Reproductive
 Endocrinology
 Practice Setting private
 Clinical Interests ovulation induction;
 endometriosis; ART
 Research Interests luteal phase
 Member Society of Reproductive Surgeons,
 Society for Assisted Reproductive
 Technology, Society of Reproductive
 Endocrinology and Infertility

Lansing

Farrah Fahimi, M.D.
 1200 E. Michigan, Suite 305
 Lansing, MI 48912
 Phone (517) 484-4900
 E-mail Ffahimi@home.com
 Specialty Certification Ob/Gyn
 Subspecialty Certification Reproductive
 Endocrinology
 Practice Setting private
 Clinical Interests ART (IVF, GIFT, ZIFT, egg
 donation, intracytoplasmic sperm injection);
 pelvic endometriosis; uterine fibroids
 Research Interests male infertility; assisted
 reproductive technologies
 Member Society of Reproductive Surgeons,
 Society for Assisted Reproductive
 Technology, Society of Reproductive
 Endocrinology and Infertility
 Comments Accepting new patients.

Mohammad Mohsenian, M.D.
 1200 E. Michigan Avenue, Suite 305
 Lansing, MI 48912
 Phone (517) 484-4900
 E-mail mmohsenian@home.com
 Specialty Certification Ob/Gyn
 Subspecialty Certification Reproductive
 Endocrinology
 Practice Setting private
 Clinical Interests ART; reproductive surgery;
 infertility
 Research Interests andrology
 Member Society of Reproductive Surgeons

Royal Oak

William Keye, M.D.
 3535 W. 13 Mile Road, Suite 344
 Royal Oak, MI 48073
 Phone (248) 551-3600
 Fax (248) 551-3616
 E-mail wkeye@beaumont.edu
 Specialty Certification Ob/Gyn

Subspecialty Certification Reproductive
Endocrinology
Practice Setting private (with full-time
position at a tertiary hospital with a free-
standing residency program) ·
Clinical Interests IVF; laparoscopy;
hysteroscopy
Research Interests IVF; menopause;
endometriosis
Member Society of Reproductive Surgeons
Comments Practice includes full-time social
worker.

Alexander Maximovich, M.D.
3535 W. 13 Mile Road, Suite 344
Royal Oak, MI 48073
Phone (248) 551-3600
Fax (248) 551-3616 ·
Specialty Certification Ob/Gyn
Practice Setting academic
Clinical Interests infertility; endometriosis; IVF
Research Interests endometriosis
Member Society of Reproductive Surgeons
Comments Operative gynecologic endoscopy
(hysteroscope, laparoscope) and operative
directed vaginal ultrasound.

John R. Musich, M.D.
Beaumont Center for Fertility & Reproductive
Medicine
3535 W. 13 Mile Road, Suite 344
Royal Oak, MI 48073
Phone (248) 551-3600
Fax (248) 551-3616
E-mail jmusich@beaumont.edu
Specialty Certification Ob/Gyn
Subspecialty Certification Reproductive
Endocrinology
Practice Setting private
Clinical Interests infertility; gynecologic/
reproductive endocrinology; repetitive
pregnancy loss
Member Society of Reproductive Surgeons

Warren

Kamran S. Moghissi, M.D.
University Center for Women's Medicine
28800 Ryan Road, Suite 320
Warren, MI 48092
Phone (313) 745-7285
Fax (313) 745-7037
E-mail kmoghiss@med.wayne.edu
Specialty Certification Ob/Gyn
Subspecialty Certification Reproductive
Endocrinology
Practice Setting academic
Clinical Interests infertility; endometriosis;
menopause
Research Interests infertility; endometriosis;
menopause
Member Society of Reproductive Surgeons

West Bloomfield

Kenneth A. Goldman, M.D.
6900 Orchard Lake Road, Suite 201
West Bloomfield, MI 48322
Phone (248) 855-7455
Fax (268) 855-7459
Specialty Certification Urology
Practice Setting private
Clinical Interests male infertility;
microsurgery; vasectomy reversal
Member Society for Male Reproduction and
Urology
Comments Fellowship training, Baylor College
of Medicine, male infertility.

Ypsilanti

Jonathan W. T. Ayers, M.D.
Ann Arbor Reproductive Medicine
4990 Clark Road, Suite 100
Ypsilanti, MI 48197
Phone (734) 434-4876
Fax (734) 434-8848
Specialty Certification Ob/Gyn
Subspecialty Certification Reproductive
Endocrinology
Practice Setting private
Clinical Interests ovulatory dysfunction; low
responder—donor oocytes
Research Interests endocrine autoimmunity
Member Society of Reproductive Surgeons

MINNESOTA

Minneapolis

Lisa D. Erickson, M.D.
Center for Reproductive Medicine
800 E. 28th Street
Minneapolis, MN 55407
Phone (612) 863-5390
Fax (612) 863-2697
Specialty Certification Ob/Gyn
Subspecialty Certification Reproductive
Endocrinology and Infertility
Practice Setting private
Clinical Interests IVF; superovulation; fertility
surgery
Member Society of Reproductive Surgeons,
Society for Assisted Reproductive
Technology, Society of Reproductive
Endocrinology and Infertility

Theodore C. Nagel, M.D.
Reproductive Medicine Center
606 24th Avenue S, Suite 500
Minneapolis, MN 55454
Phone (612) 627-4564
Fax (612) 627-4888
E-mail Nagel007@tc.umn.edu
Specialty Certification Internal Medicine;
Ob/Gyn
Subspecialty Certification Reproductive
Endocrinology

Practice Setting private
Clinical Interests IVF; polycystic ovary syndrome; hysteroscopic surgery
Research Interests blastocyst transfer vs. day three transfer; sperm chromatin structural abnormalities
Member Society of Reproductive Surgeons
Comments Academic affiliation (University of Minnesota) in a private practice setting. On-site reproductive endocrinology lab. Male evaluated on site with urologist devoted full-time to male infertility.

Jon L. Pryor, M.D.
  Center for Men's Health and Infertility
  420 Delaware Street SE
  PO Box 394 FUMC
  Minneapolis, MN 55455
  Phone (612) 625-0662
  Fax (612) 624-4430
  E-mail pryor001@tc.umn.edu
  Specialty Certification Urology
  Practice Setting academic
  Clinical Interests male infertility; vasectomy and vasectomy reversals; impotence
  Research Interests varicoceles; genetics of infertility
  Member Society for Male Reproduction and Urology
  Comments We have a very large male infertility practice and we interact closely with reproductive endocrinologists and obstetricians/gynecologists throughout the state.

J. Bruce Redmon, M.D.
  Center for Men's Health and Infertility
  PO Box 394
  FUMC University of Minnesota
  420 Delaware Street SE
  Minneapolis, MN 55455
  Phone (612) 625-0662
  Fax (612) 624-4430
  E-mail redmo001@tc.umn.edu
  Specialty Certification Internal Medicine
  Subspecialty Certification Endocrinology, Diabetes, and Metabolism
  Practice Setting academic
  Clinical Interests male fertility; male androgen deficiency; erectile dysfunction
  Research Interests semen and hormonal parameters in fertile men; therapies for male infertility; therapies for erectile dysfunction
  Comments I work closely with Dr. Jon Pryor, a urologic surgeon who shares my interest in male fertility.
  Member American Society of Andrology

Rochester

Mark A. Damario, M.D.
  Mayo Clinic
  200 First Street SW
  Rochester, MN 55905
  Phone (507) 284-3176
  Fax (507) 284-1774
  E-mail damario.mark@mayo.edu
  Specialty Certification Ob/Gyn
  Subspecialty Certification Reproductive Endocrinology
  Practice Setting private
  Clinical Interests ART; reproductive surgery
  Research Interests improving clinical outcomes of ART endometriosis
  Member Society of Reproductive Surgeons

Daniel Dumesic, M.D.
  Mayo Clinic
  200 First Street SW
  Rochester, MN 55905
  Phone (507) 284-4520
  Fax (507) 284-1774
  Specialty Certification Ob/Gyn
  Subspecialty Certification Reproductive Endocrinology
  Practice Setting academic
  Clinical Interests polycystic ovarian disease; ART; menopause
  Research Interests reproductive function in prenatally androgenzied adult female rhesus monkeys
  Member Society for Assisted Reproductive Technology

Ajay Nehra, M.D.
  Mayo Clinic
  200 First Street SW
  Rochester, MN 55905
  Phone (507) 266-4446
  Fax (507) 284-4951
  E-mail nehra.ajay@mayo.edu
  Specialty Certification Urology
  Practice Setting academic
  Clinical Interests outcome of assisted techniques; spinal cord injuries
  Research Interests genetics
  Member Society of Reproductive Surgeons, Society for Assisted Reproductive Technology, Society for Male Reproduction and Urology, Society of Reproductive Endocrinology and Infertility

Donna Session, M.D.
  Mayo Clinic
  Obstetrics & Gynecology Department
  200 First Street SW CH 3A
  Rochester, MN 55905
  Phone (507) 284-3176
  Fax (507) 284-1774
  Specialty Certification Ob/Gyn
  Subspecialty Certification Reproductive Endocrinology
  Practice Setting academic
  Clinical Interests sonohysterolgraphy; ultrasound-guided procedures; three-dimensional ultrasound
  Research Interests cell cycle; hormonal regulation of gene expression; molecular biology of spermatogenesis

Member Society for Assisted Reproductive Technology

Roseville

Russell Bierbaum, M.D.
Cryogenic Laboratories, Inc.
1944 Lexington Avenue N.
Roseville, MN 55113
Phone (651) 489-8000
Fax (651) 489-8989
E-mail rebierbaum@cryolab.com
Practice Setting private
Clinical Interests semen banking; embryo storage
Member Society for Male Reproduction and Urology

John Olson, M.D.
Cryogenic Laboratories
1944 Lexington Avenue N.
Roseville, MN 55113
Phone (651) 489-8000
Fax (651) 489-8989
E-mail jholson@cryolab.com
Specialty Certification Semen Cryobank
Practice Setting private
Clinical Interests semen cryobanking
Member Society for Male Reproduction and Urology
Comments Services: donor semen, client depositor sperm banking.

St. Paul

Ricardo Castillo, M.D.
Reproductive Medicine & Infertility Associates
360 Sherman Street, Suite 350
St. Paul, MN 55102
Phone (651) 222-6050
Fax (651) 222-5975
E-mail rcastillo@rmia.com
Specialty Certification Ob/Gyn
Practice Setting Private
Clinical Interests IVF; ultrasound; endoscopy
Member Society for Assisted Reproductive Technology

John W. Malo, M.D.
360 Sherman Street, #160
St. Paul, MN 55102
Phone (651) 268-2575
Fax (651) 268-2576
E-mail Malodiver@aol.com
Specialty Certification Ob/Gyn
Practice Setting private
Clinical Interests ART; reproductive surgery; ovulation induction
Member Society of Reproductive Surgeons

Douglas Schow, M.D.
Reproductive Medicine & Infertility Associates
360 Sherman Street, Suite 350
St. Paul, MN 55102
Phone (651) 222-6050
Fax (651) 222-5975
E-mail: schow@rmia.com
Specialty Certification Urology
Practice Setting private
Clinical Interests male infertility; microscopic vasectomy reversal; erectile dysfunction
Research Interests male infertility
Comments Dr. Schow has two warranty programs for vasectomy reversals.

Jacques P. Stassart, M.D.
Reproductive Medicine & Infertility Associates
360 Sherman Street, Suite 350
St. Paul, MN 55102
Phone (65) 222-6050
Fax (65) 222-5975
E-mail drstassart@rmia.com
Specialty Certification Ob/Gyn
Practice Setting private
Clinical Interests IVF; embryology
Research Interests cryopreservation; reduced number of embryos transferred while maintaining high pregnancy rates
Member Society for Assisted Reproductive Technology

MISSISSIPPI

Jackson

Bryan D. Cowan, M.D.
Professor & Director
Division of Reproductive Endocrinology
Department of Obstetrics & Gynecology
University of Mississippi Medical Center
2500 N. State Street
Jackson, MS 39216-4505
Phone (601) 984-5330
Fax (601) 984-5965
E-mail bcowan@ob-gyn.umsmed.edu
Specialty Certification Ob/Gyn
Subspecialty Certification Reproductive Endocrinology
Practice Setting academic
Clinical Interests IVF; fibroids; ectopic pregnancy
Research Interests implantation; fibroids
Member Society for Assisted Reproductive Technology, Society of Reproductive Endocrinology and Infertility

Randall S. Hines, M.D.
Professor & Director
In Vitro Fertilization Program
Department of Obstetrics & Gynecology
University of Mississippi Medical Center
2500 N. State Street
Jackson, MS 39216-4505
Phone (601) 984-6900
Fax (601) 984-5965
E-mail rhines@ob-gyn.umsmed.edu
Specialty Certification Ob/Gyn

Subspecialty Certification Reproductive Endocrinology
Practice Setting academic
Clinical Interests IVF; recurrent pregnancy loss; delayed puberty
Research Interests implantation; sexual differentiation
Member Society for Assisted Reproductive Technology, Society of Reproductive Endocrinology and Infertility

MISSOURI

Columbia

Gary Horowitz, M.D.
3211 S. Providence Boulevard
Columbia, MO 65203
Phone (573) 882-7199
Fax (573) 884-5619
E-mail HorowitzG@health.missouri.edu
Specialty Certification Ob/Gyn
Subspecialty Certification Reproductive Endocrinology
Practice Setting academic
Clinical Interests ART; endometriosis; chronic pelvic pain
Research Interests endometriosis; implantation; ART
Member Society of Reproductive Surgeons, Society for Assisted Reproductive Technology, Society of Reproductive Endocrinology and Infertility

L. L. Penney, M.D.
Mid-Missouri Reproductive Medicine and Surgery, Inc.
1502 E. Broadway, Suite 106
Columbia, MO 65201
Phone (573) 443-4511
Fax (573) 443-7860
Specialty Certification Ob/Gyn
Subspecialty Certification Reproductive Endocrinology
Practice Setting private
Clinical Interests endometriosis; polycystic ovarian syndrome; ART
Member Society of Reproductive Surgeons

Stephen H. Weinstein, M.D.
Division of Urology
University of Missouri Hospitals
1 Hospital Drive
Columbia, MO 65212
Phone (573) 882-1151
Fax (573) 884-7453
E-mail Weinsteins@health.missouri.edu
Specialty Certification Urology
Practice Setting academic
Clinical Interests male infertility
Research Interests varicocele
Member Society for Male Reproduction and Urology

Comments Electroejaculation also offered in our department.

Kansas City

Nezaam M. Zamah, M.D., FRCS(C), FSOGC, FACOG
University Physician Associates
4320 Wornall Road, Suite 624, Plaza I
Kansas City, MO 64111
Phone (816) 931-3040
Fax (816) 931-3545
E-mail Nzamah@cctr.umkc.edu
Specialty Certification Ob/Gyn
Subspecialty Certification Reproductive Endocrinology
Practice Setting academic/private
Clinical Interests endometriosis; tubal reanastomosis; ART (IVF/GIFT/ICSI)
Research Interests endometriosis; endoscopic surgery; contraception
Member Society of Reproductive Surgeons, Society for Male Reproduction and Urology, Society of Reproductive Endocrinology and Infertility
Comments All aspects of fertility treatments are offered. Prompt, courteous service by caring staff. New referrals are always welcome.

St. Louis

Michael J. Chehval, M.D.
621 South New Ballas Road, Suite 6002
St. Louis, MO 63141
Phone (314) 991-2626
Fax (314) 991-7950
Specialty Certification Urology
Practice Setting private
Clinical Interests male infertility
Research Interests male infertility
Member Society of Reproductive Surgeons
Comments I am in general urologic practice, but most of my publications are in the area of male infertility.

Randall R. Odem, M.D.
Division of Reproductive Endocrinology & Infertility
4444 Forest Park Avenue, Suite 3100
St. Louis, MO 63108
Phone (314) 286-2421
Fax (314) 286-2455
Specialty Certification Ob/Gyn
Subspecialty Certification Reproductive Endocrinology
Practice Setting academic
Clinical Interests infertility; ovulation induction; laparoscopy/hysteroscopy
Research Interests ovulation induction; recurrent pregnancy loss; endoscopic surgery issues
Member Society of Reproductive Surgeons
Comments I am part of a four-physician group that works out of a newly designed facility

including virtually all aspects of reproductive
endocrinology and infertility.

Valerie Ratts, M.D.
4444 Forest Park Avenue, Suite 3100
St. Louis, MO 63108
Phone (314) 286-2400
Fax (314) 286-2455
E-mail rattsv@msnotes.wustf.edu
Specialty Certification Ob/Gyn
Subspecialty Certification Reproductive
Endocrinology
Practice Setting academic
Clinical Interests polycystic ovarian syndrome
Research Interests polycystic ovarian syndrome
Member Society of Reproductive
Endocrinology and Infertility

Sherman Silber, M.D.
Director
Infertility Center of St. Louis
224 South Woods Mill Road, Suite 730
St. Louis, MO 63017
Phone (314) 576-1400
Fax (314) 576-1442
E-mail silber@infertile.com
Specialty Certification Microsurgery and
Infertility
Subspecialty Certification Reproductive
Endocrinology
Practice Setting private
Clinical Interests severe male factor infertility,
testicular sperm aspiration and extraction,
ICSI; couple infertility; vasectomy reversal
and tubal reversal
Research Interests Same as above including
research of the Y chromosome as it relates to
severe male factor
Member Society for Assisted Reproductive
Technology

Ronald P. Wilbois, M.D.
Infertility & IVF Center
3009 N. Ballas Road, Suite 359A
St. Louis, MO 63131
Phone (314) 872-9200
Fax (314) 872-9040
E-mail iivfc2@aol.com
Specialty Certification Ob/Gyn
Practice Setting private
Clinical Interests ART; reproductive surgery
Research Interests PGD/PCR/FISH
Member Society for Male Reproduction and
Urology, Society for Assisted Reproductive
Technology
Comments We are a rapidly growing center
that started in 1992. We offer all forms of
reproductive technology with two Ph.D.s for
our labs.

Daniel Williams, M.D.
4444 Forest Park Avenue, Suite 3100
St. Louis, MO 63108
Phone (314) 286-2400
Fax (314) 286-2455

Specialty Certification Ob/Gyn
Subspecialty Certification Reproductive
Endocrinology
Practice Setting academic
Clinical Interests IVF; endoscopy; ovulation
induction
Research Interests infertility treatment in
women over 40, menopause
Member Society for Assisted Reproductive
Technology; Society of Reproductive
Endocrinology and Infertility

Barry I. Witten, M.D.
621 S. New Ballas Road
Suite 2002, Tower B
St. Louis, MO 63141
Phone (314) 569-6753
Fax (314) 995-4492
E-mail wittbi@stlo.smhs.com
Specialty Certification Ob/Gyn
Subspecialty Certification Reproductive
Endocrinology
Practice Setting private
Clinical Interests IVF; general reproductive
endocrinology; microsurgery
Research Interests IVF; general reproductive
endocrinology; microsurgery
Member Society of Reproductive Surgeons

NEBRASKA

Omaha

Carolyn Doherty, M.D.
8111 Dodge Street, Suite 137
Omaha, NE 68114
Phone (888) 477-1737
Fax (402) 354-5210
Specialty Certification Ob/Gyn
Subspecialty Certification Reproductive
Endocrinology
Practice Setting private
Clinical Interests infertility; birth defects of the
reproductive tract
Member Society for Assisted Reproductive
Technology, Society of Reproductive
Endocrinology and Infertility

NEVADA

Las Vegas

Mark F. Severino, M.D.
653 Town Center Drive
Las Vegas, NV 89144
Phone (702) 341-6616
Fax (702) 341-6617
E-mail mfseverino@aol.com
Specialty Certification Ob/Gyn
Subspecialty Certification Reproductive
Endocrinology
Practice Setting academic
Clinical Interests endometriosis; uterine
fibroids; reproductive microsurgery

Research Interests estrogen and progesterone receptors
Member Society of Reproductive Surgeons

Reno

Harold C. Chotiner, M.D.
343 Elm Street, Suite 302
Reno, NV 89503
Phone (775) 788-5100
Fax (775) 788-5108
Specialty Certification Ob/Gyn
Practice Setting private
Clinical Interests reproductive surgery; habitual miscarriage
Member Society of Reproductive Surgeons

NEW HAMPSHIRE

Concord

Robert A. Sasso, M.D., FACOG
Women's Reproductive Health & Fertility
Pillsbury Building, Suite 2750
248 Pleasant Street
Concord, NH 03301
Phone (603) 228-7308
Fax (603) 228-7369
E-mail rsassco@crhc.org
Specialty Certification Ob/Gyn
Practice Setting private
Clinical Interests advanced laparoscopic surgery; infertility diagnosis and treatment; endometriosis
Member Society of Reproductive Surgeons
Comments Accreditation from the Council for Gynecologic Endoscopy.

NEW JERSEY

Camden

Joel L. Marmar, M.D.
3 Cooper Plaza, Suite 411
Camden, NJ 08103
Phone (609) 667-0404
Fax (609) 667-0085
E-mail marmar-joel@cooperhealth.edu
Specialty Certification Urology
Practice Setting private
Clinical Interests male infertility; microsurgery; vasectomy reversals and sperm aspirations
Research Interests pathophysiology of varicoceles
Member Society of Reproductive Surgeons, Society for Male Reproduction and Urology

Cherry Hill

Wesley Chodos, D.O.
2201 Chapel Avenue West, Suite 206
Cherry Hill, NJ 08002
Phone (856) 662-6662
Fax (856) 661-0661
Specialty Certification Reproductive Endocrinology
Subspecialty Certification Ob/Gyn
Practice Setting private
Clinical Interests IVF; ovulation induction; menopause
Member Society for Assisted Reproductive Technology

David Forstein, D.O.
2201 Chapel Avenue West, Suite 206
Cherry Hill, NJ 08002
Phone (856) 662-6662
Fax (856) 661-0661
Specialty Certification Reproductive Endocrinology
Subspecialty Certification Ob/Gyn
Practice Setting private
Clinical Interests IVF; ovulation induction; menopause
Member Society for Assisted Reproductive Technology

David Goldberg, D.O.
2201 Chapel Avenue West, Suite 206
Cherry Hill, NJ 08002
Phone (856) 662-6662
Fax (856) 661-0661
Specialty Certification Ob/Gyn
Subspecialty Certification Reproductive Endocrinology
Practice Setting private
Clinical Interests IVF; ovulation induction; menopause
Member Society for Assisted Reproductive Technology

Gary S. Packin, D.O.
2201 Chapel Avenue West, Suite 206
Cherry Hill, NJ 08002
Phone (856) 662-6662
Fax (856) 661-0661
Specialty Certification Reproductive Endocrinology
Subspecialty Certification Ob/Gyn
Practice Setting private
Clinical Interests ART; pelviscopic surgery; endometriosis
Research Interests polycystic ovarian syndrome; estrogen replacement therapy; ovulation induction
Member Society for Assisted Reproductive Technologies

Clifton

Mark Zavier Ransom, M.D.
1035 Route 46 East
Clifton, NJ 07013
Phone (973) 470-0303
Fax (973) 916-0488
Specialty Certification Ob/Gyn
Subspecialty Certification Reproductive Endocrinology
Practice Setting private

Clinical Interests habitual abortion; microsurgery
Research Interests luteinizing hormone and ovulation; embryo transfer techniques
Member Society for Assisted Reproductive Technology, Society of Reproductive Endocrinology and Infertility

East Brunswick

Joel W. Goldsmith, M.D.
385-C Highway 18
East Brunswick, NJ 08816
Phone (732) 613-9800
Specialty Certification Urology
Practice Setting private
Member Society for Male Reproduction and Urology

Hackensack

Stuart H. Levey, M.D.
Hackensack University Medical Plaza
20 Prosper Avenue, Suite 715
Hackensack, NJ 07601
Phone (201) 342-6600
Fax (201) 342-4222
Specialty Certification Urology
Practice Setting academic—25%, private—75%
Clinical Interests microsurgery—reversals
Member Society of Reproductive Surgeons

Hasbrouck Heights

Jose M. Colon, M.D.
Center for Reproductive Medicine
214 Terrace Avenue
Hasbrouck Heights, NJ 07604
Phone (201) 393-7444
Fax (201) 393-7410
Specialty Certification Ob/Gyn
Subspecialty Certification Reproductive Endocrinology and Infertility
Clinical Interests IVF; male infertility
Research Interests IVF
Member Society for Assisted Reproductive Technology, Society of Reproductive Endocrinology and Infertility

Peter McGovern, M.D.
214 Terrace Avenue
Hasbrouck Heights, NJ 07604
Phone (201) 393-7444
Fax (201) 393-7410
E-mail mcgovepg@cmdnj.edu
Specialty Certification Ob/Gyn
Subspecialty Certification Reproductive Endocrinology and Infertility
Practice Setting academic
Clinical Interests infertility; IVF hysteroscopic surgery
Research Interests sperm function; better methods of stimulating ovarian function; IVF
Member Society for Assisted Reproductive Technology, Society of Reproductive Endocrinology and Infertility

Irvington

Stuart Shoengold, M.D., FACS
50 Union Avenue
Irvington, NJ 07111
Phone (973) 373-3001
Fax (973) 373-4677
Specialty Certification Urology
Practice Setting Private
Clinical Interests male infertility
Member Society for Male Reproduction and Urology

Jersey City

Yale Shulman, M.D.
2255 Kennedy Boulevard
Jersey City, NJ 07304
Phone (201) 433-1057
Fax (201) 435-2716
E-mail ycshulman@aol.com
Specialty Certification Urology
Practice Setting private
Member Society for Male Reproduction and Urology

Little Silver

Miguel Damien, M.D.
200 White Road, #214
Little Silver, NJ 07739
Phone (732) 758-6511
Fax (732) 758-1048
E-mail info@eastcoastivf.com
Specialty Certification Ob/Gyn
Subspecialty Certification Reproductive Endocrinology and Infertility
Practice Setting private
Clinical Interests IVF; surgery, laparoscopy, endometriosis
Member Society for Assisted Reproductive Technology, Society of Reproductive Endocrinology and Infertility

Livingston

Satty Gill Keswani, M.D.
176 West Mt. Pleasant Avenue
Livingston, NJ 07039
Phone (973) 994-1515
Fax (973) 992-7683
E-mail sgkeswani@aol.com
Specialty Certification Ob/Gyn
Practice Setting private
Clinical Interests artificial insemination; cryo-banking
Member Society of Reproductive Surgeons

Eugene A. Stulberger, M.D.
315 East Northfield Road
Livingston, NJ 07039
Phone (973) 535-1100
Fax (973) 535-3377
Specialty Certification Urology
Practice Setting private
Clinical Interests azoospermia, microscopic

varicocele surgery; microscopic
vasovasostomy; male infertility
Research Interests all aspects of male infertility
Member Society for Male Reproduction and
Urology

Long Branch

Y. Samuel Litvin, M.D., FACS
279 3rd Avenue
Long Branch, NJ 07740
Phone (732) 222-2111
Fax (732) 229-8770
E-mail ShoreUrology@aol.com
Specialty Certification Urology
Practice Setting private
Clinical Interests male infertility; micro
epidydimal sperm aspiration; ICSI; IVF
vasectomy reversal
Member Society for Male Reproduction and
Urology

Marlton

Jerome H. Check, M.D., Ph.D.
8002E Greentree Commons
Marlton, NJ 08053
Phone (856) 751-5575
Fax (856) 751-7289
Specialty Certification Internal Medicine
Subspecialty Certification Endocrinology and
Metabolism
Practice Setting academic/private
Clinical Interests IVF embryo transfer; ovarian
management and treatment; male factor
Member Society for Assisted Reproductive
Technology, Society of Reproductive
Endocrinology and Infertility
Comments Published over 350 manuscripts in
peer review journals of infertility and
reproductive medicine in ovulatory function,
ultrasound findings, male factor, ovarian
failure, reproductive immunology, IVF-ET,
especially cryopreservation.

Robert Skaf, M.D.
South Jersey Fertility Center
512 Lippincott Drive
Marlton, NJ 08053
Phone (856) 596-2233
Fax (856) 596-2411
E-mail sjfert@erol.com
Specialty Certification Ob/Gyn
Subspecialty Certification Reproductive
Endocrinology
Practice Setting private
Clinical Interests ART; operative laparoscopy

Jung Kyo Choe, M.D.
8002 East Greentree Commons
Marlton, NJ 08053
Phone (856) 751-5575
Fax (856) 751-7289
Specialty Certification Ob/Gyn
Subspecialty Certification Reproductive
Endocrinology and Infertility

Practice Setting academic
Clinical Interests ART; polycystic ovarian
syndrome; recurrent pregnancy losses
Research Interests premature ovarian failure;
early detection of ovarian senescence; follicle-
stimulating hormone and inhibin level in
patients with ovarian failure
Member Society for Assisted Reproductive
Technology, Society of Reproductive
Endocrinology and Infertility

Grace Lee, M.D.
8002E Greentree Commons
Marlton, NJ 08053
Phone (856) 751-5575
Fax (856) 751-7289
Specialty Certification Ob/Gyn
Subspecialty Certification Reproductive
Endocrinology and Infertility
Practice Setting academic
Clinical Interests Turner's syndrome; third-
party reproduction—IVF
Member Society for Assisted Reproductive
Technology, Society of Reproductive
Endocrinology and Infertility

Millburn

Arie Birkenfeld, M.D.
Diamond Institute for Infertility &
Menopause
89 Millburn Avenue
Millburn, NJ 07041
Phone (973) 761-5600
Fax (973) 761-5100
Specialty Certification Ob/Gyn
Practice Setting private
Clinical Interests infertility; menopause
Member Society for Assisted Reproductive
Technology

Matan Yemini, M.D.
Diamond Institute for Infertility &
Menopause
89 Millburn Avenue
Millburn, NJ 07041
Phone (973) 761-5600
Fax (973) 761-5100
Specialty Certification Ob/Gyn
Practice Setting private
Clinical Interests infertility; menopause
Member Society for Assisted Reproductive
Technology

Stratford

David Sussman, D.O., FACOS
205 East Laurel Road
Stratford, NJ 08084
Phone (856) 783-5500
Fax (856) 782-7150
Specialty Certification Urology
Practice Setting private
Clinical Interests obstructive
azospermic/ejaculatory duct obstruction

Member Society for Male Reproduction and Urology

West Orange

Eric K. Scomon, M.D.
741 Northfield Avenue, Suite 206
West Orange, NJ 07052
Phone (973) 325-6100
Fax (973) 325-1616
Specialty Certification Urology
Practice Setting private
Clinical Interests male infertility; Klinefelter's syndrome; nonobstructive azoospermia
Research Interests vasectomy reversal
Member Society for Male Reproduction and Urology

Westwood

Daniel Navot, M.D.
400 Old Hook Road
Westwood, NJ 07675
Phone (201) 666-4200
Fax (201) 666-2262
Specialty Certification Ob/Gyn
Subspecialty Certification Reproductive Endocrinology
Practice Setting academic/private
Clinical Interests IVF; egg donation; induction of ovulation
Member Society for Assisted Reproductive Technology, Society of Reproductive Endocrinology and Infertility

NEW MEXICO

Albuquerque

Norman Assad, M.D.
4705 Montomery Boulevard NE, Suite 101
Albuquerque, NM 87109
Phone (505) 837-1510
Fax (505) 888-4486
Specialty Certification Ob/Gyn
Practice Setting private
Clinical Interests ART; tubal reversal
Member Society for Assisted Reproductive Technology

NEW YORK

Albany

Stuart A. Rosenberg, M.D.
319 S. Manning Boulevard
Albany, NY 12208
Phone (518) 438-1019
Fax (518) 438-0981
Specialty Certification Urology
Practice Setting private
Clinical Interests male infertility
Member Society of Reproductive Surgeons

Brooklyn

Fred Greenstein, M.D.
6300 Eighth Avenue
Brooklyn, NY 11220
Phone (718) 495-6262
Fax (718) 439-2004
E-mail Fgreenstein@pol.net
Specialty Certification Urology
Practice Setting private
Member Society for Male Reproduction and Urology

Nachum M. Katlowitz, M.D., F.A.C.S., P.C.
1407 46th Street
Brooklyn, NY 11219
Phone (718) 972-0540
Fax (718) 972-1742
E-mail nkatlowitzmd@theurologists.com
Specialty Certification Urology
Practice Setting private
Clinical Interests male infertility; male sexual dysfunction
Research Interests Web site moderator for male infertility for ATIME, an infertility support Web site; www.ATIME.org
Member Society of Reproductive Surgeons
Comments Fellowship trained in male sexual dysfunction and male infertility although there is no board certification.

George D. Kofinas, M.D., FACOG
161 Ashland Place
Brooklyn, NY 11201
Phone (718) 643-6307
Fax (718) 250-8756
Specialty Certification Ob/Gyn
Subspecialty Certification Reproductive Endocrinology
Practice Setting academic/private
Clinical Interests infertility (IVF, ovulation induction, donor eggs); infertility surgery (laparoscopy, hysteroscopy, microsurgery); endometriosis; fibroids
Research Interests endometriosis surgical treatment; gamete micromanipulation; donation of oocytes
Member Society for Assisted Reproductive Technology, Society of Reproductive Endocrinology and Infertility

Buffalo

Frank Gonzalez, M.D.
State University of New York at Buffalo
Department of Gynecology & Obstetrics
Division of Reproductive Endocrinology & Infertility
Children's Hospital of Buffalo
219 Bryant Street
Buffalo, NY 14222
Phone (716) 881-0400
Fax (716) 881-1395
E-mail Gonz85buf@sprintmail.com
Specialty Certification Ob/Gyn

Subspecialty Certification Reproductive
Endocrinology
Practice Setting academic
Clinical Interests IVF; endoscopic surgery;
polycystic ovary syndrome
Research Interests elucidation of
pathophysiology of polycystic ovary
syndrome; sperm physiology
Member Society of Reproductive Surgeons
Comments Over 10 years experience in the
care of women with reproductive endocrine
disorders and couples with infertility.

Joan Sulewski, M.D.
1275 Delaware Avenue
Buffalo, NY 14209
Phone (716) 881-0400
Fax (716) 881-1395
Specialty Certification Ob/Gyn
Subspecialty Certification Reproductive
Endocrinology
Practice Setting academic
Clinical Interests reproductive endocrinology;
surgical correction of congenital
abnormalities; menopause
Research Interests osteoporosis; hormone
replacement
Member Society of Reproductive Surgeons

Garden City

Yu-Yang Ying, M.D., P.C.
394 Old Country Road
Garden City, NY 11530
Phone (516) 248-8307
Fax (516) 248-5007
Specialty Certification Ob/Gyn
Subspecialty Certification Reproductive
Endocrinology
Practice Setting private
Clinical Interests ART; ovulation induction;
operative laparoscopy, hysteroscopy
Research Interests uterine physiology in
primates; uterine physiology of implantation;
clinical aspects of assisted reproductive
technologies
Member Society for Assisted Reproductive
Technology
Comments Certified by the Accreditation
Council for Gynecologic Endoscopy.

Great Neck

Bruce R. Gilbert, M.D., Ph.D.
900 Northern Boulevard, Suite 230
Great Neck, NY 11021
Phone (516) 487-2700
Fax (516) 487-2007
E-mail bgilbert@ppol.com
Specialty Certification Urology
Practice Setting private
Clinical Interests sperm banking; nutritional
support; complementary therapies
Research Interests molecular basis of
varicocele-related infertility; nutritional

supplementation of subfertile men;
acupuncture treatment for subfertile men
Member Society of Reproductive Surgeons

Levittown

Mitchell Essig, M.D.
MidTown Reproductive Medicine, P.C.
2920 Hempstead Turnpike
Levittown, NY 11756
Phone (516) 735-9800
Fax (516) 735-9821
Specialty Certification Ob/Gyn
Subspecialty Certification Reproductive
Endocrinology
Practice Setting private
Member Society of Reproductive Surgeons

Manhasset

Anne R. Hershlag, M.D.
Center for Human Reproduction
North Shore University Hospital
300 Community Drive
Manhasset, NY 11030
Phone (516) 562-2229
Fax (516) 562-1710
Specialty Certification Ob/Gyn
Subspecialty Certification Reproductive
Endocrinology
Practice Setting academic
Clinical Interests IVF; operative laparoscopy;
general infertility care
Research Interests IVF–related topics;
evidence-based infertility management;
sperm freezing potential
Member Society of Reproductive Surgeons
Comments This year our brand-new, state-of-
the-art, beautiful comprehensive center was
opened.

David L. Rosenfeld, M.D.
Center for Human Reproduction
North Shore University Hospital
300 Community Drive
Manhasset, NY 11030
Phone (516) 562-2229
Fax (516) 562-1710
Specialty Certification Reproductive
Endocrinology
Subspecialty Certification Ob/Gyn
Practice Setting academic
Clinical Interests infertility; reproductive
surgery; IVF
Member Society of Reproductive Surgeons

Gerald Scholl, M.D.
Center for Human Reproduction
North Shore University Hospital
300 Community Drive
Manhasset, NY 11030
Phone (516) 562-2229
Fax (516) 562-1710
Specialty Certification Ob/Gyn
Subspecialty Certification Reproductive
Endocrinology

Practice Setting academic
Clinical Interests ART
Member Society of Reproductive Surgeons

New York

Natan Bar-Chama, M.D.
   5 East 98th Street
   New York, NY 10029
   Phone (212) 241-7443
   Fax (212) 876-3246
   Specialty Certification Urology
   Practice Setting academic
   Clinical Interests male infertility
   Research Interests environmental toxins;
   genetic defects
   Member Society for Male Reproduction and
   Urology
   Comments Director, Male Reproductive
   Medicine and Surgery, Mount Sinai School of
   Medicine.

Alan S. Berkeley, M.D.
   Program for IVF, Reproductive Surgery &
   Infertility
   660 First Avenue, 5th Floor
   New York, NY 10016
   Phone (212) 263-7629
   Fax (212) 263-7853
   E-mail ASBerkeley@aol.com
   Specialty Certification Ob/Gyn
   Practice Setting academic
   Clinical Interests IVF; reproductive surgery;
   congenital anomalies
   Research Interests embryo transfer and
   multiple gestation; stimulation protocols;
   luteal support
   Member Society of Reproductive Surgeons,
   Society for Assisted Reproductive Technology
   Comments Two-year fellowship in 1970s at
   Yale, one in gynecology and one in
   reproductive endocrinology and infertility.

Ronald M. Caplan, M.D., FACOG, FACS,
FRCS(C)
   12 East 69th Street
   New York, NY 10021
   Phone (212) 517-8333
   Fax (212) 517-8275
   Specialty Certification Ob/Gyn
   Practice Setting private
   Clinical Interests videolaparoscopy;
   videohysteroscopy; photocolposcopy
   Member Society of Reproductive Surgeons

Pak H. Chung, M.D.
   New York Hospital
   Cornell Medical Center
   Center for Reproductive Medicine &
   Infertility
   505 East 70th Street
   New York, NY 10021
   Phone (212) 746-1831
   Fax (212) 746-8208
   E-mail Pakchu@mail.med.cornell.edu

Specialty Certification Ob/Gyn
Subspecialty Certification Reproductive
Endocrinology and Infertility
Practice Setting academic
Clinical Interests IVF; male factor infertility;
reproductive surgery
Research Interests steroidogenesis;
electroejaculation in men with spinal cord
injury
Member Society for Male Reproduction and
Urology

Elliot L. Cohen, M.D.
   103 East 80th Street
   New York, NY 10021-0336
   Phone (212) 288-0056
   Fax (212) 744-4539
   Specialty Certification Urology
   Practice Setting academic/private
   Clinical Interests general urology; male
   infertility
   Member Society for Male Reproduction and
   Urology

Stephen M. Cohen, M.D.
   Department of Obstetrics & Gynecology—PH
   16-79
   New York Presbyterian Hospital/Columbia
   Campus
   622 West 169th Street
   New York, NY 10032
   Phone (212) 305-8770
   Fax (212) 305-3244
   E-mail Cohenst@hermes.cpmc.columbia.edu
   Specialty Certification Ob/Gyn
   Practice Setting academic
   Clinical Interests infertility; minimal invasive
   surgery; fibroids
   Research Interests surgical treatment of
   fibroids; treatment of endometriosis;
   treatment of infertility
   Member Society of Reproductive Surgeons

Lawrence Dubin, M.D.
   137 East 36th Street
   New York, NY 10016
   Phone (212) 532-0635
   Fax (212) 481-3198
   Specialty Certification Urology
   Practice Setting private
   Clinical Interests male infertility
   Research Interests male infertility
   Member Society of Reproductive Surgeons,
   Society for Male Reproduction and Urology
   Comments Practice limited to problems of
   male infertility. Past president, Society of
   Reproductive Surgeons.

J. Francois Eid, M.D.
   428 East 72nd Street, Suite 400
   New York, NY 10021
   Phone (212) 746-5473
   Fax (212) 746-0468
   E-mail Jfeid@mail.med.cornell.edu
   Specialty Certification Urology

Practice Setting academic
Clinical Interests erectile dysfunction; anejaculation
Member Society for Male Reproduction and Urology
Comments Interest is in electroejaculation, treatment of anejaculation, spinal-cord-injured males, diabetes, and patients post-retroperitoneal lymph node dissection.

Mitchell Essig, M.D.
MidTown Reproductive Medicine, P.C.
161 Madison Avenue, 4th Floor
New York, NY 10016
Phone (212) 779-8576
Fax (212) 779-9174
Specialty Certification Ob/Gyn
Subspecialty Certification Reproductive Endocrinology
Practice Setting private
Member Society of Reproductive Surgeons

Marc Goldstein, M.D.
Weill Medical College
Department of Urology
525 East 68th Street, Box 580
New York, NY 10021
Phone (212) 746-5470
Fax (212) 746-8153
E-mail mgoldst@mail.med.cornell.edu
Specialty Certification Urology
Practice Setting academic
Clinical Interests male infertility; microsurgical vasectomy reversal and vasoepididymostomy for obstruction; microsurgical varicocelectomy
Research Interests microsurgery for repair of obstruction; pathophysiology of obstruction and varicocele
Member Society of Reproductive Surgeons

Jamie Grifo, M.D., Ph.D.
660 First Avenue, 5th Floor
New York, NY 10016
Phone (212) 263-7978
Fax (212) 263-7853
E-mail jamiegrifo@med.nyu.edu.
Specialty Certification Ob/Gyn
Subspecialty Certification Reproductive Endocrinology
Practice Setting private
Research Interests preimplantation genetic diagnosis; germinal vesicle transfer
Member Society for Assisted Reproductive Technology

Lawrence Grunfeld, M.D.
58 East 79th Street
New York, NY 10021
Phone (212) 744-1855
Fax (212) 744-2026
E-mail NYSAT@SBIVF.com
Specialty Certification Ob/Gyn
Subspecialty Certification Reproductive Endocrinology

Practice Setting private
Clinical Interests ART; reproductive surgery
Research Interests egg quality
Member Society of Reproductive Surgeons

Nachum M. Katlowitz, M.D., F.A.C.S., P.C.
67 Irving Place N., 10th Floor
New York, NY 10003
Phone (212) 253-9414
Fax (212) 254-5736
E-mail nkatlowitzmd@theurologists.com
Practice Setting private
Specialty Certification Urology
Subspecialty Certification Dysfuntion and Male Infertility
Clinical Interests male infertility; male sexual dysfunction
Research Interests Web site moderator for male infertility for ATIME, an infertility support
Web site: www.ATIME.org
Member Society of Reproductive Surgeons
Comments Fellowship trained in male sexual dysfunction and male infertility although there is no board certification.

Lisa Kump, M.D.
660 First Avenue, 5th Floor
New York, NY 10016
Phone (212) 263-0040
Fax (212) 263-7853
E-mail Lisaivf@yahoo.com
Specialty Certification Ob/Gyn—eligible
Subspecialty Certification Reproductive Endocrinology—eligible
Practice Setting academic
Clinical Interests infertility/reproductive surgeries; gynecology; IVF
Research Interests endometrium

Frederick Licciardi, M.D.
660 First Avenue
New York, NY 10016
Phone (212) 263-7754
Fax (212) 263-7853
E-mail Fredivf@aol.com
Specialty Certification Ob/Gyn
Subspecialty Certification Reproductive Endocrinology
Practice Setting academic
Clinical Interests infertility; reproductive surgery; IVF/donor egg
Research Interests embryo and egg development

Jon O. Marks, M.D.
55 East 9th Street
New York, NY 10003
Phone (212) 673-7300
Fax (212) 777-0097
E-mail jmarks@metrouro.com
Specialty Certification American Board of Urology
Practice Setting private
Clinical Interests male infertility; general urology

395

Member Society for Male Reproduction and Urology
Comments Medical Director: ReproLab 336 East 30th St., New York.

Harris N. Nagler, M.D.
Chairman, Department of Urology
Beth Israel Medical Center
Philips Ambulatory Care Center
10 Union Square East 3A
New York, NY 10003
Phone (212) 844-8900
Fax (212) 844-8921
Specialty Certification Urology
Practice Setting academic
Clinical Interests vasectomy reversal/microsurgery; microsurgical varicocelectomy; male infertility
Research Interests sexual dysfunction
Member Society of Reproductive Surgeons

Nicole Noyes, M.D.
660 First Avenue, 5th Floor
New York, NY 10016
Phone (212) 263-7981
Fax (212) 263-7853
Specialty Certification Ob/Gyn
Subspecialty Certification Reproductive Endocrinology
Practice Setting academic
Clinical Interests infertility; reproductive surgery
Member Society for Assisted Reproductive Technologies
Comments Director of Reproductive Surgery, NYU Medical Center.

Harry Reich, M.D., FACOG
16 East 60th Street
New York, NY 10022
Phone (212) 305-1068
Fax (212) 305-3244 or (570) 674-2263
E-mail hrlscp@aol.com
Specialty Certification Ob/Gyn
Practice Setting academic/private
Clinical Interests endometriosis; fibroids; adnexal mass
Research Interests endometriosis; fibroids; adnexal mass
Member Society of Reproductive Surgeons
Comments The above conditions can be treated with the laparoscopic approach rather than laparotomy.

Zev Rosenwaks, M.D.
505 East 70th Street, HT326a
New York, NY 10021
Phone (212) 746-1743
Fax (212) 746-1861
E-mail hocello@mail.med.cornell.edu
Specialty Certification Ob/Gyn
Subspecialty Certification Reproductive Endocrinology
Practice Setting academic
Clinical Interests infertility (female and male

factor); oocyte donation; age-related infertility
Research Interests preimplantation genetic diagnosis; ovarian tissue cryopreservation; human autologous endometrial co-culture
Member Society of Reproductive Surgeons

Peter J. Sarosi, M.D.
88 University Place, 9th Floor
New York, NY 10003
Phone (212) 243-5550
Fax (212) 243-0009
E-mail OFRM@aol.com
Specialty Certification Ob/Gyn
Subspecialty Certification Reproductive Endocrinology
Practice Setting private
Clinical Interests ovulation induction; IVF; oocyte donation
Research Interests resistant ovaries; gonadotropin-releasing hormone analogs
Member Society of Reproductive Surgeons

Mark V. Sauer, M.D.
Center for Women's Reproductive Care
College of Physicians & Surgeons
Columbia University
161 Ft. Washington Avenue, Room 450
New York, NY 10032
Phone (212) 305-4665
Fax (212) 305-3695
E-mail MVS9@columbia.edu
Specialty Certification Ob/Gyn
Subspecialty Certification Reproductive Endocrinology
Practice Setting academic/private
Clinical Interests assisted reproduction (IVF); oocyte donation; embryo donation
Research Interests HIV—reproduction; aging and reproduction; gamete donation
Member Society of Reproductive Surgeons, Society for Assisted Reproductive Technology, Society of Reproductive Endocrinology and Infertility

Peter N. Schlegel, M.D., F.A.C.S.
Department of Urology, Room F-907A
525 East 68th Street
New York, NY 10021
Phone (212) 746-5491
Fax (212) 746-8425
E-mail pnschleg@med.cornell.edu
Specialty Certification Urology
Practice Setting academic
Clinical Interests sperm retrieval for IVF; vasectomy reversal; varicocele
Research Interests genetics of male infertility; reactive oxygen species/sperm; germ cell transplantation
Member Society of Reproductive Surgeons
Comments See our Web site: www.maleinfertility.org/schlegel.html.

Cecilia Schmidt-Sarosi, M.D.
251 East 33rd Street

New York, NY 10016
Phone (212) 263-7566
Fax (212) 686-6614
E-mail ofrm@aol.com
Specialty Certification Ob/Gyn
Subspecialty Certification Reproductive
Endocrinology and Infertility
Practice Setting private
Clinical Interests polycystic ovarian syndrome;
endometriosis
Research Interests polycystic ovarian
syndrome; ART
Member Society for Assisted Reproductive
Technology, Society of Reproductive
Surgeons, Society of Reproductive
Endocrinology and Infertility

Mineola

Mariano Castro-Magana, M.D.
Director, Endocrine-Metabolic Diseases
Winthrop University Hospital
120 Mineola Boulevard, Suite 210
Mineola, NY 11501
Phone (516) 663-3069
Fax (516) 663-3070
Specialty Certification Pediatrics
Subspecialty Certification Pediatric
Endocrinology
Practice Setting academic/private
Clinical Interests endocrine evaluation of the
infertile male
Member Society for Male Reproduction and
Urology, Society of Reproductive
Endocrinology and Infertility

Magdalen E. Hull, M.D., M.P.H.
WCCA Winthrop University Hospital
120 Mineola Boulevard, Suite 100
Mineola, NY 11501
Phone (516) 663-3037
Fax (516) 738-6552
E-mail mhull@winthrop.org
Specialty Certification Ob/Gyn
Subspecialty Certification Reproductive
Endocrinology
Practice Setting academic
Clinical Interests infertility; endometriosis
Research Interests hormone replacement
therapy; perimenopause
Member Society of Reproductive Surgeons

Brett C. Mellinger, M.D.
WCCA Wintrop University Hospital
120 Mineola Boulevard, Suite 320
Mineola, NY 11501
Phone (516) 739-6300
Fax (516) 739-6304
E-mail bmelling@winthrop.org
Specialty Certification Urology
Practice Setting academic
Clinical Interests microsurgery; laboratory
investigations; sperm retrieval technique
Member Society for Male Reproduction and
Urology

New Hertford

Murray Nesbaum, M.D.
Ferre Institute
3945 Oneida Street
New Hertford, NY 13413
Phone (315) 724-4348
Fax (315) 724-1360
Specialty Certification Ob/Gyn
Practice Setting academic
Research Interests infertility—minority groups;
genetic counseling—cancer and reproductive
Member Society of Reproductive Surgeons
Comments Medical director responsible for
programs for lay and professional in all
aspects of reproductive health and genetic
counseling.

Port Jefferson

Daniel Kenigsberg, M.D.
Long Island IVF
625 Belle Terre Road, Suite 200
Port Jefferson, NY 11777
Phone (516) 331-7575
Fax (516) 331-1332
E-mail drkenigsberg@longislandIVF.com
Specialty Certification Ob/Gyn
Subspecialty Certification Reproductive
Endocrinology
Practice Setting private
Clinical Interests IVF; ovulation induction;
reproductive surgery
Research Interests embryo transfer—
ultrasound guided; blastocyst transfer
Member Society of Reproductive Surgeons,
Society for Assisted Reproductive
Technology, Society of Reproductive
Endocrinology and Infertility

Rochester

Grace Centola, Ph.D, HCLD
Andrology Lab
University of Rochester
Rochester, NY 14642
Phone (716) 275-2491
Fax (716) 756-5861
E-mail grace_centola@urmc.rochester.edu
Specialty Certification Andrology
Clinical Interests andrology; sperm washing;
insemination
Research Interests effects of heavy metals on
sperm function; male fertility/infertility
Member Society for Male Reproduction and
Urology

Kathleen Hoeger, M.D.
Reproductive Endocrinology and Infertility
Center
601 Elmwood Avenue
Box 685
Rochester, NY 14642
Phone (716) 275-1930
Fax (716) 756-4146
Specialty Certification Ob/Gyn

Subspecialty Certification Reproductive
Endocrinology
Practice Setting academic
Clinical Interests IVF; ovulation induction;
disorders of puberty
Research Interests polycystic ovarian
syndrome
Member Society for Assisted Reproductive
Technology, Society of Reproductive
Endocrinology and Infertility

Vivian Lewis, M.D.
Reproductive Endocrinology and Infertility
Center
601 Elmwood Avenue
Box 685
Rochester, NY 14642
Phone (716) 275-1930
Fax (716) 756-4146
E-mail Vivian_lewis@urmc.rochester.edu
Specialty Certification Ob/Gyn
Subspecialty Certification Reproductive
Endocrinology
Practice Setting academic
Clinical Interests infertility; ovulation
induction; IVF
Research Interests ovulation induction;
hormone replacement therapy
Member Society for Assisted Reproductive
Technology, Society of Reproductive
Endocrinology and Infertility

Eberhard K. Muechler, M.D.
1561 Long Pond Road
Rochester, NY 14626
Phone (716) 723-7470
Fax (716) 723-7043
E-mail EKMuechler@aol.com
Specialty Certification Ob/Gyn
Subspecialty Certification Reproductive
Endocrinology
Practice Setting private
Clinical Interests IVF; ovulation induction;
laser surgery
Member Society for Assisted Reproductive
Technology, Society of Reproductive
Endocrinology and Infertility

William Phipps, M.D.
Reproductive Endocrinology & Infertility
Center
601 Elmwood Avenue
Box 685
Rochester, NY 14642
Phone (716) 275-1930
Fax (716) 756-4146
E-mail William_Phipps@urmc.rochester.edu
Specialty Certification Ob/Gyn
Subspecialty Certification Reproductive
Endocrinology
Practice Setting academic
Clinical Interests ART
Research Interests plant estrogens
Member Society for Assisted Reproductive

Technology, Society of Reproductive
Endocrinology and Infertility

Rye

John J. Stangel, M.D.
70 Maple Avenue
Rye, NY 10580
Phone (914) 967-6800
Fax (914) 967-6208
Specialty Certification Ob/Gyn
Subspecialty Certification Reproductive
Endocrinology
Practice Setting private
Clinical Interests infertility including IVF;
pregnancy loss; polycystic ovarian
disease/syndrome; endometriosis
Research Interests polycystic ovarian
disease/syndrome; ovulation induction;
pregnancy loss
Member Society of Reproductive Surgeons

Southampton

John E. Hunt, Jr., M.D.
Hampton Gynecology & Obstetrics, P.C.
590 Hampton Road
Southampton, NY 11968
Phone (631) 283-0918
Fax (631) 287-4047
Specialty Certification Ob/Gyn
Practice Setting private
Clinical Interests infertility workup;
laparoscopy; Clomid induction of ovulation;
tuboplasty, renastomosis
Member Society of Reproductive Surgeons
Comments No IVF but in collaboration with
Long Island IVF with Dr. Daniel Kenigsberg.

Staten Island

George D. Kofinas, M.D., FACOG
1550 Richmond Avenue, Suite 204
Staten Island, NY 10314
Phone (718) 643-6307
Fax (718) 250-8756
Specialty Certification Ob/Gyn
Subspecialty Certification Reproductive
Endocrinology
Practice Setting academic/private
Clinical Interests infertility (IVF, ovulation
induction, donor eggs); infertility surgery
(laparoscopy, hysteroscopy, microsurgery);
endometriosis, fibroids
Research Interests endometriosis, surgical
treatment; gamete micromanipulation;
donation of oocytes
Member Society for Assisted Reproductive
Technologies, Society of Reproductive
Endocrinology and Infertility

Stony Brook

Richard Bronson, M.D.
Department of Obstetrics & Gynecology
Health Sciences Center, SUNY
Stony Brook, NY 11794-8091

Phone (631) 444-2737
Fax (631) 444-7740
E-mail Rbronson@mail.som.sunysb.edu
Specialty Certification Ob/Gyn
Subspecialty Certification Reproductive
Endocrinology
Practice Setting academic
Clinical Interests IVF; tubal reconstructive
surgery; recurrent pregnancy loss
Research Interests mechanisms of fertilization
failure; immunity of spermatozoa; gamete
biology
Member Society of Reproductive Surgeons
Comments Having my practice based at a
university medical center allows me to apply
new discoveries in the laboratory to my
clinical practice.

Syosset

Amir H. Ansari, M.D., FACOG, FACS, FRCS(C)
300 Bay Shore Road
No. Babylon, NY 11703
Phone (631) 586-2700
Fax (631) 586-3524
Specialty Certification Ob/Gyn
Practice Setting academic/private
Member Society of Reproductive Surgeons

Syracuse

Shawky Z. A. Badawy, M.D.
736 Irving Avenue
Syracuse, NY 13210
Phone (315) 470-7905
Fax (315) 470-7999
Specialty Certification Ob/Gyn
Subspecialty Certification Reproductive
Endocrinology
Practice Setting academic
Clinical Interests endometriosis;
hyperprolactinemia; laser surgery
Research Interests endometriosis; osteoporosis;
hyperprolactinemia
Member Society of Reproductive Surgeons

Utica

Norman F. Angell, M.D., Ph.D.
Mid-York Fertility
1656 Champlin Avenue
Utica, NY 13502
Phone (315) 797-0847
Fax (315) 797-0853
E-mail myf@borg.com
Specialty Certification Ob/Gyn
Practice Setting private
Clinical Interests infertility
Member Society of Reproductive Surgeons
Comments Andrology laboratory (semen
analysis, sperm washing, donor
insemination) in house.
Full treatment except IVF.

White Plains

Michael Blotner, M.D.
136 South Broadway, Suite 100
White Plains, NY 10605
Phone (914) 949-6677
Fax (914) 949-5758
E-mail mbjw08@pol.net
Specialty Certification Infertility
Subspecialty Certification Reproductive
Endocrinology
Practice Setting private
Clinical Interests ART; polycystic ovary
syndrome
Research Interests chlamydia
Member Society for Assisted Reproductive
Technology, Society of Reproductive
Endocrinology and Infertility

Williamsville

Philip J. Aliotta, M.D., M.H.A.
Main Urology Associates, P.C.
Brompton Professional Park
6645 Main Street
Williamsville, NY 14221
Phone (716) 631-0932
Fax (716) 631-2826
E-mail PJAMA726@aol.com
Specialty Certification Urology
Practice Setting private
Clinical Interests infertility—male; erectile
dysfunction; neurogenic bladder
Research Interests oral pharmacotherapy for
erectile dysfunction; oral therapies for
prostatic hypertrophy; therapies for
incontinence
Member Society for Male Reproduction and
Urology

John M. Wieckowski, M.D., Ph.D.
1321 Millersport Way, Suite 102
Williamsville, NY 14221
Phone (716) 634-4351
Specialty Certification Ob/Gyn
Subspecialty Certification Ph.D.—Biochemical
Pharmacology
Practice Settings private
Clinical Interests IVF
Member Society for Assisted Reproductive
Technology

NORTH CAROLINA

Chapel Hill

Gary S. Berger, M.D.
Chapel Hill Fertility Center
109 Conner Drive, Suite 2200
Chapel Hill, NC 27514
Phone (919) 968-4656
Fax (919) 967-8637
E-mail gsberger@mindspring.com
Specialty Certifications Ob/Gyn,
Epidemiology, Preventive Medicine

Subspecialty Certification Public Health
Practice Setting private
Primary Interests outpatient reproductive
surgery, sterilization reversal; ART;
comprehensive evaluation and treatment of
infertility
Research Interests outpatient reproductive
surgery, pelvic inflammatory disease and
infections in reproductive health
Member Society of Reproductive Surgeons
Comments Accreditation by the Council for
Gynecologic Endoscopy.

Stephen F. Shaban, M.D.
427 Burnett-Womack Building
Campus Box 7235
Chapel Hill, NC 27599-7235
Phone (919) 966-8217
Fax (919) 966-0098
Specialty Certification Urology
Practice Setting academic
Clinical Interests male factor evaluation and
treatment; azoospermia/microsurgical
reconstruction; surgical harvesting of sperm
for ICSI
Member Society for Male Reproduction and
Urology
Comments Intratesticular testosterone levels
and infertility; vasectomy.

John F. Steege, M.D.
Chief, Division of Advanced Laparoscopy &
Gynecologic Surgery
Department of Obstetrics & Gynecology
University of North Carolina
Campus Box 7570
Chapel Hill, NC 27599-7570
Phone (919) 966-7764
Fax (919) 966-5833
Specialty Certification Ob/Gyn
Practice Setting academic
Clinical Interests advanced laparoscopy; pelvic
pain
Research Interests laparoscopic techniques;
pain management; adhesion prevention
Member Society of Reproductive Surgeons
Comments Longest experience in central
North Carolina in advanced laparoscopic
surgical techniques and treatment of pelvic
pain.

Charlotte

Jack L. Crain, M.D.
Reproductive Endocrine Associates of
Charlotte
1918 Randolph Road
Charlotte, NC 28207
Phone (704) 343-3400
Fax (704) 343-3428
E-mail jcrain3168@aol.com
Specialty Certification Ob/Gyn
Subspecialty Certification Reproductive
Endocrinology
Practice Setting private

Clinical Interests IVF; laparoscopic surgery;
habitual abortion
Research Interests ovulation induction
Member Society of Reproductive Surgeons

Bradley S. Hurst, M.D.
Department of Obstetrics & Gynecology
Carolinas Medical Center
1000 Blythe Street
Charlotte, NC 28203
Phone (704) 355-3153
Fax (704) 355-1941
E-mail bhurst@carolinas.org
Specialty Certification Ob/Gyn
Subspecialty Certification Reproductive
Endocrinology
Practice Setting private
Clinical Interests IVF/infertility;
endometriosis; premenopausal health
Research Interests adhesion prevention;
infertility/IVF
Member Society of Reproductive Surgeons
Comments Columnist "Managing Midlife,"
published in *Rocky Mountain News*.

Michael R. O'Neill, M.D.
1718 E. 4th Street, Suite 807
Charlotte, NC 28204
Phone (704) 375-5755
Fax (704) 335-3380
Specialty Certification Urology
Practice Setting private
Clinical Interests microscopic vasovasostomy;
sperm retrieval for ICSI; evaluation of the
infertile male
Member Society for Male Reproduction and
Urology

Durham

Charles B. Hammond, M.D.
Department of Obstetrics & Gynecology
Duke University Medical Center
Box 3853
Durham, NC 27710
Phone (919) 684-3008
Fax (919) 684-6161
E-mail hammo005@mc.duke.edu
Specialty Certification Ob/Gyn
Subspecialty Certification Reproductive
Endocrinology
Practice Setting academic
Clinical Interests infertility—all causes;
menopause management; general gynecology
Research Interests menopausal efforts
Member Society of Reproductive Surgeons

Arthur F. Haney, M.D.
Duke University Medical Center
Box 2971
Durham, NC 27710
Phone (919) 684-5327
Fax (919) 681-7904
E-mail haney001@mc.duke.edu
Specialty Certification Ob/Gyn

Subspecialty Certification Reproductive Endocrinology
Practice Setting academic
Clinical Interests reproductive endocrinology and infertility; ART; endometriosis/fibroids
Research Interests leiomyomata; pelvic adhesion formation
Member Society of Reproductive Surgeons, Society for Assisted Reproductive Technology, Society of Reproductive Endocrinology and Infertility

Greenville

Clifford C. Hayslip, Jr., M.D.
East Carolina University
2305 Executive Park West
Greenville, NC 27834
Phone (252) 816-3850
Fax (252) 816-2016
E-mail hayslip@brody.med.ecu.edu
Specialty Certification Ob/Gyn
Subspecialty Certification Reproductive Endocrinology
Practice Setting academic
Clinical Interests infertility; endometriosis
Research Interests postpartum thyroid disease
Member Society for Assisted Reproductive Technology and Society for Reproductive Endocrinology

Raleigh

Mary B. Hammond, M.D.
Reproductive Consultants
2500 Blue Ridge Road, Suite 300
Raleigh, NC 27607
Phone (919) 881-7795
Fax (919) 881-7796
E-mail djcat@mindspring.com
Specialty Certification Ob/Gyn
Subspecialty Certification Reproductive Endocrinology
Practice Setting private
Clinical Interests ovulation induction; artificial insemination; IVF
Member Society of Reproductive Endocrinology and Infertility

Winston-Salem

Jeffrey L. Deaton, M.D.
Department of Obstetrics & Gynecology
Section on Reproductive Endocrinology
Wake Forest University School of Medicine
Medical Center Boulevard
Winston-Salem, NC 27157-1067
Phone (336) 716-2368
Fax (336) 716-0194
E-mail jdeaton@wfubmc.edu
Specialty Certification Ob/Gyn
Subspecialty Certification Reproductive Endocrinology
Practice Setting academic

Clinical Interests IVF; ovulation induction; male infertility
Research Interests polycystic ovarian syndrome; endometriosis; serum luteinizing hormone levels
Member Society for Male Reproduction and Urology, Society for Assisted Reproductive Technology, Society of Reproductive Endocrinology and Infertility

NORTH DAKOTA

Fargo

Steffen Christensen, M.D.
MeritCare Fertility Center
Desk #42
737 N. Broadway
PO Box 2067
Fargo, ND 58123
Phone (701) 234-2700
Fax (701) 234-2783
E-mail ChristensenSteffen@meritcare.com
Specialty Certification Ob/Gyn
Subspecialty Certification Reproductive Endocrinology
Practice Setting private
Clinical Interests IVF; chronic pregnancy loss
Member Society for Assisted Reproductive Technology

NEBRASKA

Omaha

Carolyn M. Doherty, M.D.
811 Dodge Street, Suite 237
Omaha, NE 68114
Phone (888) 477-1737
Fax (402) 354-5210
Specialty Certification Ob/Gyn
Subspecialty Certification Reproductive Endocrinology
Practice Setting private
Clinical Interests infertility; birth defect of the female reproductive tract
Member Society for Assisted Reproductive Technology, Society of Reproductive Endocrinology and Infertility

OHIO

Akron

Kevin Spear, M.D.
75 Arch Street, Suite 101
Akron, OH 44304
Phone (330) 375-4848
Fax (330) 376-4066
Specialty Certification Urology
Practice Setting academic/private
Clinical Interests male infertility; vasectomy reversal; microsurgery

Member Society for Male Reproduction and
Urology

Nicholas J. Spirtos, D.O.
Northeastern Ohio Fertility Center
468 E. Market Street
Akron, OH 44304
Phone (330) 376-2300
Fax (330) 376-4807
Specialty Certification Ob/Gyn
Subspecialty Certification Reproductive
Endocrinology
Practice Setting academic/private
Clinical Interests IVF/embryo transfer;
ovulation induction; microsurgery
Research Interests habitual abortion; luteal
phase defect/progesterone receptors; pelvic
endometriosis
Member Society of Reproductive Surgeons,
Society for Male Reproduction and Urology,
Society for Assisted Reproductive
Technology, Society of Reproductive
Endocrinology and Infertility

Cincinnati

Sherif G. Awadalla, M.D.
2123 Auburn Avenue, Suite A44
Cincinnati, OH 45219
Phone (513) 585-4400
Fax (513) 585-4595
E-mail sawadalla@aol.com
Specialty Certification Reproductive
Endocrinology
Subspecialty Certification Ob/Gyn
Practice Setting private
Clinical Interests IVF; tubal anastomosis;
laparoscopic surgery
Member Society for Assisted Reproductive
Technologies, Society of Reproductive
Endocrinology and Infertility
Comments Visit our Web site: at
www.cincinnatifertility.com.

Neeoo W. Chin, M.D.
11503 Springfield Pike, Suite 220
Cincinnati, OH 45246
Phone (513) 326-4300
Fax (513) 326-4306
Specialty Certification Ob/Gyn
Subspecialty Certification Reproductive
Endocrinology
Practice Setting private
Clinical Interests ovulation induction; female
athletes; laser reconstructive pelvic surgery
Member Society of Reproductive Surgeons,
Society for Assisted Reproductive
Technology, Society for Male Reproduction
and Urology, Society of Reproductive
Endocrinology and Infertility

Glen Hofmann, M.D.
Bethesda Center for Reproductive Health &
Fertility
619 Oak Street

Cincinnati, OH 45206
Phone (513) 569-6433
Fax (513) 569-6386
E-mail Hofmannge@aol.com
Specialty Certification Ob/Gyn
Subspecialty Certification Reproductive
Endocrinology
Practice Setting academic
Clinical Interests ovarian rescue screening; IVF
Member Society of Reproductive Surgeons,
Society for Assisted Reproductive
Technology, Society for Male Reproduction
and Urology, Society of Reproductive
Endocrinology and Infertility

James H. Liu, M.D.
Center for Reproductive Health
Eden & Bethesda Avenue
Cincinnati, OH 45229
Phone (513) 584-0955
Fax (513) 584-8916
E-mail James.Liu@uc.edu
Specialty Certification Ob/Gyn
Subspecialty Certification Reproductive
Endocrinology
Practice Setting academic
Clinical Interests menopause; ovulation
induction
Research Interests sex steroids and bone
Member Society of Reproductive
Endocrinology and Infertility

Michael D. Scheiber, M.D., MPH, FACOG
2123 Auburn Avenue, Suite A44
Cincinnati, OH 45219
Phone (513) 585-4400
Fax (513) 585-4595
Specialty Certification Ob/Gyn
Practice Setting academic/private
Clinical Interests IVF; ovulation induction;
polycystic ovarian syndrome
Research Interests IVF and embryo
implantation; polycystic ovarian syndrome;
Menopause
Member Society of Reproductive
Endocrinology and Infertility
Comments Dr. Scheiber is the national chair of
the Associate Membership of the Society of
Reproductive Endocrinology & Infertility.

Michael A. Thomas, M.D.
Center for Reproductive Health
Eden & Bethesda Avenues, 3rd Floor
Cincinnati, OH 45219
Phone (513) 584-0955
Fax (513) 584-8916
E-mail Michael.Thomas@UC.edu
Specialty Certification Ob/Gyn
Subspecialty Certification Reproductive
Endocrinology
Practice Setting academic
Clinical Interests infertility; pelvic pain;
menopause

Research Interests contraception; stress and reproductive function
Member Society of Reproductive Surgeons, Society for Assisted Reproductive Technology, Society of Reproductive Endocrinology and Infertility

Cleveland

Khalid M. Ataya, M.D.
2500 Metro Health Drive
Cleveland, OH 44109
Phone (216) 778-5990
Fax (216) 778-8847
E-mail Kataya529@aol.com
Specialty Certification Ob/Gyn
Subspecialty Certification Reproductive Endocrinology
Practice Setting academic
Clinical Interests IVF; ICSI; endometriosis
Research Interests ovary
Member Society of Reproductive Surgeons

Jeffrey M. Goldberg, M.D.
The Cleveland Clinic
9500 Euclid Avenue
Cleveland, OH 44195
Phone (216) 444-2240
Fax (216) 444-8551
E-mail goldbej@ccf.org
Specialty Certification Ob/Gyn
Subspecialty Certification Reproductive Endocrinology
Practice Setting private
Clinical Interests microsurgical tubal anastomosis; operative laparoscopy and hysteroscopy; IVF
Research Interests mini-laparotomy and local anesthesia; guided imagery in IVF; treatment of endometriosis
Member Society of Reproductive Surgeons, Society for Assisted Reproductive Technology, Society of Reproductive Endocrinology and Infertility

James M. Goldfarb, M.D.
MacDonald Hospital, 7th Floor
11100 Euclid Avenue
Cleveland, OH 44106
Phone (216) 844-3303
Fax (216) 844-3348
E-mail James.Goldfarb@UHHS.com
Specialty Certification Ob/Gyn
Subspecialty Certification Reproductive Endocrinology
Practice Setting academic/private
Clinical Interests IVF; ovulation induction; surrogate IVF
Research Interests stimulation protocols; culture conditions for IVF; the aging oocyte
Member Society of Reproductive Surgeons

Julian Gordon, M.D.
4200 Warrensville Center Road
Cleveland, OH 44122

Phone (216) 295-1010
Fax (216) 991-2210
Specialty Certification Urology
Practice Setting private
Clinical Interests microsurgery; varicocele; sexual dysfunction
Member Society for Male Reproduction and Urology

Susan Rothmann, Ph.D, HCLD, CLC
Fertility Solutions, Inc.
13000 Shaker Boulevard
Cleveland, OH 44120
Phone (216) 491-0030 x201
Fax (216) 491-0032
E-mail sarfsi@aol.com
Specialty Certification High Complexity Lab Director (HCLD)
Subspecialty Certification Certified Laboratory Consultant (CLC)
Practice Setting private
Clinical Interests andrology; client depositor gamete banking; manufacture and distribute four guided imagery tapes for fertility; lab quality control
Research Interests guided imagery; reproductive lab improvement; reproductive lab teaching/training methods
Member Society for Male Reproduction and Urology

Allen D. Seftel, M.D.
Department of Urology
11100 Euclid Avenue
Cleveland, OH 4106-5046
Phone (216) 844-7632
Fax (216) 844-4846
E-mail adsg@po.cwru.edu
Specialty Certification Urology
Practice Setting academic
Clinical Interests varicocele; vasectomy outcomes
Research Interests varicocele; Y chromosome deletions
Member Society of Reproductive Surgeons, Society for Male Reproduction and Urology

Anthony J. Thomas, Jr., M.D.
9500 Euclid Avenue
Cleveland Clinic Foundation
Cleveland, Ohio 44195
Phone (216) 444-6340
Fax (216) 445-7031
E-mail Thomasa@ccf.org
Specialty Certification Urology
Practice Setting academic
Clinical Interests microsurgery; vasectomy reversal; ICSI for male factor infertility
Research Interests role of reactive oxygen species in infertility; varicocele
Member Society of Reproductive Surgeons

Columbus

Errol Singh, M.D., FACS
3555 Olentangy River Road, Suite 1030
Columbus, OH 43214
Phone (614) 784-8765
Fax (614) 784-1153
Specialty Certification Urology
Subspecialty Certification Reproductive
Endocrinology
Practice Setting private
Clinical Interests male infertility; vasectomy
reversals—vasovasostomy; sperm retrival for
IVF
Member Society of Reproductive Medicine

Lyndhurst

Steven M. Klein, M.D.
29001 Cedar Road, #518
Lyndhurst, OH 44124
Phone (440) 646-8200
Fax (440) 646-8211
Specialty Certification Ob/Gyn
Practice Setting private
Member Society of Reproductive Surgeons

Mayfield Heights

Wulf H. Utian, M.D., Ph.D.
University Obstetrics & Gynecology
Specialties, Inc.
5850 Landerbrook Drive, Suite 300
Mayfield Heights, OH 44124
Phone (440) 442-4747
Fax (440) 449-1089
E-mail utian@menopause.org
Specialty Certification Ob/Gyn
Subspecialty Certification Reproductive
Endocrinology
Practice Setting academic/private
Clinical Interests ovarian failure
Research Interests ovarian failure; menopause
Member Society of Reproductive Surgeons

Parma

Israel Henig, M.D.
Elite Women Care
6681 Ridge Road, #302
Parma, OH 44129
Phone (440) 842-7227
Fax (440) 842-9485
E-mail Dr.Henig@msopbs.com
Specialty Certification Ob/Gyn
Subspecialty Certification Reproductive
Endocrinology
Practice Setting private
Member Society of Reproductive Surgeons

Toledo

Joseph Karnitis, M.D.
2142 N. Cone Boulevard
Toledo, OH 43606
Phone (419) 479-8830
Fax (419) 479-6005

E-mail fertilitycenterofNWohio@promedica.
org
Specialty Certification Ob/Gyn
Subspecialty Certification Reproductive
Endocrinology
Practice Setting private
Member Society for Assisted Reproductive
Technology, Society of Reproductive
Endocrinology and Infertility

Youngstown

Robert L. Collins, M.D.
900 Sahara Trail
Box 3707
Youngstown, OH 44513-3707
Phone (330) 965-8390
Fax (330) 965-8391
E-mail Robcoll@IBM.net
Specialty Certification Ob/Gyn
Subspecialty Certification Reproductive
Endocrinology
Practice Setting private
Clinical Interests ART; laparoscopic surgery;
ovulation induction
Research Interests ovulation induction;
myomas
Member Society of Reproductive Surgeons

OKLAHOMA

Oklahoma City

James F. Donovan, Jr., M.D.
920 Stanton L. Young Boulevard, WP3150
Oklahoma City, OK 73104
Phone (405) 271-6900
Fax (405) 271-3118
E-mail james-donovan@ouhsc.edu
Specialty Certification Urology
Subspecialty Certification General Surgery
Practice Setting academic
Clinical Interests male infertility; microsurgery
and reconstruction of male reproductive
organs; laparoscopy
Research Interests vascular access for dialysis
Member Society for Male Reproduction and
Urology

Gilbert G. Haas, Jr., M.D.
1000 N.Lincoln Boulevard, #300
Oklahoma City, OK 73104
Phone (405) 271-9200
Fax (405) 271-9222
Specialty Certification Ob/Gyn
Subspecialty Certification Reproductive
Endocrinology
Practice Setting private
Clinical Interests anovulation; endoscopic
surgery; male factor
Research Interests reproductive immunology;
recurrent miscarriage
Member Society of Reproductive Surgeons,
Society for Assisted Reproductive

Technology, Society of Reproductive
Endocrinology and Infertility

David Kallenberger, M.D.
3433 N.W. 56th Street, Suite 210B
Oklahoma City, OK 73103
Phone (405) 945-4701
Fax (405) 945-4728
Specialty Certification Ob/Gyn
Practice Setting private
Clinical Interests ART; reproductive surgery;
infertility
Research Interests office endoscopy
Member Society for Assisted Reproductive
Technology, Society of Reproductive
Surgeons

Eli Reshef, M.D.
3433 N.W. 56th Street, Suite 210B
Oklahoma City, OK 73112
Phone (405) 945-4701
Fax (405) 945-4728
E-mail codarsi@aol.com
Specialty Certification Ob/Gyn
Subspecialty Certification Reproductive
Endocrinology
Practice Setting private
Clinical Interests ART; operative endoscopy
(including laser); microsurgical reparative
surgery
Member Society for Assisted Reproductive
Technology, Society of Reproductive
Endocrinology and Infertility
Comments Medical Director, Bennett Fertility
Institute, Oklahoma City

Robert A. Wild, M.D., M.P.H.
920 Stanton L. Young Boulevard, WP 2410
Oklahoma City, OK 73104
Phone (405) 271-1494
Fax (405) 271-1356
Specialty Certification Ob/Gyn
Subspecialty Certification Reproductive
Endocrinology
Practice Setting academic
Clinical Interests endometriosis; polycystic
ovaries; reproductive endocrinology
Research Interests hormone and endometriosis;
polycystic ovaries; endometriosis;
epidemiology
Member Society of Reproductive Surgeons

Tulsa

Donald Tredway, M.D.
Tulsa Center for Fertility & Women's Health
1145 S. Utica, Suite 1209
Tulsa, OK 74014
Phone (918) 584-2870
Fax (918) 587-3602
Specialty Certification Ob/Gyn
Subspecialty Certification Reproductive
Endocrinology
Practice Setting private

Clinical Interests polycystic ovarian syndrome;
male infertility
Research Interests hirsutism; polycystic
ovaries
Member Society of Reproductive Surgeons

Stanley G. Prough, M.D.
Tulsa Center for Fertility & Women's Health
1145 S. Utica, Suite 1209
Tulsa, OK 74104
Phone (918) 584-2870
Fax (918) 587-3602
E-mail Sprough@Hillcrest.com
Specialty Certification Ob/Gyn
Practice Setting private
Clinical Interests polycystic ovarian syndrome;
endometriosis
Research Interests blastocyst culture; embryo
co-culture
Member Society of Reproductive Surgeons,
Society for Assisted Reproductive Technology
Comments Tulsa Center for Fertility &
Women's Health is a full-service fertility
center with an active and quite successful in
vitro fertilization program.

OREGON

Bend

David B. Redwine, M.D.
2190 N.E. Professional Court
Bend, OR 97701
Phone (541) 382-8622
Fax (541) 383-0021
E-mail endo@scmc.org
Specialty Certification Ob/Gyn
Practice Setting private
Clinical Interests endometriosis; laparoscopic
surgery
Research Interests surgical treatment of
endometriosis
Member Society of Reproductive Surgeons

Eugene

Paul Kaplan, M.D.
Women's Care Fertility Center
590 Country Club Parkway, Suite A
Eugene, OR 97401-6037
Phone (541) 683-1559
Fax (541) 683-1709
Specialty Certification Ob/Gyn
Practice Setting private
Clinical Interests infertility/assisted
reproductive technologies; endometriosis;
polycystic ovarian syndrome
Research Interests subcutaneous hMG/hCG;
controlled ovarian hyperstimulation/
intrauterine insemination; blastocyst culture
Member Society of Reproductive Surgeons

Portland

Kenneth A. Burry, M.D.
University Fertility Consultants

1750 S.W. Harbor Way, Suite 100
Portland, OR 97201-5133
Phone (503) 418-3700
Fax (503) 418-3708
E-mail burryk@ohsu.edu
Specialty Certification Ob/Gyn
Subspecialty Certification Reproductive
Endocrinology
Practice Setting academic
Clinical Interests IVF; endometriosis; pre- and
post-menopause
Research Interests IVF; hormone management
of menopause; endometriosis
Member Society of Reproductive Surgeons,
Society for Assisted Reproductive
Technology, Society of Reproductive
Endocrinology and Infertility

Eugene F. Fuchs, M.D.
1750 S.W. Harbor Way, #230
Portland, OR 97201
Phone (503) 525-0071
Fax (503) 224-7925
E-mail Fuchsef@aol.com or Fuchse@ohsu.edu
Specialty Certification Urology
Practice Setting academic
Clinical Interests vasectomy reversal;
TESE/ICSI; male infertility
Research Interests sperm retrieval and
cryopreservation; long-term results of
vasectomy reversal
Member Society of Reproductive Surgeons

John S. Hesla, M.D.
Portland Center for Reproductive Medicine
2222 N.W. Lovejoy Street, Suite 404
Portland, OR 97210
Phone (503) 274-4994
Fax (503) 274-4946
Specialty Certification Ob/Gyn
Subspecialty Certification Reproductive
Endocrinology
Practice Setting private
Clinical Interests IVF; endometriosis;
polycystic ovarian syndrome
Research Interests IVF; ovarian physiology
Member Society of Reproductive Surgeons

Phillip E. Patton, M.D.
University Fertility Consultants
1750 S.W. Harbor Way, Suite 100
Portland, OR 97201-5133
Phone (503) 418-3700
Fax (503) 418-3708
E-mail pattonp@ohsu.edu
Specialty Certification Ob/Gyn
Subspecialty Certification Reproductive
Endocrinology
Practice Setting academic
Clinical Interests IVF; recurrent pregnancy loss
Research Interests ovarian hyperstimulation;
menopause
Member Society of Reproductive Surgeons

PENNSYLVANIA

Abington

Stephen G. Somkuli, M.D., Ph.D.
1245 Highland Avenue, Suite 404
Abington, PA 19001
Phone (215) 887-2010
Fax (215) 887-3291
Specialty Certification Ob/Gyn
Subspecialty Certification Reproductive
Endocrinology
Practice Setting private
Clinical Interests IVF; primary and secondary
infertility; endometriosis
Research Interests Integrins and implantation;
reproduction after cancer; lupus and
reproduction/hormones
Member Society for Male Reproduction and
Urology, Society for Assisted Reproductive
Technology, Society of Reproductive
Endocrinology and Infertility
Comment Visit our Web site: www.abington-
repromed.com.

Jay S. Schinfeld, M.D.
1245 Highland Avenue, Suite 404
Abington, PA 19001
Phone (215) 887-2010
Fax (215) 887-3291
Specialty Certification Ob/Gyn
Subspecialty Certification Reproductive
Endocrinology
Practice Setting private
Clinical Interests IVF; primary and secondary
infertility; endometriosis
Research Interests integrins and implantation;
reproduction after cancer; lupus and
reproduction/hormones
Member Society for Male Reproduction and
Urology, Society for Assisted Reproductive
Technology, Society of Reproductive
Endocrinology and Infertility
Comment Visit our Web site: www.abington-
repromed.com.

Allentown

Bruce I. Rose, Ph.D., M.D.
Infertility Solutions, P.C.
2200 Hamilton Street, Suite 105
Allentown, PA 18104
Phone (610) 776-1217
Fax (610) 776-4149
E-mail www.infertility.solution.com
Specialty Certification Ob/Gyn
Subspecialty Certification Reproductive
Endocrinology
Practice Setting private
Clinical Interests sperm problems; advanced
reproductive technologies; polycystic ovarian
syndrome; sperm and ovarian
cryopreservation
Research Interests sperm function tests; sperm
physiology; mycoplasma

Member Society of Reproductive Surgeons, Society for Assisted Reproductive Technology, Society for Male Reproduction and Urology, Society of Reproductive Endocrinology and Infertility
Comments One of the strengths of this practice lies in the close integration of clinical and laboratory aspects of care. A second strength is our ability to provide a personalized experience for our patients even for complex procedures.

Bethlehem

Ha-Lin Christina Lee, M.D.
95 Highland Avenue, Suite 100
Bethlehem, PA 18017
Phone (610) 868-8600
Fax (610) 868-8700
E-mail Familyfertility@enter.net
Specialty Certification Ob/Gyn
Subspecialty Certification Reproductive Endocrinology
Practice Setting private
Clinical Interests IVF/ICSI (ICSI); blastocyst culture; donor/gestational surrogacy
Member Society for Assisted Reproductive Technology

Bryn Mawr

Guy T. Bernstein, M.D.
245 Bryn Mawr Avenue
Bryn Mawr, PA 19010
Phone (610) 525-2515
Fax (610) 527-6586
E-mail gtbmd@aol.com
Specialty Certification Urology
Practice Setting private
Clinical Interests medical and surgical treatment of male factor infertility including varicocele repair, microsurgical reconstruction, and vasovasostomy
Member Society for Male Reproduction and Urology
Comments I am in private practice in a suburb of Philadelphia and an assistant professor at Jefferson Medical College. I work with a number of reproductive endocrinologists in the Philadelphia area.

William H. Pfeffer, M.D.
130 S. Bryn Mawr Avenue, D-Wing, Suite 1000
Bryn Mawr, PA 19010
Phone (610) 527-0800
Fax (610) 527-9868
E-mail Pfefferw@MLHS.org
Specialty Certification Ob/Gyn
Subspecialty Certification Reproductive Endocrinology
Practice Setting private
Clinical Interests fertility treatment; endometriosis; surgery
Member Society of Reproductive Surgeons

Elkins Park

Michael D. Birnbaum, M.D., PC
8380 Old York Road, Suite 200
Elkins Park, PA 19027
Phone (215) 886-9116
Fax (215) 887-7077
E-mail babymaker@home.com
Specialty Certification Ob/Gyn
Practice Setting private
Clinical Interests endometriosis and pelvic pain; polycystic ovarian syndrome and related problems; operative laparoscopy
Member Society of Reproductive Surgeons

Hershey

William C. Dodson, M.D.
PO Box 850
Hershey, PA 17033
Phone (717) 531-8478
Fax (717) 531-6286
E-mail wdodson@psghs.edu
Specialty Certification Ob/Gyn
Subspecialty Certification Reproductive Endocrinology
Practice Setting academic
Clinical Interests ovulation induction; ART
Research Interests superovulation and intrauterine insemination
Member Society for Assisted Reproductive Technology, Society of Reproductive Endocrinology and Infertility

Richard Legro, M.D.
PO Box 850
Hershey, PA 17033
Phone (717) 531-8478
Fax (717) 531-6286
E-mail rsll@psu.edu
Specialty Certification Ob/Gyn
Subspecialty Certification Reproductive Endocrinology and Infertility
Clinical Interests polycystic ovary syndrome; fertility
Research Interests polycystic ovary syndrome
Member Society of Reproductive Endocrinology and Infertility

Meadow Brook

Arthur Castelbaum, M.D.
1650 Huntingdon Pike, Suite 154
Meadow Brook, PA 19046
Phone (215) 938-1515
Fax (215) 938-8756
Specialty Certification Reproductive Endocrinology
Practice Setting private
Clinical Interests laparoscopy; hysteroscopy; IVF
Member Society for Assisted Reproductive Technologies, Society of Reproductive Endocrinology and Infertility

Martin F. Freedman, M.D.
    1650 Huntingdon Pike, Suite 154
    Meadow Brook, PA 19046
    Phone (215) 938-1515
    Fax (215) 938-8756
    E-mail Info@northernfertility.com
    Specialty Certification Reproductive
    Endocrinology
    Practice Setting private
    Clinical Interests IVF; ovulation induction;
    pelvic endometriosis
    Research Interests embryo cryopreservation
    Member Society of Reproductive Surgeons

Philadelphia

Frances R. Batzer, M.D.
    815 Locust Street
    Philadelphia, PA 19107-5507
    Phone (215) 922-2206
    Fax (215) 922-3777
    E-mail frances@womensinstitute.org
    Specialty Certification Ob/Gyn
    Subspecialty Certification Reproductive
    Endocrinology
    Practice Setting private
    Clinical Interests ovulation induction;
    transvaginal ultrasound pelvic evaluation
    Research Interests ovarian tissue preservation
    Member Society of Reproductive Surgeons,
    Society for Assisted Reproductive
    Technology, Society of Reproductive
    Endocrinology and Infertility

Stephen L. Corson, M.D.
    815 Locust Street
    Philadelphia, PA 19107-5507
    Phone (215) 922-2206
    Fax (215) 627-7554
    E-mail stephen@womensinstitute.org
    Specialty Certification Ob/Gyn
    Subspecialty Certification Reproductive
    Endocrinology
    Practice Setting private
    Clinical Interests endoscopy; ART; uterine
    anomalies
    Research Interests endoscopy; ART; uterine
    anomalies
    Member Society for Reproductive Surgeons,
    Society for Assisted Reproductive
    Technology, Society of Reproductive
    Endocrinology and Infertility

Gregory T. Fossum, M.D.
    834 Chestnut Street, Suite 300
    Philadelphia, PA 19107
    Phone (215) 955-5000
    Fax (215) 923-1089
    E-mail Gregory.Fossum@mail.TJU.edu
    Specialty Certification Ob/Gyn
    Subspecialty Certification Reproductive
    Endocrinology
    Practice Setting academic
    Clinical Interests infertility surgery; ovulation
    induction; IVF

Research Interests menorrhagia; surgery;
follicular development
Member Society for Male Reproduction and
Urology

Benjamin Gocial, M.D.
    815 Locust Street
    Philadelphia, PA 19107-5507
    Phone (215) 922-2206
    Fax (215) 922-3777
    E-mail ben@womensinstitute.org
    Specialty Certification Ob/Gyn
    Practice Setting private
    Clinical Interests minimally invasive surgery;
    ART
    Research Interests minimally invasive surgery,
    ART
    Member Society for Assisted Reproductive
    Technology

Jacqueline Gutman, M.D.
    815 Locust Street
    Philadelphia, PA 19107
    Phone (215) 922-2206
    Fax (215) 922-3777
    E-mail Jackie@womensinstitute.org
    Specialty Certification Ob/Gyn
    Subspecialty Certification Reproductive
    Endocrinology
    Clinical Interests IVF; ovulation disorders;
    third-party reproduction (oocyte donation,
    gestational carrier)
    Research Interests factors impacting success of
    IVF; stress and infertility; insulin resistance
    and polycystic ovarian disease

Irvin H. Hirsch, M.D.
    Jefferson University Urology Associates
    833 Chestnut East, Suite 703
    Philadelphia, PA 19107
    Phone (215) 955-1000
    Fax (215) 923-2275
    E-mail Irvin.Hirsch@mail.TJU.edu
    Specialty Certification Urology
    Practice Setting academic
    Clinical Interests reproductive rehabilitation;
    microsurgery
    Research Interests spinal cord injury
    Member Society of Reproductive Surgeons

Maureen P. Kelly, M.D.
    815 Locust Street
    Philadelphia, PA 19107-5507
    Phone (215) 922-2206
    Fax (215) 922-3777
    E-mail maureen@womensinstitute.org
    Specialty Certification Ob/Gyn
    Subspecialty Certification Reproductive
    Endocrinology
    Practice Setting private
    Clinical Interests complex ovulation induction;
    ART—donor oocyte specific interest;
    cyropreservation
    Research Interests ART; IVF/donor
    egg/gestational carrier

Member Society for Assisted Reproductive Technology, Society of Reproductive Endocrinology and Infertility

Luigi Mastroianni, Jr., M.D.
University of Pennsylvania Medical Center
3400 Spruce Street, 106 Dulles Building
Philadelphia, PA 19104-4283
Phone (215) 662-2970
Fax (215) 349-5512
E-mail LMastroianni@Obgyn.upenn.edu
Specialty Certification Ob/Gyn
Subspecialty Certification Reproductive Endocrinology
Practice Setting academic
Clinical Interests ART; fertility issues
Research Interests ethical issues in reproductive medicine
Member Society of Reproductive Surgeons

Pasquale Patrizio, M.D.
University of Pennsylvania Medical Center
3400 Spruce Street, 106 Dulles Building
Philadelphia, PA 19104-4283
Phone (215) 662-2977
Fax (215) 662-3535
E-mail Ppatrizio@obgyn.upenn.edu
Specialty Certification Ob/Gyn
Subspecialty Certification Reproductive Endocrinology and Infertility
Practice Setting academic
Clinical Interests IVF and ICSI; epididymal and testicular sperm aspiration
Research Interests genetics of male infertility; germ cell development; embryo development
Member Society for Assisted Reproductive Technology, Society for Male Reproduction and Urology, Society of Reproductive Endocrinology and Infertility

Steven J. Sondheimer, M.D.
University of Pennsylvania Medical Center
3400 Spruce Street, 106 Dulles Building
Philadelphia, PA 19104
Phone (215) 662-2978
Fax (215) 662-3535
E-mail Ssondheimer@obgyn.upenn.edu
Specialty Certification Ob/Gyn
Subspecialty Certification Reproductive Endocrinology
Practice Setting academic
Clinical Interests infertility; reproductive endocrinology; gynecology
Research Interests infertility; contraception; cyclic mood disorder
Member Society of Reproductive Surgeons

Pittsburgh

Miguel A. Marrero, M.D.
1050 Bower Hill Road, Suite 304
Pittsburgh, PA 15243
Phone (412) 572-6565
Fax (412) 572-6591
E-mail mammdpc@aol.com

Specialty Certification Ob/Gyn
Subspecialty Certification Reproductive Endocrinology
Practice Setting private
Clinical Interests endometriosis; uterine leiomyomas; IVF
Research Interests Activation mechanism of progesterone receptor
Member Society for Assisted Reproductive Technologies

Joseph S. Sanfilippo, M.D.
Allegheny General Hospital
323 East North Avenue
Pittsburgh, PA 15212
Phone (412) 359-1900
Fax (412) 359-5133
Specialty Certification Ob/Gyn
Subspecialty Certification Reproductive Endocrinology
Practice Setting academic
Clinical Interests operative laparoscopy; assisted reproductive technologies; endometriosis
Research Interests Phase III and IV clinical trials—endometriosis
Member Society of Reproductive Surgeons

Upland

Albert El-Roeiy, M.D.
Crozer Chester Medical Center
One Medical Center Boulevard
Upland, PA 19013
Phone (610) 447-2727
Fax (610) 447-6549
E-mail aelroeiy@crozer.org
Specialty Certification Reproductive Endocrinology and Infertility
Practice Setting academic
Clinical Interests polycystic ovarian disease; infertility; male infertility
Research Interests polycystic ovarian disease and insulin resistance
Member Society for Assisted Reproductive Technology, Society of Reproductive Endocrinology and Infertility

Wayne

Abraham Munabi, M.D.
950 West Valley Road, Suite 2401
Wayne, PA 19087
Phone (610) 964-9663
Fax (610) 964-0536
Specialty Certification Reproductive Endocrinology
Subspecialty Certification Ob/Gyn
Practice Setting private
Clinical Interests donor egg, IVF, surrogacy, donor embryo; preimplantation genetic diagnosis; donor insemination, ICSI
Member Society for Assisted Reproductive Technology, Society of Reproductive Endocrinology and Infertility

Michael Sobel, D.O.
950 West Valley Road, Suite 2401
Wayne, PA 19087
Phone (610) 964-9663
Fax (610) 964-0536
Specialty Certification Ob/Gyn
Subspecialty Certification Reproductive
Endocrinology
Clinical Interests donor egg, IVF, ICSI,
surrogacy, donor embryo; preimplantation,
genetic diagnosis, donor insemination;
surgical procedures
Member Society for Assisted Reproductive
Technology

West Reading

Jeffrey B. Frank, M.D.
301 South 7th Avenue, Suite #245
West Reading, PA 19611
Phone (610) 374-2214
Fax (610) 374-8852
E-mail davedonn@aol.com
Specialty Certification Ob/Gyn
Practice Setting private
Clinical Interests general infertility; IVF;
intracytoplasmic sperm injection
Research Interests egg freezing; co-culture;
assisted hatching
Member Society of Reproductive Surgeons
Comments Visit our Web site: www.
infertilitypa.com

Vincent A. Pellegrini, M.D.
301 South 7th Avenue, Suite 245
West Reading, PA 19611
Phone (610) 374-2214
Fax (610) 374-8852
E-mail davodonn@aol.com
Specialty Certification Ob/Gyn
Practice Setting private
Clinical Interests general infertility; IVF; ICSI
Research Interests egg freezing; co-culture;
assisted hatching
Member Society of Reproductive Surgeons,
Society for Assisted Reproductive
Technology, Society of Reproductive
Endocrinology and Infertility
Comments Visit our Web site:
www.infertilitypa.com.
Although I am not a board-certified
reproductive endocrinologist, my practice has
been almost totally infertility/endocrine since
1983. Started our private practice IVF
program in 1986.

RHODE ISLAND

Providence

David Keefe, M.D.
Women & Infants Hospital
101 Dudley Street
Providence, RI 02905
Phone (401) 453-7500

Fax (401) 453-7599
E-mail Dkeefe@wihri.org
Specialty Certification Ob/Gyn
Subspecialty Certification Reproductive
Endocrinology
Practice Setting academic
Clinical Interests IVF infertility
Research Interests aging and infertility;
improving IVF outcomes; reducing triplet
gestations
Comments I also direct the laboratory for
reproductive medicine at the Woods Hole
Marine Biological Laboratory.

Mark Sigman
2 Dudley Street, Suite 175
Providence, RI 02905
Phone (401) 421-0710
Fax (401) 421-0796
E-mail msigman@lifespan.org
Specialty Certification Urology
Practice Setting academic
Clinical Interests male infertility
Research Interests growth factors involved in
spermatogenesis
Member Society for Male Reproduction and
Urology

SOUTH CAROLINA

Columbia

Edward E. Moore, M.D.
1410 Blanding Street, Suite 205
Columbia, SC 29201
Phone (803) 779-6320
Fax (803) 779-6323
E-mail eemoore@aol.com
Specialty Certification Ob/Gyn
Practice Setting private
Clinical Interests infertility; endometriosis;
tubal anastomosis
Research Interests gonadotropins/ovulation
Member Society of Reproductive Surgeons
Comments Certified endoscopic surgeon.

Greenville

Michael R. Hoffman, M.D.
One Caledon Court
Greenville, SC 29615
Phone (864) 232-9456
Fax (864) 232-9468
Specialty Certification Ob/Gyn
Practice Setting private
Clinical Interests endoscopy; endometriosis;
fibroids
Member Society of Reproductive Surgeons

Thomas M. Price, M.D.
890 W. Faris Road, Suite 470
Greenville, SC 29605
Phone (864) 455-8488
Fax (864) 455-8489
E-mail tprice@ghs.org

Specialty Certification Ob/Gyn
Subspecialty Certification Reproductive
Endocrinology
Practice Setting academic
Clinical Interests infertility; hormone
replacement therapy
Research Interests sex steroid receptors; body
fat distribution; hormone replacement
therapy
Member Society for Assisted Reproductive
Technology, Society of Reproductive
Endocrinology and Infertility

Mt. Pleasant

Robert Kaufmann, M.D.
  Southeastern Fertility Center, P.A.
  1375 Hospital Drive
  Mt. Pleasant, SC 29464
  Phone (843) 881-3900
  Fax (843) 881-4729
  E-mail robkauf13@aol.com
  Specialty Certification Ob/Gyn
  Subspecialty Certification Reproductive
  Endocrinology
  Practice Setting private
  Member Society for Assisted Reproductive
  Technology, Society of Reproductive
  Endocrinology and Infertility

Grant W. Patton, Jr., M.D.
  Southeastern Fertility Center, P.A.
  1375 Hospital Drive
  Mt. Pleasant, SC 29464
  Phone (843) 881-3900
  Fax (843) 881-4729
  Specialty Certification Ob/Gyn
  Practice Setting private
  Clinical Interests infertility, primarily IVF and
  IUI
  Member Society of Reproductive Surgeons

TENNESSEE

Chattanooga

John Lucas, M.D.
  1751 Gunbarrel Road
  Chattanooga, TN 37421
  Phone (423) 899-0500
  Fax (423) 499-5521
  Specialty Certification Ob/Gyn
  Subspecialty Certification Reproductive
  Endocrinology and Fertility
  Practice Setting private
  Clinical Interests infertility surgery; IVF
  Member Society for Assisted Reproductive
  Technology

Johnson City

Samuel S. Thatcher, M.D., Ph.D., FACOG
  Center for Applied Reproductive Science
  Medical Center Office Building
  408 North State of Franklin Road, Suite 31
  Johnson City, TN 37604

Phone (423) 461-8880
Fax (423) 461-8887
E-mail thatcher@ivf-et.com
Specialty Certification Reproductive
Endocrinology
Practice Setting private
Clinical Interests ART; polycystic ovarian
syndrome
Research Interests ovarian aging; polycystic
ovarian syndrome; early development
Member Society of Reproductive
Endocrinology and Infertility

Kingsport

Pickens A. Gantt, M.D.
  2204 Pavilion Drive, Suite 307
  Kingsport, TN 37660
  Phone (423) 392-6330
  Fax (423) 392-6053
  Specialty Certification Ob/Gyn
  Subspecialty Certification Reproductive
  Endocrinology
  Practice Setting private
  Clinical Interests antiaging; menopause and
  natural hormones; IVF
  Research Interests IVF; endometriosis
  Member Society of Reproductive Surgeons,
  Society for Assisted Reproductive
  Technology, Society of Reproductive
  Endocrinology and Infertility

Knoxville

Michael C. Doody, M.D., Ph.D.
  220 Ft. Sanders W. Boulevard
  Knoxville, TN 37922
  Phone (423) 531-3011
  Fax (423) 531-7582
  Specialty Certification Ob/Gyn
  Subspecialty Certification Reproductive
  Endocrinology
  Practice Setting private
  Clinical Interests infertility, management;
  laparoscopic surgery; reproductive
  endocrinology
  Research Interests diagnostic tools in infertility;
  statistical analysis of clinical trials
  Member Society of Reproductive Surgeons

Jeffrey A. Kennan, M.D.
  1928 Alcoa Highway, Suite 201
  Knoxville, TN 37920
  Phone (865) 544-8800
  Fax (865) 544-6581
  E-mail jkennan@mc.utmck.edu
  Specialty Certification Ob/Gyn
  Subspecialty Certification Reproductive
  Endocrinology
  Practice Setting private
  Clinical Interests reproductive technologies/
  IVF; reproductive surgery; male factor
  infertility

Research Interests endometriosis; ovulation induction
Member Society of Reproductive Surgeons

Edward D. Kim, M.D.
1924 Alcoa Highway, Box U-11
Knoxville, TN 37920
Phone (865) 544-9254
Fax (965) 544-9716
E-mail ekim@mc.utmck.edu
Specialty Certification Urology
Practice Setting academic
Clinical Interests male infertility; vasectomy reversals; varicoceles
Research Interests nerve grafting during radical prostatectomy; male infertility genetics
Member Society for Male Reproduction and Urology

I. Ray King, M.D.
1925 Ailor Avenue
Knoxville, TN 37921
Phone (423) 524-2000
Fax (423) 524-4693
E-mail gyn@knoxnews.infi.net
Specialty Certification Ob/Gyn
Practice Setting private
Member Society of Reproductive Surgeons

Memphis

Raymond Weehan Ke, M.D.
956 Court Avenue, Room D328
Memphis, TN 38163
Phone (901) 448-8480
Fax (901) 448-8782
E-mail rke@utmem.edu
Specialty Certification Ob/Gyn
Subspecialty Certification Reproductive Endocrinology
Practice Setting academic
Clinical Interests IVF; polycystic ovarian syndrome
Research Interests vascular effects of estrogen
Member Society for Assisted Reproductive Technology, Society of Reproductive Endocrinology and Infertility

William Kutteh, M.D., Ph.D.
909 Ridgeway Loop Road.
Memphis, TN 38120-4020
Phone (901) 767-6868
Fax (901) 683-2231
E-mail wkutteh@utmem.edu
Specialty Certification Ob/Gyn
Subspecialty Certification Reproductive Endocrinology and Immunology
Practice Setting private
Clinical Interests recurrent pregnancy loss; unexplained infertility; ART
Research Interests recurrent pregnancy loss; immunologic aspects of infertility
Member Society for Assisted Reproductive Technology, Society of Reproductive

Surgeons, Society of Reproductive Endocrinology and Infertility

Nashville

Esther Eisenberg, M.D.
Vanderbilt University Medical Center
1211 22nd Ave. South
Nashville, TN 37232-2519
Phone (615) 322-6576
Fax (615) 343-4902
E-mail esther.eisenberg@mcmail.vanderbilt.edu
Specialty Certification Ob/Gyn
Subspecialty Certification Reproductive Endocrinology
Practice Setting academic
Clinical Interests polycystic ovarian syndrome; ovulation induction/ovulatory dysfunction; endometriosis
Research Interests menopause; endometriosis
Member Society for Assisted Reproductive Technology, Society of Reproductive Endocrinology and Infertility

George A. Hill, M.D.
2400 Patterson Street, Suite 319
Nashville, TN 37203
Phone (615) 321-4740
Fax (615) 320-0240
Specialty Certification Ob/Gyn
Subspecialty Certification Reproductive Endocrinology
Practice Setting private
Clinical Interests IVF; tubal microsurgery; endoscopic surgery
Member Society of Reproductive Surgeons

Jaime M. Vasquez, M.D.
326 21st Avenue North
Nashville, TN 37203
Phone (615) 321-8899
Fax (615) 321-8877
E-mail drvasquez@mindspring.com
Specialty Certification Ob/Gyn
Subspeciality Certification Reproductive Endocrinology
Practice Setting private
Clinical Interests ART, egg donation, surrogacy; endometriosis, pelvic pain; salpingitis, tubal disease, tubal reversal
Research Interests oocyte quality, poor ovarian reserve; advanced reproductive age; male infertility
Member Society of Reproductive Surgeons

Glenn Weitzman
2400 Patterson Street, Suite 319
Nashville, TN 37203
Phone (615) 321-4740
Fax (615) 320-0240
E-mail gweitzman@nashvillefertility.com
Specialty Certification Ob/Gyn

Subspecialty Certification Reproductive
Endocrinology
Practice Setting private
Clinical Interests IVF; ART; tubal
reanastomosis; operative laparoscopy
Member Society of Reproductive Surgeons,
Society for Assisted Reproductive
Technology, Society of Reproductive
Endocrinology and Infertility

Christine Whitworth, M.D.
2400 Patterson Street, Suite 319
Nashville, TN 37203
Phone (615) 321-4740
Fax (615) 320-0240
Specialty Certification Ob/Gyn
Subspecialty Certification Reproductive
Endocrinology and Infertility
Practice Setting private
Clinical Interests IVF; ART; tubal
reanastomosis; operative laparoscopy
Member Society for Assisted Reproductive
Technology, Society of Reproductive
Endocrinology and Infertility

TEXAS

Austin

Maya B. Bledsoe, M.D., FACE
1111 Research Boulevard, #485
Austin, TX 78759
Phone (512) 338-8181
Fax (512) 338-8375
Specialty Certification Internal Medicine
Subspecialty Certification Endocrinology
Practice Setting private
Research Interests female infertility; male
infertility; thyroid disease
Member Society for Male Reproduction and
Urology
Comments I am a reproductive medicine
specialist, active in American Association of
Clinical Eudocrinologists. I was trained by
Dr. Emil Steinberger.

Thomas C. Vaughn, M.D.
3705 Medical Parkway, Suite 402
Austin, TX 78705
Phone (512) 451-0149
Fax (512) 451-0977
Specialty Certification Ob/Gyn
Subspecialty Certification Reproductive
Endocrinology
Practice Setting private
Clinical Interests IVF; general infertility;
reconstructive surgery
Research Interests superovulation; adhesion
prevention
Member Society of Reproductive Surgeons,
Society for Assisted Reproductive
Technology, Society for Male Reproduction
and Urology, Society of Reproductive
Endocrinology and Infertility

Carrollton

H. Jane Chihal, M.D., Ph.D.
4325 North Josey Lane, Suite 100
Carrollton, TX 75010
Phone (972) 394-9544
Fax (972) 492-7198
E-mail hjchihal@aol.com
Specialty Certification Reproductive
Endocrinology
Practice Setting private
Clinical Interests hormone replacement
therapy; endometriosis; polycystic ovarian
syndrome
Member Society of Reproductive Surgeons

Dallas

John D. Bertrand, M.D.
8305 Walnut Hill, #10
Dallas, TX 75231
Phone (214) 363-7801
Fax (214) 363-5906
E-mail docjdb@home.com
Specialty Certification Ob/Gyn
Practice Setting private
Clinical Interests endoscopy; controlled
ovarian hyperstimulation; IVF; IUI
Member Society of Reproductive Surgeons
Comments Diagnostic hysteroscopy in office;
operative hysteroscopy.

Diana M. Bookout, M.D.
8160 Walnut Hill, Suite L006
Dallas, TX 75231
Phone (214) 345-7575
Fax (214) 345-8344
E-mail Bookout@PHSCare.org
Specialty Certification Ob/Gyn
Practice Setting private
Clinical Interests ART/infertility; gynecology
Member Society for Assisted Reproductive
Technology

Bruce R. Carr, M.D.
Department of Obstetrics & Gynecology
UT Southwestern Medical Center
5323 Harry Hines Boulevard
Dallas, TX 75390-9032
Phone (214) 648-4747
Fax (214) 648-8066
E-mail bcarr@mednet.swmed.edu
Specialty Certification Ob/Gyn
Subspecialty Certification Reproductive
Endocrinology
Practice Setting academic
Clinical Interests polycystic ovarian disease;
leiomyoma; infertility
Research Interests androgen excess;
menopause
Member Society of Reproductive
Endocrinology and Infertility

Samuel J. Chantilis, M.D.
8160 Walnut Hill Lane, Suite 320
Dallas, TX 75231

Phone (214) 363-5965
Specialty Certification Ob/Gyn
Subspecialty Certification Reproductive Endocrinology
Practice Setting private
Clinical Interests IVF; oocyte donation; operative hysteroscopy and laparoscopy
Research Interests clinical drug trials
Member Society for Male Reproduction and Urology, Society of Reproductive Surgeons, Society for Assisted Reproductive Technology, Society of Reproductive Endocrinology and Infertility

Brian M. Cohen, M.B.Ch.B., M.D., FACOG, FRCOG
National Fertility Center of Texas, P.A.
7777 Forest Lane, Suite C-63
Dallas, TX 75230
Phone (972) 566-6686
Fax (972) 566-6670
E-mail natlfert@flash.net
Specialty Certification Reproductive Endocrinology
Practice Setting private
Clinical Interests IVF with blastocyst culture; recurrent miscarriage; operative hysteroscopy
Member Society of Reproductive Surgeons
Comments Director, Women's Minimal Access Surgery Center at Columbia University. Dr. Cohen is renowned for his pioneering work in the field of gynecologic microsurgery and is an international expert in the field of infertility.

Ali Guerami, M.D.
8160 Walnut Hill Lane, Suite 208
Dallas, TX
Phone (214) 345-6963
Fax (214) 345-7140
Specialty Certification Ob/Gyn
Subspecialty Certification Reproductive Endocrinology
Practice Setting private
Clinical Interests IVF and third-party reproduction; ovulation dysfunction; menopause
Research Interests steroid hormone metabolism
Member Society for Assisted Reproductive Technology, Society of Reproductive Endocrinology and Infertility

Samuel P. Marynick, M.S., M.D., FACP, FACE, HCLD
3707 Gaston Avenue, Suite 325
Dallas, TX 75246
Phone (214) 828-2444
Fax (214) 821-5015
E-mail Samm@baylordallas.edu
Specialty Certification Internal Medicine
Subspecialty Certification American Board of Bioanalysts
Practice Setting private

Clinical Interests ART; IVF and embryo transfer; male infertility; ovulation disorders
Research Interests related pregnancy loss; embryo toxins; decreased spermatogenesis disorders
Member Society for Male Reproduction and Urology, Society for Assisted Reproductive Technology, Society of Reproductive Endocrinology and Infertility
Comments I evaluate the husband and wife simultaneously to seek to decipher the cause(s) of the couple's infertility.

J. Michael Putman, M.D.
3707 Gaston, #410
Dallas, TX 75246
Phone (214) 823-2692
Fax (214) 887-8244
Specialty Certification Ob/Gyn
Practice Setting private
Clinical Interests IVF; operative endoscopy; general infertility
Research Interests endometriosis
Member Society of Reproductive Surgeons

Alfred J. Rodriguez, M.D.
7777 Forest Lane, Suite 236-C
Dallas, TX 75230
Phone (972) 566-4500
Fax (972) 566-6861
E-mail ajr236@airmail.net
Specialty Certification Ob/Gyn
Practice Setting private
Clinical Interests ART (IVF); habitual aborter; endometriosis
Research Interests male factor infertility
Member Society of Reproductive Surgeons

Ft. Worth

Alan Johns, M.D.
3700 Rufe Snow
Ft. Worth, TX 76180
Phone (817) 284-1152
Fax (827) 284-1973
E-mail delbert1l@aol.com
Specialty Certification Ob/Gyn
Practice Setting private
Clinical Interests laparoscopic reconstructive pelvic surgery; endometriosis
Research Interests endometriosis; postoperative adhesion prevention
Member Society of Reproductive Surgeons

Houston

Samuel L. Attia, M.D., P.A.
6624 Fannin, Suite 1460
Houston, TX 77030
Phone (713) 790-0557
Fax (713) 790-0592
Specialty Certification Urology
Practice Setting private
Clinical Interests microsurgery; impotence
Member Society for Male Reproduction and Urology

John E. Bertini, Jr., M.D., FACS
1315 Saint Joseph Parkway, Suite 1502
Houston, TX 77002
Phone (713) 650-1502
Fax (713) 751-1633
E-mail jbert1024@aol.com
Specialty Certification Urology
Practice Setting private
Clinical Interests spinal cord injury and
infertility; vasovasostomy; electroejaculation
Research Interests Sidenofil and spinal cord
injury
Member Society for Male Reproduction and
Urology

Sandra Carson, M.D.
6550 Fannin, #801
Houston, TX 77030
Phone (713) 798-8484
E-mail scarson@bcm.tmc.edu
Specialty Certification Ob/Gyn
Subspecialty Certification Reproductive
Endocrinology
Practice Setting academic
Clinical Interests spontaneous abortion;
preimplantation diagnosis; ectopic pregnancy
Research Interests spontaneous abortion;
preimplantation diagnosis; ectopic pregnancy
Member Society for Assisted Reproductive
Technology, Society of Reproductive
Endocrinology and Infertility

James C. Chuong, M.D.
7515 S. Main Street, Suite 580
Houston, TX 77030
Phone (713) 794-0070
Fax (713) 794-0010
E-mail chuong@cooperinstitutearm.com
Specialty Certification Ob/Gyn
Subspecialty Certification Reproductive
Endocrinology
Practice Setting private
Clinical Interests IVF, IUI, and sperm washing;
infertility workup; infertility surgery, using a
microscope and laser including tuboplasty
(untie the tubes) and myomectomy (removal
of tumor of the uterus)
Member Society of Reproductive Surgeons

Randall C. Dunn, M.D.
7550 Fannin
Houston, TX 77054
Phone (713) 512-7826
Fax (713) 512-7829
Specialty Certification Ob/Gyn
Subspecialty Certification Reproductive
Endocrinology
Practice Setting private
Clinical Interests IVF procedures; laparoscopic
surgery
Member Society of Reproductive Surgeons

Robert R. Franklin, M.D.
Ob/Gyn Associates, P.A.
7550 Fannin

Houston, TX 77054
Phone (713) 512-7000
Fax (713) 512-7845
Specialty Certification Ob/Gyn
Practice Setting private
Clinical Interests endometriosis; polycystic
ovarian syndrome; infertility surgery
Research Interests endometriosis
Member Society of Reproductive Surgeons

George M. Grunert, M.D.
7550 Fannin
Houston, TX 77054
Phone (713) 512-7851
Fax (713) 512-7853
E-mail grunert@icsi.net
Specialty Certification Ob/Gyn
Practice Setting private
Clinical Interests infertility; IVF;
preimplantation genetic diagnosis
Research Interests preimplantation genetic
diagnosis; improvement in ART;
neuroendocrinology
Member Society of Reproductive Surgeons
Comments Dr. Grunert has been director of
the IVF program at the Women's Hospital of
Texas and the Obstetrical and Gynecological
Association of Houston since 1984. His
practice encompasses the study and
treatment of infertility, menstrual disorders,
reproductive endocrinology, repeated
miscarriage, menopausal management, and
all aspects of total care for women.

Robert Franklin, M.D.
Ob/Gyn Associates, PA
7550 Fannin
Houston, TX 77054
Phone (713) 512-7000
Fax (713) 512-7845
Specialty Certification Ob/Gyn
Subspecialty Certification Reproductive
Endocrinology
Practice Setting private
Clinical Interests endometriosis; polycystic
ovarian syndrome; infertility surgery
Research Interests Endometriosis
Member Society of Reproductive Surgeons

Dolores J. Lamb, Ph.D., HCLD
Baylor College of Medicine
Scott Department of Urology
One Baylor Plaza, Room 440E
Houston, TX 77030
Phone (713) 798-6266
Fax (713) 798-5577
E-mail dlamb@loww.urol.bcm.tmc.edu
Specialty Certification American Association of
Bioanalysis
Subspecialty Certification National Registry in
Clinical Chemistry
Practice Setting academic
Clinical Interests andrology—laboratory
evaluation of the male; ICSI

Research Interests genetic basis of male infertility; steroid regulation of reproductive tumor growth; molecular biology of genitourinary defects
Member Society for Male Reproduction and Urology
Comments division of male reproductive surgery and medicine

Larry I. Lipshultz, M.D.
6560 Fannin, Scurlock Tower #2100
Houston, TX 77030
Phone (713) 798-6163
Fax (713) 798-6007
E-mail larryl@bcm.tmc.edu
Specialty Certifications Urology, American College of Surgeons
Practice Setting academic
Clinical Interests male infertility—diagnosis and treatment; microsurgical treatment of male infertility; sexual dysfunction
Research Interests genetic causes of male infertility; environmental toxins and infertility; New diagnostic tests in male infertility
Member Society of Reproductive Surgeons

Dorothy J. Roach, M.D.
530 Wells Fargo Drive, Suite 116
Houston, TX 77090
Phone (281) 444-4784
Fax (281) 444-0429
E-mail droach@dbmed.net
Specialty Certification Ob/Gyn
Subspecialty Certification Reproductive Endocrinology
Practice Setting private
Clinical Interests ART; ovulation induction; reproductive surgery
Member Society for Assisted Reproductive Technology, Society of Reproductive Endocrinology and Infertility
Comments Director of a freestanding IVF center in suburban North Houston since 1995.

Cecilia T. Valdes, M.D.
7550 Fannin
Houston, TX 77054
Phone (713) 512-7064
Fax (713) 512-7829
Specialty Certification Ob/Gyn
Subspecialty Certification Reproductive Endocrinology
Practice Setting private
Clinical Interests IVF; laparoscopic surgery
Member Society of Reproductive Surgeons

Ronald L. Young, M.D.
6550 Fannin, Smith Tower, Suite 901
Houston, TX 77030
Phone (713) 798-8726
Fax (713) 798-7575
E-mail ronaldy@bcm.tmc.edu
Specialty Certification Ob/Gyn

Practice Setting academic
Clinical Interests fertility; menopause
Research Interests menopause; contraception; fertility
Member Society of Reproductive Surgeons

Katy

Jacob Tal, M.D.
1260 Pin Oak, Suite 110
Katy, TX 77494
Phone (28) 392-8180
Fax (281) 392-7911
E-mail jtal@compassuet.com
Specialty Certification Ob/Gyn
Practice Setting Private
Clinical Interests ovulation induction; recurrent pregnancy losses (early)
Member Society of Reproductive Endocrinology and Infertility

San Angelo

Lourell E. Sutliff, M.D.
225 E. Beauregard
San Angelo, TX 76093
Phone (915) 658-1511
Fax (915) 481-2386
Specialty Certification Ob/Gyn
Subspecialty Certification Reproductive Endocrinology
Practice Setting private
Clinical Interests medical-surgical infertility; satellite IVF program
Member Society of Reproductive Surgeons

San Antonio

Joseph R. Garza, M.D.
7940 Floyd Curl Drive, Suite 900
San Antonio, TX 78229
Phone (210) 616-0680
Fax (210) 616-0684
E-mail docgarza@aol.com
Specialty Certification Ob/Gyn
Practice Setting private
Clinical Interests IVF/embryo transfer; microsurgery/laser surgery; recurrent pregnancy loss
Research Interests endometriosis; polycystic ovarian disease
Member Society of Reproductive Surgeons
Comments Interest in donor oocytes, ICSI, embryo cryopreservation, reproductive endocrinology.

J. Ricardo Loret de Mola, M.D.
The University of Texas Health Science Center at San Antonio
Department of Obstetrics & Gynecology
7703 Floyd Curl Drive
San Antonio, TX 78229-3900
Phone (210) 567-6121
Fax (210) 567-4958
E-mail loretdemola@uthscsa.edu
Specialty Certification Ob/Gyn

Subspecialty Certification Reproductive
Endocrinology and Infertility
Practice Setting academic
Clinical Interests IVF; oocyte donation;
conservative treatment of uterine fibroids
Research Interests role of growth factors in the
pathophysiology of myomas
Member Society for Male Reproduction and
Urology, Society for Assisted Reproductive
Technology, Society of Reproductive
Endocrinology and Infertility

Temple

Jose F. Pliego, M.D.
Department of Obstetrics & Gynecology
Scott & White Hospital and Clinic
2401 S. 31st Street
Temple, TX 76508
Phone (254) 724-2738
Fax (254) 724-8344
E-mail jpliego@swmail.sw.org
Specialty Certification Ob/Gyn
Subspecialty Certification Reproductive
Endocrinology
Practice Setting private
Clinical Interests all areas of reproductive
endocrinology and infertility
Member Society of Reproductive Surgeons
Comments We have an active IVF/ICSI
program and perform donor IUI.

Waco

Stephen H. Corwin, M.D.
2911 Herring Avenue, Suite 310
Waco, TX 76708
Phone (254) 755-4500
Fax (254) 755-4510
Specialty Certification Urology
Practice Setting academic/private
Member Society for Male Reproduction and
Urology
Comments I am a clinical associate professor
of the Family Practice Department of
Community Medicine at the University of
Texas Southwestern Medical Center, 1989 to
present.

Webster

Vicki Schnell
Center of Reproductive Medicine
450 Medical Center Boulevard, #202
Webster, TX 77598
Phone (281) 332-0073
Fax (281) 332-1860
E-mail schnellv@gte.net
Specialty Certification Ob/Gyn
Subspecialty Certification Reproductive
Endocrinology and Infertility
Practice Setting private
Clinical Interests donor egg program; ICSI;
IVF
Research Interests GnRH analogues; tubal
factor infertility; blastocyst transfers

Member Society of Reproductive Surgeons,
Society for Male Reproduction and Urology,
Society for Assisted Reproductive
Technology, Society of Reproductive
Endocrinology and Infertility

The Woodlands

Jon M. R. Rawson, M.D., Ph.D.
Woodlands Fertility Center
1001 Medical Plaza Drive, Suite 280
The Woodlands, TX 77380
Phone (281) 363-4445
Fax (281) 292-4419
Specialty Certification Ob/Gyn
Practice Setting private
Clinical Interests reproductive endocrinology
and infertility; tubal microsurgery and
sterilization reversal; endometriosis
Research Interests tubal microsurgical
advancements; endometriosis
Member Society of Reproductive Surgeons
Comments See our Web site:
FERTILITYFOCUS.com. Clinical Faculty,
baylor College of Medicine, Division of
Reproductive Endocrinology and Infertility.

UTAH

Salt Lake City

Harry H. Hatasaka, M.D.
University of Utah
Department of Obstetrics & Gynecology
50 North Medical Drive, Suite 2B200
Salt Lake City, UT 84132
Phone (801) 581-4172
Fax (801) 585-2388
Specialty Certification Ob/Gyn
Subspecialty Certification Reproductive
Endocrinology
Practice Setting academic
Clinical Interests infertility;
hyperandrogenism; endometriosis
Research Interests polycystic ovarian
syndrome; ART; recurrent pregnancy loss
Member Society for Assisted Reproductive
Technology, Society of Reproductive
Endocrinology and Infertility

Kirtly Parker James, M.D.
Department of Obnocology/Gynocology
University of Utah Health Sciences Center
Salt Lake City, UT 84132
Phone (801) 581-3834
Fax (801) 585-5146
Specialty Certification Ob/Gyn
Subspecialty Certification Reproductive
Endocrinology
Practice Setting academic
Clinical Interests menopause; infertility;
ovulatory disorders
Research Interests menopause
Member Society for Assisted Reproductive

Technology, Society of Reproductive
Endocrinology and Infertility

C. Matthew Peterson, M.D.
50 North Medical Drive
Salt Lake City, UT 84132
Phone (801) 581-6880
Fax (801) 585-2388
Specialty Certification Ob/Gyn
Subspecialty Certification Reproductive
Endocrinology and Infertility
Practice Setting academic/private
Clinical Interests IVF; polycystic ovarian
syndrome; donor egg IVF
Research Interests oocyte maturation; IVF;
ovarian cancer
Member Society of Reproductive Surgeons,
Society for Assisted Reproductive
Technology, Society of Reproductive
Endocrinology and Infertility
Comments The only IVF center in Utah
abiding by all SART, CLIA, and CAP
standards for IVF.

VERMONT

Burlington

John R. Brumsted, M.D.
Fletcher Allen Health Care
111 Colchester Avenue
Burlington, VT 05401
Phone (802) 847-4754
Fax (802) 847-5677
E-mail John.Brumsted@vtmednet.org
Specialty Certification Ob/Gyn
Subspecialty Certification Reproductive
Endocrinology
Practice Setting academic
Clinical Interests endometriosis
Member Society of Reproductive Surgeons

Julia V. Johnson, M.D.
The University of Vermont
1 South Prospect Avenue
Burlington, VT 05401
Phone (802) 847-1400
Fax (802) 847-8433
E-mail julia.johnson@vtmednet.org
Specialty Certification Ob/Gyn
Subspecialty Certification Reproductive
Endocrinology
Practice Setting academic
Clinical Interests menopause; infertility;
reproductive endocrinology
Research Interests menopause/hormone
replacement therapy
Member Society for Assisted Reproductive
Technology, Society of Reproductive
Endocrinology and Infertility
Comments Director, Division of Reproductive
Endocrinology.

Cynthia Sites, M.D.
The University of Vermont

Fletcher Allen Health Care
1 South Prospect Street
Burlington, VT 05401
Phone (802) 847-1400
Fax (802) 847-8433
E-mail csites@200.uvm.edu
Specialty Certification Ob/Gyn
Subspecialty Certification Reproductive
Endocrinology
Practice Setting academic
Clinical Interests reproductive endocrinology;
menopause
Research Interests hormone replacement and
heart disease
Member Society for Assisted Reproductive
Technology, Society of Reproductive
Endocrinology and Infertility

VIRGINIA

Arlington

Michael DiMattina, M.D.
46 S. Glebe Road, #301
Arlington, VA 22204
Phone (703) 920-3890
Fax (703) 892-6037
E-mail DominionFertility@erols.com
Specialty Certification Ob/Gyn
Subspecialty Certification Reproductive
Endocrinology
Practice Setting private/academic
Clinical Interests IVF; infertility; male factor
Research Interests implantation; multiple
pregnancy
Member Society of Reproductive Surgeons,
Society for Assisted Reproductive
Technology, Society of Reproductive
Endocrinology and Infertility

Charlottesville

B. G. Bateman, M.D.
Northridge Clinic
2955 Ivy Road, Suite 304
Charlottesville, VA 22903
Phone (804) 243-4590
Fax (804) 293-6409
Specialty Certification Ob/Gyn
Subspecialty Certification Reproductive
Endocrinology
Practice Setting academic
Clinical Interests endoscopic surgery; ART
Research Interests endometriosis
Member Society of Reproductive Surgeons

Stuart S. Howards, M.D.
University of Virginia Hospital
PO Box 800 422
Charlottesville, VA 22908
Phone (804) 924-9559
Fax (804) 982-3652
E-mail ssh4e@virginia.edu
Specialty Certification Urology
Practice Setting academic

Clinical Interests male infertility
Research Interests varicocele; vasectomy
reversal
Member Society for Male Reproduction and
Urology

Fairfax

Nancy Durso, M.D.
3020 Hamaker Court, #500
Fairfax, VA 22031
Phone (703) 204-9600
Fax (703) 204-9605
E-mail nmdmd@erols.com
Specialty Certification Ob/Gyn
Practice Setting private
Clinical Interests infertility; pelvic pain;
polycystic ovaries
Member Society of Reproductive Surgeons
Comments Personalized, cost-effective care for
infertility including advanced reproductive
technologies.

David S. Saffan, M.D.
3020 Hamaker Court, #500
Fairfax, VA 22031
Phone (703) 204-9600
Fax (703) 204-9605
E-mail dsaffan@erols.com
Specialty Certification Ob/Gyn
Practice Setting private
Clinical Interests IVF/ICSI; endometriosis;
operative hysteroscopy
Member Society of Reproductive Surgeons

Mechanicsville

Lonny Green, M.D.
8228 Meadow Bridge Road
Mechanicsville, VA 23116
Phone (804) 730-5023
Fax (804) 282-6671
Specialty Certification Urology
Practice Setting private
Clinical Interests male infertility
Member Society for Male Reproduction and
Urology

Norfolk

David Archer, M.D.
Eastern Virginia Medical School
601 Colley Avenue
Norfolk, VA 23507
Phone (757) 446-7444
Fax (757) 446-8998
E-mail archerdf@evms.edu
Specialty Certification Ob/Gyn
Subspecialty Certification Reproductive
Endocrinology
Practice Setting academic
Clinical Interests menopause; contraception
Research Interests menopause; contraception

Susan A. Ballagh, M.D.
Jones Institute for Reproductive Medicine
601 Colley Avenue

Norfolk, VA 23507-1627
Phone (757) 446-7100
Fax (757) 446-8998
E-mail ballagsa@evms.edu
Specialty Certification Ob/Gyn
Practice Setting academic
Clinical Interests laparoscopy/hysteroscopy:
alternatives to hysterectomy; recurrent
miscarriage and infertility; endometriosis
Research Interests contraception; menopause;
endometriosis
Member Society of Reproductive Surgeons,
Society of Reproductive Endocrinology and
Infertility

William E. Gibbons, M.D.
Jones Institute for Reproductive Medicine
601 Colley Avenue
Norfolk, VA 23507
Phone (757) 446-8934
Fax (757) 446-8998
E-mail Gibbonwe@evms.edu
Specialty Certification Ob/Gyn
Subspecialty Certification Reproductive
Endocrinology
Practice Setting academic
Clinical Interests infertility; polycystic ovarian
syndrome; menopause
Research Interests preimplantation genetic
diagnosis
Member Society of Reproductive Surgeons,
Society for Assisted Reproductive
Technology, Society of Reproductive
Endocrinology and Infertility

Suheil J. Muasher, M.D.
Jones Institute for Reproductive Medicine
601 Colley Avenue
Norfolk, VA 23507
Phone (757) 446-7116
Fax (757) 446-8998
E-mail MuasheSJ@evms.edu
Specialty Certification Ob/Gyn
Subspecialty Certification Reproductive
Endocrinology and Infertility
Practice Setting academic
Clinical Interests IVF; ovulation induction;
surgery for congenital anomalies of
reproductive tract
Research Interests stimulation protocols for
IVF; improving IVF success rates; treatment
of low responders
Member Society for Assisted Reproductive
Technologies, Society of Reproductive
Endocrinology and Infertility
Comments My primary interest is to improve
IVF success rates and to simplify the
procedure and to develop new technologies.

Richmond

Michael G. Edelstein, M.D.
Fertility Institute of Virginia
10710 Midlothian Turnpike, Suite 331
Richmond, VA 23235

Phone (804) 379-9000
Fax (804) 379-9031
E-mail fertdoctor@aol.com
Specialty Certification Ob/Gyn
Subspecialty Certification Reproductive
Endocrinology
Practice Setting private
Clinical Interests IVF, GIFT, ICSI, assisted
hatching; laser laparoscopy, microsurgery;
ovulation induction; male factor infertility
Research Interests recurrent miscarriage
treatment
Member Society of Reproductive Surgeons,
Society for Assisted Reproductive
Technology, Society of Reproductive
Endocrinology and Infertility

Joseph G. Gianfortoni, M.D.
7603 Forest Avenue, Suite 204
Richmond, VA 23229
Phone (804) 673-2273
Fax (804) 285-3109
Specialty Certification Ob/Gyn
Subspecialty Certification Reproductive
Endocrinology
Practice Setting private
Clinical Interests IVF; endometriosis;
polycystic ovaries
Member Society of Reproductive Surgeons,
Society for Assisted Reproductive
Technology, Society of Reproductive
Endocrinology and Infertility
Comments Comprehensive fertility services.
Seeing private patients for over 18 years with
16+ years of IVF experience.

Sanford M. Rosenberg, M.D.
7603 Forest Avenue, Suite 301
Richmond, VA 23229
Phone (804) 285-9700
Fax (804) 285-9745
E-mail Eggdoc96@aol.com
Specialty Certification Ob/Gyn
Subspecialty Certification. Reproductive
Endocrinology
Practice Setting private
Clinical Interests IVF; laser laparoscopy; tubal
microsurgery, fibroids, endometriosis
Research Interests pelvic adhesions; male
factor infertility; ovulation induction
Member Society of Reproductive Surgeons

Geof Tidey, M.D.
7603 Forest Avenue, Suite 301
Richmond, VA 23229
Phone (804) 285-9700
Fax (804) 285-9745
Specialty Certification Ob/Gyn
Subspecialty Certification Reproductive
Endocrinology
Practice Setting private
Clinical Interests IVF; endometriosis;
laparoscopic/hysteroscopic surgery
Research Interests failure to ovulate

Member Society for Assisted Reproductive
Technology, Society of Reproductive
Endocrinology and Infertility

Williamsburg

Roger E. Schultz, M.D.
500 Strawberry Plains Road
Williamsburg, VA 23185
Phone (757) 253-0051
Fax (757) 229-9526
E-mail schultz@erols.com
Specialty Certification Urology
Practice Setting private
Clinical Interests general urology; uro-
oncology; male fertility
Member Society for Male Reproduction and
Urology

WASHINGTON

Bellevue

Barry C. Stewart, M.D.
1310 116th Avenue, Suite B
Bellevue, WA 98004
Phone (206) 215-3200
Specialty Certification Ob/Gyn
Practice Setting private
Clinical Interests optimization of IVF cycle
success; diagnosis of lack of fertility (reasons
for); recurrent pregnancy loss
Research Interests adhesion prevention at
surgery; Treatment of endometriosis with
GnRH-a
Member Society of Reproductive Surgeons
Comments We are a full-service reproductive
endocrinology center sensitive to the needs
and desires of our patients. Dr. Stewart is also
a clinical associate professor of obstetrics and
gynecology at the University of Washington
School of Medicine.

Seattle

Richard E. Berger, M.D.
University of Washington Medical Center
Department of Urology, Box 356510
1959 N.E. Pacific Street
Seattle, WA 98195
Phone (206) 543-3270
Fax (206) 543-3272
E-mail rberger@u.washington.edu
Specialty Certification Urology
Practice Setting academic
Clinical Interests vasectomy reversal, prostatitis
Research Interests prostatitis; vasectomy
reversal
Member Society for Male Reproduction and
Urology

Victor Fujimoto
Department of Ob/Gyn—Reproductive
Endocrinology
4225 Roosevelt Way N.E., Suite 305
Seattle, WA 98105

Phone (206) 543-0670
Fax (206) 685-7818
E-mail fudgie@u.washington.edu
Specialty Certification Ob/Gyn
Subspecialty Certification Reproductive
Endocrinology
Practice Setting academic
Clinical Interests ART
Research Interests noninvasive treatment of
uterine fibroids
Member Society of Reproductive
Endocrinology and Infertility, Society for
Assisted Reproductive Technology
Comments I am on faculty staff at the
University of California, San Francisco.

Lee Hickok, M.D.
1101 Madison, Suite 1500
Seattle, WA 98104
Phone (206) 215-3200
Fax (206) 215-6590
E-mail staff@repromed.com
Specialty Certification Ob/Gyn
Practice Setting private
Clinical Interests IVF; Mullerian anomalies;
microsurgery
Research Interests ultrasound; adhesion
prevention
Member Society for Assisted Reproductive
Technology

Brenda Houmard
Department of Ob/Gyn—Reproductive
Endocrinology
4225 Roosevelt Way N.E., Suite 305
Seattle, WA 98105
Phone (206) 543-0670
Fax (206) 685-7818
E-mail bhoumard@u.washington.edu
Practice Setting academic
Clinical Interests reproductive endocrine
disorders
Research Interests molecular regulation of
ovarian aging
Member Society of Reproductive
Endocrinology and Infertility

S. Samuel Kim
Department of Ob/Gyn—Reproductive
Endocrinology
4225 Roosevelt Way N.E., Suite 305
Seattle, WA 98105
Phone (206) 543-0670
Fax (206) 685-7818
E-mail medssk@u.washington.edu
Specialty Certification Ob/Gyn
Subspecialty Certification Reproductive
Surgery and Infertility
Practice Setting academic
Clinical Interests ART (especially ovarian
cryopreservation); endoscopic surgery;
menopause
Research Interests ovarian cryopreservation;

ovarian reserve; fertility conservation for
cancer patients
Member Society of Reproductive Surgeons,
Society for Assisted Reproductive
Technology, Society for Male Reproduction
and Urology

Gerard S. Letterie, M.D.
Center for Fertility & Reproductive
Endocrinology
Virginia Mason Medical Center
1100 9th Avenue
Seattle, WA 98110
Phone (206) 223-6190
Fax (206) 341-0596
E-mail gerard.letterie@vmmc.org
Specialty Certification Ob/Gyn
Subspecialty Certification Reproductive
Endocrinology
Practice Setting private
Clinical Interests IVF; congenital anomalies of
the reproductive tract; gonadal dysgenesis
Research Interests early embryo development;
low-dose stimulation protocols
Member Society for Assisted Reproductive
Technology, Society of Reproductive
Endocrinology and Infertility

Lorna Marshall, M.D.
Center for Fertility & Reproductive
Endocrinology
Virginia Mason Medical Center, XII-FC
1100 9th Avenue
Seattle, WA 98101
Phone (206) 223-6190
Fax (206) 341-0596
E-mail obslam@vmmc.org
Specialty Certification Ob/Gyn
Subspecialty Certification Reproductive
Endocrinology
Practice Setting private
Clinical Interests ART; operative endoscopy;
polycystic ovaries
Research Interests reproductive ethics;
reproductive technologies; menopause
Member Society for Assisted Reproductive
Technology, Society of Reproductive
Endocrinology and Infertility

R. Dale McClure, M.D.
Virginia Mason Medical Center
1100 9th Ave.
Seattle, WA 98111
Phone (206) 223-6179
Fax (206) 223-7650
Specialty Certification urology
Practice Setting academic
Clinical Interests male reproductive problems;
microsurgery—vasectomy reversals, sperm
aspirations; varicocele
Research Interests sperm function testing
Member Society of Reproductive Surgeons,
Society for Male Reproduction and Urology

Robert McIntosh, M.D.
   1101 Madison, Suite 1500
   Seattle, WA 98104
   Phone (206) 215-3200
   Fax (206) 215-6590
   E-mail staff@repromed.com
   Clinical Interests IVF; new fertility procedures
   Research Interests lecture on medical ethics on infertility
   Member Society of Reproductive Surgeons, Society for Assisted Reproductive Technology

Donald E. Moore, M.D.
   4225 Roosevelt Way N.E., Suite 101
   Seattle, WA 98105
   Phone (206) 598-4225
   Fax (206) 598-6081
   Specialty Certification Ob/Gyn
   Subspecialty Certification Reproductive Endocrinology
   Practice Setting academic
   Clinical Interests general infertility; IVF
   Research Interests infection and infertility; fallopian tube disease
   Member Society of Reproductive Surgeons
   Comments Our group of specialists has a large, active, and successful IVF program as well as general infertility.

Don Smith, M.D.
   1101 Madison, Suite 1500
   Seattle, WA 98104
   Phone (206) 215-3200
   Fax (206) 215-6590
   E-mail staff@repromed.com
   Specialty Certification Ob/Gyn
   Practice Setting private
   Clinical Interests reproductive surgery
   Research Interests gynecologic endoscopy
   Member Society of Reproductive Surgeons, Society for Assisted Reproductive Technology

Michael R. Soules, M.D.
   4225 Roosevelt Way N.E., Suite 305
   Seattle, WA 98105
   Phone (206) 543-4693
   Fax (206) 685-7818
   E-mail msoules@u.washington.edu
   Specialty Certification Ob/Gyn
   Subspecialty Certification Reproductive Endocrinology
   Practice Setting academic
   Clinical Interests infertility; reproductive endocrinology; ART
   Research Interests reproductive aging; cryopreservation of ovarian tissue
   Member Society of Reproductive Surgeons

Barry C. Stewart, M.D.
   Pacific Gynecology Specialists
   1101 Madison Street, Suite 1500
   Seattle, WA 98104-3551
   Phone (206) 215-3200
   Fax (206) 215-6595
   Specialty Certification Ob/Gyn

Practice Setting private
Clinical Interests optimization of IVF cycle success; diagnosis of lack of fertility (reasons for); recurrent pregnancy loss
Research Interests adhesion prevention at surgery; treatment of endometriosis with GnRH-a
Member Society of Reproductive Surgeons
Comments We are a full-service reproductive endocrinology center sensitive to the needs and desires of our patients. Dr. Stewart is also a clinical associate professor of obstetrics and gynecology at the University of Washington School of Medicine.

Wayne D. Weissman, M.D., P.S.
   1221 Madison, Suite 1210
   Seattle, WA 98104
   Phone (206) 292-6488
   Fax (206) 623-2436
   Specialty Certification Urology
   Practice Setting private
   Clinical Interests microsurgery, TESE, MESA; ICSI varicocele specialist
   Member Society of Reproductive Surgeons, Society for Male Reproduction and Urology

Tacoma

R. Z. McLees, M.D.
   3582 Pacific Avenue
   Tacoma, WA 98405
   Phone (253) 475-5433
   Specialty Certification Ob/Gyn
   Practice Setting private
   Clinical Interests IVF; ICSI
   Research Interests sex selection
   Member Society for Assisted Reproductive Technology, Society of Reproductive Endocrinology and Infertility
   Comments We have been specializing in high-tech fertility treatments since the early 1980s, well before specialty board, and have done much primary research.

WEST VIRGINIA

Charleston

Tamer Yalcinkaya, M.D.
   830 Pennsylvania Avenue, Suite 304
   Charleston, WV 25302
   Phone (304) 388-1515
   Fax (304) 388-1570
   E-mail tamer.yalcinkaya@Camcare.com
   Specialty Certification Ob/Gyn
   Subspecialty Certification Reproductive Endocrinology
   Practice Setting academic
   Clinical Interests hyperandrogenism and polycystic ovarian syndrome; tubal disease, endometriosis; ART
   Research Interests role of GABA in the ovary; travaginal ultrasound and ectopic pregnancy; endoscopic surgery
   Member: Society for Assisted Reproductive

Technology, Society of Reproductive
Endocrinology and Infertility

WISCONSIN

La Crosse

Paul D. Silva, M.D.
  Fertility Clinic
  Gundersen/Lutheran Medical Center
  1836 South Avenue
  La Crosse, WI 54601
  Phone (608) 782-7300
  Fax (608) 791-6611
  E-mail Asstorsv@GundLuth.org
  Specialty Certification Ob/Gyn
  Subspecialty Certification Reproductive
  Endocrinology
  Practice Setting private
  Clinical Interests IVF; GIFT; reversal of tubal
  sterilization
  Research Interests laparoscopic procedures;
  polycystic ovarian syndrome; endometriosis
  Member Society for Assisted Reproductive
  Technology, Society of Reproductive
  Endocrinology and Infertility

Madison

Wolfram Nolten, M.D.
  H4/568 CSC UWHC
  600 Highland Avenue
  Madison, WI 53792
  Phone (608) 263-9221
  Fax (608) 262-9289
  E-mail wenolten@facstaff.wisc.edu
  Specialty Certification Internal Medicine
  Subspecialty Certification Endocrinology
  Practice Setting academic
  Clinical Interests male infertility; diabetes;
  endocrine
  Research Interests male infertility

Marshfield

Michael C. Sellen, M.D.
  1000 N. Oak
  Marshfield, WI 54449
  Phone (715) 387-5235
  Fax (715) 387-5240
  E-mail SeelenM@MFLDCLIN.edu
  Specialty Certification Urology
  Practice Setting academic/private
  Clinical Interests fertility; cancer; pediatrics
  Member Society for Male Reproduction and
  Urology, Society of Reproductive
  Endocrinology and Infertility

Waukesha

Matthew A. Meyer, M.D.
  721 American Avenue, Suite 304
  Waukesha, WI 53188
  Phone (414) 549-2229
  Fax (414) 549-1657
  E-mail mattm@exec.pc

Specialty Certification Ob/Gyn
Practice Setting private
Clinical Interests ART (IVF, ICSI, blastocyst);
ultrasound; donor oocyte
Research Interests minimizing costs of ART
ovarian cryopreservation
Member Society for Assisted Reproductive
Technology

WYOMING

Casper

Sam T. Scaling, M.D.
  940 E. 3rd, Suite 211
  Casper, WY 82601
  Phone (307) 577-4226
  Fax (307) 577-4229
  Specialty Certification Ob/Gyn
  Practice Setting private
  Clinical Interests infertility evaluation and
  treatment
  Member Society of Reproductive Surgeons

CANADA

BRITISH COLUMBIA

Stacy Elliott, M.D.
  Vancouver Sperm Retrieval Clinic
  Echelson-5
  855 West 12th Avenue
  Vancouver, BC V52 1M9
  Phone (604) 875-8282
  Fax (604) 875-8249
  E-mail doc@scisexualhealth.com
  Specialty Certification Sexual Medicine
  Practice Setting academic
  Clinical Interests sperm retrieval and
  anejaculation; disability and fertility; all
  sexual medicine
  Research Interests spinal cord injury and
  fertility; sexual rehabilitation
  Member Society for Male Reproduction and
  Urology
  Comments Only do ejaculatory dysfunction
  and resultant male infertility. Only
  multidisciplinary (urology/sexual
  medicine/gynecology) sperm retrieval clinic
  in western Canada (not general male
  infertility clinic).

Mark Nigro, M.D., FRCP
  Vancouver Sperm Retrieval Clinic
  Echelon-5
  855 West 12th Avenue
  Vancouver, BC V52 1M9
  Phone (604) 872-8252
  Fax (604) 875-8249
  E-mail doc@scisexualhealth.com
  Specialty Certification Urology
  Practice Setting academic
  Clinical Interests sperm retrieval and

ejaculation; disability and fertility; all sexual medicine
Research Interests spinal cord injury and fertility; sexual rehabilitation
Member Society for Male Reproduction and Urology
Comments Only do ejaculatory dysfunction and resultant male infertility, only multidisciplinary (urology/sexual medicine/gynecology) sperm retrieval clinic in western Canada (not general male infertility clinic).

NOVA SCOTIA

Bruce C. Dunphy, M.D.
5980 University Avenue, Room G2141
Halifax, Nova Scotia
Canada B3H4N1
Phone (902) 420-6645
Fax (902) 425-1125
Specialty Certification Ob/Gyn
Subspecialty Certification Reproductive Endocrinology
Practice Setting academic
Clinical Interests assisted reproduction; tubal surgery; operative endoscopy
Research Interests outcome studies; continuing professional education
Member Society of Reproductive Surgeons

ONTARIO

Robert W. Hudson, M.D., Ph.D., FRCPC
Department of Medicine, Division of Endocrinology
Queen's University
Stuart Street
Etherington Hall
Kingston, Ontario
Canada K7L 3N6
Phone (613) 533-2973
Fax (613) 533-6574
E-mail hudsonr@post.queensu.cg
Specialty Certification Internal Medicine
Subspecialty Certification Endocrinology
Practice Setting academic
Clinical Interests andrology—male infertility; the aging male; testosterone replacement
Research Interests testicular function; varicocele—hormone abnormalities in the aging male
Member Society for Male Reproduction and Urology

B. Norman Barwin, M.B., Ch.B., M.D., F.R.C.O.G., F.A.C.O.G., F.S.O.G.C.
Fertility Centre
770 Broadview Avenue
Ottawa, Ontario
Canada K2A3Z3
Phone (613) 728-5104
Fax (613) 728-3497

E-mail barwin@nakcon.ca
Specialty Certification Reproductive Physiology
Subspecialty Certification Fellow of Royal College of Ob/Gyn (UK)
Practice Setting private
Clinical Interests infertility, premenstrual syndrome, menopause; reproduction endocrinology; andrology
Research Interests IUI and donor insemination; ovulation induction; menopause and andropause studies
Member Society for Male Reproduction and Urology, Society of Reproductive Endocrinology and Infertility
Comments Past president of Canadian Fertility Society; current president of Infertility Awareness Association of Canada (IAAC).

Arthur Leader, M.D.
Ottawa Hospital
510-737 Parkdale Avenue
Ottawa, Ontario
Canada K1Y 1J8
Phone (613) 761-4427
Fax (613) 761-5417
E-mail aleader@ottawahospital.on.ca
Specialty Certification Ob/Gyn
Subspecialty Certification Reproductive Endocrinology
Practice Setting academic
Clinical Interests andrology; ART; health economics
Research Interests clinical studies on male infertility
Member Society for Male Reproduction and Urology

QUEBEC

Michel Thabet
5600 Boulevard des Galeries #401
Quebec City, Quebec
Canada G2K 2H6
Phone (418) 260-9555
Fax (418) 260-9556
E-mail nathab@globetrotter.qc.ca
Specialty Certification Urology
Subspecialty certification Andrology
Practice Setting private
Clinical Interests male infertility; ART; vasovasostomy
Research Interests clinical varicocele vasourostomy, epididymal marker and glucosidose-P34
Member Society of Reproductive Surgeons, Society for Male Reproduction and Urology

Tugas Tulandi, M.D., F.R.C.S.(C), FACOG
McGill Reproductive Center
687 Pine Avenue West

Montreal, Quebec
Canada H3A 1A1
Phone (514) 842-1231 x1391
Fax (514) 843-1448
Specialty Certification Ob/Gyn
Practice Setting academic

Clinical Interests reproductive/endoscopic surgery; endometriosis; preservation of fertility
Research Interests endometriosis, adhesions; endometrial ablation
Member Society of Reproductive Surgeons

CANADIAN IN VITRO FERTILIZATION (IVF) CENTERS

The following list of IVF centers and the services they offer comes from the membership directory of the Canadian Fertility and Andrology Society. That directory also includes a list of all individual members of the society. It is available from the Canadian Fertility and Andrology Society, 2065 Alexandre de Seve, Suite 409, Montreal, Canada H2L 2W5, phone (514) 524-9009, fax (514) 524-2163.

Again, the authors do not intend to imply endorsement of the clinics listed in this book. In all cases, you should use the same careful deliberation that you normally would employ when choosing a physician or medical clinic.

ALBERTA

Foothills Regional Fertility Program
1620–29th Street NW, #300
Calgary, Alberta, T2N 4L7
Phone (403) 284-5444
Fax (403) 284-9293
Assisted hatching; embryo cryopreservation; epididymal sperm aspiration; gestational carrier; intracytoplasmic sperm injection; IVF, ovum donor

BRITISH COLUMBIA

University of British Columbia IVF Program
Willow Pavilion, 2nd Floor
855 W. 12th Avenue
Vancouver, British Columbia, V5Z 1M9
Phone (604) 875-5113
Fax (604) 875-5124
E-mail fwilson@interchange.cbc.ca
Embryo cryopreservation; IVF

Genesis Fertility Centre
555 12th Avenue West
Vancouver, British Columbia, V5Z 3X7
Phone (604) 879-3032
Fax (604) 875-1432
E-mail gensis@iatronet.net
Web site www.iatronet.net/genesis
Assisted hatching; embryo cryopreservation; epididymal sperm aspiration; intracytoplasmic sperm injection; IVF

MANITOBA

Heartland Fertility & Gynecology Clinic
701-1661 Portaga Avenue
Winnipeg, Manitoba R3J 3T7
Phone (204) 779-9988
Fax (204) 779-8877

Total gynecological coverages therapeutic donor insamination; hyperstimulation; IVF; known egg donation

NEW BRUNSWICK

George L. Dumont Hospital
330 University Avenue
Manetow, New Brunswick, E1C 2Z3
Phone (506) 857-3884
Fax (506) 852-4197

NOVA SCOTIA

IWK Grace Health Centre
Department Obstetrics/Gynecology
5850/5890 University Avenue
PO Box 3070
Halifax, Nova Scotia, B3J 3G9
Phone (902) 420-3180
Fax (902) 420-3056
Embryo cryopreservation; epididymal sperm aspiration; IVF; sperm hyaluronidase testing

ONTARIO

C.A.R.E Health Resources
649 Queensway West
Mississauga, Ontario, L5B 1C2
Phone (905) 897-9600
Fax (905) 897-9614
E-mail jtcare@aol.com
Embryo cryopreservation; epididymal sperm aspiration; IVF ovum donor

London Health Sciences Centre
Reproductive Endocrinology & Infertility Program
339 Windermere Road
London, Ontario, N6A 5A5
Phone (519) 663-2966

Fax (519) 663-3938
Web site www.lhsc.on.ca/programs/infertility
Assisted hatching: embryo cryopreservation;
epididymal sperm aspiration;
intracytoplasmic sperm injection; IVF

2F2Fertility Clinic
McMaster Hospital
1200 Main Street West, Box 2000
Hamilton, Ontario, L8N 3Z5
Phone (905) 521-5080
Fax (905) 521-2609
Web site www.cmh.on.ca/indext.htm
Cryopreservation; oocyte donation

Markham Fertility Centre
377 Church Street
Markham, Ontario, L6B 1A1
Phone (905) 472-8856
Fax (905) 472-4130
Web site www.markhamfertilitycentre.com

Goal Program/Fertility Center
737 Parkdale Avenue, #510
Ottawa, Ontario, K1Y 1J8
Phone (613) 761-4100
Fax (613) 761-5462/(613) 761-4678
E-mail fertrn@civich.ottawa.on.ca
Embryo cryopreservation; epididymal sperm
aspiration; intracytoplasmic sperm injection
IVF

IVF Canada
2347 Kennedy Road, Suite 304
Scarborough, Ontario, M1T 3T8
Phone (416) 754-8742
Fax (416) 321-1239
E-mail info@ivfcanada.com
Assisted hatching; embryo cryopreservation;
epididymal sperm aspiration; gestational
carrier; intracytoplasmic sperm injection; IVF;
ovum donor; sperm hyaluronidase testing

Life Program
Toronto East General Hospital
825 Coxwell Avenue
Toronto, Ontario, M4C 3E7
Phone (416) 469-6590
Fax (416) 469-6503
Assisted hatching; embryo cyropreservation;
epididymal sperm aspiration;
intracytoplasmic sperm injection; IVF ovum
donor

ISIS Regional Fertility Centre
7145 West Credit Avenue, Building #3
Mississauga, Ontario, L5N 2J7
Phone (905) 816-9822
Fax (905) 816-9833
Assisted hatching; embryo cryopreservation;
epididymal sperm aspiration;
intracytoplasmic sperm injection IVF, ovum
donor; sperm hyaluronidase testing

Reproductive Biology Unit (RBU) & In Vitro
Fertilization (IVF) Unit

Toronto General Hospital
200 Elizabeth Street, 6EN-231
Toronto, Ontario, M5G 2C4
Phone (416) 340-3213 (RBU); (416) 340-3214
(IVF); (416) 340-4713 (IVF List)
Fax (416) 340-3292
Embryo cryopreservation IVF ovum donor
(anonymous); sperm hyaluronidase testing

Success Through Assisted Reproductive
Technologies (START)
655 Bay Street, 18th Floor
Toronto, Ontario, M5G 2K4
Phone (416) 506-0805
Fax (416) 506-0680
Assisted hatching; embryo cryopreservation;
epididymal sperm aspiration; gestational
carrier; intracytoplasmic sperm injection; IVF;
ovum donor

Toronto Centre for Advanced Reproductive
Technology
150 Bloor Street West, Suite 210
Toronto, Ontario, M5S 2X9
Phone (416) 972-0110
Fax (416) 972-0036
E-mail tcart@online.com
Assisted hatching; embryo cryopreservation;
epididymal sperm aspiration; gestational
carrier; intracytoplasmic sperm injection IVF;
ovum donor; sperm hyaluronidase testing

Toronto Fertility Institute
66 Avenue Road
Toronto, Ontario, M5R 3N8
Phone (416) 964-8501
Fax (416) 963-9931
E-mail khamsi@ica.net
Embryo cryopreservation; gestational carrier;
intracytoplasmic sperm injection IVF; ovum
donor

QUEBEC

Fertility Clinic Hospital St-Luc
264 Rene Levesque Boulevard
Montreal, Quebec, H2Z 1P1
Phone (514) 281-2141
Fax (514) 281-6133
IVF; intracytoplasmic sperm injection;
epididymal sperm aspiration

Procrea Bio Sciences Inc.
1100 Beaumont Avenue, Suite 305
Ville Mont-Royal, Quebec, H3P 3H5
Phone (514) 345-8535
Fax (514) 345-8978
E-mail Procrea@interlink.net
Web site www.procrea.qc.ca
Embryo cryopreservation IVF;
intracytoplasmic sperm injection; epididymal
sperm aspiration

Reproductive Centre
McGill University

Royal Victoria Hospital
687 Pine Avenue West
Montreal, Quebec, H3A 1A1
Phone (514) 843-1650/(514) 843-1496
Assisted hatching; embryo cryopreservation;
epididymal sperm aspiration;
intracytoplasmic sperm injection; IVF, ovum
donor

SASKATCHEWAN

Division of Reproductive Endocrinology &
Infertility

Royal University Hospital
Department of Obstetrics Gynecology,
College of Medicine
University of Saskatchewan
103 Hospital Drive
Saskatoon, Saskatchewan, S7N 0W8
Phone (306) 966-8623
Fax (306) 966-8040
E-mail artus.rei@usask.ca
Web site www.usask.ca/medicine/obgyn/
artus
Gestational carrier; IVF

RESOURCES

Infertility Services

American Association of Tissue Banks
1350 Beverly Road, Suite 220A
McLean, VA 22101
(703) 827-9582
Supplies list of AATB-associated
sperm banks in United States and
Canada. Send stamped, self-
addressed envelope.

American College of Obstetricians and Gynecologists Resource Center
409 12th Street SW
Washington, DC 20024-2188
(202) 638-5577
This national organization of ob/gyns
has a resource center that can
provide patient education
pamphlets, lists of ob/gyns in
certain areas of the country, and
answers to basic questions about
infertility and women's health.

American Society for Reproductive Medicine
1209 Montgomery Highway
Birmingham, AL 35216-2809
(205) 978-5000
The national organization of fertility
specialists provides general
information about infertilty and
patient pamphlets.

American Society of Andrology
PO Box 15171
Lenexa, KS 66285-5171
(913) 541-9077
Refers patients to andrologists across
the country.

American Urological Association, Inc.
1120 North Charles Street
Baltimore, MD 21201
(301) 727-1100
Provides patient information
pamphlets and the name of a
physician/officer of the association
who can supply information about
specific questions as well as a
possible referral to a local
urologist.

DES Action USA
Long Island Jewish Medical Center
(East Coast Office)
New Hyde Park, NY 11040
(516) 775-3450
DES Action USA (West Coast Office)
2845 24th Street
San Francisco, CA 94110
(415) 826-5060
Provides education and support to
mothers, daughters, and sons
exposed to the drug
diethylstilbestrol (DES)

Endometriosis Association
8585 North 76th Place
Milwaukee, WI 53223
1-800-992-3636 (in the United States)
1-800-426-2363 (in Canada)
Furnishes information on local
support groups, crisis call
assistance, and education and
research programs regarding
endometriosis.

Fertilitext
1-900-PREGNANT
A national telephone service
  providing recorded information
  and live consultation about fertility
  treatment and specialists.

*National Society of Genetic
  Counselors*
233 Canterbury Drive
Wallingford, PA 19086
(215) 872-7608
Provides information on genetic
  counseling services and referrals.

*Planned Parenthood Federation of
  America*
810 Seventh Avenue
New York, NY 10019
(212) 541-7800
Provides referral to a local Planned
  Parenthood affiliate that may
  supply infertility diagnosis and
  counseling.

Resolve, Inc.
1310 Broadway
Somerville, MA 02144
(617) 623-0744
This national self-help group for
  infertile couples provides physician
  and IVF referrals, literature about
  many aspects of infertility, a
  newsletter, and telephone
  counseling. It has support groups
  across the country.

SHARE
(Source of Help in Airing and
  Resolving Experiences)
Joseph Health Center
300 First Capitol Drive
St. Charles, MO 63301
(314) 947-6164
Supplies information packets on
  miscarriage, stillbirth, ectopic

pregnancy, and neonatal (near-
  birth) death; a bibliographic
  listing of books, articles, and audio-
  visual material on grieving; a
  bimonthly newsletter; a listing of
  parents in an outreach groups;
  and a support group referral
  list.

Adoption Services

Child Welfare League of America
440 First Street NW, Suite 310
Washington, DC 20001
(202) 638-2952
Publishes *The National Adoption
  Resource Directory*, listing adoption
  agencies across the country.

Latin American Parent Association
PO Box 72
Brooklyn, NY 11234
(718) 236-8689
Provides information about adopting
  babies from Latin America.

National Adoption Center
1500 Walnut Street, Suite 701
Philadelphia, PA 19102
1-800-TOADOPT or (215) 735-9988
Web site: www.adopt.org
Promotes adoption opportunities for
  children throughout the country,
  particularly those with special
  needs.

*National Adoption Information
  Clearinghouse*
11426 Rockville Pike, Suite 410
Rockville, MD 20852
(301) 231-6512
Web site: www.calib.com/naic
Provides fact sheets, articles, and
  information about films and
  videotapes on adoption; a
  computerized list of books and

written materials on adoption; a directory of adoption agencies and other adoption resources; and information on state and federal laws on adoption.

National Council for Adoption
1930 17th Street NW
Washington, DC 20009-6207
(202) 328-1200
As association of private adoption agencies that provides information, publications, and resource listings on adoption.

North American Council on Adoptable Children
970 Raymond Avenue, #106
St. Paul, MN 55114-1149
(612) 644-3036
Web site: www.nacac.org
A national support group for adoptive parents that specializes in placing older, handicapped, or minority children.

OURS, Inc
3333 Highway 100 North
Minneapolis, MN 55422
(612) 535-4829
This national support group provides information about licensed adoption agencies with a focus on foreign adoptions.

International Adoption

Adoptive Families of America
(800) 372-3300

International Concerns Committee for Children
(303) 494-8333

National Adoption Hotline
(202) 328-8072

Specific Adoption Laws
A country-by-country guide can be found at travel.stage.gov/ children's_issues_html#adoption

INTERNET RESOURCES

The Internet can be a valuable resource for in-depth, timely information about infertility available in the privacy of your own home. Search the word "infertility" on a search engine and you will come up with more than 20,000 "hits," or pages. This vast network of data has made it easy to find answers to nearly any fertility question. At the same time, what's out there is largely unregulated. Some sites are rife with misinformation, while others sell fraudulent products. Fertility patients must consider the source to help them determine whether the information is accurate or credible.

If a couple has gone through a fertility workup and has a diagnosis, they can assist their fertility specialist by visiting reputable Web sites and learning about symptoms, treatments, medications, and the latest studies about their condition. Many fertility patients who use the Internet to research information also join online support groups. Conversing, even electronically, with others who face similar challenges and frustrations can be comforting, although some people find they end up spending inordinate amounts of time researching fertility issues and chatting online.

Online information can enhance a couple's medical care but should not be used as a doctor substitute. General answers to common problems are helpful guidelines, but only a qualified doctor can provide specific answers to individual problems. Nevertheless, the Internet has evolved into an important tool to help patients retrieve the most up-to-date information and to help improve communication between doctors and patients.

Professional organizations have become important disseminators of well-researched fertility information on the World Wide Web. Here are some comprehensive sites:

www.inciid.org   The International Council for Infertility Information
Dissemination (INCIID, pronounced "inside") is "dedicated to helping infertile couples explore their family-building options, including treatment, adoption, and choosing to live child-free." This site offers both basic and advanced articles about specific topics, dozens of fact sheets, bulletin boards run by experts, and chat rooms.

www.resolve.org   The Resolve home page shows couples where to start to determine whether they have a fertility problem and how to choose a fertility specialist, and provides connections to local chapters around the country.

www.asrm.com   The American Society for Reproductive Medicine home page includes such resources as FAQs (Frequently Asked Questions), fact sheets, and patient information booklets.

www.womens.health.com/health_center/infertility/index.html
The Women's Health Initiative's learning center can help couples who are dealing with infertility and feelings of frustration. This site has extensive information on a variety of fertility topics.

www.noah.cuny.edu/pregnancy   NOAH is a team effort from the City University of New York, the Metropolitan Library Council, the New York Academy of Medicine, and the New York Public Library. It has reviewed links to many health topics, and includes large sections on infertility and adoption issues at the AskNOAHAboutPregnancy site. The links jump to other links on a range of medical and nonmedical subjects, and is a good place to start fertility research.

www.cdc.gov/nccdphp/drh/arts/   This is an important federal government site for IVF patients since it provides the success rates for all clinics that have registered with the Society of Assisted Reproductive Technology. Unfortunately, the published data from the Centers for Disease Control is about three years old and may not represent current IVF success rates.

Other sites provide a more personable touch to Web information. About.com, which touts itself as The Human Internet, provides Web pages run by individuals on a wide variety of topics, including infertility. Infertility with Tracy Morris at infertility.about. com/health/infertility offers a full-service site, including recent articles, forums, live chat, a contact guide, and free newsletter, as well as links to related sites on About.com The FertilityPlus site at www.fertilityplus.com provides fertility FAQs and information by patients for patients on beginning fertility issues, advanced fertility issues, infertility newsgroups, fertility resource lists, and even fertility humor.

For more information about the fertility treatments available at the Chapel Hill Fertility Center (directed by Dr. Berger), go to www.fertility-center.com/ staff.html or www.chapelhillfertility.com/Clinical&NursingStaff.htm. For the most up-to-date information on male fertility treatments available at the Cornell Institute for Reproductive Medicine (run by Dr. Goldstein), go to www.maleinfertility.org. For the most timely success rates at Cornell's IVF program, go to www.ivf.org.

Newsgroups are discussion forums to post and share information. Typically, they are not moderated, and must be visited each day to read the latest postings. Accessing a newsgroup requires special software called a newsreader, which usually is included in browsers such as Microsoft's Outlook Express and Netscape's Messenger. Most newsgroups have a core of active participants, and offer a place to find a real, live person to answer questions. The following newsgroups are devoted to some aspect of infertility:

alt.infertility   The largest of all infertility newsgroups.

misc.health.infertility   Another general infertility newsgroup.

alt.infertility.primary   This newsgroup deals primarily with primary infertility.

alt.infertility.secondary   A newsgroup for secondary infertility.

alt.infertility.pregnancy   A place to discuss pregnancy after fertility treatments.

alt.infertility.surrogacy   Information about surrogate and gestational carriers.

alt.support.pco   Discussions about polycystic ovarian syndrome (PCOS) and how it relates to infertility.

alt.support.des   Discussions about diethystilbestrol (DES) and how it relates to infertility.

alt.support.endometriosis   Discussions about endometriosis and how it relates to infertility.

alt.adoption   Discussions about adoption issues.

alt.adoption.agency   Another place to discuss general adoption issues.

soc.support.pregnancy.loss   A newsgroup to help support women who have lost a pregnancy.

Bulletin boards, also known as message boards or forums, are similar to newsgroups but are smaller and more tightly focused. They are generally easier to access and read, and are usually not moderated. Besides bulletin boards found on the Web, large online services such as America Online and CompuServe also offer bulletin boards that relate to fertility topics. Many local Resolve groups also have fabulous bulletin boards. The following bulletin boards relate to some aspect of infertility:

www.fertilitext.org and www.ihr.com/infertility are two excellent bulletin boards found at the INCIID Web site. Other bulletin boards are available on a variety of specific topics, and patients can search through thousands of postings for information about diseases, clinics, and even individual doctors.

In AOL's "Health" area, a search for "infertility" will guide you to three main resources: infertility, experts, and chat groups. Chat groups provides a schedule of chat programs, subjects, and schedule times. Also available are connections to treatments, clinics, drugs, and books at Amazon.com.

CompuServe's Family Forum has two topics, Fertility and Adoption/Foster Care, that provide pertinent discussions for fertility patients.

WebMD has message boards on Infertility and Reproduction, including Open Discussion, Secondary Infertility, and Treatment Options. Pregnancy message boards include Common Complications, including prenatal care, miscarriage, and ectopic pregnancies, and Open Discussion, including high-risk pregnancy.

Mailing lists on the Web provide lively discussions on virtually any and every fertility topic. To subscribe to a mailing list requires sending an e-mail message to an Internet address and then following the instructions. Every day, information from the mailing list will arrive automatically by e-mail on the list's topic. Moderated mailing lists help ensure that only relevant posts are forwarded, and are preferable to unmoderated mailing lists. The following is a sampling of mailing lists that deal with some aspect of infertility:

BabyOne—Primary Infertility

To sign on, go to www.onelist.com/subscribe.cgi/BabyOne

B2—BabyTwo
An unmoderated list for secondary infertility. Mail to: listserv@maelstrom.stjohns.edu. Type in message body: subscribe babytwo firstname lastname

Domestic Adoption
Mail to: listserv@sjuvm.stjohns.edu. Type in message body: subscribe adoption firstname lastname

Donor Insemination Support
Mail to: external-majordomo@postofc,corp.sgi.com. Type in message body: subscribe di-support

Endometriosis
Mail to: listserv@listserv.dartmouth.edu. Type in message body: subscribe witsendo yourname

Fortility
For women over age forty. Mail to: fortility-request@columbia.edu. Type in message body: subscribe

IF-Adopt—Adoption During or After Fertility Treatments
To sign on, go to www.onna.org/community/sisterlists.html

MFI Male Factor Infertility
An unmoderated list pertaining to male factor infertility. To sign on, go to www.onna.org/community/sisterlists.html

MAI—Miscarriage After Infertility
Mail to: listserv@listserv.acsu.buffalo.edu. Type in message body: subscribe mai

Mothers Via Egg Donation
For women interested in an egg donation program. Mail to: tasc@surrogacy.com. Type in subject line: send mved application

Multiple Miscarriages
For women who have had multiple miscarriages. Mail to: tasc@surrogacy.com. Type in subject line: send mm application

Pregnancy After Infertility
Mail to: pal-list-request@cyberclick.com. Type in message body: subscribe. To sign on, go to www.onelist.com/subscribe.cgi/PAI

Parents Through ART (Assisted Reproduction Techniques)
Mail to: tasc@surrogacy.com. Type in subject line: send pta application

Surrogate Mothers
Mail to: tasc@surrogacy.com. Type in subject line: send sm application

WAW—Wanting and Waiting
For patients who want to share information and receive emotional support while trying to conceive. Mail to: wantingandwaiting-subscribe@makelist.com

GLOSSARY

Abortion   premature termination of a pregnancy; may be induced or spontaneous (miscarriage)

Acquired immune deficiency syndrome (AIDS)   a fatal disease caused by a virus that destroys the immune system's ability to fight off infection

Acrosome   the packet of enzymes in the sperm's head that allow sperm to dissolve a hole in the coating around the egg, which allows the sperm to penetrate and fertilize the egg

Acrosome reaction   chemical change that enables a sperm to penetrate an egg

Adhesion   a union of adjacent organs by scar tissue

Adrenal glands   the endocrine glands on top of each kidney

Aerobic bacteria   bacterial organisms that require relatively high concentrations of oxygen to survive and reproduce

Agglutination   clumping together, as of sperm, often due to an infection, inflammation, or antibodies

Amenorrhea   absence of menstruation

Amniocentesis   aspiration of amniotic fluid from the uterus, usually performed at three to three and a half months of pregnancy, to test a fetus for genetic abnormalities

Anaerobic bacteria   bacterial organisms that survive in relatively low oxygen concentrations

Androgens   male sex hormones

Andrologist   a specialist who treats sperm problems

Anovulation   absence of ovulation

Antibody   a protective agent produced by the body's immune system in response to a foreign substance

Antigen   any substance that induces the formation of an antibody

Antisperm antibodies   antibodies that can attach to sperm and inhibit movement of sperm or fertilization

Artificial insemination (AI)   placement of a sperm sample inside the female reproductive tract (see also intracervical insermination, intrauterine insemination, intratubal insemination)

Aspiration   suctioning of fluid, as from a follicle

Assisted hatching   procedure done during in vitro fertilization cycle to open a small section of the embryo's wall before it is transferred to the uterus to help with implantation

Asymptomatic   without any symptoms

Autoantibodies   antibodies formed against one's own tissues

Autoimmunity   an immune response against one's own tissues

Azoospermia   absence of sperm

Bacteria   microscopic, single-celled organisms that can cause infections of the genital tract

Basal body temperature (BBT)   the temperature taken at its lowest point in the day, usually in the morning before getting out of bed

Biopsy   a fragment of tissue removed for study under the microscope

Blood-testis barrier   barrier that separates sperm from the bloodstream

Bromocryptine (Parlodel) a drug that reduces levels of the pituitary hormone prolactin

Cannula a hollow tube used, for example, to inseminate sperm artificially

Capacitation process by which sperm become capable of fertilizing an egg

Catheter a flexible tube used for aspirating or injecting fluids

Cauterize to destroy tissue with heat, cold, or caustic substances usually to seal off blood vessels or ducts

Cervix the lower portion of the uterus into that opens into the vagina

Cervicitis inflammation of the cervix

Chlamydia a type of bacteria that is frequently transmitted sexually between partners or from an infected mother to her newborn child; the most common sexually transmitted bacterial disease

Chorionic villus sampling (CVS) taking a biopsy of the placenta, usually at the end of the second month of pregnancy, to test the fetus for genetic abnormalities

Chromosome threads of DNA in a cell's nucleus that transmit hereditary information

Clomiphene citrate (Clomid, Serophene) a fertility pill that stimulates ovulation through release of gonadotropins from the pituitary gland

Colposcopy examination of the cervix through a magnifying telescope to detect abnormal cells

Condom a device that fits over the penis to prevent pregnancy and sexually transmitted infections

Congenital defect a birth defect

Conization surgical removal of a cone-shaped

portion of the cervix, usually as treatment for a precancerous condition

Corpus luteum ("yellow body") formed in the ovary following ovulation, it produces progesterone

Cryocautery cautery by freezing

Cryptorchidism failure of one or both testicles to descend into the scrotum

Cul-de-sac pouch located at the bottom of the abdominal cavity between the uterus and rectum

Culdoscopy examination of the internal female pelvic organs through an incision in the vagina

Cyst a sac filled with fluid

Danazol (Danocrine) a synthetic androgen frequently prescribed for endometriosis

Deoxyribonucleic acid (DNA) the combination of amino acids in the cell's nucleus that make up the chromosomes, which transmit hereditary characteristics

Diethystilbestrol (DES) a synthetic estrogen (originally prescribed to prevent miscarriages) that caused malformations of the reproductive organs in some who were exposed to the drug during fetal development

Dilatation and curettage (D&C) an operation that involves stretching the cervical opening to scrape out the uterus

Donor insemination artificial insemination with donor sperm

Dysfunction abnormal function

Ectopic pregnancy pregnancy located outside of the uterus

Egg (ovum) the female reproductive cell

Egg donation donation of an egg by one woman

to another woman who attempts to become pregnant by in vitro fertilization

Ejaculate the sperm-containing fluid released at orgasm

Ejaculatory ducts the male ducts that contract with orgasm to cause ejaculation

Electrocautery cauterization using electrical current

Embryo the developing baby from implantation to the second month of pregnancy

Embryologist a specialist in embryo development

Embryo transfer placing a laboratory-fertilized egg into the uterus

Endocrine gland an organ that produce hormones

Endometrial biopsy removal of a fragment of the lining of the uterus for study under the microscope

Endometriosis growth of endometrial tissue outside of its normal location in the uterus

Endometritis inflammation of the endometrium

Endometrium the inner lining of the uterus

Epididymis the tightly coiled, thin-walled tube that conducts sperm from the testicles to the vas deferens

Epididymitis inflammation of the epididymis

Estradiol the principal estrogen produced by the ovary

Estrogens female sex hormones

Fallopian tubes ducts that pick up the egg from the ovary; where a sperm normally meets the egg to fertilize it

Fecundability the ability to become pregnant

Fetus the developing baby from the second month of pregnancy until birth

Fertilization union of male gamete (sperm) with the female gamete (egg)

Fibroid (myoma or leiomyoma) a benign tumors of the uterine muscle and connective tissue

Fimbria the fingerlike projections at the end of the fallopian tube nearest the ovary that capture the egg and deliver it into the tube

Fimbriaplasty plastic surgery on the fimbria of a damaged or blocked fallopian tube

Fluoroscope an imaging device that uses X rays to view internal body structures

Follicle a fluid-filled sac in the ovary that releases an egg at ovulation

Follicle-stimulating hormone (FSH) the pituitary hormone that stimulates follicle growth in women and sperm formation in men

Fructose produced by the seminal vesicles, the sugar that sperm use for energy

Gamete a reproductive cell; the sperm in men, the egg in women

Gamete intrafallopian transfer (GIFT) combining eggs with sperm outside of the body and immediately placing them into the fallopian tubes to achieve fertilization

Gardnerella a bacteria that may cause a vaginal infection

Genes the unit of heredity, composed of DNA; the building blocks of chromosomes

Gestation sac the fluid-filled sac in which the fetus develops, visible by an ultrasound exam

GIFT see Gamete intrafallopian transfer

Gland an organ that produces and secretes essential body fluids or substances, such as hormones

Gonadotropins the hormones produced by the pituitary gland that control reproductive function; follicle-stimulating hormone (FSH) and luteinizing hormone (LH)

Gonadotropin-releasing hormone (GnRH) the hormone produced and released by the hypothalamus that controls the pituitary gland's production and release of gonadotropins

Gonads organs that produce the sex cells and sex hormones; testicles in men and ovaries in women

Gonorrhea a sexually transmitted disease caused by the bacteria *Neisseria gonococcus* that can lead to infertility

Granuloma a ball of inflamed tissue, commonly formed after vasectomy due to sperm leaking from the vas deferens

Habitual abortion repeat miscarriages

Hamster test a test of the ability of a man's sperm to penetrate a hamster egg stripped of its outer membrane, the zona pellucida. Also called Hamster zona-free ovum (HZFO) test or sperm penetration assay (SPA)

Hemizona assay a laboratory test of the ability of sperm to penetrate into a human egg; first the egg is split in half, then one half is tested against the husband's sperm and the other half against sperm from a fertile man

Hirsuitism excessive hair growth

Hormone a substance, produced by an endocrine gland, that travels through the bloodstream to a specific organ, where it exerts its effect

Host uterus procedure a woman carries to term a pregnancy produced by an infertile couple through in vitro fertilization. Also called gestational carrier.

Hostile mucus cervical mucus that impedes that natural progress of sperm through the cervical canal

Human chorionic gonadotropin (hCG) the hormone produced early in pregnancy to keep the corpus luteum producing progesterone; may be injected to stimulate ovulation and progesterone production Human menopausal gonadotropin (hMG) a combination of luteinizing and follicle-stimulating hormone used to induce multiple ovulation in various fertility treatments

Hydrotubation injection of fluid, often into the fallopian tubes to determine if they are open

Hyperandrogenism excessive production of androgens in women, frequently a cause of hirsutism and also associated with polycystic ovarian disease (PCOD)

Hyperprolactinemia excessive prolactin in the blood

Hyperstimulation excessive stimulation of the ovaries that can cause them to become enlarged

Hypothalamus the endocrine gland at the center of the brain that produces gonadotropin-releasing hormone and controls pituitary function

Hypothyroidism underactivity of the thyroid gland

Hysterectomy surgical removal of the uterus

Hysteroscopy examination of the inner cavity of the uterus through a fiber-optic telescope inserted through the vagina and cervical canal

Hysterosalpingogram (HSG) an X-ray examination of the uterus and fallopian tubes

Immune system the body's defense against injury or invasion by a foreign substance or organism

Immunoglobulins a class of proteins endowed with antibody activity; antibodies

Immunosuppressive drug a drug that interferes with the normal immune response

Immunotherapy a medical treatment for an immune system disorder that involves transfusing blood cells into a woman who has had recurrent miscarriages

Implantation attachment of the fertilized egg to the uterine lining, usually occurring five to seven days after ovulation

Impotence inability of a man to achieve an erection or ejaculation

Infertility inability of a couple to achieve a pregnancy or to carry a pregnancy to term after one year of unprotected intercourse

Inflammation a response to some type of injury such as infection, characterized by increased blood flow, heat, redness, swelling, and pain

Intracervical insemination (ICI) artificial insemination of sperm into the cervical canal

Intracytoplasmic sperm injection (ICSI) direct injection of a single sperm into an egg

Intratubal insemination (ITI) artificial insemination of sperm, which have been washed free of seminal fluid, into the fallopian tubes

Intrauterine insemination (IUI) artificial insemination of sperm, which have been washed free of seminal fluid, directly into the uterine cavity

In utero while in the uterus during early development

In vitro fertilization (IVF) (literally, "in glass") fertilization outside the body in a laboratory; the term "test tube baby" is inaccurate since fertilization occurs in a small circular dish, not a test tube

Karyotype a chromosome analysis

Klinefelter's syndrome a chromosome abnormality that prevents normal male sexual development and causes irreversible infertility due to the presence of an extra female (X) chromosome

Laparoscopy examination of the pelvic organs through a small telescope called a laparoscope

Laparotomy a surgically opening of the abdomen

Leiomyoma (fibroid) a benign tumor of the uterus

Leydig cells the cells in the testicles that make testosterone

LH surge the sudden release of luteinizing hormone (LH) that causes the follicles to release a mature egg

Luteal phase postovulatory phase of a woman's cycle; the corpus luteum produces progesterone, which in turn causes the uterine lining to secrete substances to support the implantation and growth of the early embryo

Luteal phase defect (LPD) inadequate function of the corpus luteum that may prevent a fertilized egg from implanting in the uterus or may lead to early pregnancy loss

Luteinized unruptured follicle (LUF) syndrome the failure of a follicle to release the egg even though a corpus luteum has formed

Luteinizing hormone (LH) the pituitary hormone that causes the testicles in men and ovaries in women to manufacture sex hormones

Menarche the time when a woman has her first menstrual period

Menopause the time when a woman stops having menstrual periods

Metrodin (Pure FSH) an injectable drug consisting of pure follicle-stimulating hormone used to stimulate ovulation

Microsurgery reconstructive surgery performed under magnification using delicate instruments and precise techniques

Miscarriage spontaneous abortion

Morphology the study of form, such as assessing the shape of sperm during semen analysis

Motility motion, such as the forward swimming motion of healthy sperm

Mucus secretion from a gland that can be watery, gellike, stretchy, sticky, or dry; fertile mucus is watery and stretchy

Mycoplasma an infectious agent that falls structurally between a virus and a bacterium

Myomectomy surgical removal of a uterine fibroid tumor

Obstetrician-gynecologist (ob-gyn) a physician who specializes in the treatment of female disorders and pregnancy

Oligomenorrhea infrequent and irregular menstrual cycles

Oligospermia a low sperm count

Ovarian cyst a fluid-containing enlargement of the ovary

Ovarian reserve the number of responsive follicles remaining in the ovary and the ability of the ovary to produce good-quality eggs

Ovarian wedge resection surgical removal of a portion of a polycystic ovary to produce ovulation

Ovary the female gonad; produces eggs and female hormones

Ovulation release of the egg from the ovary

Pap smear removal of cells from the surface of the cervix to study microscopically

Parlodel see bromocryptine

Patent open; for example, fallopian tubes should be patent after a sterilization reversal operation

Pelvic cavity the area surrounded by the pelvic bone that contains the uterus, fallopian tubes, and ovaries in women, and the prostate gland and seminal vesicles in men

Pelvic inflammatory disease (PID) inflammation of any of the female pelvic organs, usually due to infection from a sexually transmitted disease

Penis the male organ of sexual intercourse

Pergonal see human menopausal gonadotropin

Pituitary gland the endocrine gland at the base of the brain that produces the gonadotropins luteinizing hormone and follicle-stimulating hormone, which in turn stimulate the gonads to produce sex cells and hormones

Polycystic ovarian disease (PCOD) a condition found among women who do not ovulate, characterized by multiple ovarian cysts and increased androgen production

Polyp a growth or tumor on an internal surface, usually benign

Postcoital test (PCT) microscopic examination of a woman's cervical mucus at the fertile time of the cycle to determine the number and motility of sperm following intercourse

Pre-embryo a fertilized egg in the early stage of development prior to cell division

Progesterone the female hormone produced by the corpus luteum after ovulation, that prepares the uterine lining for implantation of a fertilized egg and helps maintain the pregnancy

Prolactin the pituitary hormone that in high amounts stimulates milk production

Prostate gland the male gland encircling the urethra that produces one third of the fluid in the ejaculate

Prostaglandins a group of hormone like chemicals that have various effects on reproductive organs; so named because they were first discovered in the prostate gland

Reproductive endocrinologist an ob-gyn who specializes in the treatment of hormonal diseases that affect reproductive function

Reproductive surgeon an ob-gyn or urologist who specializes in the surgical correction of anatomical disorders that impair reproductive function

Retrograde ejaculation ejaculation backward into the bladder instead of forward through the urethra

Salpingectomy surgical removal of the fallopian tubes

Salpingitis inflammation of one or both fallopian tubes

Salpingitis isthmica nodosa an abnormal condition of the fallopian tube where it attaches to the uterus, characterized by nodules

Salpingostomy an operation to open a blocked fallopian tube

Scrotum the sac containing the testicles, epididymis, and vas deferens

Semen the fluid containing sperm and secretions from the testicles, prostate, and seminal vesicles that is expelled during ejaculation

Semen analysis laboratory examination of semen to check the quality and quantity of sperm

Seminal vesicles the paired glands at the base of the bladder that produce seminal fluid and fructose

Seminiferous tubules in the testicles, the network of tubes where sperm are formed

Septum a wall that divides a cavity in half, such as a uterine septum

Sertoli cells the cells in the testicles that provide nourishment to the early sperm cells

Sexually transmitted disease (STD) a disease caused by an infectious agent transmitted during sex

Sperm male gamete or reproductive cell

Sperm bank a place where sperm are kept frozen in liquid nitrogen for later use in artificial insemination

Sperm count the number of sperm in the ejaculate (when given as the number of sperm per milliliter, it is more accurately known as the sperm concentration or sperm density)

Sperm penetration assay (SPA) see hamster test

Spermicide an agent that kills sperm

Sterilization a surgical procedure (such as tubal ligation or vasectomy) designed to produce infertility

Sterilization reversal a surgical procedure used to undo a previous sterilization operation and restore fertility

Superovulation stimulation of multiple ovulation with fertility drugs; also known as controlled ovarian hyperstimulation (COH)

Surrogate mother a woman who becomes artificially inseminated with a man's sperm and carries the pregnancy for an infertile couple, who adopt the baby after its birth (the man being the biologic father of the child)

Testicle the male gonad; produces sperm and male sex hormones

Testicular biopsy the removal of a fragment of a testicle for examination under the microscope

Testosterone the primary male sex hormone

Thyroid gland the endocrine gland in the front of the neck that produces thyroid hormones, which regulate the body's metabolism

Tocolytic a drug that relaxes smooth muscles

and therefore interferes with uterine contractions; frequently used to stop premature labor

Total effective sperm count an estimate of the number of sperm in an ejaculate capable of fertilization; total sperm count x percent motility x percent forward progressive motility x percent normal morphology

Toxin a poison produced by a living organism, such as by some bacteria

Tubal ligation surgical sterilization of a woman by obstructing or "tying" the fallopian tubes

Tuboplasty plastic or reconstructive surgery on the fallopian tubes to correct abnormalities that cause infertility

Tumor an abnormal growth of tissue that can be benign or malignant (cancerous)

Ultrasound (US) use of high-frequency sound waves for creating an image of internal body parts

Ureaplasma a microorganism similar to mycoplasma (see mycoplasma)

Urethra the tube through which urine from the bladder is expelled

Urologist a physician who specializes in the surgical treatment of disorders of the urinary tract and male reproductive tract

Uterus the womb; female reproductive organ that nourishes the fetus until birth

Vagina the female organ of sexual intercourse; the birth canal

Vaginitis inflammation of the vagina

Varicocele varicose vein in the scrotum

Vas deferens the tubes that conduct sperm and testicular fluid to the ejaculatory ducts

Vasectomy surgical sterilization of a man by interrupting both vas deferens

Vasectomy reversal surgical repair of a previous vasectomy for a man who wants to regain his fertility

Vasogram an X-ray study of the vas deferens

Venereal disease see sexually transmitted disease

Virus a microscopic infectious organism that reproduces inside living cells

Zona pellucida the protective coating surrounding the egg

Zygote an egg that has been fertilized but not yet divided

Zygote intrafallopian transfer (ZIFT) in vitro fertilization with a transfer of the zygote into the fallopian tube; a combination of in vitro fertilization and gamete intrafallopian transfer (GIFT)

Index

Note: Page references in *italics* indicate illustrations and captions

A&D Ointment, 300
abortion, 22, 26, 35, 164, 249; spontaneous (*see* miscarriage)
abortion pill, 150
abscesses: dental, 70; and PID, 19
acquired immune deficiency syndrome. *See* AIDS
acrosome, 10, 99, 115
acrosome reaction, 10, 29, 118
ACTH (adrenocorticotropic hormone), 145
Actifed, 302
activin, 150–51
Actos, 145–46
acupressure, 320, 321
acupuncture, 320, 321, 322–23, 324
adenocarcinoma, 31
adenomyosis, 77, 89, 166
adenosis, 74–75, 76
adhesions, 77, 108, 109, 110, 111; sitz baths for, 325; surgery to remove, 156, 161, 164, 194, 196. *See also* scarring
adnexa, 77
adoption, 271, 275–83; vs. donor insemination, 245–46; embryo adoption, 336; host uterus and, 251; questions to consider, 284–85; resources, 430–31; surrogacy and, 252, 254, 255
adrenal gland disorders, 58; tumors, 103, 144
adrenal gland function, 147; herbs for, 323, 328; suppressing, 144–45
adrenal hormones. *See* androgens; cortisol; DHEAS; testosterone
adrenaline, 291

adrenocorticotropic hormone (ACTH), 145
Advanced Reproductive Care (ARC) Network, 64
age: egg donation and, 247; and fertility decline, 34–35, 337, 339; host uterus and, 252; IVF and, 49, 208–9, 223, 311–12, 338, 339; pregnancy and, 338–39; secondary infertility and, 311–12. *See also* older women
agglutination, 101, 103
AID (artificial insemination by donor). *See* donor insemination
AIDS, 21, 67, 82, 240, 243
alcohol, 35, 43, 44, 45, 50, 172, 299, 313
Aldactone, 29, 145
alfalfa extract, 324
alpha blockers, 29
alternative therapies, xix, 317–30; carnitine supplements, 327; herbal treatments, 323–24, 325, 326, 328–30; for men, 326–30; mind/body therapy, 321–22; naturopathy, 324–25; potential dangers, 328–30; success rates, 320; TCM, 322–24, 326; for women, 322–25
AMA (American Medical Association), 63
amenorrhea, 24, 39, 40, 136–37, 143, 323. *See also* premature menopause
American Academy of Adoption Attorneys, 279
American Association of Oriental Medicine, 322
American Association of Tissue Banks, 241, 429
American Bar Association, surrogacy guidelines, 340

exercise and, 33, 38, 39–40, 49;
herbs for, 324; prolactin and,
139–40; relaxation techniques for,
320; stress and, 38, 39–40, 49. *See
also* amenorrhea
menstruation: pain with, 71, 89;
treatments to prevent, 135, 142
MESA (microsurgical epididymal
sperm aspiration), 227
metals, 47
Metamucil, 299
metformin, 145
methionine, 324
methotrexate, 167
methoxychlor, 47
Metrodin, 58; for men, 148; for
women, 133, 134, 137, 138, 140, 191,
201, 212, 214. *See also* pure FSH
microadenomas, 141
Microdot technique, 181–82
micromanipulators, 224
microscope, 94, 157
microsurgery, 109, 157; to clear
blockages, xviii, 58, 112, 119,
179–80; vs. laparoscopy, 162, 163; to
repair fallopian tubes, 112, 156, 157;
to repair varicoceles, xviii, 160, 169,
170, 313; for sperm extraction,
227–28; sterilization reversals, 16,
24–25, 156, 157–59, 181–82, 313. *See
also* surgery
microsurgical epididymal sperm
aspiration (MESA), 227
mifepristone, 150
migraines, 128
Milk of Magnesia, 299
mind/body therapy, 321–22
mineral supplements, 49, 50, 150, 324,
327, 328
Minipress, 29
miscarriage, 25–26, 297; among older
women, 35, 337; antisperm
antibodies and, 28; bacterial
infections and, 20; chemical
exposure and, 47; cloning and, 333;
detecting, 135, 202; emotional

issues, 264; IVF and, 221; previous
history of, 52, 291, 301; questions to
ask about, 284; signs of, 201;
smoking and, 46; stress and, 320;
support groups, 264; therapies to
prevent, 142, 201–4, 213, 291
moxibustion, 323
MRI (magnetic resonance imaging),
89, 141, 196
MS (multiple sclerosis), 199
mucus, cervical. *See* cervical mucus
multiple pregnancy, 290, 341–42; egg
donation and, 247; hormone
treatments and, 127, 130, 132; IVF
and, 217, 219, 221, 338, 341; PGD
and, 345
multiple sclerosis, 199
multiple sex partners, 22–23, 35, 46
mumps, 93
muscular dystrophy, 345
mycoplasma, 18, 20, 83, 155, 156
Mylanta, 300
Mylicon, 300

Naferelin, 138. *See also* GnRH agonists
narcotics, 172
National Advisory Board for Ethics
and Reproduction, 230
National Center for Health Statistics,
63
National Institute of Child Health and
Human Development, 48
National Institutes of Health (NIH),
334
National Survey of Family Growth,
307
National Toxicology Program (NTP),
47
naturopathy, 324–25
nausea, during pregnancy, 295, 302,
303, 304
Nd-YAG laser, 194
neisseria, 83. *See also* gonorrhea
neural tube defects, 302
NGU (non-gonococcal urethritis),
19–20

ABOUT THE AUTHORS

GARY S. BERGER, M.D. is unique in being certified in the medical specialities of Obstetrics and Gynecology, Preventive Medicine, *and* Epidemiology. He was one of the first American infertility specialists to bring female microsurgery techniques from England and has developed a technique of outpatient tubal sterilization reversal. He also reported the first birth following intratubal insemination. Dr. Berger has directed a private infertility practice, the Chapel Hill Fertility Center, for more than twenty years, and is Clinical Associate Professor of Obstetrics and Adjunct Associate Professor of Maternal and Child Health at the University of North Carolina. He is also a charter member of the Society of Reproductive Surgeons.

After receiving his medical degree from the University of Rochester, Dr. Berger was an intern at Duke University and a resident at Johns Hopkins and the University of North Carolina. He also trained in epidemiology in the U.S. Public Health Service at the Centers for Disease Control and obtained a Master of Science degree in Public Health from the University of North Carolina.

Dr. Berger is the author or editor of eleven medical books and has written more than 160 articles for physicians on various subjects in the area of reproductive health. This is his first book written for the lay public.

MARC GOLDSTEIN, M.D., is Professor of Reproductive Medicine and Urology at the Weill Medical College at Cornell University, Co-Executive Director of the Cornell Institute of Reproductive Medicine, and Surgeon in Chief of Male Reproductive Medicine and Surgery at the New York Weill-Cornell Medical Center. He is also a Staff Scientist with the Population Council's Center for Biomedical Research, located on the campus of Rockefeller University.

Dr. Goldstein has written more than one hundred-seventy medical articles in journals textbooks and is the author of the *Surgery of Male Infertility*, the first textbook dedicated exclusively to that subject, and the *Atlas of the Surgery of Male Infertility*. He is on the editorial board of the medical journal *Microsurgery and Journal of Andrology*..

In addition, Dr. Goldstein is listed in the books *Best Doctors in America 2001* and *How to Find the Best Doctors, New York Metro Area, 2001*, as well as in *America's Top Doctors*.

A summa cum laude graduate of the College of Medicine, State University of New York–Downstate Medical Center in Brooklyn, New York, Dr. Goldstein worked as a resident in general surgery at Columbia Presbyterian Hospital in New York and was trained in urology at the Downstate Medical Center. He continued his postgraduate training in reproductive physiology at the Population

Council, Center for Biomedical Research, and at the Rockefeller University Hospital. He is a board-certified urologic surgeon and member of half a dozen national medical societies dealing with male fertility and reproduction. More information about his practice can be found at www.maleinfertility.org.

MARK FUERST has been a freelance journalist for more than two decades. His articles have appeared in popular consumer magazines such as *Family Circle* and *Woman's Day*, and he has written articles on infertility for *Baby Talk*, *Good Housekeeping*, *Woman's World*, and United Features Syndicate. As a staff writer for *Medical World News*, he covered several infertility conferences and wrote numerous articles on infertility. He is also the coauthor of *Computer Phobia*, *Sports Injury Handbook*, *Golf Injury Handbook*, *Tennis Injury Handbook*, *Tone-A-Metrics* and the upcoming *Tell Me Where It Hurts*.

Mr. Fuerst earned a biology degree from Dickinson College and a master's degree in journalism from the University of Missouri at Columbia. He is a member of the National Association of Science Writers and is a past president of the American Society of Journalists and Authors.